MACROECONOMICS

KEYNESIAN, MONETARIST,
AND MARXIST VIEWS

Howard J. Sherman
University of California, Riverside

Gary R. Evans
Harvey Mudd College

HARPER & ROW, PUBLISHERS, New York
Cambridge, Philadelphia, San Francisco,
London, Mexico City, São Paulo, Sydney

Dedicated to the memory of
WESLEY C. MITCHELL

This book is presented
with love
to
Sonia Evans
and
Barbara Sinclair

Sponsoring Editor: David J. Forgione
Project Editor: Jo-Ann Goldfarb
Designer: T. R. Funderburk
Production Assistant: Debi Forrest Bochner
Compositor: Com Com Division of Haddon Craftsmen, Inc.
Printer and Binder: R. R. Donnelley & Sons Company
Art Studio: Fine Line Illustrations, Inc.

MACROECONOMICS: Keynesian, Monetarist, and Marxist Views
Copyright © 1984 by Harper & Row, Publishers, Inc.

All rights reserved. Printed in the United States of America. No part of this book may be used or reproduced in any manner whatsoever without written permission, except in the case of brief quotations embodied in critical articles and reviews. For information address Harper & Row, Publishers, Inc., 10 East 53d Street, New York, NY 10022.

Library of Congress Cataloging in Publication Data

Sherman, Howard J.
  Macroeconomics : Keynesian, monetarist, and Marxist views.

  Includes bibliographical references and index.
  1. Macroeconomics. I. Evans, Gary R., 1946–
II. Title.
HB172.5.S5237 1984   339   83-18364
ISBN 0-06-046109-8

BRIEF CONTENTS

Detailed Contents v
Preface xiv

Part One DETERMINATION OF INCOME AND EMPLOYMENT 1

CHAPTER 1 Say's Law: Supply Calls Forth Its Own Demand 3
CHAPTER 2 The Historical-Institutional Critique of Say's Law 12
CHAPTER 3 The Circular Flow: A National Accounting Framework 29
CHAPTER 4 Say's Law and the Classical View 43
CHAPTER 5 The Critical Analysis of Say's Law 58
CHAPTER 6 Money: From $MV = PT$ to $IS\text{-}LM$ 79

Part Two BEHAVIOR OF MACROECONOMIC BUILDING BLOCKS 105

CHAPTER 7 The Growth of Government 107
CHAPTER 8 Consumption 131
CHAPTER 9 Investment 155
CHAPTER 10 Income Distribution 182
CHAPTER 11 The Rate of Profit 204

Part Three GROWTH AND BUSINESS CYCLES: CAUSES OF UNEMPLOYMENT 223

CHAPTER 12 The Dynamic Framework: Conditions for Steady Growth 225
CHAPTER 13 Classical and Keynesian Cycle Theories 244

CHAPTER 14 Demand-Side Cycle Theories: Marxist, Post Keynesian, and Institutionalist Views 257
CHAPTER 15 Supply-Side and Combined Cycle Theories: Marxist and Conservative Views 268

Part Four MODERN MONETARY THEORIES 285

CHAPTER 16 The Return of Monetarism 287
CHAPTER 17 Modern Nonmonetarist Monetary Theories 306
CHAPTER 18 Monetary Theories of the Business Cycle 329

Part Five INFLATION 343

CHAPTER 19 Demand-Pull and Cost-Push Inflation 343
CHAPTER 20 Profit-Push Inflation: Monopoly Power 361
CHAPTER 21 International Aspects of Inflation and Unemployment 378

Part Six THE ROLE OF GOVERNMENT 399

CHAPTER 22 The Endogenous Shaping of Government Policies 401
CHAPTER 23 Fiscal Policy 416
CHAPTER 24 Monetary Policy 440
CHAPTER 25 Direct Controls and Public Employment 471
CHAPTER 26 Public Ownership 479

Index 487

DETAILED CONTENTS

Preface xiv

Part One DETERMINATION OF INCOME AND EMPLOYMENT 1

CHAPTER 1 **Say's Law: Supply Calls Forth Its Own Demand** 3
   The Physiocrats 5
   Malthus's Theory of Gluts 6
   Say's Law 7
     The Refinement of Say's Law 8
     Critique and Defense of Say's Law 9

CHAPTER 2 **The Historical-Institutional Critique of Say's Law** 12
   Production for the Market 13
   Regular Use of Money 15
   Production for Private Profit 18
   Conclusion: The Three Conditions of Overproduction 19
   Capitalism and the Business Cycle 19
     Cycles in the U.S. Economy 21
     The Timing and Typing of Business Cycles 24
   Summary 28

CHAPTER 3 **The Circular Flow: A National Accounting Framework** 29
   The Circular Flow of the Gross National Product 29
   Net National Product 32
   National Income 33
   Personal and Disposable Income 33
   Savings and Investment 36
   The Concept of Value Added 38
   Gross National Product in Real Terms 39

Potential Gross National Product   40
Per Capita GNP   40
Net Economic Welfare   41
Summary   42
Glossary of Symbols   42

CHAPTER 4 **Say's Law and the Classical View**   43
The National Production Function   44
The Labor Market   45
The Determination of Real Output   49
The Commodity Market   49
The Determination of the Price Level   51
Summary of Classical Model   52
Summary   54

APPENDIX 4A   Complete Model of the Classical Theory   55

CHAPTER 5 **The Critical Analysis of Say's Law**   58
Equilibrium of Aggregate Supply and Demand   58
A Keynesian Model   60
The Consumption Function   61
The Investment Function   61
The Market for Savings and Investment   63
The Role of Expectations in Creating a Disequilibrium   65
Unemployment Equilibrium   67
Developments in the Labor and Commodity Markets   67
Keynes's Rejection of the Classical Argument   70
The Importance of Considering Aggregate Demand   71
American Keynesianism and the "Keynesian Cross"   72
Marx's Critique of Say's Law   75
Summary   77

CHAPTER 6 **Money: From $MV = PT$ to $IS\text{-}LM$**   79
Definitions of Money   80
The Genesis of Modern Monetary Theory: The Equation of Exchange   81
Economic Distress and the Triumph of Keynes   82
Other Motives for Demanding Money   83
Slippage in the Connection Between Money and Expenditures   85
A Keynesian Explanation of the Behavior of Velocity   86
Further Refinements in Keynesian Theory   87
The $IS\text{-}LM$ Model   88
The Use of $IS\text{-}LM$ for Analysis   93
An Increase in the Money Supply   93
A Reduction in the Propensity to Consume or Invest   94
A Rise in the Speculative Demand for Money   95
The Classical Case: No Speculative Demand for Money   95
A Critique of $IS\text{-}LM$ 96

Neo-Keynesians Versus Post Keynesians 97
Summary 98
APPENDIX 6A The Money Inventory and Portfolio Theories 99

Part Two BEHAVIOR OF MACROECONOMIC BUILDING BLOCKS 105

CHAPTER 7 **The Growth of Government** 107
    Trends in Government Spending 107
        Federal Versus State and Local 107
        Trends in Government Revenues 112
        Tentative Conclusions on Government Spending 115
    Government Finance 117
    The Federal Reserve System 117
        Discount Window Policy 120
        Changing Reserve Requirements 120
        Open Market Operations 121
    Summary 122
APPENDIX 7A The Government Multiplier 122
APPENDIX 7B Federal Reserve Operations 128
CHAPTER 8 **Consumption** 131
    Keynes's View of Consumption 132
    The Relative Income Hypothesis 134
    The Life Cycle Hypothesis 134
    The Permanent Income Hypothesis 135
    Conclusions from Neoclassical-Keynesian Theories 136
    The Class Income Hypothesis 138
    Cyclical Behavior of Consumption and Income 139
    Behavior of the Propensity to Consume 142
    Cycle Patterns of the 1920s and the 1930s 144
        Explanation of the Cyclical Behavior of Consumers 144
        Long-run Trends 149
    Summary 150
APPENDIX 8A: Consumption Function Estimates 151
CHAPTER 9 **Investment** 155
    The Major Categories of Investment 156
        Plant and Equipment Investment 157
        Residential Construction Investment 157
    Theory of Investment 158
        Other Investment Functions 161
    Cyclical Patterns of Investment and Profits 162
        Timing in Different Industries 164
    Inventory Investment 166

viii   DETAILED CONTENTS

    Investment and Interest Rates   169
      Long-run Trend in Interest Rates   171
      Long-run Trend in Investment   171
    Summary   172
APPENDIX 9A: Determination of Investment   173
APPENDIX 9B: Depreciation and Replacement   173
APPENDIX 9C: The Investment Multiplier   176
APPENDIX 9D: The Cyclical Behavior of Investment   180
CHAPTER 10 **Income Distribution**   182
    Present U.S. Income Distribution   182
    Framework and Definitions   183
    Problems with Measuring Profits, Wages, and Productivity   185
    Theories and Controversies   187
    Cyclical Changes in Income Distribution, 1921–1938   188
    Long-run Changes from the 1950s to the 1980s   189
    The Wage Share, 1949–1970   190
    The Wage Share, 1970–1980   192
    Theories of the Wage Share, Wages, and Productivity   194
    Output, Capacity, and Unemployment   198
    Summary   200
APPENDIX 10A: Regression Analysis of the Wage Share   200
CHAPTER 11 **The Rate of Profit**   204
    Behavior of the Profit Rate and the Profit Share   205
      The Profit Share   208
      Capacity Utilization and the Profit Rate   210
      Ratio of Potential Output to Capital and the Rate of Profit   212
      Tentative Conclusions on the Three Components   216
    Summary   218
APPENDIX 11A: Analysis of the Components of the Profit Rate   219

Part Three   GROWTH AND BUSINESS CYCLES: CAUSES OF UNEMPLOYMENT   223

CHAPTER 12 **The Dynamic Framework: Conditions for Steady Growth**   225
    Classical Supply-Side Theory   226
    Keynes on Saving and Growth   229
    Neoclassical Growth Theory   230
    Modern Supply-Side Growth Theory   232
    Marx: Equilibrium (or Simple Reproduction)   234
    Marx: Growth (or Expanded Reproduction)   235
    Post Keynesian Growth Models   236
    Summary   236
APPENDIX 12A: Classical Supply-Side Growth Model   237
APPENDIX 12B: Domar's Growth Model and the Razor's Edge   238

APPENDIX 12C: Solow's Growth Theory 240
APPENDIX 12D: A Marxist Growth Model 241
CHAPTER 13 **Classical and Keynesian Cycle Theories** 244
 The Natural Rate of Unemployment 244
 Other Neoclassical Theories of Unemployment 246
 Wesley Clair Mitchell and John Maynard Keynes 249
 The Simplest Keynesian Model 250
  Workings of the Model 252
 Summary 252
APPENDIX 13A: A Formal Model of the Simplest Keynesian Theory 252
CHAPTER 14 **Demand-Side Cycle Theories: Marxist, Post Keynesian, and Institutionalist Views** 257
 Underconsumptionist Theories 257
 Marx and Underconsumption 259
 A Realization Theory 261
  Government and Demand 264
  Money, Credit, and Demand 264
  International Demand 264
 Summary 265
APPENDIX 14A: The Formal Realization Model 265
APPENDIX 14B: A Simpler Demand Model 266
CHAPTER 15 **Supply-Side and Combined Cycle Theories: Marxist and Conservative Views** 268
 Overinvestment Theories 268
 Supply-Side Marxism: The Reserve Army Theory 270
 Supply-Side Marxism: Organic Composition Theory 274
 A Combined Production-Realization Theory: The Two-Horned Dilemma 275
 Evaluation of the Combined Model 277
 Summary 279
APPENDIX 15A: A Reserve Army Model 279
APPENDIX 15B: A Very Simple Overinvestment Model 280
APPENDIX 15C: Actual Behavior at Different Stages of the Average Cycle 281
APPENDIX 15D: The Combined Model in Equations: A Production-Realization Model 282

Part Four   MODERN MONETARY THEORIES   285

CHAPTER 16 **The Return of Monetarism** 287
 The Declining Importance of Money 287
 The Phillips Curve 288
 The Crowding-Out Hypothesis 289
 Monetarist Tenets 291
 Basic Criticisms of Monetarism 292
 The Primary Monetarist Model 293

Expectations 296
Expectations and the Monetarist "Transmission Mechanism" 296
Money and Real Values 298
Money and Real Interest Rates 299
The Distribution of Money-Stimulated Spending on Prices and Output 300
The Monetarist Approach to the Phillips Curve 301
The Futility of Discretionary Monetary Policy 302
Monetarists' Interpretations of Inflation 303
The Monetarist Attitude About Fiscal Policy 303
Monetarist Recommendations 304
Summary 304

CHAPTER 17 **Modern Nonmonetarist Monetary Theories** 306
Reasons for the New Criticism 306
Four Nonmonetarist Schools of Thought 307
Main Arguments of the Critics 308
Uncertainty and Its Effects upon the Financial Markets 308
   The Problem of Uncertainly in Investment Decisions:
      The Unstable Investment Function 309
   The Unstable Demand for Borrowed Funds and Disequilibrium 310
   Uncertainty and the Connection Between Monetary "Rules"
      and Volatile Interest Rates 311
The Possibility of a Permanent Leakage in the Expenditure Stream 312
The Problem of Defining Money 314
   Recent Evidence of the Problem of Defining Money 314
Credit Matters More Than Money 315
Interest Rates Matter More Than Money 316
   The Wealth Effects and Portfolio Effects of Interest Rate Changes 317
   The Sectoral Effects of Interest Rate Changes 318
The Endogenous Money Supply: Money Can't Be Controlled 318
   The Long-run Relationship 319
   The Legacy 319
   The Short-run Endogenous Money Supply 321
   The Effect of Credit Stabilization Policies
      and the Endogenous Money Supply 322
   The Looseness of Control 323
   Discount Borrowing and the Federal Funds Market 323
   Attracting Funds to High-Yield Liabilities 324
A Summary of the Institutional Explanation 324
The Relationship Between Money and Spending 325
Marxist View of Money 326
Summary 327

CHAPTER 18 **Monetary Theories of the Business Cycle** 329
The Fisherian-Monetarist Theory of the Business Cycle 330
   The Modern Monetarist Variation 332

Irving Fisher's Debt-Deflation Theory of Business Cycles 334
Hyman Minsky's Financial Business Cycle Theory 335
  The Boom 337
  The Bust 339
Contrasting the Two Types of Monetary Theory 340
An Integration of Real and Monetary Factors: Marxist and Other Theories 340
Summary 342

Part Five INFLATION 343

CHAPTER 19 Demand-Pull and Cost-Push Inflation 345
The Keynesian Framework 345
Inflation in Wartime 346
Inflation in Business Expansions 348
Monetary Contributions to Demand-Pull Inflation 349
  Stagflation: Inflation During Stagnation 351
Cost-Push Theories 354
  Cost-Push Inflation as an Explanation for Stagflation 358
Summary 359
Suggested Readings 360

CHAPTER 20 Profit-Push Inflation: Monopoly Power 361
The Increase of Monopoly Power 361
Monopoly Power and Administered Prices 364
  Prices of Automobiles, Oil, and Food 367
Explanation of Price Behavior 368
Monopoly and Profit Rates 370
  Monopoly Profit Rates over the Cycle 373
Summary 376
Suggested Readings 376

APPENDIX 20A: Monopoly in a Cycle Model 377

CHAPTER 21 International Aspects of Inflation and Unemployment 378
Theory of Business Cycle Spread 378
  Investment and the Spread of Cycles 380
  Behavior of Investment and Trade in the Great Depression 381
  Facts of U.S. Export and Import Cycles from 1949 to 1980 383
Imperialism and Multinational Firms 385
Inflation and Monopoly in Western Europe and Japan 387
Concentration by Multinational (or Global) Firms 389
  Profits and Multinational Firms 391
  Stagflation and the Multinationals 392
Rise and Decline of the U.S. Empire 393
Shortages 396
Summary 397

Part Six THE ROLE OF GOVERNMENT 399

CHAPTER 22 The Endogenous Shaping of Government Policies 401
   Conservative View of Government 401
   The Liberal View: Keynesians and Pluralists 403
   The Radical or Marxist View 404
      The Importance of Class 406
      How Economic Power Determines Political Results 408
   Class Background of Political Leaders 410
   The Structural Bases of Control 411
   Qualifications to the Class Analysis 412
   Feedback Mechanisms of Control 414
   Summary 415

CHAPTER 23 Fiscal Policy 416
   The Conservative View of Fiscal Policy 416
   The Liberal View 417
   Supply-Side Fiscal Policy 419
   The Radical View of Fiscal Policy 421
   Limitations of Liberal Fiscal Policy 422
   Administrative Constraints 422
   Political Constraints 423
   Economic Constraints 427
   Automatic Stabilizers 428
   Cyclical Behavior of Government Revenue 429
   Government Spending over the Business Cycle 431
   Cyclical Behavior of Government Deficits 434
   Conflicting Interpretations of the Fiscal Data 436
   Summary 437

APPENDIX 23A An Endogenous Model of Fiscal Policy 438
APPENDIX 23B Deficits and Balanced Budgets 438

CHAPTER 24 Monetary Policy 440
   Monetary Tools 442
   Monetary Policy Between 1946 and 1951 443
   Interest Rate Stabilization Policies, 1952–1970 444
   Monitoring Monetary Aggregates, 1970–1979 445
   The Volcker Plan—October 1979 447
      The Volcker Decision 451
   Strict Monetarist Policies 453
      The Theoretical Justification for Strict Monetarism 455
   Discretionary Monetarism 456
   The Criticism of Monetarist Policies 457
   Monetary Eclecticism 458
   Controlling Interest Rates 459
   Controlling Wide Aggregates and Credit 460

Some Criticisms of the Nonmonetarist Policies 461
The Problem of Simultaneously High Rates of Infation, Interest Rates, and Unemployment 462
The Need for Monetary and Fiscal Policy Coordination 462
Radical Monetary Policy 463
Summary 464

APPENDIX 24A Targets of the Federal Reserve System 465

CHAPTER 25 **Direct Controls and Public Employment** 471
Wage-Price Controls 471
Controls, Inefficiency, and Corruption 473
Controls and Income Distribution 474
The Liberal Solution to Stagflation 475
Public Employment 476
Problems with Public Employment and Price Controls 477
The Choices of Planning Modes 477
Summary 478

CHAPTER 26 **Public Ownership** 479
Macro Balance Under Planning 479
Growth Cycles and Central Planning 481
Macro Balance Under Decentralized Public Ownership 482
Other Problems of Public Ownership 483
Summary 486

Index 487

PREFACE

This book is intended to present a new, alternative perspective in the field of macroeconomics. Therefore, in addition to the usual review of the literature in the area, this book also presents the original research findings of the authors themselves, particularly in the monetary and cycle areas. We believe that this approach should enhance the book's value by making it more interesting to students and even keeping instructors awake by introducing them to some new material.

DIFFERENCES FROM PREVIOUS APPROACHES

This book differs in many ways from most books on macroeconomics. Rather than pretending there is only one truth, this book explicitly presents several points of view: the neoclassical-Keynesian view dominant in the United States, the monetarist view, the supply-side view, Post Keynesian views, institutionalist views, and Marxist views.

Most macroeconomics texts confine themselves to quite arid theory and, perhaps, some econometrics. In this book, Wesley Mitchell's descriptive approach to the empirical data, especially his description of the cyclical movements of capitalism, is used extensively. Formal econometric methods are also used, but very sparingly. This book makes use of theory and extensive empirical data (including the authors' own research results), but it also paints the broad picture of the historical evolution of capitalist institutions.

Most macroeconomic texts present static models of equilibrium at a given time or comparisons of different equilibria. This book tries to present a comprehensive model of the *dynamics* of the capitalist business cycle and long-run economic changes. It is the authors' belief, based on many years of teaching, that a fully dynamic theory of the economy is the only way to give students an interesting and realistic view of the problems of unemployment and inflation.

Macroeconomics is not a game, and it is about people, not about numbers. We do not believe that economists should ever recommend more unemployment of human beings as a "cure" for inflation or anything else. Therefore, the main focus of this book is not on imaginary equilibria or steady growth situations, but on the existing reality of large-scale unemployment and inflation—and how to end both of them.

Finally, most macroeconomic texts treat government as external to the economic system, able to do whatever is rationally determined to be necessary by wise, impartial economists. This book presents a political-economic model that explains the influence of the economic system in determining government policies, followed by the reciprocal influence of government policies on the economy.

In summary, this book covers the same subjects as most macroeconomic texts, but with a totally different approach and emphasis. Most texts pretend to be above the battle, present mainly theory with a little econometrics, and are mostly static equilibrium-oriented. This book explicitly presents the different warring views, adds very considerable historical and institutional material in a whole political-economic system, and is mostly oriented to a dynamic model of the system.

THE PLAN OF THE BOOK

Part One of this book presents a framework and introduction to different points of view. Chapter 1 presents Say's law. Chapter 2 asks: Under what conditions are unemployment and inflation possible? What kind of institutions give rise to these possibilities? Chapter 2 traces economic institutions from feudalism to capitalism in this light. Chapter 3 describes the circular flow of money and output, as well as the national income accounts. Chapters 4, 5, and 6 present the formal debate on Say's law between its defenders (classical, neoclassical, monetarist, and supply-side economists) and its critics (Keynes, Keynesians of various types, institutionalists such as Veblen, and Marxists of various types).

Part Two presents the behavior of government, consumption, investment, income distribution, and the rate of profit over the business cycle and over the long run under the institutional conditions existing in the United States from the 1920s to the present. In each case, the traditional theories are presented, along with the authors' own theoretical view and empirical research.

Part Three presents various theories of growth and business cycles, ranging from monetarist and Keynesian to underconsumptionist and other Marxist theories. Part Four presents the recent development of monetary theory, including both monetarist and antimonetarist views, and then discusses the role of money and credit in the business cycle.

Part Five discusses various theories of inflation. It presents the usual Keynesian and monetarist views of demand-pull inflation and the role of money. It discusses the many varieties of cost-pull theories, based on wage-push, rising raw material prices, and other cost factors. It emphasizes the important role of monopoly in causing profit-push inflation and in exacerbating unemployment. It examines the changing international situation of the United States and how this affects both inflation and unemployment.

Part Six presents theoretical views and factual data on the role of government fiscal, monetary, and direct control policies. The theoretical interpretations range from Keynesian and monetarist views of policy to Marxist views of policy.

THE USE OF APPENDIXES

Appendixes are used for all the more technical econometric data and mathematical models. In this way, the text is uncluttered and readable by any intermediate student. Yet the appendixes also allow the book to be used for graduate courses in macroeconomics. They also include some of the authors' own theoretical contributions that may be of some interest to other economists.

ACKNOWLEDGMENTS

We are very grateful for the excellent editing and typing done by Kaylyn Gary, Shirlee Pigeon, and Poinka Wong. We are grateful for the financial support given by the University of California, Riverside, Committee on Research, and for the research funding by Harvey Mudd College, Claremont.

For research assistance, we wish to thank Richard Beason, Hans van Otterloo, and Paul Dylan Sherman. We are grateful to Victor Perlo for a prompt reply to a request for information. We most profoundly appreciate the very constructive criticisms of chapters and articles, on which this book was built, made by Samuel Bowles, Robert Chernomas, James Devine, James Earley, Mason Gaffney, Herbert Gintis, Robin Hahnel, David Laibman, Gary Langer, John A. Miller, Philip Mirowski, Frank Munley, Seiichi Nagashima, Nei-Pew Ong, Robert Pollin, Howard Wachtel, Helmut Wagner, Thomas Weisskopf, Andy Winick, and Ken Woodward.

We also wish to thank the graduate students of Economics 201A at the University of California, Riverside, for many useful comments. We especially wish to thank Robin Hahnel and the two journals for letting us use some (completely rewritten) parts of two articles: Robin Hahnel and Howard J. Sherman, "Income Distribution and the Business Cycle," *Journal of Economic Issues* 16 (March 1982), pp. 49–73; and Robin Hahnel and Howard J. Sherman, "The Profit Rate over the Business Cycle," *Cambridge Journal of Economics* 6 (June 1982), pp. 185–194. Some of the ideas in this book first appeared in Howard J. Sherman, "A Marxist Theory of Business Cycles," *Review of Radical Political Economics* 11 (Spring 1979), pp. 1–23.

Howard J. Sherman
Gary R. Evans

Part One

DETERMINATION OF INCOME AND EMPLOYMENT

Chapter 1

SAY'S LAW: SUPPLY CALLS FORTH ITS OWN DEMAND

In the year of the American Revolution, 1776, a popular Scottish moral philosopher made a contribution to the literary world that was as important as it was durable. The man was Adam Smith, and his book was called *An Inquiry into the Nature and Causes of the Wealth of Nations*.[1] The ideas within the pages of this encyclopedic masterpiece defined the ethos that was to dominate Western economic development. Smith's quintessential thoughts still today constitute the core of mainstream American economic doctrine.

As the title of his book suggests, Adam Smith wanted to know what was responsible for the growth of national wealth. The book summarizes the results of his personal inquiry into this matter.

As a scholar in moral philosophy, Smith established the logical foundation for his work by identifying what he thought was essential human nature. He developed an image of humans as materialistic, egoistic, selfish, and primarily motivated by the pursuit of their own self-interest. As an example of his arguments, Smith declared that

> . . . Man has almost constant occasion for the help of his brethern, and it is in vain for him to expect it from their benevolence only. He will be more likely to prevail if he can interest their self-love in his favor, and show them that it is for their own advantage to do for him what he requires of them . . .

[1] Adam Smith, *An Inquiry into the Nature and Causes of the Wealth of Nations* (New York: Random House [Modern Library]: 1965; orig. pub. 1776).

It is not from the benevolence of the butcher, the brewer, or the baker that we expect our dinner, but from their regard to their own interest.[2]

This was not a normative argument. Smith did not advocate these sorts of primal drives and instincts. He simply believed from his own observation that people were unavoidably driven by their own self-interest.

Given these assumptions about human nature, Smith then outlined what he regarded as the best economic social structure for directing these individual drives to an end that promotes general social welfare and national economic growth. Smith wanted to resolve the paradox that a nation of people in pursuit of their individual self-interest could behave in a way that allowed *all* to benefit mutually. The appropriate social structure, he argued, should include competitive markets and the private ownership of property.

In such a world, the producers who owned private productive property could advance themselves by making profits only if they provided to the public what the public desired to have. Public "votes" on what would be produced nationally were exercised in the marketplace. Socially desired goods and services were purchased at a price that allowed profits to accrue to the producer, but unwanted items went unsold, forcing the producer to pay a penalty. The presence of competition ensured that producers would strive to produce by using efficient means that involved low costs because consumers would buy from producers who sold at the lowest price. This drive for efficiency expedited the implementation of new technologies, which, in turn, caused national wealth to grow.

With this social arrangement, the paradox is resolved. Each producer "neither intends to promote the public interest, nor knows how much he is promoting it." Instead, "he intends only his own gain, and he is in this, . . . , led by an invisible hand to promote an end which was no part his intention."[3]

Adam Smith's "invisible hand" excited the intellectual world of the early nineteenth century.[4] His logical system provided fuel for the intense political effort to overthrow all feudal remnants and replace them with modern capitalist institutions in Europe and elsewhere.

Not all were convinced by Smith's logic, however. Many, such as the Socialist critics, saw misery in the place of harmony. A market system, they argued, would preserve and promote a severe inequality of wealth. The dispassionate producers described by Adam Smith would instead be powerful exploiters, using their wealth and political power to suppress wages, isolate workers, and ensure that their class privileges were inaccessible to the multitude of laboring poor.[5]

The possibility of another fundamental economic problem was recognized by some critics of Smith. They asked, "Would such a system be prone to crisis?" What would happen if producers simply produced too much for the market—if the demand for produced goods was insufficient? The answer, they feared, would be a general economic breakdown, replete with

---

[2] *Ibid.*, p. 14.
[3] *Ibid.*, p. 423.
[4] Moreover, his work is much richer and more flexible than our brief exposition could indicate. See E. K. Hunt, *History of Economic Thought, A Critical Perspective* (Belmont, Calif.: Wadsworth, 1979), chap. 3.
[5] See, *ibid.*, chap. 7.

high unemployment, financial distress, and ruination. The theoretical answer to these many fears, which denies their validity, is referred to as Say's law.

In the sections that follow, both the criticisms that argue that economic breakdown is possible in market economies and the rebuttal, Say's law, will be presented. In a discussion of this controversy, it is appropriate to start with an early intellectual group that feared occasional disruption in the economy. This group is called the Physiocrats.

THE PHYSIOCRATS

The Physiocrats[6] were a group of French social reformers who wrote in the eighteenth century. Their ideas substantially influenced Adam Smith and the nineteenth-century classical economists. Few economists in the classical era wrote their opinions without giving some credit to the Physiocrats for their useful ideas.

Motivated by scientific studies that discovered the flow of blood through the body, the Physiocrats began to perceive the French economy as a sort of organic social mechanism characterized by a circular flow of goods and services in one direction and by money payments in the other. In 1758, François Quesnay illustrated this circular flow in his famous *Tableau Economique.* A collaborator, Marquis de Mirabeau, popularized Quesnay's contribution shortly thereafter.[7] Quesnay divided society into industrial and agricultural classes. He felt that if an insufficient percentage of all revenues did not flow to the agricultural class, the economy would atrophy.

This belief came from the notion that any increase in economic net output (production beyond base production requirements) could occur only in the agricultural sector. To intellectuals living in a backward agricultural country, it was obvious that in farming you could extract far more output than the amount of input used in production. For example, if you sowed 10 bushels of grain, you might harvest 50. Hence agriculture was obviously very productive.

In manufacturing, on the other hand, the case was less clear. In manufacturing, natural resources did not reproduce themselves "in kind" (there is no way to sow a shoe and reap three shoes). Instead, resources were transformed into something qualitatively different. Wood became a house, or iron became a cannon. The Physiocrats could not see how this expanded net output. As far as they were concerned, what was being put in was identical to what was coming out—it was merely altered in appearance and use. Their logical error was later exposed by the development of labor and utility theories of value.

Given, however, that the Physiocrats held this point of view, they argued that if consumption expenditures on products from the agricultural sector diminished below a certain level, then the strength and vitality of the *entire* economy would suffer. Only the agricultural sector promoted economic growth.[8] If funds to this sector were inadequate, then the sector could

---

[6]Cf. Joseph J. Spengler, "The Physiocrats and Say's Law of Markets," *The Journal of Political Economy* 53 (1945), pp. 25–46.

[7]Cf. Ronald L. Meek, ed., *The Precursers of Adam Smith* (London: Dent, 1973). Quesnay's *Tableau* is reproduced on p. 124.

[8]See *ibid.,* p. 321.

not employ the resources (including new technology) that would allow for the expansion of economic output. To use their own analogy of the human body, if the flow of blood is restricted to the foot, the body might survive, but the entire organism might be crippled.

MALTHUS'S THEORY OF GLUTS

A very influential criticism of Smith's argument was developed by Thomas Robert Malthus.[9] Malthus, remembered historically for his controversial *Essay on the Principle of Population,* was a respected and influential political economist in the classical era. His principal economic work, *Principles of Political Economy,*[10] was published in 1820.

In the history of ideas, Malthus provides a sort of a bridge between the naive reasoning of the Physiocrats and the refined analysis of John Maynard Keynes. (Keynes is discussed at length in Chapter 5.) Malthus believed, in opposition to Smith, that there could be too much saving. Malthus argued that there is a limit to how much capital can be profitably invested at a given time with given technology. If the level of savings exceeds that amount, then some saved funds will not be lent because there will be no ready borrowers. These funds, therefore, are not spent and fall from circulation. The payments flow in the economy is disrupted, and the economy suffers. Furthermore, fully anticipating one of the fundamental arguments of John M. Keynes a century later, Malthus believed that the level of economic activity was determined by the level of demand: "General wealth, like particular portions of it, will always follow effectual demand."[11]

Like the Physiocrats, Malthus used class divisions in society to provide insights into patterns of spending behavior. Malthus divided society into three classes: landlords, laborers, and capitalists. These three classes earned rents, wages, and profits respectively. The spending patterns of these three classes varied. Because workers were so destitute, they tended to spend all their income for the consumption of goods and services. Landlords were prodigals, spending a good part of their rental income on luxuries and servants, providing direct employment for large numbers of people. Malthus approved of this:

> It is also very important to observe, that menial servants are absolutely necessary to make the resources of the higher and middle classes of society efficient in the demand for material products. No persons possessing incomes above five hundred pounds a year, would be inclined to have such houses, furniture, clothes, carriages and horses, and such eatables and drinkables in their houses as they have at present, if they were obliged to sweep their own rooms, brush and wash their own furniture and clothes, clean their own carriage and horses, and had none but themselves to make a demand for eatables and drinkables.[12]

Capitalists, on the other hand, were very niggardly. Driven by an insatiable desire to accumulate wealth, they spent little for consumption and saved a great deal:

---
[9]The explanation that follows of Malthus's theory of gluts drew heavily from E. K. Hunt, *op. cit.,* pp. 74–79.
[10]Thomas R. Malthus, *Principles of Political Economy* (New York: Kelley, 1968; orig. pub. 1820).
[11]*Ibid.,* p. 363.
[12]*Ibid.,* p. 408.

> The great object of their [capitalists'] lives is to save a fortune, both because it is their duty to make a provision for their families, and because they cannot spend an income with so much comfort to themselves, while they are obliged perhaps to attend a counting-house for seven or eight hours a day.[13]

This propensity to save on the part of capitalists was the origin of occasional problems in the economy, Malthus thought. When profits were high, a sizable income flowed to the capitalist class, which guaranteed a high level of savings. Capitalists, through investment, would try to convert these savings to demand for physical capital, but eventually there would be obstacles to this effort.

First, if technology did not change, their new machines financed by investment could not be productively employed unless a growing labor force could use them. The labor force, however, was restricted by population growth. To put this another way, with a given technology, the ratio of capital to labor (K/L) used in production was fixed. If the labor force grows at some rate, this fixes the maximum growth rate for employable capital. If a high rate of savings were capable of financing a growth rate in capital in excess of this maximum, then a general glut would appear in the economy. Since no additional capital could be productively employed, savings had no outlet, and *effectual demand* would atrophy, causing a slump in the economy.

Second, Malthus argued, if new technologies allow capital to *replace* labor, then some labor will be unemployed (having been replaced by machines). Although this might lower costs for the producer, some part of the labor force would lose their income and consequently reduce their spending, again reducing effectual demand and again causing economic distress.

SAY'S LAW

As mentioned before, the intellectual response to these theoretical arguments about possible defects in capitalism falls under the rubric "Say's Law." Most classical economists endorsed the harmony of Smith's "invisible hand," and they felt compelled to defend the ideal against attacks that suggested the system was flawed.

In England, the people most responsible for popularizing Say's law were a small group of political economists associated with the famous English economist David Ricardo. This brilliant man was the leading exponent of British classical liberalism, the set of political and economic ideas that gave sanctity to proposals for a world based upon free trade.

Ricardo's circle included J. R. McCulloch, James Mill, and Jane Marcet. Marcet's publications were quite popular, and she was probably the person most responsible for promoting popular acceptance of Say's law. According to some scholars, on certain grounds it might even be argued that James Mill *originated* Say's law.[14] J. B. Say himself wrote some of the seminal components of this law in the 1803 edition of his *Traité*. It was the much-revised second edition of his manuscript, published in 1819, that contained a comprehensive theory.

---

[13]*Ibid.,* p. 400.
[14]Cf. Spengler, *op. cit.*

Six years before, in a book entitled *Commerce Defended,* James Mill basically asserted what is now regarded as Say's law. According to Mill, there was no possibility of inadequate demand for all goods in an economy either because of underinvestment or underconsumption.

The classical formulation of Say's law states that *supply calls forth its own demand*. In other words, according to Mill, the act of production itself creates a level of income sufficient to purchase all that has been produced. The sum of all rents, wages, and profits will equal the value of all production and will be used to buy that production. The aggregate value of income payments is identical to the value of all things produced for sale, so the income is sufficient to demand all that is supplied. Therefore, no matter how much could be produced at full employment, market forces ensured that all labor resources available for use would be employed.

Say himself had argued that an excess of a single product might be produced, but markets would correct that short-run difficulty. Such maladjustments were sure to be corrected as soon as competition could force capital to switch from one industry to another. In a typical statement, Ricardo argued, "Too much of a particular commodity may be produced, of which there may be said to be such a glut in the market as not to repay the capital expended on it; but this cannot be the case with all commodities."[15] Savings will always find an outlet as investment because people will not forgo the yield offered by investment. Say essentially asserted that there are always abundant opportunities for investment.

Say's method of analysis was far more consistent with mainstream classical analysis than that of the renegade Malthus. Malthus had continued the Physiocrats' tradition of using an analysis of the different spending habits of different classes to derive his theory of crisis. Say, in contrast, continued the Smithian tradition of regarding the economy as an aggregate of atomistic individuals who were recipients of income and simultaneously consumers and savers.

Both Say and Mill thought that a high level of savings was healthy and desirable for an economy and could present no problems. Both rejected the use of the analysis of the spending habits of different classes. Most importantly, the logic of their argument is *that the level of production determines the level of demand.* This is in direct contrast to the Physiocratic-Malthusian proposition that the distribution of income between classes determines the pattern of consumption and the level of demand, which, in turn, determines the level of production.

The Refinement of Say's Law

The kernel of truth in Say's law is the platitude that every purchase constitutes a sale and that every sale means some money income to someone, which may be used for more purchases. Ricardo wrote: "No man produces but with a view to consume or sell, and he never sells but with an intention to purchase some other commodity which may be useful to him or which may contribute to future production. By purchasing them, he necessarily becomes

---

[15]David Ricardo, *The Principles of Political Economy and Taxation* (London: Gonner, Bell and Sons, 1891), p. 276.

either the consumer of his own goods, or the purchaser and consumer of the goods of some other person."[16]

David Ricardo correctly claimed that what today might be referred to as "Say's identity" was valid: the value of production will always equal the value of income.[17] But Say's law, in its denial of theories of crisis, claims more than that. Say's *identity* might hold for an economy with a 50 percent unemployment rate. Say's *law* claims that supplying the market through production creates an equal income *and* that income causes an equal demand. Therefore, there is sufficient demand at full employment, so there can be *no* involuntary unemployment.

As economists gradually refined Say's law, it became more apparent that the key to supporting this logical argument was emphasis on the role played by *flexible prices and interest rates.* The key to Malthus's argument was that he assumed implicitly the generalization that prices and interest rates do not adjust to changes in consumption patterns, new technologies, variations in the capital stock, and changing perceptions about the opportunities for gains from the employment of capital. Malthus was describing a system that was unrealistically inflexible in defiance of Smith's unrealistically fluid and ever-adjusting markets.

Gradual refinements in theory by later economists like J. S. Mill, Alfred Marshall, the marginalists (e.g., Jevons and Walras), and the monetary theorists allowed Say's law to be developed into a logically intact comprehensive package, stressing the role played by flexible prices and interest rates. In the more refined theory, this flexibility automatically adjusts demand to supply, with the result that full employment is the natural state of the economy (though external shocks may temporarily disrupt it).

Critique and Defense of Say's Law

The critics have not relented in their attacks on Say's law. Their ideas have also transcended the inadequacies of Malthus's argument. There have been institutionalist demonstrations—by economists like Thorstein Veblen and Wesley Mitchell—that the abstract formulation of Say's law ignores the historically specific institutions of capitalism that cause deficient demand. These criticisms are developed in the next chapter.

Then, after a chapter developing the national accounting framework of analytic categories, Chapter 4 offers the fully developed defense of Say's law. This model is stated in modern categories, but it is based on the classical view of Say's law with a number of neoclassical refinements. This model of the economy attempts to demonstrate that involuntary unemployment is impossible because at any level of supply—including the full employment level of supply—flexible prices and interest rates allow demand to adjust to that level.

One of the earliest critics of Say's law was Marx; Marx retained and refined the analysis of the different incomes and spending habits of different classes. John Maynard Keynes exploded the controversy wide open again with his brilliant attack upon the principles inherent in Say's law during the Great Depression of the 1930s. The criticisms by Keynes

---

[16] *Ibid.,* p. 273.
[17] Cf. Mark Blaug, *Economic Theory in Retrospect* (Homewood, Ill.: Irwin, 1968), chap. 5, p. 113.

are given in a complete analytic model in Chapter 5, followed by the analytic framework of Marx. These models, showing the weaknesses of Say's law, also set the stage for the development of most of the Keynesian and Marxist theories in the rest of the book.

From the time that Keynes wrote through the 1940s, 1950s, and 1960s, most economics textbooks began their macroeconomic exposition with an explanation of the fallacies of Say's law. It became so commonplace and accepted that it would seen odd to spend as much time on it as we do here. This is very necessary, however, because Say's law has been revived in the last 10 or 15 years as a major weapon of a resurgent conservative economics. Both Milton Friedman's monetarist school and the modern adventure into *supply-side economics* make Say's law a major building block. It is the rock on which these economists build, and its strength or weakness is vital to an evaluation of these schools.

The extraordinary upsurge in monetarist and supply-side economics is reflected in the fact that many macroeconomics books now imply the correctness of Say's law, though in a very much refined and sophisticated version. This is evident from the fact that modern economic texts—for the same reasons that Adam Smith did—primarily look at the functioning of an equilibrium economic mechanism and the long-term trends of a stable, growing economy. Given the acceptance of Say's law, there can be no such thing as a business cycle of boom and bust structurally inherent in the capitalist economy. Therefore, they treat the business cycle, if at all, in a few pages. When explaining unemployment or inflation, they do not examine inherent, institutional reasons for excess or deficient demand (such as Keynes examined), but rather look at external shocks to a well-functioning private enterprise economy. The monetarists, of course, perceive the main barrier to smooth progress to be the monetary policy of the government, which they believe has been more harmful than helpful. Other conservative theories will emphasize external barriers to smooth progress, such as the power of labor unions or the power of Arab oil kingdoms and the Organization of Petroleum Exporting Countries (OPEC) cartel.

Even some of those who claim to be descendents of Keynes, such as the neo-Keynesians in the United States, tend to present arguments quite similar to the monetarist and supply-side views, even though they differ on specific policy mechanisms. As Paul Samuelson announced some years ago, there is a grand synthesis in the United States of neoclassical and neo-Keynesian theory. When neo-Keynesian economics dominated theory, the neo-Keynesians believed that government must intervene to correct some problems (also usually caused by external shocks, such as war or Arab oil cartels or Soviet grain purchases). Government actions, however, would be swift and easy to design, so the economy would then perform exactly as Adam Smith had expected. In this dominant view, Say's law operates with a little help from the government. The monetarists, on the other hand, see Say's law always operating except when government takes a wrong step. The result is that in the books written by both schools in the United States, the focus is on an economy operating in equilibrium or in stable growth. The problems of the economy are seen as brief, externally caused, and easy to correct. These books assume stability as the norm whereas fluctuations are an exception. The emphasis is then on the proper stabilization policies for an economy that tends to be self-correcting, but may need a little help in the very short run.

On the contrary, almost all Post Keynesians (such as Joan Robinson), institutionalists (such as Wesley Mitchell), and Marxists (such as Michal Kalecki) see the institutions of capitalism themselves leading to recessions and depressions, as well as to inflation. The investigation of these internal mechanisms of the system, which lead to our major problems of inflation and involuntary unemployment (declared impossible by Say's law), is central to the work of these schools of thought. The Post Keynesians assert that John Maynard Keynes also agrees with their position. Exactly contrary to the monetarists, the Post Keynesians and other critical theorists would even insist that the money supply itself is *endogenously*—that is, internally—determined (an issue that we will investigate in great detail).

Therefore, the focus of this book is *not* stability or equilibrium growth, but the fluctuations of the capitalist economy known as business cycles. We believe that the most important features of macroeconomic reality are these recurrent bouts of large-scale involuntary unemployment plus a long-run, structurally determined trend toward inflation. These features are the norm, and stability is the exception. This book will examine stabilization policy in the context of this stop-go economy. In the presentation, the full range of opinions will be presented, from the dominant conservative theories to the liberal and radical alternative theories.

Chapter 2

THE HISTORICAL-INSTITUTIONAL CRITIQUE OF SAY'S LAW

The classical and neoclassical economists typically formulate Say's law in an ahistorical manner, good for all times and places. If there is economic production of any amount of supply, an income is generated to those who produce it, and that income becomes a demand to buy the supply. But there are actually some hidden assumptions about institutional arrangements. It often sounds as if they are discussing simpler, precapitalist arrangements—and some of the classical and early neoclassical economists had a preference for discussing a Robinson Crusoe economy.

Say's law would apply to Robinson Crusoe's economy, in which a few individuals produced for their own direct use and there was no money and no exchange. Say's law also applies to a large degree, as we shall see in detail, to most earlier precapitalist economies. For various reasons, as feudal economy may have poverty, unemployment for a long period of time, and vast amounts of human misery, but neither Robinson Crusoe nor feudal economies have problems that are traceable to a lack of effective demand.

When the isolated manorial estates of feudalism are replaced by highly integrated private enterprise economies, however, these capitalist economies have three features that are relevant to the issue posed here:

1. Production for a market.
2. The regular use of money in the market.
3. Production for private profit.

Chapter 2 THE HISTORICAL-INSTITUTIONAL CRITIQUE OF SAY'S LAW

These three institutional features introduce the possibility of deficient aggregate demand and the possibility of large-scale involuntary unemployment, which invalidates Say's law.

PRODUCTION FOR THE MARKET

It was characteristic of the private enterprise economy that was fully developed in England by the end of the eighteenth century that most production was solely directed toward its sale on the market. This was hardly ever true of earlier societies. In the most primitive societies, almost all productive activity was directed to production of food by mere gathering or growing of fruit and vegetables or hunting of animals by the collective unit of all the males and/or females of the tribe. Naturally, the produce was usually consumed in roughly equal proportions by these same tribal members or their families. Even at a later stage (characterized by agriculture and herding), production was for use, not sale; none of the Indian tribes of the Americas, not even the Aztecs, bought or sold land or produced crops to sell for a profit to others. In fact:

> For the red man soil existed only in order to meet the necessities of life, and production, not profit, was the basis of his economy . . . Unemployment was certainly never a problem in the Indian communities of early America.[1]

Since there was little division of labor within the tribe, there was little, if any, trade among its members. In fact, very little commerce was transacted between the most primitive tribes, and that "was virtually restricted to materials small in bulk and precious for their decorative or magical qualities."[2] Even a relatively more advanced society such as the Inca Empire of South America still was based on a self-sufficient economic unit consisting of a few families, called the *ayllu,* whose only external economic relation was the work-service tax owed to the state and paid in agricultural produce or work on government projects.[3] In fact, all over the world for thousands of years almost all economic systems—whether tribal or feudal—were based on relatively self-sufficient agricultural units.

In the Roman Empire there was a great deal of trade, but most of it was in luxury goods[4] and did not affect the self-sufficiency of the basic agricultural unit, the slave-run plantation (though a lack of surplus could bring starvation to large numbers of city dwellers). As one author says:

> . . . notwithstanding the phenomenal expansion of trade and industry the vast masses inside the Empire still continued to win their livelihood from the soil. Agriculture remained throughout antiquity the most usual and most typical economic activity, and land the most important form of wealth.[5]

---

[1] John A. Crow, *The Epic of Latin America* (Garden City, N.Y.: Doubleday, 1948), p. 54.
[2] Grahame Clark, *From Savagery to Civilization* (London: Cobbett Press, 1946), p. 96.
[3] See Crow, *op. cit.,* pp 26–29.
[4] See the brief account in F. W. Walbank, *The Decline of the Roman Empire in the West* (London: Cobbett Press, 1956), pp. 11–13.
[5] *Ibid.,* p. 18.

Rome did have unemployment among the urban proletariat, most of whom were former peasants forced off the land by the competition of slavery. This was a long-run phenomenon caused by the complete lack of mass markets, not a cyclical breakdown of the market.

Feudal England lacked both extensive trade and towns because the primitive level of technology made impossible the supply of large urban populations and even greatly restricted trade between the villages. As a result, in the England of that day

> Towns developed slowly; each group of burgesses solved their local problems on their own initiative and in their own time. Even in 1377 not much more than eight percent of the population were townsmen, and only a minority of these had independent dealings with continental markets.[6]

Of course, in the later medieval period there were areas of more highly developed industrial production, such as Flanders and northern Italy, and even relatively backward England carried on a systematic wool trade with Flanders. Yet these were exceptions to the general rule of the feudal economy and may be considered early signs pointing to the beginning of the end of that economy.

During the Middle Ages market institutions as we know them today were not well developed. If there happened to be surplus production from the slave or feudal estate, then it might be marketed in return for foreign luxury items for the lord of the estate, but it was not a matter of life and death for the economic unit. If the surplus found no market, the manor was still supplied with its necessities for that year and could and would continue the process of production for next year's needs.

What could disturb such economically self-sufficient societies were only those catastrophes that were more or less "external" to the economy, namely, the vicissitudes of nature (such as droughts, plagues, or floods) or the whims of human beings (such as government interference, war, or revolution). These phenomena could and did depress production (and bring about famines) both in various randomly spaced intervals and seasonally because of the special seasonal sensitivity of agriculture. Such economies could not, however, conceivably face the problem of lack of effective demand for all commodities, which is a serious frequent problem in market economics. The problem of lack of demand could not exist because the economic unit directly consumed most of the products of its own land and could do without trade altogether.

In the transitional period, in the England of the sixteenth, seventeenth, and eighteenth centuries, the majority of the people still lived on the land; but more and more products, both agricultural and industrial, were delivered to the marketplace. There was increasing long-run unemployment in this period because peasants were removed from agricultural production much more rapidly than employment grew in capitalist industry—but the unemployment was not cyclical.

By the end of the eighteenth century, the private enterprise system of production for the market embraced most of the economic activity. Production of commodities for the market was no longer a matter of accident as it had been, but was one of the most essential features of the private enterprise system. In the nineteenth century, one business entrepreneur might

---

[6]Marion Gibbs, *Feudal Order* (London: Cobbett Press, 1949), pp. 7–8.

own a factory producing millions of shoes, but the whole family of the entrepreneur could consume only a few of these. The shoes had to be sold in order to buy other consumer goods for the entrepreneur's family, to pay wages to those working for the business, and to replace and expand the plant and equipment of the business.

In earlier economic systems, the self-sufficient economic unit—or the artisan producing a trickle of handmade items for known customers—could not possibly be troubled by lack of demand for its products. When almost all that was produced by the economic unit was consumed by it, lack of demand was not going to be a problem. But in the industrialized private enterprise system, the specialized business person produces only for the market and cannot continue production if there is no demand for his or her products in the market. This, then, is the first main institutional feature of the private enterprise economy of the late eighteenth century. It was one of three conditions making possible the beginning of large-scale, cyclical unemployment at that time.

REGULAR USE OF MONEY

A second institutional feature that is necessary before there can be a deficiency of aggregate demand is the regular use of money in exchange, which takes the place of the barter system of exchanging goods for goods. Many economists have concentrated on this as the sole necessary condition for the possibility of a lack of effective demand; but that is because they imply the first condition, production for exchange in the market, in the second condition, the regular use of money in exchange. The two conditions might be presented in a single formal statement, but it is analytically useful to separate them.

Among the most primitive tribes, where there is very little trade, exchange is conducted by barter. In slightly more advanced societies, though barter is still the only mode of exchange, certain commodities, such as cows or horses, may be used as "money" in the sense that the values of all other commodities are calculated in terms of them. Only when there is a large volume of trade will there begin to grow up a system more like that of the modern monetary economy, usually with a certain amount of the precious metals becoming the known equivalent of certain amounts of all other commodities. At a still later period, the metals are stamped into coins, originally with the purpose of more conveniently figuring amounts and facilitating the exchange of goods.

The use of money, however, brings many new complications onto the economic scene. In the Roman Empire, for example, vast amounts of money were needed by the government to support wars of expansion, large standing armies, police and bureaucracy, and an unfavorable balance of trade (owing to the importing of luxuries from the East). The emperors were eventually forced to the expedient of debasing their coins by clipping or by contamination with baser metals. As the government debased the coins and as production declined in the later days of the empire, the amount that could be bought with the coins declined rapidly; in other words, a catastrophic inflation occurred.[7]

---

[7] See Walbank, *op. cit.*, pp. 42–43, 51–52.

In spite of the Romans' financial troubles and difficulties in the use of money, they were *not* confronted with the modern problem of "too many" commodities in the market relative to the money demand for them. Regular use of money was *not* enough by itself to usher in the menace of a lack of aggregate demand so long as most of the Roman economy was still contained in self-sufficient agricultural units.[8] The luxury trade in the empire did suffer from the extreme inflation, but only as one more affliction in addition to colonial wars and slave revolts, the extreme inefficiency of employing slave labor, and the Roman citizen's attitude that any participation in the work process was degrading (because work was only for slaves). Moreover, since most of the people still lived on the land, the relatively small amount of trade and commerce that did exist was not absolutely necessary to the continued functioning of most of the economy. This is not to deny that trade was essential to the preservation of the empire as a political unit and for the existence of higher culture in large urban centers, especially Rome. Rome was an importer of grain from Egypt and North Africa, as well as of wine and various fruits from Gaul, to mention only some of the more important imports. When this trade declined in the second century, the Roman cities suffered and also declined, but the agricultural units continued, though in new forms and on an even more self-sufficient basis.

With the breakup of the Roman Empire, trade suffered a considerable decline; in early feudalism the pattern was overwhelmingly that of the isolated, self-sufficient manor. Barter, therefore, grew in importance, and the use of money declined. On each manor, in return for the lord's "protection," the serf provided all the necessary articles of consumption and services needed by the lord, his family, and his retinue. In the later medieval period, however, technology began to improve, and industry and commerce slowly began to revive and reach new heights in Western Europe. The widespread trade of the later medieval period eventually led to the replacing of barter by a money economy; at the same time, as noted in the preceding section, production was increasingly designed for sale on the market rather than for use at home.

With the increased use of money, exchange in the market required the use of money as an intermediary. If the holder of money, for whatever reason, decided to hold it and abstain from using it for purchase, the demand for market commodities was lower than it otherwise would have been. Some goods availble for sale on the market would remain unsold.

Early classical economists denied that the introduction of money into exchange could cause problems. For example, David Ricardo contended that "productions are always bought by productions, or by services; money is only the medium by which the exchange is effected."[9] It is true that one function of money is to facilitate the exchange of commodities, but it has other uses as well. *In the modern economy the seller obtains only money for commodities, which money the seller may or may not use at a later time to buy other commodities;* in the meantime, money may be used for the storage of value for future use. It is thus possible for a person to buy or sell without doing the opposite action at the same time. It is not always the case that all buyers will immediately use their money to buy what they want. There is,

---

[8]See *ibid.,* p. 18.
[9]David Ricardo, *The Principles of Political Economy and Taxation* (London: Gonner, Bell and Sons, 1891 ed.), p. 275.

Chapter 2 THE HISTORICAL-INSTITUTIONAL CRITIQUE OF SAY'S LAW

therefore, no inherent necessity in a money economy that sellers should find buyers for all commodities brought to market.

The problem is not an aggregate lack of money in the economy. While the poor, who wish to buy goods, have no money; the rich, who have money, may be reducing their spending. The chain of circulation may then be broken at any point at which the flow of money is slowed in its movement. The reduction of the flow of circulation, like the reduction of the volume of water flowing in a stream, causes a slowdown in the movement of products by this means. Although it is basically true that commodities exchange for commodities even after the introduction of money, the mere necessity of the money bridge makes all the difference in the world. If the bridge is absent, finished commodities may pile up in warehouses while potential consumers are unable to buy them. Only money can make a possible consumer into an actual buyer in the private enterprise system. Thus, the use of money makes possible the lack of aggregate effective or monetary demand for commodities, so it is a precondition of the business cycle.

An *excess* of supply in this economic system does not mean that everyone is fully satisfied. In every recession or depression there are millions of poor people who would be happy to have more goods and services. Therefore, the problem is not overproduction of the total commodities of a society in the absolute sense that the supply is greater than what people want or desire; rather the problem is that there may be "too many" commodities on the market *relative* to the monetary or "effective" demand for them. The term *effective demand* simply means desire combined with money because desire or need without money has no effect under capitalism.

An additional problem in the sphere of money may arise from the use of tokens or paper money. The government may always cause some degree of inflation by merely starting its printing presses turning out more paper money. The economies of Europe, for example, were brought to their knees by the spectacular collapse of the French and English finance markets in the early eighteenth century. Excessive printing of paper money by these two governments resulted in a wild speculation in financial securities. The ensuing collapse destroyed numerous fortunes, escalated unemployment, and caused economic distress for nearly a decade.

An additional complication arises from the fact that money may merely be used as a unit of account for indebtedness—that is, in the form of credit. The use of credit intensifies all money problems because not only may a person sell something and not immediately purchase something else, but it is also possible to sell something and not recieve the proceeds of the sale for some time. If Brown owes Smith, and Smith owes Johnson, and Johnson owes Martin, then a break anywhere along this chain of credit circulation will be disastrous for all the later parties in the chain. Moreover, the chain in the modern private enterprise economy is usually circular in nature, so that the reverberations reach the starting point and may begin to go around again. This does not, of course, explain why the chain should ever break in the first place.

It has been argued here that no problem of deficient effective demand was possible before money and credit institutions became the usual way of doing business. Does this mean that these institutions are sufficient to explain recessions and depressions? We know that money and credit existed in ancient Rome and in the sixteenth to eighteenth centuries in Western Europe, yet the financial disturbances of those times do not seem to have been the same phenomena as the modern type of economic downturn. It is true that after the development of money and credit, every catastrophic natural happening or violent political event might be reflected in a sudden distrust of monetary institutions and a panic in the financial markets. For example, when the English fleet was burned by the Dutch in 1667 and also when in 1672 Charles II stopped payments from the Exchequer, there were sudden runs on the London banks. In the eighteenth century, financial crises resulted from the Jacobite conspiracy in 1708, the bursting of the South Sea Bubble (a stock speculation) in 1720, the fighting with the Young Pretender in 1745, the aftermath of the Seven Years War in 1763, and the disturbances caused by the American revolutionary war.[10]

Wesley Mitchell comments, however, that these panics were unlike the modern business contractions both in cause and effect. First, they originated in "external" causes rather than in the endogenous mechanism that operates (as we shall see) under capitalism. Second, they resulted in only limited depressions in a few trades. He concludes that the first truly general industrial depression of the modern type appeared as late as 1793 in England.[11]

Distress in the financial sector has been a key causal factor in most depressions, but that is not always the case. Usually, the more serious downturns have involved one form of financial catastrophe or another. The contribution of the financial sector to economic distress will be reviewed in later chapters.

PRODUCTION FOR PRIVATE PROFIT

Two necessary conditions have been examined—(1) production for the market and (2) the regular use of money—which must be present if a business contraction occurs in which demand fluctuates below the full employment level of supply. Yet at least one more institutional condition is necessary before it can be said that a downturn may be caused by the fact that total demand is not equal to total supply in an economy. The third condition is the existence of private ownership of production facilities and production for private profit.

In an economy based on private ownership of individual competing units, the sum of their decisions to produce may not equal the sum of decisions by other individuals and businesses to spend—that is, to consume and invest. If the sum of the value of outputs is greater than the sum of the monetary or effective demand, then there is not enough revenue to cover the costs of production and an additional profit for the private entrepreneur. This criterion is decisive because if the private entrepreneur is not making a profit, the entrepreneur will reduce or discontinue production, machinery will stand idle, and many, if not all, of the workers of that enterprise will be unemployed.

No economists ever spent more time discussing the profit motive as the central motivation for all production than did the classical economists. Yet, except in the case of Malthus, the fact that production might prove unprofitable does not often seem to have entered their discussions of business declines; therefore, they reached the conclusion of the impossibility

---

[10]See the discussion of all these events in W. C. Mitchell, *Business Cycles* (Berkeley: University of California Press, 1913), pp. 583–584.
[11]*Ibid.*

of a contraction caused by lack of profitability in the private enterprise system. Actually, the possibility always exists that the production of commodities may outpace the demand for commodities *at a price sufficient to cover costs and also yield a profit.*

CONCLUSION: THE THREE CONDITIONS OF OVERPRODUCTION

In summary, Say's law—that aggregate demand will always come to equal aggregate supply—will indeed hold true in an economy of self-sufficient economic units or in a nonmonetary economy or in an economy that is not run for private profit. It is difficult to disentangle these elements completely in any given historical situation, yet it does seem that all three of these institutional features must be present for the modern type of business contraction to appear. For example, even with the regular use of money, the problem of lack of aggregate demand did not become crucial in the ancient Roman economy with its self-sufficient agrarian units. On the other hand, it is *possible* to have deficient aggregate demand and general unemployment in any economy where production is undertaken (1) for exchange in the market, (2) through the intermediary of a monetary unit, *and* (3) for the purpose of making private profit for the individual enterprise. But these necessary conditions for the *possibility* of deficient demand and involuntary unemployment have not been demonstrated to be sufficient to explain the actual occurrence of these phenomena.

CAPITALISM AND THE BUSINESS CYCLE

In precapitalist societies there were economic depressions, but these resulted from natural phenomena or political conflicts affecting supplies. Under modern capitalism, it will be shown, there is a recurring business cycle of expansion followed by recession or depression—and this cycle has endogenous (that is, internally generated) causes. Before we go further, it is necessary to define the terms *capitalism, recession, depression,* and *business cycles.*

Capitalism is an economic system in which raw materials, plant, and equipment—called physical capital and bought with money capital—are owned by a relatively small number of private individuals. These capitalists hire for wages a large class of workers, who own no capital (or negligible capital), to do the actual work of production. The capitalists own the product. They sell the product in the market in exchange for money. This amount of money (based on the value of the product produced by the workers) is normally higher than their costs of production, so the difference is pocketed as the capitalists' private profit.

A recession is a mild depression. The distinction is rather arbitrary. In both, production in the economy shrinks rather than rises for some period of time, such as two quarters. The unemployment rate also rises. If the unemployment rate is very high, say in excess of 10 percent, or there is a high number of bankruptcies, people begin to refer to the slump as a depression. To avoid repeating the phrase "recession or depression" every time, this text will usually use the neutral word *contraction*. Similarly, to avoid the use of the loaded term *prosperity* (because not everyone is prosperous), a business upturn is described as an *expansion*.

The modern business cycle may be defined as the recurrent expansion and contraction of economic activity. The business cycle is located primarily in industry rather than in agriculture, and the contraction is characterized by a lack of profitability in almost all areas of industry at once. Arthur Burns and Wesley Mitchell, in their extensive discussion of business cycles, define the cycle as follows:

> Business cycles are a type of fluctuation found in the aggregate economic activity of nations that organize their work mainly in business enterprises: a cycle consists of expansions occurring at about the same time in many economic activities, followed by similarly general . . . contractions . . . this sequence of changes is recurrent but not periodic . . .[12]

Burns observes that the problem of business cycles is "inseparable from the problem of how a capitalist economy functions."[13] And Mitchell argues thus:

> . . . the total number of past business cycles may well be less than a thousand. For business cycles are phenomena peculiar to a certain form of economic organization which has been dominant even in Western Europe for less than two centuries, and for briefer periods in other regions.[14]

Clearly, Mitchell believes that the business cycle has endogenous causes within the capitalist system.

The internally generated business cycle appears to have made its first appearance in England—and then only at the end of the eighteenth century. The periods of economic crisis before that time were easily attributable to external or purely political events. It does appear that the British business cycle of the nineteenth century was an indigenous product of British economic development. The vast British trading network, however, reached every other country in the world; therefore, in every other country the cycle must be partly a product of diffusion from England as well as of independent evolution. That does *not* mean, of course, that England has remained unaffected by the consequent development of other countries or that it is the country that is least influenced by present-day international events.

The business cycle is found in all capitalist countries, but the forms of the cycle are much influenced by international events and national peculiarities. There is a similar progression of cycle phases in country after country. Yet no two cycles are exactly the same; they differ in cause, duration, industrial scope, intensity, and importance of various aspects and also in how rapidly they spread from one country to another. The most highly developed industrial countries, such as England, France, and Germany, have closely linked and coincident cycles. In the nineteenth century, however, the less developed and mainly agricultural countries, such as czarist Russia, Brazil, and China, diverged quite considerably from the international pattern.[15]

---

[12] Wesley Clair Mitchell and Arthur F. Burns, *Measuring Business Cycles* (New York: National Bureau of Economic Research, 1946), p. 3.

[13] Arthur Burns, "Introduction" to W. C. Mitchell, *What Happens During Business Cycles* (New York: National Bureau of Economic Research, 1951), p. vii.

[14] W. C. Mitchell, *Business Annals* (New York: National Bureau of Economic Research, 1926), p. 47.

[15] Wesley C. Mitchell and W. L. Thorp, *Business Annals* (New York: National Bureau of Economic Research, 1926), p. 93.

Wesley Mitchell found that the modern business cycle began in England in 1793; in the United States in 1796 (influenced by England); in France in 1847; in Germany in 1857; and in 1888 to 1891 in czarist Russia, Argentina, Brazil, Canada, South Africa, Australia, India, Japan, and China. After 1890, the business cycle assumed a truly international character with regard to major cycles. It also seems significant that there are no records of recurrent cycles in the less developed countries prior to that period, for these countries were mainly agricultural and did *not* have the capitalist institutions specified in the three conditions discussed earlier. After 1890, when the European economies came to dominate the rest of the capitalist world through colonization, trade, and investment, the cycle became more and more pronounced in the less developed countries. In the 1929 crash, every country in the world felt the impact and went into a depression period (excepting only the USSR). Again, in 1938 most countries suffered a relapse together. In Western Europe and Japan, recessions in the United States did *not* cause major downturns in the 1950s and 1960s. In the downturn of 1973 to 1975, however, these countries joined the U.S. economic contraction—and again in the period 1980 to 1982 all these countries joined the United States in a decline.

Cycles in the U.S. Economy

When a country is in its early stages of industrial development, it is difficult to be independent of foreign influences. Likewise, when a country is small and unable to be self-sufficient, it is usually dependent on foreign supply and demand. In the beginning of the nineteenth century, the United States was both immature industrially and limited in its main centers of commerce and industry to the small area along its Atlantic coast. Therefore, the United States at that period was very susceptible to foreign influences in its economy, especially to the trade and investment of the United Kingdom. The basic direction of influence was surely from the rapidly developing industry of the United Kingdom outward to the less developed industry and commerce of the United States. When depressions developed in England, they often led to depressions in America because of the decline in British imports from America. In the few instances where the American decline began first, the reduction of British investment opportunities may have spread the depression to England.

Investment in the United States brought big profits, but had great risks attached to it and was subject to violent swings according to the decisions of foreign investors. All the other features of the U.S. economy also were typical of a less developed country, including the following characteristics of that period. Two-thirds or more of all U.S. produce was agricultural. Most enterprises, whether farm or handicraft, were one-person proprietorships. Much work was done at home, and shop windows were often merely that part of the home that fronted on the street. There were few urban wage workers because there were but few shops of more than one person (with perhaps an apprentice). Markets were limited to the local area. Most families in agriculture were completely self-sufficient. There were large unclaimed and unexplored areas. There was much barter, little use of money, and an undeveloped and inefficient banking system. By far the most important section of capital was engaged in commerce—and largely foreign commerce at that. Since it lacked the necessary conditions, the U.S. economy of the early period (at least until 1837) did not have internally generated cycles.[16]

In the period of 1837 to 1860, foreign influences were somewhat less important, and business cycles were partly the result of internal generation. If not dominant, however, foreign influences certainly played an often decisive part in U.S. development. For example, the British financial panic of 1847 led directly to the moderate U.S. depression of 1848.

The period from the Civil War to the end of the nineteenth century was the period in which the United States reached industrial maturity. By the end of that period the corporate form of business was predominant; only a sixth of all output was agricultural; agriculture itself was more commercial and market-directed; the factory system with thousands of workers replaced the small handicraft shops and the home production of almost all articles; the United States had a system of heavy industry, which was as complex and interrelated as any in the world; organized management faced a growing union movement; money had replaced barter in every aspect of the economy; markets were national or international in scope; the frontier had ended; and commerce provided only a small part of the national income. Since it now had the conditions of advanced capitalism, the U.S. economy generated its own cycles, but still interacted closely with Western European cycles.

In the United States in the twentieth century, foreign relations have dominated the domestic economy only in the major wars, the First World War, the Second World War, the Korean War, and the Vietnam War. Otherwise, domestic internal mechanisms have dominated the U.S. business cycle, though military spending and international trade and investment have obviously played a significant role. Major declines in the U.S. economy, such as the Great Depression of the 1930s or the severe recessions of 1975 and 1982, have severely hurt the rest of the world. The mild recessions that the U.S. economy undergoes every three or four years do not have a major effect on most of the world though they obviously hurt some specific trading partners. It should be noted that even "mild" recessions do increase human misery for millions of U.S. workers by involuntary idleness, drastic declines in income, and pessimism and alienation, which lead to higher rates of divorce, crime, and suicide.

Certainly, the most catastrophic economic event of the twentieth century has been the Great Depression. Actually, the Great Depression, which lasted from 1929 until World War II, consisted of two related depressions. The first and most awful phase of the depression began in late 1929 with the famous stock market crash of that year and ended in 1933 with a complete collapse of the nation's banking system. In between was a real estate market crash, a horrendous decline in national output, and a severe price deflation. National income fell 30 percent in those four years, causing unemployment to rise from 3.2 percent of the labor force to 24.9 percent. The number of unemployed workers swelled from 1.5 million to 12.8 million. Wholesale prices fell over 30 percent in the same period. Investment dropped an

---

[16]The material in this section has been culled from several standard texts, the best of which by far, with respect to data, is Maurice W. Lee, *Economic Fluctuations* (Homewood, Ill.: Irwin, 1955), pp. 109–240, 563–622; also see W. B. Smith and A. H. Cole, *Fluctuations in American Business, 1790–1860* (Cambridge, Mass.: Harvard University Press, 1935); with respect to analysis, some of the following sections rely heavily upon R. A. Gordon, *Business Fluctuations,* 3d ed. (New York: Harper & Row, 1961).

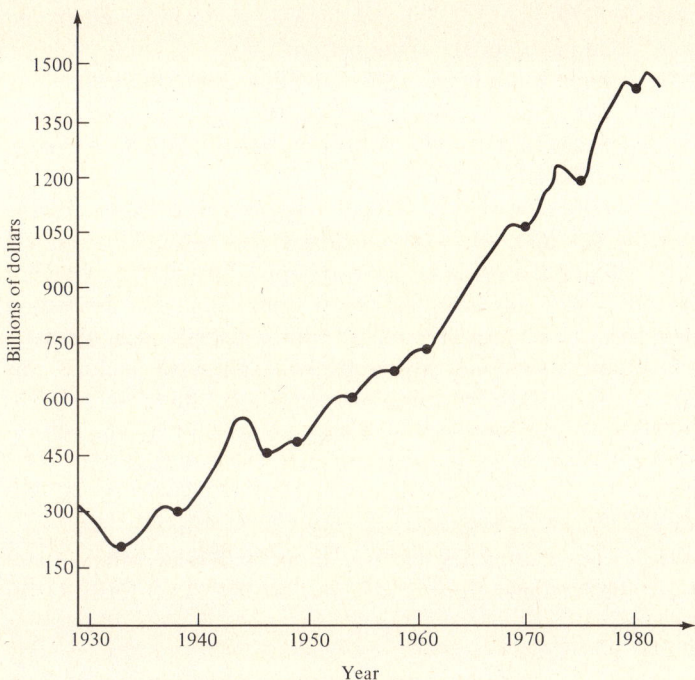

Figure 2.1 Gross National Product (GNP), 1929–1982, in Constant 1972 Dollars
NOTE: Dots represent troughs of business cycles.
SOURCE: U.S. Department of Commerce.

amazing 88 percent. Some key industries were devastated. Iron, lumber, and auto production fell 59 percent, 58 percent, and 65 percent respectively. Hardship was endemic.[17]

There was a sluggish recovery between 1933 and 1937 although the economy never even recovered to the level achieved in 1929 during this period, and unemployment remained high. A second slump began in 1937. A full recovery was not to be experienced until World War II and the resulting demand for military hardware finally restored the economy.

After the enormous expansion of the U.S. economy in World War II, the late 1940s, the 1950s, and the 1960s were characterized by moderate growth rates and four minor recessions. They were also characterized by two very large "limited" wars in Korea and Vietnam, which maintained a high level of military spending in the economy. The military spending led to a high rate of inflation in both wars. At the end of the Vietnam War, however, the inflation continued. It has continued ever since, increasing in expansions, but declining very slowly in contractions. In addition to continued inflation, the 1970s and early 1980s have been characterized by much lower growth rates, severe recessions, and higher rates of unemployment.

Figure 2.1 shows the performance of the real gross national product or GNP (economic

[17] A graphic description of the Great Depression is provided by Lester Chandler, *America's Greatest Depression, 1929–1941* (New York: Harper & Row, 1970). All statistics are from this book.

output adjusted for inflation) since 1929. Figure 2.2 shows the level of unemployment, and Figure 2.3 shows the consumer price index for the same period.

As can be seen, the Great Depression was a far more serious economic setback than any recession since. The 1950s and the 1960s were a time of relative stability—by most criteria these were the two most stable decades in the nation's history. Price inflation, however, became endemic by the end of the 1960s.

As the inflation accelerated into the 1970s, the contractions became more severe, and the modern phenomenon of *stagflation* (simultaneous high unemployment and inflation) made its appearance. The economy moved into the 1980s with the unhappy combination of record high inflation and the most severe contraction since the Great Depression. The depression of 1982 temporarily reduced inflation, but at the cost of 12 million unemployed, almost 2 million discouraged workers who gave up and no longer actively sought work, and millions more involuntarily reduced to part-time work. Among the unemployed, there were significantly higher rates of divorce, crime, physical and mental disease, and general human misery.

The Timing and Typing of Business Cycles

Most of the work on the timing of business cycles has been done by Wesley Mitchell and the research agency he created, the National Bureau of Economic Research (NBER). In

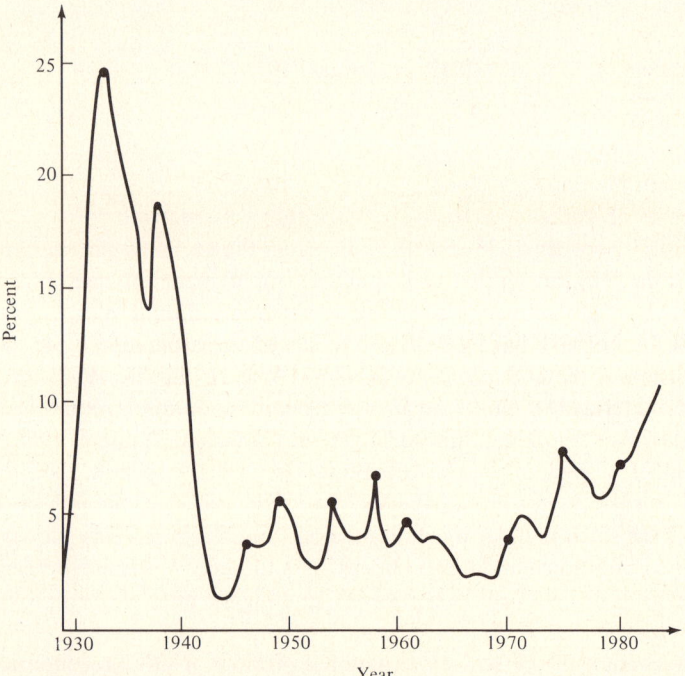

Figure 2.2 Unemployment as a Percent of the Labor Force, 1929–1982
NOTE: Dots represent troughs of business cycles.
SOURCE: U.S. Department of Commerce.

Chapter 2 The Historical-Institutional Critique of Say's Law

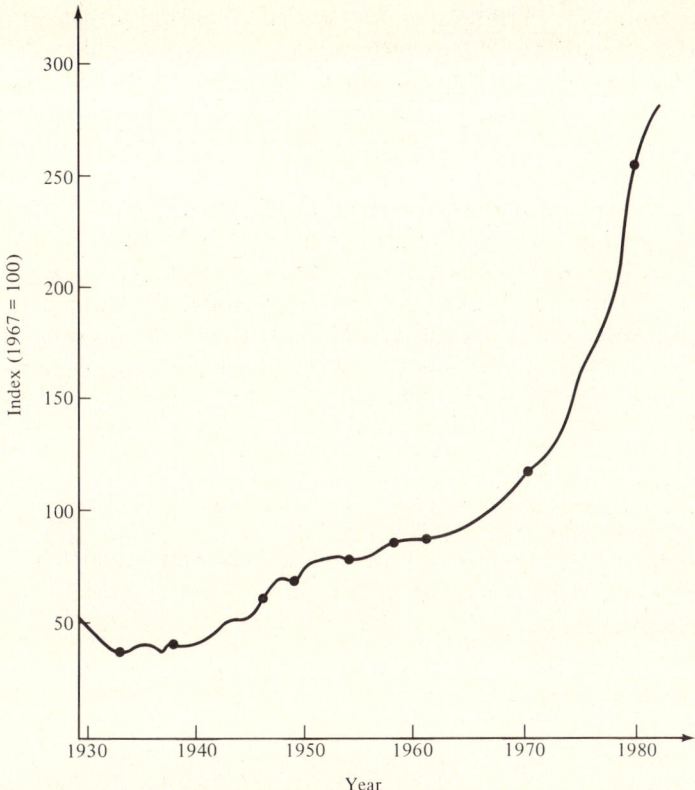

Figure 2.3 Consumer Price Index, 1929–1982
NOTE: Dots represent troughs of business cycles.
SOURCE: U.S. Department of Commerce.

accordance with his definition, Mitchell dates business cycles by the times when most business activity is at its lowest point (this is a *trough*) or its highest point (this is a *peak*). To do this, he examined hundreds of series, as well as the business news in many newspapers in earlier years. This procedure of dating cycles has continued to be practiced by the NBER. The U.S. Department of Commerce seems to accept the word of the NBER for when the U.S. economy is "officially" in an expansion or contraction. The NBER findings for cyclical expansions (from initial trough to peak) and contractions (from peak to final trough) are given in Table 2.1. The average contraction is one year and seven months. The average expansion in peacetime is two years and three months. The average wartime expansion is much longer: five years and four months.

There are some weaknesses in the present NBER dating method. Whereas Mitchell examined every scrap of available evidence, the NBER at present uses a more limited set of indicators. By its rough rule, a contraction is declared whenever the gross national product (GNP) declines for at least two quarters, and an expansion is declared whenever the GNP

Table 2.1

BUSINESS CYCLE EXPANSIONS AND CONTRACTIONS IN THE UNITED STATES, 1854 TO 1981

Business Cycle Reference Dates		Duration in Months	
		Contraction (from Peak to Trough)	Expansion (from Trough to Peak)
Trough	Peak		
December 1854	June 1857	(X)	30
December 1858	October 1860	18	22
June 1861	April 1865	8	<u>46</u>
December 1867	June 1869	32	18
December 1870	October 1873	18	34
March 1879	March 1882	65	36
May 1885	March 1887	38	22
April 1888	July 1890	13	27
May 1891	January 1893	10	20
June 1894	December 1895	17	18
June 1897	June 1899	18	24
December 1900	September 1902	18	21
August 1904	May 1907	23	33
June 1908	January 1910	13	19
January 1912	January 1913	24	12
December 1914	August 1918	23	<u>44</u>
March 1919	January 1920	7	10
July 1921	May 1923	18	22
July 1924	October 1926	14	27
November 1927	August 1929	13	21
March 1933	May 1937	43	50
June 1938	February 1945	13	<u>80</u>
October 1945	November 1948	8	37
October 1949	July 1953	11	<u>45</u>
May 1954	August 1957	10	39
April 1958	April 1960	8	24
February 1961	December 1969	10	<u>106</u>
November 1970	November 1973	11	36
March 1975	January 1980	16	58
July 1980	July 1981	6	12

NOTE: Underscored figures are the wartime expansions (Civil War, World War I, World War II, Korean War, and Vietnam War).
SOURCE: National Bureau of Economic Research, Inc., as reported in U.S. Department of Commerce, *Business Conditions Digest* (February 1982), p. 104.

rises for at least two quarters. Even with a sophisticated, weighted analysis of several indicators, any choice of a single date must be somewhat mechanical and arbitrary.

Another problem is that this timing procedure ignores the issue of whether there are really different types of cycles. Various economists have distinguished at least four main types of business cycle. First, there is the very long-run cycle of approximately 60 years, named for N. D. Kondratieff, the economist who first investigated this cycle. The idea that economic activity tends to rise for about 30 years and then fall for about 30 years is intriguing. It was first fully developed by Joseph Schumpeter.[18] Schumpeter associated each long expansion with a major innovation, such as the railroad or the automobile. The theory is revived every time that economists perceive a long period, such as the present, when there is low growth and severe recessions. Some Marxists have been particularly attracted to it in recent years.[19] The problems with accepting this cycle theory include these: (1) there has been time for only a few such cycles, so the evidence is very scanty; (2) there is enormous controversy among this theory's proponents as to the proper dates (there are simply no neat 30-year rises and 30-year declines); and (3) there is disagreement among its proponents over the mechanisms of its expansion and contraction, and none of the explanations have persuaded most economists.

The second alleged type of cycle is a 15-year cycle, called the Kuznets cycle, after Simon S. Kuznets.[20] The Kuznets cycle's timing is usually associated with the swings of the construction industry. Third, there is alleged to be a cycle of about 10 years, commonly called the Juglar cycle after Clement Juglar. The Juglar cycle is associated with major depressions, which cause vast declines in investment in plant and equipment. There were severe recessions or depressions about every 10 to 12 years in the nineteenth century, but this has been far more variable in the twentieth century, perhaps owing to wars or other new factors.

Finally, there is a cycle of about 3 or 4 years (the NBER average peacetime cycle is 46 months in total), commonly called a Kitchin cycle after Joseph Kitchin. These shorter cycles are frequently viewed as mild cycles associated with the rise and fall of inventories. There are many cycle theories based on the rise and fall of investment in inventories. There are many other cycle theories based on the rise and fall of investment in plant and equipment. It is noticeable that the various theories mostly involve the same factors, so one cannot say that there are entirely different theories for the Kitchin and Juglar cycles. Furthermore, in practice, as we shall see in a later chapter on investment, the difference between the behavior of these two categories of investment in the two types of cycles is not totally different in kind, but only marginally and quantitatively different. Shorter cycles see a larger rise and decline of investment in inventories, but also considerable rise and decline of plant and equipment investment. Longer cycles witness more fluctuations in plant and equipment investment, but also considerable fluctuations in inventory investment. The details are not important here, but will be explained in later chapters.

---

[18] See Joseph A. Schumpeter, *Business Cycles: A Theoretical, Historical, and Statistical Analysis of the Capitalist Process* (New York: McGraw-Hill, 1939).

[19] See Ernest Mandel, *Long Waves of Capitalist Development* (London: Cambridge University Press, 1980).

[20] For introduction to Kuznets, Juglar, and Kitchin cycles, see James Gapinski, *Macroeconomic Theory* (New York: McGraw-Hill, 1982), chap. 4.

SUMMARY

Say's law applies to some extent to precapitalist economic systems, but it does not apply to capitalism—according to the institutionalist critique—because of three institutional features of capitalism: (1) commodities are exchanged in the market rather than remaining in self-sufficient economies; (2) money and credit are used rather than barter; and (3) production is for private profit rather than for the use of an individual or community. The result is that there are recurrent periods of expansion and excess demand, as well as recurrent periods of contraction and deficient demand; this pattern of boom and bust is called the business cycle. According to the NBER dating, the average peacetime expansion has lasted 27 months, the contractions have lasted 19 months, and the whole cycle has averaged 46 months. Most cyclical downturns in the United States are relatively mild, though causing much human suffering, but major depressions do occur at unpredictable intervals. The mechanisms underlying severe depressions seem to be somewhat the same as those for recessions though one major difference is the amount of monetary collapse observed in major depressions (as we shall see in later chapters).

The next chapter sets up an analytic and accounting framework for examining the macroeconomy in a systematic fashion. Then the systematic defense of Say's law by the neoclassical economists and the systematic attacks on it by Keynesian and Marxist economists are explored. These important debates provide a framework for beginning to investigate the dynamics of the economy in the following parts.

Chapter 3

THE CIRCULAR FLOW: A NATIONAL ACCOUNTING FRAMEWORK

In the preceding chapters, Say's law, which says that aggregate supply automatically calls forth its own demand, was examined. Then the argument was investigated that this law does not hold true under modern capitalist institutions although it may have been true in some precapitalist societies. The next two chapters will move to a formal and systematic defense and critique of the possibility of deficient (or excess) demand in a capitalist society. To do a systematic and formal analysis, however, we must begin with the national accounting terminology and conceptual framework within which the argument will be conducted.

It is appropriate to begin with the U.S. national income accounts, as presented by the U.S. Department of Commerce (the national accounts of most capitalist countries are similar). These accounts arose in their present form because of the need for precise information in the Great Depression. Their original formulation and development were much influenced by the theoretical concepts of John M. Keynes, whose main theoretical work appeared about the same time. After these accounts and concepts are presented, a critique of some of their weaknesses is provided.

THE CIRCULAR FLOW OF THE GROSS NATIONAL PRODUCT

Gross national product (GNP) is defined as the total value of all the finished goods and services produced by a nation in a particular period, such as a year. Each good or service is valued at its market selling price. The market pricing system thus provides a yardstick by means of which totally different and otherwise unrelated items can be compared and aggregated. As long as the price of each item is set, it is possible to aggregate, as a sum of prices times quantities, such different items as apples, automobiles, haircuts, and umbrellas—the result being called the gross national product.

The main concept represented by national income accounting is a two-way circular flow of money in the circulation process. Money moves as income (or costs of supply) from business to households. This includes the flow of wages and salaries to workers, profits and interest to capitalists, and rents to landlords.

$$\text{HOUSEHOLDS} \xleftarrow{\text{(income, costs of supply)}} \text{BUSINESS}$$

There is a return flow of dollars of spending (such as spending by consumers), constituting the demand for products.

$$\text{HOUSEHOLDS} \xrightarrow{\text{(spending, demand)}} \text{BUSINESS}$$

When government and international trade are included, the flows are similar, but more complex. On the demand side, GNP may be measured in terms of total spending. The four kinds of spending are consumer spending, investment spending, government spending, and net export spending. The term *investment* here refers only to actual spending by corporations and other businesses for means of production, that is, for new plants (factories and other construction), new equipment (machinery and other tools), and increases in inventories. *Inventories* consist of stocks of raw materials, semifinished materials in the manufacturing process, and finished products not yet sold. Investment, in the sense used in this book, does not include acquisition of shares (or any debt instrument) from a business to an individual or from one individual to another. Likewise, *government spending* includes only purchases of goods and services, *not* transfers of money from government to individuals for any other reason, such as unemployment compensation. Finally, *net exports* measures the money demand from the sale of U.S. exports minus the money outflow from purchases of imports by residents of the United States.

The gross national product, when calculated from the demand side, is thus by definition stated to be

$$GNP = \text{spending} = \text{consumption} + \text{investment} + \text{government} + \text{net exports} \quad (3.1)$$

or
$$Y^g = C + I^g + G + (X - M) \quad (3.2)$$

where Y^g is gross national product, C is consumer spending, I^g is gross investment spending, G is government spending, X is exports, and M is imports. As will be seen from what follows, the term *gross* refers to the inclusion of replacement spending for depreciated plant and equipment.

The equation just given states an identity, equal because of definition. The four spending flows are defined as being exhaustive of all spending flows. Moreover, the definitions include all intended, planned, before-the-fact, *ex ante* spending. They also include, however, all unintended, unplanned, after-the-fact, *ex post* spending. For example, suppose business *intends* to invest $1 million in new plant and equipment. Suppose the same business is also unable to sell $200,000 worth of finished goods. Then these finished goods are considered to be *unintended* inventory investment. Therefore, this business's total *investment spending* will be $1.2 million for that time period, composed of both intended and unintended investment.

This equality of product to spending, therefore, is purely a statistical or accounting device. It exists by definition because national income accountants do not distinguish between intended and unintended investment in inventories. In the national income accounts, aggregate supply and demand are always equal because an excess of actual supply over planned demand results in the accumulation of unwanted inventories. As these unwanted goods pile up, the accountants include them as part of the inventory on hand. But all accumulation of inventories is defined as *investment*. So total spending on both consumption and investment (intended and unintended) must equal the total supply of all products (including those sold and not sold). Of course, when speaking theoretically in later chapters, we will argue that intended or planned spending may be more or less than the intended or planned supply of goods and services at present prices. That does not, however, change the accounting identity of supply (income) and demand (spending) in the actual data of the national income accounts.

On the income side, the payments by business include wages, salaries, and fringe benefits to workers, profit and interest to capitalists, rent to landlords, indirect business taxes to government (mostly sales taxes), and depreciation. Depreciation payments are defined to be the cost that arises from wear and tear—as well as obsolescence—of plant and equipment. Businesses measure depreciation according to rules issued by the U.S. government, stating how long the useful lifetime of different types of plant and equipment is.

This cost or income side of the gross national product is sometimes called the gross national income (or GNI).

$$GNI = \text{income} = \text{wages} + \text{salaries} + \text{fringe benefits} + \text{rent} + \text{profit} + \text{interest} + \text{indirect business taxes} + \text{depreciation} \quad (3.3)$$

All the items are costs, except profits, which are the residual after all costs are paid. Profits include both corporate and unincorporated business profits.

As a simplification and first approximation, unless stated otherwise, the term *wages* will be used here to refer to wages plus salaries plus fringe benefits. Also as a simplification and first approximation, unless stated otherwise, the term *profits* will be used here to refer to profits plus rent plus interest. Then the gross national income can be written as

$$GNI = \text{wages} + \text{profits} + \text{indirect business taxes} + \text{depreciation} \quad (3.4)$$

or

$$Y^g = W + \Pi + T^i + D \quad (3.5)$$

where Y^g is gross national product, W is wages, Π is profits, T^i is indirect business taxes, and D is depreciation. The same symbol is used for GNI and GNP because they must always be equal.

Keynes and his followers have mainly concentrated on exceedingly detailed examinations

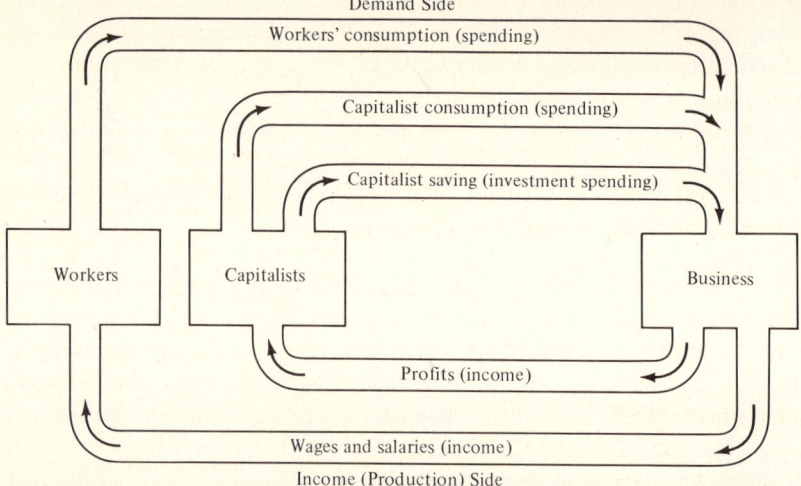

Figure 3.1 Income and Spending

NOTE: The role of government, exports and imports, and depreciation are omitted. Assumes workers do no saving. Assumes businesses pay out all net income in the form of *profits* (including dividends, rent, and interest). Assumes all savings are invested, a simplifying assumption, which will be dropped when we leave accounting and go to analysis.

of the spending or demand side. Equation 3.2 receives the emphasis in the Keynesian approach. Keynes treated income as very important, but seldom differentiated among types of income. Marx concentrated on the cost of production or income side. Marx treated demand as very important, but seldom differentiated among types of demand in any detail. Marx's approach is drastically different from Keynes's approach to national income accounts, but the detailed differences are not discussed here.[1] Supply-side economics tends to emphasize the production side. Attention in the following text will be given to both sides. Equation 3.5 is as close as it is possible to get to an income or production-side approach with U.S. national income accounts. An elementary flow diagram with simplifying assumptions represents the relationship between spending and income in Figure 3.1.

NET NATIONAL PRODUCT

Net national product (NNP) is equal to gross national product minus depreciation:

$$NNP = GNP - \text{depreciation} \tag{3.6}$$

---

[1]The differences are clearly spelled out in Anwar Shaikh, "National Income Accounts and Marxian Categories" (June 1978), an unpublished paper from Economics Department, New School for Social Research. The differences between U.S. and Soviet income accounting are discussed in Howard Sherman, *The Soviet Economy* (Boston: Little, Brown, 1969), pp. 120, 251.

Chapter 3   The Circular Flow: A National Accounting Framework

It follows that on the spending side

$$NNP = \text{consumption} + \text{net investment} + \text{government} + \text{net exports} \quad (3.7)$$

or
$$Y^n = C + I + G + (X - M) \quad (3.8)$$

where Y^n is net national product and I is net investment. Net investment is defined as gross investment minus depreciation. On the income side

$$NNP = \text{wages} + \text{profits} + \text{indirect business taxes} \quad (3.9)$$

or
$$Y^n = W + \Pi + T^i \quad (3.10)$$

The net national product is a useful concept when comparing two economies to see what is actually available for use after depreciation of productive assets. The fact that one economy may have more depreciation than another means that it produces less product after subtracting depreciation. Therefore, the comparison should be net of depreciation.

NATIONAL INCOME

The *national income* is defined to be the total income of the nation in a year's time going to all economic classes of the population, including both wages and profits. It does not include indirect business taxes (mainly sales taxes) because these taxes are paid by business to government before anyone receives any income from the sales. So, on the spending side:

$$\text{national income} = \text{consumption} + \text{net investment} + \text{government} + \text{net exports} \\ - \text{indirect business taxes} \quad (3.11)$$

In terms of incomes received, then:

$$\text{national income} = \text{wages} + \text{profits} \quad (3.12)$$

or
$$Y = W + \Pi \quad (3.13)$$

where Y is national income. These are wages and profit income before personal income taxes.

PERSONAL AND DISPOSABLE INCOME

The government imposes various taxes on the national income but also adds to the income stream many kinds of welfare payments. Therefore, the total of payments to all classes in production (i.e., the national income) is not the amount of income that households actually have at their disposal. Households' income comes from production *plus* various welfare payments *minus* various taxes.

In order to proceed from national income to income that actually goes to people (i.e., *personal income*), we must make various additions and subtractions. First, corporate profits do not go directly to any individual; corporate profits must be subtracted from national income in the process of determining the personal income actually going to individuals.

Second, individuals pay out of their wage income certain compulsory contributions for social insurance to the government (these are payments for what is usually called *social security*); these also must be subtracted from the national income. Third, individuals make various payments of interest on loans to financial institutions and to government; these also must be subtracted to find personal income.

On the positive side, the government makes many *transfer* payments that transfer income to individuals (not for present services), thus adding to personal income. These transfers include unemployment compensation, farm subsidies, business subsidies, and social security benefits. Second, corporations pay dividends out of profits. Third, a great many individuals receive interest payments from the government or from corporations. All such payments must be added to the national income if we wish to calculate personal income. Totaling all the additions and subtractions from national income, the result is personal income. The procedure is indicated by the following unwieldy equation:

$$\text{personal income} = \text{national income} - \text{corporate profits} - \text{interest paid by individuals} - \text{social security taxes} + \text{government transfer payments} + \text{dividends} + \text{personal interest income} \qquad (3.14)$$

Finally, there is *disposable personal income*, which is the amount of money at the disposal of individuals and households for spending on consumption or for personal saving. In order to find this quantity, we must deduct *personal income taxes*, which are the taxes an individual or household must pay in proportion to its yearly income. The result is expressed as

$$\text{disposable personal income} = \text{personal income} - \text{personal income taxes} \qquad (3.15)$$

Consumers may now spend and save out of disposable personal income. If consumption expenditures are subtracted, we arrive at personal saving. Table 3.1 shows the national income accounts for 1981. As can be seen, gross national product can be regarded as either aggregate demand or aggregate cost. The left side of the table shows the sources of aggregate demand. The total of all four categories equals gross national product. The total also equals the total level of aggregate demand *if* it is assumed that the entirety of the category called *inventory change* was *planned inventory change*. Businesses intentionally allow their inventories to grow. Any growth in inventories that is intentional is called a planned change in inventories. If there is an unintentional growth in inventories, such as an unwanted buildup on the lots of auto dealers because of disappointing sales, this is called an *unplanned* change in inventories. Since any such buildup represents a deficiency of aggregate demand, it should not be included in total demand. Unfortunately, there is no easy way of telling how much of a change in inventories is planned or unplanned.

The right-side column shows the division of gross national product into payments that cover costs of production (including the government's costs of operation). Wages, unincorporated business income, rental income, dividends, interest income, and net transfer payments—all constitute *income* and add up to the category called *national income*, which is shown in Table 3.2. Net transfer payments include all direct payments received by private individuals and businesses from the government (such as social security, unemployment compensation, and welfare) minus contributions to social security.

To these income payments are added depreciation and indirect business taxes (primarily sales taxes). Depreciation is a cost of production because it is the estimate of the value of

Table 3.1

NATIONAL INCOME ACCOUNTS FOR 1981 (BILLIONS OF DOLLARS)

Aggregate Demand			Costs of Production	
Consumption		$1858	Wages	$1637
Durable goods	232		Unincorporated business	135
Nondurable goods	743		Rent	34
Services	883		Dividends from profits	61
Investment (gross)		451	Interest	309
Nonresidential fixed	329		Net transfer payments	229
Residential fixed	106		Depreciation	322
Inventory change	16		Indirect business taxes and transfers and statistical discrepancy	198
Government purchases		591	Equals	
Federal	230		Gross national product	$2925
State and local	361			
Net Exports		26		
Exports	367			
Imports	341			
Equals				
Gross national product		$2925		

SOURCE: U.S. Department of Commerce, *Survey of Current Business*.

worn-out productive resources, and yet it does not contribute to actual income. Indirect business taxes reflect the fact that there is a difference between market price for all items, which is reflected in GNP, and prices received by producers to provide income. This difference is primarily explained by sales taxes. They do not contribute to income directly, but, for national income account purposes, must still be regarded as a cost of production.

Finally, in the collection of data for the national income accounts, some mistakes are unavoidably made. The right column will not exactly match up with the left column. The difference, which is usually less than 1 percent of GNP, is called the statistical discrepancy.

As can be seen in Table 3.1, in the national income accounts, the right column equals the left because both add up to GNP (including the statistical discrepancy). Again, this does not imply in any sense that the economy is always in equilibrium (or that Say's law is being statistically demonstrated). A disequilibrium, in which the value of production exceeds demand, will appear as a large growth in inventory change. Even though the economy is truly in disequilibrium, these accounts will not show that.

Table 3.2 shows national income and how it is broken into the subordinate categories of personal income and disposable personal income. A flow diagram showing the circulation of GNP when government is present is shown in Figure 3.2.

Figure 3.3 shows the behavior of the various components of GNP since 1955. As can be seen, consumption is responsible for between 62 and 64 percent of GNP, and government purchases explains about 20 percent. Net exports, which are sometimes negative, seldom contribute more than 1 percent to GNP. Investment contributes a little over 15 percent.

Table 3.2

NATIONAL INCOME ACCOUNTS FOR 1981 (BILLIONS OF DOLLARS)

National and Personal Income

Gross national product	$2925	
− Depreciation (capital consumption allowances)		−$322
= Net national product	= 2603	
− Indirect business taxes and transfers (mostly sales taxes)		− 260
= National income	= 2343	
− Corporate profits		− 189
− Net interest payments		− 215
− Contributions to social security		− 239
+ Government transfer payments		+ 321
+ Personal interest income		+ 309
+ Dividends and business transfers		+ 73
= Personal income	= 2403	
− Personal income taxes		− 388
= Disposable personal income	= 2015	
− Personal consumption		−1858
= Personal saving	= 157	

SOURCE: U.S. Department of Commerce, *Survey of Current Business.*

SAVINGS AND INVESTMENT

It is necessary to distinguish between the concepts of wealth, capital, and investment. *Wealth,* the broader concept, is the total holding by everyone of all durable consumer goods *plus* the ownership of natural resources *plus* the total holding of the entire stock of capital (including inventories). Wealth is not measured in the national income and product accounts. A high level of production certainly implies that a large stock of wealth exists in the form of productive capital. The national accounts, however, measure only the value of the flow of production and, hence, income. They are not designed to measure the holding of wealth or capital. *Capital* is defined as the total value of all existing buildings and factories, machines and equipment for production, and inventories.

Investment may then be defined simply as the *change* in capital, its increase or decrease within a year or some other period. This means that any individual investment that does not increase the amount of capital, such as the purchase of old shares of stock by one individual from another, does not count as net investment for the nation. Even if a corporation sells new stock, the proceeds do not become net investment in the economy until the corporation actually uses the money to purchase new factories, equipment, or inventories. In other words, the investment discussed here is not mere financial dealing or individual investment of money, but the physical expansion of the nation's economic capacity. More specifically, this year's investment consists of new construction, new producer's durable equipment, and the change in business inventories.

Investment is the *flow* of spending for these new producer goods in one time period, such

Chapter 3 THE CIRCULAR FLOW: A NATIONAL ACCOUNTING FRAMEWORK

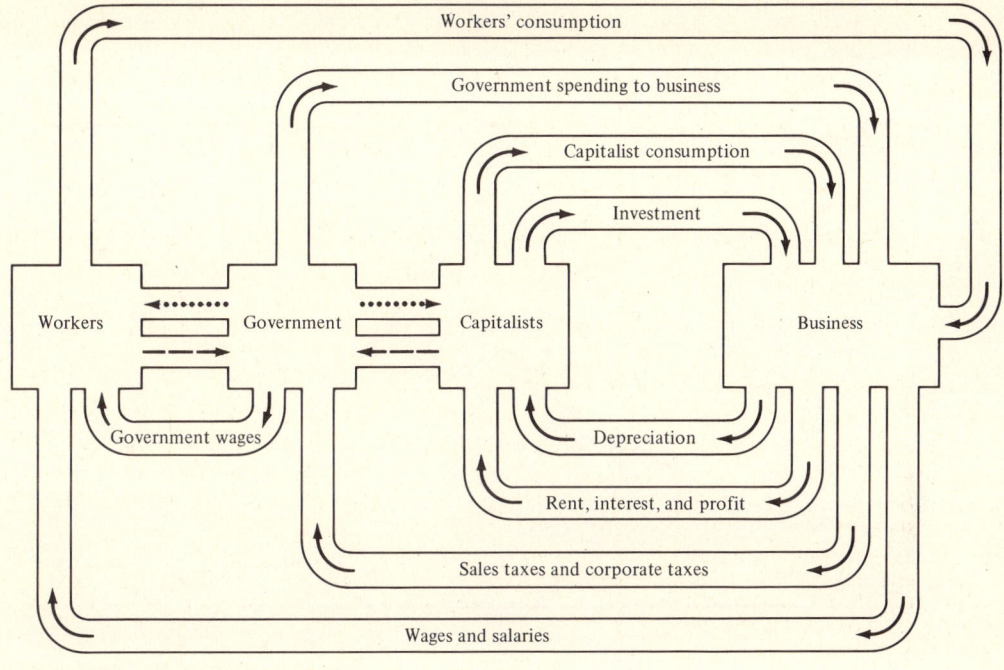

Figure 3.2 The Circulation of GNP (Flow of Dollars)
NOTE: Imports and exports are omitted.

as a year. *Capital,* on the other hand, is a *stock* of goods at a particular time, such as January 1. So investment measures the change in the stock of capital from the beginning of one year to the beginning of the next year.

Only one more distinction in this area of analysis needs to be made. The total investment in the economy is called *gross investment.* It includes both *net investment,* or investment to expand productive capacity, and *replacement investment,* or investment needed to replace the depreciation of present productive capacities.

In macroeconomics, savings has a special meaning. Most of our national product goes for consumption—that is, the aggregate purchase of consumer goods and services by all U.S. households. Whatever part of disposable personal income is not used for consumption is defined as personal saving. Whatever part of profits that is not used to pay dividends is part of gross business savings. Gross business savings also include depreciation funds put aside by business. Hence

$$S = PS + GBS \qquad (3.16)$$

where S is savings, PS is personal savings, and GBS is gross business savings.

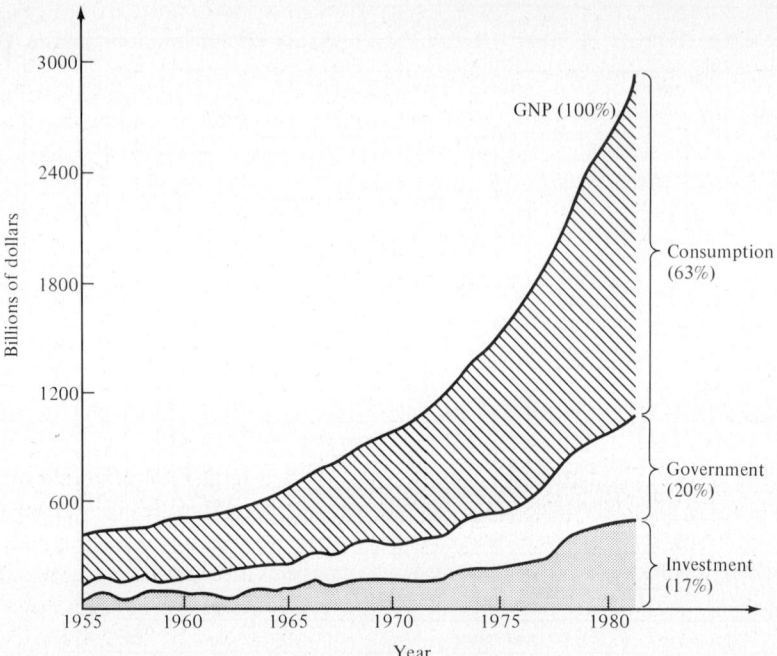

Figure 3.3 GNP and its Components 1955–1981
NOTE: Percentage figures are for 1981. *Government* means government purchases of goods and services. *Investment* includes gross investment (16%) and net exports (1%) which is exports minus imports.
SOURCE: U.S. Department of Commerce.

THE CONCEPT OF VALUE ADDED

The GNP of the United States, as reported by the U.S. Department of Commerce, includes only final products. It avoids counting the value of the same product more than once when this product appears (within the same year) at various intermediate stages of the production process. Suppose *both* the value of all steel produced and the value of all the automobiles produced were counted in GNP. Since a great deal of steel is used in automobile production, we would be counting the value of that steel twice, once by itself and once as a principal ingredient in automobiles.

One correct procedure is to include only the *value added* by labor in each industry—that is, the increase in the worth of the product in the production process of that industry beyond the worth of the raw materials bought from other industries. Therefore, the value added by labor to the raw material in the steel industry would be counted. Then the value added by labor in making automobiles out of the steel would also be counted. But the value of the steel, or any other product from another industry, used by the auto industry would not be counted again. The whole calculation of gross product may be illustrated as follows:

$$\text{gross product in steel and auto industry} = \text{steel (value added by labor in the form of wages + rent + interest + profit + depreciation)} + \text{auto (value added by labor in the form of wages + profits + rent + interest + depreciation)} \quad (3.17)$$

Note that the value of autos does not include the value of steel used by the auto industry.

Notice that depreciation represents value added by previous labor. We must emphasize once more that the costs of the raw materials bought and used up in both industries are *not* included in the gross product of either industry. In both cases, the values produced by other industries are not included; only the values produced by this industry are included. The value added is thus less than the revenue in each industry by exactly the amount of goods and materials bought from other industries.

GROSS NATIONAL PRODUCT IN REAL TERMS

To know whether a change in GNP reflects a change in national welfare, one must determine whether the change was due to a change in the economic measuring rod (prices) or a change in the *real* quantity of goods and services produced. If the national product doubles in money value but the price level has also doubled, then the real product—the goods and services available to the nation—has remained the same. Or, if GNP in current prices has risen 5 percent but the overall price level has risen 3 percent, physical output has increased by only about 2 percent.

In calculating GNP, the government must begin with current prices. But if one wants to make comparisons between years when price changes have occurred, the money value of GNP can be deflated by dividing the current value by an index showing how much prices have changed:

$$\frac{\text{prices} \times \text{quantity produced}}{\text{price index}} = \text{real (or deflated) GNP} \quad (3.18)$$

The U.S. Department of Commerce compiles price indexes for the many components of GNP. It also deflates each component by its index. Each index is constructed from the price changes that have occurred in the items that make up that component. By the choice of a base year, such as 1929 (1929 = 100), against which all price changes are measured, deflated GNP data can be made comparable over the years.

The three most important price indices compiled by the government are the consumer price index (CPI), the producer price index (PPI, formerly called the wholesale price index), and the implicit price deflator (IPD).

The consumer price index is designed to represent the price behavior of those goods that are purchased by consumers. The producer price index represents goods purchased by manufacturers and other producers. Each of these two price indices uses a "market basket" of goods weighted to represent accurately the average purchasing behavior of the typical consumer and producer. The implicit price deflator is used specifically to adjust nominal GNP for inflation and would be the price index used in equation 3.18 (given earlier). There is a separate IPD for each of the major categories of GNP (for example, a consumption IPD), and the IPD for GNP is weighted to reflect the relative importance of these categories to GNP.

All these indices are constructed by using the following formula:

$$\text{price index in year } X = \frac{\text{weighted average of prices in year } X}{\text{weighted average of prices in base year}} \quad (3.19)$$

In mathematical terms, the formula is

$$PI_x = \frac{\sum_{i=1}^{n} A_i P_{ix}}{\sum_{i=1}^{n} A_i P_{iB}} \quad (3.20)$$

where PI_x is the price index in year X, A_i represents each of the n weights, and P_{ix} and P_{iB} represent each of the n prices in year X and the base year respectively. The choice of the base year in the construction of any price index is arbitrary.

The performance of the consumer price index was shown in Chapter 2 in Figure 2.3.

POTENTIAL GROSS NATIONAL PRODUCT

Many times, part of the nation's productive capacity goes unused. Factories may stand idle or be only partially used while millions of unemployed workers search for jobs. During such periods, economists can calculate the approximate *potential* output that would obtain *if* the unemployed laborers could be put to work and *if* the factories not being utilized could be used to full capacity. The difference between potential and actual output is a widely used measure of the economic costs of recessions and depressions. (This difference does not include the costs in human suffering, such as feelings of failure, mental illness, divorce and child abuse, and even suicide in a few cases.)

Potential real national income or output will be represented by the symbol Z. The U.S. government provides data on the ratio of actual output to potential output (Y/Z), which is called the ratio of capacity utilization (the weaknesses of this index are discussed in a later chapter). Knowing the actual output (Y) and the ratio of capacity utilization (Y/Z), one may calculate the potential full-capacity output (Z).

PER CAPITA GNP

The actual GNP in real terms is often used as a reflection of national welfare. But suppose one wants to know the welfare not for the nation but for each individual. If China has the same national product as England, then the average Chinese is much worse off than the average English person because of the tremendous difference in population. Therefore, to measure the individual welfare, one must divide the GNP of a nation by the number of its population. This result is the per capita GNP. Notice, however, that per capita GNP is only an average; it does not say anything about how the GNP is distributed among individuals. A country with very low per capita income may have some very rich individuals.

NET ECONOMIC WELFARE

Finally, suppose GNP is deflated by price rises and by population increases. Is the resulting real per capita GNP a good measure of individual human welfare? More and more economists are coming to the conclusion that it is *not* necessarily a good welfare measure.

On the one side, there are some goods and services not included in the GNP because they are not given a value in the market. For example, the work of housewives is not counted in the GNP. Yet many women (and some men) work long, hard hours in the home, and their labor equals about one-fourth of the official GNP value. This exclusion is very inconsistent because a maid's labor is counted in the GNP to the amount of her salary, yet if the maid marries the owner of the house, then the maid's labor is no longer counted, and GNP is reduced. The reason for this exclusion is probably the sexist idea that women don't really work very hard (since most housework is done by women) plus the notion current in our capitalist society that services are valuable only if they are sold in the market.

On the other side, many costs to the public are not subtracted from the GNP even though they are caused by the production of the GNP. For example, production and use of cars and trucks cause air pollution. This pollution costs the public in terms of health, such as eye and respiratory diseases and even property damage, for example, harm to trees and plants. Thus, the GNP should be reduced by the amount of this damage.

Moreover, some large portion of the GNP is composed of wasteful or harmful goods that reduce or do not increase human welfare; this portion should not be included in the GNP. For example, cigarettes are part of the GNP, but they are harmful to health, according to the U.S. government. Advertising "service" is part of the GNP, but a large part of it is pure propaganda or misinformation. The largest single expenditure that produces neither consumer goods nor expansion of industry is military spending, yet all of those billions of dollars spent to stockpile bombs and tanks are included in the GNP. It has even been argued that most military production does *not* increase public security since it is either wasteful or unnecessary. If national product is to be calculated in terms of human welfare, then a strong case may be made for excluding all or most military production.

It might also be noted that some projects benefit the public beyond the cost shown in the GNP. For example, a dam built by the government for water and power (and counted in the GNP at cost) may also produce recreation and beauty.

Therefore, a new measure is needed, and some economists have argued for *net economic welfare* (NEW) to replace the official GNP. NEW would equal GNP but in addition would (1) *add* all unpaid labor (e.g., homemakers' labor), (2) *add* unpriced benefits (e.g., recreation from dams), (3) *subtract* unpriced costs (e.g., pollution from industry and cars), and (4) *subtract* all harmful and wasteful products (e.g., cigarettes and bombs and most advertising).

SUMMARY

It was apparent at the end of the Great Depression that there was a need for data so that the performance of the economy could be evaluated. Consequently, the U.S. national income accounts were developed. These useful accounts reflect the fact that income and production follow a circular flow through the economy. They are used to show how income is disaggregated and are also used to show the components of spending. In addition, they can be adjusted for inflation and for the size of the population.

Gross national product, the measure of the market value of all final goods and services in the economy, provides a measure of national output intended for the market. Many critics believe that is an inaccurate measure of welfare, however. It does not include nonmarket labor and considers wasteful spending to have the same value as spending that actually contributes to national welfare.

GLOSSARY OF SYMBOLS

Important symbols used throughout this book include the following:

$Y=$ national income (or output) in constant dollars
$C=$ consumption spending in constant dollars
$I=$ net private domestic investment in constant dollars
$W=$ all labor income, including wages and salaries, in constant dollars
$\Pi=$ all property income, including profit, rent, and interest, in constant dollars
$K=$ the stock of capital in constant dollars
$N=$ the amount of labor employed in hours
$X=$ exports in constant dollars
$M=$ imports in constant dollars
$G=$ government purchases of goods and services in constant dollars
$Z=$ potential output if capacity were fully utilized in constant dollars
$P=$ the price level, meaning the GNP price deflator, unless stated otherwise

Chapter 4

SAY'S LAW AND THE CLASSICAL VIEW

As noted briefly in Chapter 1, the dominant classical view holds that unemployment and economic distress are accidents caused by factors external to the economy. They are always minor and temporary. The capitalist economy, if left to itself, will always automatically come back to full employment and stable prices in a short time. *Say's law states that any supply of goods will generate sufficient income to produce the level of demand necessary to clear the market.* Therefore, there can never be overproduction of goods relative to demand for any length of time. Every supply of output leads to income, which leads to an equal amount of demand.

James Mill, J. B. Say, and other classical economists presented three arguments to claim that competition in the capitalist system always restores full employment at equilibrium. (The term *equilibrium* means that supply equals demand.) First, it was claimed that, even if supply of goods were temporarily greater than demand, this imbalance would quickly be cured by competition. Under competitive conditions the excess supply of output would quickly cause prices to drop. At the new, lower prices, demand would automatically rise to equal the supply.

Second, it was claimed that all income not spent for consumption would always be invested. If more money were saved than invested, competition among lenders would cause the rate of interest to fall. Moreover, a lower rate of interest stimulates investment, which rises until it equals the amount of saving. Thus, the total spending for consumer and investment goods would always rise to equal the total amount of goods produced.

The third and final classical argument is that, even if prices don't drop and the supply of goods is temporarily excessive, this causes only temporary unemployment. The unemployment causes competition among workers, which leads to lower wages. The lower wages stimulate capitalists to demand more labor (since it's cheaper), which restores full employment. Therefore, the classical economists concluded that the capitalist system would automatically restore full employment with stable prices after any temporary dislocation.

The belief that the economy automatically reaches equilibrium at full employment implies some very particular behavioral assumptions about the markets for products, labor, and money, as well as about the relations between these three markets. Specifically, in the first case, if demand in the commodity market falls short of supply, (1) competition among sellers will cause a drop in prices, and then (2) demand will be stimulated to increase, and (3) supply will fall until equilibrium is reached. In the second case, if investment demand is temporarily less than the supply of saving, (1) competition among lenders will cause a drop in the interest rate (or price of borrowing money), and then (2) investment will be stimulated to increase, and (3) saving will decline until equilibrium is reached. Finally, as the argument goes, if the demand for workers in the labor market is less than their supply, (1) competition among workers will cause a drop in wages, and then (2) demand for labor will be stimulated (although some workers may withdraw from the market) until (3) equilibrium is reached—at full employment of the workers still in the market. These behavioral assumptions imply that all buyers and sellers have perfect information, act rationally, are able to move without cost, and meet no monopoly barriers in any market.

The remainder of this chapter is devoted to presenting a formal model that represents Say's law. The model, which is a popular modern pedagogical tool, is designed to represent the salient features of the mainstream classical point of view. The model as it is constructed was *not* developed by the classical economists themselves. It was, in fact developed by some of the early Keynesian critics of the classical point of view and was thought to represent the classical position faithfully.[1]

The model represents Say's law because it displays a natural tendency toward an equilibrium where there is no unemployment. This simplified model is designed to demonstrate the *essence* of the full-employment argument. The model assumes perfect competition in at least the labor market and ignores the role played by the government and the foreign sector. Such a model is terribly unrealistic, but it is only designed to represent an *ideal.* Conservative classical and neoclassical economists *advocate* perfect competition and a very small role for government (and in the United States, they note, the foreign sector does not have a large net effect upon the economy).

The model allows the determination of the level of real output, the amount of labor used in production, and the general price level when the money supply is given. An attachment to the general model also allows the determination of savings, investment, consumption, and the real interest rate.

THE NATIONAL PRODUCTION FUNCTION

This short-run model employs a national production function where the level of real output (GNP) is a function of the amount of labor used in production. The model recognizes that

---

[1] The model is similar in many features to the theory of Pigou, which was criticized by Keynes as a representative of the "classical" point of view. See A. C. Pigou, *Theory of Unemployment* (London: Macmillan, 1933); also A. C. Pigou, *Industrial Fluctuations* (London: Macmillan, 1927).

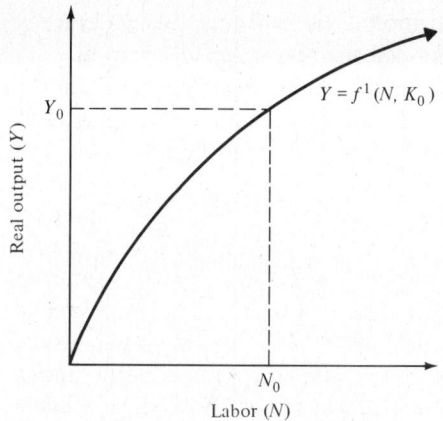

K_0 = given level of capital, that is, a constant

Figure 4.1 The National Production Function

capital is also used in production, but the capital stock is regarded as fixed in the short run. The production function may be expressed with the equation

$$Y = f^1 (N, K_0) \qquad (4.1)$$

where Y is the level of real national output (GNP), N is the amount of labor used in production (the level of employment), f^1 is a positive function, and K_0 is the capital stock that is fixed. In this function there is a positive relationship between output and labor employed. A graph of this function is shown in Figure 4.1. It is assumed that labor yields diminishing returns when the capital stock is fixed, which is why the function has a concave shape.

In Figure 4.1, the level of production is determined by the amount of labor used. In the graph, N_0 allows the production level Y_0.

THE LABOR MARKET

In this model, it is in the labor market that output and employment are determined. The amount of labor employed is determined by the supply function of labor in conjunction with the demand function for labor. The supply of labor is a function of the real wage. At a higher real wage, workers will supply more labor because the disutility of working is more fully overcome by the greater reward. At lower real wages, workers choose more leisure.

The supply function of labor is

$$N_s = f^2 (W) \qquad (4.2)$$

where N_s is the supply of labor, W is the real wage rate, and f^2, the relationship between the two, is positive. The higher the real wage rate, the higher is the amount of labor supplied to the market.

The demand for labor (N_d) is also treated as a function of the real wage, where there is an inverse relationship between the demand for labor and the real wage:

$$N_d = f^3 (W) \tag{4.3}$$

where f^3 is a negative function.

In neoclassical microeconomic theory, the demand for any factor input to production, including labor, is determined by the input's marginal physical product. In production theory, producers will demand that amount of labor where the marginal product of labor is equal to the real wage. In other words, producers choose the level of labor, N_0, where

$$W = MPP\ (N_0) \tag{4.4}$$

In this equation, $MPP\ (N_0)$ represents the marginal physical product of labor when N_0 labor is being used. This is because producers employ a factor input like labor up to the point where its real marginal cost (W) is equal to its real marginal return (MPP). (This is explained in greater detail in Appendix 4.A).

The marginal physical product of labor can be determined from the production function. Since the production function actually represents the *total* product of labor for all levels of N, then the *slope* of the production function identifies the marginal physical product of labor for all levels of N.

A hypothetical demand curve for labor is shown in Figure 4.2. When the real wage is on the vertical axis and labor is on the horizontal axis, then the labor demand curve is simply the marginal physical product line taken from the slope of the production function. The derivation of two arbitrarily chosen points on the labor demand curve is shown in Figure 4.2. When 3 units of labor are used in production, the marginal physical product of labor is equal to 1 (because the slope of the production function equals 1 at that point). This is represented by point *a* on the production function, and this allows the determination of point *a* on the demand for labor curve. That point on the demand curves simply reflects the fact that if the real wage is 1 unit, then 3 units of labor will be demanded. This is because the marginal physical product of labor is one when 3 units are employed, and this must be equal to the real wage.

Point *b* on both graphs shows the determination of a second point on the labor demand curve. Eight units of labor will be employed only if the real wage drops to 0.5 because the marginal physical product of labor is only 0.5 when that much labor is employed.

It may seem as if the details of the determination of the labor demand curve are being overstressed, but a very important point must be understood. *The location of the demand curve for labor is not arbitrary.* In this model it is fixed by the physical features of the production function, which in turn means that its location is determined by the state of technology that sets the shape of the production function. This is an important theoretical point because it implies that if there is a disturbance in the labor market, it will not be due to an arbitrary shift in the curve of the demand for labor, which represents the decisions of capitalists.

The usual classical (and Keynesian) theories are portrayed as models of equilibrium. If, and only if, there is equilibrium, the supply and demand for labor are equal. Therefore:

$$N_d = N = N_s \qquad (4.5)$$

where N is the equilibrium level of labor.

These three independent equations (4.2, 4.3, and 4.5) have only three independent variables, namely, the real wage, the demand for labor, and the supply of labor. Therefore, they are solvable (by substituting equations 4.2 and 4.3 into 4.5). The solution is shown in Figure 4.3(b) where the result is an equilibrium real wage and an equilibrium amount of labor

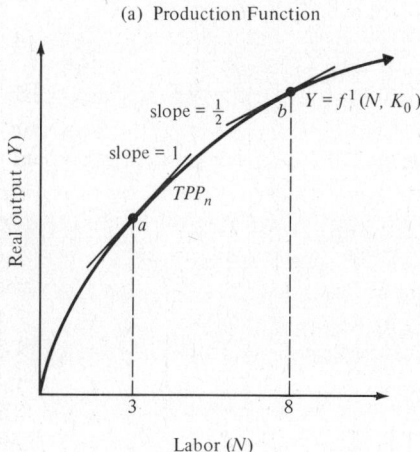

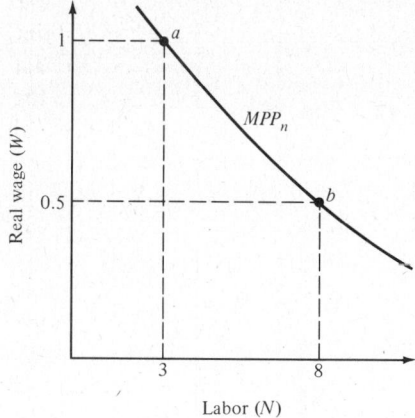

TPP_n = total physical product of labor (production function)
MPP_n = marginal physical product of labor (labor demand)
K_0 = given level of capital (a constant)
f^1 = a positive function

Figure 4.2 The Determination of the Labor Demand Curve

employed. Since that point is on both the demand curve and supply curve of labor, there are —according to the classical economists—*no* involuntarily unemployed workers when equilibrium is reached. Unemployment leads to lower wages, which reduces supply of labor and increases demand for labor, so equilibrium is restored with full use of all available labor. There is automatic "full employment."

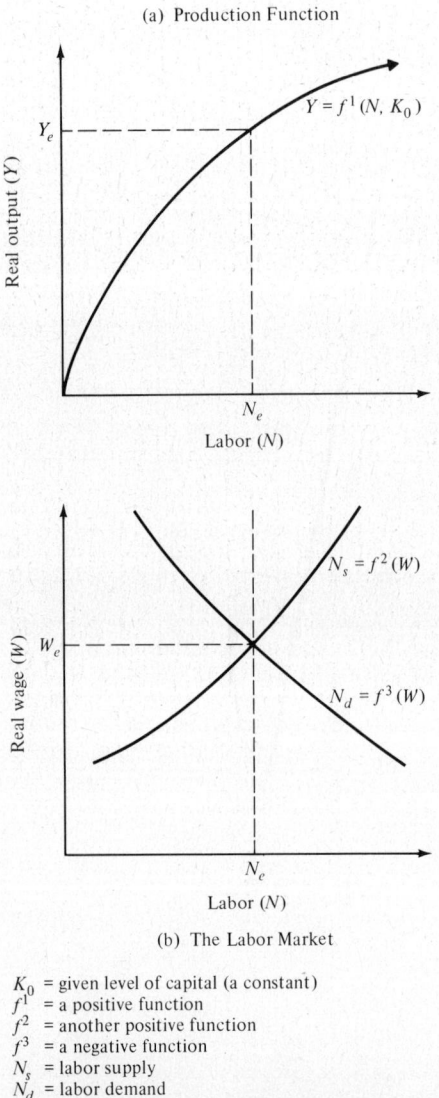

K_0 = given level of capital (a constant)
f^1 = a positive function
f^2 = another positive function
f^3 = a negative function
N_s = labor supply
N_d = labor demand

Figure 4.3 The Determination of the Level of Production

THE DETERMINATION OF REAL OUTPUT

In Figure 4.3, the production function is graphed along with the labor market equations in a two-quadrant graph. Knowing the equilibrium amount of employment (N_e), the production function leads directly to the equilibrium level of national output (Y_e). Therefore, the equilibrium level of national output is directly determined by supply and demand in the labor market—and the production function. The supply and demand for labor are both functions of the real wage, assumed to equal the marginal product of labor. The marginal product of labor at full employment determines the equilibrium output.

THE COMMODITY MARKET

The classical vision of the economy can be represented by a flow diagram showing the flow of incomes and expenditures through the economy (see Figure 4.4). In this simple example, there are no government and no foreign trade. The economy is divided into two sectors: (a) businesses, who generate income and are the recipients of spending, and (b) consumers, who receive income and either spend or save that income. Saved income finds its way into the financial markets, where it is used for investment (a form of spending). All the spending and income flows in Figure 4.4 represent dollar movements through the economy. Say's law essentially says there are no *leakages* in this payment flow.

By definition, income received from the supply of production (Y_s) may be used for consumption or for saving. Saving is defined as all income (or output) minus consumption. Therefore, in equation form,

$$Y_s = C + S \tag{4.6}$$

where Y_s is the supply of net national product or national income, C is consumption, and S is saving. In this elementary model there are no government spending, no taxing, and no international trade.

The level of expenditures or aggregate demand (Y_d) in the economy will consist of the sum of consumption and investment.

$$Y_d = C + I \tag{4.7}$$

where I is net investment.

If there is an equilibrium where the level of output equals the level of spending, then:

$$Y_s = Y = Y_d \tag{4.8}$$

$$C + S = C + I \tag{4.9}$$

and
$$S = I \tag{4.10}$$

In other words, at equilibrium, the output demanded equals the output supplied, consumption plus saving equals consumption plus investment, and saving equals investment. The

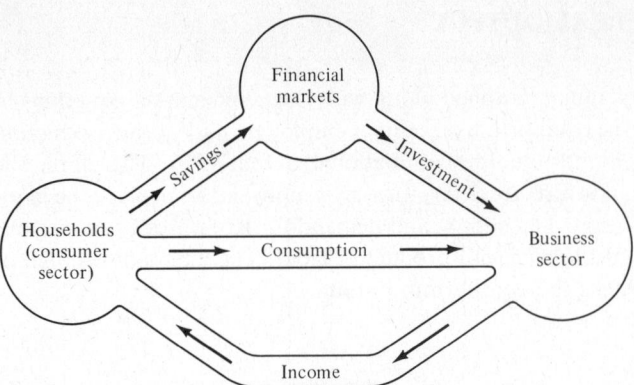

Figure 4.4 The Flow of Income in the Classical Model

classical model, however, does *not assume* that this equilibrium is *necessarily at full employment*. It *proves* that equilibrium is at full employment by its behavioral assumptions about the various markets. These assumptions include the equality of supply and demand in the labor market by the real wage, as well as the equality of saving and investment by the rate of interest.

According to the classical (and neoclassical) theory, the interest rate reflects market evaluations about the relative importance of present and future consumption. Therefore, the interest rate determines what percentage of income goes into present consumption versus saving and lending for future returns. In functional form, the saved proportion of income (S/Y) is a function of the interest rate (r);

$$\frac{S}{Y} = f^4(r) \tag{4.11}$$

There is a positive relationship (the function, f^4) between S/Y and r because a higher interest rate causes people to save more.

Assume that investors borrow all the money they invest. The higher the interest rate, the less they will borrow. So the invested proportion of income and the interest rate are inversely related.

$$\frac{I}{Y} = f^5(r) \tag{4.12}$$

where f^5 is a negative function. As the interest rate rises, the proportion of national income invested declines because it costs investors more to borrow money.

The saving function and the investment function are shown together in Figure 4.5. Together, they determine the equilibrium interest rate and the proportion of income that is saved and invested at equilibrium. Thus, the proportion saved (S/Y) equals the proportion invested (I/Y). There are only two independent variables (r and $S/Y = I/Y$) in these

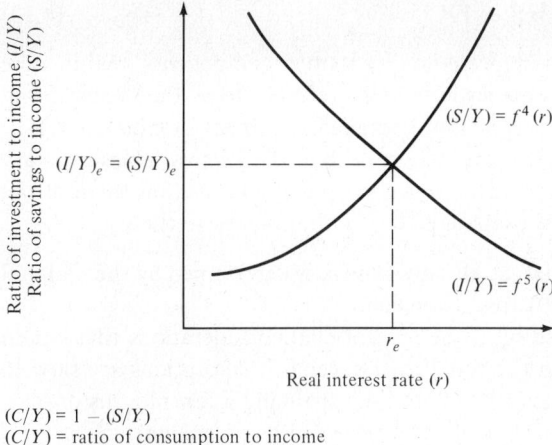

$(C/Y) = 1 - (S/Y)$
(C/Y) = ratio of consumption to income
f^4 = a positive function
f^5 = a negative function
e = equilibrium level

Figure 4.5 The Determination of the Proportion of Income Going to Savings, Investment, and Consumption

two independent equations (4.11 and 4.12), so it is possible to find the equilibrium solution (indicated graphically by the point where they cross).

It was shown above that the level of output or real income is determined in the labor market, which sets equilibrium employment. The level of employment translates into a level of output by means of the production function. Only then, given the level of aggregate output (Y) and given the saving ratio (S/Y), can the level of saving (S) be determined. Knowing saving and output, one obviously knows the level of consumption ($C = Y - S$). The point is that output is determined on the supply side in the labor market and production process, and it is merely divided into saving (or investment) and consumption according to the rate of interest, which represents preferences for present versus future consumption and attitudes about investment.

THE DETERMINATION OF THE PRICE LEVEL

So far only *real* values have been determined in this model. In the classical model, the fixing of the price level, which allowed the determination of *nominal* levels of spending and income, was essentially determined by the amount of money in circulation.

The classical economists regarded the *nominal* level of aggregate demand as equal to the amount of money (M) in the economy times its rate of circulation (or velocity, V) through the economy; so MV = nominal aggregate demand.

The rate of circulation, called *velocity,* was equal to the number of times a typical dollar was spent on final goods and services. This means, of course, that

$$MV = YP \tag{4.13}$$

where YP is the nominal national income represented by its two components, real income (Y) and the general price level (P). This equation is often referred to as the "equation of exchange." (The equation of exchange is given more detailed treatment in Chapter 6.)

This little tautology has no analytic value at all where each of the four variables can vary to an unlimited extent. The classical economists, however, put limitations on three of the variables that gave life to the equation of exchange. The limitations were these:

1. Real output (Y) has a given value that, as already shown, is determined by the national production function and the supply and demand for labor.
2. Velocity (V) is primarily determined by those institutional considerations that would aid or impede the flow of money through the economy. Since such institutions are slow to change over time, it follows that over short periods of time spanning a few months or even years, velocity would be relatively stable and could be regarded as a constant.
3. The money stock (M) was controlled by regulatory authorities.

The first qualification was a conclusion from the real part of this model, and the other two are assumptions. Given this, the only unknown in the equation of exchange is the price level. Given income and velocity, the price level will depend upon the amount of money provided by the monetary authorities:

$$P = \frac{V_0}{Y_0} M \tag{4.14}$$

where V_0 and Y_0 are given constants in the time period considered. Hence, nominal values are determined by the money supply.

Figure 4.6 shows the relation of prices and output with the money supply fixed. In this graph, each of the two hyperbolas shows the relationship between the level of prices and real output, given some level of the money stock. The real level of output (Y_e) is given by conditions in the labor market. When the money supply is M_a, the level of prices will be P_a. If the money supply is increased to M_b, the level of prices will be P_b. It is important to see that variations in the money supply affect *only* the price level. This was a commonly held opinion among many classical economists.

More output causes lower prices because the total flow of money ($M_0 V_0$) is fixed, so the same money flow must be spread over more commodities. Lower output would cause higher prices because the same money flow is spread over fewer goods. Supply-side economists emphasize this relationship when they argue that successful incentives to increase output will eventually lower prices (or at least reduce inflation), assuming a constant or very slowly growing money supply.

SUMMARY OF CLASSICAL MODEL

In Figure 4.7, the entire classical model is shown. It traces the lines of causation from the labor market to the money and commodity markets. Say's law results from the model because

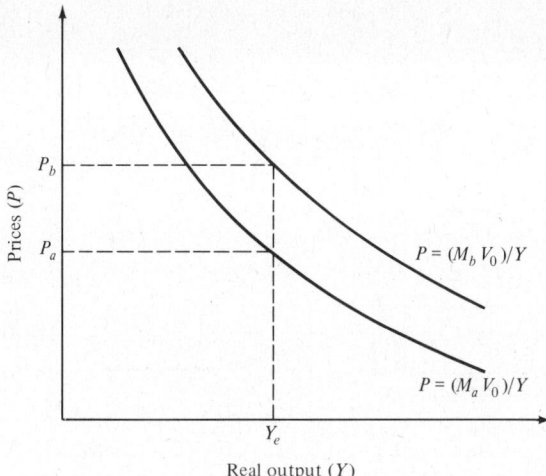

Y_e = equilibrium real output (determined in the labor market)
V_0 = velocity of money (a constant)
M = money (determined by the monetary authorities)

Figure 4.6 The Determination of the Price Level Using the Equation of Exchange

labor demand and supply are always equilibrated by the price of labor (wages). Output is determined by the labor market and the production function. Once output is determined, prices are determined by the money supply and fixed money velocity. The flexible interest rate determines the composition of consumption and savings and hence investment, given the preference of people for present versus future income.

This model has some interesting implications. The production function is fixed by technology, and the demand for labor is determined by the production function. Is there any way in this model for the level of real output and employment to drop?

Refer to Figure 4.8. In the labor market graph, the labor supply curve is shifted upward. This might occur if workers develop a preference for more leisure. They will supply more labor only at a higher real wage than before. As can be seen, the real wage and the price level both rose, but the level of employment and output both drop (to N_u and Y_u), where u indicates a level below the full employment level, that is, a level with unemployment.

If the original levels of output (Y_e) and employment (N_e) were considered "full employment," then full employment has been lost, and the economy has slipped into a recession. The cause, however, can be attributed to the *voluntary* shift in the labor supply curve. Some economists in the classical tradition argued that statistically measured unemployment might be *voluntary* unemployment. The economy is still in equilibrium, but workers are demanding wages that are too high if they are dissatisfied with the level of employment. If they want employment to grow, they themselves are the obstacle. They must be willing to lower their wage demands (which would have the effect of lowering the supply curve). It must be remembered in this model that a reduction in employment and output cannot be caused by a shift in the labor *demand* curve. It is fixed because it is the marginal product curve.

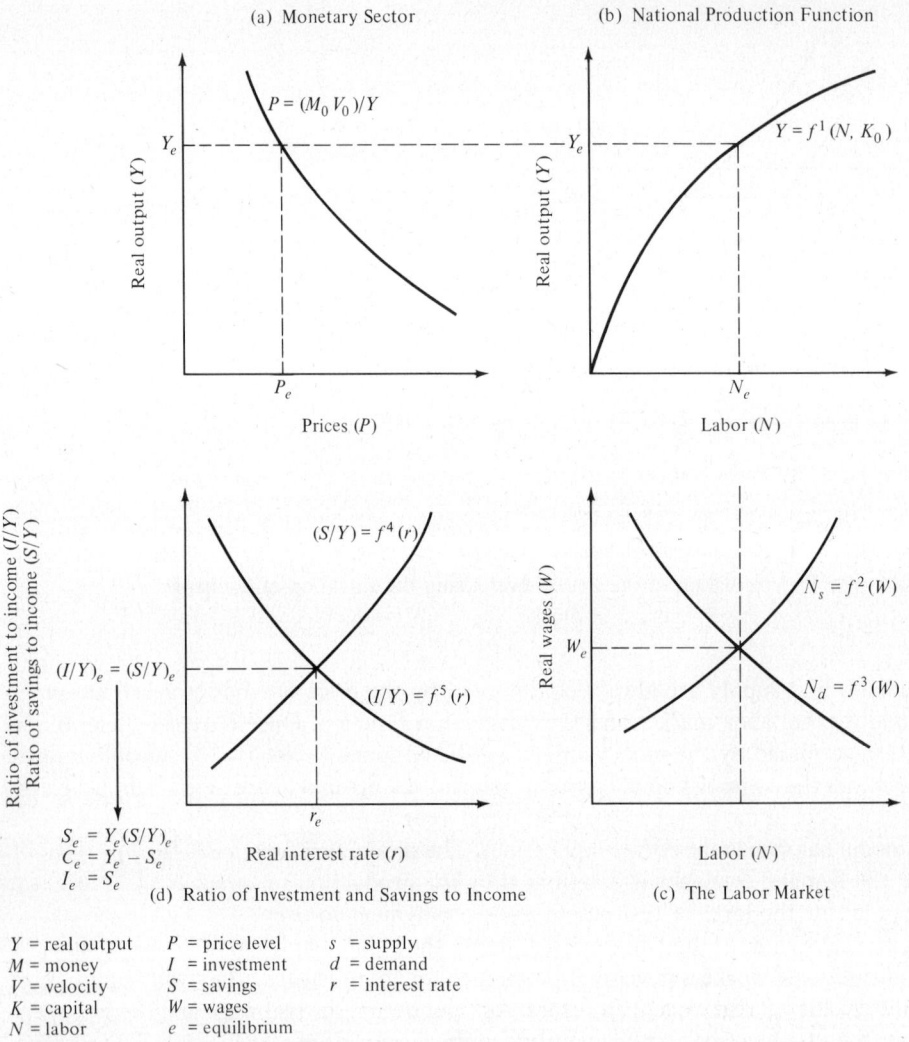

Figure 4.7 The Full Classical Model

SUMMARY

This chapter presented a model that contains the salient argument of mainstream classical economic theory. It presents the conclusion of Say's law that the economy will operate at a full employment equilibrium if labor itself does not impose an obstacle. In this more refined sense of Say's law, all markets have a tendency to work toward equilibrium because of competitive pressures and flexible wages, prices, and interest rates. In the labor market, all workers who desire to be employed at the prevailing wage rate are employed. Furthermore, it is workers who, in the labor-leisure choice, *determine* the wage rate. Therefore, if the detached observer sees any unemployment, it is voluntary unemployment.

The model that produced this result assumed perfect competition, no government, and a

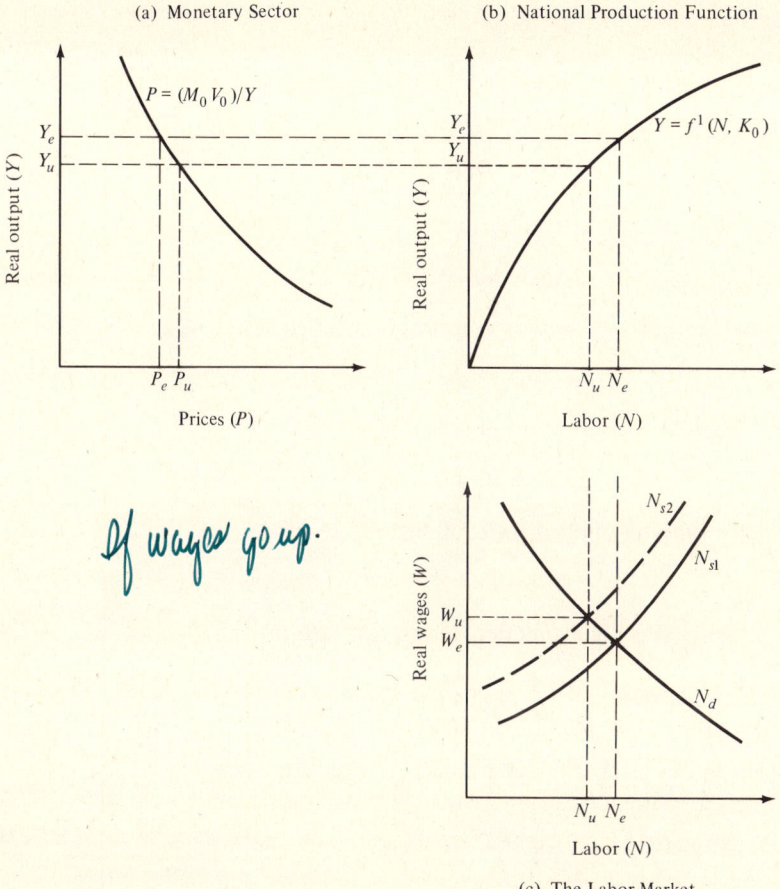

Figure 4.8 The Effect of a Shift in the Labor Supply Curve

given technology. The labor supply curve determines the level of employment and output. The money supply determines the price level. Attitudes about savings and investment determine the composition of aggregate demand. Most of the assumptions and arguments of this model are critiqued in the next chapter.

APPENDIX 4A

Complete Model of the Classical Theory

The complete classical model is repeated here:

Production (Y) is a function of labor (N) and capital (K).

$$Y = f^1(N, K_0) \tag{4A.1}$$

Labor supply (N_s) is function of the real wage (W).

$$N_s = f^2(W) \qquad (4A.2)$$

Labor demand (N_d) is function of the real wage.

$$N_d = f^3(W) \qquad (4A.3)$$

Labor demand equals labor supply, at equilibrium.

$$N_d = N = N_s \qquad (4A.5)$$

Output supplied (Y_s, or real income) equals consumption (C) plus saving (S).

$$Y_s = C + S \qquad (4A.6)$$

Output demanded (Y_d) equals consumption plus investment.

$$Y_d = C + I \qquad (4A.7)$$

Output demanded equals output supplied, at equilibrium.

$$Y_s = Y = Y_d \qquad (4A.8)$$

Average propensity to save (S/Y) is a function of interest rate (r).

$$\frac{S}{Y} = f^4(r) \qquad (4A.11)$$

The average propensity to invest (I/Y) equals function of interest rate.

$$\frac{I}{Y} = f^5(r) \qquad (4A.12)$$

Money (M_0, a given) times velocity (V, constant) equals output times price (P).

$$M_0 V_0 = YP \qquad (4A.13)$$

For the convenience of the reader, these equations are numbered the same as those in the Chapter 4, except that an A is added to indicate Appendix. The missing numbers are equations not directly necessary in the full model (because they are included in or implied in equations that are stated).

Notice that the production function and labor market equations (4A.1, 4A.2, 4A.3 and 4A.5) can be solved together to determine the equilibrium level of output! Through the rest of the model, this given level of output will then determine the levels of consumption, saving, investment, and price. The commodity and finance markets (equations 4A.6, 4A.7, 4A.8, 4A.11 and 4A.12) only determine the proportion of that given output that will go into consumption and investment (saving). The equation of exchange (4A.13) only determines the price level, based on that given output level.

In this model, it is important to understand that the labor demand curve was the marginal product of labor curves. The argument depended upon the proposition that

$$W = MPP_n \tag{4A.4}$$

where W is the real wage rate and MPP_n is the marginal product of labor.

This result comes from neoclassical microeconomic theory, where it is argued that producers want to maximize profits. They will, therefore, maximize the following constrained function:

$$\text{Maximize } \Pi = P_y Y - (P_n N + P_k K) - \lambda \, (Y - f\,[N,\,K]) \tag{4A.14}$$

where $(P_n N + P_k K)$ is cost, $P_y Y$ is revenue, λ is the Lagrangian constraint, Y is the level of output, P_y is the price of output, P_n is the price of labor, P_k is the price of capital, and $f(N,K)$ is the production function.

Assume that the level of capital (K) is fixed in the short run. To obtain two first-order conditions for cost minimization, one must take the following two derivatives and set them equal to zero.

$$\partial \Pi / \partial N = -P_n + \lambda \, \partial f / \partial N = 0 \tag{4A.15}$$

$$\partial \Pi / \partial Y = P_y - \lambda = 0 \tag{4A.16}$$

Substituting (4A.16) into (4A.15) produces this result:

$$\partial f / \partial N = P_n / P_y \tag{4A.17}$$

The left-hand expression is defined to be the marginal product of labor, and the right-hand expression is the real wage. Equation (4A.13), therefore, is derived from the first order conditions for profit maximization. This whole neoclassical approach to marginal productivity has been strongly attacked in a vast literature in the last decade.

Chapter 5

THE CRITICAL ANALYSIS OF SAY'S LAW

John Maynard Keynes (1883–1946) is perhaps the most important economist of the first half of the twentieth century. His background does not appear to be that of a radical or an earthshaker. Born into a respected English family and educated in the best British schools, Keynes worked for His Majesty's Civil Service and the Bank of England, edited the *Economic Journal,* and wrote careful treatises on Indian finances and formal logic as well as on the general problems of money. Keynes was always considered one of the establishment in cultural, governmental, and financial circles, yet he rocked the establishment both in England and the United States by demolishing the myth of Say's law and automatic full employment.

Say's law had been attacked by such unorthodox economists as Malthus and Marx. Keynes, however, attacked it in detail, using the respectable academic tools of the classical and neoclassical economists. In his most famous book,[1] written at the depths of the Great Depression, he exposed a fatal flaw in the classical model and showed that the equilibrium level of the economy might be either at a point of heavy unemployment or at overly full employment and inflation.

EQUILIBRIUM OF AGGREGATE SUPPLY AND DEMAND

Keynes used the idea of an equilibrium of the forces of aggregate supply and demand as an important analytical tool for understanding the level of output and employment. *Aggregate supply* is defined as the total output that business produces and plans to sell. *Aggregate*

---

[1] John Maynard Keynes, *The General Theory of Employment, Interest, and Money* (New York: Harcourt Brace Jovanovich, 1936).

demand is defined as the total dollar amount of final goods and services that consumers, business people, government, and foreigners *plan* to buy from the business sector. *Equilibrium* exists when planned aggregate demand equals planned aggregate supply at present prices.

Accountants investigating the modern economy typically make supply and demand equal in their calculations, but that is only by including unwanted and unplanned accumulation of inventories as part of "demand." When aggregate supply actually exceeds the level of demand, business inventories in the form of unsold goods begin to accumulate. Therefore, the following relationship exists:

$$\text{supply} = \text{demand} + \text{change in inventories} \tag{5.1}$$

Planned spending is defined as all spending except the spending on unintended and unwanted increases in inventories. Planned supply and planned demand will be equal only when the economy is *at equilibrium. Equilibrium* means that buyers' and sellers' desires exactly agree at present prices. If, however, 1000 bushels of ripe tomatoes go unsold, then the supply at present prices is greater than the planned demand, so there is no equilibrium.

The problem may be explained another way by saying there is equilibrium only if consumption plus planned investment are equal to consumption plus saving. *Saving* is defined as the difference between income and planned consumption spending. Keynes argued that equilibrium is maintained only if saving out of income is just equal to planned investment spending.

A flow diagram of economic equilibrium was shown in the previous chapter in Figure 4.4. A modification to that same diagram showing the possibility of a disequilibrium is presented in Figure 5.1. This diagram allows the possibility of "financial hoarding," where some monetary savings that flow into financial markets do not immediately flow back out as funds used to finance investment.

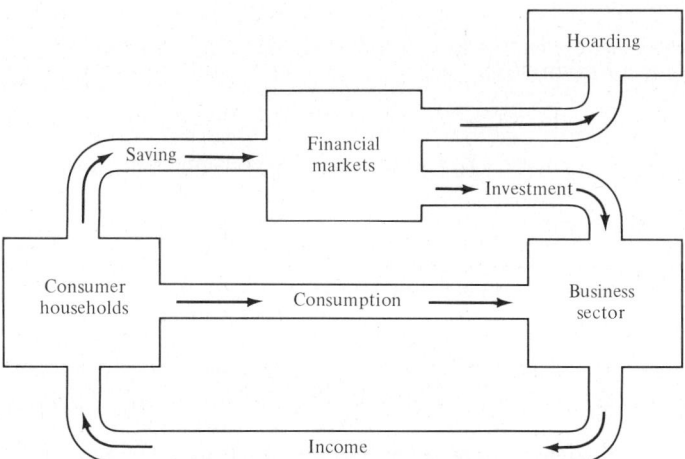

Figure 5.1 Income and Demand Flow Diagram Showing the Possibility of Financial Hoarding

The flow diagram in Figure 5.1 does *not* assume that savings equals intended investment. It assumes that

$$\text{savings} = \text{investment demand} + \text{financial hoarding} \tag{5.2}$$

Savings will equal investment, and the economy will be in equilibrium only when hoarding equals zero. Any hoarding constitutes a leakage from the spending stream.

Financial hoarding does not necessarily imply behavior like sticking money in a mattress or saving pennies in a jar. If people accumulate money in their checking account and refuse to spend it or if banks hold deposits that are not lent or if people use money to buy up financial assets in speculative frenzy, financial hoarding occurs. Remember that, in economics, *investment* always means actually spending on plant, equipment, and materials—it does *not* mean merely depositing money in a bank or buying someone else's shares of stock. More detailed examples of financial hoarding are provided in later sections, and investment is discussed in Part Two.

If saved funds do not find an outlet as investment, aggregate demand will be less than aggregate supply, and the economy will be in disequilibrium. If this condition persists, the conditions for an economic crisis are present.

Disequilibrium here means simply that the total money demand for all goods is different from the value of all goods at present prices. When demand is less than supply, inventories accumulate, and capitalists lose money, so they cut back on production and fire workers. The economy may reach equilibrium again only at a much lower level of supply, when a vast number of workers are unemployed.

A KEYNESIAN MODEL

Keynes was not always a careful writer, and he was unclear in many of his crucial arguments. As is typical of many seminal works, his written contributions to economic thought have been subjected to substantial amounts of "interpretation." The model that follows is another such interpretation and is, one hopes, faithful to Keynes's own view on essential matters.

As in the classical model, the output supplied (Y_s) or national income equals by definition the consumer spending (C) plus all saving (S).

$$Y_s = C + S \tag{5.3}$$

The level of expenditures or aggregate demand (Y_d) equals intended consumer spending plus intended investor (I) spending.

$$Y_d = C + I \tag{5.4}$$

If there is equilibrium, where output supplied equals aggregate demand, then savings equals investment:

$$Y_s = Y = Y_d \tag{5.5a}$$

$$S = I \tag{5.5b}$$

Keynes's great achievement was to show that there might be a disequilibrium that could lead to a later equilibrium with unemployment and price instability.

THE CONSUMPTION FUNCTION

Keynes's consumption function relates aggregate consumption to aggregate income.

$$C = f^1(Y) \tag{5.6}$$

where there is a positive relationship (the function, f^1) between consumption and income. Since consumption plus saving equal income, the saving function equals income minus the consumption function.

$$S = Y - f^1(Y) \tag{5.7}$$

This is quite unlike the classical function, which emphasizes the interest rate. Later Keynesians use both income and the interest rate.

Keynes gives particular attention to deducing the psychological bases for the decision of households to save or consume at different economic levels. Consumer demand is determined for the most part by the level of national income. His reasoning about consumer behavior is based on certain broad psychological assumptions: (1) At a very low income level, the average individual still needs some minimum consumption and, therefore, will spend all his or her income on consumption and may even dip into savings or go into debt to spend more than his or her whole current income on consumption. (2) As the individual's income rises, a smaller percentage of it is needed to cover minimum needs, so at some break-even point he or she reaches an equality of income received and consumption spending. (3) As income rises to a very high level, consumption needs and desires may be filled through the use of a smaller portion of income, so an increasing percentage may be saved. Therefore, as income rises, the proportion of income spent on consumption declines.

Keynes called the average ratio of aggregate consumption to aggregate income the *average propensity to consume:*

$$APC = \frac{C}{Y} \tag{5.8}$$

The ratio of the *change* in consumption to a change in income is called the marginal propensity to consume;

$$MPC = \frac{\Delta C}{\Delta Y} \tag{5.9}$$

Note the psychological approach embedded in this terminology; it will be criticized at a later point when consumption functions are discussed in detail.

THE INVESTMENT FUNCTION

Keynes sees investment as a function of the *marginal efficiency of capital,* defined as the expected rate of return on capital. This expected rate of return is inversely related to the size of the capital stock. Keynes looks at both the expected flow of revenue and the expected flow of costs. He stresses that expectations are affected by "animal spirits," confidence, and many other unquantifiable variables. On the cost side, Keynes, like the classical economists, stresses the rate of interest as the price of borrowing saved income. On the revenue side, unlike the classical economists, he emphasizes the importance of demand or national income.

Thus, investment is a function of the interest rate, national income, and certain expectations about future sales, prices, interest rates, and so forth.

$$I = f^2 (Y, r, E) \tag{5.10}$$

where f^2 is a function, r is the interest rate, and E represents expectations. The functional relationship between investment and income is positive, while the relationship between investment and the interest rate is negative. The complicated impact of changes in expectations will be shown later. Some Keynesians would make investment a function of the level of national income; most would make it a function of the change in national income. Keynes himself emphasized not only national income, but also the importance of expectations of future revenues and future costs, so the investment decision is often characterized by uncertainty about the future.

The relationship between the marginal efficiency of capital schedule and the investment schedule is shown in Figure 5.2. The *marginal efficiency of capital* was the expected yield or rate of return on a new capital stock.

If we consider the case of capital that would be productive forever (no physical depreciation), the yield on capital (*MEC*) will equal the return from capital (Π) divided by the price of capital (P_k):

$$MEC = \frac{\Pi}{P_k} \tag{5.11}$$

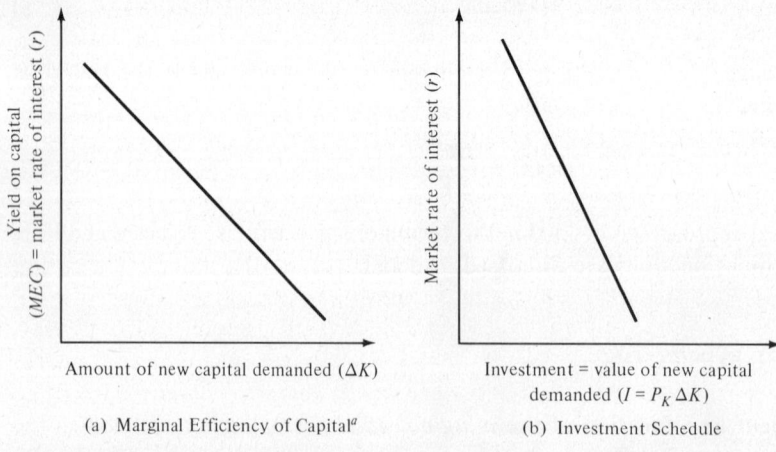

(a) Marginal Efficiency of Capital[a] (b) Investment Schedule

P_K = price of capital

Figure 5.2 Marginal Efficiency of Capital Schedule
[a]$MEC = r$ only at equilibrium.

P_k is expected to rise as the capital stock rises since investors will bid up the price of capital. The return (Π) will fall because a declining marginal product of capital will make each unit of capital added less productive. This implies that there is a negative relationship between the *MEC* and the quantity of capital. It is assumed that producers will expand their capital stock until the *MEC* is equal to the market interest rate. Therefore, *if there is equilibrium,* the *MEC* schedule also shows the relationship between the market interest rate and the quantity of capital demanded by investors. This relationship is shown in Figure 5.2(a).

If the quantity of capital demanded (ΔK) is multiplied times the price of capital, the resulting product, which is the level of investment, can be charted as the investment schedule. This is shown in Figure 5.2(b).

It is important to understand that the MEC schedule and the investment demand schedule are not the same thing. There is a subtle difference. The MEC schedule shows the relationship between the rate of return on capital (equal to the interest rate in equilibrium) and the *amount* of new capital demanded (ΔK). The investment schedule shows the relationship between the interest rate and the *value* of new capital demanded ($P_k \, \Delta K$), which is defined as investment. Also, it is important to understand that as ΔK rises with lower interest rate, P_k will rise with it; and the product of the two ($P_k \, \Delta K$), which is investment, will reflect both changes.

Even if capital has a finite life, the results are essentially the same. Instead of using equation 5.11 to calculate the *MEC*, we would have to use a discounting formula.

$$P_k = \sum_{i=1}^{t} \frac{\Pi_i}{(1+MEC)^i} \qquad (5.12)$$

In this equation, which would have to be solved for *MEC*, t represents the number of years in the life of the capital asset, and Π_i represents the expected return in each year. In this more complicated formula, *MEC* will still fall as P_k rises and Π_i drops with a larger capital stock.

THE MARKET FOR SAVINGS AND INVESTMENT

As was shown in Chapter 4, the classical economists regarded the interest rate as the variable that produced the equilibrium between savings and investment. Keynes denied this. His denial was based upon the belief that some portion of savings could be retained in the form of money rather than lent directly or indirectly to investors. Money, Keynes argued, normally provides the holder with absolute *liquidity,* which is the ability to exercise "immediate command over goods in general." Bonds aren't as liquid as money because they can't be used to buy goods or even other financial assets directly. Money can. Because money is liquid—and that has value to someone possessing wealth—some amount of money will often be retained from savings. (Keynes considered a number of reasons why people would hold money as a form of saved wealth. These reasons are discussed extensively in Chapter 6.)

Three things acted together to determine the status of the financial market:

1. The level of savings, as determined by the marginal propensity to consume.
2. The marginal efficiency of capital, which determines the investment schedule.
3. The proportion of savings that is held in the form of money, which was ignored by the classical economists.

Figure 5.3 represents a Keynesian financial model. The negatively sloped investment schedule is determined by the marginal efficiency of capital. Savings, shown here as being insensitive to interest rates, is determined by the marginal propensity to save $(1-MPC)$. The interest rate is *not* determined by the equilibrium of savings and investment (at point b). The actual supply of funds provided to the finance markets is, in this case, less than savings and is represented by the *SF* line. *The difference between the supply of funds and savings is the amount of savings held in the form of money and not supplied to the finance markets.* At equilibrium interest rate r_e, the amount of money held in this way is represented by distance a. As can be seen in the model, the equilibrium interest rate, when there is one, is determined where investment and the supply of funds are equal.

The graph, as drawn, shows that the amount of money held is larger at low interest rates. When yields on alternatives to money are low, the liquidity offered by money justifies holding large amounts of it.

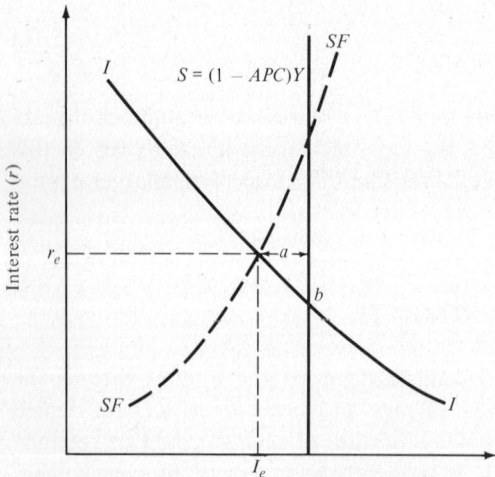

Investment (I), savings (S), supply of funds (SF)

S = savings
Y = income
APC = average propensity to consume
SF = supply of funds to the market
a = amount of money withdrawn for savings for liquidity purposes
b = where savings and investment are equal
e = equilibrium level

Figure 5.3 Equilibrium in the Finance Market

The graph also shows the possibility that the supply of funds may be greater than the level of savings at very high interest rates. This is possible only if money balances held from previous savings are used to purchase financial assets when yields are exceptionally attractive (this might be called "dishoarding").

Keynes regarded the "liquidity preference" of individuals, which determines the location of the SF line in Figure 5.3, to be very sensitive not only to interest rates, but also to many other variables, including potentially volatile expectations about future interest rates, price levels, and so forth. This implies that the supply of funds schedule in Figure 5.3 can shift around quite a bit and might shift dramatically with a sudden change in these expectations.

THE ROLE OF EXPECTATIONS IN CREATING A DISEQUILIBRIUM

Keynes gave considerable emphasis to the role of expectations in explaining economic performance and in explaining the recurrent crises that afflict capitalist market economies. His use of the expression "animal spirits" to describe the formation of expectations is perhaps unfortunate because the use of this term has occasionally engendered undeserved ridicule. In the use of it, Keynes simply meant that the guesses that are made about the economic future are not only the consequence of reason, but also of intuition, emotions, peer pressure, and other imprecise forces. Because this is so, expectations about the future returns from investment decisions might be biased—perhaps grossly so. Various world political and economic events might occasionally generate unjustified optimism or pessimism. If a certain turn of events transformed a consensus of optimism to a consensus of pessimism, regardless of the underlying rationality of these attitudes, very serious economic disruptions could occur.

Consider, for example, the situation in the late 1920s. There is considerable evidence that until 1929 the public mood was very optimistic—probably unreasonably optimistic.[2] Investors might have imagined that investment projects were likely to yield very lucrative returns. Such expectations would have generated a high investment schedule. Likewise many consumers might have felt very secure, believing they would keep their jobs and perhaps even experience a robust rise in their standard of living. Their level of consumption might have been fairly high.

Then in the autumn of 1929 the stock market crashed, the first incident in a chain of economic calamities. It is conceivable that this shocking event burst the optimistic bubble and replaced it with confusion, fear, and gloomy pessimism. (It is vital to emphasize that the stock market crash itself and the resulting change in expectations did *not* come out of the clear blue sky, but were the results of changes in real, objectively measured factors.) Such a dramatic change in expectations could severely affect both the supply of funds and investment schedules. One possible outcome is shown in Figure 5.4.

For a period of time the investment demand curve might collapse, as is demonstrated by the movement of the investment curve from position I_1 to position I_2 in Figure 5.4. This might be because the expected future revenue stream (the Π in equations 5.11 and 5.12) is

---

[2]See John K. Galbraith, *The Great Crash: 1929* (Boston: Houghton Mifflin, 1972).

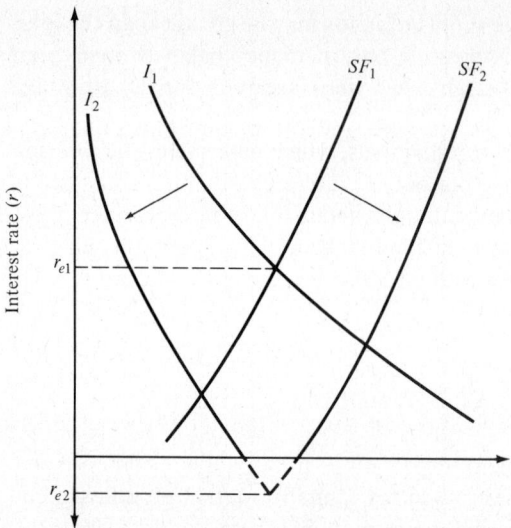

SF = supply of funds
I = investment
r = interest rate
e = equilibrium level

Figure 5.4 Disequilibrium in the Finance Markets Due to a Sudden (Pessimistic) Change in Expectations
NOTE: Supply of funds due to the finance markets equals savings minus money withdrawn for liquidity purposes.

deflated: estimates of future demand, sales prospects and even price stability might turn much more pessimistic. This might be due to a wait-and-see attitude or, in an extreme case, to outright panic.

Simultaneously, the supply of funds might move sharply outward because of a sudden rise in savings, as is represented by the movement of the supply of funds curve from SF_1 to SF_2 in Figure 5.4. Consumers, motivated by fear and an impending sense of insecurity, might defer consumption, especially of expensive items, to allow savings to accumulate. These savings might possibly offset a future income loss. These savings can take any form. The holders of saved funds would have probably been inclined to hold them in money form, either in checking accounts or currency, in the late 1920s.

The impact upon the economy is therefore twofold. The rising level of savings detracts from consumption, potentially creating a disequilibrium problem if the saved funds cannot be absorbed as investment. Additionally, to the extent that saved funds are "hoarded" as money and neither used for consumption nor channeled into investment, there is a leakage from aggregate demand which endangers the economy.

The more pervasive the switch in attitude, the more likely it is that at least one, if not both, of these schedules of savings and investment will shift substantially. As Figure 5.4 shows, the shifts could be so great that there is no equilibrium of the supply of funds and investment at a positive interest rate. Although negative interest rates are a theoretical possibility (banks would pay borrowers to borrow and charge interest to depositors!), they are an institutional impossibility; there is no organizational structure that would allow them to exist. There is, instead, a serious disequilibrium where the level of savings exceeds the level of investment.

The net effect of all of this is the "financial hoarding" illustrated in Figure 5.1. Considering the impact upon the entire economy, since aggregate output supplied (national income) equals consumption and savings,

$$Y_s = C + S \tag{5.3}$$

and since aggregate demand equals consumption and investment,

$$Y_d = C + I \tag{5.4}$$

when savings exceeds investment,

$$S > I \tag{5.13}$$

aggregate supply exceeds aggregate demand:

$$Y_d < Y_s \tag{5.14}$$

This is the general macroeconomic disequilibrium condition that can cause a recession. If there are attendant disturbances in the economy, such as numerous bankruptcies or a collapse of the financial system, then an economic depression is possible.

UNEMPLOYMENT EQUILIBRIUM

The first symptom of disequilibrium would be an undesired buildup in inventories. Soon after, output would be restricted by producers to bring inventories under control and match the new lower level of demand. There might be a decline in prices, which could cause more disturbances in the financial markets (because debtors find it harder to honor old debt obligations).

Eventually, because of the sharp declines in income, the flow of funds into savings will eventually drop, and the savings schedule will move back toward the origin. This is shown in Figure 5.5.

As can be seen, the interest rate is very low, as are the levels of savings and investment, when compared to levels of the past. At this low level, however, the economy is back in equilibrium. Savings and investment are equal, as is the level of aggregate demand and aggregate supply. Because income has fallen, however, the economy has returned to equilibrium at a *lower* income-output level than existed prior to the change in expectations. Unfortunately, the economy might stabilize at this level with high unemployment.

DEVELOPMENTS IN THE LABOR AND COMMODITY MARKETS

There was no place in the classical model, which was based on Say's law, for any of this to occur. Since the demand for labor was a function only of labor productivity and the wage

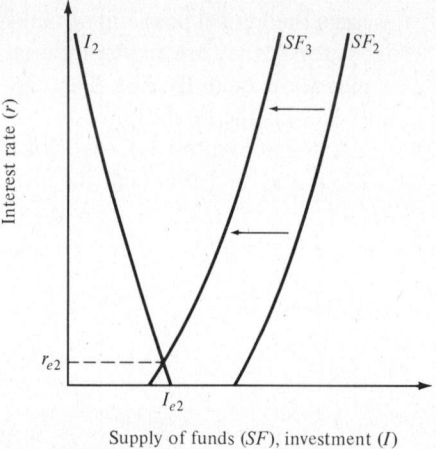

e = equilibrium level
SF = savings less money withdrawn for liquidity

Figure 5.5 Equilibrium in the Financial Markets When There Is an Unemployment Equilibrium

rate, the level of national output and the amount of labor actually employed were determined by the placement of the labor supply curve, which workers controlled.

The graphical version of the classical model is reproduced from Chapter 4 in Figure 5.6. Suppose there is a situation where a low level of national output and high unemployment exists. According to the classical model, unemployment exists when the supply of labor exceeds the demand for it. In Figure 5.6, this disequilibrium condition exists only when the real wage is too high—at level W_u in Figure 5.6. There is no other way that unemployment can be explained with this model.

This perspective encouraged many of the classical economists to insist that high unemployment and low output existed primarily because the real wage was too high. Such a problem can be overcome, they insisted, if only workers would agree to a nominal wage reduction, causing a drop in their real wage.

Indeed, the very conservative bias of the classical model is apparent when it is used to analyze this issue. The production function in graph(a) of Figure 5.6 is fixed by technology, as is the demand function for labor (since it is the marginal physical product of labor curve derived directly from the production function). In this model, capitalists passively choose a production level where the marginal product of labor equals the real wage. If the economy is at an equilibrium at a low level of production, that can be attributed to a "lazy worker" supply function, where the N_s supply curve is close to the vertical axis. (In such a case, workers might be said to have a high preference for "leisure.") If there is unemployment, workers are keeping real wages too high, and their refusal to drop nominal wages is the cause of the unemployment. Hence, because they could do something about it, workers are "voluntarily" unemployed.

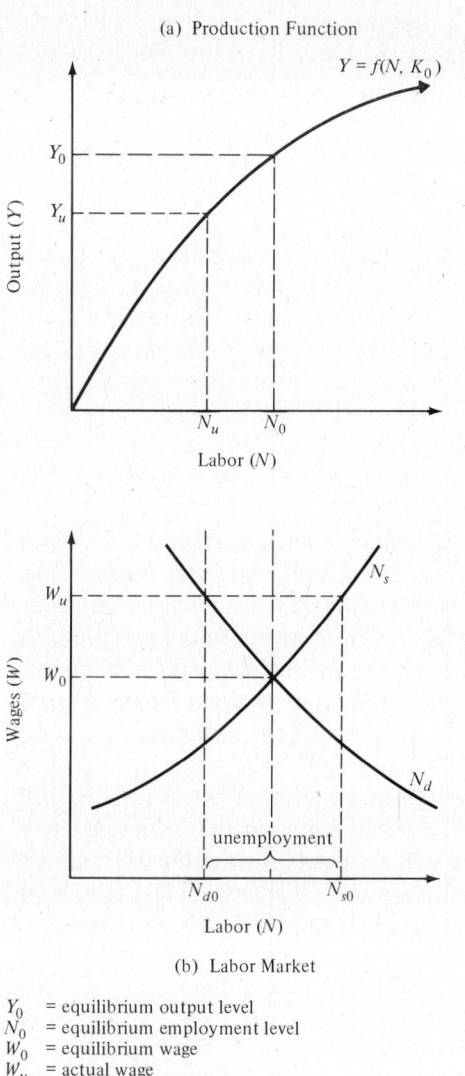

Y_0 = equilibrium output level
N_0 = equilibrium employment level
W_0 = equilibrium wage
W_u = actual wage
Y_u = actual level of output
N_u = actual level of employment
N_{d0} = actual labor demanded at W_u
N_{s0} = actual labor supplied at W_u
K_0 = capital (a constant)

Figure 5.6 Unemployment in the Classical Model

KEYNES'S REJECTION OF THE CLASSICAL ARGUMENT

Keynes (and later Keynesians) agreed that if certain institutional forces fixed wages at a level that was too high (above what would otherwise be the equilibrium in a competitive market), unemployment might result. In the original Keynesian analysis this, however, was not the *only* potential cause of unemployment. Therefore, recessions need not always (or ever) be attributed to the refusal of workers to lower their wages.

Keynes didn't comment on the specific "classical" model presented here, but he did comment upon one very similar to this developed by A. C. Pigou.[3] It is apparent from his writings that Keynes rejects outright the classical version of the demand for labor. Keynes agrees with the classical economists that the demand for labor is partly determined on the cost side, so it is partly a function of the real wage rate and productivity. But Keynes's major contribution is to point out the obvious fact that the demand for labor is also partly determined by the demand for output (in other words, *aggregate demand*). Thus, where the classical economists could say that labor demand is a function of the marginal productivity of labor, Keynes says it is also a function of aggregate demand.

Although the productivity of labor has considerable impact upon the demand for labor, equally if not more important is the impact of *expectations about sales of the products that labor manufactures.* If businesses are optimistic about sales (and have falling inventories), this optimism will tend to increase the demand for labor. If forecasts of future prospects are rapidly reversed, or if inventories suddenly build unexpectedly, the demand for labor suddenly might collapse. Keynes's opinion on this matter probably came from the observation that when he saw people fired or laid off, it was not due to changes in the marginal product of labor, but because of a drastic change in sales forecasts.

Although Keynes accepted the classical production function ($Y =$ function of N, K_0), his approach implies that we must turn its use in the chain of causation exactly upside down. The classical line of causation starts with a full-employment equilibrium in the labor market and says that, given the production function, that amount of labor would produce an equilibrium at the full-employment level of output. Keynes begins at the other end. Consumer demand plus investment demand require a certain level of output. That level of output, given the production function, will require a certain level of labor. Thus, in Figure 5.7, we have turned around the production function to read:

$$N = g(Y, K_0) \qquad (5.15)$$

where g is a positive function. The productivity relationship remains the same, but the direction of causation is reversed. This explains how labor demand is partly a function of output demanded and partly a function of labor productivity. Figure 5.7 illustrates the fact that, if labor productivity remains constant, a decline in output demanded will reduce employment.

---

[3]See J. M. Keynes, *The General Theory,* chap. 19. Pigou's model, which is very similar to the classical model criticized in this chapter, is developed in A. C. Pigou, *Theory of Unemployment* (London: Macmillan, 1933).

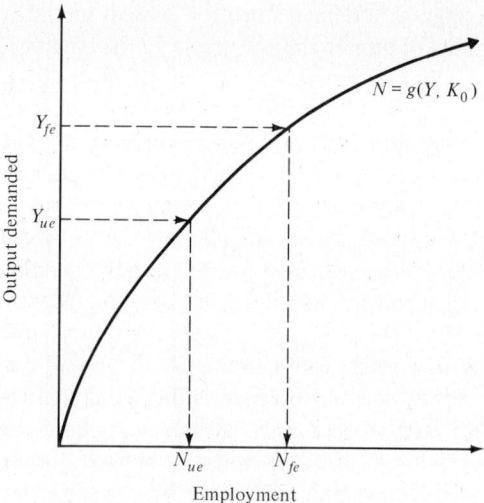

Y_{fe} = full employment level of output
Y_{ue} = unemployment equilibrium level of output
K_0 = given amount of capital
N_{fe} = full employment level of labor employed
N_{ue} = unemployment equilibrium level of labor employed

Figure 5.7 Effect of Decline in Output Demanded on the Employment of Labor

THE IMPORTANCE OF CONSIDERING AGGREGATE DEMAND

Considering only marginal productivity, all neoclassical economists conclude that the appearance of unemployment must mean that workers are getting a wage above the market (supply and demand) level. Therefore, the workers could be fully employed if they would accept a lower wage. Keynes, however, was not willing to concede that lowering workers' wages would restore full employment. To propose reducing wages during a period of economic distress, Keynes insisted,

> is tantamount to assuming that the reduction in money-wages will leave demand unaffected. There may be some economists who would maintain that there is no reason why demand should be affected, arguing that aggregate demand depends on the quantity of money multiplied by the income-velocity of money . . . Whilst no one would wish to deny the proposition that a reduction in money-wages *accompanied by the same aggregate effective demand as before* will be associated with an increase in employment, the precise question at issue is whether the reduction in money-wages will or will not be accompanied by the same aggregate effective demand as before . . .[4]

---

[4]*Ibid.*, pp. 258, 259.

As is pointed out in this quotation, nominal aggregate demand in the classical model is a monetary phenomenon, determined by the product of money times velocity in the equation of exchange (described in Chapter 4). Keynes did not accept this approach because of his belief that money could be either spent or held for liquidity purposes at the user's discretion. Aggregate demand was determined by the level of spending by businesses, governments, and consumers. Since the income of the latter group is determined mostly by wages earned, any variation in the wage rate will affect aggregate demand. Under the right circumstances it would cause aggregate demand to *drop*. If this happened, unemployment would be made *worse* by cutting wages rather than better. Not only is unemployment not necessarily the fault of workers demanding high wages; lowering wages won't necessarily cure unemployment—indeed, it might cause unemployment to rise.

There are *two* separate effects. Lower wages for all workers will increase product per dollar of labor cost, so it will increase employment if output demanded remains the same. This is the effect discussed exclusively by all neoclassical economists and by all business people as an argument for lowering wages. But lower wages for all workers will also reduce output demanded, which will reduce employment if productivity remains the same. This is the effect discussed by all trade unionists as an argument for higher wages. What Keynes did point out was (a) the existence of both effects and (b) that if the demand effect is greater, the net effect of reduction of wages is to reduce employment (which will further reduce aggregate wages and aggregate demand).

Keynes emphatically argued that, in considering the behavior of the economy, one must always consider the impact of aggregate demand. Since markets, in Keynes's opinion, did not always handily solve these problems, it was necessary to stimulate the market occasionally by artificial means. The most direct means would be through a high level of government purchasing in the economy. These Keynesian practical solutions are discussed in later chapters.

AMERICAN KEYNESIANISM AND THE "KEYNESIAN CROSS"

As the original Keynesian model became better understood, the *demand side* orientation of the model became strongly emphasized. Gradually, economists developed a pedagogical model (used for teaching Keynesian principles) that stressed the role of aggregate demand in determining the equilibrium level of income. This model, called the "Keynesian cross" was popularized in the 1950s by American economists in their textbooks.

In these models, the role of money and interest rates in the economy was de-emphasized. The model tried to demonstrate that variations in national spending could be attributed primarily to autonomous spending shocks. A Keynesian cross model is shown in Figure 5.8.

In this model, at equilibrium, aggregate supply and aggregate demand are equal. This level is "demand determined" and equal to the sum of consumption (C), investment (I), and government spending (G) along the equilibrium locus (the 45° line) that equates expenditures and income. The values of these components are determined in the following way:

$$C = a + (MPC)\ YD \tag{5.16}$$

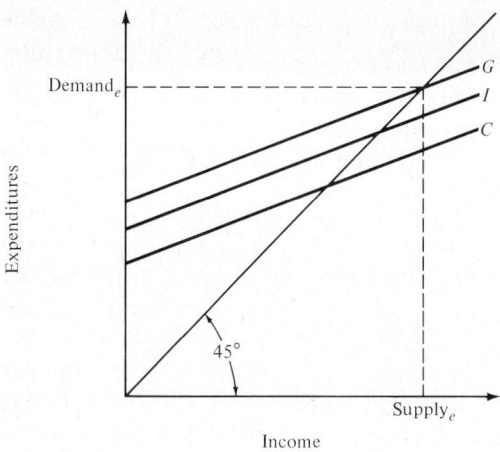

C = consumption
I = investment
G = government
e = equilibrium level

Figure 5.8 Diagram of a Keyensian Cross

where a is some constant, MPC is the Keynesian "marginal propensity to consume," and YD is disposable income after taxes. By definition:

$$YD = Y - T(Y) = (1-T)Y \qquad (5.17)$$

where T is the tax rate and Y is national income (GNP). Savings is the residual after consumption spending is subtracted:

$$S = YD - C \qquad (5.18)$$

where S is savings. Government spending equals taxes plus deficits:

$$G = T(Y) + D \qquad (5.19)$$

where G is government spending and D is deficit borrowing when the government runs a deficit. As an equilibrium position: investment equals all saving minus deficit borrowing:

$$I = S - D \qquad (5.20)$$

where I is investment.

Equation 5.16 is the Keynesian consumption function. Savings, in equation 5.18, is treated as a residual remaining after consumption. All income not consumed is kept in a box at home or deposited in a savings institution or used to purchase a financial asset. Equation 5.19 acknowledges that government spending must be financed by taxes or a deficit, which must be borrowed from savings. Equation 5.20 sets investment equal to all savings left over after the deficit has been financed (this is an equilibrium condition).

Income is the sum of the components of aggregate demand:

$$Y = C + I + G \tag{5.21}$$

The feature that gave this model its *demand side* was the proposition that investment and government spending decisions were not determined by saving. Investment decisions depended upon prospects for future profits, given the capital stock, capital price, interest rates, and expectations about future sales. Government spending was simply determined by the fiscal authorities. Therefore the I and the G in equation 5.21 have given values that determine the level of income. If equation 5.17 is substituted into equation 5.16, the result is

$$C = a + (MPC)(1-T)Y \tag{5.22}$$

If this is substituted into equation 5.21, the resulting equation (with I_0 and G_0 being set as constants) allows the determination of income.

$$Y = I_0 + G_0 + a + (MPC)(1-T)Y \tag{5.23a}$$

which reduces to:

$$Y = \frac{a + I_0 + G_0}{[1 - MPC(1-T)]} \tag{5.23b}$$

For example, if it is assumed that

$$a = \$10 \text{ billion} \tag{5.24}$$

$$MPC = 0.80 \tag{5.25}$$

$$T = 0.25 \tag{5.26}$$

and investors decide to spend $12 billion and the government decides to spend $42 billion, then

$$Y = \frac{10 + 12 + 42}{[1 - 0.80(0.75)]} = \$160 \text{ billion} \tag{5.27}$$

Solving for the other equations in the system produces the following results:

$$YD = (1-T)Y$$
$$120 = 0.75(160) \tag{5.17}$$

$$C = a + (MPC)YD$$
$$106 = 10 + 0.8(120) \tag{5.16}$$

$$S = YD - C$$
$$14 = 120 - 106 \tag{5.18}$$

$$G = TY + D$$
$$42 = 0.25(160) + 2 \tag{5.19}$$

$$I = S - D$$
$$12 = 14 - 2 \tag{5.20}$$

$$Y = C + I + G$$
$$160 = 106 + 12 + 42 \tag{5.21}$$

In the Keynesian cross diagram, the consumption line represents equation 5.16. The investment and government lines reflect the view that they are not determined by saving. If a higher level of nominal income were desired and justified, this could be accomplished by increasing government expenditures. This would shift the G line on the "Keynesian cross" upward; the initial spending stream would be multiplied as it flows through the economy until a higher and again stable level of employment and income was again achieved. The resulting deficit would be financed by an increase in savings that itself was the consequence of higher incomes.

In this model, equation 5.23b—considering the change in each variable—shows that the change in income will be equal to a multiple of the original change in autonomous government spending.

$$\Delta Y = \frac{1}{[1-MPC\ (1-T)]} \times \Delta G \qquad (5.27)$$

The middle expression of equation 5.27 is the famous Keynesian *multiplier*. New savings will be generated because of higher income:

$$\Delta S = (1-MPC)(1-T)\Delta Y \qquad (5.28)$$

New tax revenues will also be generated because of higher income:

$$\Delta TR = T(\Delta Y) \qquad (5.29)$$

where TR is new tax receipts.

Combining equations 5.27, 5.28, and 5.29 produces the result that new savings and the new tax revenues, *which accrue from the new higher levels of income,* will exactly equal the original level of government borrowing.

$$\Delta S + \Delta TR = \Delta G \qquad (5.30)$$

Because of this result, this model gives the impression that exogenous (external to the economy) increases in government spending in effect pay for themselves. Consequently, the importance of the monetary impact of government spending was substantially de-emphasized. The de-emphasis of the monetary impact of government spending eventually led to severe criticism of the model from both conservative and liberal economists. The Cambridge Keynesian economist Joan Robinson declared the model to be naive because it grossly simplified the complexity of the true Keynesian model. As will be seen in Chapter 16, the conservative monetarists criticized this model because of its neglect of the financial implications of government spending.

MARX'S CRITIQUE OF SAY'S LAW

Long before Keynes wrote, Karl Marx (1818–1883) made the same critical attack on Say's law; he also showed logically that capitalism is subject to recurrent attacks of mass unemploy-

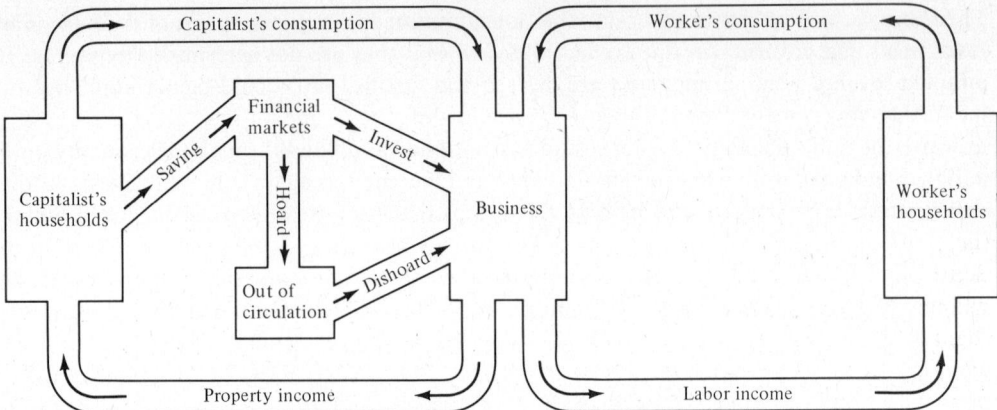

Figure 5.9 Income Flow—Marxist Picture (Private Domestic Sector Only)

ment.[5] Unlike Keynes, however, he argues that the capitalist diseases of unemployment and inflation cannot be cured by reforms but only by replacing capitalism completely with the new economic system of socialism.

Marx's distinctive contribution to income determination analysis is to point out the very different demand behavior resulting from workers' wage income and from capitalists' property income. This distinction is shown in Figure 5.9.

Marx divides income into two flows:

$$\text{labor income } (W) + \text{property income } (\Pi) = \text{national income } (Y) \qquad (5.31)$$

Labor income here includes all income earned from labor, such as piecework wages, hourly wages, and salaries. Property income includes all the unearned income deriving from ownership of property, such as profits from ownership of capital, rent from ownership of land, and interest from ownership of money. Marx argued that all property income is derived directly or indirectly from the labor done by workers.

The important point for macroeconomics is that workers' wages and capitalists' property income reveal very different spending patterns. On the one hand, most workers' income is in the lower-income categories. Thus, most of workers' income is spent for consumption whereas very little, if any, is saved. For simplicity, Marx considers that the low wages of debt-ridden poor workers are balanced by the higher wages of better-paid workers. Therefore, Marx assumes that aggregate wages just equal the consumer spending of workers:

$$\text{wage income} = \text{workers' consumption} \qquad (5.32)$$

The data in later chapters will indeed indicate that the average worker—the average of poorly paid and better paid, in good times and bad times—saves almost nothing.

Capitalists, on the other hand, receive very high incomes from profits, rent, and interest.

---

[5] Karl Marx, *Capital* (Chicago: Charles Kerr, 1903, first published 1867).

Therefore, as will be shown in later chapters, capitalists do save large parts of their income. As a result, the pattern of spending from capitalist income shows two flows. Capitalists not only spend on consumer goods, including luxuries, but also save some of their income:

$$\text{capitalist consumption} + \text{capitalist saving} = \text{property income} \tag{5.33}$$

What happens to capitalists' savings? In what forms do they save? A large part of their savings will be invested for profit. The capitalist buys stocks and bonds in corporations, and the corporations invest the money in factories, equipment, and inventories of goods on hand. Some of the money is invested indirectly through deposits in banks and insurance companies, who lend it to corporations, who use it to buy capital goods. It happens periodically, however, that there are no more profitable ways to invest the remaining amounts of capitalist saving. In that case, some of capitalist savings are not profitably invested but are held idle in banks or other hoards. As a general proposition,

$$\text{capitalist investment} + \text{capitalist hoarding} = \text{capitalist saving} \tag{5.34}$$

Of course, in a year with very high profit expectations, capitalists may invest beyond their current income by lowering their saving hoards or dishoarding.

Marx thus agrees with Keynes that saving may be greater than planned investment (causing unemployment) or saving may be less than planned investment (causing inflation). Marx, however, stresses that these problems arise because of (1) the distribution of income under capitalism and (2) the behavior of capitalists seeking profits. Marx stressed that the classical economists of his era were largely ahistorical, so they ignored the important new institutions of capitalism: production for the market, production for private profit, and pervasive use of money.

SUMMARY

The Great Depression was a complex historical event. The causes of the Great Depression were even more complex. It would be misleading to insist that Keynes identified unstable or volatile investment and savings functions as the "cause" of the depression. Keynes's observations on the depression and the economy were far more profound and complicated than those ideas presented here. Since Keynes's arguments were partly dynamic disequilibrium arguments, they cannot easily be represented in a simple static model. In later chapters, another conventional model called the *IS-LM* model often used to represent Keynes is presented, as well as the simplest "Keynesian" cycle model by Samuelson. But both of these are only pale reflections of Keynes's thought and misrepresent it in some ways. This chapter merely captures some of the salient arguments that are Keynesian in origin, which are used to deny Say's law at a theoretical level. The example of the Great Depression was used because Keynes's theoretical contributions to economics came partly as a response to the depression. It is no coincidence that Keynes's major works, most of which were published in the 1930s, were oriented to explaining the behavior of the overall economy and were concerned with such things as the level of national output or unemployment.

Keynes's conspicuous contribution to economic theory was to demonstrate as a logical possibility that an economy could suffer from a recurring serious problem of involuntary unemployment. Furthermore, the unemployment could have *endogenous* causes, meaning that it is the result of economic behavior on the part of people *within* the normal operation of the capitalist type of economy.

The occasional disequilibrium leading to unemployment could be caused by either a very unstable investment function, unstable consumption function (which affects savings behavior adversely), or both. The instability was due to the extreme sensitivity of these functions to changes in expectations. Expectations, in turn, could occasionally be very volatile and prone to sudden reversals, so a small change in the underlying economic conditions could lead to a large decline.

Given that an endogenous disequilibrium could disturb the economy, Keynes's second major contribution was to show that an economy could return to equilibrium at less than full employment. Savings and investment would equalize at low levels, as would aggregate demand and supply. Appeals to workers to lower their wages to stimulate demand for their services might be ineffective because aggregate demand could drop when aggregate worker income drops. The real cause of unemployment was not workers' reluctance to lower their wages, but an unstable demand function for labor's services.

The Marxist explanation presented in this chapter is similar to that of Keynes except that it emphasizes the distribution of income among the economic classes. Capitalists do most of the saving in the economy. If income distribution shifts in their favor and if there are not ample investment outlets for their savings, then there will be a drop in aggregate demand. Marx did not believe there would be equilibrium at any level, but rather a continuing process of change with disequilibrium at various levels of unemployment.

Up to this point, the role of the financial sector of the economy, which is very important in all these arguments, has only superficially been described. All during the classical and early Keynesian era, a debate over monetary theory raged on as a component of the more general controversy discussed so far. The debate over the role of the financial sector in economic instability is presented in the next chapter.

Chapter 6

MONEY: FROM $MV=PY$ TO $IS\text{-}LM$

Modern monetary policy has a rich and interesting legacy. Some of the fundamental ideas that are still believed today are centuries old, yet refinements to theory continue, producing insights and attitudes that have drastically changed the character of monetary theory.

The Keynesian revolution of the 1930s certainly accelerated innovation in monetary theory while at the same time changing the direction and methods of inquiry. New questions were asked; and new answers, provided. The field has become much more "scientific" in the sense that the bulk of research effort is now concerned with empirically verifying established hypotheses.

One might think that the amount of effort spent in refining monetary theory would have advanced knowledge on these matters to such a state that there would be a general consensus among economists about appropriate monetary policy. Unfortunately, such is not the case. There is perhaps more discord at the present than ever before. The intensity of current debates brings memories of the famous debates in England that occurred more than 150 years ago during the time of David Ricardo. Strangely enough, many modern arguments are essentially unaltered from their counterparts at that time.

That this is so is understandable. Because applied monetary policy involves the use of government power to influence behavior in private markets, monetary theory has profound political and philosophical implications. Some theories propose relatively interventionist policies whereas others trust the efficacy of unfettered free financial markets. In many cases, two theories that appear in opposition may both be structurally correct; policies based on these theories would "work" according to the plan envisioned by the theorists. The source of the opposition is to be found in the fact that the implementation of "working" policies will have different impacts upon interest groups and the rights of different individuals to act in the economic environment in the way they desire. For example, businesses typically favor laissez-faire policies because profit opportunities are more abundant whereas certain consumer and union groups favor interventionist policies because they believe they promote economic stability. Since the theories are as much political as economic, they are bound to differ.

So instead of having a body of knowledge that might be referred to as "monetary theory," we may perhaps find it more appropriate to refer to monetary theories. There is no consensus, and many of the ideas that influence policy today are directly contradictory, as will be seen further on.

This chapter will discuss some of the monetary theories that were popular prior to and during the period dominated by Keynesian economic theory. The chapter begins by introducing the equation of exchange and then follows with the Keynesian critique. The popular *IS-LM* model is explained next, and the chapter concludes with a discussion of important early modifications made to the theory by William Baumol and James Tobin. This will complete the discussion of the "early" monetary models that shaped economic thinking from the 1920s through the 1950s.

Because "modern" (post-1960) monetary theories use elaborate modifications of the theories discussed in this chapter and rely to some extent on material developed in the next nine chapters, discussion of these theories will be resumed in Part Four of this book. This chapter, in effect, discusses the theoretical *foundation* of modern monetary theory.

DEFINITIONS OF MONEY

When monetary theory is discussed, it is often implied or assumed that there is a clear understanding about what money actually is. Money is easy to define in terms of its functions. The conventional definition of *money* declares money to be anything that serves as (1) a medium of exchange, (2) a unit of account, and (3) a store of value.

A financial asset is a *medium of exchange* when it can be used directly to finance purchases of goods and services and to repay debts. If something has to be converted into a means of payment before it can be used to buy something, it is not money. This is the primary feature that distinguishes money from other financial assets like Treasury bills and those passbook accounts at savings and loan associations that must be kept a certain time (or can only be converted with a penalty).

Prices of goods, services, and financial assets are denominated in the monetary unit of account. The *unit of account* for American money is the dollar (and fractions of the dollar like the cent), and all prices are denominated in this unit of account.

Money is very convenient. It allows modern economies to transcend the requirements of barter because it eliminates the need for simultaneous exchange when trade takes place. Under a barter system, one might have to trade strawberries for squash. In a monetary system, one sells strawberries for money, then retains the money until one desires to make an expenditure. For money to serve this useful function, it must be a *store of value*. It must, in other words, represent a given amount of purchasing power over time. Inflation tends to undermine this last function of money because during inflation money gradually loses its purchasing power.

Designating a list of financial assets that serve these functions is not as easy as it might seem. Federal Reserve notes (paper money) and coins are surely included because they are *legal tender,* which means that the law requires anyone to accept them for payment. Checking accounts at banks and other financial institutions are also included because most payments made today are made by check. There are a number of financial assets, however, that fall into a gray area. They include, for example, the now popular money market mutual funds, which allow limited checking privileges. Economists cannot agree on whether assets such as these should be counted as money.

The modern controversy over what should and should not be counted as money will be explained in depth in Chapter 17 after suitable groundwork has been established for the discussion. For the purposes of this chapter, assume that money consists of coin, currency, and checkable deposits (checking accounts) at banks and other financial institutions.

THE GENESIS OF MODERN MONETARY THEORY: THE EQUATION OF EXCHANGE

An attitude prevailing among some theorists today is that there is a distinct and understandable relationship between the amount of money supplied by monetary authorities and the level of nominal spending in the economy. Such an attitude insists that the supply of money is exogenous to the economy and controlled by a regulatory agency and that the connection between money and spending is stable and predictable.

The device that is often used to demonstrate this proposition at the pedagogical level is the so-called *equation of exchange.* Simply stated, it says that the money stock times its rate of circulation in the economy is equal to the flow of spending on final goods and services:

$$MV = PY \tag{6.1}$$

In this identity equation, P should be thought of as the general price level. Y is the real value of all final goods produced in a single year. (Statistically, P would be represented by the implicit price deflator for gross national product, and Y would be gross national product in constant dollars.) M is the statistically measured money stock (however defined). Velocity (V) represents the number of times on the average that a single dollar is spent on final goods and services in a given year. Not too much importance should be imputed to the notion that velocity is a rate of circulation of money. Money doesn't flow through the economy like water down a chute. Most money exists as mere bookkeeping entries, and a good part of it sits unused (out of circulation) for long periods of time. More useful notions of the meaning of velocity will be introduced later.

The equation of exchange is a mere identity—a tautology. It simply reflects the truism that the value of all final goods and services sold and transferred to the ultimate users (PY) were paid for by money transfers in the opposite direction (MV). In its simplest form as a mere truism, the identity is not a behavioral equation, and it explains very little about the connection between money and expenditures. Only when additional information or supplementary models are supplied does the equation begin to tell useful stories.

The equation of exchange is often attributed to Irving Fisher, one of the true pioneers in modern monetary theory. The historical legacy is somewhat unclear, however, because the equation of exchange is implicit in a long string of monetary theories, reaching back through Mill and Ricardo to David Hume. Fisher is a good starting point, nonetheless, because his early works established an approach where the level of the money stock is the singular important variable that affects the level of spending in a market economy.[1]

In Fisher's paradigm, if velocity is constant or changes slowly, then all sudden money increases are reflected as increases in nominal national output. The distribution of the effect between prices and real output is indeterminate, of course, without knowing more about the state of capacity utilization and other things. If the economy is operating at full capacity, then the impact will primarily be felt in prices.

Velocity was not constant in Fisher's model nor in any other of any importance, but its behavior was not explained by any variable that also influenced the money stock. Velocity might change because institutional changes could expedite or retard the flow of payments through the economy, and hence it was determined by spending habits and the structure of financial institutions. Velocity would, therefore, be slow to change, and most significant changes would depend upon innovations in the payments mechanism.

Fisher was part of the classical tradition that believed that resources were normally being fully utilized in a developed free market economy. According to the classical tradition, the market worked in such a way that resources would automatically be used by profit-maximizing businesses if their cost of use was exceeded by the value of their contribution to social wealth. Once the scale of resource use reached the point where this was no longer true, the resource was being fully utilized, and no further exploitation would take place. This is consistent with the equilibrium in the Say's law model presented in Chapter 4. When true for all resources, including labor, the economy would be operating at full capacity or full employment. The level attainable was limited by such constraints as the size and skill level of the labor force, availability of resources, the state of technology, the consumption desires of the population, and so forth.

This belief in the "invisible hand" was fervently subscribed to by Fisher and most others in his discipline prior to the 1930s. The Y component of gross national product was being maximized at most times, so anything but the most modest and gradual increases in the money supply would cause a rise in prices.

To economists in the tradition of Irving Fisher, money mattered only in the sense that ample amounts were needed to lubricate the wheels of trade. Since output was determined by real factors in the economy such as the state of technology and the supply of labor and other resources, variations in the money stock primarily influenced the price level. Extreme increases in the money supply would cause an unwanted inflation, and decreases would cause a deflation.

ECONOMIC DISTRESS AND THE TRIUMPH OF KEYNES

The Great Depression not only traumatized the real world, but it also traumatized economic theory. Models explaining the connection between money and the real economy were obvi-

---

[1] Irving Fisher, *The Purchasing Power of Money* (New York: Kelley, 1963; orig. pub. 1911).

ously deficient because they neither predicted nor explained the collapse. A paradigm centered on the equation of exchange or some similar construction would have found it impossible to give a decent explanation of the catastrophe that had beset the world. An intellectual vacuum was created by the turn of events, and into that void stepped the notable English economists of the period, the most eminent among them being John Maynard Keynes.

Keynes was part of a group of who were investigating the demand for money balances.[2] They wanted to reexplore the question of what people did with their money. Implicit in the classical version of the equation of exchange is the notion that money is held to finance transactions and for no other reason. Money, in the classical view, is only necessary because in a market economy receipts are not simultaneous with, or the same size as, expenditures, so purchasing power must temporarily be held in some medium of exchange.

The classical forms of the demand equation for money simply reflected this idea. The simplest demand equation was expressed as

$$Md = kPY = kQ \qquad (6.2)$$

Md represents the demand for money, and PY, as before, represents nominal expenditures or income (Q). Since prices (P) times quantity of output (Y) must equal the total flow of goods and services actually sold (at their present price or money value), this flow must equal by definition the amount of national income (Q) actually expended. At equilibrium, of course, all national income is expended. The proportion of income that is demanded as money balances is represented by the constant coefficient k. Here, the demand for money is simply a linear function of nominal GNP. The linear coefficient, (k), captures the relationship between money and spending. Therefore, it is the reciprocal of the velocity coefficient in the equation of exchange so long as it is assumed that there is an equilibrium equality between the demand and supply of money.

It is important to make clear what the *demand for money* actually represents. In the classical view, it is simply the aggregate amount of money that people require for all of their transactions—given the velocity or speed at which the payment mechanism works. The *demand for money* may be thought of as the desired money *inventory* that people and businesses want to hold (out of a given income and wealth).

The simplest classical model of money demand (necessary for all transactions) is not very profound, nor does it offer any startling revelations about the economy. As will be seen further on, however, with a few Keynesian modifications, the model will come to life and reveal some interesting insights.

OTHER MOTIVES FOR DEMANDING MONEY

The theory of demand presented by the classical economists might be conveniently labeled the "transactions demand" for money. Keynes believed that there were other motives than financing transactions for holding money. Keynes developed these ideas into the now famous

---

[2] See A. C. Pigou, "The Value of Money," *Quarterly Journal of Economics* (1917–1918), for an example of early work in this area.

classification of motives for holding (demanding) money: the *transactions motive,* the *precautionary motive,* and the *speculative motive.*[3]

The transactions motive for holding money is compatible with the Fisherian view of the role of money in a market economy. Money is used because it is necessary to facilitate transactions. The amount of money held will roughly correspond to the level of income in the economy. By inference, if new money balances are acquired, they would be used for transactions, preserving the rough proportionality between the money stock and spending flows.

The other two motives recognize that money can be held indefinitely as a financial asset, similar in many respects to more obvious financial assets like bonds and bills. The precautionary demand for money made use of the proposition that knowledge about the future is quite uncertain. Consumers and especially businesses can never be certain about the frequency and magnitude of receipts (or income). Many types of expenditures (such as for medical bills) are unforeseen as well. For that reason, businesses and consumers can be expected to keep a certain amount of cash on hand at all times to meet unforeseen contingencies. What solvent business, for example, would like to find itself in a situation of being unable to meet its payroll because of an unanticipated temporary shortfall in cash receipts? It is important to acknowledge that such a precautionary nature exists, but it is far more important, according to Keynes, to recognize that the amount of money held for this motive might fluctuate substantially as public opinion or forecasts of future events changed over time.

The speculative motive also relies heavily upon the notion that the future is uncertain. People who hold their wealth in the form of financial assets are never quite certain about the future value and yield of these assets. The performances of the stock market from 1928 to 1930 and of the bond market from 1979 to 1982 demonstrate the potential fragility of some "safe" assets. In a period of price stability, money offers no yield, which is a disadvantage, but its nominal value is certain. Therefore, it can be classified as a low-yield riskless asset. Most sophisticated savers, including businesses, will diversify their financial assets. In a portfolio of financial assets, money might have an important place because its nominal value is certain and it is readily available to finance the acquisition of another financial asset if an unexpected favorable opportunity presents itself.

For example, suppose the modern-day stock market trader foresees an unexpected climb in stock market prices. In that case, present stock values are a bargain. Having all wealth tied up in nonmoney securities might prevent the possibility of taking advantage of this bargain if those securities are illiquid or must be sold at a loss (they may have declined in value, for example, when equity prices rose). Sophisticated stock market traders, knowing this, will at times desire to have a good percentage of their portfolio tied up in money.

Cyclically, as the value of securities in a portfolio rises, the owner can be expected to liquidate some, taking profits and holding the cash proceeds until another buying opportunity presents itself. This holding of cash is what Keynes referred to as the speculative demand for money. Suppose, for example, a speculator believes that the economy has just reached bottom and will soon expand. Suppose she holds a $100 Treasury bond with a 10 percent

---

[3] These are introduced in John M. Keynes, *The General Theory of Employment, Interest, and Money* (New York: Harcourt Brace Jovanovich, 1936), pp. 195–198.

interest rate on its face. If interest rates have fallen to 8 percent, she would be able to sell the bond at a considerable profit. The speculator would then *hold the money* until interest rates went back up again. Then she could buy the same bond much more cheaply.

SLIPPAGE IN THE CONNECTION BETWEEN MONEY AND EXPENDITURES

Keynes called his theory of demand for money the theory of "liquidity preference." He theorized that all income is divided into consumption and savings by the recipients. The amount saved must be held in the form of a financial asset. Since different assets offer different degrees of liquidity and since money offers perfect liquidity, the amount actually held in cash will depend upon the recipient's *liquidity preference*.[4] Alternative financial assets offer positive yields, but there is risk associated with holding them because of the uncertain course of future interest rates. Their deviation from expected levels could cause capital losses. Anticipations about the level of future interest rates depend upon the present level of rates, so the demand for nontransactions money balances will vary with current interest rates.[5]

If such a proposition is true, the stable relationship between money and expenditures is substantially disturbed. Consumers hold cash not only for transactions purposes, but also because there is a liquidity-yield trade-off that influences the composition of their wealth in such a way that they might desire to hold money as a form of financial wealth. Accordingly, Keynes argued, under certain circumstances, the relationship between changes in the money supply and the level of spending in the economy becomes very inexact and occasionally unpredictable. If, for example, the liquidity preference of the public is rising when the money supply is increased, the effect of an expansion in money will be substantially diluted.[6] The public, in effect, would be hoarding more cash and not spending it. The connection between money and income becomes more enigmatic.

This latter point can be clarified with an example. The source of the accumulation of financial wealth is savings, that portion of money receipts that are not used for consumption. Savings is a flow. As illustrated in Figure 6.1, this flow, which always originally is in a money form, can either be converted into a nonmoney financial asset through the purchase of a security, or it may remain in money form, with the saver building up an unused money inventory.

The allocation of this flow between money and other financial assets will be determined, in part, by the level of interest rates and expectations about future interest rates. If interest rates are low, but are expected to rise, more of this flow will be diverted into a money form than would otherwise be the case. The reason is obvious; the speculator wants to avoid capital losses and wants to be able to have enough liquidity to take advantage of low security prices that are expected in the future.

Suppose recent economic events (such as volatile security markets) make the sensitivity of the speculative demand for money to interest rate changes rather high. Suppose, addition-

---

[4]Keynes, *op. cit.*, p. 166.
[5]*Ibid.*, pp. 201, 202, 208.
[6]*Ibid.*, pp. 173, 207, 208.

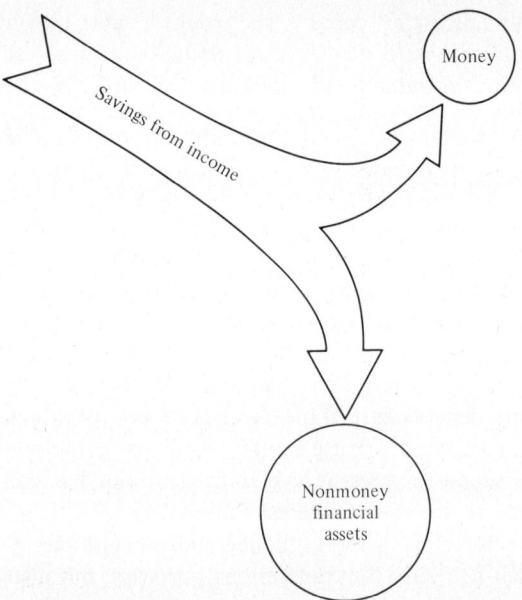

Figure 6.1 Savings Are Held in a Form of Financial Wealth, Either as Money or a Nonmoney Financial Asset, Such as a Bond

ally, that the economy is depressed. What would be the effect of a larger supply of money in this situation? Would it stimulate the economy? The larger supply of money would be accompanied by lower interest rates as credit conditions became easier. Businesses would be the recipients of new spending. If the proceeds are spent, which presumeably they would be, the economy is stimulated.

But what about the activity of the rest of the economy? If interest rates have dropped and the demand for speculative balances is very sensitive to this, a good part of the savings flow will be diverted into unused cash balances. The impact of this will *decrease* the level of spending, which tends to offset the original stimulus.

A KEYNESIAN EXPLANATION OF THE BEHAVIOR OF VELOCITY

One way of expressing this sort of Keynesian argument is to say that the the velocity of money is unstable.[7] Since velocity is simply the ratio of nominal GNP to the money stock, any set of circumstances that causes GNP to remain flat or fall when the money stock rises will cause velocity to fall. Any variable that affects the demand for money will usually affect velocity because variations in the demand for money will normally also affect GNP.

---

[7] For an interesting discussion of how to view these issues in terms of the behavior of velocity, see Bryon Higgins, "Velocity: Money's Second Dimension," in Federal Reserve Bank of Kansas City, *Economic Review* (June 1978), pp. 1–15.

This insight means that velocity (V) can be regarded from a new perspective when considering its contribution to the demand version of the equation of exchange:

$$Md = (1/V)GNP \qquad (6.3)$$

This variation of equation 6.2 simply reflects the fact that the coefficient (k) linking the demand for money to the level of expenditures is the reciprocal of velocity. Any variable that changes the velocity of money will automatically change the demand for money. Similarly, any variable except income (GNP) that changes demand for money must change velocity.

In the examples mentioned earlier, it was said that Keynes hypothesized that the demand for speculative money (MSD) was a function of the level of interest rates (r), where there is an inverse relationship (a negative function, g) between the two:

$$MSD = g(r) \qquad (6.4)$$

This goes back to our example of the speculator who wishes to hold money in liquid form when interest rates are very low and then will put the money into other financial assets when interest rates rise. This implies that velocity is also a function of the interest rate,

$$V = h(r) \qquad (6.5)$$

where there is a positive relationship (the function, h) between the two variables. If interest rates rise, the demand for speculative money will drop. These money balances become transaction balances and are spent, raising GNP and the velocity of money.

FURTHER REFINEMENTS IN KEYNESIAN THEORY

The profundity of Keynes's contribution to monetary theory was probably matched by the ambiguity with which he presented it in *The General Theory*. The Keynesian model provides numerous hints and insights, but is left with gaping holes in crucial explanations, combined with contradictory arguments here and there. Much of what has been presented here as Keynesian theory has relied upon recent interpretations of Keynes. In Keynes's original writings, it is not made perfectly clear why consumers hold money as a speculative financial asset. The original Keynesian model that explains this relies upon the idea that a saver fears a capital loss due to falling bond prices during a period of rising interest rates or upon the notion that *liquidity* in and of itself offers some utility to wealth holders.[8]

If it can be accepted that a speculative demand for money might actually exist, the relationship between money and income (spending) will indeed periodically be unstable. Is it possible then, one might ask, to clarify the exact nature of the relationship between money and income, preferably in the form of a model?

---

[8]The bonds-money nature of the Keynesian model is pointed out by John Hicks, *Economic Perspectives* (Oxford: Clarendon Press, 1977), chapter 3.

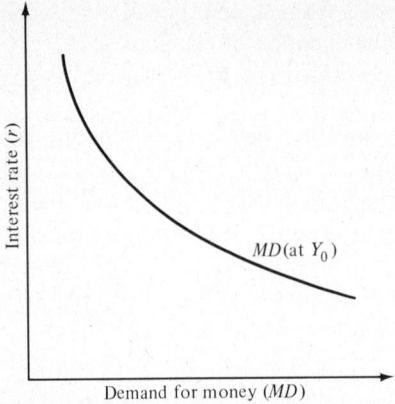

Y = income (GNP)
Y_0 = a given level of income

Figure 6.2 The Demand for Money as a Function of the Level of Interest Rates, Given Some Level of Income

THE *IS-LM* MODEL

Certainly, the most significant and fruitful attempt to do this followed *The General Theory* one year later. In his famous essay "Mr. Keynes and the Classics," John Hicks developed the first version of *IS-LM* theory.[9] The *IS-LM* theory was dominant in mainstream economic thought from at least 1950 to 1975, so it is well worth a full discussion. On the other hand, the reader must be warned that since the mid-1970s, its grip on economists has been weakened; many economists (including John Hicks) have now repudiated it for reasons given in a later section. The reasons include questions as to whether it accurately represents Keynes and as to whether it accurately represents reality.

In the *IS-LM* model, the demand for money is a function of both the level of income and the level of interest rates. Given any level of income, the demand for money can be represented by Figure 6.2. The demand for money rises as interest rates fall because of the speculative motive (for holding money).

Figure 6.3 shows four money demand functions associated with the four levels of income. Also shown is the level of the money supply, which is controlled by the monetary authorities. From the graph, four equilibrium points can be identified where the supply of, and demand for, money are equal. *Each indicates the unique interest rate associated with a given level of income where the money market is in equilibrium.* For example, point *b* indicates that, given

---

[9]John Hicks, "Mr. Keynes and the 'Classics' (1937)," reprinted in John Hicks, *Critical Essays in Monetary Theory* (Oxford: Clarendon Press, 1967), pp. 126–142.

For a precise, modern explanation of *IS-LM* analysis combined with empirical support for the model, see David Laidler, *The Demand for Money: Theories and Evidence* (Scranton: International Textbook, 1969).

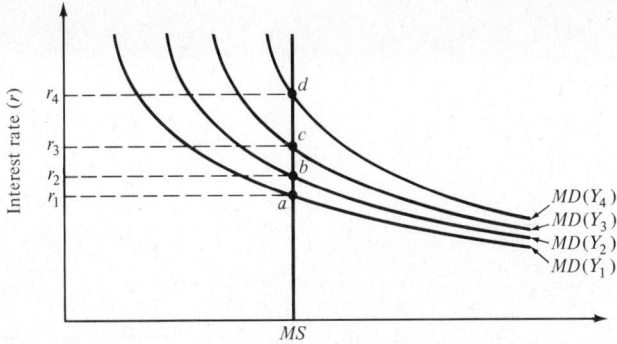

Demand for money (MD), supply of money (MS)

Y = income (GNP)

Figure 6.3 The Demand for Money at Four Levels of Income and Four Equilibrium Interest Rates, Given the Money Supply

the money supply shown, if the level of income in the economy is Y_2, the interest rate will be r_2.

Given a continuum of such money demand functions, it is possible to establish the locus that maps the equilibrium interest rate to given levels of income, given a certain money supply. At all points on the locus of equilibrium points, the demand for money equals the supply. The result is the *LM* function, which is shown in Figure 6.4; equilibrium points *a* through *d* are the same as those represented in Figure 6.3.

What effect will a change in the money supply have upon the *LM* curve? The answer to this question can be seen in Figure 6.5. An increase in the money supply (from MS_1 to MS_2) is shown. Given this increase, lower interest rates will be associated with given levels of income. The *LM* curve will drop. The opposite occurs if the money supply contracts.

The *IS* function, the second major component of the *IS-LM* model, represents all interest rate and income combinations where savings equals investment. In the *IS-LM* model, both investment and savings are assumed to be functions (*f* and *g*) of the levels of income and interest rates:

$$I = f(Y, r) \tag{6.6}$$

$$S = g(Y, r) \tag{6.7}$$

where I is investment, S is savings, Y is income, and r is the interest rate. The relationship between savings and the interest rate is positive, between investment and the interest rate is negative, and both savings and investment are positively related to income.

Graphs showing both savings schedules and investment schedules are shown in Figure 6.6. The schedules show the relationship between savings and the interest rate and investment and the interest rate. These must be a separate schedule for each level of income because a growth in income causes each schedule to shift right.

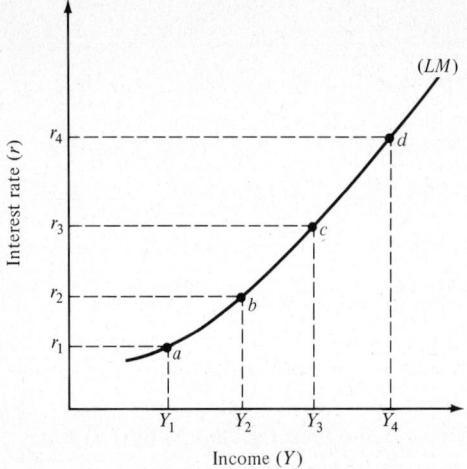

LM = equilibrium locus for money supply and demand

Figure 6.4 The LM Function: A Locus Where the Supply of, and Demand for, Money Are Equal

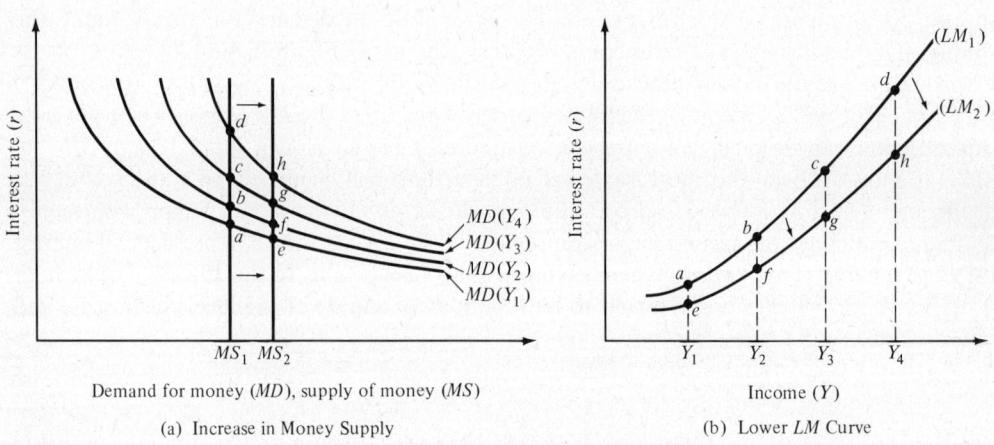

(a) Increase in Money Supply

(b) Lower LM Curve

Figure 6.5 An Increase in the Money Supply Lowers the LM Curve

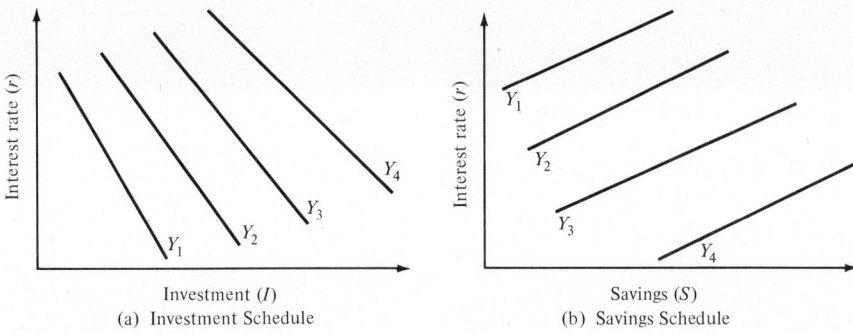

Y = income (GNP)

Figure 6.6 Savings and Investment Schedules as a Funtion of the Level of Interest Rates for Four Levels of Income

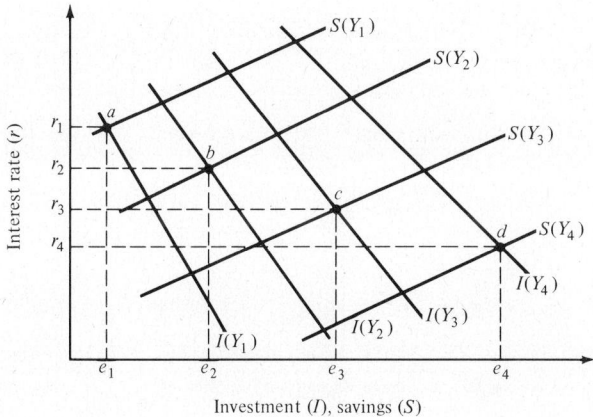

Y = income

Figure 6.7 Savings and Investment Schedules Superimposed on the Same Graph, with Equilibrium Points Shown

In Figure 6.7 the two graphs are superimposed. *At each level of income* there will be a unique interest rate that equilibrates savings and investment. Point *b*, for example, identifies the interest rate (r_2) that equilibriates savings and investment (at e_2) at income level Y_2. Three other equilibrium points are also shown.

If the entire continuum of income were considered, the resulting locus of intersections would define the corresponding combinations of income and interest rates where savings and investment are in equilibrium. This is the *IS* curve, which normally has a negative slope. The *IS* curve derived from Figure 6.7 is shown in Figure 6.8.

Combining the *IS* and *LM* functions, the result, shown in Figure 6.9, provides the

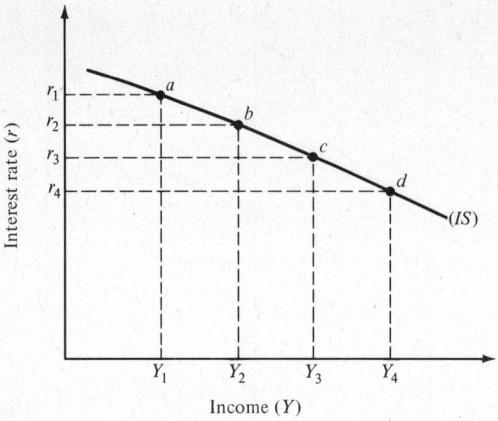

IS = equilibrium locus for savings and investment

Figure 6.8 The *IS* Curve

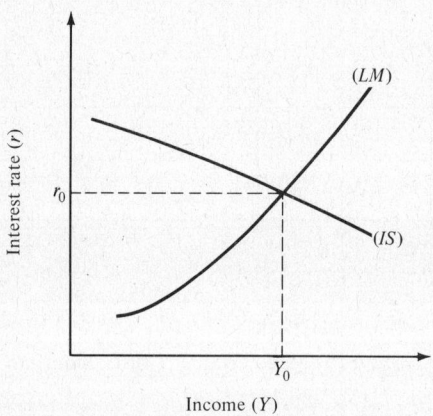

LM = equilibrium locus for money supply and demand
IS = equilibrium locus for savings and investment

Figure 6.9 The Complete *IS-LM* Model

equilibrium level of interest rates and income. It assumes a given equilibrium between savings and investment and between money supplied and money demanded.

Once the model is constructed, the analyst can evaluate the impact upon output of a collapse in the investment schedule, changes in the propensity to save, increases in the money stock, and so forth. Not only does the model give a clear picture of the sort of complex relationships that exist in a financial economy, it is also a pedagogical masterpiece. Probably millions of *IS-LM* graphs have gone up on chalkboards as teaching tools.

THE USE OF *IS-LM* FOR ANALYSIS

Quite a number of interesting results are obtained when the *IS-LM* equilibrium model is used to analyze things like changes in the supply of money. A number of examples are shown further on. Although it is normally assumed that the *IS* curve has a negative slope, some writers argue that it might be positively sloped in some special instances. That case, however, is too rare and adds too much complexity to be shown here, so we will stick to the usual negatively sloped *IS* curve.

AN INCREASE IN THE MONEY SUPPLY

Figure 6.10 shows the effect of an increase in the money supply. In 6.10(a) the money supply is increased from MS_a to MS_b. A single money demand curve for a given level of income is also shown. As can be seen, for any given level of income (such as that represented by the

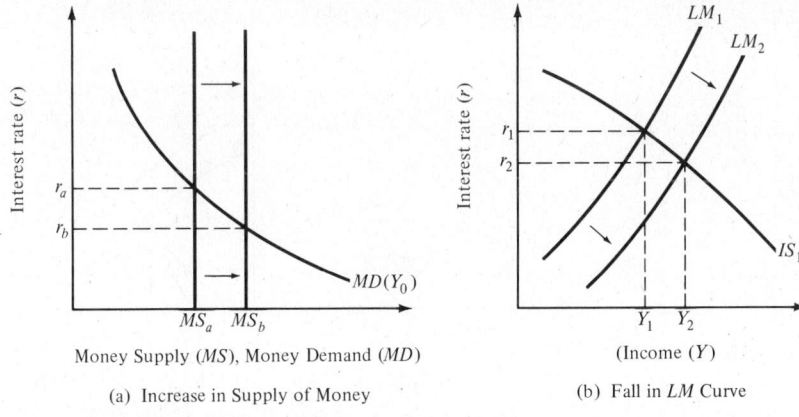

(a) Increase in Supply of Money

(b) Fall in *LM* Curve

LM = equilibrium locus for money supply and demand
IS = equilibrium locus for savings and investment

Figure 6.10 The effect of an Increase in the Supply of Money

money demand curve), interest rates will be lower. At income level Y_0, the interest rate drops from r_a to r_b when the money supply is increased.

Since the interest rate drops for all levels of income, this implies that the *LM* curve shifts downward, as is shown in 6.10(b). Nominal income grows (from Y_1 to Y_2). With the normal assumption of the negatively sloped *IS* curve, interest rates fall.

A REDUCTION IN THE PROPENSITY TO CONSUME OR INVEST

If there is either a decrease in the average propensity to consume (lowering the consumption-income ratio and raising the savings-income ratio) or a reduction in the desire to invest, the effect will be the same. This is shown in Figure 6.11.

Figure 6.11(a) shows the effect upon the savings schedule of a drop in consumption at income level Y_0 (the drop in consumption causes a rise in savings since savings is the residual left over from consumption). Savings rises (shifts right) from S_a to S_b. The effect is to lower the equilibrium interest rate associated with any income level, such as Y_0. This shifts the *IS* curve down, as shown in Figure 6.11(c).

Figure 6.11(b) shows the effect of a reduction in investment at any given level of income. In the graph, investment shifts from I_a to I_b, which causes the equilibrium interest rate to drop from r_a to r_b. Since this result would be true for all levels of income, this reduction in investment also shifts the *IS* curve downward, as shown in Figure 6.11(c).

When we refer to Figure 6.11(c), it can be seen that this decrease in consumption (increase in savings) or decrease in investment causes *both* interest rates and income to fall. It should be noted that the interest rate decline is the effect and not the cause of the decline in investment or rise in savings.

This result is interesting because it confirms the Keynesian argument that reductions in the level of aggregate demand (either consumption or investment) will reduce the equilibrium

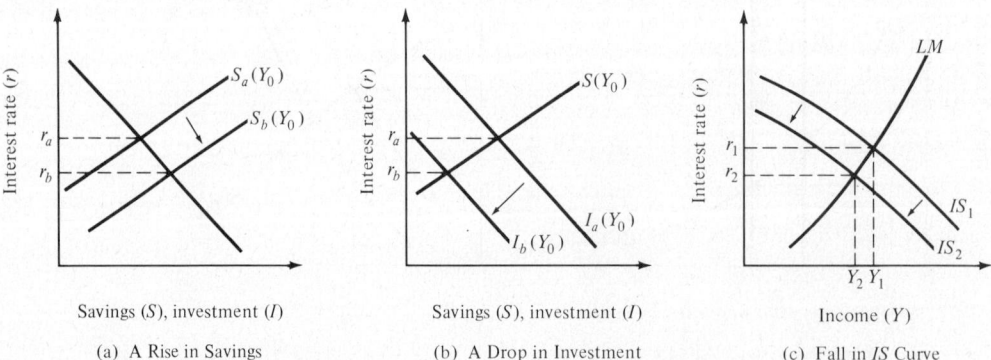

(a) A Rise in Savings (b) A Drop in Investment (c) Fall in *IS* Curve

LM = equilibrium locus for money supply and demand
IS = equilibrium locus for savings and investment

Figure 6.11 The Effect of a Reduction in Propensity to Consume or Invest

level of income. Increases in either category of spending will, of course, produce exactly the opposite result.

A RISE IN THE SPECULATIVE DEMAND FOR MONEY

The effect of a rise in the speculative demand is shown in Figure 6.12. In Figure 6.12(a), the rise in the demand for money at income level Y_0 is shown as a shift in the money demand schedule from MDa to MDb. As can be seen, the supply and demand for money will be equal for all income levels at higher interest rates. This implies that the LM curve shifts upward, as is shown in Figure 6.12(b).

Again this confirms the Keynesian result that the level of aggregate demand (income) will drop if there is a rise in the demand for money as a financial asset to be held and not spent.

THE CLASSICAL CASE: NO SPECULATIVE DEMAND FOR MONEY

When it is assumed that there is only a transactions demand for money, then the demand for money is not sensitive to interest rates. Such a situation is represented in Figure 6.13(a). The demand for money is simply a function of the level of income and is hence represented as a perfectly vertical line. Therefore, if a certain amount of money is supplied by the monetary authorities (MS in Figure 6.13[a]), then income must grow until the demand for money equals that supply. This is shown as income level Y_0 in Figure 16.13(a). Equilibrium income is then established at that level.

This implies that the LM curve is perfectly vertical at income level Y_0, as is shown in Figure 16.13(b). Shifts in the IS function merely influence the interest rate and are the only

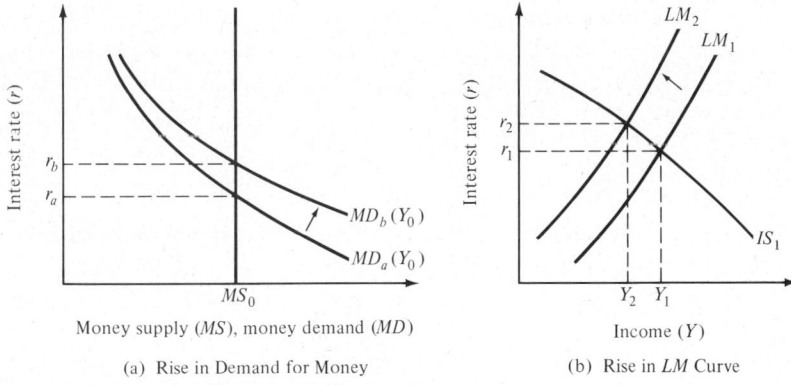

(a) Rise in Demand for Money (b) Rise in LM Curve

LM = equilibrium locus for money supply and demand
IS = equilibrium locus for savings and investment

Figure 6.12 The Effect of a Rise in the Speculative Demand for Money

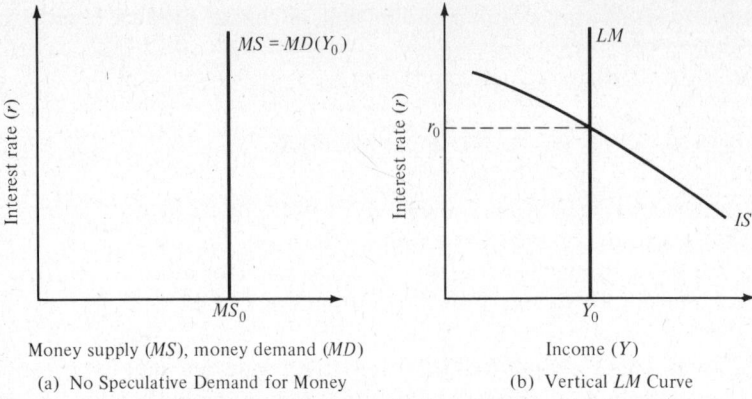

(a) No Speculative Demand for Money (b) Vertical LM Curve

LM = equilibrium locus for money supply and demand
IS = equilibrium locus for savings and investment

Figure 6.13 The Effect of No Speculative Demand for Money

thing that influence the interest rate. The amount of money supplied is the *only thing* that influences the level of nominal income. This is perfectly consistent with the classical model presented in Chapter 4. In that model, real output was determined by labor supply and demand. The price level was determined by the money supply, and nominal output was the product of the two. Savings and investment determined the interest rate without affecting the level of output and were the only things that affected the interest rate.

When the *IS-LM* and the classical models are compared, it is easy to see what critical assumption causes them to produce such different results; the assumption is that the demand for money is or is not sensitive to the level of interest rates. In the *IS-LM* model with the assumption of the speculative demand for money, the demand for money is sensitive to interest rates. Therefore, the analyst does get the normal Keynesian results that variations in aggregate demand cause variations in income and that interest rates are not only influenced by savings and investment decisions, but by the money supply and demand as well.

A CRITIQUE OF *IS-LM*

The issues are (1) whether or not *IS-LM* truly captures the spirit of Keynes and (2) whether or not it correctly represents reality. First, in the *IS-LM* model, one is left with the impression that almost *any* problem regarding the level of national output can be solved by monetary authorities. A collapse of the investment schedule can be completely offset by an increase in the money stock, for example, resulting in restored national income, albeit at lower interest rates. Keynes certainly did not believe that an increase in the money supply could restore the economy after a collapse in investment.[10]

---

[10]Keynes, *op. cit.,* pp. 164, 173, 217–219, 295–296.

Second, the model also describes equilibrium conditions (and it is nearly impossible to get the model *out* of equilibrium). As mentioned in Chapter 5, however, a good part of the Keynesian explanation involves the notion of serious noncorrecting *disequilibrium,* such as the disequilibrium between savings and investment. Keynes's argument (and the real world) is dynamic whereas the *IS-LM* model is static. Third, the model makes no use of the important essential part played by expectations in Keynesian crisis theory. Fourth, as Hicks later acknowledged,[11] the economics of *The General Theory* was depression (or crisis) economics whereas *IS-LM* models a flexible economy where adjustments to crisis can be easily and expeditiously made—so depression never occurs. Fifth, the *IS-LM* model assumes a purely exogenous money stock, which is questionable (see Chapter 17).

Finally, the *IS-LM* model, and the neo-Keynesians who use it, emphasizes that rigidities —inflexible prices, wages, and interest rates—may prevent full employment; but these rigidities can be cured by government stimulus to investment while weakening unions to hold down wages. Many of the Post Keynesians argue that this overlooks Keynes's insight that lower wages mean lower demand, which reduces employment.

NEO-KEYNESIANS VERSUS POST KEYNESIANS

By the mid-1950s, the "Keynesian" school had clearly split into two warring factions. One faction constituted what Paul Samuelson called "the neoclassical-Keynesian synthesis"; they might be called neoclassical-Keynesians or, for short, neo-Keynesians. These neo-Keynesians are mostly in the United States, and most of them have tended to move back toward classical, right-wing laissez-faire policies. They make use of the *IS-LM* model as the essential truth of Keynesian economics. They argue that Say's law does not work only because of the imperfections or rigidities in the market system. In the commodity market, prices are not flexible enough downward—because of both monopoly and government interference. In the money market, there is the rigidity of the interest rate at the low level of the liquidity trap.

Most of all, however, they tend to emphasize that the problem is caused by rigid wages in the labor market—caused by unions, minimum wage laws, safety laws, and other government interference. If only all government regulations and interference were removed and if all unions were destroyed, then wages would be flexible downward. The lower wages would restore full employment while the pure functioning of the market would solve all other problems. In the meantime, any lack of demand can be solved by an infusion of government spending or a cut in taxes (recently, more popular), after which the market will again take over. Because they call themselves Keynesian, but are closer to the classicals in much of their analysis and policy recommendations, Joan Robinson calls them "Bastard Keynesians."

On the other side, there is the school called Post Keynesian. This terminology is somewhat confusing because the Post Keynesians claim to be (and probably are) closer to the original writings of Keynes than are the neo-Keynesians. The Post Keynesians point out that the heart of Keynes's achievement was his refutation of Say's law by means of consideration of the possible lack of aggregate demand in a monetary, capitalist economy.

---

[11]Hicks, *Economic Perspectives,* p. 83.

They do not dispute the existence of rigidities in each of the markets: commodity, money, and labor. What they emphasize, however, is that even if these rigidities were removed, there would still *not* necessarily be full employment equilibrium. If interest rates were flexible downward, interest rates still could not go below zero, but the expected profit rate could go below zero—in which case, no investment. If prices freely fluctuated downward as demand declined, this would reduce the flow of business income, leading to even less investment.

Joan Robinson, the leading Post Keynesian, emphasizes that flexible wages downward in a depression must lower income. Moreover, reduced wages lowers income for precisely those people with the highest ratio of consumer spending to income. Therefore, even if profit income increased equally to the decline in wages, consumer demand would decline. For these reasons, reduction of wages may not cure a depression, but may even make it worse. The exact result depends on the exact pattern of time lags in responses of consumers and investors, considered in later chapters.

Finally, it should be noted that there are other differences between the two schools, particularly in the area of monetary analysis. Like the monetarists, many neo-Keynesians think the money supply is set by government, so any problem is attributable to government. Post Keynesians, as discussed in Chapter 17, believe the money supply is determined by internal economic forces.

SUMMARY

Prior to the Keynesian era, the mainstream classical tradition relied heavily upon the equation of exchange to explain the performance of nominal income (GNP). The equation said that money (M) times its relocity (V) equals, in equilibrium, the price level (P) times the quantity of output (Y)—that is, the flow of money equals the flow of goods and services. Real output was determined by the operation of the free market, and the price level was primarily determined by the amount of money in circulation. Velocity, the rate of money circulation through the economy, was thought to be reasonably stable.

As economists began to investigate the demand for money, it became apparent that variations in the demand for money might substantially disturb the connection between the money stock and the level of aggregate demand. From this fruitful discovery came the early contributions of Keynes, refined by Hicks's comprehensive *IS-LM* model. (Further refinements came with the development of money inventory models and portfolio theory models. These models are presented in Appendix 6A.)

The contributions of Keynes, Hicks, and those who followed in their tradition were substantial. Among other things, they provided numerous theoretical reasons why the relationship between money and the level of spending might be unstable or difficult to predict. Their writings had a distinct "demand-side" emphasis. Velocity could rise and fall because money holdings could vacillate substantially in response to expectations, interest rates, technological innovation, and a host of other parameters that either move cyclically or have a trend as the economy moves through time.

No longer could the equation of exchange provide a meaningful picture of the true relationship between money and spending. The introduction of the notion that people and business might be inclined to hold money as a financial asset and that these holdings might be volatile challenged the paradigm that stretched back over a century.

This was hardly the end of the controversy, however. For a considerable time, macroeconomic theory was dominated by the analysis of demand behavior in the economy. The next five chapters will review many of the theoretical and empirical arguments about the determination of the components of aggregate demand.

For a period of time Keynesian monetary theory and the analysis of aggregate demand tended to dominate macroeconomic theory. The intellectual challenge to the equation of exchange did not go unanswered, however, and a new group of economists called monetarists devoted a tremendous effort in the attempt to salvage what had seemed to become a theoretical anachronism. With this effort, the whole monetary controversy reemerged in full force. An in-depth discussion of the debate is provided in Part Four, the section on modern monetary theory.

Appendix 6A

The Money Inventory and Portfolio Theories

THE MONEY INVENTORY

A very significant contribution to money demand theory was made by William Baumol in 1952.[12] Baumol pointed out that cash balances held by either consumers or businesses should be regarded as a sort of inventory that will be allowed to fluctuate. The inventory is necessary because receipts and disbursements are never simultaneous in a real economy. Transaction costs make it prohibitive to hold nonmoney balances in such a way to ensure that they can be converted to money at the time they are required, even when there is perfect knowledge about the timing of future disbursements. Given that perfect knowledge is seldom present, uncertainty about future disbursements additionally compels one to hold "precautionary balances."

These money inventories can be manipulated up and down in response to developments in the economy. Figure 6A.1 provides an illustration. If, for example, the desire to reduce money inventories as a percent of income or receipts becomes pervasive in the economy, then the level of spending (and income) will rise without a corresponding increase in the nominal measure of money stock. Velocity will rise.

Baumol gives some suggestions about why money inventories might fluctuate. If there are economies of scale with large cash holdings, then as wealth grows over time, velocity might rise as well (the money-income ratio would be a negative function of wealth). Additionally,

---

[12]William J. Baumol, "The Transactions Demand for Cash: An Inventory Theoretic Approach," *Quarterly Journal of Economics* (November 1952).

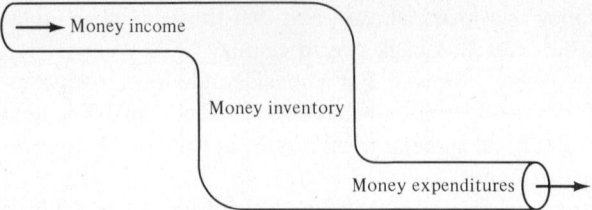

Figure 6A.1 The Money Inventory

NOTE: All money income intially becomes part of the money inventory. Money expenditures, continuing the payments stream, will therefore consist of money income plus any reduction in inventory or minus any addition to inventory. This money flow is analogous to the flow of a river into and out of a large, controlled reservoir.

if payments can be lumped together because of innovations in bill-paying procedures, money can be employed more economically, dropping the demand for money and increasing demand for other financial assets. This insight might explain recent consumer cash economizing as credit cards are used to purchase and bills are all paid at the same time.

Baumol gave no attention to the role of interest rates or price expectations in his inventory model, but models including these as key parameters would have no difficulty incorporating the inventory approach.

James Tobin[13] elaborated on Baumol's model, arguing that even the *transactions* demand for cash might be sensitive to *interest rates*. Tobin, like Baumol, argued that money is needed because receipts and disbursements are not simultaneous. Were there no transaction costs of converting financial assets to money, then all transactions inventory could be held in yield-bearing form. As payments become due, a conversion could be made to money and payment could be made. High transaction costs, however, will override the benefits of holding paper wealth in a nonmoney form.

Tobin argues, though, as yields on money substitutes rise, some of the high transaction costs would be exceeded by the benefits of holding yield-bearing assets. Hence cash holdings would drop as yields on substitutes rise.

A PORTFOLIO THEORY MODEL

Models investigating the original speculative motive for holding money inventories dramatically improved with the refinement of portfolio theory. An early contribution was made by John Hicks,[14] but the first comprehensive modern explanation of portfolio theory was made by James Tobin.[15] Tobin clarifies why people would hold "the non-interest-bearing obligations of the government instead of its interest bearing obligations."

---

[13]James Tobin, "The Interest Elasticity of the Transaction Demand for Cash," *The Review of Economics and Statistics* (August 1956).

[14]John Hicks, "A Pure Theory of Portfolio Selection," *Critical Essays in Monetary Theory* (Oxford: Clarendon Press, 1967).

[15]James Tobin, "Liquidity Preference as Behavior Towards Risk," *Review of Economic Studies* (February 1958).

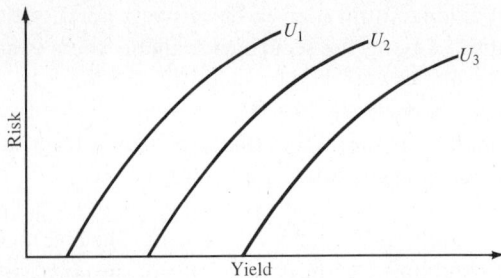

$U_3 > U_2 > U_1$
U = level of utility

Figure 6A.2 Subjective Risk-Yield Trade-off Curves (Indifference Curves) Representing Different Levels of Utility

When Keynes discussed the demand for money, the role played by risk did not clearly emerge. He relied heavily upon the notion of the *liquidity premium,* which, although clearly defined, is difficult to measure or determine theoretically. The *liquidity premium* is the value imputed to any final asset because of its ease of conversion into a medium of exchange. Keynes argued that holders of wealth will adjust portfolios until the returns (at the margin) on all assets are *equal.* These returns consisted of the sum of yield plus carrying cost plus liquidity premium.[16]

Portfolio theory does not argue that *returns* are marginally equal on portfolio assets. Instead, each wealth holder encounters an objective risk-yield trade-off for each combination of assets in the financial portfolio. Bonds contribute high yield but high risk. Money contributes no yield but also no risk. Various proportions of bonds and money (or money and other yield-bearing assets) provide different combinations of risk and yield. Holders of *investment balances* will subjectively choose that risk-yield combination that maximizes their utility. This will differ from saver to saver because the degree of risk aversion (generally, the desire to avoid risk) varies. Savers do not try to maximize yield alone because the future yield stream is uncertain. The saver must consider a probability distribution for yield, which, given that if yields change security values change as well, implies a probability distribution for capital gain and loss as well. Obviously, if the yield on any nonmoney asset changes, this changes the objective risk-yield trade-off for the entire portfolio, and the saver will adjust the financial assets in the portfolio to a new optimum choice. Since money is one of those assets, the demand for money will change.

The model relies upon the notion that wealth holders have a utility function that is sensitive to both yield and risk. The subjective trade-off between yield and risk, given any level of satisfaction, can be represented by indifference curves such as those shown in Figure 6A.2. Each one (such as the level of utility marked U_1) shows that higher risk offers the same level of satisfaction only if associated with higher yield—indeed, the substitution between risk and yield requires ever greater proportions of yield to compensate for increasing risk.

---

[16]Keynes, op. cit., pp. 226–227.

The portfolio manager is going to try to maximize utility, given objective risk and yield options available with the purchase of securities. Among the securities available there is an objective correlation between risk and yield; securities with higher yields involve more risk. Risk is difficult to define, but most models use something like the variance or standard deviation of a security's price. Presumably, a high variance implies that a security's price has been volatile, presenting a greater probability of a given capital gain or loss.

A two-asset portfolio model is shown in Figure 6A.3. Quadrant I demonstrates that a low-yield security offers a yield of 2 percent and that the other offers 10 percent. The portfolio will yield between 2 percent and 10 percent, depending upon the composition of the portfolio. Yield line *ab* represents the yield associated with the percentage of the portfolio in the

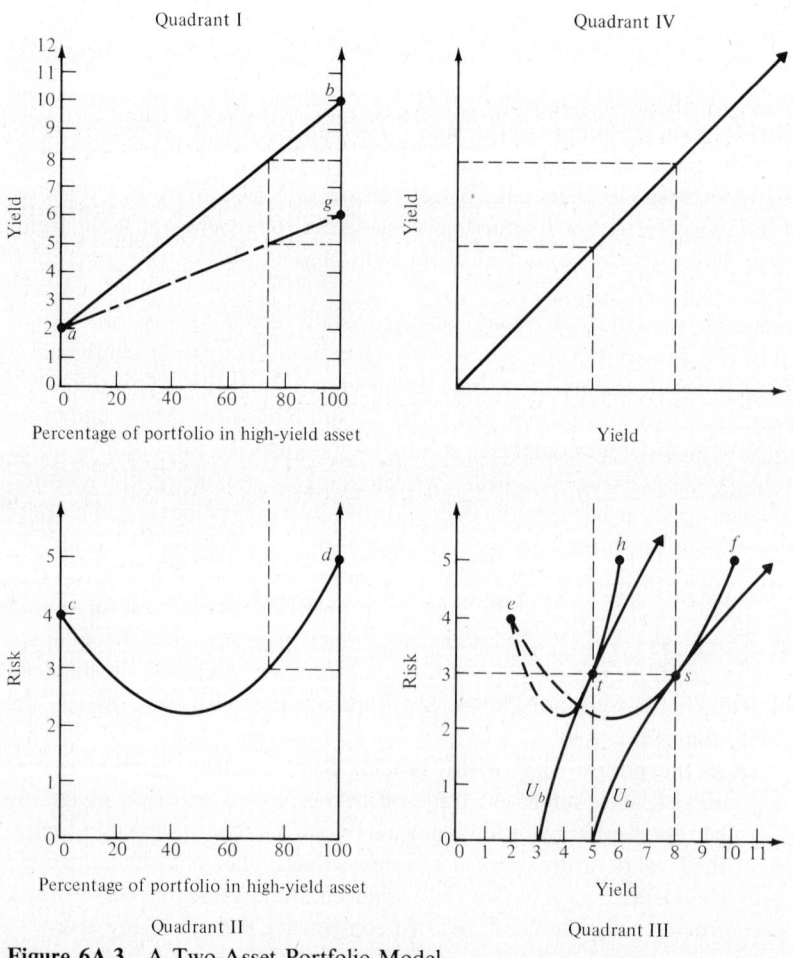

Figure 6A.3 A Two-Asset Portfolio Model

high-yield asset. Portfolio yield $= aY_1 + (1-a) Y_2$, where a is the percentage of the portfolio in the high-yield asset.

Quadrant II demonstrates the risk associated with the composition of the portfolio. As can be seen, the low-yield asset has a variance of 4, and the high-yield asset has a variance of 5. The sag in the risk line demonstrates the benefit of diversification; if two assets of given risk are combined in a portfolio, the resulting portfolio risk will, for some combinations, be lower than the lowest risk on any single asset.

The combinations of yield and risk provided by this portfolio are represented by the *objective* risk-yield trade-off line *ef* shown in quadrant III. The extreme points show the results of no diversification. Point *e*, for example, demonstrates that yield will be 2 percent and risk will be 4 if all funds are tied up in the low-yield asset.

The dotted portion of the objective trade-off line is suboptimal; there are portfolio combinations that offer higher yields *and* lower risks than the combinations (such as point *e*) represented by that portion of the trade-off line. This is because of the benefits of diversification.

Lines U_a and U_b are the *subjective* indifference curves discussed earlier. The goal of the maximizer is to choose a point along the indifference curve that is the furthest removed from the vertical axis.

The portfolio manager will be maximizing his or her objective where the subjective trade-off between risk and yield (marginal rate of substitution) is equal to the objective trade-off (the slope of the *ef* trade-off line). This is point *s* on indifference line U_a. At that choice point, the level of risk will be 3 and the yield 8 percent. About 75 percent of the portfolio is invested in asset 2.

In this model, it can be seen that a demand for each of the two financial assets exists. Both are a function of yield and risk. If yield or risk on either asset changes, the quantity demanded of both assets will change.

It seems intuitive that the demand for an asset will rise when the yield on that asset rises and will fall when yield falls. A quick glance at Figure 6A.3, however, indicates that this positive demand relationship *is not necessarily* a property of this model. Suppose the yield on the risky asset drops from 10 percent to 6 percent. This is represented by line *ag* on Figure 6A.3(a). Suppose risk is unaffected. The resulting objective trade-off line is represented by curve *eh* in Figure 6A.3(c).

It is possible to draw a legitimate indifference locus that intersects the new trade-off line at a point that leaves the composition of the portfolio completely unaffected! Indifference locus U_b is such a curve because it intersects *eh* at point *t*, leaving about 75 percent of the portfolio still invested in the high-risk asset. The measure of risk is still 3, but the portfolio yield has dropped from 8 to 5 percent.

Finally, by inspection, it is apparent that it would even be possible to draw an intersection point above point *t* on the objective trade-off line, which would produce the unexpected result that the demand for an asset will *rise* as its yield *falls!*

Such a result is not completely counterintuitive. Suppose a portfolio manager is trying to achieve a given rate of return in this two-asset world. If the yield on the high-yield asset comes down, the yield on the entire portfolio will come down. The investor can maintain his or her portfolio yield somewhat by moving *in favor* of the asset that has declined in value, so long as he or she is willing to undertake a higher risk. The outcome is ambiguous because income and substitution effects act as countervailing forces. As the yield on a high-yield asset drops, the substitution effect makes this asset less attractive. On the other hand, this drop in yield lowers income, and the saver might wish to preserve income by buying *more* of the high-yield asset.

It should be obvious that the portfolio model can be used to explain the demand for money. Money would be an asset with very low yield and very low risk (perhaps zero in both case). With this application, the portfolio model demonstrates that because of the competing power of income and substitution effects, the relationship between yield on alternative assets and the demand for money is ambiguous.

The model does show that the demand for money will change in some *direction,* and one might argue that it is possible for the substitution effect to transcend the income effect consistently when money is involved, making the sensitivity of money demand to interest rates persistently negative. Resolution of this proposition then becomes an empirical matter.

Part Two

BEHAVIOR OF MACROECONOMIC BUILDING BLOCKS

Chapter 7

THE GROWTH OF GOVERNMENT

The behavior of the private sector can be understood in this era only if one first understands the growth of government.

TRENDS IN GOVERNMENT SPENDING

Aside from the jumps in spending during the first and second world wars, total government spending (federal, state, and local) has risen fairly continuously in the twentieth century. Total government spending was 7.7 percent of GNP in 1902, rising to 8.1 percent in 1913 on the eve of World War I. It continued to rise to 20.5 percent in 1940 after the New Deal. After World War II, total government spending was 24.7 percent in 1950, 30.0 percent in 1960, and 34.1 percent in 1970.[1] Thus, it generally rose through conservative as well as liberal administrations. Although government spending was only a small influence in 1902 at 7.7 percent, at 34.1 percent of GNP it implies a whole new stage of capitalism in symbiosis with government. Fiscal policy can and does change the distribution of income, the allocation of resources, the inflation rate, and the course of the business cycle.

Federal Versus State and Local

When most people think of the growth of government spending, they think of federal spending. In wartime, that is correct, but otherwise it is much less true. Federal spending

---

[1] See Roger L. Ransom, "In Search of Security: The Growth of Government in the United States, 1902–1970," *University of California, Riverside Working Papers* no. 40 (January 1980).

was only 1 percent of GNP in 1929 before the Great Depression. During the Second World War, government spending (almost all military) rose to the incredible height of 42 percent of GNP in 1944, thereby producing full employment. Trends since then are shown in Table 7.1.

Total government spending rose enormously in the 1949 to 1980 period, but not much of that was due to the federal government. Most of the rise in spending was done by state and local governments, whose spending almost doubled in the period as a percentage of GNP. In this period, federal government purchases of goods and services actually *declined* from 12.5 to 8.4 percent of GNP. Total federal spending did rise, but not because of more purchase of goods and services.

The figures in Table 7.1 have important implications. Federal expenditures have grown slightly even though federal purchases of goods and services have dropped because of the growing importance of transfer payments, especially social security. Transfer payments simply transfer income from those being taxed to the recipients of government payments. With such expenditures, the government does not purchase anything produced nor make any claim upon the nation's economic resources. Because of this, the federal government's purchases of goods and services are the correct measure of the federal government's contribution to aggregate demand rather than federal expenditures.

In the recent controversy over the size and relative importance of the federal government, the interpretation of the trend in government size and economic importance depends upon the reviewer's perspective. Because higher expenditures require higher taxation, critics of large government countered that government is growing too rapidly even though a good part of the taxes are returned in the form of transfer payments. Supporters of a large and active government, on the other hand, point out that the federal government's relative contribution to aggregate demand (as reflected in purchases of goods and services) has dropped sharply, approaching the level seen prior to World War II. If the government contribution to aggregate demand is regarded as a stabilizing force in the economy, then that stabilizing force has been dramatically reduced in recent years.

What things the federal government does spend on besides goods and services is examined in later sections, but it is worth noting that one item is federal grants-in-aid to state and local

Table 7.1

GOVERNMENT SPENDING (AS PERCENTAGE OF GNP)

Cycle	Federal Spending	State and Local Spending	Total Spending	Federal Purchases of Goods and Services
1949–1954	18.5%	7.6%	26.1%	15.1%
1954–1958	17.7	8.6	26.2	13.5
1958–1961	18.9	9.8	28.7	12.8
1961–1970	19.6	11.5	31.1	11.8
1970–1975	20.8	14.0	34.8	8.5
1975–1980	22.0	14.2	36.2	7.4

SOURCE: U.S. Department of Commerce, *Business Conditions Digest* (May 1981).

Table 7.2

COMPONENTS OF GOVERNMENT SPENDING, 1902–1970[a]

Year	Total[b]	Military	Education	Health	Social Security	Interest or Debt
1902	100%	18.1%	15.7%	3.6%	0 %	6.0%
1913	100	13.4	18.0	3.4	0	5.3
1927	100	10.7	20.0	3.8	0	12.0
1940	100	10.2	13.9	3.6	0.1	7.6
1950	100	30.7	13.7	3.9	1.0	6.9
1960	100	34.8	12.8	3.5	7.1	6.2
1970	100	26.9	16.8	4.1	10.8	5.5

[a] Components are given as percentages of total spending.
[b] Total means federal, state, and local spending.
SOURCE: U.S. Bureau of the Census, *Historical Statistics of the United States, Colonial Times to the Present*, bicentennial ed., Part 2, Series Y533–Y566, pp. 1120–1121. A similar table is presented and discussed in detail in Roger L. Ransom, "In Search of Security: The Growth of Government in the United States, 1902–1970," *University of California, Riverside Working Papers* no. 40 (January 1980).

governments. In the cycle of 1954 to 1958, federal grants were only 0.8 percent of GNP.[2] They rose continually, however, till federal grants in the 1970 to 1975 cycle were 3.0 percent of GNP. Since this money is spent by state and local governments and is not spent by the federal government, it should really be subtracted when one is comparing federal spending to state and local spending. Moreover, it should also be subtracted from total government spending when one is comparing that to GNP because otherwise it is double-counted, once as a federal expenditure and once more when state and local governments spend it. With that correction, total federal spending would remain almost constant as a percentage of GNP in the entire period, and total spending would rise only by the amount of state and local spending.

Types of Spending. Naturally, the most interesting question is, What does government spend its money upon? Table 7.2 shows the main components of government spending for selected years.

Education had its highest percentage of government spending in the 1920s, but its share has declined since then. Government spending for health has remained at about the same low share of government spending during the whole century. Social security begins in the 1930s and reaches 10 percent of government spending by 1970. It is very questionable, however, whether social security spending should be in the category of "government" spending. The government has never paid a penny for social security out of general revenues. All payments to date have come from the special tax called the social security "contribution."

The military share in Table 7.2 is grossly understated, as shown further on, because it counts only the officially recorded spending on "defense" (note that no government spends on "offense"). Even in the restricted official definition of military "defense," the military share

---

[2] John Ray, Jr., *Government Fiscal Policy in the United States, 1949–19751* (Ph.D. diss., University of California, Riverside, 1981).

is the largest single share in recent decades, and it accounts for most of the jump in government spending from the 1930s to the 1950s, 1960s, and 1970s.

On the average for the period of 1949 to 1975, total federal purchases of goods and services were 10.5 percent of GNP, but federal *non*military purchases of goods and services were only 2.1 percent of GNP. For the same 1949 to 1975 period, federal military purchases of goods and services were 8.4 percent of GNP.[3] The Reagan administration's spending plans for the early 1980s will greatly raise the percentage of government spending going to the military as a share of the budget and as a share of GNP.

Federal spending other than purchase of goods and services was 8.8 percent of GNP on the average for the 1949 to 1975 period. This other spending *does* include welfare, social security, and unemployment compensation, *but* it also includes interest on the public debt, which is almost entirely paid to the wealthy. It includes a lot of welfare to the rich, specifically subsidies to farmers (a majority of all farm subsidies go to the 20 percent richest farmers[4]) and subsidies to a very long list of businesses.

Military Spending. It was noted that military spending is the largest single item in the U.S. budget. Conservatives in the early 1980s intend a vast increase in it, projecting well over a trillion dollars in expenditures during President Reagan's first term in office. To measure the full extent of the military impact on the economy, it is interesting to note that the U.S. Department of Defense is the largest planned economy in the world today outside of the USSR. It spends more than the net income of all U.S. corporations. It has 470 major and 6,000 lesser installations, owns 30 million acres of land, spends over $250 billion a year (a figure that will steadily rise), and uses 22,000 primary contractors and 100,000 subcontractors.[5] Some key areas of the economy are especially affected. As early as 1963, before the U.S. entry into the Vietnam War, studies show that 36 percent of the output of producers' durable goods were purchased directly or indirectly by the federal government, mostly for military use.

How big is U.S. military spending? It certainly includes all the official Department of Defense spending, but it goes considerably beyond that. How far is controversial, but the most careful study to date includes half of all "international affairs" spending, veterans' benefits, atomic energy and space appropriations (mostly military-related), and 75 percent of the interest on the public debt (since at least 75 percent of the debt was used to pay for wars). Other things that are too hard to get exact data on are major parts of the budget for research and development, the CIA, and other intelligence agencies—and, of course, the deaths, wounds, and alienation of young Americans. For the five quantifiable items in military spending, James Cypher adds up the grand total of $1.7 *trillion* from 1947 through 1971—enough to buy our entire gross national product for 1969 and 1970.[6]

---

[3] See *ibid.,* chap. 8.

[4] See James Bonnen, "The Effect of Taxes and Government Spending on Inequality," in R. Edwards, M. Reich and T. Weisskopf (eds.), *The Capitalist System* (Engelwood Cliffs, N.J.: Prentice-Hall, 1972), pp. 235–243.

[5] See U.S. Defense Department documents reported in Seymour Melman, *Pentagon Capitalism* (New York: McGraw-Hill, 1970).

[6] See James Cypher, *Military Expenditures and the Performance of the Post-war Economy, 1947–1971* (Ph.D. diss., University of California, Riverside, 1972), chap. 2. Also see James Cypher, "Capitalist Planning and Military Expenditures," *Review of Radical Political Economics* 6 (Fall 1974), pp. 1–19.

Yet this amount of direct military spending (even if it includes the things we can't quantify) still underestimates the impact of military spending on the U.S. economy. There is a very large indirect or secondary effect on (1) additional consumer goods from the spending of those who receive military dollars and (2) additional investment in plant, equipment, and inventories by military industries. Economists measure the secondary effects of military spending by the *government multiplier,* which measures the ratio of the total increase in all spending to every dollar of increase in government spending. Estimates of the multiplier from military spending range from about $1.85 to $3.50 of total spending for every dollar of military spending.

The most important measure of military spending is as a percentage out of the whole gross national product (GNP). From 1947 to 1971 it ranged, in Cypher's estimates,[7] from a low of 10.1 percent of GNP in 1948 to a high of 21.9 percent in the Korean War year of 1952. For the whole 1947 to 1971 period, direct military spending averaged 13.2 percent of GNP according to this estimate. Military spending also has powerful indirect effects when it is respent by those who receive it, so its total effect is much larger than its direct percentage of GNP (these effects are discussed more precisely with reference to the government multiplier in Appendix 7A of this chapter). It has been estimated that the indirect effects may equal the direct effects, so direct military spending of 13.2 percent of GNP might generate 26.4 percent of GNP.[8]

Big business benefits strongly from the high level of military spending. On the aggregate level, it is used to protect U.S. investments abroad, to get the economy out of recessions, and to prevent a major depression; but there is an additional incentive for the individual defense contractor. This incentive is based on the fact that the rate of profit is very high in military production and that most of these profits go to a few very large firms. Almost all military contracts go to some 205 of the top 500 corporations, and just 100 of them get 85 percent of all military contracts.

Military profits are mostly understated because, in reporting to the government, the military firms overstate their costs. Because they do not operate under competition but in a close relationship with the Pentagon, they probably overstate costs more than most firms. Thus, they allocate costs of other parts of their business to military contracts and add in all sorts of other unrelated costs. They also make many hidden profits through the use of complex subcontracting procedures to subsidiaries, unauthorized use of government-owned property, and getting patents on research done for the government.

Still, a study by the General Accounting Office (GAO) of the U.S. government had definitely spelled out their high profit rates.[9] First, the GAO asked 81 large military contractors by questionnaire what their profit rates were for 1966 through 1969. The replies, which were limited by self-interest, still admitted an average profit rate of 24.8 percent—much higher than nonmilitary profits in the same industries. But spot checks by GAO showed that

---

[7]*Ibid.,* chap. 2.
[8]See James Cypher, "Capitalist Planning and Military Expenditures," *Review of Radical Political Economics* 6 (Fall 1974), pp. 1–19; but for a somewhat different view, see L. J. Griffin, M. Wallace, and J. Devine, "The Political Economy of Military Spending," *Cambridge Journal of Economics* 6, no. 1 (March 1982), pp. 1–14, which also has a good review of the literature.
[9]See Government Accounting Office reports fully discussed by Cypher, *Military Expenditures* (Ph.D. diss.), *op. cit.,* chap. 5.

Table 7.3

FEDERAL PERSONAL INCOME TAX, LEGAL VERSUS ACTUAL RATES (1966)

Income Range	Tax Rate (%) in Law	Tax Rate (%) of Adjusted Family Income Actually Paid
$ 0–4,999	0.0– 9.2%	3.1%
$ 5–9,999	9.2–15.4	5.8
$ 10–14,999	15.4–19.1	7.6
$ 15–19,999	19.1–22.2	8.7
$ 20–24,999	22.2–25.2	9.2
$ 25–49,999	25.2–37.7	9.9
$ 50–99,999	37.7–51.6	13.4
$100–499,999	51.6–66.3	15.3
$500–999,999	66.3–68.2	14.1
$1 million and over	68.2–69.9	12.4

SOURCES: Tax rate in law from Internal Review Service Income Tax Tables. Actual rates paid from Joseph Pechman and Benjamin Okner, *Who Bears the Burden?* (Washington, D.C.: Brookings, 1974), p. 59. These data are also discussed in a very useful and interesting unpublished paper by Marcus D. Pohlmann, "The American Welfare State: Public Assistance or Conduit Colonialism?" (Departments of Political Science and Urban Studies, College of Wooster, Wooster, Ohio).

these profit rates were still very much underreported. So the GAO did its own audit of the books of 146 main military contractors. The study found that the profit rate of these contractors was a fantastic 56.1 percent rate of return on invested capital!

Trends in Government Revenues

The federal personal income tax is, in the law, a *progressive tax,* that is, a tax with higher rates on higher incomes. Most other taxes, such as sales taxes and social security taxes and property taxes, are regressive; that is, higher percentages of income are paid in taxes by the poor than by the rich. Yet even the federal personal income tax is not as progressive as it looks according to its rates because of loopholes allowing the rich (but not the poor) to avoid taxes.

One example of a loophole is the fact that capital gains, that is, gains from sale of stock or other property, are taxed at lower rates than income from labor. For a wealthy family with an income *over* $1 million a year, the average savings from this tax loophole by itself was $641,000 *each year* in 1972 (it has gone up since then). Rich families (a half million to a million a year) saved $165,000 a year on this one loophole in 1972. Middle-class families (in the income range of $20,000 to $25,000) saved only $120 a year, whereas lower-income working families (earning $5,000 to $10,000) saved an average of only $8 from this loophole.[10]

This and other loopholes leads to a huge discrepancy between legal tax rates (before loopholes) and actually paid tax rates, shown in Table 7.3.

[10] See Philip Stern, *The Rape of the Taxpayer* (New York: Vintage Books, 1974), p. 94.

Table 7.4

FEDERAL REVENUES, 1954–1975[a]

Cycle	Total Revenue	Personal Income Tax	Corporate Income Tax	Social Security Tax	Other
1954–1958	18.2%	8.2%	4.8%	2.5%	2.7%
1958–1961	18.5	8.4	4.3	3.2	2.6
1961–1970	19.2	8.7	4.0	4.3	2.3
1970–1975	19.6	9.0	3.2	5.7	1.7

[a] As percentages of GNP.
SOURCE: U.S. government data, reported in John Ray, Jr., *Government Fiscal Policy and the Business Cycle in the United States, 1949–1975* (Ph.D. diss., University of California, Riverside, 1981).

Table 7.3 shows that the personal tax rates, before loopholes, are very progressive. Actually paid tax rates are much less progressive and actually decline in the two highest categories. When this slightly progressive tax is combined with all the highly regressive taxes in the federal, state, and local systems, the result—according to a careful and elaborate study by Pechman and Okner—is slightly regressive overall.[11] The very poor, in the third percentile of the population of taxpayers, actually paid 35.6 percent of their income in all taxes. From the tenth to the nineteenth percentile of population, the actually paid tax rates are somewhat lower and almost constant, varying from a high of 26.1 percent at the thirtieth percentile to a low of 25.0 percent at the ninetieth percentile. The ninety-fifth percentile pay an actual tax rate of only 24.1 percent! The people in the top 1 percent are still far below the poor at an actual rate of 28.6 percent of income (but, remember, the people in the top 1 percent of the population have much earnings not even counted as "taxable income," namely, tax-exempt interest on municipal bonds).

The only thing that has changed since this survey is that various "reforms" have made the tax system far more regressive. After an enormous increase in tax breaks for the rich in the Reagan tax plan of 1981 (including tax breaks in corporate, estate, and gift taxes as well as in personal income taxes), future studies will probably find that the overall effect of all U.S. federal, state, and local taxes is quite regressive, taking higher percentages of income from the poor and the middle class than from the rich!

How have government revenues moved in recent decades? Table 7.4 shows the movements of the main federal revenue sources as percentages of GNP.

Total federal revenues have continually increased from cycle to cycle in this period as a percentage of GNP though the percentage rose only by 1.4 percent of GNP all the way from the cycle 1954–1958 to the cycle 1970–1975. The personal income tax also rose continuously as a percentage of GNP, but the whole rise was only 0.8 percent of GNP. Social security taxes rose continuously and rapidly, a rise of 3.2 percent of GNP. On the contrary, the corporate income tax *declined* as a percent of GNP continuously and strongly, a decline of 1.6 percent of GNP. The corporate tax provided 23 percent of all federal revenue in 1948,

---

[11] Joseph Pechman and Benjamin Okner, *Who Bears the Burden?* (Washington, D.C.: Brookings, 1974), p. 51.

but it is predicted—after the Reagan cuts—to reach only 7 percent by 1987. Thus, the federal tax burden shifted away from corporations and toward the regressive social security tax—which movement was greatly accelerated by the tax changes of the early 1980s.

The trend in state and local revenues is also very interesting, as revealed in Table 7.5.

State and local revenues have risen very rapidly in this period. Personal income taxes as well as sales taxes have risen much more rapidly than GNP, and federal grants-in-aid have taken an enormous upward jump. Corporate profit taxes remain tiny at the state and local levels. Sales taxes, which remain the largest single part of state revenues, are very regressive, with the poor paying the highest percentage.

Finally, Table 7.6 presents a comparison of federal deficits with state and local deficits.

In the first two cycles (1949–1958, mostly during the Eisenhower administration), the federal government had a surplus on average. In the next two cycles (1958–1970), there was a small deficit on average. Since 1970, the average deficit has become larger and larger. State and local finances progressed in exactly the opposite direction. State and local governments averaged some small deficits during the first three cycles (1949–1961), then had a growing surplus (which has continued into the 1980s). The state and local surpluses are due to the fact that the federal government has borne the main burden of recessions and depressions—and the federal government has given increasing grants-in-aid to states and localities. The differing directions of federal and state and local finances have resulted in deficits for the total of all governments, but fairly small ones on the average. (In the 1982 depression, most states also had deficits, while the federal deficit increased enormously.)

Obviously, an additional dollar of government spending tends to increase demand, but an additional dollar of taxation tends to reduce demand. A surplus shows a net depressing effect on demand whereas a deficit has a net stimulating effect on demand (unless deficit financing leads to high enough interest rates to offset the increased dollars, an issue discussed in later chapters).

Table 7.5

STATE AND LOCAL REVENUES, 1954–1975[a]

Cycle	Total Revenue	Indirect Business Taxes (Mostly Sales)	Personal Income Tax	Corporate Profit Tax	Federal Grants-in-Aid	Other
1954–1958	8.3%	5.6%	1.1%	0.2%	0.8%	0.6%
1958–1961	9.6	6.1	1.3	0.2	1.3	0.7
1961–1970	11.6	6.8	1.8	0.3	1.8	0.9
1970–1975	14.8	7.7	2.7	0.4	3.0	1.0

[a] As a percentage of GNP.
SOURCE: U.S. government data, reported in John Ray, Jr., *Government Fiscal Policy and the Business Cycle in the United States, 1949–1975* (Ph.D. diss., University of California, Riverside, 1981).

Table 7.6

GOVERNMENT DEFICITS[a]

Cycle	Federal Surplus (or Deficit)	State and Local Surplus (or Deficit)	Total Government Surplus (or Deficit)
1949–1954	0.1	−0.2	−0.1
1954–1958	0.2	−0.3	−0.2
1958–1961	−0.5	−0.2	−0.7
1961–1970	−0.4	0.1	−0.3
1970–1975	−1.2	0.8	−0.4
1975–1980	−2.3	1.0	−1.3

[a] As a percentage of GNP.
SOURCE: U.S. Department of Commerce, *Business Conditions Digest* (May 1981).

Tentative Conclusions on Government Spending

Government spending has certainly grown in this century, mostly since 1929. Federal government spending has mainly expanded in two areas. The largest single growth factor in federal spending has been military spending. The other large growth factor since the Great Depression has been social security, but it must always be remembered that not a single dollar for social security has ever come out of general revenues up until this time—so it has had no effect at all on the deficit. None of the national debt, now over a trillion dollars, can be attributed to social security; most of the national debt can be attributed to military spending.

Federal spending for actual goods and services has actually declined as a percentage of gross national product since 1949, and total federal spending has not risen much as a percentage of GNP. But state and local government spending has just about doubled. The total government spending at all levels has grown to over 35 percent of GNP.

Why has government grown? The issue may be different for military and nonmilitary spending. Some writers emphasize that military spending has grown because the United States has become an imperial superpower—and, some would add, is locked in combat with another superpower. Other economists argue that military spending has grown to support the economy.[12]

Aside from social security, spending for welfare, health, and education rose relative to GNP in the 1930s and 1940s. Health, education, and welfare payments have continued to grow absolutely, but declined as a percentage of GNP in the 1950s and again in the 1970s. This growth may be partly the result of a growth in the strength of labor out of the frustrations of the Great Depression. Partly, however, it may represent an attempt by capitalism to buy peace with labor through alleviation of the worst of poverty and unemploy-

---

[12] See Cypher, "Capitalist Planning . . . ," *op. cit.*, pp. 18–19.

ment.[13] This reform tendency was represented by the Democrats in the New Deal and in the Great Society of the 1960s. It has been under assault by those parts of the capitalist class supporting the far right in the Republican party. The partial truce between capital and labor brought about by the reform periods has been shattered by the assault on health, education, and welfare payments by the Reagan administration. All these conclusions, however, are very tentative and controversial among economists. Each of the preceding views will be discussed in detail in Chapter 23 on fiscal policy.

Everyone is aware that government spending is a very major component of demand. But, of course, government receipts are almost as high. So government also absorbs a huge part of income, thereby reducing demand. Only the deficit spending represents a stimulus (aside from monetary effects). There is no question that government deficit spending directly affects aggregate demand—and indirectly affects consumer demand and investment demand—in very significant ways.

Government also affects consumption and investment through the monetary system because it regulates and influences both consumer credit and investment credit. This relationship is discussed in the next section.

Another area of influence of government spending and taxation is its impact on income distribution, which, in turn, has effects on consumption and investment. Who receives the money that government spends? Does government spending mainly go to the poor in the form of welfare? It was demonstrated earlier that that is *not* the case. Much spending goes into military production, where profits from the taxpayers' money are two or three times what they are in civilian fields. Social security payments mostly come from social security taxes on workers, so they do not change the pattern of income distribution very much. Government also increases inequality by its subsidies to business in many areas, such as shipbuilding, and in its subsidies to rich farmers. Almost all the interest on the national debt goes to the very rich, so it also increases inequality.

Most previous studies (cited earlier) have indicated that the net effect of all taxation has a very slight regressive effect on income distribution because some mildly progressive taxes are canceled out by many regressive taxes. With the massive tax shifts of the Reagan administration toward less taxation of the rich and the corporations, however, future studies will probably find that the U.S. tax system is now very significantly regressive in its overall net effect. Not enough data are yet available to test this hypothesis.

There are many other ways in which government affects income distribution. For example, the fact that it is easier to cheat on the income tax if you have a high, property-based income results in a shift toward the rich. The fact that the antitrust laws are so seldom enforced puts a great deal of profit into corporations at the expense of consumers. The fact that labor laws have dealt harshly with labor unions (since the Taft-Hartley Act of 1947) has lessened the

---

[13]See the very thorough and provocative discussion of these issues in Samuel Bowles, "The Keynesian-Welfare State and the Post-Keynesian Political Containment of the Working Class," *Socialist Review* (forthcoming). Also see Herbert Gintis and Samuel Bowles, "The Welfare State and Long-term Economic Growth: Marxian, Neoclassical, and Keynesian Approaches," *American Economic Review* 72 (May 1982), pp. 341–345.

bargaining power of labor. This is one reason for the decline of labor unions as a percentage of the work force since 1947, as will be seen in Part Five.

GOVERNMENT FINANCE

The federal government is the single largest spending entity in the world today. As such, its financial operations are very complicated. In recent years, the federal government has tended to spend more than it receives in revenues. The difference, which is the deficit that was described in Table 7.6, has to be financed.

When the government runs a deficit, the deficit must be financed by government borrowing. When the government borrows, it sells U.S. Treasury securities to the general public and to financial institutions. The three major types of securities are U.S. Treasury bills, notes, and bonds. These differ primarily in their maturities. Bills typically have maturities of 13, 26, or 52 weeks. Notes have maturities of between 1 and 5 years, and bonds have maturities of over 5 years.

The gross public debt of the federal government has exceeded a trillion dollars since 1981 and is growing rapidly. Of this amount, over $750 billion is represented by bills, notes, and bonds. (The remainder is called nonmarketable debt, most of which is possessed by foreign, state, and local governments and by other agencies of the U.S. government. The small publicly held savings bonds are also included in this category.) These marketable securities (bills, notes, or bonds) are sold and resold in a very competitive secondary market that registers billions of dollars of transactions daily. The interest rates of these securities, which are determined by the forces of supply and demand, are watched around the world as the bellwether interest rates in the American financial markets.

The operation of this huge market has a considerable impact upon the condition of the American economy. This is discussed extensively in later chapters.

THE FEDERAL RESERVE SYSTEM

All large governments have a government-controlled central bank to assist in the management of financial affairs. In the United States, that role is performed by the Federal Reserve System.

The Federal Reserve System was created in 1913 as primarily a reserve depository for member commercial banks. Under any banking system, banks retain a small percentage of their assets in a money form as reserves against their deposits and other liabilities. This enables them to meet unexpected deposit drains, instills confidence in the public that they will be able to do so, and is usually required by law. Prior to the creation of the Federal Reserve System, banks kept their reserves partly in their own vaults and partly on deposit at larger banks. When there were deposit drains on small banks, they were often compelled to withdraw their reserves from larger banks, which threatened the ability of the large banks to retain their own reserves. Recurring financial crises and bank failure led to the conclusion that reserves should be held by a semipublic agency. Additionally, the agency should have the power to make reserve loans to troubled banks during times of crises.

On December 23, 1913, President Woodrow Wilson signed the Federal Reserve Act establishing the Federal Reserve System (Fed). It was the government's answer to the banking failures and monetary panics of the early 1900s. The Fed is the central bank of the United States, corresponding to the Bank of England or the Bank of France. Its original purposes were to give the country a currency flexible enough to meet its needs and to improve the supervision of banking. Today, however, these form only a part of broader and more important objectives, which include maintaining price stability, fostering a high rate of economic growth, and promoting a high level of employment.

Federal Reserve functions are carried out through 12 Federal Reserve banks and their 24 branches, but there is also central coordination by the Board of Governors of the Federal Reserve in Washington, D.C. The board of governors consists of 7 members appointed by the president and confirmed by the Senate. One of the board's duties is to supervise all Fed operations. The board participates in all the principal monetary actions of the Fed. It has full authority over changes in the legal reserve requirements of member banks (within the limits prescribed by Congress). The board "reviews and determines" interest rates of the individual Federal Reserve banks, and it has the authority to establish the maximum rates of interest member banks may pay on savings and other time deposits. In addition, the board is responsible for the regulation of stock market credit.

The presidents of the 12 regional Federal Reserve banks are *not* publicly elected or appointed; they are usually conservative bankers.[14] The president of each Federal Reserve bank is appointed by the board of directors of that bank. Each board of directors has 9 members, *6 of whom (Class A and Class B) are elected directly by the member banks* (usually on the advice of the state bankers' association, their lobbying group). The other three directors (Class C)

> are supposed to be representative of a broader public. In fact, they represent the same narrow interests as the others: twenty-nine of the thirty-six current Class C directors are executives or directors of corporations, mostly large.[15]

The House Banking Committee of the U.S. Congress surveyed all the 108 directors (12 Federal Reserve banks times 9 directors) and concluded that the directors are "representative of a small elite group which dominates much of the economic life of this nation."[16] These directors of the regional Federal Reserve banks included *no* women, *no* labor union members or worker representatives, *no* consumer organization members, *no* small farmers, and only two blacks. What is more incredible is that the Federal Reserve has existed 63 years and has had 1088 persons on its regional boards of directors, but *none* have been

---

[14] See the excellent article by Congressman Henry Reuss (then chairman of the House Committee on Banking, Currency, and Housing), "A Private Club for Public Policy," *The Nation* (October 16, 1976), pp. 370–372.
[15] *Ibid.*, p. 371.
[16] Quoted in *ibid.*, p. 371.

women, *none* have been workers or consumer representatives, and only four have been blacks.

There is also a Federal Open Market Committee (FOMC), which has the important function of buying and selling government bonds on the open market. The FOMC is composed of the seven members of the Board of Governors of the Federal Reserve (mostly conservative economists and big business representatives) plus five presidents of the regional Federal Reserve banks (the 12 presidents take turns on the FOMC, but they are all bankers). These are the people who determine the major part of U.S. monetary policy.

The Federal Reserve System has since evolved into a powerful central bank capable of taking discretionary actions that can profoundly affect the economy. The Board of Governors of the Federal Reserve and the Federal Open Market Committee now consider it part of their mandate to attempt to implement policies that will, among other things, control inflation, promote real growth, and stabilize international financial conditions.

The policy makers realize that they can't directly control these things, of course, but they hope to influence them by controlling or influencing the level of interest rates, growth of the money stock or other monetary aggregates, credit conditions, and so forth. The priority given to what "matters" the most in these control operations has varied over the years, with interest rates receiving most attention a decade ago and narrowly defined money aggregates (such as M1) getting primary emphasis now.

It's still the case, of course, that banks are required to keep an amount equal to a certain percentage of their liabilities (including customer deposits) on deposit at a Federal Reserve Bank. The deposit is simply a special sort of checking account. The deposit is a liability of the Federal Reserve Bank and an asset of the customer member bank in the same way that a checking account is a liability of the bank issuing the account and an asset of the customer possessing the checkbook. When funds are transferred between private banks and a Federal Reserve Bank, the transaction is recorded as a change in reserves. A bank's reserves at the Fed constitute its "balance" with that agency.

The ultimate constraint upon the private banking system's ability to provide credit to the economy is the level of reserves that those banks have on deposit. When a bank makes a new loan, creating an asset for itself, it usually gives the proceeds to the borrower by creating or adding to a checking account—creating a "demand deposit" liability. As any introductory economics text points out, this is how money is created in our modern American world, for demand deposits are part of the money supply. The bank is able to create the liability (and hence make the loan) only if it has or is able to place sufficient reserves on deposit to cover the liability. Because of this, the Federal Reserve System can at least loosely control the rate of deposit creation (or money creation) and lending by controlling the rate at which it allows reserves in the banking system to grow.

Aside from having a great deal of regulatory power over American banks, because most banks must keep reserves at a Federal Reserve Bank, the Federal Reserve System has three important policy tools that it can use to influence the economy: setting reserve requirements, discount window policy, and open market operations. The latter is by far the most important policy tool and is literally used daily by the Federal Reserve System to carry out its objective.

For readers unfamiliar with the way the Federal Reserve System manages its reserves, examples are provided in Appendix 7B. If the reader is unfamiliar with this topic, Appendix 7B should be read prior to reading the next three sections.

Discount Window Policy

Banks and certain other financial institutions have the right to borrow reserves from the Federal Reserve System. This is called *discount window* borrowing, and the interest rate charged on such loans is the *discount rate* that occasionally receives attention in the financial press.

Although the reserve loans are supposedly for "emergencies," banks routinely borrow from the Federal Reserve System when they are short of funds. The Federal Reserve discourages this practice when it becomes excessive or when a single bank relies upon such loans too often, but usually the reserves are made available for borrowing when the demand is there.

The borrowing of reserves adds reserves to the banking system, of course, and this allows banks to expand their loans and increase the money supply. Because loan credit becomes more easily available, such borrowing can exert downward pressure on interest rates. A reduction in such borrowings has the opposite effect.

The Federal Reserve System implements its discount window policy primarily by raising or lowering the discount rates. Given that interest rates on most heavily traded financial securities rise and fall continuously, the board of governors does not use this tool too often. Whereas Treasury bill rates move up and down daily, the discount rate often remains unchanged for months. In recent years, the discount rate has been below market rates for bank reserves (banks can lend and borrow reserves among themselves in the so-called federal funds market), so the prevailing discount rate does not seem to "ration" borrowed funds as most interest rates do. Instead, the occasional changes in the discount rate simply serve as a signal to the financial markets that the Federal Reserve System is altering (if only subtly) its policy. For example, if the discount rate is raised, it might be a signal that the Fed intends to "tighten up," slowing the growth rate of money and credit.

Discount window policy, however, has been used very little in recent years. Although changes in the discount rate occasionally cause a brief flurry in the financial markets, they tend to be generally ignored and have little apparent impact.

Changing Reserve Requirements

The actual size of required reserve deposits against bank liabilities depends upon the size and type of liability. For example, after 1976, banks were required to keep 7 percent of all demand deposits up to $2 million on reserve with higher and higher percentages for amounts greater than that. For any demand deposit amount in excess of $400 million, an amount equal to 16.25 percent was required to be on deposit as reserve. The reserves on time deposits depend upon maturity and are lower than the requirement on demand deposits. For example, large deposits maturing between 30 and 179 days required a 6 percent reserve whereas large deposits maturing in over 4 years require only 1 percent.

By raising or lowering these reserve requirements, the Federal Reserve System can strongly influence the level of bank liabilities (and hence the level of credit supported by these liabilities). For example, if, given any level of reserves already on deposit at the Federal Reserve Banks, reserve requirements are lowered, this would allow banks to expand their lending and hence their liabilities, making more credit available, increasing the money supply, and lowering interest rates.

Again, however, the board of governors has not used this policy tool in recent years, although reserves on most liabilities were standardized in 1980. The board has, in recent years, extended reserve requirements to liabilities not previously included. By 1987, certain liabilities of nonbank financial institutions will even have reserve requirements imposed against them.

Open Market Operations

Open market operations involve the buying and selling of securities—almost always, U.S. Treasury debt instruments. If the Federal Reserve System buys a Treasury bill from a member bank, it pays for the bill by increasing the bank's reserves. If the bill is purchased from a nonbank private party, a check from the Federal Reserve System is given to that party. When deposited in a private bank, the check is sent to the Federal Reserve System for redemption. The Federal Reserve System honors its obligation by increasing the depositing bank's reserves by the amount of the check. Hence, the purchase of a Treasury security either from a bank or another private party causes reserves to rise. The sale of a security in an open market operation has exactly the opposite effect; reserves will contract.

In addition to reserves, open market operations affect nominal interest rates. If the Federal Reserve System purchases securities in large enough numbers, because the securities are bought and sold in competitive markets, this demand will force the price of securities up. Since security values and yields move inversely, interest rates on the grade of securities purchased will drop. If such purchases continue for a time, arbitrage in the financial markets will cause other interest rates to drop "in sympathy" with the purchased securities.

In summary, an open market purchase of U.S. Treasury securities by the Federal Reserve System will increase bank reserves while dropping interest rates. The higher level of reserves will allow banks to expand their loans, increasing liabilities until all reserves are committed. Since the liabilities increased are normally demand deposits, the money stock grows as well. So interest rates drop while reserves, loans (credit), bank liabilities, and usually the money supply all grow. An open market sale will have the exact opposite effect.

Given all of this, it is easy to see why the Federal Reserve System places such emphasis on open market operations. Since such operations systematically affect interest rates, the money supply, and bank lending, they are very powerful tools. Open market operations are discussed in greater detail in Appendix 7B.

The operation of the Federal Reserve System is discussed very extensively in Chapter 24, where we present conservative, liberal, and radical views of the correct monetary policies to follow.

SUMMARY

Government spending has a considerable impact upon economic behavior in America. The relative importance of government expenditures has grown since World War II although the federal government's contribution to aggregate demand (its purchases of goods and services) has dropped sharply. The growth in expenditures can be explained primarily by the growth of military spending. In recent years, social security has also increased, but it comes from social security funds, not from general tax revenues.

The largest single category for government spending is for military spending. This absorbs more than 25 percent of spending by all governments. Such spending is likely to be permanently entrenched because it provides so many jobs and such lucrative compensation for corporations that benefit from military spending.

Although the taxation system in the United States is supposed to be progressive, because of numerous tax loopholes, it is only slightly so. Between individuals and corporations, the tax burden in the United States at the federal level is shifting away from corporations at the expense of individuals. The tremendous rise in social security taxes over the last 30 years is responsible for the largest increase in the tax burden at the federal level. At the state and local levels, all categories of taxation have increased substantially since the Korean War.

Federal government deficits have also shown a growing trend over the years. When the government runs a deficit, the U.S. Treasury must sell securities, usually in the form of bills, notes, or bonds. The U.S. Treasury debt now exceeds $1 trillion and is still growing rapidly. There is now a huge market for Treasury debt instruments, and the yields on these securities have a considerable impact upon world finance markets.

The Federal Reserve System, a quasi-public agency dominated by bankers and conservative corporate executives, is the nation's central bank. Created as a depository for bank reserves, it now has the responsibility for implementing monetary policy in the United States. To accomplish its goals, it can use the discount window policy, can change reserve requirements, and can use open market operations. In recent years, the Federal Reserve System has almost exclusively used the latter, buying and selling Treasury securities on a daily basis for the purpose of influencing the money supply, interest rates, and credit conditions in general.

Appendix 7A

The Government Multiplier

The obvious objectives of government fiscal policy are to *increase* the net flow of demand during depressions by increasing spending and lowering taxes and to *reduce* the net flow of demand during inflation by reducing spending and raising taxes. Not only the direct effects but also the secondary effects of these policies are important. For example, in a depression it is hoped that increases in government spending will mean more income to businesses or individuals and that this, in turn, will lead to further increases in private consumption and investment.

The secondary effects of a government expenditure may be quantified in terms of the government multiplier. The *government multiplier* is the ratio of increase in national income to an increase in government spending. Why will national income increase by more than the amount of government spending?

Take the very simple assumption that consumption reacts in a given ratio to an increase in income (whereas investment remains constant). This means every increase in income from government automatically leads to a certain increase in consumption spending. This spending means a further, though smaller, increase in income, some of which will be spent for a second round of consumption, and so forth.

The process by which the government multiplier allegedly increases income may be seen in a numerical example. Assume (1) a certain increase in government spending with (2) a given marginal propensity to consume and (3) that the increase in government spending takes place without any change in tax receipts. Under these simple assumptions, the result may be seen in Table 7A.1.

Suppose this is a period of some unemployment. The U.S. government spends $1000 (as shown in Table 7A.1) to hire some workers to help build a school or a battleship. The $1000 is paid to the workers, who have a marginal propensity to consume (MPC) of 80 percent. Therefore, they spend $800 and save $200. The $800 is spent to buy consumer goods. The

Table 7A.1

HOW THE GOVERNMENT MULTIPLIER WORKS

Increase in Government Spending	Increase in Consumption	Increase in National Income	Increase in Saving
$1000		$1000	
0	$ 800	$ 800	$ 200
0	$ 640	$ 640	$ 160
0	$ 512	$ 512	$ 128
0	$ 410	$ 410	$ 102
0	$ 328	$ 328	$ 82
—	—	—	—
—	—	—	—
—	—	—	—
Total Increase in Government Spending	Total Increase in Consumption	Total Increase in National Income	Total Increase in Saving
$1000	$4000	$5000	$1000

ASSUMPTIONS:
1. Suppose government increases its spending by $1000 (whereas private investment does not change).
2. Also suppose a marginal propensity to consume of ⅘, or 80 percent.

owners and workers who receive the $800 also have an MPC of 80 percent, so they will respend $640 and save $160.

After enough rounds of spending, the entire $1000 has been saved. If all the consumer spending is added together, it equals $4000. The initial government spending ($1000) plus the consumer spending ($4000) resulting from it provides the total increase in national income ($5000).

If the $1000 increase in government spending is a one-time injection of new spending, then the totals at the bottom of Table 7A.1 represent only temporary additions to consumption, saving, and national income. After these one-time increases are realized, however, total spending will eventually return to its original level. But if the $1000 increase is a new, stepped-up rate of government spending that continues through several subsequent periods, the totals represent the rise from the old, lower levels to the new, higher levels of spending flows, which will persist in each future period.

From this description of how the multiplier works, it should be clear that if less is saved out of each increment to income, then each increment to consumption spending will be larger. In other words, if the marginal propensity to save declines, the subsequent increases in consumption and income will be larger.

The multiplier formula is just a shortcut for finding where the process of Table 7A.1 ends without repeating the calculation a great many times. Because the formula works equally well for an initial increase *or* decrease in government spending, it can be stated more generally as *changes* rather than increases or decreases. By definition:

$$\text{government multiplier} = \frac{\text{change in income}}{\text{change in government}} = \frac{\Delta Y}{\Delta G} \qquad (7A.1)$$

where Y is income and G is government spending.

Movement from one equilibrium to another equilibrium position is assumed. Therefore, at the end of the process, the change in saving must equal the change in government spending (so $G = S$, where S is saving). Substituting saving for government, we get this result:

$$\text{government multiplier} = \frac{\text{change in income}}{\text{change in saving}} = \frac{\Delta Y}{\Delta S} \qquad (7A.2)$$

or, by simple mathematical manipulation,

$$\text{government multiplier} = \frac{1}{(\text{change in saving})/(\text{change in income})} = \frac{1}{(\Delta S)/(\Delta Y)} \qquad (7A.3)$$

The denominator of this fraction is nothing but the marginal propensity to save. So the formula to remember is just

$$\text{multiplier} = \frac{1}{MPS} \text{ or } \frac{1}{1-MPC} \qquad (7A.4)$$

Notice that the marginal propensities to save (*MPS*) and consume (*MPC*) always add up to exactly 1.0, so *MPS* equals one minus *MPC*.

Look again at the example in Table 7A.1. It has been established that *total increase in income = increase in government × the multiplier*. In this example, the increase in government spending is $1000. What is the multiplier? The *MPC* is ⅘, so the MPS is ⅕. The multiplier must equal 1 divided by ⅕, which is 5. So it may be calculated that

$$\text{total increase in income} = \$1000 \times 5 = \$5000 \tag{7A.5}$$

This demonstrates how the multiplier is used to find the end result of government spending.

Of course, if the multiplier is reduced, then the government spending has less effect. At one extreme, if the multiplier is just 1, the change in income is just equal to the change in government spending. At the other extreme, if the multiplier approaches infinity, any small change in government spending will cause an infinite change in income.

Of course, the value of the multiplier is controlled by the *MPC* or *MPS*. If the *MPC* falls, so does the multiplier (because less is respent out of each increase in income). A multiplier of only 2 means an *MPC* of only ½. A multiplier of only 1 means everything is saved and the *MPC* is zero. But a multiplier of infinity means all income is immediately respent for consumption, the *MPC* is 1, and the *MPS* is zero.

The government multiplier may also be derived from a formal model, which gives some further insights into its assumptions. The first assumption is that, in equilibrium, the supply of output (Y) will equal consumer demand plus investment demand plus government demand. (Net exports are ignored for simplicity.)

$$Y = C + I + G \tag{7A.6}$$

The second assumption is that consumption is a function of income. Using the simplest linear function:

$$C = a + bY \tag{7A.7}$$

where a and b are constants, and b is assumed to be between zero and 1. (In this simple model, the consumption function is based upon *gross national product* (Y) rather than *disposible income* (Y minus taxes). In more complicated models where disposable income is used, the multiplier is weighted by the *tax rate*. See equation 5.27 in Chapter five for an example of the complicated multiplier.) The third assumption of this simplest model is that *investment* is a constant (k):

$$I = k \tag{7A.8}$$

because the investment multiplier will be discussed separately in Chapter 9.

Government spending is set outside of the model by the government:

$$G = G_0 \tag{7A.9}$$

where G_0 is given by exogenous factors, that is, factors external to the model.

If equations 7A.7, 7A.8, and 7A.9 are substituted into 7A.6, the result is

$$Y = a + bY + k + G_0 \tag{7A.10}$$

Suppose there is an exogenously caused change in the level of government spending to a new permanent level (G_1). Define $\Delta G = G_1 - G_0$. To see the effect of this change, take the first differences of all the components of the equation, and then divide every component by the change in government spending. Thus:

$$\frac{\Delta Y}{\Delta G} = \frac{\Delta a}{\Delta G} + \frac{\Delta b Y}{\Delta G} + \frac{\Delta k}{\Delta G} + \frac{\Delta G}{\Delta G} \tag{7A.11}$$

Since a and k are constants, their change is zero. Of course, $\Delta G/\Delta G = 1$. Therefore:

$$\frac{\Delta Y}{\Delta G} = 0 + \frac{\Delta b Y}{\Delta G} + 0 + 1 \tag{7A.12}$$

or, getting rid of the zeros

$$\frac{\Delta Y}{\Delta G} - \frac{\Delta b Y}{\Delta G} = 1 \tag{7A.13}$$

or, combining the like terms

$$\frac{(1-b)\Delta Y}{\Delta G} = 1 \tag{7A.14}$$

Therefore

$$\frac{\Delta Y}{\Delta G} = \frac{1}{1-b} \tag{7A.15}$$

So the government multiplier is $1/(1-b)$ or $1/(1-MPC)$.

Of course, the government multiplier ratio is an artificial concept because it does not take into account all the changing factors and complications involved. The first qualification is the fact that the second, third, and fourth rounds of spending do not occur instantaneously; it takes time before income is respent for consumption. Long or varying time lags make it much more difficult to speak of an exact multiplier. Second, the multiplier explained here assumes that investment is a given constant and is not affected by changes in income. As will be shown in Chapter 9, however, there is probably a close connection between investment and the change in income. If this is so, changes in government spending, as well as the secondary changes in consumer spending, may directly affect investment. However, government spending may have negative psychological effects on investment if it is thought to take away funds by taxation or to compete by means of cheaper products. At any rate, government spending is likely to have some direct or indirect effect on investment, and as a result investment may not legitimately be considered a constant in this regard.

The third major set of qualifications regarding the government multiplier arises from the fact that MPC does not remain constant, yet it is the very rock on which the multiplier theory is founded. It does not remain constant because, for one thing, consumption is actually influenced by many factors other than income. The marginal propensity to consume also varies because there are different leakages from the process at different times. For example, the effect of an increase in government spending on national income may be partly siphoned off by the levy of higher taxes or merely by automatic movements into higher tax brackets. Furthermore, it may happen that increased spending for imports removes some portion of income from the domestic multiplier process. For all these reasons, MPC may change too often for any accurate prediction of the multiplier beyond a short period of only one or two rounds of the process.

The fourth and last qualification has to do with how the government spending is financed. If the government takes back through taxation the same amount that it spends, then there is no net addition to consumer spending, only the initial government spending is added to the economy, and the multiplier will be only 1. The national income will increase only by the amount of the increase in government spending. To see this point more clearly, you will find it useful to examine the tax multiplier.

The government multiplier for a decrease in taxes is always one less than the multiplier for an equal increase in spending. For example, if the marginal propensity to consume is two-thirds and if all other complications are ignored, then the multiplier for government spending is three; but the multiplier from decreased taxation is only two. The reason is very simple: if the government spends an extra billion dollars, that billion is part of national income in addition to the secondary consumer spending. If taxes go down by a billion dollars, the same additional consumer spending may be generated, but the original billion of decreased taxation is certainly not an addition to national income, though it leaves a billion more disposable income, in the hands of individuals.

Since the multiplier from a change in government spending is always just one greater than the multiplier from a change in taxes, it follows that new government spending financed by equal new taxation will always have a net multiplier of exactly one. In other words, if an increase of government spending is financed by an equal increase in taxes, the total effect may simply be that there is an increase in government product, but no change in private product or private income. The increase in national income is just equal to the new government spending, but because of the taxation, there are no secondary effects on private spending; this principle is called the *balanced budget multiplier.*

Of course, the balanced budget multiplier rests on a good many unrealistic assumptions. It must include all the assumptions of the simple government spending multiplier: that private investment stays constant, that all the rounds of consumer spending occur instantaneously, and that the marginal propensity to consume remains constant. Furthermore, it must be assumed that the *MPC* is the same for income received from government spending and for additional disposable income owing to a decrease in taxes. This means, for one thing, that the average income level of people receiving money from the government and people paying taxes must be about the same. Moreover, the time lags in government spending and government taxation must be the same, so that the amounts involved are actually equal, assuming we can predict the exact effect of a lowering of tax rates. Finally, the whole argument assumes that there is enough unemployment slack for all the increased spending to create more product. If there is full employment, the increased government spending could only produce more money income along with an inflation of prices, not more product or real income.

If an increase of government spending is financed by the sale of government bonds, which is the so-called deficit spending, the effect on the private economy depends on how the bondholders would have used the money if they had not loaned it to the government. If they would have used it all for consumption or investment anyhow, then there is no net stimulation to the private economy; that is, the multiplier is just one. If they would have used only a small percentage of it for consumption or investment, then the government spending has a very powerful net effect on the private economy.

Finally, the most inflationary method of financing government spending is to cause the money supply to grow (as shown in the next appendix) because this withdraws nothing from the private sector either by taxation or borrowing. Thus, in a deep depression a government may sometimes finance expenditures by creating money whereas at full employment it will attempt to use only taxation. The impact and use of borrowing falls between these two extremes.

Appendix 7B

Federal Reserve Operations

The impact of the manipulation of bank reserves by the Federal Reserve System can best be shown with T-account examples. A T-account reflects the financial status of a business. The account is simply a list of the business assets, debts (liabilities), and net worth (equity). In a T-account, all assets are listed in the column on the left side of the T-account. All debt (liabilities) and net worth (equity) are listed on the right side. Since net worth is, by definition, equal to the value of assets minus debts (liabilities), the two sides of the T-account are equal in value.

Reserves held by the Federal Reserve System for member banks are liabilities of the Federal Reserve System and are assets of private banks. The loans made by private banks are assets. The customers' deposits in banks, such as demand deposits, are liabilities. Both entities own government securities, which are assets.

In a simplified example, suppose that the only bank liability is demand deposits and the reserve requirements against those demand deposits is 10 percent. These demand deposit liabilities are money, by definition.

Suppose the T-accounts that follow represent the status of the Federal Reserve System and the entire private banking system. The private banking system's T-account represents the sum of all assets, liability, and equity categories for all private banks. All figures are in billions of dollars.

FEDERAL RESERVE SYSTEM		PRIVATE BANKING SYSTEM	
Assets	Liabilities & Equity	Assets	Liabilities & Equity
$20 Government bills	$10 Reserves 10 Equity	$10 Reserves 80 Loans 20 Government bills	$100 Demand deposits 10 Equity

As can be seen, the private banking system has checking account (demand) deposits of $100 billion, which is the money supply. The banks are required to hold $10 billion in reserves at the Fed, which are recorded as private banking system assets and Fed liabilities. The private banking system possesses some U.S. Treasury bills, on which interest is earned, and has $80 billion in loans, both of which are assets.

Now suppose the Fed buys $5 billion in government bills from the PBS. This is called an *open market operation,* which adds to the nation's money supply, as will be seen further on. The initial impact is as follows:

FEDERAL RESERVE SYSTEM		PRIVATE BANKING SYSTEM	
Assets	Liabilities & Equity	Assets	Liabilities & Equity
$25 Government bills	$15 Reserves 10 Equity	$15 Reserves 80 Loans 15 Government bills	$100 Demand deposits 10 Equity

As can be seen, the Fed "paid" for the bills by crediting the private banking system with $5 billion in reserves. On the asset side of the private banking system T-account, their bills declined by $5 billion, and their reserves grew by the same. The liability side of the PBS account was unaffected.

Since the private banking system is only required to hold $10 billion in reserves, it has excess reserves of $5 billion. Because this is so, it can make new loans. When the private banks make loans, they "create" a demand deposit entry in the borrower's checking account. For example, if a borrower borrows $10,000, the bank may tell the borrower that she simply has $10,000 in her checking account that wasn't there before. In this way, money, which is primarily a bookkeeping entry, is created.

In the example being used here, the final result of the open market operation is as follows (the Fed T-account is the same as earlier); but the T-account of the private banking system has changed as follows:

PRIVATE BANKING SYSTEM	
Assets	Liabilities & Equity
$15 Reserves 130 Loans 15 Government bills	$150 Demand deposits 10 Equity

The private banking system expanded *both* loans and demand deposits by $50 billion. This is the same act, not two separate events—when a loan is created, a demand deposit is simultaneously created. When demand deposits reached $150 billion, the banks had to stop lending because all reserves were once again required reserves.

In this example, the Fed provided $5 billion to the private banking system in an open market operation, which resulted in an expansion of the money supply of $50 billion.

Chapter 8

CONSUMPTION

Consumption is, by far, the largest category of aggregate demand. Year after year consumption absorbs between 60 percent and 65 percent of total GNP. Over 90 percent of personal disposable income is absorbed by consumption. Obviously, the behavior of consumption will have considerable impact upon the behavior of aggregate demand.

In the national income accounts, consumption is divided into three categories: (1) consumer nondurable goods, (2) consumer durable goods, and (3) services. In 1982, the $1971 billion spent on consumption was divided into $243 billion for durable goods (12 percent), $762 billion of nondurable goods (39 percent), and $966 billion (49 percent) for services. As can be seen from these figures, the demand for services is now the most important category of consumption. Services have slowly grown in relative importance over the last 30 years at the expense of consumption of nondurable goods. In 1955, for example, services constituted only 40 percent of consumption whereas the demand for nondurable goods contributed to 48 percent of consumption. The relative roles of these two categories have been almost exactly reversed since that time.

Despite the change in its composition, consumption as an aggregate category has been fairly stable. Figure 8.1 shows the behavior of consumption as a percentage of GNP from 1952 to 1980. As can be seen, this ratio has never been below 61.5 percent and never above 64.5 percent. Furthermore, no trend is evident. As will be seen later in this chapter, however, consumption behavior can still potentially play a large role in business cycles. Consumption is such a large category that a drop of only 1 percent in a given year will amount to a drop of over $20 billion in aggregate demand if it is not offset elsewhere.

This chapter examines the various interpretations of consumer behavior by economists since J. M. Keynes. Additionally, it examines the empirical data on the behavior of consumer demand over the business cycle.

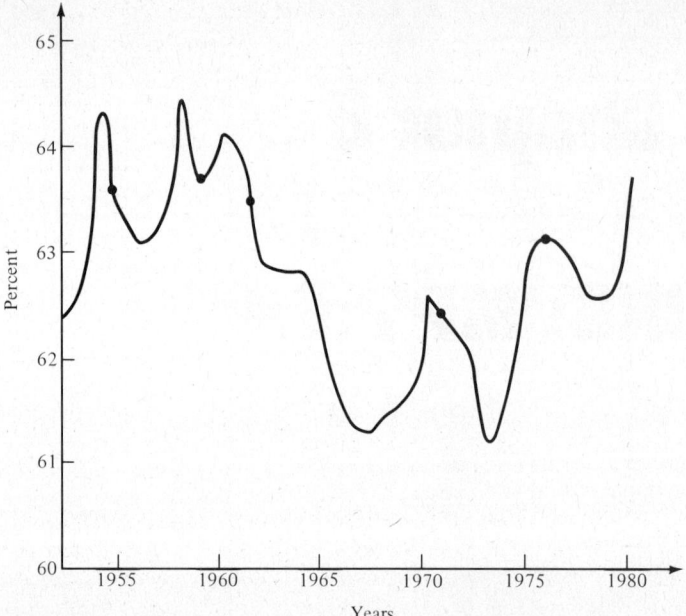

Figure 8.1 Consumption as a Percentage of GNP, 1952–1980
NOTE: Dots represent troughs of business cycles.
SOURCE: U.S. Department of Commerce.

KEYNES'S VIEW OF CONSUMPTION

Keynes saw a need for a description of the behavior of consumer demand in the aggregate. Previous neoclassical writers talked only about individual consumers because Say's law made it unnecessary to discuss aggregate demand. Keynes saw aggregate consumer behavior in terms of psychology. He stated the "fundamental psychological law" that "men are disposed, as a rule and on the average, to increase their consumption as their income increases, but not by as much as the increase in their income."[1] He argued that people have a certain habitual consumption expenditure or standard of living out of a given level of income. If a person's income rises, he or she will—at first—continue the same standard of living, so the person will save more. In the long run, that person may slowly adjust his or her consumption upward—but saving would still tend to rise somewhat faster than consumption.

Since Keynes explained consumption in terms of psychological propensities, almost all economic textbooks today define the ratio of consumption to income as the *average propen-*

---

[1]John Maynard Keynes, *General Theory of Employment, Interest, and Money* (New York: Harcourt Brace Jovanovich, 1936), p. 96.

sity to consume or APC. The ratio of additional consumption to additional income is called the *marginal propensity to consume* or MPC. As is pointed out later on, it is not psychological propensities alone, but also many objective factors (such as the distribution of income) that determine the ratio of consumption to income. Moreover, the psychological propensities are by no means innate or eternally unchanging. Our present psychology of all-out consumerism (the more, the better) is shaped and determined by our cultural environment, including family background, religion, education, and indoctrination by the advertising media. To call the result a purely psychological propensity is misleading. That terminology is used here only because it is so widespread, but there is always the implicit proviso that the propensity (APC or MPC) is socially conditioned and constrained by the objective facts.

The "Keynesian" consumption function is shown in beginning economics textbooks in its simplest, straight-line form:

$$C = a + bY \tag{8.1}$$

where C is aggregate consumption, Y is income (whether national or personal or disposable is discussed further on), a is a positive constant, and b is a positive constant between zero and 1. In this case, b is the marginal propensity to consume; since it is a constant, the relation is linear. Since the constant a indicates a positive consumption level even when income is zero, the average propensity to consume (APC) must decline as income rises. Keynes himself had a far more complex perspective, as indicated by his belief that the marginal propensity to consume (MPC) was also likely to decline as income rises.

The so-called Keynesian Revolution generated a plethora of empirical research on consumption behavior. Cross-sectional studies of different families earning different levels of income in a given year confirmed the view that the average propensity to consume falls (and the average propensity to save rises) as the income level rises. Poor families had a very high APC, and wealthy families had a low APC. Studies of monthly or quarterly time-series data for aggregate consumption and income for relatively short time periods (i.e., less than or equal to a whole business cycle) also seem to confirm that the APC falls as income rises—whereas the APC rises when income falls.

Later studies, however, covered much longer time periods, taking each ten years as one point or each business cycle as one point. In these long-run time-series data, it was found that the average propensity to consume (C/Y) remained constant over time even though income rose by many times its original level. By the end of the 1950s, three new neoclassical-Keynesian theories had emerged to account for these seemingly contradictory facts.

The debate over the long-run behavior of the ratio of consumption to income (APC) is very important. Keynes suspected that the APC might gradually fall as a nation became more prosperous. In time, this might have dire implications. If the APC declines over time, the ratio of savings to income would have to grow. All such savings would have to find suitable investment outlets. The relative importance of investment would continue to grow. If, at times, there were simply not enough suitable investment outlets to absorb the growing fund of savings, the economy might be very prone to recession.

THE RELATIVE INCOME HYPOTHESIS

The relative income hypothesis, developed by James Duesenberry,[2] is closest to Keynes's original intuition. Duesenberry explained both the cross-sectional result that the APC falls as income rises and the long-run time-series result that the APC is roughly constant by arguing that consumers are not so much concerned with their absolute level of consumption as with their consumption relative to the rest of the population. A person with a lower-than-average income, according to Duesenberry, will tend to have a higher-than-average ratio of consumption to income because he or she is trying to keep up with a national average consumption standard with a below-average income. On the other hand, a person with a higher-than-average income will have a lower ratio of consumption to income because it takes a smaller proportion of his or her income to buy the standard consumption bundle. As long as income distribution is stable, there is no reason for the ratio of consumption to income to change as income grows along the trend line. Only if income distribution changes would relative positions change, so only in that case would the long-run APC change.

Duesenberry also explained the short-run time-series result that the APC declines as income rises in expansion and increases as income falls in contraction. He argues that present consumption is influenced by previous peak levels of consumption (so it is not reversible in time). Given the habit of a certain peak level of consumption, it is more difficult for a family —when a recession reduces its income—to reduce its level of consumption once attained than to reduce the proportion of income saved. When there is a new recovery, APC will slowly fall to its long-run average as families regain their old peak standard of living.

THE LIFE CYCLE HYPOTHESIS

The life cycle hypothesis, developed by Ando and Modigliani in the early fifties,[3] explains the cross-sectional results by arguing that people's psychological propensity to save out of income is greater in the middle years of their lives than in the early and late years. Ando and Modigliani argue that at any point in time a higher-than-proportionate number of middle-aged people will be found in higher-than-average income brackets. At the same time, a higher-than-proportionate number of young and old will be found in lower-than-average income brackets.

In addition, the life cycle hypothesis explanation of both short-run and long-run aggregate time-series data hinges on the return to the pre-Keynesian assumption that consumption behavior is fundamentally determined by estimated total wealth, net worth, or present value. It also hinges on the belief that estimates of total wealth behave differently from income over the cycle. Since estimated total wealth increases at the same rate as total income in the long

---

[2] James Duesenberry, *Income, Saving, and the Theory of Consumer Behavior* (Cambridge, Mass.: Harvard University Press, 1949).
[3] A. Ando and Franco Modigliani, "The Life Cycle Hypothesis of Saving: Aggregate Implications and Tests," *American Economic Review,* 53 (March 1963), pp. 55–84.

run and since consumption is a constant function of estimated total wealth according to the life cycle hypothesis, consumption should increase at the same rate as income in the long run, making APC roughly constant in long-run time series.

In the short run, the market value of wealth in property—and, therefore, the present value of income from property—falls less rapidly than aggregate income during recessions.[4] Since consumption is based on the present value of income, holders of wealth in property will maintain their consumption and not let it fall as rapidly as their current labor income falls. Consequently, this is a factor tending to raise APC in contractions while letting APC fall again to its long-run level in expansions. All the arguments and alleged facts in the life cycle hypothesis have been defended and attacked in numerous articles.[5]

THE PERMANENT INCOME HYPOTHESIS

The permanent income hypothesis of Milton Friedman explains the constancy of the APC in the long-run time series as an accurate reflection of the "true" constancy of the relationship between estimates of *permanent income* and desired levels of *permanent consumption*.[6] Permanent income is determined by total expected wealth during a person's lifetime. Friedman explains the apparent deviation from this relationship in the cross-sectional and short-run time-series data (in which APC falls as income rises) as a kind of statistical optical illusion in which the "true" behavioral relations between permanent consumption and permanent income are "disguised."

There is *transitory income*, which is defined to be income received by accident or windfall in a single period. This transitory income will not affect our long-run estimate of permanent income. Yet the transitory income and *transitory consumption* are inevitably measured as part of *observed income* and *observed consumption*. At any point in time, given the definition of transitory income, there will be a higher-than-proportionate number of individuals with high transitory income found in high observed income brackets. Similarly, there will be a higher-than-proportionate number of individuals with low transitory incomes in low observed income brackets. Friedman assumes the propensity to consume out of transitory income is less than out of permanent income because people know they must return to their permanent level, so the APC would *appear* to decline as income rises in any cross-sectional study. Similarly, since recession years are characterized by a lower-than-average ratio of transitory income to observed income whereas boom years have a higher-than-average ratio of transitory income to observed income, the APC would *appear* to decline as income rises in short-run time series as well.

[4]See Michael K. Evans, *Macroeconomic Activity* (New York: Harper & Row, 1969), p. 37.
[5]See, e.g., defense by Franco Modigliani, "The Consumption Function in a Developing Economy and the Italian Experience," *American Economic Review* 65 (December 1975), pp. 825–842. See, e.g., attack by Betsy Buttrell White, "Empirical Tests of the Life Cycle Hypothesis," *American Economic Review* 68 (September 1978), pp. 547–560. Also see, e.g., Alan Blinder, "Intergenerational Transfers and Life-Cycle Consumption," *American Economic Review* 66 (May 1976), pp. 87–93.
[6]Milton Friedman, *A Theory of the Consumption Function* (Princeton, N.J.: Princeton University Press, 1957).

Friedman's consumption function says that permanent consumption (C_P) equals a constant (k) times permanent income (Y_P), so

$$C_P = kY_P \tag{8.2}$$

where k is constant in the short run, but changes slowly in the long run. It (k) changes in response to changes in long-run interest rates (r); the utility functions (U) of people, including their ages, family composition, and changing preferences; and the ratio (w) of present physical assets to total wealth. Thus

$$k = f(r, U, w) \tag{8.3}$$

but all of these factors change very slowly.

CONCLUSIONS FROM NEOCLASSICAL-KEYNESIAN THEORIES

All three of the neoclassical-Keynesian theories still base themselves primarily on assumptions about psychological propensities to consume out of income. All three of them still see the fluctuations in the average propensity to consume (C/Y) as *"a result of departures from the long-run average rate of growth of income"*[7] (emphasis in the original). Much of neoclassical-Keynesian literature thus explains the particular relationship of consumption and income over the short-run cycle mainly by the psychological preferences of all individuals. These long-run preferences are modified by unexpected income fluctuations,[8] previous peak income, age, interest rates, or expected permanent wealth. (All economists agree that there may be exogenous effects by government tax policies[9] or changes in exchange rates that affect imports.)

The relative income and permanent income hypotheses—and to a lesser extent the life cycle hypothesis—all predict similar results. The predicted results are shown in Figure 8.2.

Both the predicted actual behavior of income and its long-run trend are shown in the top of the graph, and the predicted actual behavior of consumption is below that. Consumption is more closely a function of the *trend* in income, staying at about 65 percent of the trend, than it is a function of cyclical actual income. If these hypotheses are true, one would expect the ratio of consumption to income (APC) to decline during expansions and grow during contractions.

Most neoclassical-Keynesian theories—particularly the permanent income and life cycle hypotheses—lead to a very clear contradiction with one of Keynes's chief conclusions. Keynes argued that the average propensity to consume declines at higher-income levels. Therefore, Keynes stressed that more inequality, a higher proportion of income to the rich and a lower proportion to the poor, would tend to lower consumer demand. The implication

---

[7] Paul Wonnacott, *Macroeconomics* (Chicago: Irwin, 1974), pp. 343–344.

[8] See, e.g., Lewis J. Rosen, "Stock Market Capital Gains and Consumption Expenditures," *Journal of Finance* 28 (December 1973), p. 1379.

[9] See, e.g., Michael Boskin, "Taxation, Saving, and the Rate of Interest," *Journal of Political Economy* 86 (April 1978), pp. 503–527.

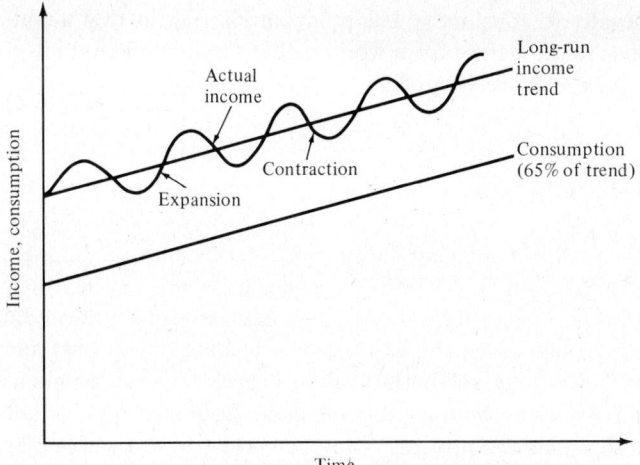

Figure 8.2 The Relationship Between Consumption, the Income Trend, and Actual Income as Explained by the Relative and Permanent Income Hypotheses
NOTE: The data here are purely hypothetical.

is that, if it is necessary to increase consumer demand to eliminate unemployment, then there should be greater equality of income.

The conservative neoclassical-Keynesians—such as Friedman—argue against Keynes's thesis and their theories are designed in part to remove that thesis from the accepted "Keynesian" doctrine. For example, Alan Blinder argues thus:

> In the early Post Keynesian days it was commonly assumed, presumably on the basis of Keynes' own intuition, . . . that equalization of the income distribution would increase consumption. With . . . the ascendancy of the Friedman (1957) and Modigliani and Brumberg (1954) models of consumer behavior, this view fell into disrepute in academic circles.[10]

He states that the "modern" or Friedman view "does not accord very well with intuition," especially the intuition of "those not schooled in macroeconomics."[11] It is clear that, for Blinder, *macroeconomics* means only the viewpoint of neoclassical-Keynesians; it does not include the viewpoint of Keynes, the Post Keynesians, or Marxists.

Whereas Keynes argued that the average propensity to consume falls at higher-income levels, the three neoclassical-Keynesian theories discussed earlier all deny this basic finding. They argue that the short-run or cross-sectional results can be explained by other, temporary factors. It follows that a change in the distribution of income, in the eyes of these theorists,

---

[10] Alan S. Blinder, "Distribution Effects of the Aggregate Consumption Function," *Journal of Political Economy* 83, no. 3 (1975), pp. 447–448.
[11] *Ibid.*, p. 448.

will *not* change the average propensity to consume.[12] The policy implication is that a shift in income distribution from the poor to the rich or from workers to capitalists will not lower consumer demand, so it will not have a depressing effect.

THE CLASS INCOME HYPOTHESIS

Marx always stressed that class relationships under capitalism restrict consumer demand. He wrote ". . . the majority of the population, the working people, can only expand their consumption within very narrow limits."[13] Keynes did not put it in class terms, but he did emphasize that increasing inequality may widen the gap between income (or output) and consumer demand. Keynes said: "Since I regard the individual propensity to consume as being (normally) such as to have a wider gap between income and consumption as income increases, it naturally follows that the *collective* propensity for a community as a whole may depend . . . on the distribution of incomes within it."[14]

Both Post Keynesians and modern Marxists (such as Michael Kalecki,[15] Joan Robinson,[16] or Sidney Weintraub[17]) have argued that consumer demand is strongly affected by the distribution of income. The poor have high marginal propensities to consume, that is, a high ratio of additional consumption out of additional income. The rich have much lower marginal propensities to consume. Therefore, if the rich get a higher share of income and the poor a lower share than in the previous period, the marginal propensity to consume for the whole country will decline.

Capitalists, who receive profits from ownership of property and shares of corporate stocks, mostly have very high incomes. Even after consuming many luxuries, they are able to save and have a low propensity to consume. Workers, who earn wages and salaries from labor, have a much lower average income. Workers are, on the average, not able to save because they must consume all or almost all their income to meet basic needs.

The class income hypothesis stresses the lower marginal propensity to consume out of profits than out of wages. This implies that a shift of income from workers to capitalists will cause a lower average propensity to consume for the whole society. A shift of income from capitalists to workers would raise the propensity to consume. For policy purposes, this means that policies (such as those of the Reagan administration in 1981) that shift income from poor and workers to rich capitalists will restrict consumer demand.

Although a few models have used this distinction in forecasting,[18] most neoclassical-

---

[12]See *ibid.* Also see, e.g., Philip Musgrove, "Income Distribution and the Aggregate Consumption Function," *Journal of Political Economy* 88 (June 1980), pp. 504–525.

[13]Karl Marx, *Theories of Surplus Value* (Moscow: Progress Publishers, 1952, first pub. 1903) p. 492.

[14]John M. Keynes, "Mr. Keynes on the Distribution of Incomes and 'Propensity to Consume': A Reply," *Review of Economics and Statistics*, 27 (August 1939), p. 129.

[15]Michael Kalecki, *Theory of Economic Dynamics*, 2d ed. (London: Allen and Unwin, 1965; first pub. 1935).

[16]See discussion of Joan Robinson in Alfred Eichner and J. A. Kregel, "An Essay on Post-Keynesian Theory: A New Paradigm in Economics," *Journal of Economic Literature* 13 (December 1975), pp. 1293–1314.

[17]Sidney Weintraub, *An Approach to the Theory of Income Distribution* (Philadelphia: Chilton, 1958).

[18]See, e.g., James Duesenberry et al., *The Brookings Quarterly Econometric Model of the United States* (Chicago: University of Chicago Press, 1965).

Keynesians build their analysis on the psychological propensity to consume of a single individual rather than the behavior of groups. This view is closely related to the tendency of neoclassical-Keynesians to take psychological propensities as a given exogenous fact as if people were born with such propensities. Even if they would acknowledge some environmental influences on consumers, such as advertising, they still believe that it is not the job of economists to investigate such social influences.

Contrary to the neoclassical-Keynesians, institutionalists emphasize that the consumer behavior of different individuals and classes is neither innate nor outside of the economist's proper jurisdiction. Institutionalists, such as Thorstein Veblen or John Kenneth Galbraith,[19] have shown how consumer behavior is dictated by the social environment. In the view of the class income hypothesis, the main shifts in the average propensity to consume over the cycle must be explained, not merely by psychological propensities with social origins, but by objective shifts in class income distribution. It should always be remembered that the aggregate consumer *propensity to consume* is (1) socially conditioned and (2) affected by the class distribution of income.

CYCLICAL BEHAVIOR OF CONSUMPTION AND INCOME

What is the actual behavior of consumption as income rises and falls? In Chapter 2, when the actual history of U.S. cycles was examined, the most comprehensive chronology of the business cycle was found to be that by Wesley Mitchell[20] and his followers at the National Bureau of Economic Research (NBER).[21] In spite of its deficiencies (discussed in Chapter 2), this chronology of *cycle peaks,* when most business activity is highest, and *cycle troughs,* when most business activity is lowest, is still the best available, so it is used here. In Chapter 2, the monthly peaks and troughs were given from 1854 to 1980. The quarterly peaks and troughs for the last six cycles are shown in Table 8.1.

All the cyclical data in this book are quarterly data, calculated for these six cycles. According to the method developed at the National Bureau of Economic Research (NBER), the cycle is divided into nine stages. Stage 1 is the initial trough, stage 5 is the peak, and stage 9 is the final trough. Stages 2, 3, and 4 divide the expansion into an equal number of quarters. Stages 6, 7, and 8 divide the contraction into an equal number of quarters.

The level of an economic variable, such as national income, is then calculated at each stage. It is expressed as a percentage of its average level over the whole cycle. The average level over the whole cycle is called the *cycle base,* and it always equals 100 because it is exactly 100 percent of the average of all the values of the variable over the cycle.

Since every cycle base equals 100 and since each stage is expressed as a percentage of its base, it is legitimate to average several cycles together. Thus, the cycle pattern for national

---

[19]John Kenneth Galbraith, *The New Industrial State* (Boston: Houghton Mifflin Co., 1967).
[20]Wesley Mitchell, *What Happens in Business Cycles* (New York: National Bureau of Economic Research, 1951).
[21]See Wesley Mitchell and Arthur Burns, *Measuring Business Cycles* (New York: National Bureau of Economic Research, 1946). Also see, e.g., Geoffrey Moore and Julius Shiskin, *Indicators of Business Expansions and Contractions* (New York: National Bureau of Economic Research, 1967).

Table 8.1

CYCLE DATES

	Trough	Peak	Trough
Cycle 1	1949.4	1953.3	1954.3
Cycle 2	1954.3	1957.3	1958.2
Cycle 3	1958.2	1960.2	1961.1
Cycle 4	1961.1	1969.4	1970.4
Cycle 5	1970.4	1973.4	1975.1
Cycle 6	1975.1	1980.1	1980.3

NOTE: 1949.4 means the fourth quarter of 1949. Cycle dates are quarterly.
SOURCE: National Bureau of Economic Research, reported in U.S. Department of Commerce, *Business Conditions Digest* (February 1982).

Table 8.2

LEVELS OF NATIONAL INCOME AND CONSUMPTION

LEVELS AS PERCENTAGE OF CYCLE BASE

	Average Trough	Expansion			Average Peak	Contraction			Average Trough
Stage	1	2	3	4	5	6	7	8	9
National income	87.4	92.0	99.8	105.4	107.1	106.6	105.2	104.2	103.9
Consumption	89.6	93.0	99.0	104.4	106.6	106.7	106.3	106.2	106.7

NOTE: This table represents an average of six cycles, from 1949 through 1980, in quarterly data and in constant 1972 dollars.
SOURCES: National income data from U.S. Department of Commerce, *National Income and Product Accounts, 1926 to 1974* (Washington, D.C.: U.S. Government Printing Office, 1975) plus *Survey of Current Business,* issues from 1975 to 1981. Consumption data from U.S. Department of Commerce, *Business Conditions Digest* (April 1981).

income and consumption for the average of the six most recent cycles is shown in Table 8.2 and in Figure 8.3.

These data show that national income in real terms (adjusted for inflation) rose in the average expansion by 19.7 percentage points and fell in the average contraction by 3.2 percentage points. The small decline in the average contraction was due to the very mild contractions of the 1950s and the 1960s. The contraction of 1975 was twice as strong (a fall of 6.7 points).

For aggregate national consumption in real terms, the expansions and contractions are not as strong as for national income. On the average, consumption rose only 17 points to the peak and fell only 0.4 percentage points to its lowest level in the contraction. Again, this small average decline was due to the mild contractions of the 1950s and the 1960s. During those contractions, real consumer spending actually continued to rise, though more slowly than in the expansions. Real consumption spending declined 1.6 percentage points in the more severe recession of 1975.

Although the simplest NBER method allows an examination of the levels of each variable

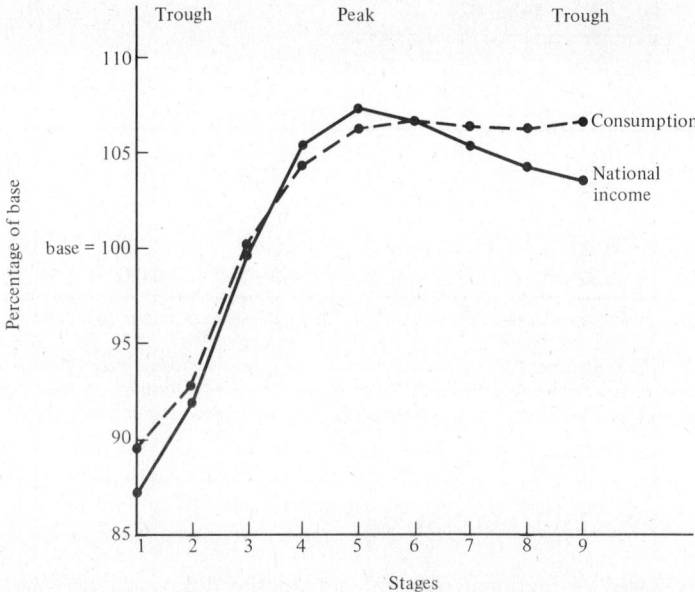

Figure 8.3 National Income and Consumption
NOTE: This figure represents an average of six cycles from 1949 to 1980, in quarterly data and in constant 1972 dollars.
SOURCES: National income data from U.S. Department of Commerce, *National Income and Product Accounts, 1926 to 1974* (Washington, D.C.: U.S. Government Printing Office, 1975); plus *Survey of Current Business,* issues from 1975 to 1981. Consumption data from U.S. Department of Commerce, *Business Conditions Digest* (April 1981).

at nine stages of the cycle, economists usually want to examine monthly rates of change rather than levels. To do that, one has only to go a few steps farther. First, take the difference between the levels of each two adjoining stages. Second, divide by the number of months from the midpoint of the first stage to the midpoint of the second.

As an example, the monthly change in national income and consumption from stage to stage of the business cycle is examined in Table 8.3.

From Table 8.3, it is clear that in the average cycle expansion, national income rose, but it rose more and more slowly as it approached the peak. Second, in the average expansion period, total real consumption rose, but it rose more and more slowly as it approached the peak. Third, in the first half of the average expansion, consumption grew much more slowly than national income, but in the last half of expansion it grew about the same rate or slightly faster.

In the average contraction, national income fell all the way to the trough, but fell more slowly in the last stages of contraction. Consumption continued rising slightly right after the peak, then fell for a few stages, but started to rise again before the end of contraction. Again, the average is deceiving because real consumption rose in the mild contractions of the 1950s and the 1960s, but fell in the 1975 and 1980 contractions.

Table 8.3

CHANGES IN NATIONAL INCOME AND CONSUMPTION

Change from Stage to Stage, per Month, as Percentage of Cycle Base

	Expansion				Peak	Contraction		
Stages	1–2	2–3	3–4	4–5	5–6	6–7	7–8	8–9
National income	0.54	0.51	0.31	0.20	−0.22	−0.60	−0.32	−0.08
Consumption	0.41	0.37	0.32	0.23	0.05	−0.30	−0.03	0.27

NOTE: This table represents an average of six cycles from 1949 through 1980, in quarterly data and in constant 1972 dollars.
SOURCES: National income data from U.S. Department of Commerce, *National Income and Product Accounts, 1926 to 1974* (Washington, D.C., U.S. Government Printing Office, 1975) plus *Survey of Current Business,* issues from 1975 to 1981. Consumption data from U.S. Department of Commerce, *Business Conditions Digest* (April 1981).

BEHAVIOR OF THE PROPENSITY TO CONSUME

Consumption is not directly based on national income, but on the disposable personal income. The amount of disposable personal income is less than national income because it is after deduction of all retained corporate profits and of all taxes (though it includes all subsidies and welfare payments to individuals). Disposable income also fluctuates less than national income because taxes usually rise and fall faster than income whereas welfare and subsidies are usually countercyclical (as will be seen in Part Six).

The average propensity to consume out of disposable personal income (ratio of consumption to disposable personal income) was an average of 0.92 in the first cycle (1949–1954) and was an average of 0.91 in the last cycle (1975–1980). Thus, it has had no trend in this period and has been fairly stable in the long run. The average propensity to consume out of national income was only 0.81 in the period 1975–1980. The difference is due to the fact that some of national income is taxed by government and some is profits retained by corporations.

Disposable personal income is usually used by economists to predict consumption because its relation to consumption is normally more stable than that of national income to consumption. In Appendix 8A the marginal propensity to consume out of disposable personal income is estimated for the period 1949 to 1980 to be between 0.90 and 0.84, depending on the method of estimation.

The cyclical pattern of the average propensity to consume, that is, the ratio of consumption to income at each stage of the cycle is shown in Table 8.4 and Figure 8.4. On either definition, the average propensity to consume falls in the expansion (because income rises faster than consumption) and rises throughout the contraction (because income falls faster than consumption). The APC out of disposable personal income is far more stable than the APC out of national income over the cycle. The reason is that consumption is remarkably stable, while disposable personal income is more stable than national income for the reasons given earlier.

Table 8.4

AVERAGE PROPENSITY TO CONSUME (APC)

Change from Stage to Stage, per Month, as Percentage of Cycle Base

Stages	Expansion				Peak	Contraction		
	1–2	2–3	3–4	4–5	5–6	6–7	7–8	8–9
APC from disposable personal income	−0.04	−0.03	−0.02	−0.04	0.03	0.02	0.02	0.09
APC from national income	−0.17	−0.15	0.00	0.02	0.25	0.29	0.29	0.34

NOTE: This table represents an average of six cycles from 1949 to 1980, in quarterly data and in constant 1972 dollars.
SOURCES: National income data from U.S. Department of Commerce, *National Income and Product Accounts, 1926 to 1974* (Washington, D.C.: U.S. Government Printing Office, 1975) plus *Survey of Current Business,* issues from 1975 to 1981. Consumption data plus personal disposable income data from U.S. Department of Commerce, *Business Conditions Digest* (April 1981).

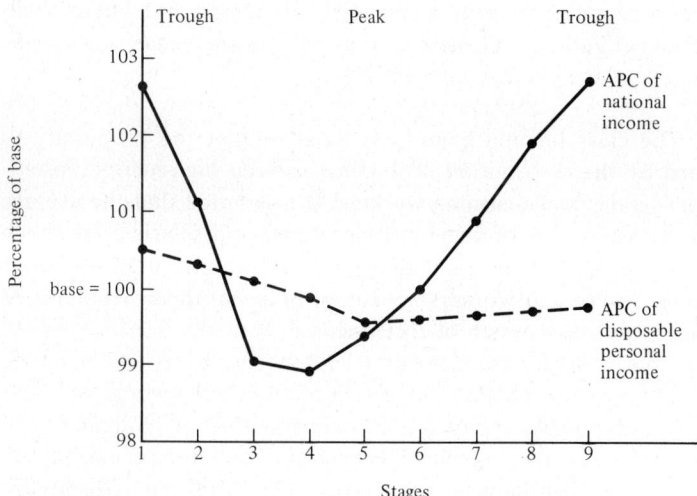

Figure 8.4 Average Propensity to Consume (APC)
NOTE: This figure represents an average of six cycles from 1949 to 1980, in quarterly data and in constant 1972 dollars.
SOURCES: National income data from U.S. Department of Commerce, *National Income and Products Accounts, 1926 to 1974* (Washington, D.C.: U.S. Government Printing Office, 1975); plus *Survey of Current Business,* issues from 1975 to 1981. Consumption data plus personal disposable income data from U.S. Department of Commerce, *Business Conditions Digest* (April 1981).

CYCLE PATTERNS OF THE 1920s AND THE 1930s

The scanty data from the 1920s and 1930s indicates the same type of pattern. Wesley Mitchell[22] found that, in the average expansion of the four cycles of 1921 to 1938, the national income rose by 22.5 percent (of its average level over the cycle) from initial trough to peak. But consumption rose only by 15.0 percent, so the average propensity to consume declined in the average expansion.

Similarly, in the average contraction from peak to final trough in those same four cycles, from 1921 to 1938, national income fell by 17.6 percent, whereas consumption fell by only 9.9 percent. Therefore, in the average contraction in the 1920s and the 1930s, the average propensity to consume rose.

Explanation of the Cyclical Behavior of Consumers

Why does the average propensity to consume fall in the expansion, and why does it rise in the contraction? The relative income hypothesis explains this behavior as the slow adjustment of spending habits to changing income. The propensity to consume rises in contractions because consumers remember their peak income and try to keep spending at the peak level.

The permanent income hypothesis explains the rising propensity to consume in contractions as a result of consumers' viewing their lower incomes as only temporary. These dominant views (which are neoclassical and neo-Keynesian) thus explain the behavior in terms of the psychological preferences of the average consumer.

Shifts in Class Income. The class income hypothesis assumes that the propensity to consume is partly determined by the distribution of income between high-income, profit-making capitalists and lower-income, wage-earning workers. It is asserted that the average and marginal propensities to consume out of wage income (wages and salaries) are much higher than out of nonwage or profit income (including profit, rent, and interest). Wage income is mostly at low income levels, and workers need it all to live at the usual standard of living. Capitalists may save and invest much of their income.

Various studies have found this to be the case. For example, Lawrence Klein in 1962 found that the marginal propensity to consume (MPC) out of disposable wage income was 0.85 whereas the MPC out of disposable profit (nonwage) income was 0.40 in Holland in the period from 1947 to 1954.[23] He found similar results in England in the same period.[24] Klein and Goldberger found an MPC out of disposable wages of 0.62 and an MPC out of disposable profit of only 0.46 for the United States from 1929 to 1952.[25] Most interestingly, Milton Friedman cites a number of studies from 1890 to 1950 in the United States showing the same

---

[22]Mitchell, *op. cit.,* pp. 154–155.
[23]Lawrence Klein, *An Introduction to Econometrics* (Englewood Cliffs, N. J.: Prentice-Hall, 1962), p. 228.
[24]*Ibid.,* p. 230.
[25]Lawrence Klein and A. S. Goldberger, *An Econometric Model of the United States, 1929–1952* (Amsterdam: North Holland Publishing Co., 1955), p. 51.

result.[26] Friedman's own study for the United States finds an APC of 0.77 for (nonfarm) business owners and an APC of 0.96 for (nonfarm) employees.[27]

Canadian data in a 1969 study found that in Canada the MPC from labor income was much higher than the MPC from nonlabor income.[28] British data in a 1980 study show that the MPC from wage and salary income is above the MPC from self-employment and unearned income.[29] Another British study in 1980 reported an MPC of wage income equal to 0.837 whereas the MPC of nonwage income is only 0.228.[30] In Appendix 8A, the data for the period 1949 to 1980 for the United States also reveal a higher MPC for all "wages" (or labor income) than for "profits" (or property income).

The estimates differ for different countries, different times, different definitions of "wages" and "profits," and even different regression methods (as shown in Appendix 8A). In every case, however, the APC and MPC for workers are higher than that for capitalists. The APC for workers approaches 1.00 in most studies whereas that for capitalists is much lower.

How does this fact help explain the decline of aggregate APC for all income recipients in expansions and the rise of aggregate APC in contractions? If there is a shift in income distribution from (high APC) workers to (low APC) capitalists in expansions, this would help explain why aggregate APC falls. A shift back from capitalists to workers in share of income in contractions would help explain the rise of aggregate APC. Table 8.5 and Figure 8.5 examine the evidence of the last six cycles.

The wage share of national income (W/Y) moves in the same direction as the average propensity to consume out of national income (C/Y) in seven of the eight cycle segments of the average cycle. They move down together in early expansion. They move up together slightly in late expansion and move up together strongly in the early contraction. *Wages* is defined as all employee compensation here; this definition presents many problems, which are examined in great detail in Chapter 10 on income distribution.

Regardless of definition, all indicators of the split between wages and nonwage ("profit") income show that the share going to wages declines in the first half of expansion. This is one cause of the decline in the aggregate propensity to consume. For example, assume the APCs given by Milton Friedman, 0.96 for workers' wages and 0.77 for capitalist profits. Assume wages and profits are each $100 billion. Then consumption = 0.96($100) + 0.77($100) = $173 billion, so APC = $173/200 = 0.87.

Now suppose, as income expands, that the expansion increases only the profit share. So wages still equal $100 billion, but profit grows to $150 billion. Then consumption = 0.96($100) + 0.77($150) = $211.5 billion, so APC declines to = $211.5/250 = 0.85. Thus, a declining wage share helps explain a declining aggregate APC.

---

[26]Milton Friedman, *A Theory of the Consumption Function* (Princeton, N.J.: Princeton University Press, 1957), pp. 69–79.

[27]*Ibid.*, p. 69.

[28]E. Burmeister and P. Taubman, "Labor and Non-Labor Income Saving Propensities," *Canadian Journal of Economics* 2 (1969), pp. 1–15.

[29]P. Arestis and C. Driver, "Consumption out of Different Types of Income in the U.K.," *Bulletin of Economic Research* 32 (1980), pp. 23–36.

[30]A. J. Murfin, "Savings Propensities from Wage and Non-wage Income," *Warwick Economic Research Papers* no. 174 (1980).

Table 8.5

AVERAGE PROPENSITY TO CONSUME (APC)

CHANGE FROM STAGE TO STAGE, PER MONTH, AS PERCENTAGE OF CYCLE BASE

	Expansion				Peak	Contraction		
Stages	1–2	2–3	3–4	4–5	5–6	6–7	7–8	8–9
APC from national income	−0.17	−0.15	0.0	.02	0.25	0.29	0.29	0.34
Wage share of national income	−0.18	−0.01	0.9	.10	0.27	0.28	0.07	−.07

NOTE: This table represents an average of six cycles from 1949 to 1980, in quarterly data and in constant 1972 dollars.

SOURCES: National income data from U.S. Department of Commerce, *National Income and Production Accounts, 1926 to 1974* (Washington, D.C., U.S. Government Printing Office, 1975) plus *Survey of Current Business,* issues from 1975 to 1981. Consumption data plus personal disposable income data from U.S. Department of Commerce, *Business Conditions Digest* (April 1981).

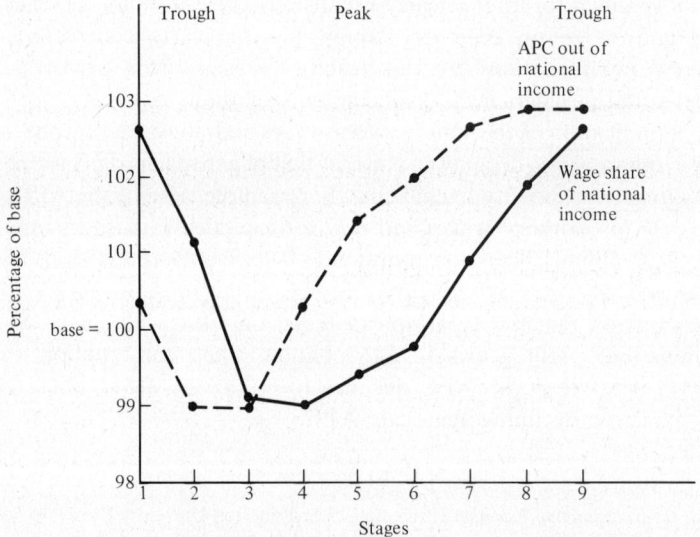

Figure 8.5 Average Propensity to Consume and the Wage Share

NOTE: This figure represents an average of six cycles from 1949 to 1980, in quarterly data and in constant 1972 dollars.

SOURCE: U.S. Department of Commerce, *Business Conditions Digest* (April 1981).

Table 8.6

CONSUMER DEBT TO INCOME

CHANGE FROM STAGE TO STAGE PER MONTH, AS PERCENTAGE OF CYCLE BASE

	Expansion				Peak	Contraction		
Stage	1–2	2–3	3–4	4–5	5–6	6–7	7–8	8–9
Debt to income	0.04	0.32	0.47	0.50	0.35	−0.14	−0.05	−0.67

NOTE: This table represents an average of six cycles, from 1949 to 1980, in quarterly data and in constant 1972 dollars.
SOURCE: Consumer installment debt as a ratio of personal income from U.S. Department of Commerce, *Business Conditions Digest* (June 1981).

Shifts in Credit. Consumer demand is also a function of the amount of credit. In every expansion, consumer credit rises. In fact, even the ratio of consumer debt to income rises rapidly in the expansion. This happens because consumer optimism about future income encourages consumers to borrow increasing amounts. At the same time, the optimism of lenders allows consumers to borrow more. This means that consumer demand throughout the expansion is pushed higher than it would have been without credit.

Consumer debt has undoubtedly played a major role in sustaining the level of consumption in recent decades. This is made evident by the very rapid growth of consumer debt from 1950 to the present in the United States. Since credit allows consumers to spend beyond their incomes, in the absence of such credit expansion, Keynes's suspicion of a consistently declining APC might have actually transpired.

Table 8.6 and Figure 8.6 show the typical behavior of consumer debts as a ratio to income.

Table 8.6 does reveal the rise of consumer debt as a percentage of income in the average expansion. On the other hand, in the average economic contraction, credit is restricted, thereby reducing consumption. Specifically, the ratio of consumer debt to income usually continues to rise in early contraction because consumers desperately search for more credit. Then, however, as the recession or depression intensifies, the ratio of consumer debt to income declines considerably because lenders refuse to give more credit and consumers become more cautious. The restriction of credit thus further depresses consumer demand in the constraction.

A very thorough study by Philip Klein finds that consumer credit has intensified the business cycle because consumer credit has "fluctuated much more widely . . . than has aggregate economic activity in the United States."[31] He notes that its impact is increasing as the percentage of consumer debt to income keeps increasing. Yet he is careful to point out that "cyclical fluctuations do not stem primarily from consumer credit changes. . . . For one thing, business cycles were a factor in economic life long before consumer credit assumed much significance."[32]

---

[31]Philip A. Klein, *The Cyclical Timing of Consumer Credit, 1920–67* (New York: National Bureau of Economic Research, 1971), p. 59.
[32]*Ibid.*, p. 2.

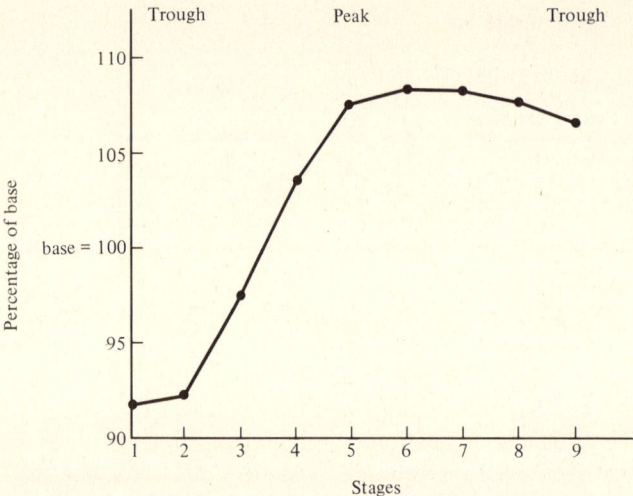

Figure 8.6 Ratio of Consumer Debt to Personal Income
NOTE: This figure represents an average of six cycles from 1949 to 1980, in quarterly data and in constant 1972 dollars.
SOURCE: U.S. Department of Commerce, *Business Conditions Digest* (June 1981).

Government Spending and Tax Shifts. Higher government spending and lower taxes may stimulate consumption. Obviously, the stimulus will be greater if more of the spending increases and more of the tax cuts go to the poor because they have a higher marginal propensity to consume. Likewise, lower government spending (particularly to the poor) and higher taxes (particularly on the poor) will reduce consumer spending.

A later chapter (Chapter 23) will reveal that government spending tends to increase in contractions and to decrease (or rise more slowly) in expansions. The reason is that welfare to the poor rises with unemployment, and welfare to the rich also rises when there is lower demand (for example, subsidies to rich farmers rise in every contraction). On the other side, if there is no inflation, then income taxes tend to fall as a percentage of income in a contraction whereas they will rise as a percentage of income in an expansion. This happens even if there are no legislative changes in income taxes because people will move into lower tax brackets in contractions and into higher tax brackets in expansions. Of course, if inflation continues during a contraction, then income recipients may move into even higher tax brackets in a contraction.

In the absence of inflation, however, it will normally be the case that the existing government programs and tax structures will automatically tend to stimulate consumption much more in contractions than in expansions. The government may also choose to make further changes that will increase these tendencies.

In addition to the direct effects of government spending and taxation, whether automatic or by discretionary policy, there are considerable indirect effects. These indirect effects

Table 8.7

TREND IN CONSUMER DEBT TO INCOME

Cycle	Average During Entire Cycle
1949–1954	6.8%
1954–1958	9.3
1958–1961	10.2
1961–1970	12.2
1970–1975	13.2
1975–1980	13.8

SOURCE: Consumer installment debt as a ratio of personal income from U.S. Department of Commerce, *Business Conditions Digest* (June 1981).

are measured by the government "multiplier," which was examined in an appendix in Chapter 7.

Long-run Trends

In addition to the short-run cyclical swings that may affect consumer demand, there are also some important long-run trends that have had major influences on consumption. First, government has been increasing the amount of spending for both social programs and military programs, as we saw in Chapter 7. This spending, with its indirect multiplier effect, has put a floor under consumption to some extent—certainly, much more of a floor than existed in the 1930s.

Second, consumer debt rose greatly in the 1920s, then fell enormously during the Great Depression. Since the Second World War there has been a steady increase in consumer debt, both absolutely and relative to income. Many new forms of credit have made it easier to obtain and use. The U.S. economy runs much more on credit now than it did in any earlier period. As long as credit keeps expanding, it is a long-run stimulating force for consumer demand (though it may also feed inflation). Any faltering of credit, however, will be strongly felt in this more fragile and vulnerable economy. The exact magnitude of the increases in consumer debt can be seen in Table 8.7.

Table 8.7 shows a slow but steady trend toward an increased ratio of consumer debt to the income of consumers ever since 1949. In fact, ignoring cyclical fluctuations, it has been growing since the 1920s. The largest component of consumer debt is automobile credit; it is also the most volatile component and has been growing most rapidly. Whereas disposable personal income grew 5 times from 1929 to 1967, outstanding automobile credit grew 17 times![33]

Third, a long-term trend toward more equal distribution of income would increase the average propensity to consume whereas a long-term trend toward more inequality would

---

[33] *Ibid.*, p. 59.

decrease the average propensity to consume. Unfortunately, the factual record in this area is highly controversial among economists. The official statistics tend to indicate no great long-run changes since detailed data began in the early 1900s. Using their own definitions, some conservatives have found a long-run shift in income from rich capitalists toward the poor and workers. Using different definitions, some radicals have found a long-run shift in income distribution from the poor and workers toward rich capitalists.

Finally, the inflationary trend of the last few decades has probably also affected the marginal propensity to consume. When a consumer knows that prices will fall in the future, as was the case in part of the Great Depression of the 1930s, then the rational thing to do is to hoard one's money and wait to spend it at a later time when it will buy more goods and services. On the other hand, when consumers know (or expect) that prices will keep rising in the future, as has been the case in the last decade, then a rational consumer will try to spend a larger portion of his or her income immediately before the buying power of the dollar decreases still further.

These, of course, are both cumulative processes. The expectation of future price declines, based on present ones, reduces consumer spending, which brings greater price and output declines. The expectation of more inflation in the future, based on past and present inflation, causes more rapid consumer spending, which in turn feeds the inflation. Thus, these long-term trends are not easily reversed for this reason alone (and for other reasons).

SUMMARY

Keynes was one of the first economists in the modern era to give such considerable attention to aggregate consumption behavior. Consumption is by far the largest component of aggregate demand. Keynes described consumption as being motivated by psychological propensities influenced primarily by the level of income.

When it was discovered that the behavior of consumption was more stable and less cyclical than income, a series of hypotheses were offered to explain this behavior. The relative income hypothesis suggested that consumption behavior depended, in part, upon the standard of living experienced by the consumer's peers. If a consumer experienced a sudden windfall income gain, his or her consumption out of that income might be low, given that he or she was wealthier than his or her peers. On the other hand, if *all* consumers experience a gradual income gain, their consumption might tend to rise as a constant proportion of income.

The life cycle hypothesis argues that consumption habits vary over the life span and depend more upon total wealth than income. This is similar to the permanent income hypothesis, which suggests that consumption is more closely related to permanent income than to annual or quarterly transitory income.

All three of these orthodox hypotheses make the prediction that the average propensity to consume will be cyclical in the short run—falling during expansion and rising during contractions—but a constant proportion of the long-run trend in income. The orthodox theories are not alone, however. The class income hypothesis also explains the cyclical behavior of the APC. This hypothesis claims that the average propensity to consume is higher for capitalists than for workers. During an expansion, income distribution shifts in favor of capitalists. Since they have a lower APC, the overall APC falls. The reverse happens during a contraction.

Cyclical evidence using NBER methods was presented, confirming the expected behavior of consumption over the cycle. Additional evidence was presented supporting the class income hypothesis.

The role of credit in the behavior of consumption was also investigated. It is likely that credit conditions contribute to the cyclical behavior of the APC and additionally might help support the trend.

Since consumption is more steady than income, when variations in income are caused by some other factor, such as erratic investment behavior, then consumption has a stabilizing influence on business cycles. Steady consumption habits dampen booms and soften recessions. On the other hand, if consumption itself exhibits erratic behavior because of shifts in the distribution of income or changes in consumer credit conditions, the amplitude of the business cycle may be intensified.

In addition to government and consumption, the third major component of aggregate demand in the business cycle is investment. The behavior of investment is investigated next.

Appendix 8A

Consumption Function Estimates

In the text of each chapter, only the NBER cyclical analysis is presented. The regression and correlation results are relegated to appendixes for two reasons. First, the technical level of these discussions is higher than that of the rest of the book. Second, because of the many weaknesses of time-series regressions explained further on, the reader should not put much faith in these results.

FUNCTIONAL RELATION BETWEEN CONSUMPTION AND INCOME

Consumption and income have each been described over the business cycle. What is their functional relationship? To determine this, the NBER analysis is insufficient, so correlation and regression analysis is necessary. The data are quarterly, in billions of constant dollars, from 1949.1 to 1980.4. Real aggregate consumption and real personal disposable income are both from U.S. Department of Commerce, *Business Conditions Digest* (April 1981). Ordinary least squares analysis finds

$$C_t = 125.4 + \underset{(201.3)}{0.90} Y_{t-1} \qquad R^2 = 0.99 \qquad (8A.1)$$

where C is consumption, where Y is disposable income, and where the figure in parenthesis is the T statistic, which measures statistical significance (capital T is used because lowercase t refers to time). With the number of cases and variables used in most equations in this book, the T statistic indicates that the regression coefficient is statistically significant at the 0.01 confidence level if T is greater than 2.7. The 0.01 confidence level means, roughly, that such a coefficient would be found by chance only one time in 100 when the actual coefficient was zero. By convention, in this book, *statistically significant* means significant at the 0.01 confidence level unless otherwise stated.

The regression coefficient of consumption on income, that is, the MPC out of national income, is positive and statistically significant. Note that it (0.83) is lower than most estimates because it is out of national income rather than personal disposable income. National income is used so that the results will be comparable with the results from wages and profits, which are divisions of national income. Use of national income stresses the fact that retained corporate profit is 100 percent saved and none of it is consumed.

The symbol R^2 is the square of the correlation coefficient, R. The coefficient R^2 is called the *coefficient of determination* and is commonly said to state how much of the variance of the dependent variable is "explained" by the independent variable. Here, income is said to "explain" 99 percent of the variance in consumption.

Notice that equation 8A.1 assumes a simple time lag of one quarter. The empirical data do show a time lag between income and consumption because (1) after a business receives income, it does not pay it out immediately, and (2) after an individual receives income, he or she does not spend it all immediately. The assumption of a constant time lag, however, is incorrect. The time lag changes both secularly and over the cycle, so one should *not* assume that it correctly predicts the future time lag. Other problems and weaknesses of this regression estimate are examined further on.

Relation Between Consumption and Class Distribution of Income

To test the relationship of consumption to wages (W) and profits (Π), the data for the entire period of 1949 to 1980 were used in an ordinary least squares regression and the result was

$$C_t = 104.3 + \underset{(36.9)}{0.99 W_{t-1}} + \underset{(0.3)}{0.13 \Pi_{t-1}} \qquad R^2 = 0.99 \qquad (8A.2)$$

where W is "wages" and Π is "profits." Wages and profits were derived as follows. The national income comes from U.S. Department of Commerce data cited in Table 8.2. The wage share (the percentage that all employee compensation is of national income) is given in U.S. Department of Commerce, *Business Conditions Digest* (April 1981). The national income multiplied by the wage share gives *wages* whereas the entire residual is called *profits*. The difficult problems and weaknesses in these definitions are discussed in a later chapter (Chapter 10) on income distribution.

The MPC for wages is higher than the MPC for profits though the exact MPCs are accidents depending on definitions and time periods covered. The correlation is over 0.99, and the coefficient for wages is significantly greater than zero. The coefficient for profits is *not* significantly different from zero, but that does not harm the hypothesis that the MPC for wages is higher than the MPC for profits.

The Weaknesses of Regression and Correlation

The results of equations 8A.1 and 8A.2—in terms of high and significant correlations—seem to be very impressive. But it is useful to stop and point out the many problems and dangers of using regression methods, especially ordinary least squares regression. A large number of problems with all regression methods have been noted by such well-known economists as J. M. Keynes.[34] First, there is always the problem of the quality of the data, the biases in reporting them, and the particular definitions used by various governments. As was noted, this is especially the case with data on wages and profits.

Second, there is also the problem that a strong, statistically significant relation (a high R^2 and a high T) between one variable and another merely shows that their movements are associated with each other. It says nothing about whether there is a relation of cause and effect. If the relation exists, it says nothing about what the direction of the causation is. Moreover, the correlation may be due to the fact that both variables are affected by a third variable and have no particular direct relation to each other. Thus, a high correlation does *not* mean that the relation will necessarily continue in the future.

Third, most economic variables have long-run time trends that move together. If it is desirable to examine the short-run cyclical relations of particular variables, it is necessary to remove their long-run trends. One way to remove the trend is to look at *first differences*, for example, not C_t and Y_t, but $\Delta C = C_t - C_{t-1}$ and $\Delta Y = Y_t - Y_{t-1}$. In that method, there is no time trend, and the estimates merely compare the quarterly movements of consumption with the quarterly movements of income. To eliminate the trend, in all further regressions in this book we will use comparisons of first differences.

Another major problem of time series is autocorrelation.[35] The problem is that almost all economic variables move up together in expansions and down together in contractions, many have the same trends, and all tend to influence each other. For example, consumption may be and is affected by income (and other variables) from many past periods. In that case, present consumption will be closely correlated with previous consumption (and residuals between observed and estimated values will have a systematic pattern). To measure autocorrelation, the Durbin-Watson statistic is used. The Durbin-Watson statistic shows *no* autocorrelation if it is exactly 2.00 and no statistically significant autocorrelation in a range around 2.00. (In the cases used in this book, there is no significant autocorrelation in the range between 1.50 and 2.50.) The Durbin-Watson statistic will be indicated by the symbol DW and will be shown with all equations that follow.

For equation 8A.1, the regression of consumption on lagged income, the Durbin-Watson statistic was 0.16. For equation 8A.2, the regression of consumption on wages and profits, the Durbin-Watson statistic was 0.17. Both of these DW statistics are miserable, showing a very significant amount of autocorrelation. Therefore, the high correlations and apparently significant regressions of equations 8A.1 and 8A.2 are not to be trusted at all. They do

---

[34] See Michael Phelps, "Laments, Ancient and Modern: Keynes on Mathematical and Econometric Methodology," *Journal of Post-Keynesian Economics* 11 (Summer 1980), pp. 482–493.

[35] For a discussion of the problem of autocorrelation and methods of removing it, see Robert Pindyck and Daniel Rubinfeld, *Econometric Models and Economic Forecasts,* 2d ed. (New York: McGraw-Hill, 1976), pp. 152–168.

describe past reality, but they do *not* necessarily show cause and effect, and they do *not* necessarily show a statistically significant basis for prediction.

Fortunately, when first differences are used to remove the time trend, this method also removes much of the autocorrelation in many cases. Therefore, this is another reason why it is very useful that equations in the book will be estimated on the first differences of each variable. This correction—the use of first differences—removes some of the trend and autocorrelation problems, but still leaves all the other weaknesses of any regression method.

Adjusted Estimate of Consumption and Income

The problem of finding the right time lag has been mentioned earlier. One way of describing the relationship more accurately is to acknowledge that consumption is actually influenced by income at several previous periods, the so-called distributed lag function. Therefore, it is best to calculate a lag distributed over several quarters with both of the variables used as first differences.

For 1949 through 1980, using the same data as in equation 8A.1, we get this result.

$$\Delta C_t = \underset{(8.3)}{0.53 \Delta Y_t} + \underset{(3.2)}{0.21 \Delta Y_{t-1}} + \underset{(0.5)}{0.03 \Delta Y_{t-2}} + \underset{(0.8)}{0.05 \Delta Y_{t-3}} + \underset{(0.3)}{0.02 \Delta Y_{t-4}} \quad (8A.3)$$

For this equation, DW equals 2.15, which is not significant. When the regression coefficients are all added together, the sum is 0.84, which represents perhaps the best estimate of the marginal propensity to consume for this period. Notice that only the first two lagged first differences of the national income variable are statistically significant. After the second period back, the lagged variables do not have enough influence to be statistically significant and slowly fade toward zero.

Adjusted Consumption and Class Income

It is still more complex to use first differences and distributed lags for the relation between consumption and labor income and property income.[36] To make it meaningful would require testing several different definitions of labor and property income, including some data not readily available (such as wages and profits after all taxes). This task must await some new research project.

---

[36]For other alleged technical problems in relating consumption to class incomes, see Evans, *op. cit.*, pp. 44, 45.

Chapter 9

INVESTMENT

Investment is the key variable in the dynamics of capitalism. *Investment* is defined as the expenditure of money on new plant and equipment construction and on the increase of inventories (*inventories* include stocks of raw materials, semifinished goods, and finished goods). Investment means millions of workers constructing factories and building machines. Investment means that eventually the new factories can employ millions more workers. It is the means of growth of the economy, as well as the means of employing workers.

Investment is also central to business cycle theory because it fluctuates violently, far more violently than the consumer goods sector. For example, in the four cycles from 1921 through 1938, real consumption rose only 15 percent in the average expansion, whereas real gross investment rose 55 percent! In those same four cycles, real consumption fell in the average contraction by only 10 percent (even though the average is dominated by the Great Depression) whereas real gross investment fell by 49 percent.[1]

Similarly, in the six cycles from 1949 to 1980, investment was again much more violent in its fluctuations than was consumption. In those six cycles, real consumption rose 17 percent in the average expansion while real gross (nonresidential) investment rose 25 percent. In the average contraction of those six cycles, real consumption actually rose on an average of 0.1 percent (with three increases and three decreases in the six contractions) while real gross investment fell by an average 7 percent.[2]

Net investment fluctuates far more than gross investment. For the six cycles from 1949 to 1980, the average expansion of real net investment (nonresidential) was 49 percent; and its average contraction, at 36 percent.[3] *Net investment* is defined as gross investment minus the amount used to replace depreciated plant and equipment. But this means that estimates

---

[1] Wesley Mitchell, *What Happens During Business Cycles* (New York: National Bureau of Economic Research, 1951), pp. 154–155.
[2] Derived from U.S. Department of Commerce, *Business Conditions Digest* (April 1981).
[3] Depreciation data from U.S. Department of Commerce, *National Income and Product Accounts to 1974* (1976) and *Survey of Current Business,* 1975 to 1981.

of net investment always involve guesses as to how much of total investment was for replacement and how much was brand-new. In practice, economists just assume that replacement always equals depreciation. In the section on depreciation, however, it will be seen that replacement may not always equal depreciation; moreover, it will be demonstrated that calculation of depreciation is itself a tricky business. For these reasons, all estimates of net investment—including the ones given here—are highly suspect. For the most part, this chapter will use the more trustworthy data on gross investment.

THE MAJOR CATEGORIES OF INVESTMENT

The major categories of investment are inventory investment, plant and equipment investment (including nonresidential construction), and residential construction investment. These categories often behave quite differently from each other, so it is useful to examine some of their characteristics separately.

The mild business cycles of the 1950s and the 1960s were sometimes referred to as "inventory investment cycles" by some economists. This is because for some of the mild cycles about 90 percent of the drop in GNP during contractions was explained by a decline in inventory investment. Apparently, as consumption growth rates slowed in the early stages of recessions, business inventories rose to undesirable levels. Businesses would trim their inventories down by laying off employees and cutting back on production; consequently, the resulting recession would correspond with a decline in inventories. Any *change* in inventory is regarded as inventory investment (or disinvestment, if the change is negative).

It should be remembered that there is an important difference between *intended* and *unintended* inventory investment. Intended investment reflects any change in inventories that producers, wholesalers, and retailers actually desire. For example, as their sales grow, if they want their inventories to remain at a roughly constant proportion of sales, then they will also allow their inventories to grow. During a period of enthusiastic optimism, they may even temporarily want their inventories to grow faster than sales.

On the other hand, if sales register a disappointing drop, inventories will also grow under these circumstances. Auto inventories provide a good example of this phenomenon. When auto sales initially register a slump, as they have in recent years, dealers, who may have ordered new cars months before, find a growing number of unsold cars on their lots. This is obviously unintended investment. Because such a phenomenon truly represents a deficiency in aggregate demand, *unintended* inventory investment is not a component of aggregate demand. Unfortunately, there is no easy and reliable way to separate intended and unintended inventory investment.

Because sales are rising, intended inventory investment rises when the economy is surging ahead in a boom. In the initial stages of a slump, because goods are still flowing into businesses from old orders, there is unintended inventory investment, which is accompanied by a decline in sales.

Plant and Equipment Investment

The importance of plant and equipment investment should be obvious. This kind of investment adds directly to the nation's productive capital stock. It is undoubtedly the most important component of aggregate demand that contributes to long-term economic growth. There is a very strong correlation between the ratio of plant and equipment investment to GNP and economic growth rates among the world's economies. In the United States, this type of investment is almost always between 9 percent and 11 percent of GNP and is remarkably stable. During the Great Depression, however, this category of aggregate demand initially collapsed to nothing. In fact, in 1933, *net* private domestic investment (which subtracts for depreciation of existing plant and equipment) was a *negative* $6.1 billion, an amount equal to 12 percent of GNP in that year.

It is felt by some economists that the level of plant and equipment investment in the United States is too low for strong future economic growth. Supply-side economists make this argument and insist that tax cuts will provide the necessary incentive to cause this category to grow. Tax cuts, they argue, will provide both corporations and individuals with more funds for investment while simultaneously allowing them to keep more of the future rewards of such investment. Critics of these supply-side arguments point out that such arguments ignore the fact that there is no investment if there is no expectation of demand. It also ignores the fact that governments invest heavily in capital (for example, freeways, airports, computers, office buildings, hydroelectric projects, irrigation facilities, and so forth) and that new technologies must be developed before new investment is feasible. Such technologies will not be forthcoming if education is damaged by the supply-siders' zeal to cut government spending.

Residential Construction Investment

Until the mid-1970s, residential construction investment was an inconspicuous and relatively stable component of aggregate demand, contributing, on the average, to about 5 percent of aggregate demand. In the recessions of 1970 and 1975, this component fell to about 3.5 percent of GNP. The industry ran at fairly high capacity during the three decades after World War II, allowing the construction in the early 1970s in excess of 2 million new dwellings per year. To obtain a house at a reasonable cost was a middle-class American dream and one that was being realized.

Since 1975 this has been the industry most severely affected by the ailing American economy. In the early 1980s the industry was truly operating at a depression level at between 20 and 30 percent of capacity. No longer is the industry inconspicuous—when suffering the most, this industry adds hundreds of thousands to the unemployment rolls, leaves billions of dollars in resources unutilized, and is contributing to a serious housing shortage in the United States. Housing ownership as an automatic privilege for the middle class is no longer taken for granted. Throughout 1981 and 1982, families that were potential first-time home buyers with income below $40,000 could not qualify for home loans in most large East Coast and West Coast cities. Ironically, homes sat vacant at two-thirds their previous value in the depressed upper Midwest. Even homeowners who had purchased homes were having difficulty. Both payments delinquencies and foreclosure rates were at record high levels (since 1953, when the records were originated) in the summer of 1982.

There is no doubt about the reason for the depression in residential construction investment. Record high mortgage interest rates were to blame. Typically, more than 80 percent of a new home's mortgage (the buyer's collateralized debt) is financed by a long-term (typically 30-year) loan. A 1 percent rise in the interest rate for such loans can increase the monthly payment for a typical home in a city like Los Angeles by more than $100 per month. Considering that rates throughout 1982 were almost 9 percentage points above the equivalent rates a decade earlier and that homes were more than twice as expensive, it is no wonder that home sales were depressed. For example, in the summer of 1982, a $100,000 home in Los Angeles required a monthly payment of $1,414, including taxes and insurance, after a 5 percent down payment on a Veterans' Administration loan. To qualify for such a loan, a family would have to have an annual gross income that exceeded $50,000.

Distress in the housing industry has important linkage effects in the economy. Lumber-growing regions, such as the Pacific Northwest, are severely affected. Financial institutions, especially savings and loans, suffer from the high delinquency and foreclosure rates. They are also squeezed by the fact that many of their old loans are earning low interest whereas their deposits pay much higher current market rates. Because of the latter problem, lenders for home loans are tending to offer new types of loans that place the burden of interest rate uncertainty on the homeowner instead of on the lending institution.

Reasons for the high interest rates that have so severely damaged housing and other industries are discussed extensively in Chapters 16, 17, 18, and 24.

THEORY OF INVESTMENT

What determines the level of plant and equipment investment each year? It is determined by available financial and physical resources, as well as by the expectation of profit. If the resources are available, but capitalists expect losses, they will not invest. These expectations are subjective, highly volatile, and very uncertain because they are based on guesses about the future. Almost everything affects business expectations, so different economists have stressed different factors.

The theory of the accelerator, that investment demand is derived from the change in output demanded, has been around for a long time. Its earliest appearance in a formal business cycle model is in the 1930s. Paul Samuelson[4] argued that the level of investment is a function of the change in consumer demand. It is a truism that, in the long run, if technology is unchanged, increased demand must be met by more capital investment. Samuelson assumed that, in the short run, more consumer demand would improve expectations and motivate investors. A formal equation would be this:

---

[4]Paul Samuelson, "Interactions Between the Multiplier Analysis and the Principle of Acceleration," *Review of Economic Statistics* 21 (May 1939), pp. 75–78.

$$I_t = v(C_{t-1} - C_{t-2}) \tag{9.1}$$

where I is net investment, C is consumption, and v is a positive constant (known as the accelerator coefficient).

Samuelson's accelerator coefficient reflects the notion that, given an unchanging technology in the short run, the ratio of capital to consumption is roughly a fixed constant (equal to the accelerator coefficient):

$$v = \frac{K}{C} \tag{9.2}$$

where K represents capital (remember that capital is a stock of producers' goods, not a flow over time). This implies that a given capital (a stock of producers' goods) is necessary to produce any given amount of consumer goods (a flow in a certain time period). This theory assumes that the value of v is determined by technology. Any technological improvement increasing the productivity of capital would lower the value of v.

Since the ratio of capital to consumption must be a constant, when consumption changes, then the ratio of the change in capital to the change in consumption must also be equal to the same constant:

$$v = \frac{\Delta K}{\Delta C} \tag{9.3}$$

Since investment is defined as the change in capital,

$$I = \Delta K \tag{9.4}$$

the investment function in equation (9.1) is derived from the relation of capital to output of consumer goods with a time lag.

This equation has a time lag between changes in consumer demand and investment activity because (1) capitalists must first recognize changes in consumption demand, (2) they must find funds and make concrete decisions to invest, and (3) the spending on new plant and equipment generally takes as long as the actual construction work takes. The exact length of the time lag is a complex question, as shall be seen later.

Equation (9.1) has many deficiencies. Perhaps the most obvious is that investment demand rests not only on demand for new investment goods in the consumer goods industries, but also on demand for new investment goods in the investment goods industries themselves. To take account of this fact, the more sophisticated accelerator theories make investment a function of changes in both consumer demand and investment demand:

$$I_t = v[(C_{t-1} - C_{t-2}) + (I_{t-1} - I_{t-2})] = v(Y_{t-1} - Y_{t-2}) \tag{9.5}$$

where Y is net national product or national income. (Government and net exports are assumed to be zero in this elementary model.) But consumer demand plus investor demand equals total output demanded, so investment becomes a function of changes in total output demanded. At the present time, because of the many weaknesses of equation 9.1 discussed later, most Keynesian econometric studies link investment and output in far more complex ways.[5]

In the first place, naive accelerator models have been replaced by flexible accelerator models, in which optimal capital stock is viewed as a function of many previous levels of output rather than of current output alone. Furthermore, considerable attention has been focused on the most appropriate lag structure for the flexible accelerator. Different views of the appropriate lag structure range from geometrically declining weights to many more complex forms.[6]

Modern Keynesian econometric approaches to investment have also attempted to combine sophisticated accelerator theories with theories of the cost of capital. Accelerator theories emphasize output and capital stock, which are deemed the principal determinants of the marginal efficiency of investment schedule. The other theories emphasize variables such as the interest rate and cash flow, which figure prominently in the marginal cost of funds schedule. Here the work of Jorgenson and Hall[7] and Grilliches and Wallace[8] figures prominently in estimating accelerator functions that take into account "user cost of capital" with the problem of lag structure prominently in mind.

All the accelerator models have a singular feature. If the accelerator coefficient has a value that falls into a particular range (the range depends upon the actual structure of the model), the path of net national product (Y_t) will be cyclical. Why this is so is fairly easy to see. Suppose that investment is simply a function of the change in consumer demand (as in equation 9.1). If consumer demand rises in the early expansion at a rising pace, then investment rises rapidly. If, however, the growth of consumer demand merely slows down, then investment will begin to decline. This happens because investment is assumed to be a function of the *change* in consumer demand, not its *level*. In the most dramatic case, if consumer demand remains at a high level, but does not change, then investment will be zero. Thus, investment is very sensitive to any weakness in consumer demand and investment is very unstable. A model demonstrating the cyclical behavior caused by the accelerator coefficient is shown in Appendix 9D.

Samuelson's model, like all accelerator cycle models, also assumes a multiplier mechanism. So a reduction of investment—through the mechanism of lower consumer spending—leads to a multiplied effect in lower income. This further lowers consumer demand, thus setting off a contraction.

It is clear, however, that the accelerator type of investment function (even when based on output rather than just consumption) has many defects—and that *no* economist agrees with it in its simplest form. First, the investment response to changes in demand exhibits a

---

[5] See Dale Jorgenson, "Econometric Studies of Investment Behavior: A Survey," *Journal of Economic Literature* 9, no. 4 (1971), pp. 1111–1147.

[6] See Robert M. Solow, "On A Family of Lag Distributions," *Econometrica* 28, no. 2 (April 1960), pp. 393–406. Also see Michael Evans, *Macroeconomic Activity: Theory, Forecasting, and Control* (New York: Harper & Row, 1969). Also see F. de Leeuw, "The Demand for Capital Goods by Manufactures: A Study of Quarterly Time Series," *Econometrica* 30, no. 3 (July 1962), pp. 407–423.

[7] Dale Jorgenson and M. Hall, "Capital Theory and Investment Behavior," *American Economic Review* 53, no. 2 (May 1963), pp. 247–259.

[8] Z. Grilliches and N. Wallace, "The Determinants of Investment Revisited," *International Economic Review* 6, no. 3 (September 1965), pp. 311–329.

changing time lag over the cycle, so *no* fixed time lag is really appropriate. Second, the accelerator coefficient itself changes over the cycle because of changes in business expectations as to profits. Third, the accelerator is lower in recovery because of unused capacity. Fourth, at the peak the accelerator is physically limited by the capacity of the capital goods industries. Fifth, in the trough, aggregate disinvestment is limited by the amount of depreciation in each year. Sixth, this investment function leaves out variables other than aggregate demand. In particular, it omits changes in the cost of labor, machines, and raw materials, as well as the cost of borrowing capital, all of which affect profit and profit expectations, which, in turn, affect investment. Seventh, this investment function treats monopoly and competitive sectors the same, which is incorrect.[9] Eighth, this investment function omits specific consideration of government and international demand.

In spite of all these deficiencies, the accelerator has been used in many cycle models because it represents a powerful truth in addition to allowing for rather simple mathematics.

Other Investment Functions

To overcome some of the obvious deficiencies of the accelerator, an economist may start with the more general proposition that capitalists invest because they *expect* to make a profit. This proposition does not necessarily nullify the narrow technological argument of the accelerator (that investment is required to expand output), but includes it as one possible predictive element. Economists have considered long lists of variables that might affect expectations of future profits, including stock prices, unfilled orders, changes in sales, and recent profit performance. Robert Eisner's extensive study found that investment is "clearly related . . . closely to current and past sales changes and profits."[10] Many other studies have found a clear correlation of investment and profits in time-series data.

One study also found a close relationship between the changes in the *rate* of profit and changes in business investment, but with a varying time lag.[11] Few other studies, however, have directly considered the rate of profit. Eisner[12] finds that the rate of profit is not related to investment; in fact, he finds that it is negatively correlated (but not statistically significant). Eisner's results, however, in this respect are dubious because (1) he uses annual data whereas quarterly data are required for the proper sensitivity, and (2) he uses the same time lag for profits and profit rates, which may be an incorrect approach.

Another set of variables consists of those reflecting the flow of money and credit available to the firm. This set includes variables such as total profits,[13] interest rates, cash flow, debt-asset ratio, and other measures of liquidity.[14] It may be that all the studies finding

---

[9]See the excellent discussion of this point in Malcolm C. Sawyer, *Macroeconomics in Question: The Keynesian-Monetarist Orthodoxies and the Kaleckian Alternative* (Armonk: M.E. Sharpe, 1982), chap. 2.

[10]Robert Eisner, *Factors in Business Investment* (Cambridge, Mass.: Ballinger, for N.B.E.R., 1978), p. 171.

[11]See Howard Sherman and Thomas Stanback, "Cyclical Behavior of Profits, Appropriations, and Expenditures: Some Aspects of the Investment Process," *Proceedings of the American Statistical Association* 59 (September 1962), pp. 274–286.

[12]Eisner, *op. cit.*, p. 108.

[13]Adrian Wood, *A Theory of Profits* (Cambridge: Cambridge University Press, 1975).

[14]See Evans, *op. cit.*, chap. 5.

significant relations between investment and total profits really reflect the availability of funds rather than expectations. Data presented further on indicate that total profits do affect investment mainly through the availability of funds (though they *may* also affect expectations). For this purpose, total "profits" may be defined to include corporate profits, noncorporate profits, rental income, and the interest income of financial capitalists—in short, all property income. (Other available funds include depreciation allowances and credit to business, discussed later.)

In addition to total profits, investment is also affected by expectations of future *rates* of profit on investment. These future expectations are reflected mainly in the past and present ratios of total profit to total capital investment. The rational investor's expectations must be influenced by the *rate* of return on his or her investment rather than by the absolute level of profits. If both total profits and the rate of profit are included in the investment function, the result should better approximate reality.

$$I_t = f(\Pi_{t-1}, \ldots, \Pi_{t-n}; \frac{\Pi_{t-1}}{K_{t-1}}, \ldots, \frac{\Pi_{t-1}}{K_{t-2}}) \tag{9.6}$$

where Π is total profits, K is total capital, and f is a functional relationship.

CYCLICAL PATTERNS OF INVESTMENT AND PROFITS

How does investment move over the business cycle? How do profits and profit rates move over the business cycle? Using the NBER-Commerce Department turning points and the NBER method of analysis,[15] we show the cyclical patterns of investment, profits, and profit rates in Table 9.1 and Figure 9.1.

Investment (nonresidential) rose in the average expansion and declined in the average contraction.

It may be noted in passing that residential *investment* behaves differently with a different cycle, usually longer, than nonresidential investment. Theoretically, residential investment should be looked at more as a very durable consumer good for most buyers, though as an investment in rents or as a speculative investment for other buyers. There is a considerable literature on residential investment, which cannot be discussed here.[16]

The data on investment (in Table 9.1) clearly show that in the average expansion investment rises first fairly slowly, then very rapidly—but slows more and more as it approaches the peak. In the average contraction, it falls slowly, then very rapidly.

---

[15] Wesley Mitchell and Arthur Burns, *Measuring Business Cycles* (New York: National Bureau of Economic Research, 1946).

[16] A pioneering article was C. D. Long, "Long Cycles in the Building Industry," 51 *Quarterly Journal of Economics* (May 1939), pp. 371–403. Also see J. M. Guttentag, "The Short Cycle in Residential Construction," *American Economic Review* 51 (June 1961), pp. 292–308. Also see Manuel Gottlieb, "Long Swings in Urban Building Activity," *43rd Annual Report of the NBER* (New York: NBER, 1963). Also see Francisco Arcela and Allan Metzler, "The Markets for Housing and Housing Services," *Journal of Money, Credit and Banking* 5 (February 1973), pp. 78–99.

Chapter 9 INVESTMENT 163

Table 9.1

INVESTMENT, PROFITS, AND PROFIT RATES

Change from Stage to Stage, per month, as Percentage of Cycle Base

	Expansion				Peak	Contraction		
Stages	1–2	2–3	3–4	4–5	5–6	6–7	7–8	8–9
Gross investment	0.25	0.66	0.52	0.46	−0.11	−0.91	−0.74	−0.87
Total profits	0.97	0.56	0.12	−0.08	−0.94	−1.47	−0.51	0.44
Profit rate on capital	0.78	0.28	−0.20	−0.40	−1.15	−1.67	−0.71	0.20

NOTE: This table represents an average of six cycles, from 1949 through 1980, in quarterly data, and in billions of constant 1972 dollars.
SOURCES: *Gross investment* means gross private domestic investment, nonresidential, from U.S. Department of Commerce, *Business Conditions Digest* (*BCD*) (April 1981). *Total profits* equal national income minus wages. National income from U.S. Department of Commerce, *National Income and Product Accounts, 1929–1974* (*NIPA*, pub. 1977) and *Survey of Current Business* (*SCB*). *Wages* equal national income times compensation of employees as percentage of national income, from *BCD* (April 1981). *Profit rate on capital* equals ratio of total profits to capital. *Capital* from 1948 to 1974 interpolated quarterly from annual data of total producers' durable equipment plus total nonresidential structures, from U.S. Department of Labor, Bureau of Labor Statistics, Bulletin 2034, *Capital Stock Estimates for Input-Output Industries* (1979). *Capital* from 1975 to 1980 adds net investment of each quarter. *Net investment* equals gross investment minus depreciation. *Depreciation* equals capital consumption allowances with capital consumption adjustment, minus residential depreciation, from *NIPA* and *SCB*.

Total profits rose most rapidly in the initial recovery, then rose more and more slowly. In the stage *before* the cycle peak, total profits fell slightly in the average expansion. Total profits fell rapidly in the first half of contraction, then fell more slowly. Total profits even rose somewhat in the stage just before the cycle trough. Profits are thus a leading indicator of cycle turns. Whereas investment turns are roughly coincident with cycle peaks and troughs, our data for 1949 to 1980 indicate that total profits lead turns in investment (and the cycle) by one to two quarters. We noted earlier the theoretical reasons for this time lag of investment behind its determinants.

The rate of profit on capital rises very rapidly at the initial stage of the average expansion. It then slows a little. In the last part of expansion, it falls, leading the downturn in total profits by a whole stage. In the average contraction, the rate of profit falls very rapidly, then falls less rapidly. It turns up again just before the cycle trough. The rate of profit is thus another leading indicator of cycle turns; it turns even earlier than total profits. Our data for 1949 to 1980 show that the rate of profit leads investment (and the cycle) by about three-quarters on the average.

Why does the rate of profit decline even before total profits in expansions? The answer is because its denominator is the capital stock, which is continually rising in that period. When total profit (its numerator) slows down its growth by enough, then the rate of profit on capital must actually decline!

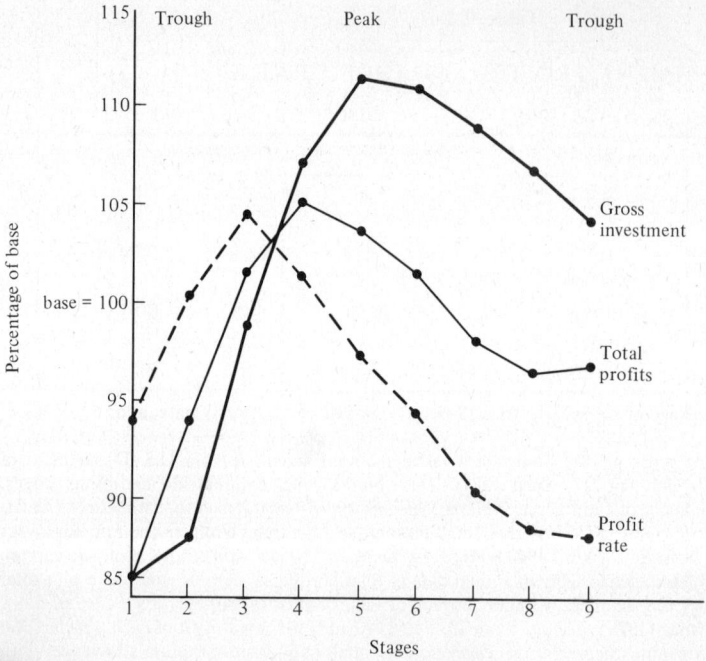

Figure 9.1 Investment, Profits, and Profit Rates
NOTE: This figure represents an average of six cycles, from 1949 through 1980, in quarterly data and in constant 1972 dollars, as percentage of cycle base.
SOURCES: *Gross investment* means gross private domestic investment, nonresidential, from U.S. Department of Commerce, *Business Conditions Digest (BCD)* (April 1981). *Total profits* equal national income minus wages. National income from U.S. Department of Commerce, *National Income and Product Accounts, 1929–1974* (*NIPA*, pub. 1977) and *Survey of Current Business (SCB)*. *Wages* equal national income times compensation of employees as percentage of national income, from *BCD* (April 1981). *Profit rate on capital* equals ratio of total profits to capital. *Capital* from 1948 to 1974 interpolated quarterly from annual data of total producers' durable equipment plus total nonresidential structures, from U.S. Department of Labor, Bureau of Labor Statistics, Bulletin 2034, *Capital Stock Estimates for Input-Output Industries* (1979). *Capital* from 1975 to 1980 adds net investment of each quarter. *Net investment* equals gross investment minus depreciation. *Depreciation* equals capital consumption allowances with capital consumption adjustment, minus residential depreciation, from *NIPA* and *SCB*.

Timing in Different Industries

There is some correlation between aggregate investment and profits and profit rates. But no simple aggregate function can explain investment very fully and accurately. The reason is that there are vast differences in timing in each industry. All industries do *not* have rising profit rates to the same point, nor do all industries have rising investment in the entire expansion and falling investment in the entire contraction. Most business activity expands and declines with different timing in different industries. In his study of 794 different indicators of economic activity over the business cycle, Mitchell discovered this: "During the 4 stages of expansion, 74, 77, 78, and 69 percent of all series characteristically rise; during the 4 stages of contraction, 68, 77, 76, and 63 percent characteristically fall."[17]

The same phenomenon is shown for sales, profits, profit rates, and investment according to the *diffusion indexes* published by the U.S. Department of Commerce (in the *Business Conditions Digest*). A diffusion index simply measures the *percentage* of industries with a rise in some indicator, such as profits. For example, a diffusion index of 69 means that 69 percent of the industries have rising profits. Examination of such diffusion indexes indicate that the percentage of industries with rising sales or rising profits rises in the early and mid-expansion, but then the *percentage* with rising sales or rising profits declines even while the *aggregate* sales or profits is still rising.[18] So the economy does not fall apart all at once with no prior sign like the one-horse shay; there are advance signs for those who can read them.

Though the timing is very different, the sequence of events in every expansion is approximately the same in most industries. Total sales are rising in expansion, then rise more slowly (while the diffusion index may start falling). At this point, both the profit margin on sales and the profit rate on capital begin to decline as an early warning signal.[19] Later, total profits begin to fall in most industries—while the diffusion index of sales is clearly declining. Still, later, new capital appropriations for expansion by businesses, the first indication of new investment decisions, begin to decline. Finally, at the business cycle peak, total sales and net investment begin an absolute decline. This sequence of events is repeated in the contraction in reverse.

Another reason why aggregate investment functions are unsatisfactory is the fact that the time lags are lengthy and they change in different cycles. On the average, total profits lead investment by one to two quarters whereas profit rates lead investment by about three quarters. But some important differences were observed between the period of the 1950s and the 1960s and the period of the 1970s. In the rapid growth of the 1950s and the 1960s, recovery was strong, and contractions were mild. In the 1970s, recoveries of investment in early expansion were weaker; and the declines in investment, profits, and profit rates in contractions were much steeper. The total profit, through its impact on available funds, had the greater impact on investment in the 1950s and the 1960s. If the funds were available, investors were usually optimistic enough. The profit rate had the greater impact on investment in the 1970s because expectations became more uncertain and optimistic expectations became even more important.

Nevertheless, in spite of all of these complications, all the data indicate that total profits and profit rates do influence net investment. This bears out the pioneering work by Michael Kalecki,[20] which has been followed by most Post Keynesians and Marxists in its emphasis on the role of profits and profit rates. Of course, there are many other influences—such as the role of credit—which we will discuss later.

---

[17]Wesley Mitchell, *What Happens During Business Cycles* (New York: National Bureau of Economic Research, 1951), p. 76.
[18]See Bert Hickman, "Diffusion, Acceleration, and Business Cycles," *American Economic Review* 49 (September 1959), pp. 535–565.
[19]The facts in this paragraph on the individual industries are from Sherman and Stanback, *op. cit.,* pp. 274–286.
[20]Michael Kalecki, *Theory of Economic Dynamics* (New York: Monthly Review Press, 1954).

INVENTORY INVESTMENT

The discussion has so far been built on the behavior of investment *as if* all investment were solely in equipment and factory construction. Aggregate investment is actually composed of the increase in plant construction, increase in equipment, *and* the increase in inventories.

Changes in inventory investment play a very important role in most business cycles. For example, in the five business cycles from 1919 through 1938, the average change in inventory investment accounted for 23.3 percent of the average rise in gross national product in expansions and 47.5 percent of the decline in gross national product in contractions. In the same period, changes in construction and producer's durable equipment together accounted for an average of only 20.5 percent of the rises and 37 percent of the declines.[21] This finding was confirmed for the postwar period when changes in inventories again constituted very large percentages of the cyclical changes in gross national product.[22]

If the longer and more severe or "major" depressions and expansions are examined, it appears that much of the decline or rise is in investment in plant and equipment. When the shorter, less severe, "minor" recessions and expansions are examined, however, most of the decline or rise is in inventory investment. During the five cycles from 1919 through 1938 for cycle phases (the whole expansions or the whole contraction) of 8 months to a year, the change in inventory investment was 96 percent of the change in gross national product; for cycle phases of 1.5 to 2.5 years, the change in inventory investment was 47 percent of the change in gross national product; and for cycle phases of 3.75 to 4.17 years, the change in inventory investment was only 19 percent of the change in gross national product.[23]

In the period since the Second World War, the same phenomena are observed. Shorter periods show more importance of inventory investment whereas changes over longer periods show more importance of changes in plant and equipment investment.[24] It seems that the adjustment of inventories to cyclical changes in production is carried out more rapidly than that of plant and equipment though the latter must make a very large adjustment if the phase lasts long enough.

What is the cyclical behavior of inventories? In most of the prosperity phase, both inventory stocks and inventory investment, which is the increase in stocks, are rising and continue to rise up to the cycle peak. In this period, demand is greater than supply; consequently, product and sales increase, and inventory investment rises in order to reach the desired ratio of inventory to sales. This is a kind of acceleration principle; that is, if the stock of inventory is determined by the level of sales, then investment in inventory is determined by changes in sales.

Of course, inventory investment is not determined by a purely mechanical relationship to the change in sales. The real issue is always the expectation of profits. For one thing, prices

---

[21] See Moses Abramowitz, *Inventories and Business Cycles* (New York: National Bureau of Economic Research, 1950), p. 5.

[22] See Thomas M. Stanback, Jr., *Post-war Cycles in Manufacturers' Inventories* (New York: National Bureau of Economic Research, 1963), p. 6. Also see the very useful data in Alan S. Blinder, "Inventories and the Structure of Macro Models," *American Economic Review* 71 (May 1981), Table 1, p. 12.

[23] Abramowitz, *op. cit.*, pp. 481–482.

[24] Stanback, *op. cit.*, p. 6.

Table 9.2

INVENTORIES-SALES RATIO AND INVENTORY INVESTMENT[a]

Change from Stage to Stage, per Month, as Percentage of Cycle Base

Stages	Expansion				Peak	Contraction		
	1–2	2–3	3–4	4–5	5–6	6–7	7–8	8–9
Ratio of inventories to sales	−0.66	−0.13	0.05	0.18	0.49	0.60	0.35	0.57
Inventory investment	4.27	1.63	−0.35	−0.20	−4.66	−2.60	−3.03	−3.97

[a] *Inventory investment* means the net change in business inventories. To avoid negative numbers, inventory investment was raised by a constant $20 billion in every quarter. This reduces the observed percentage rate of change, but leaves the same cyclical pattern.
NOTE: This table represents an average of six cycles, from 1949.4 through 1980.3, in quarterly data and in billions of constant 1972 dollars.
SOURCE: U.S. Department of Commerce, *Business Conditions Digest* (October 1981).

are rising in this phase of the cycle; as a result, holding inventories provides the possibility of more profit by selling the goods at an enhanced value. Therefore, some inventories will be acquired on a purely speculative motive. There is also a time lag between the change in sales and the acquiring of inventories. Consequently, inventory investment continues approximately up to the peak of the cycle.[25]

The actual behavior of inventory investment (the change in inventories) and the ratio of inventories to sales from 1949 to 1980 are examined in Table 9.2 and Figure 9.2.

Table 9.2 shows that net inventory investment, the change in business inventories, rises very rapidly in the first half of expansion. Capitalist entrepreneurs are very optimistic in this period, so they rapidly increase their inventories of goods on hand—including raw materials for more production and finished goods for more sales. In the second half of expansion, capitalists are more cautious in their purchases (though still increasing them). Therefore, purchases do not keep up with sales, so there is a slight decline in net inventory investment. In the entire contraction period, on the other hand, inventory investment declines rapidly because capitalists are very pessimistic about future sales.

These movements of inventory investment are mirrored in the ratio of inventories to sales. In the recovery from recession, during the early part of the expansion, sales are booming so inventories fall behind. Therefore, the ratio of inventories to sales falls in the early expansion. As the expansion progresses, sales growth slows up a little, while inventories continue to grow. So the ratio of inventories to sales rises a little and and reaches its desired level. In the contraction, the ratio of inventories to sales rises fairly rapidly and goes way beyond the desired level. The reason is that, even though inventory investment has a very rapid decline,

---

[25] Abramowitz, *op. cit.*, pp. 470–475; Stanback, *op. cit.*, p. 17.

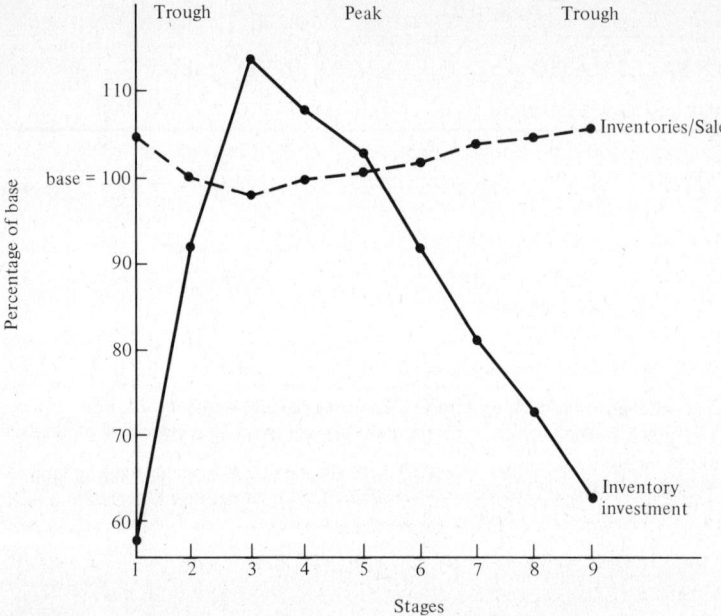

Figure 9.2 Inventory Investment and Inventories-Sales Ratio
NOTE: This figure represents an average of six cycles, from 1949 through 1980, in quarterly data and in constant 1972 dollars, as percentage of cycle base.
SOURCE: U.S. Department of Commerce, *Business Conditions Digest* (October 1981).

sales fall even faster! So the rising ratio of inventories to sales in the recession is a sure symptom of economic illness.

In the first part of the contraction, the amount of inventory investment declines rapidly as a result of falling sales. Yet the level of inventories does continue to rise! In other words, investment is declining, but it is still positive. There is *no* planned inventory investment at this point. There is unplanned inventory investment because goods already ordered cannot be sold and pile up. In the period 1919 to 1938, the annual data indicate that inventories continue to accumulate after each cyclical peak for from 6 to 12 months.[26] In the period since 1945, the quarterly data indicate that inventories continue to rise for 1 to 8 months after each cycle peak.[27] In the last half of the contraction, inventory investment continues to decline, and it becomes negative, so there is a big decline in the amount of inventories on hand. Yet, as shown earlier, the amount of sales declines even faster, so the inventory to sales ratio keeps rising.

It may be noted that, whether or not interest rates affect investment in plant and equipment, they seem to have no effect on inventory investment. An article published in 1981 says:

---

[26]See Abramowitz, *op. cit.,* pp. 107–109.
[27]See Stanback, *op. cit.,* p. 17.

"We find no strong, systematic influence of real interest rates on inventory investment ... the conventional literature ... has consistently failed to uncover an influence of interest rates on inventory investment."[28]

There are those who argue that overstocked inventories at the end of expansion are an independent factor causing part of the decline and, in fact, in short or "minor" cycles, may be the sole factor causing decline.[29] Since investments both in inventories and in plant and equipment show a significant decline at about the same time, however, we may suspect that many of the same factors cause the decline of both categories of investment. To some extent, inventory investment—like other investment—may be affected by the profit squeeze caused by rising costs and less rapidly rising demand.

Less profits mean both less funds with which to purchase inventories and less optimistic expectations for the use of inventories. To some extent also, the decline in the increase of sales will eventually affect inventory investment. There is, however, a very considerable time lag before increased production allows the adjustment of inventories to approach the desired ratio to sales. Furthermore, the beginnings of price decline after the peak will cause a collapse of the speculative motive for holding inventories. Finally, when sales do begin an absolute decline, planned inventory investment may be pushed downward till it is quite negative.

Both Marx and Keynes argue that the length of time necessary to reduce inventories to their desired level is an important factor in determining the duration of the depression.[30] Yet this does not mean that inventory investment in the recovery increases for some reason different from that for other investment. It seems better to consider inventory investment as reacting to most of the same factors as plant and equipment investment, with the actual role of inventories being greater the shorter the cycle, and the role of plant and equipment being greater the longer the cycle. Of course, all fluctuations—and especially the shorter—would be much less severe if there were no inventory fluctuations.

INVESTMENT AND INTEREST RATES

This section first examines how the interest rate behaves over the business cycle. Then it asks the controversial question, Does the interest rate have a significant affect on investment decisions?

There are a huge number of different interest rates on different kinds of loans. Most rates do move in the same direction, however, so they are all reflected in the cyclical pattern of the bank rate on short-term business loans, shown in Table 9.3 and Figure 9.3.

The interest rate on bank loans to business rises in most of the expansion because there

---

[28]Louis J. Maccini and Robert J. Rossana, "Investment in Finished Goods Inventories," *American Economic Review* 71 (May 1981), p. 21.

[29]See Lloyd A. Metzler, "Nature and Stability of Inventory Cycles," *Review of Economics and Statistics* 23 (August 1941), pp. 113–129; Metzler, "Business Cycles and the Modern Theory of Employment," *American Economic Review* 36 (June 1946), pp. 278–291; Metzler, "Factors Governing the Length of Inventory Cycles," *Review of Economics and Statistics* 29 (February 1947), pp. 1–15.

[30]See Karl Marx, *Capital,* vol. 3 (Chicago: Charles H. Kerr, 1909), pp. 576–577. See John M. Keynes, *General Theory of Employment, Interest, and Money* (New York: Harcourt Brace Jovanovich, 1936), p. 317.

Table 9.3

BANK RATE OF INTEREST ON SHORT-TERM BUSINESS LOANS

Change from Stage to Stage, per Month, as Percentage of Cycle Base

	Expansion				Peak	Contraction		
Stages	1–2	2–3	3–4	4–5	5–6	6–7	7–8	8–9
Interest Rate	−0.82	0.42	1.24	2.00	0.21	2.45	−0.58	−6.43

NOTE: This table represents an average of six cycles, from 1949 through 1980, in quarterly data.
SOURCE: U.S. Department of Commerce, *Business Conditions Digest* (August 1981).

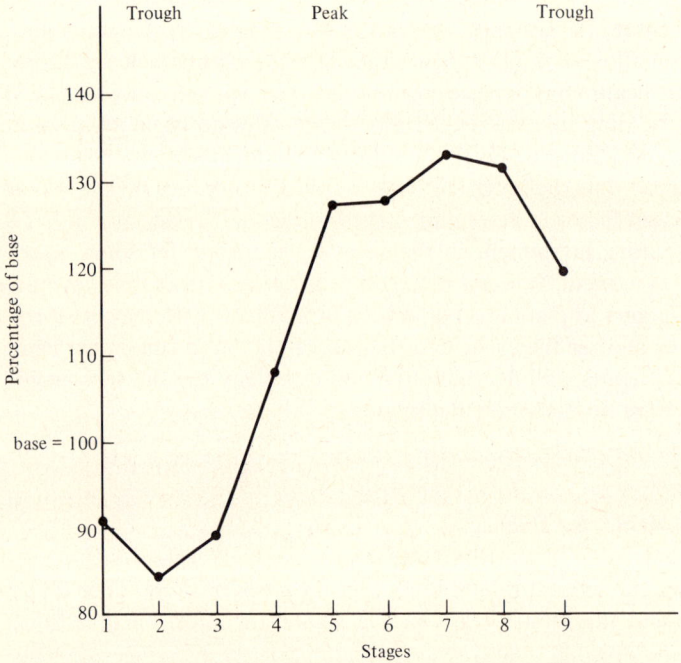

Figure 9.3 Bank Rate of Interest on Short-term Business Loans
NOTE: This figure represents an average of six cycles, from 1949 through 1980, in quarterly data and in constant 1972 dollars, as percentage of cycle base.
SOURCE: U.S. Department of Commerce, *Business Conditions Digest* (August 1981).

is a growing demand for loans. It continues to rise in the first half of the average contraction (but not in all contractions) because businesses in trouble want even more loans, whereas bankers do not want to make loans due to the risk. In the last half of contraction, interest rates finally drop because the outlook is too gloomy for most investment projects. The drop continues into the beginning of the recovery because more funds are still available than is the demand for them.

In the 1940s and the 1950s, numerous studies found little or no empirical evidence of the impact of interest rates on investment.[31] This led to a sharp debate, with pro and con theoretical arguments and empirical studies. This whole debate is now obsolete because of changed conditions. In the 1940s and the 1950s, interest rates were relatively low and stable. Interest rates are now much higher and quite volatile. These long-run historical trends have greatly changed the the situation, making interest rates extremely important to business.

Long-run Trend in Interest Rates

Interest rates were very low in the Great Depression, and rates of 2.5 percent were still common in the late 1940s. The interest rate has had an upward trend since then. In the six cycles since 1949, the interest rate on short-term bank loans to business averaged 3.3 percent from 1949 to 1954, 4.1 percent from 1954 to 1958, 4.9 percent from 1958 to 1961, 6.0 percent from 1961 to 1970, 8.0 percent from 1970 to 1975, and finally 10.1 percent from 1975 to 1980.[32] It was over 17 percent in early 1980. Of course, these averages hide the fact that small businesses pay much higher rates than big business. But even big business had to pay very high interest rates by the early 1980s.

Long-run Trend in Investment

Investment grew quite rapidly in the 1950s and the 1960s, but its growth rate has declined in the 1970s and 1980s. The average growth of investment from one cycle to the next (in terms of the average level of gross private domestic nonresidential investment in each cycle) was 0.38 per month from the 1949–1954 cycle to the 1954–1958 cycle. There was no change to the next very brief cycle. Then there was a rapid rise in the 1960s of 0.63 per month from the 1958–1961 cycle average to the 1961–1970 cycle average. But after that, the investment growth slipped to 0.36 per month from the 1961–1970 cycle average to the 1970–1975 average level. Finally, from the average level of the 1970–1975 cycle to the average level of the 1975–1980 cycle, growth was only 0.16 per month.[33]

What caused the rapid growth of the 1950s and the 1960s, and what caused the much weaker growth of the 1970s and the early 1980s? The brief answer is that business downturns got worse. There were many more quarters of contraction relative to expansion in the later period. Also the declines of 1973–1975 and of the early 1980s were more severe. The greater duration and severity of contractions in the 1970s and the early 1980s are reflected in much higher average rates of unemployment, much lower rates of use of capacity, less growth of productivity, higher rates of bankruptcies, declines in real wages, and more suicides, divorce, and crime, as well as less investment.

---

[31]See John R. Meyer and Edwin Kuh, *The Investment Decision* (Cambridge, Mass.: Harvard University Press, 1957), pp. 181–189.
[32]Data derived from U.S. Department of Commerce, *Business Conditions Digest* (August 1981).
[33]Data derived from U.S. Department of Commerce, *Business Conditions Digest* (April 1981).

To say, however, that less investment was due to more long and severe contractions only pushes the problem back one step. Why did contractions get worse in the 1970s and the early 1980s? A full explanation would involve this whole book. Only a few of the main factors are listed here. Interest rates did go higher, but—as shown in Part Four—there is good reason to believe that credit and interest rates themselves are determined endogenously by economic movements. A major reason for the increase in interest rates was, of course, inflation. Inflation, which is discussed in Part Five, also harms investment growth by making the future much more unpredictable. With varying rates of inflation, how can business predict costs and prices? This extreme uncertainty must surely have adverse effects on investment because expected profit rates become impossible to predict. The continued growth of monopoly power, discussed in Chapter 20, has also probably reduced investment because monopolists have less incentive to update equipment or increase production and would rather use their profits to buy up other companies.

Chapter 21 shows that international relations were exceedingly favorable for the U.S. economy in the 1950s, but became far less favorable by the 1970s. Chapter 7 also emphasized that federal government spending—mostly military—was very high in the Korean War in the 1950s and in the Vietnam War in the 1960s. In the 1970s, military spending was rising absolutely, but declining as a percentage of GNP until the Reagan administration.

SUMMARY

Investment is an important variable, with strong fluctuations. It is clearly affected by total sales, total profits, and the rate of profit. Total profits—and also credit—are important because they represent the availability of funds. The profit rate is important because it—and many other hard-to-quantify factors—affect the expectations of investors for future profits.

In shorter cycles, most of the fluctuation is in inventories. In longer cycles, most of the fluctuation is in plant and equipment. Inventories and plant and equipment investment are mainly affected by the same factors, those that influence the availability of funds and expectations (in Appendix 9B, it is revealed that the same factors also influence replacement investment).

The long-run trends in inflation, interest rates, rising monopoly, a less favorable international situation, and less government support for demand have all caused a slower growth of investment. The long-run rise in business debt means greater vulnerability to bankruptcy.

Investment is important, not only for its direct effects on national income and production, but also for its indirect effects. The workers who build new plant and equipment receive additional income, most of which they respend on additional consumer goods, causing a further increase in national income. So an investment multiplier can be calculated, very similar to the government multiplier discussed in an earlier chapter (see Appendix 9C for details).

APPENDIX 9A

Determination of Investment

Many theories emphasize the importance of sales as a stimulant to investment. Others emphasize the need for funds, which come from profit, rent, and interest income (as well as credit). Still others emphasize the importance of the expected rate of profit as a stimulus to investors. All of these three are interrelated and must be tested together.

Keeping in mind the limitations of any regression technique, we feel that it is still worth presenting the result for the years 1949 to 1980[34] (using the first differences of all the variables):

$$\Delta I_t = -.78 + \underset{(9.49)}{0.15\Delta Y_t} + \underset{(3.47)}{0.09\Delta \Pi_{t-2}} + \underset{(2.86)}{0.67\Delta} \frac{\Pi_{t-3}}{K_{t-3}} \tag{9A.1}$$

$$R^2 = 0.55 \qquad\qquad DW = 1.75$$

These findings show that the tests do not reject our hypothesis that output or sales (Y), total profits (Π), and the rate of profit (Π/K) all play an important role in the determination of investment. In the years from 1970 to 1980 taken alone, when investment and profit rates both fluctuated more strongly than in the 1950s or the 1960s, the correlation for the whole equation was considerably higher (still using first differences of the variables):

$$\Delta I_t = -.87 + \underset{(6.20)}{0.14\Delta Y_t} + \underset{(2.82)}{0.08\Delta \Pi_{t-2}} + \underset{(3.17)}{1.92\Delta} \frac{\Pi_{t-3}}{K_{t-3}} \tag{9A.2}$$

$$R^2 = 0.68 \qquad\qquad DW = 1.78$$

The rate of profit appears to have played a stronger role in the 1970s, when expectations became more uncertain.

APPENDIX 9B

Depreciation and Replacement

So far it has been assumed that the income allotted to the depreciation allowance is always exactly balanced by the spending on replacement investment. Yet we have advanced no reason, other than initial simplicity of exposition, for accepting this assumption. Moreover, the importance of the matter is indicated by the fact that depreciation averages 50 percent

---

[34] Data from the same sources as in Table 9.1.

or more of gross investment. For example, Kuznets[35] found that depreciation (that is, capital consumption) was 63 percent of gross expenditures on construction and producers' durables during the period of 1919 to 1928. In this section, therefore, we analyze the different movements of depreciation and replacement investment.

In fact, in any unplanned economy, there must be continuous small random differences between depreciation and replacement. An excess of depreciation allowance over replacement spending means more funds available for net investment, but a net loss to demand at the time *if* the funds are not invested. Vice versa, if replacement is greater than depreciation allowances, this increases total demand *if* it does not cut down the funds used for net investment. We must also recognize that in practice it is difficult to distinguish between replacement and net investment. Much investment takes the guise of replacement of old capital by new innovations.

In each business expansion, a great deal of replacement is hurried into place long before the old capital has fully depreciated. Thus, in expansion, replacement investment tends to rise rapidly regardless of physical depreciation. On the contrary, in each recession or depression, there is no desire to maintain a high level of output, so many "necessary" replacements are postponed. Thus, in contraction there is a decline of replacement investment regardless of the behavior of depreciation (within limits discussed later). Therefore, the very strong cyclical behavior of gross investment is partly due to the cyclical fluctuation of net investment in new plant, equipment, and inventories, but it is also partly due to the cyclical fluctuation of replacement investment. Unfortunately, there are no available aggregate data to separate net investment and replacement except by the false assumption that replacement equals depreciation.

Depreciation, on the other hand, proceeds serenely, changing little in business expansion and contraction (except by changes in the law). In an expansion, this source of saving falls behind replacement investment. In a recession or depression, this source of saving may be far greater than the replacement investment in this period. In fact, since depreciation is related to aggregate capital accumulated in many previous years, it declines only very slightly except in very long depressions. For example, in the four cycles from 1921 to 1938, depreciation of all business capital fell an average of only one-half of one percent of its cycle average during the contractions, and even that drop was largely due to the weight of the Great Depression (the 1929–1932 decline).[36]

In the period of 1949 to 1980, depreciation in constant dollars rose at almost the same pace in recessions as in expansions.[37] There was simply no cyclical pattern to depreciation, but a mostly smooth increase. If, as we suspect, replacement investment was rushed in expansions and postponed in contractions, then replacement was greater than depreciation in expansions and much less than depreciation in contractions.

Most new investment is made during expansions, so the average time of purchase of capital

---

[35] See the discussion in R. A. Gordon, "Investment Opportunities in the United States," *Business Cycles in the Post-War World* (New York: Oxford University Press, 1952), p. 293.

[36] See W. C. Mitchell, *What Happens During Business Cycles* (New York: National Bureau of Economic Research, 1951), p. 142.

[37] Derived from depreciation data in U.S. Department of Commerce, *National Income and Product Accounts to 1974* (1976) and *Survey of Current Business*, 1975 to 1980.

will be somewhere between the midpoint of prosperity and the cycle peak; the average machine will wear out some fixed time after that date. Suppose that prosperity lasts five years and that the depression lasts another five years. If the average machine is bought in the third year of prosperity and lasts ten years, then the spending for its replacement will not take place until the next boom period. On these assumptions the process of replacement intensifies the business cycle because replacement spending exceeds depreciation saving in each expansion and depreciation saving exceeds replacement spending in each contraction.[38]

Both Marx and Keynes[39] observed that the duration of the depression may depend to some extent on the lifetime of machinery since when it begins to wear out, some of the funds of the corporation may begin to be used for replacement investment. Thus, R. A. Gordon[40] finds the length of cycles influenced by the fact that spending on new construction has declined in relation to spending on new producers' durables from over 300 percent in the nineteenth century to about 80 percent in the 1946–1950 period. Since producers' durables have a shorter lifetime than construction, this would lead us to expect shorter and more frequent cycles.

There are, however, many reasons why replacement "needs" may be far from a mechanical function of previous investment. In addition to all the technical factors, there is the fact that firms are as strongly influenced by their expectations when making replacements as when making net investments. Even such apparently technical factors as the life span of the machinery become quite flexible when the very standard of scrapping is influenced by business expectations. Accordingly, after a depression begins, firms hold back on replacement; but when a period of prosperity seems to be already under way, they may spend for replacement much sooner than necessary.

If a business cycle is to result purely from periodic replacement,[41] then the useful economic life of capital goods must be a fixed time and must be "external" to other business conditions. If this is not so, then most replacement investment must be only a secondary factor intensifying cycle movements in either direction. J. S. Bain[42] shows that the economic lifetime of a machine is a function not merely of its physical wear and tear, but also of rates of obsolescence and available replacements, scrap values, operating and maintenance costs, and rates of interest. Moreover, both the present and expected values of each of these factors are important, and each is systematically influenced by the changing business expectations over the cycle. Therefore, replacement is often postponed as not "needed" until recovery, at which time the economic life of the machine is quickly found to be finished.

We conclude that the need for physical replacement, called forth at the end of a lengthy depression, probably has an effect on the duration of a contraction, but it is not a very simple relationship. We also find that depreciation allowances have grown at a roughly unchanging rate. Replacement investment, on the contrary, appears to move as an effect of the business

---

[38]See, for a full statement of this theory, Johan Einarsen, *Reinvestment Cycles* (Oslo: J. Chr. Gundersens Boktrykkeri, 1938).

[39]See J. M. Keynes, *General Theory of Employment, Interest, and Money* (New York: Harcourt Brace Jovanovich, 1936), p. 317; Karl Marx, *Capital,* vol. 2 (Chicago: Charles H. Kerr, 1909), p. 211.

[40]Gordon, *op. cit.,* p. 291.

[41]See Einarsen, *op. cit.*

[42]Joe S. Bain, "The Relation of the Economic Life of Equipment to Reinvestment Cycles," *Review of Economics and Statistics* 21 (May 1939), pp. 79–88.

cycle, speeding up in expansion and slowing or declining in contraction. Therefore, the cyclical fluctuations of replacement investment do intensify cyclical swings. In other words, replacement investment is moved to expand and decline by most of the factors affecting net investment, but probably somewhat more mildly.

APPENDIX 9C

The Investment Multiplier

Some economists believe that Keynes's most important conceptual contribution to macroeconomics is the consumption function and that the most important analytic tool to come out of the Keynesian dissection of consumption is the multiplier. The *multiplier* expresses the relation between the initial increase (or decrease) in one of the components of aggregate demand and the total increase (or decrease) in national income caused by it. The initial spending change may come from any one of the components of aggregate demand, but investment spending is the most volatile. Investment spending characteristically rises sharply or falls drastically during cyclical fluctuations. Its fluctuations are usually of much greater amplitude than those of consumption.

Obviously, it is vital that government policy makers know how any change in spending, whether in direct government spending or in private investment encouraged by government spending, will affect national income. This question first received considerable attention during the 1930s, when New Deal politicians debated ways of combating the depression.

Government spending was covered in Chapter 7, so the focus here is on the effects of changes in investment spending. In precise terms the *investment multiplier* may be defined as the ratio of change in national income to change in investment. This is more than a definition; there is alleged to be a causal relationship running from change in investment spending to change in income. Change in investment usually causes a larger change in income and output because some of the money spent on investment will be *respent* by its recipients for additional consumption.

Assume that during a period with some unemployment a firm decides to construct a large new factory. This sudden increase in investment spending will increase the incomes of the contractors who supply the necessary machinery and materials and will provide jobs and wages for previously unemployed workers. Now assume that the initial increase in spending and income is $1000. The recipients of this income will immediately respend most of it for consumer goods, which will result in new income for businesspeople and workers in the consumer goods industries. These income recipients will, in turn, spend much of their new income on more consumer goods. Exactly how much additional spending occurs in each round will depend on the marginal propensity to consume of the income recipients. But it is already clear that any additional consumer spending must mean that the total income generated will be more than the original $1000 of investment spending.

The easiest way to see how the multiplier is supposed to work is to study a numerical example. In the example in Table 9C.1, only some initial change in investment and a certain

Table 9C.1

HOW THE MULTIPLIER WORKS

Number of Rounds of Spending	Increase in Investment	Increase in Consumption	Increase in National Income	Increase in Saving
0	$1000	—	$1000	—
1	0	$ 800	800	$ 200
2	0	640	640	160
3	0	512	512	128
4	0	410	410	102
5	0	328	328	82
6	0	262	—	66
—	0	—	—	—
—	—	—	—	—
—	—	—	—	—
—	—	—	—	—
—	—	—	—	—
—	—	—	—	—
Infinite Number of Rounds of Spending	Total Increase in Investment	Total Increase in Consumption	Total Increase In National Income	Total Increase in Saving
	$1000	$4000	$5000	$1000

ASSUMPTIONS:
1. Suppose an increase in investment of $1000.
2. Also suppose a marginal propensity to consume of ⅘, or 80 percent.

marginal propensity to consume need be assumed. One thousand dollars of investment becomes $1000 of income when it is spent. It is assumed that 80 percent, or $800, of that income is respent on consumption, which means another $800 of national income going to other individuals. They will then spend 80 percent, or $640, of *that* income, and so it goes. In the first round, 20 percent, or $200, leaks out into saving, and in the second round, 20 percent of the remaining income, or $160, leaks out into saving. The process ends only when the last $1 of the increased income is saved. At that point the whole $1000 of investment has been saved, but there already have been many rounds of consumption spending in between. In this example the total of all the rounds of consumption spending (or respending) will eventually approach $4000, and national income will approach a level that is $5000 higher than before.

If investment returns to its old level after completion of the factory, the entire process will then work in reverse. Therefore, when the multiplier is used as an analytical tool, it is necessary to distinguish between a one-time injection of new investment spending and a rise in the level of new investment spending that is sustained over a long period of time.

If the $1000 increase in investment is considered as a one-time injection of new spending, then the totals at the bottom of Table 9C.1 represent only temporary additions to consumption, saving, and national income. After these one-time increases are realized, however, total spending will eventually return to its original level. But if the $1000 increase is a new, stepped-up rate of investment spending that continues through several subsequent periods, the totals represent the rise from the old, lower levels to the new, higher levels of spending flows, which will persist in each future period.

From this description of how the multiplier works, it should be clear that if less is saved out of each increment to income, then each increment to consumption spending will be larger. In other words, if the marginal propensity to save declines, the subsequent increases in consumption and income will be larger.

The multiplier formula is just a shortcut for finding where the process of Table 9C.1 ends without repeating the calculation a great many times. Because the formula works equally well for an initial increase *or* decrease in investment, it can be stated more generally as changes rather than as increases or decreases. By definition:

$$\text{multiplier} = \frac{\text{change in income}}{\text{change in investment}} = \frac{\Delta Y}{\Delta I} \qquad (9C.1)$$

Movement from one equilibrium to another equilibrium position is assumed. Therefore, at the end of the process, the change in saving must equal the change in investment. Substituting saving for investment, the result is:

$$\text{multiplier} = \frac{\text{change in income}}{\text{change in saving}} = \frac{\Delta Y}{\Delta S} \qquad (9C.2)$$

or, by simple mathematical manipulation,

$$\text{multiplier} = \frac{1}{(\text{change in saving})/(\text{change in income})} = \frac{1}{(\Delta S)/(\Delta Y)} \qquad (9C.3)$$

Lo and behold! The denominator of this fraction is nothing but the marginal propensity to save. So the formula to remember is just

$$\text{multiplier} = \frac{1}{MPS} \text{ or } \frac{1}{1 - MPC} \qquad (9C.4)$$

because the marginal propensities to save (*MPS*) and consume (*MPC*) always add up to exactly 1.0.

Look again at the example in Table 9C.1. It has been established that *total increase in income = increase in investment × the multiplier*. In this example, the increase in investment is $1000. What is the multiplier? The *MPC* is ⅘, so the *MPS* is ⅕. The multiplier must equal 1 divided by ⅕, which is 5. So it may be calculated that

$$\text{total increase in income} = \$1000 \times 5 = \$5000 \qquad (9C.5)$$

This demonstrates how the multiplier is used to find the end result of investment spending.

Notice that if the multiplier is reduced, then the investment spending has less effect. At one extreme, if the multiplier is just 1, the change in income is just equal to the change in investment. At the other extreme, if the multiplier approaches infinity, any small change in investment will cause an infinite change in income.

Of course, the value of the multiplier is controlled by the *MPC* or *MPS*. If *MPC* falls, so does the multiplier (because less is respent out of each increase in income). A multiplier of only 2 means an *MPC* of only ½. A multiplier of only 1 means everything is saved and the *MPC* is zero. But a multiplier of infinity means all income is immediately respent for consumption, the *MPC* is 1, and the *MPS* is zero.

The investment multiplier may also be derived from a formal model, which gives some further insights into its assumptions. The first assumption is that, in equilibrium, the supply of output (Y) will equal consumer demand plus investment demand (ignoring government and foreign trade for the moment):

$$Y = C + I \qquad (9C.6)$$

The second assumption is that consumption is a function of income. Using the simplest linear function:

$$C = a + bY \qquad (9C.7)$$

where a and b are constants, and b is assumed to be between zero and 1. The third assumption of this simplest model is that investment is an exogenously given variable:

$$I = I_0 \qquad (9C.8)$$

where I_0 is given by exogenous factors, that is, factors external to the model.

If equations 9C.7 and 9C.8 are substituted into 9C.6, the result is:

$$Y = a + bY + I_0 \qquad (9C.9)$$

Suppose there is an exogenously caused change in the level of investment to a new permanent level (I_1). We define $\Delta I = I_1 - I_0$. To see the effect of this change, we take the first differences of all the components of the equation and then divide every component by the change in investment. Thus:

$$\frac{\Delta Y}{\Delta I} = \frac{\Delta a}{\Delta I} + \frac{\Delta bY}{\Delta I} + \frac{\Delta I}{\Delta I} \qquad (9C.10)$$

Since a is a constant, its change is zero. Of course, $\Delta I/\Delta I = 1$. Therefore:

$$\frac{\Delta Y}{\Delta I} - \frac{\Delta bY}{\Delta I} = 1 \qquad (9C.11)$$

Adding the like terms and dividing by $1-b$, the final result is:

$$\frac{\Delta Y}{\Delta I} = \frac{1}{1-b} \qquad (9C.12)$$

So the investment multiplier is $1/1-b$.

There are some obvious weaknesses or, at least, qualifications that must be kept in mind when the multiplier theory is used. First, so far the time element has been ignored; it takes a certain amount of time before income received is respent for consumption and still more time before the second and third and later rounds of respending may occur. If the time lag happens to be very long or varies widely, a much more complicated multiplier will be needed to get a realistic answer to the change in income for one year.

Second, it has been assumed that *MPC* remains constant until the process is completed. In reality, *MPC* often changes and is affected by many psychological and institutional factors. For example, the accumulated savings of World War II greatly increased the propensity to consume in the immediate postwar years.

Moreover, saving is not the only leakage from the income stream. Higher or lower taxes will also change *MPC* out of national income. Furthermore, if purchases of imports (e.g., Toyotas) increase, there will be a leakage from domestic consumer spending. Thus, the domestic *MPC* may change too often to permit accurate prediction of the multiplier for more than a few months in the future.

Third, the multiplier formula assumes that investment will remain the same while consumption and national income are expanding rapidly. Obviously, the simple multiplier theory cannot be used if further changes in investment are to be considered.

For all of these reasons, the conclusion is that whereas the multiplier is a helpful explanatory device, it cannot be relied on for an exact estimate.

APPENDIX 9D

The Cyclical Behavior of Investment

As is shown in equation 9D.1 (which repeats equation 9.1 in the chapter), Samuelson's accelerator model treats investment as a function of the change in consumption.

$$I_t = v \ (C_{t-1} - C_{t-2}) \tag{9D.1}$$

This is because it is assumed that the capital-to-consumption ratio is constant, as is shown in equation 9D.2 (which repeats equation 9.2 in the chapter).

$$v = K/C \tag{9D.2}$$

and because by definition investment is equal to a change in the capital stock, as is shown in equation 9D.3 (which repeats equation 9.4 in the chapter).

$$I = \Delta K \tag{9D.3}$$

This implies that if there is a one-time increase in consumption, investment must also rise, "accelerating" the increase in national income (Y). If consumption then stabilizes at the new level (without declining), then no further increase in the capital stock is necessary. Therefore investment falls to zero, causing income to decline. This is shown in Table 9D.1. Assume that the accelerater (the capital-to-consumption ratio) is two, and, for purposes of simplification, that consumption is autonomous.

At time period one consumption rises from 100 to 110, causing income to rise. Consump-

Table 9D.1

THE CYCLICAL BEHAVIOR OF INVESTMENT

Time	ΔC_t	C_t	K_t	I_t	Y_t	ΔY_t
0	0	100	200	0	100	0
1	10	110	200	0	110	10
2	0	110	220	20	130	20
3	0	110	220	0	110	−20
4	0	110	220	0	110	0

ASSUMPTIONS:
1. $v = 2.0$
2. $Y = C + I$
3. C is autonomous

tion stabilizes at this rate hereafter. In the subsequent time period (two) investment rises (see equation 9D.1) "accelerating" income to 130 from 110. In time period three, with the capital stock at the required 220, capital stabilizes and investment falls to zero. This causes a *fall* in income of 20. Finally, as is seen in the far-right column, a business cycle has occured.

Chapter 10

INCOME DISTRIBUTION

Income distribution is of the greatest importance in macroeconomics because it has a very strong influence on consumer demand, on investment behavior, and even on the behavior of government. It was shown earlier that a higher share of wages in the national income means a higher propensity to consume. It was also shown that higher profits tend to produce more investment because funds are more readily available. Furthermore, it was mentioned in the last chapter—and will be demonstrated in Part Six—that the unequal distribution of income is reflected in the unequal distribution of political power in the United States.

On the other side, a high level of consumer and investment demand means a high level of demand for labor; so it will be shown in this chapter that income distribution itself is affected by the level of demand. And, of course, government also has effects on income distribution in an enormous number of ways. For example, government determines the recognition of trade unions, governments have employed armed force against trade unions, other governments have encouraged trade unions, government may give subsidies to the poor or may give subsidies to the rich or to big business, and government may tax the poor or may tax the rich. The United States government affects the distribution of income in the United States by these methods and by many other methods. Thus, income distribution both affects all the other major variables in the macroeconomy and is also affected by them.

PRESENT U.S. INCOME DISTRIBUTION

The facts of income distribution in the United States are well known and need be mentioned here only briefly. In 1977, the lowest 20 percent of families by income had only 5 percent of all income whereas the top 20 percent of families had 42 percent of all income. The top 5 percent of families had 16 percent of all income or as much as the bottom 40 percent of families.[1] There has been very little change in the overall individual distribution of income, that is, among all families and individuals, in the twentieth century in the United States.

Let us examine the *functional* distribution of income, that is, distribution according to source of income, or the functional relation of the income receiver to the economy. The top 1 percent of Americans by income own between 57 percent and 75 percent of all corporate stock according to various highly respectable estimates.[2] These few people earning most of the corporate profits may be termed "capitalists." They also receive most of the interest income from bonds and most of the rental income from things such as oil wells. Of those people with incomes over $1 million a year in 1971, over 95 percent of those incomes came from ownership of property and money.[3] At the other end of the spectrum, people earning under $10,000 a year made over 90 percent of their income from labor, so they may be called "workers."

In 1977, total reported property income was $396 billion (including business proprietors' income, rental income, corporate profits before taxes, and net interest income); we shall show later that this total was greatly understated. If all other income were labor income (which we shall show that it was not), then labor income was $990 billion by official definitions. The ratio of property income to labor income (called the rate of exploitation by Marx) was 40 percent. It would be much higher if we made all the proper corrections for overstatement of *labor income* and understatement of *property income*.

The relative importance of workers and other functional recipients of income has drastically changed over the course of American history. In 1780 (excluding slaves) only 20 percent of all people in the economy were wage and salary workers, 80 percent were self-employed, and less than 1 percent were managers and officials. By 1969, 84 percent were wage and salary workers, only 9 percent were self-employed, and 7 percent were managers and officials.[4] There are no official data on the number of capitalists.

FRAMEWORK AND DEFINITIONS

For the moment, we make use of the official U.S. national income categories, leaving a criticism of them to the next section. All variables are in real terms, that is, constant dollars. Let *wages* (W) be defined to include all wage income, salary income, fringe benefits, bonuses, and commissions. Let *profit* (Π) be defined to be all the rest of national income, namely, corporate profits, noncorporate profits, rent, and interest. Then, of course, the national income (Y) equals wage plus profits.

---

[1] U.S. Department of Commerce, *Statistical Abstract of the United States* (Washington, D.C.: U.S. Government Printing Office, 1978), p. 395.
[2] Robert Lampman, James D. Smith, and Stephen D. Franklin, reported in U.S. Department of Commerce, *Statistical Abstract of the United States* (Washington, D.C.: U.S. Government Printing Office, 1978), p. 110.
[3] See Samuel Bowles and Herbert Gintis, *Schooling in Capitalist America* (New York: Basic Books, 1975), p. 90.
[4] See Michael Reich, "The Evolution of the U.S. Labor Force," in R. Edwards, M. Reich, and T. Weisskopf (eds.), *The Capitalist System* (Englewood Cliffs, N.J.: Prentice-Hall, 1972), pp. 174–183.

$$Y = W + \Pi \tag{10.1}$$

It also follows that the wage *share* (W/Y) plus the profit share (Π/Y) equal one.

$$\frac{W}{Y} + \frac{\Pi}{Y} = 1 \tag{10.2}$$

Thus, if either the wage share or the profit share is known, so is the other one.

A third way of measuring income distribution between classes is what Marx called the *rate of exploitation,* which—in its closest equivalent in national income terms—is profit divided by wages (Π/W). The rate of exploitation, by this definition, equals the profit share divided by the wage share.

$$\frac{\Pi}{W} = \frac{\Pi/Y}{W/Y} \tag{10.3}$$

From equations (10.2) and (10.3), if the wage share or the profit share is known, then the rate of exploitation is known. Therefore, income distribution by class may be described here by the wage share because that is the most convenient context for discussing hourly wages and productivity, but the movements of the rate of exploitation and the profit share are clearly implied. Any statement about the wage share (W/Y) can be restated in terms of the profit share (Π/Y) or the rate of exploitation (Π/W).

If both the numerator and denominator of the wage share are divided by the number of hours of labor expended in the entire economy (N), an interesting set of relationships may be seen:

$$\text{wage share} = W/Y = \frac{W/N}{Y/N} = \frac{\text{real hourly wage}}{\text{productivity per labor hour}} \tag{10.4}$$

Since we are using *real* wages, the top part of this ratio is now the real hourly wage (W/N). Since we are using *real* income or output, the bottom part of the ratio is the productivity of labor per hour (Y/N). So the income share of workers is equal to the real hourly wage divided by the productivity of labor. Obviously, the wage share rises if the hourly wage rises or if productivity declines or both, all other things being constant. The wage share falls if the hourly wage falls or if productivity rises or both, all other things being constant. Throughout the discussion of the wage share, an attempt will be made to explain its movements by explaining the movements of its two components: (1) real hourly wages and (2) the product per labor hour.

The term *productivity* or *labor productivity* used in this chapter just means the total product (in terms of real national income) divided by the number of hours of labor; it is an average product-labor ratio. Its changes may reflect not only changes in the amount of labor, but also changes in the quality of labor, changes in capital, changes in technology or in the availability of natural resources—in short, anything that affects output or employment. This is very different from the usual neoclassical term *marginal productivity of labor,* which is supposed to measure the marginal output of labor *with all other factors held constant.* The simpler product-labor ratio, with other factors changing, is more appropriate to the short-run macro behavior discussed here (and, anyhow, quarterly data on the marginal product are not available).

PROBLEMS WITH MEASURING PROFITS, WAGES, AND PRODUCTIVITY

In our earlier chapter on the national income accounts, there was a discussion of the biases present in the official definition of national product. The biases are no less when it comes to dividing the product or income between wages (all labor income in theory) and profits (all property income in theory). In the first place, the Internal Revenue Service always finds more illegal nonreporting of profits than of wages. This does not necessarily mean that workers are more honest than capitalists. The U.S. tax system makes it much easier to hide property income (which is not withheld at the source) than labor income (part of which is withheld for taxes before it is even paid).

Second, there are very few legal tax loopholes available for labor income. The law is filled with legal tax loopholes for property incomes of both individuals and businesses. As noted in Chapter 9, corporate taxes are a steadily decreasing percentage of the whole revenue. To note all the legal loopholes would require a long book, so we give just a few examples. Interest on state and municipal bonds is not taxable, so it is not reported as income. Only 40 percent of capital gains (increases in value of property and stock) is counted as income. The "cost" of "depreciation" keeps increasing year by year, simply because of changes in the law, so the profit after "cost" is greatly reduced. Estimates of the worth of these tax loopholes range from $100 billion to $200 billion.

Though many guesses are involved, it is possible that the total of property income that is illegally not reported plus that which is legally not reported (by tax loopholes) could be equal to the entire amount that is reported.

On the other hand, what is officially called *wages* is greatly overstated. It includes managerial salaries. Many managers' salaries are actually large amounts of profits in disguise as labor salaries because they can then be counted as corporate "costs." Moreover, wages include *fringe benefits,* which also cover in disguise much profit income in forms such as three martinis at business lunches for executives or use of an airplane by executives to go to football games for "public relations." All these executive payments are really profits, so they should not be counted as labor income.

Moreover, employers' contributions to social security are clearly a tax on profits, so that amount should be in before-tax profits. Instead, by a bookkeeping convention, this amount is part of before-tax wages! As an indication of how major some of these items are, if this one change is made (treating capitalists' contributions to social security as part of before-tax profits), then there is no change in the wage share in the last 30 years. The wage share (with this one correction) was 0.68 in 1948 and was 0.69 in 1977.[5]

Finally, since more and more self-employed petty entrepreneurs and small farmers are

---

[5]Samuel Bowles and Herbert Gintis, "The Crisis of Liberal Democratic Capitalism," *Politics and Society* 11 (1982), p. 71.

going bankrupt and becoming workers, the percentage of people earning wages and salaries keeps going up. A correction should also be made for this change in calculating the wage share because it goes to a larger and larger percentage of the people. This is a major change over a long period because wage and salary earners have risen from 20 percent to well over 90 percent—and the rise was steep even in the last 30 years.

There have been many attempts at careful corrections of the official national income accounts to reach a more unbiased set of categories (from a pro-labor view), but these remain controversial to most economists.[6] The national income categories are used here only because they are (1) readily available, (2) familiar to most economists, and (3) biased against all pro-labor conclusions. Therefore, when one can use these data and still come to pro-labor policy conclusions, these conclusions are more persuasive.

The bias is strongest in absolute comparisons at a given time. For example, the ratio of property income to labor income stated earlier would be perhaps twice or three times as high as the official statistics if we corrected for all the biases mentioned earlier. In data on long-run trends, however, there may be much less bias because—in a comparison of the growth of two things—there will be a bias in the trend if, and only if, there is an *increase* in the bias over time. Unfortunately, in this area there is some evidence of that. There are more and more tax loopholes, for example, legal changes allowing faster and faster "depreciation" for tax purposes. Managers are growing in numbers, and their salaries are increasing by leaps and bounds, with a good number over $1 million a year. For this reason, it is necessary to be extracautious about presenting trend data.

Finally, data on purely cyclical fluctuations will be biased if, and only if, there is a systematic increase in bias at certain points in the cycle. By testing many different definitions, we found very little change in cyclical results. So the bias seems least in the data we use most.

Another category of data that are very unreliable and biased are the data on *productivity*, the ratio of product to labor hours. Many writers have pointed out that productivity has a roughly defined meaning for manufacturing output, but is ambiguous for other sectors. For example, how is the "productivity" of a lawyer defined? Since the usual definitions give a lower productivity in the service sectors than in manufacturing, a shift to services may mean less apparent productivity. This shift is occurring, so it may explain some of the apparently lower productivity growth rates of recent years. On the other hand, this shift from manufacturing to services has been occurring continuously for some time. It does not reverse itself in different parts of the cycle. Therefore, the purely cyclical pattern of productivity should not be much affected by it. In fact, we shall see that the cyclical pattern of productivity has remained the same in different periods. It has had stronger declines in recent contractions, which may be related to this long-run shift.

---

[6]See the excellent paper by Anwar Shaikh, "National Income Accounts and Marxian Categories," mimeographed (New York: New School for Social Research, December 1978). Also see the extremely useful articles by Victor Perlo, "Book Review of Simon Kuznets, *Shares of Upper Income Groups in Income and Savings,*" in *Science and Society* 25 (Spring 1954), pp. 168–173; and Victor Perlo, "The New Propaganda of Declining Profit Shares and Inadequate Investment," *Review of Radical Political Economics* 8 (Fall 1976), pp. 53–64.

THEORIES AND CONTROVERSIES

Long-run. Neoclassical economists explain income distribution according to the theory of *marginal productivity*. In this theory, the wage of labor equals the additional product of the last worker. The profit or "return to capital" equals the additional product of the last machine. Critics argue that the profit goes to human capitalists, not to the machines.

Marxists explain income distribution by the theory that all the value of output is attributable to labor, including present labor and the previous labor that went to build machines and factories. Capitalists take part of this product as their profit because of their power through the institution of ownership. Neoclassical economics implies that each functional class gets what it deserves whereas Marx argues that profit comes from the exploitation of labor.

Fortunately, we need only keep these issues in mind but need not resolve them in macroeconomics. For one thing, both theories assume long-run equilibrium to get their results. We are concerned with situations where supply and demand are usually unequal. We are mainly concerned with why—in those disequilibrium situations—the distribution of income changes in certain systematic ways and what the impact of these changes is.

Factually, there is an argument whether the share of labor income in all income is decreasing, increasing, or constant. The conclusion is totally dependent on the biases mentioned earlier and on how we adjust to remove biases. There is also a raging dispute on whether the rate of growth of labor productivity is declining or not. This again depends on what definitions are used.

Short-run or Cyclical Movements. Does the wage share (or profit share) increase or decrease in expansions? Does the wage share (or profit share) increase or decrease in recessions and depressions? What is the behavior of the two components of the wage share: labor productivity and real hourly wages? *Why* do the wage share and its components behave the way they do? After examining the facts, we will look at the theoretical explanations in some detail, but here it is worth briefly highlighting some of the major theories and controversies.

One theory, often espoused by trade unionists and underconsumptionists, may be called the *wage lag* theory. In this view, in a business expansion, productivity always rises faster than real wages per hour; therefore, the wage share falls throughout the expansion. In a contraction, real wages per hour again lag behind the movement in productivity—that is, both fall—but productivity falls faster. Therefore, the wage share rises in every contraction (even though real wages are falling). Why? Most argue that in an expansion, rapidly improving technology raises productivity. Real wages are held down by the institutional arrangements of capitalism, that is, (1) fixed wage contracts for a year or two, (2) opposition to raising wages by capitalist-controlled media, and (3) opposition to raising wages by capitalist-controlled governments.

In a more general sense, the wage lag theory argues that changes in income distribution are dominated by the simple institutional fact that the capitalist employer owns the product. If, as is always true in expansions, there is increasing productivity, then the employer automatically owns the increased product. To gain merely the same share of the increased product as they had before the increase, workers must struggle and bargain and play catch-up. It is thus not surprising that in an expanding economy the share going to wages normally declines.

As we shall see, most of the wage lag theories would also give similar arguments for the reverse process in contractions. Therefore, they expect the wage share to rise in contractions (even though the real wage is declining).

Another set of theories emphasizes the hiring and firing practices of capitalists at different levels of the use of capacity. One group emphasizes that when the economy declines, rational capitalists hesitate to fire skilled workers because it may be hard to hire them back—this is the theory of *labor hoarding*. Another group emphasizes that some kinds of overhead workers, such as maintenance workers, cannot be fired just because output declines—this is called the *overhead labor theory*. Either way, we could explain a rising wage share in contractions by an apparent decline of productivity per worker (and vice versa in expansions).

A quite different theory comes from those who agree that the wage share falls in early and mid-expansion, but emphasize the fact that it begins to rise again in late expansion. Similarly, the wage share may rise in most of the contraction, but starts to fall again in late contraction. This theoretical explanation is called the *reserve army* theory because it emphasizes unemployment; Marx called the unemployed the "reserve army of labor." These theorists claim that in late expansion the reserve army of unemployed is depleted; this gives employed workers more bargaining power with bosses to raise the wage share. In late contraction, the reserve army of unemployed is swelled by millions of new unemployed workers; this huge surplus supply of labor weakens labor's bargaining position, so the wage share declines.

None of these theories is lightly held, and there is much hard fighting over them because of their implications for the causes of economic downturns and, consequently, policy decisions. Does a falling wage share cause less consumer demand, leading to a recession or depression? Trade unionists argue that a falling wage share does cause a lower propensity to consume, so wages should be raised for this reason. Does a rising wage share mean less profits, causing a fall in investment, which leads to a recession or depression? The Wall Street business establishment often argues that a rising wage share does lower profits and investment, so the wage share should be lowered for this reason. This chapter first examines the facts and then gets back to these theories.

CYCLICAL CHANGES IN INCOME DISTRIBUTION, 1921–1938

Wesley Mitchell had much less data than are available today, but he does present a few suggestive figures on income distribution in the four cycles between 1921 and 1938.[7] These figures are mostly dominated by the cycle of the Great Depression, which peaked in 1929 and reached its nadir in 1933. For the *average* expansion of these four cycles, national income rose by 22.5 percent of its average cycle base whereas total employee compensation rose only 19.8 percent. Therefore, the wage share (W/Y) declined in the average expansion of the 1920s and the 1930s. The decline in the wage share is also shown more dramatically by the fact

[7]Wesley Mitchell, *What Happens During Business Cycles* (New York: National Bureau of Economic Research, 1951).

that in the average expansion phase of the same four cycles, net profits of all U.S. corporations rose 199.2 percent!

In the average contraction phase of these four cycles, national income fell by 17.6 percent of its cycle average whereas total wages fell by only 13.0 percent. Therefore, the wage share (W/Y) rose in the average contraction of the 1920s and the 1930s. Again, the rise in the wage share in the average contraction is emphasized by the fact that net profits of all U.S. corporations fell 174.6 percent!

LONG-RUN CHANGES FROM THE 1950s TO THE 1980s

What has happened in the period from 1950 to the present? There have been several long-run changes that have drastically changed the economic environment from the mild cycles of the 1950s and the 1960s to the deeper crises of the 1970s and the 1980s. First, the 1950s and the 1960s were characterized by wars, including the aftermath of World War II, the cold war, the Korean War, and the Vietnam War. There were high levels of military spending (as shown in Chapter 7). This military spending declined in the 1970s as a percentage of GNP though there is at present an attempt by President Reagan to revive the cold war and increase military spending. Second, in 1950, the United States was totally dominant in production and trade whereas now it faces serious competition from Japan and Western Europe (as we shall see in detail in Part Five). Third, President Nixon used wage-price controls to hold down wages while allowing prices to rise (as we shall see in detail in Part Six). (Note that the real weekly wage has not increased since 1965 except for cyclical phases.) Fourth, there has been an enormous increase in monopoly—by measures such as conglomerate merger—which has been one of the causes of the acceleration in price inflation (as we shall show in Part Five). Since monopoly is not under competitive pressure to innovate, it may also result in less investment—which leads to less growth of productivity. As a result of all these factors, contractions of the 1970s were deeper, unemployment was greater, and the relatively unfavorable conditions for labor resulted in long periods of declining real wages and a declining wage share.

The four cycles from 1949 to 1970 were dominated by wars, very high military spending, high demand for U.S. goods and services from the war-devastated countries of Europe and Asia, and relatively little competition from abroad. The result was relatively mild cycles and high levels of employment, so there were relatively favorable conditions for high wages for labor. Therefore, this was a period of long-run trends of rising productivity and rising real hourly wages.

Some of the specific reasons for the declines in the growth of real hourly wages and productivity in the 1970s probably include (1) inflation outrunning nominal wages (which we investigate in Part Four); (2) government attempts to hold down wages—such as Nixon's Pay Board—or to hold down the whole economy, supposedly to reduce inflation (which we investigate in Part Six); and (3) less innovation embodied in new investment as a result of weaker demand. These long-run changes are the context in which the cyclical movements of the two periods become intelligible. Some economists have seen the 1970s as the beginning of a long-cycle Kondratieff downturn, but that label doesn't seem to make it any easier to explain the long-run trends we have noted.

The effects of these long-run changes can be seen very clearly in a few statistics comparing the 1950s and the 1960s with the period of the 1970s. For one thing, the official unemployment rate from 1949 to 1970 was 4.7 percent, but rose to 6.3 percent in the period from 1970 to 1980.[8] By 1982, about 12 million people (near 11 percent) were unemployed. Capacity utilization averaged 84 percent in the earlier period, but fell to 82 percent in the 1970s—and was 68 percent in part of 1982.[9]

In the average *contraction* of the four cycles from 1949 to 1970, real hourly wages rose by 0.17 percent per month, labor productivity rose by 0.07 percent per month, total real wages fell only -0.16 per month, and real national income fell only -0.26 per month. In the average *contraction* of the two cycles of the 1970s, all the variables decline: real hourly wages fell -0.04 percent per month, productivity declined -0.18 per month, total real wages fell -0.28 percent, and real national income fell at -0.43 percent per month.[10] Thus, the recessions of the 1970s were far more severe than the recessions of the 1950s and the 1960s.

THE WAGE SHARE, 1949–1970

The period from 1949 to 1970 had relatively mild cyclical downturns and relatively low unemployment. Since there were plenty of markets and incentive to produce, there was a high rate of growth of investment and a high rate of growth of productivity. These were very favorable conditions for labor, so there was a trend toward rising hourly wages. From 1950 to 1965, the real weekly earnings of all production workers in private industry (in constant 1977 dollars) rose from $133.83 to $183.21.[11]

These long-run trends are partly reflected in the cyclical movements of the four cycles shown in Table 10.1 and Figures 10.1 and 10.2.

In this period of relatively mild downturns and fairly strong growth, the wage share declined only in the first half of expansion, then rose in the last half of expansion and most of the contraction. It declines again only in the last stage of contraction, on the eve of recovery. To understand these movements, let us recall that the wage share (W/Y) is defined as the ratio of wages (W) to national income (Y). The wage share (W/Y) equals the real hourly wage (W/N, ratio of real wages to labor hours) divided by productivity (Y/N, ratio of real income to labor hours). If productivity is constant, higher real hourly wages mean a higher wage share of income. If real hourly wages are constant, higher productivity means a lower wage share out of income.

Notice that, in theory, the monthly change in the wage share must equal the monthly change in real hourly wages minus the monthly change in productivity. In Table 10.1 this is only roughly and approximately true because each variable has a different cycle base, so

---

[8] See U.S. Department of Commerce, *Business Conditions Digest* (March 1982).
[9] Capacity utilization in manufacturing calculated by Federal Reserve Board, reported by U. S. Department of Commerce, *Business Conditions Digest* (August 1981).
[10] Same sources as in Table 10.1.
[11] Data from Council of Economic Advisors, *Economic Report of the President* (Washington, D. C.: Government Printing Office, 1982), p. 277.

Table 10.1

WAGE SHARE, HOURLY WAGES, AND PRODUCTIVITY, 1949–1970

Change from Stage to Stage, per Month, as Percentage of Cycle Base

	Expansion				Peak	Contraction		
Stages	1–2	2–3	3–4	4–5	5–6	6–7	7–8	8–9
Wage share	−0.19	−0.01	0.15	0.13	0.30	0.12	0.06	−0.08
Real hourly wages	0.16	0.16	0.23	0.24	0.20	0.09	0.18	0.23
Productivity	0.34	0.17	0.08	0.11	−0.10	−0.03	0.12	0.31

NOTE: This table represents an average of four cycles, in quarterly data and in constant 1972 dollars.
SOURCES: Wage share (W/Y) means "compensation of employees as percentage of national income," from U.S. Department of Commerce, *Business Conditions Digest (BCD)* (April 1981). Real national income (Y) from U.S. Department of Commerce, *Survey of Current Business,* various issues from 1950 to 1981. Real total wages (W) equal real national income (Y) times wage share (W/Y). Real hourly wages (W/N) are total real wages (W) divided by total number of labor hours (N), *BCD* (April 1981). Productivity (Y/N) is real national income (Y) divided by labor hours (N).

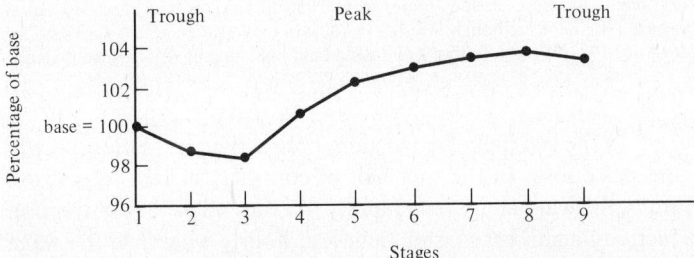

Figure 10.1 The Wage Share (Ratio of Wages to National Income, or W/Y), 1949–1970
NOTE: This figure represents an average of four cycles, in quarterly data and in constant 1972 dollars, as percentage of cycle base.
SOURCES: Wage share *(W/Y)* means "compensation of employees as percentage of national income," from U.S. Department of Commerce, *Business Conditions Digest (BCD)* (April 1981). Real national income *(Y)* from U.S. Department of Commerce, *Survey of Current Business,* various issues from 1950 to 1981. Real total wages *(W)* equal real national income *(Y)* times wage share *(W/Y)*.

the percentage changes are not perfectly comparable. It happens to be exactly true only in a few phases. For example, in the change from stage 4 to stage 5, the monthly change in the wage share (0.13 percent of its cycle base) just equals the monthly change in real hourly wages (0.24 percent of its cycle base) minus the monthly change in productivity (0.11 percent of its cycle base).

Because of the relatively mild downturns in 1949 to 1970, real hourly wages continued to rise in the average downturn though more slowly than they rose in expansions. Why does the wage share ever decline when real hourly wages are rising? The answer is that it declines when productivity rises even faster than real hourly wages.

In the first half of the average contraction, productivity rose more rapidly than hourly

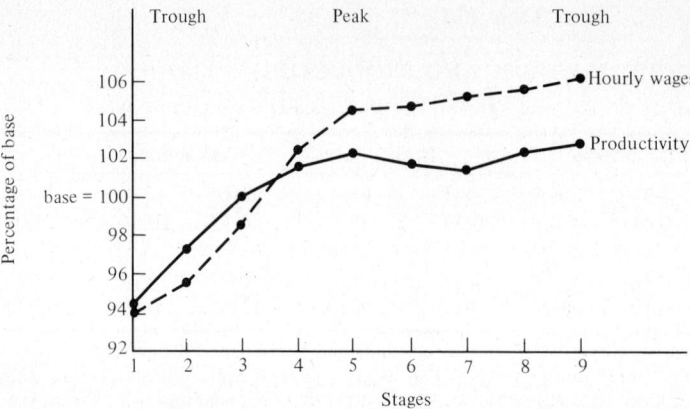

Figure 10.2 Productivity (Ratio of National Income to Labor Hours) and Real Hourly Wages (Ratio of Wages to Labor Hours), 1949–1970
NOTE: This figure represents an average of four cycles, in quarterly data and in constant 1972 dollars, as a percentage of cycle base.
SOURCES: Wage share (W/Y) means "compensation of employees as percentage of national income," from U.S. Department of Commerce, *Business Conditions Digest (BCD)* (April 1981). Real national income (Y) from U.S. Department of Commerce, *Survey of Current Business,* various issues from 1950 to 1981. Real wages (W) equal real national income (Y) times wage share (W/Y). Real hourly wages (W/N) are total real wages (W) divided by total number of labor hours (N), BCD (April 1981). Productivity (Y/N) is real national income (Y) divided by labor hours (N).

wages, so the wage share declined. In the last half of expansion, productivity rose more slowly than hourly wages, so the wage share rose. In the first half of contraction, real wages rose while productivity fell, so naturally the wage share rose rapidly. At the end of the contraction —as a sign of recovery—productivity again rose faster than real hourly wages, so the wage share fell.

Why did productivity rise so rapidly in the beginning of expansion, and why did productivity fall in the first half of contraction? Various theoretical explanations are examined later, but it is worth stressing one factor that can*not* be the cause. Technology causes a very slow growth of average productivity each year. But technology cannot explain the very rapid growth in the recovery period, nor can technological advance explain why productivity actually fell in the first half of contraction.

THE WAGE SHARE, 1970–1980

The period from 1970 to 1980 was much less favorable to workers; it included periods of severe recession and severe inflation. The result was that average weekly earnings of production workers in all private industry *fell* from $183.21 in 1970 to $171.13 in 1981 (in constant 1977 dollars).[12] The cyclical behavior of the wage share and its components in this period is in Table 10.2 and Figures 10.3 and 10.4.

[12]*Ibid.,* p. 277.

Table 10.2

THE WAGE SHARE, 1970–1980

CHANGE FROM STAGE TO STAGE, PER MONTH, AS PERCENTAGE OF CYCLE BASE

	Expansion				Peak	Contraction		
Stages	1–2	2–3	3–4	4–5	5–6	6–7	7–8	8–9
Wage share (W/Y)	−0.16	−0.05	−0.04	0.05	0.21	0.61	0.10	−0.03
Hourly wage (W/N)	0.14	0.12	0.03	−0.07	0	0.03	−0.06	−0.16
Productivity (Y/N)	0.29	0.16	0.07	−0.12	−0.20	−0.54	−0.16	0.20

NOTE: This table represents an average of two cycles, in quarterly data and in constant 1972 dollars.
SOURCES: Wage share (W/Y) means "compensation of employees as percentage of national income," from U.S. Department of Commerce, *Business Conditions Digest (BCD)* (April 1981). Real national income (Y) from U.S. Department of Commerce, *Survey of Current Business,* various issues from 1950 to 1981. Real total wages (W) equal real national income (Y) times wage share (W/Y). Real hourly wages (W/N) are total real wages (W) divided by total number of labor hours (N), *BCD* (April 1981). Productivity (Y/N) is real national income (Y) divided by labor hours (N).

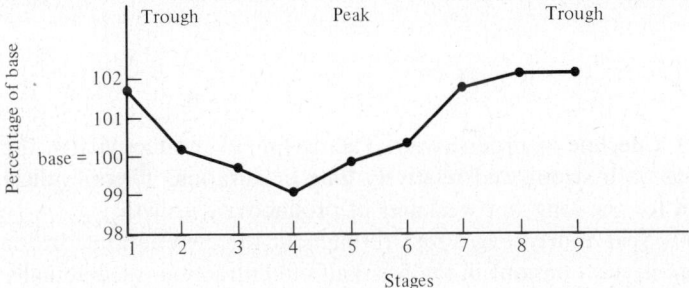

Figure 10.3 The Wage Share (Ratio of Wages to National Income), 1970–1980
NOTE: This figure represents an average of two cycles, in quarterly data and in constant 1972 dollars, as percentage of cycle base.
SOURCES: Wage share *(W/Y)* means "compensation of employees as percentage of national income," from U.S. Department of Commerce, *Business Conditions Digest (BCD)* (April 1981). Real national income *(Y)* from U.S. Department of Commerce, *Survey of Current Business,* various issues from 1950 to 1981. Real total wages *(W)* equal real national income *(Y)* times wage share *(W/Y)*.

This table reveals a very different picture in the 1970s from what was found in the 1950s and the 1960s. The wage share *falls* in most of the average expansion except in the last brief stage. This happens because, in most of the expansion, the productivity of labor rises faster than the real hourly wage of labor! In the last stage of expansion, the hourly wage started falling. Yet the wage share rose slightly because productivity fell more than hourly wages.

The wage share rose considerably in most of the average contraction of the 1970s, falling very slightly in the last stage. But unlike the situation in the 1950s and the 1960s, the wage

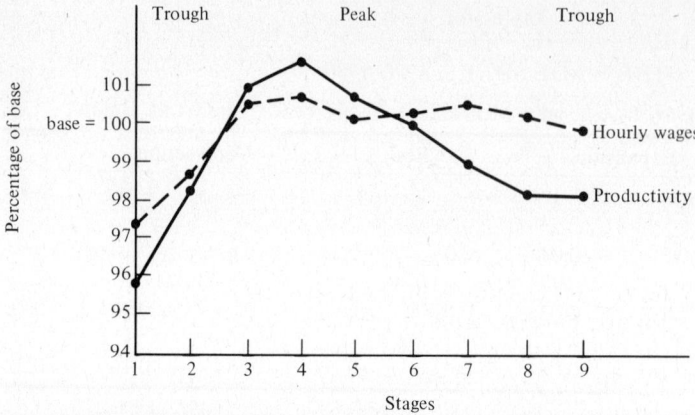

Figure 10.4 Productivity (Ratio of National Income to Labor Hours) and Real Hourly Wages (Ratio of Wages to Labor Hours), 1970–1980
NOTE: This figure represents an average of two cycles in quarterly data and in constant 1972 dollars, as percentage of cycle base.
SOURCES: Wage share (W/Y) means "compensation of employees as percentage of national income," from U.S. Department of Commerce, *Business Conditions Digest (BCD)* (April 1981). Real national income (Y) from U.S. Department of Commerce, *Survey of Current Business*, various issues from 1950 to 1981. Real total wages (W) equal real national income (Y) times wage share (W/Y). Real hourly wages (W/N) are total real wages (W) divided by total number of labor hours (N), *BCD* (April 1981). Productivity (Y/N) is real national income (Y) divided by labor hours (N)

share rose mostly because of a decline in productivity. The decline of productivity in the contractions of the 1970s was both strong and relatively long in duration. These cyclical declines were a major reason for the long-run weakness of productivity growth.

In the 1950s and the 1960s, real hourly wages rose throughout the contractions. In the 1970s, real hourly wages were nearly constant in the first half of contraction, then actually fell in the last half of contraction. The wage share rose only because of the swift decline of productivity. All national income fell so much that workers' wages fell considerably although their percentage of national income rose. These significant declines in real hourly wages for the first time since World War II brought pain to workers' families and began to rock the political boat. In addition to the pain caused by falling real hourly wages, all these contractions also caused workers the misery of heavy unemployment.

THEORIES OF THE WAGE SHARE, WAGES, AND PRODUCTIVITY

First, the various factors affecting (according to different theories) hourly wages and labor productivity must be stated in a systematic listing. Then it may be shown which factors are most important at which phase of most cycles (or the average cycle, remembering that the average hides some significant differences).

The real hourly wage (W/N) is determined by industrial relations (or "class conflict" in

Marxist terminology) between capitalists and workers in the framework of capitalist relations of production within given economic conditions. These conditions include (1) the demand for labor, which is a function of the demand for products—and is also reflected in capacity utilization. The real hourly wage is also (2) in part a function of the supply of labor reflected in the degree of unemployment. The wage bargain is also in part a function of (3) the power of labor unions and of (4) the degree of business monopoly power, the power of business directly in the labor market, and the influence of business on the public through the media. The real wage per hour is also influenced by (5) the power and tactics of the capitalist state. This factor includes institutional structures, such as recognition of unions and enforcement of fixed labor contracts for a given period of time. Finally, (6) international events, such as wars or international shifts of economic power, affect the wage bargain.

The productivity of labor (Y/N) is affected by industrial relations (or class conflict) in a fight over speedup by the bosses versus slowdown by the workers. The conditions influencing the outcome of this struggle include (1) demand for labor, reflected in output and capacity utilization; (2) the supply of labor, reflected in the rate of unemployment; (3) strength and militancy of unions; (4) power of business monopoly; (5) actions of the capitalist stage; and (6) international conditions. These influences are similar to those on the real hourly wage. In addition, however, labor productivity is also affected by (7) technology (an important long-run factor) and by (8) the degree of optimal use of capacity and labor, which will differ at different levels of capacity utilization.

Most economists would agree that all these factors have some effect; the highly controversial issue is; Which ones should be emphasized? Some have put the strongest emphasis on the effect of higher employment or lower employment on labor's bargaining position.[13] Others have emphasized that the capitalist cannot fire some types of workers, such as bookkeepers or maintenance workers (called "overhead" workers) or other specially trained workers, even when output drops.[14] The important factors are different at different phases of the business cycles, so it is necessary to look concretely at each phase.

Early Expansion. We must explain why, in the first half of the expansion the wage share declines, or—as the *wage lag* theory accurately stresses—why hourly wages rise very slowly and productivity rises very rapidly.

First, in this period, demand for labor is rising, and unemployment is declining. This raises the real hourly wage a little. Yet the increase is so small that we must explain why it is not more because it does *not* rise in proportion to the decline in unemployment. Second, part of the answer to the slowness of growth of real wages (and decline in labor's share of income) is the fact that unemployment is still high and the memories of the previous recession are very sharp. Since wages are rising a little, employed workers are not yet militant enough to demand still higher wages (even though their share of output is falling). The psychology of

---

[13] Raford Boddy and James Crotty, "Class Conflict and Macro-Policy," *Review of Radical Political Economics* 7 (Spring 1975). Also see Andrew Glyn and B. Sutcliffe, *British Capitalism, Workers, and the Profit Squeeze* (London: Penguin Books, 1972).

[14] See Thomas Weisskopf, "Marxian Crisis Theory and the Rate of Profit in the Postwar U.S. Economy," *Cambridge Journal of Economics* 3 (December 1979), pp. 341–378. Also see Joseph Steindl, *Maturity and Stagnation in American Capitalism* (New York: Monthly Review, 1952).

workers is strongly affected by their previous experiences with unemployment as well as by the present situation. Third, wage contracts are fixed at the old levels. It takes time before the next bargaining period is reached. Until there are changes forced through bargaining, all of the increase in product automatically goes to the capitalist employer because the employer owns the product under capitalism. Fourth, prices are rising, so it is extra difficult to raise *real* wages. Fifth, the government, the media, and "public opinion" are all opposed to further wage increases when wages (and prices) are rising.

The main reason for the falling wage share is the rapid rise in productivity. First, rising productivity might be due to technological improvements. The problem with that thesis is that technology improves productivity at best at a snail's pace per year, but we are talking about large increases in productivity in a few months. So technology may be one small contributor, but *not* the main one. Second, neoclassical economists might say the use of capacity in the economy was way below the point of lowest average cost, so it is rising toward that point. Unfortunately, most real life studies find fairly constant costs (beyond a certain minimum size) over a broad range of levels of production.[15] Again, this might be a small factor, but not a major one.

Third, the hypotheses of labor hoarding and overhead labor seem to explain much of the increase in productivity. The *labor hoarding* hypothesis says that when output declines, employers do not fire skilled workers in proportion to the decline, so the employers do not need to hire skilled workers in proportion to the expansion.[16] Employers may have spent some money to train the skilled workers, and they are afraid it will be difficult to hire them back. So as long as employers think that a decline will soon be over, they keep many more skilled workers than needed, so that product per labor hour declines. In the expansion period, those same workers will be more fully utilized (and no more need to be hired for some time), so product per labor hour rises rapidly.

The *overhead labor* hypothesis is a variant of the labor hoarding process. It is not all skilled workers who are retained out of proportion, but rather those workers who constitute a necessary overhead regardless of the level of production (within broad limits). Such *overhead workers* would include maintenance workers, accountants and bookkeepers, security people, lawyers, many kinds of secretarial help, some engineers, some executives, and so forth. In the expansion, these overhead workers are already present, so they need not be hired in the early expansion. Therefore, the apparent or measured product per labor hour for the average of all workers will rise rapidly.

Late Expansion. In the last stage of expansion, the wage share has risen in all of the last six cycles. In the four mild cycles of the 1950s and the 1960s, real hourly wages continued to rise to the peak while productivity also rose, but more slowly. In the two cycles of the

---

[15] See J. S. Bain, "Price and Production Policies," *A Survey of Contemporary Economics,* ed. Howard S. Ellis (New York: McGraw-Hill, 1948), p. 140.

[16] Charles Schultze, "Short-Run Movements and Income Shares," in National Bureau of Economic Research, *The Behavior of Income Shares, Studies in Income and Wealth,* vol. 27 (Princeton, N.J.: Princeton University Press, 1964).

1970s, real hourly wages fell in the last stage before the peak, but productivity fell even more. What causes these movements?

First, the major hypothesis that seems to explain some of the rise in labor's share and slowdown of productivity is the hypothesis of the depletion of the *reserve army* of unemployed. In the later stages of expansion, unemployment (the reserve army of labor) declines, so fewer and fewer workers are competing for new jobs. Since there is less competition among workers and less fear of losing jobs, worker militancy increases—as reflected in the fact of increasing numbers of strikes. Workers are thus able to raise the labor share of income by getting higher wages and holding back speedup (i.e., limiting productivity growth).

Since what is under discussion is *real* hourly wages, it is not sufficient to determine what forces might raise nominal wages (i.e., wages expressed in current dollars). If workers are able to get higher nominal wages, why can't capitalists simply raise prices enough so that real wages remain the same? This would leave the *shares* of capitalists and workers unaffected by higher nominal wages. Of course, capitalists always wish to raise their prices. Whether they can do so or not depends on many factors.

At this point in the cycle, the most important influence is perhaps the limitation of demand by consumers, investors, and government. It was shown (in Chapter 8) that the growth of consumer demand is slowing down, partly because of the decline of the wage share in early expansion and mid-expansion. It was shown (in Chapter 9) that the growth of investment demand is slowing down, mostly because the prospects of future high profit rates are dimming, based on weakening present profit rates. Chapter 7 revealed the vast importance of government demand. In Part Six it will be shown that government policy has tended to dampen demand (including its own spending) at this point in recent cycles.

A second reason for the slowdown or decline in productivity fits the usual neoclassical theory. It is the argument that production may be rising beyond the optimal use of capacity, so it will bring diminishing returns or lower productivity. Since capacity utilization, however, has mostly stayed far below any possible optimal level, this reason seems unpersuasive.

Third, thousands of new, small, and inexperienced firms come crowding into the market at this point. Their entry undoubtedly does lower average productivity.

Early Contraction. First, in the early stages of the downturn, employment remains fairly high. Employers are hoarding skilled labor and all overhead labor. Therefore, measured productivity declines very rapidly (even though technology is *not* running backward).

Second, at the same time, fixed labor contracts prevent any rapid decline in real hourly wages. Third, the government, the media, and "public opinion" are much more sympathetic to labor's resistance to wage cuts than they were to higher wages.

In summary, the fact that wage rates decline very slowly while productivity rapidly declines explains the rising wage share.

Late Contraction. First, by late contraction, employers fire every possible worker who is not absolutely essential, even some of the skilled workers and overhead workers. Therefore, product per worker hour may finally rise again at the cycle trough.

Second, rapidly rising unemployment worsens the bargaining power of workers, lowers their militancy, and reduces the number of strikes. Therefore, real hourly wages may fall.

As a result of rising productivity and lower real wages, the wage share has declined toward the end of most contractions.

OUTPUT, CAPACITY, AND UNEMPLOYMENT

The theories reported in the preceding sections implicitly involve the level of output, the degree of capacity utilization, and the rate of unemployment among the determinants of income distribution. For example, at lower levels of output, there is less use of capacity relative to potential full capacity, so there is more labor hoarding and there are more overhead workers relative to production. These determinants are portrayed in Table 10.3 and Figure 10.5. Their long-run behavior was discussed earlier; here their cyclical behavior is examined.

Although some cycles are more severe than others, the cyclical pattern remains the same for each of these three variables in all cycles. Real national income and the degree of capacity utilization rise in every expansion (more and more slowly as the peak is approached) and fall in every contraction. Unemployment falls in every expansion (more slowly as the peak is approached) and rises rapidly in every contraction.

Capacity utilization is defined to mean the ratio of capacity actually utilized to the potential full amount of capacity available. Conceptually, capacity utilization could also be defined as actual output from capacity actually utilized (Y) to the potential output that could be produced at full capacity (Z). A good index would have to be based on a very careful

Table 10.3

OUTPUT, UNEMPLOYMENT, AND CAPACITY UTILIZATION

Change from Stage to Stage, per Month, as Percentage of Cycle Base

Stages	Expansion				Peak	Contraction		
	1–2	2–3	3–4	4–5	5–6	6–7	7–8	8–9
Real national income	0.54	0.51	0.31	0.20	−0.22	−0.60	−0.32	−0.08
Unemployment	−1.36	−1.79	−0.59	−0.19	3.28	5.18	5.18	4.55
Capacity utilization	0.63	0.49	0.09	0.01	−0.92	−1.60	−1.04	−1.20

NOTE: This table represents an average of six cycles, from 1949 through 1980, in quarterly data and in constant 1972 dollars.
SOURCES: Unemployment rate of all workers, from U.S. Department of Commerce, *Business Conditions Digest* (*BCD*) (March 1982). Capacity utilization in manufacturing from Federal Reserve Board, reported in *BCD* (August 1981). Real national income from U.S. Department of Commerce, *Survey of Current Business,* issues from 1950 to 1981.

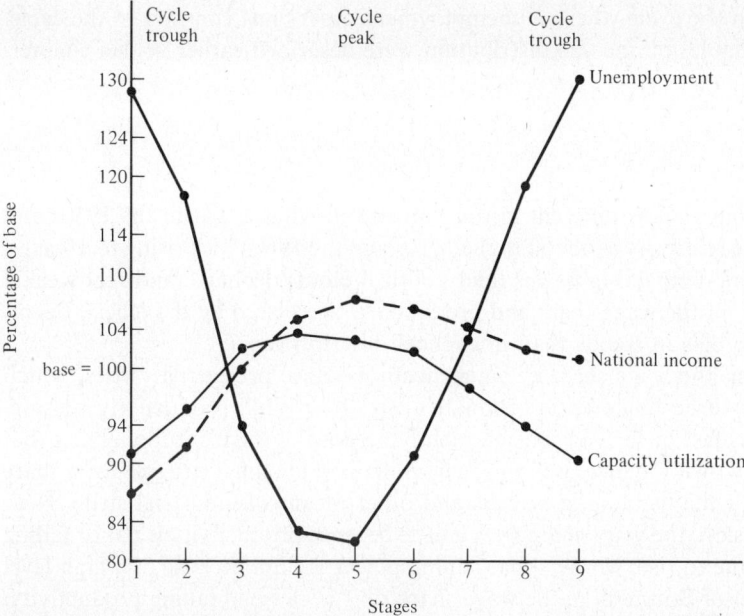

Figure 10.5 Real National Income, Unemployment, and Capacity Utilization
NOTE: This figure represents an average of six cycles, from 1949 through 1980, in quarterly data and in constant 1972 dollars, as percentage of cycle base.
SOURCES: Unemployment rate of all workers, from U.S. Department of Commerce, *Business Conditions Digest (BCD)* (March 1982). Capacity utilization in manufacturing from Federal Reserve Board, reported in *BCD* (August 1981). Real national income from U.S. Department of Commerce, *Survey of Current Business,* issues from 1950 to 1981.

estimate of what the highest possible use of capacity would be if industry operated at the point of lowest average cost. Actually, the reported ratio depends on how capitalists report Z (potential output at full capacity) or Y/Z (the ratio of output from capacity utilized to potential output at full capacity) when they report to the U.S. government in the questionnaires filed by a sample of U.S. corporations. Moreover, the index of the ratio of capacity utilization (Y/Z) for manufacturing prepared from firm reports by the Federal Reserve Board has other limitations. For example, the index omits any factories that are completely idle. Nevertheless, the Federal Reserve Board index seems to be the best available, so it is used here.

It must also be noted that the U.S. Labor Department's rate of total unemployment is seriously deficient because it leaves out "discouraged" workers and part-time employees who desire and cannot obtain full-time employment. Detailed adjustments and corrections to both of these series would greatly raise the unemployment rate, but the adjustments are complex and controversial so they are not made here.

Even with all the definitional problems, the cyclical pattern of the three variables given here is clear enough for the present purpose: real national income and capacity utilization move up and down with the cycle whereas unemployment moves just contrary to the cycle. The effects of these variables on income distribution were described earlier in this chapter.

SUMMARY

Income distribution behavior was different in the 1970s from what it was in the 1950s and the 1960s. Workers were relatively better off in the 1950s and the 1960s with rising real wages, but in the 1970s workers' bargaining power (and political clout) declined, and real weekly wages fell. All the data on the wage share and productivity are biased by the official definitions, but there is more bias in trends than in cyclical descriptions.

In most of expansion, the wage share declines mostly because productivity rises, which is mainly due to falling overhead labor proportionate to all labor. While productivity is rising, real wages do not rise as fast in early expansion mainly because of the institutional fact that capitalists automatically own the increased product while workers must struggle for a share of that increase through the bargaining process and other means of industrial strife. Near the cycle peak of expansion, the wage share rises a little because productivity is flat or falling while real wages continue to rise; workers' bargaining power is high because of a high level of employment. In most of contraction, the wage share rises because of falling productivity, owing mainly to a rising percentage of overhead labor to all labor. Finally, at the end of the contraction, the wage share begins to fall again because of the weakness of labor owing to high unemployment.

APPENDIX 10A

Regression Analysis of the Wage Share

The cyclical behavior of the wage share was investigated in the text, but regression can provide some additional information on its relations to unemployment and capacity utilization. The many weaknesses of regression analysis of time series need not be repeated here, but it must be emphasized especially here that the testing is limited to linear assumptions. Many authors would argue that these relations are nonlinear, so the results do not necessarily test some of the most important hypotheses. Much additional research needs to be done to make clearer what variables are involved and what the forms of those relationships are.

Since the behavior of these relations changed so drastically over time, only the data for 1970 to 1980 are used here. In order to look at changes, we examine how the first differences of each variable are related to each other. The three explanatory variables are real national income, the unemployment rate, and the degree of capacity utilization. Both real income and capacity utilization cannot be used in the same equation because they are not independent of each other. Therefore, real national income is used to represent all the demand factors because it reflects a greater range of economic activity than capacity utilization—and because capacity utilization is less well defined (but it may be noted that using capacity utilization rather than real income gives the same results).

For 1970 to 1980 (data from same sources as in Tables 10.1 and 10.3), using first differences of the variables, we find:

$$\Delta \frac{W_t}{Y_t} = 0.24 - \underset{(8.35)}{10.03 \Delta Y_t} - \underset{(4.00)}{0.37 \Delta U_{t-1}} \tag{10A.1}$$

$$R^2 = 0.67 \qquad DW = 1.91$$

where W is wages, Y is real national income, and U is the unemployment rate. The change in the wage share is negatively influenced by the change in real national income and negatively influenced by the change in unemployment (with a time lag). The relationships are statistically significant and "explain" 67 percent of the variance of the wage share.

In other words, the wage share tends to decline when output expands and tends to rise during contractions of output. At the same time, when unemployment is declining, after a time lag there is a tendency for the wage share to rise (as it does near the cycle peak). When unemployment rises in a contraction, there is a tendency—after a time lag—for the wage share to fall (as it does near the cycle trough). Theory says that a long time lag should be expected. In other functional forms that were tested, the strongest relation of the wage share to unemployment is with a three-quarter time lag. In conclusion, the association of the wage share with output is stronger for the early expansion and mid-expansion and for the early contraction and mid-contraction whereas the association with unemployment is stronger in late expansion and late contraction.

If capacity utilization is substituted for output, the results are just about the same (except that the overall correlation slips to $R^2 = 0.46$). There is a strongly significant negative relation of the wage share to capacity utilization ($T = 5.31$) with no time lag. When capacity utilization is rising rapidly in early expansion and mid-expansion, the wage share falls. When capacity utilization is falling rapidly in early contraction and mid-contraction, the wage share rises.

DETERMINANTS OF HOURLY WAGES

These three determinants of the wage share—output, capacity utilization, and unemployment—may affect either of the components of the wage share: hourly wages or productivity. When these relations of the three explanatory variables with hourly wages were tested—in every possible combination, in many functional forms, and with every possible time lag—*no* statistically significant association of real hourly wages with real national income, with capacity utilization, or with the unemployment rate was found during the 1950s, the 1960s, or the 1970s (or over the whole period).

In the 1950s and the 1960s, the real hourly wage generally had a slightly negative relation (*not* statistically significant) to real national income and capacity utilization. This was because, in the relatively mild recessions of those years, the real hourly wage rose slightly whereas, of course, income and capacity utilization fell. In the 1970s, the real hourly wage had a slightly positive relation (*not* statistically significant) to national income and capacity utilization because hourly wages tended to rise a little in business expansions and fall a little in business contractions. The hourly wage had very little consistent relation with unemployment, even with a time lag.

These results indicate that the explanatory variables did *not* affect the wage share through the hourly wage rate, but rather through their effects on productivity. The labor hoarding and overhead labor theories discuss only productivity, so they are strengthened by this result. The unemployment hypothesis (or reserve army theory), however, sometimes paints a picture in which lower unemployment causes higher wage rates and higher unemployment causes lower wage rates. This causal relation does not appear significant in these data though it has an appeal in theory. The effect of the reserve army of unemployed must operate through labor productivity, which is more difficult to explain.

DETERMINANTS OF PRODUCTIVITY

For the period of 1970 through 1980 (data from the same sources as in Tables 10.1 and 10.3), using first differences of the variables, we find:

$$\Delta \frac{Y_t}{N_t} = -0.15 + \underset{(9.78)}{0.04 \Delta Y_t} + \underset{(4.62)}{0.42 \Delta U_{t-1}} \qquad (10A.2)$$

$$R^2 = 0.73 \qquad DW = 2.02$$

where Y is real national income, N is number of labor hours, and U is the unemployment rate. There is a strong, positive, and significant relation of the change in labor productivity to the change in real output and the change in unemployment (with a time lag). The variances of the explanatory variables together "explain" almost three-fourths of the variance in productivity.

If capacity utilization is substituted for real national income, then it also shows a strongly positive and statistically significant ($T = 5.65$) relation to labor productivity. The overall correlation for the equation, however, is less than with real income (R^2 drops to 0.49).

In other words, when real national income and capacity utilization are rising in early expansion and mid-expansion, labor productivity rises rapidly (because, for one thing, overhead workers are more fully utilized). With a considerable time lag, falling unemployment slows down the growth in labor productivity toward the cycle peak (because the approach to full employment gives workers more bargaining power, which they use to resist speedup).

When real national income and capacity utilization fall in early contraction and mid-contraction, there is a rapid fall in labor productivity (because, for one thing, the proportion of overhead workers to output must rise). With a considerable time lag near the end of contraction, the rising unemployment rate deprives workers of the power to resist, so labor productivity stops falling (and may actually rise).

Having reached these conclusions, we must reemphasize that regression does not say anything about cause and effect. Moreover, equations 10A.1 and 10A.2 have some specific limitations and weaknesses. The time lag for the unemployment effect is not easily fixed. For different time periods, the time lag varied from one to three quarters; there is no theory that says it must be constant over time in different cycles or even within one cycle. Second, the form of these relationships is more likely nonlinear rather than the simple linear form shown here. Third, the wage share is not only influenced by output, unemployment, and capacity utilization; the wage share also influences these variables. Thus, a more complete test would have to be based on a set of simultaneous equations in one model.

Chapter 11

THE RATE OF PROFIT

The rate of profit is the key to business activity because the current and past rate of profit influences business expectations and investment. The rate of profit, in turn, is affected by almost everything else in the capitalist system.

Let total *profits* be defined by the symbol Π. The *rate of profit* is defined here as the ratio of profit (Π) to capital (K), so the rate of profit is Π/K. One way of analyzing the behavior of rate of profit is to analyze its components. Define Y as national income. By definition the rate of profit may be written as the profit share of income (Π/Y) times the ratio of output to capital (Y/K):

$$\frac{\Pi}{K} = \frac{\Pi}{Y} \cdot \frac{Y}{K} \qquad (11.1)$$

Some theories concentrate on the profit share; others, on the output to capital ratio.

In looking at actual business activity, we must recognize that actual output (Y) hardly ever equals the potential output (Z), which might be produced at full utilization of capacity. The ratio between actual output and potential full-capacity output is defined to be the "capacity utilization ratio" or Y/Z. If we include this factor, the rate of profit may be written as the profit share (Π/Y) times the capacity utilization ratio (Y/Z) times the ratio of potential full-capacity output to capital (Z/K):

$$\frac{\Pi}{K} = \frac{\Pi}{Y} \cdot \frac{Y}{Z} \cdot \frac{Z}{K} \qquad (11.2)$$

This is true by definition, but provides the basic framework used here. These three components of the profit rate—the profit share, the capacity utilization ratio, and the potential output-capital ratio—each represent the factors stressed by one group of economists.[1]

---

[1] This insight comes from an excellent article by Thomas Weisskopf, "Marxian Crisis Theory and the Rate of Profit in the Postwar U.S. Economy," *Cambridge Journal of Economics* 3 (December 1979), pp. 341–378.

One group of theories (e.g. the reserve army theory) stresses the influence of the profit share. Toward the end of expansion, a high level of employment causes rising wages, which reduces the profit share. Toward the end of contraction, a large amount of unemployment causes falling wages, which restores the profit share.[2] In Chapter 10, it was shown how the profit share is also influenced by the degree of labor hoarding, by the degree of utilization or underutilization of overhead labor, by fixed wage contracts, by labor laws, and by every other factor affecting the power of labor versus capital.

Second, some explanations of profit rate behavior (e.g. any demand-oriented theory) stress the influence of capacity utilization. When less capacity is utilized, it means—in this view—that there is insufficient demand for products at present prices.[3] The limits of demand are set by the level and distribution of income under capitalism. When less capacity is utilized, capitalists obviously make less profit per unit of capital invested in the capacity to produce. Lower use of capacity also means less full use of overhead labor. On the revenue side, lower use of capacity means less ability of capitalists to raise prices; they must hold down prices or even reduce prices to sell their goods. In a recovery, increasing demand leads to higher capacity utilization, which raises the rate of profit.

Third, some theorists emphasize the potential, full-capacity output-capital ratio. They argue that, if there is rapid growth approaching full use of capacity, then the ratio of output produced to capital utilized may be reduced by shortages, bottlenecks, disproportions, and inefficient operations.[4] A lower ratio of output to capital (at a given level of capital utilization and a given profit share of output) must mean less output per unit of capital. If, on the other hand, growth is slowed or there is actual decline, then there are plenty of raw materials, skilled labor, and so forth, so a given unit of capital has the potential to produce more.

To evaluate these theories, we must see what actually happens to the profit rate and to each of the three components. Then the component threads can be woven together into a unified theory.

BEHAVIOR OF THE PROFIT RATE AND THE PROFIT SHARE

The profit rate on capital (Π/K) and the profit share of national income (Π/Y) are described in Table 11.1 and Figure 11.1.

In the average of the four cycles from 1949 to 1970, the profit rate on capital rose rapidly in the first half of expansion, declined in the last half of expansion, declined very rapidly in the first half of contraction, and declined less rapidly toward the end of contraction. In the average expansion of the two cycles of 1970 to 1980, the rate of profit on capital rose rapidly at first, then more slowly, then declined a little before the peak—setting the stage for a recession. In the average contraction of these two cycles, the rate of profit declined very

---

[2] See R. Boddy and J. Crotty, "Class Conflicts and Macropolicy," *Review of Radical Political Economics* 7 (Spring 1975), pp. 1–17.
[3] See Paul Sweezy, *Theory of Capitalist Development* (New York: Monthly Review, 1958). Also see Paul Baran and Paul Sweezy, *Monopoly Capital* (New York: Monthly Review, 1966).
[4] See Weisskopf, *op. cit.*, p. 341.

Table 11.1

THE PROFIT RATE ON CAPITAL (Π/K)

CHANGE FROM STAGE TO STAGE, PER MONTH, AS A PERCENTAGE OF CYCLE BASE

	Expansion				Peak	Contraction		
Stages	1–2	2–3	3–4	4–5	5–6	6–7	7–8	8–9
Average of four cycles (1949–1970)	0.85	0.25	−0.44	−0.41	−1.24	−0.84	−0.75	−0.08
Average of two cycles (1970–1980)	0.64	0.36	0.28	−0.38	−0.98	−2.09	−1.89	0.76

SOURCES: *Profit* equals national income − wages. National income in constant dollars from U.S. Department of Commerce, *Survey of Current Business* (1949–1980). Wages equals national income times ratio of employee compensation to national income, from U.S. Department of Commerce, *Business Conditions Digest* (*BCD*) (April 1981). Capital in 1949 is producers' equipment plus nonresidential structures, from U.S. Department of Labor, *Capital Stock Estimates for Input-Output Industries* (1979), Bulletin 2034, p. 29. Capital after 1949 is cumulative amount of net investment. Net investment is nonresidential, gross, private, domestic investment in constant dollars, from *BCD* (April 1981), minus depreciation of same from *Survey of Current Business* (1949–1980).

rapidly for most of the contraction, then rose before the trough—setting the stage for recovery.

This behavior of the profit rate is explained in the next few sections on the basis of the behavior of its three components. But it is necessary here to warn the reader about the biases in the data. In the previous chapter, the many biases in official estimates of *profits,* defined here as all nonwage income, were discussed in detail. The biases in the official definition of profits reduce its apparent long-run growth trend for the reasons detailed in the last chapter.

Measurement of capital is even more ambiguous and biased. Since it is a heterogeneous collection of machines and structures, there is a huge and controversial literature over the meaning of any measure of it. Here the official data on its dollar value were used, as deflated by the government. Whenever there is such rapid inflation as occurred in part of this period, it is well to be skeptical about the results of deflating any data, particularly an aggregation as complex as this one. All the measures of real capital for this period show it rising; there is great controversy over how fast it rises, even among those who agree that this aggregate has a meaning.

Since *capital* always rose in this period whereas *profits* had a downward bias, there is a downward bias in the trend of profit rates. Even with a downward bias, there is no falling trend to the official rate of profit in this period. For five-year averages, the rate of profit on stockholders' equity (capital minus liabilities) for all U.S. manufacturing corporations *after taxes* was 11.6 percent (1950–1954), 11.0 percent (1955–1959), 10.0 percent (1960–1964), 12.6 percent (1965–1969), 11.5 percent (1970–1974), and 14.2 percent (1975–1980).[5]

Over a longer period of time, the lack of a trend is even more apparent though it always

---

[5] See Council of Economic Advisors, *Economic Report of the President* (Washington, D. C.: Government Printing Office, 1982), p. 331.

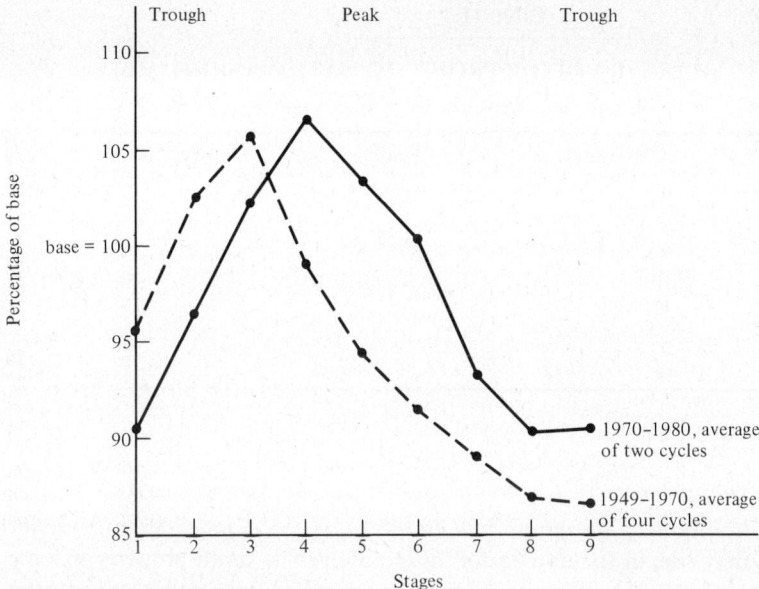

Figure 11.1 The Rate of Profit

NOTE: This figure represents an average of four cycles (1949–1970) and of two cycles (1970–1980), in quarterly data and as a percentage of cycle base.

SOURCES: *Profit* equals national income minus wages. National income in constant dollars from U.S. Department of Commerce, *Survey of Current Business* (1949–1980). Wages equal national income times ratio of employee compensation to national income, from U.S. Department of Commerce, *Business Conditions Digest (BCD)* (April 1981). Capital in 1949 is producers' equipment plus nonresidential structures, from U.S. Department of Labor, *Capital Stock Estimates for Input-Output Industries* (1979), Bulletin 2034, p. 29. Capital after 1949 is cumulative amount of net investment. Net investment is nonresidential, gross, private, domestic investment in constant dollars, from *BCD* (April 1981), minus depreciation of same from *Survey of Current Business* (1949–1980).

depends at what date it begins or ends. If we use averages over whole cycles (so as to avoid beginning or ending at a peak or trough), the profit rate on stockholders' equity in all U.S. manufacturing corporations *before taxes* was just 3.8 percent in the cycle covering part of the Great Depression (1933–1938). The same profit rate jumped to 16.2 percent in the profitable years of the Second World War (1938–1945). It rose to 17.8 percent in the prosperous recovery from war, when there was a huge demand (1945–1949). It jumped again to 24.3 percent in the Korean War (1949–1954), then began to fall as military demand slackened to 21.0 percent in the cycle 1954–1958 and to 17.3 percent in the cycle 1958–1961. Then, with the impact of the Vietnam War, the profit rate before taxes rose to 19.3 percent (1961–1970 average).[6]

As explained earlier, the long-run trends are affected by various biases. Yet the major rises (in wars) and declines (in the Great Depression) are reflected by all measures of profit rates.

---

[6]See U.S. Internal Revenue Service, *Statistics of Income, Corporate Income Tax Returns* (Washington, D. C.: Government Printing Office, 1935–1975).

Table 11.2

THE PROFIT SHARE (RATIO OF PROFIT TO NATIONAL INCOME)

Change from Stage to Stage, per Month, as a Percentage of Cycle Base

	Expansion				Peak	Contraction		
Stages	1–2	2–3	3–4	4–5	5–6	6–7	7–8	8–9
Average of four cycles, 1949–1970	0.43	−0.01	−0.35	−0.31	−0.70	−0.30	−0.15	0.16
Average of two cycles, 1970–1980	0.50	0.13	0.12	−0.18	−0.66	−1.22	−1.02	0.12

SOURCE: Profit share (Π/Y) equals 1 minus wage share (W/Y). Wage share from U.S. Department of Commerce, *Business Conditions Digest* (April 1981).

Moreover, *the cyclical pattern of the profit rate is the same for a wide range of definitions*.[7] The economist may use, in the numerator, corporate profits or all property income, before taxes or after taxes, manufacturing or total profits, various adjustments for inventories, depreciation, or inflation. In the denominator, *capital* may be measured as equity or total assets and with many kinds of adjustments. On any of these definitions, profit rates rise rapidly in early expansion, slow or fall before the peak, fall rapidly in early contraction, and slow or rise before the trough.

The Profit Share

Profits are defined here as all nonwage national income, so profits equal national income minus wages:

$$\Pi = Y - W \qquad (11.3)$$

Therefore, the profit share (Π/Y) must equal 1 minus the wage share:

$$\frac{\Pi}{Y} = 1 - \frac{W}{Y} \qquad (11.4)$$

Since the wage share was explored in great detail in the preceding chapter, the profit share has been explained because it is determined by the same factors.

The behavior of the profit share is shown in Table 11.2 and Figure 11.2. Note that the biases in the data were covered in detail in the previous chapter in discussing the wage share, so these biases need not be repeated here.

There is a striking difference in the expansions of the two periods. In the average expansion of the four cycles (1949–1970), the profit share turned down even before mid-expansion. In

---

[7] See Howard Sherman, *Profits in the United States* (Ithaca: Cornell University Press, 1968).

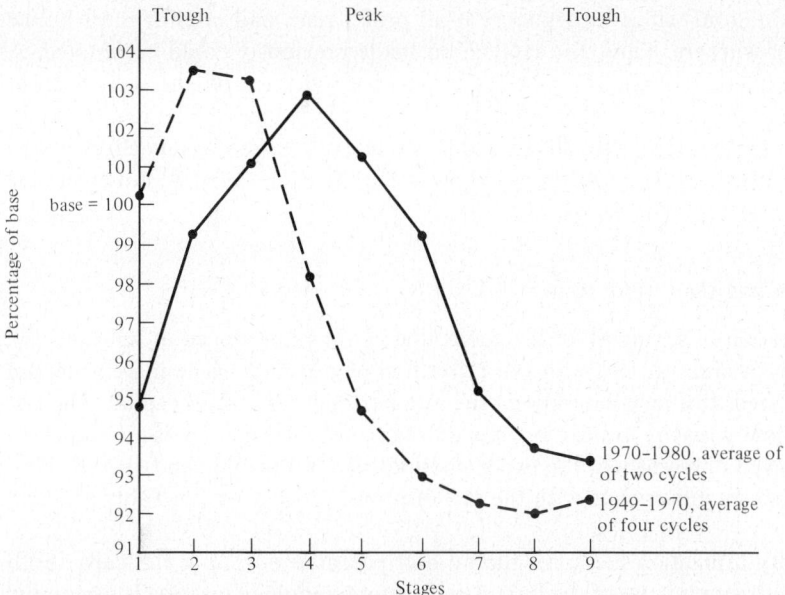

Figure 11.2 The Profit Share (Ratio of Profit to National Income)
NOTE: This figure represents an average of four cycles (1949–1970) and of two cycles (1970–1980), in quarterly data and as a percentage of cycle base.
SOURCE: Profit share (Π/Y) equals 1 minus wage share (W/Y). Wage share from U.S. Department of Commerce, *Business Conditions Digest* (April 1981).

the average expansion of the two cycles (1970–1980), the profit share rose till just before the peak. In the average contraction of both periods, the profit share fell most of the time, then rose just before the trough.

This distinctive behavior of the profit share (Π/Y) is very similar to that of the profit rate (Π/K). Both ratios turn down before the peak by a much longer time lead in the 1950s and the 1960s than in the 1970s. Both ratios stop falling much or even rise in the last stage of contraction, heralding the recovery. The milder cycles of the 1950s and the 1960s witnessed an early decline of the profit share and the profit rate, but the pace of decline was slow even in contraction. The stronger cycles of the 1970s were marked by a longer and more rapid rise of profit rate and profit share in expansions (contrary to some myths), followed by more rapid declines. Since profits fluctuate more than income or capital, these two ratios must always move in the same direction most of the time.

Does this mean that changes in the profit share of income are the main cause of changes in profit rates on capital? Certainly, if the profit share of output declines, there must be a negative influence on the rate of profit. If the profit share rises, there must be a positive influence on the rate of profit.

Since profit is defined here as all nonwage income, the ratio of profit to wages must also move in the same direction as the ratio of profit to income. The ratio of profit (here defined as all profit, rent, and interest) to wages (here defined as all labor income) is very similar to

Marx's rate of exploitation—since he argues that all profit, rent, and interest must be the result of the labor of workers. Thus, the same point made previously could be restated. A fall in the rate of exploitation (Π/W) must be a negative influence on the rate of profit whereas a rise in the rate of exploitation must be a positive influence on the rate of profit.

There is no question that the profit share or the rate of exploitation has an effect on the profit rate. Before reaching any conclusions as to how much effect, however, we must examine the other two components of the profit rate.

Capacity Utilization and the Profit Rate

If there is no expectation of selling all of the goods that could be produced at full capacity, then a capitalist will produce at less than full utilization of capacity. Since there is capital that is not being utilized, this naturally lowers the rate of profit per unit of capital. The last chapter discussed how capacity utilization moved over the cycle, but it is necessary to examine how it behaved differently in the two subperiods of 1949 to 1970 and 1970 to 1980 —and also to compare its movements with the rate of profit. This is done in Table 11.3 and Figure 11.3.

In theory, capacity utilization measures the ratio of potential output at full-capacity to actual output; it is a direct measure of the lack of perfect functioning of a capitalist economy. The practical problems of measurement are many, but they were discussed in the previous chapter, so need not be repeated here.

In the 1949–1970 period, in the average business expansion, the use of capacity rises very rapidly at first—exactly as the rate of profit rises. In the second half of business expansion, the use of capacity is almost constant whereas the rate of profit is falling. Thus, lack of capacity utilization limits the rate of profit, but it cannot cause the actual decline of the profit rate. If the profit share is declining, however, the constant capacity utilization—reflecting a fairly constant demand—does explain why prices are limited and cannot be raised to offset any wage increases. In the business contraction, the ratio of capacity utilization declines all

Table 11.3

CAPACITY UTILIZATION

Change from Stage to Stage, Per month, As Percentage of Cycle Base

Stages	Expansion				Peak	Contraction		
	1–2	2–3	3–4	4–5	5–6	6–7	7–8	8–9
Average of four cycles, 1949–1970	0.85	0.53	−0.04	0.04	−1.54	−1.21	−1.30	−0.69
Average of two cycles, 1970–1980	0.20	0.40	0.39	−0.06	−0.40	−1.39	−1.53	−2.22

SOURCE: Capacity utilization for manufacturing (FRB), U.S. Department of Commerce, *Business Conditions Digest* (August 1981).

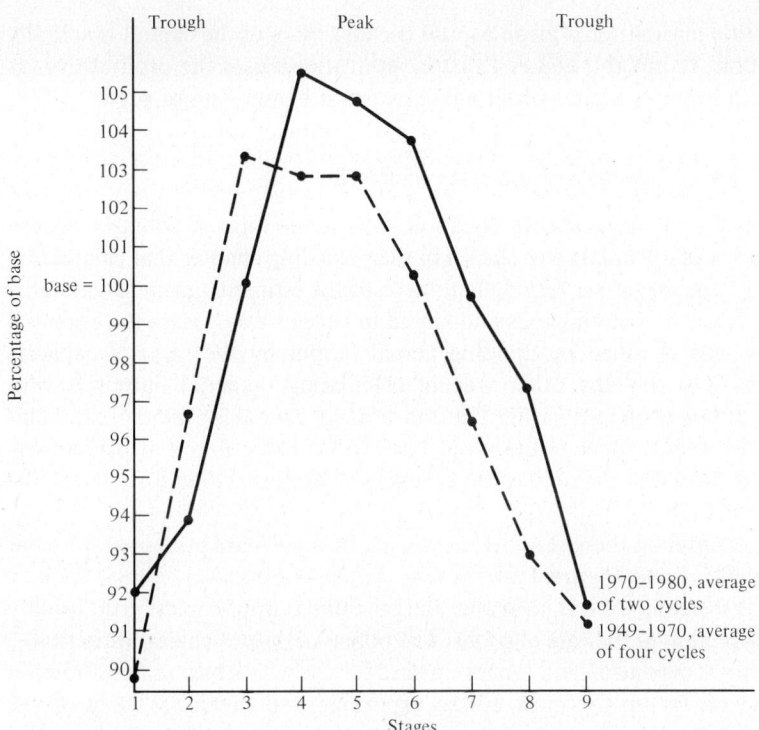

Figure 11.3 Capacity Utilization (Ratio of Actual to Potential Output)
NOTE: This figure represents an average of four cycles (1949–1970) and of two cycles (1970–1980), in quarterly data and in constant 1972 dollars, as a percentage of cycle base.
SOURCE: Capacity utilization for manufacturing (FRB), U.S. Department of Commerce, *Business Conditions Digest* (August 1981).

the time. It may thus be a major explanation of the decline of the rate of profit in the contraction—except that the rate of profit does turn up again just before the trough whereas capacity utilization does not (though it slows its decline).

In the 1970–1980 period, the difference is that capacity utilization continues a sharp rise for over three-quarters of the expansion—but so does the rate of profit in this period. Capacity utilization again declines very rapidly for the whole business contraction, whereas the rate of profit again declines for most of the contraction, but rises just before the trough. That rise in the profit rate at the end of contraction, therefore, might be accounted for by the rise in the profit share (or fall in the wage share) but *not* by the continued decline in capacity utilization.

Since higher demand causes more use of capacity, there is a relation between capacity utilization and real national income. The data indicate that capacity utilization does rise rapidly in the early stages of output expansion, but it then reaches a plateau and is steady or slightly declining while output and income are still slowly rising. The relationship, therefore, appears to be nonlinear. In Appendix 11A, regression analysis does indicate a significant, but nonlinear relation between capacity utilization and national income or output.

In turn, capacity utilization affects the rate of profit in two ways. Higher capacity utilization directly raises the rate of profit on a given capital because more of the capital is actually being used for production. Indirectly, higher capacity utilization raises the profit share (as seen in the last chapter), and the higher profit share causes a higher rate of profit.

Ratio of Potential Output to Capital and the Rate of Profit

The third component of the rate of profit (in equation 11.2) is the ratio of potential output at full capacity to the stock of capital. It was shown in the preceding chapter that calculating potential output at full employment is a very difficult task, so the estimates given by capitalist entrepreneurs of their capacity are ambiguous and biased in various ways. Here the potential output at full capacity was obtained by dividing actual output by the ratio of capacity utilization. Neither this way nor any other way of calculating potential output is very satisfactory. Moreover, it was explained earlier that the stock of capital is even more difficult to measure and that its meaning is open to question. The ratio of two dubious measurements to each other—potential output to capital—must be taken with great skepticism and is the weakest indicator used here.

For completeness in examining these theories, however, the results are presented for what they are worth in Table 11.4 and Figure 11.4.

Assuming this data is meaningful, it is clear that the potential output-capital ratio usually moves in the opposite direction to the rate of profit. The potential output-capital ratio moves down for the whole business expansion and moves upward for the whole business contraction whereas the profit rate moves up for most of the expansion and down for most of the contraction. Thus, it cannot explain most of the movements of the rate of profit though it

Table 11.4

RATIO OF POTENTIAL OUTPUT TO CAPITAL (Z/K)

CHANGE FROM STAGE TO STAGE, PER MONTH, AS PERCENTAGE OF CYCLE BASE

	Expansion				Peak	Contraction		
Stages	1–2	2–3	3–4	4–5	5–6	6–7	7–8	8–9
Average of four cycles, 1949–1970	−0.48	−0.28	−0.03	−0.15	0.55	0.60	0.72	0.49
Average of two cycles, 1970–1980	−0.33	−0.25	−0.10	−0.14	0.39	0.73	0.53	0.97

SOURCES: Capital in 1949 is producers' equipment plus nonresidential structures, from U.S. Department of Labor, *Capital Stock Estimates for Input-Output Industries* (1979), Bulletin 2034, p. 29. Capital after 1949 is cumulative amount of net investment. Net investment is nonresidential, gross, private, domestic investment in constant dollars, from *Business Conditions Digest* (*BCD*) (April 1981), minus depreciation of same from *Survey of Current Business* (1949–1980). Potential output (Z) equals output (Y) divided by capacity utilization (Y/Z). Output is real national income in constant dollars from U.S. Department of Commerce, *Survey of Current Business* (1949–1980). Wages equal national income times ratio of employee compensation to national income, from U.S. Department of Commerce, *BCD* (April 1981). Capacity utilization for manufacturing (FRB), from U.S. Department of Commerce, *BCD* (August 1981).

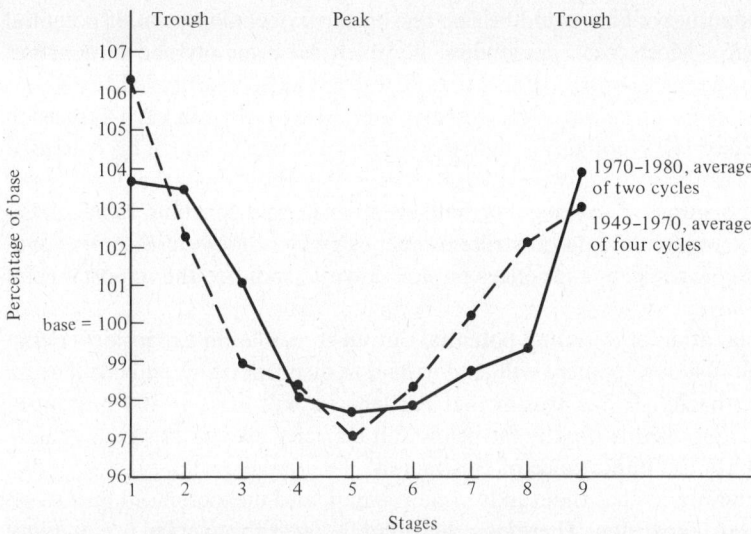

Figure 11.4 Ratio of Potential Output to Capital
NOTE: This figure represents an average of four cycles (1949–1970) and of two cycles (1970–1980), in quarterly data and in constant 1972 dollars, as a percentage of cycle base.
SOURCES: Capital in 1949 is producers' equipment plus nonresidential structures, from U.S. Department of Labor, *Capital Stock Estimates for Input-Output Industries* (1979), Bulletin 2034, p. 29. Capital after 1949 is cumulative amount of net investment. Net investment is nonresidential, gross, private, domestic investment in constant dollars, from *Business Conditions Digest (BCD)* (April 1981), minus depreciation of same from *Survey of Current Business* (1949–1980). Potential output *(Z)* equals output *(Y)* divided by capacity utilization *(Y/Z)*. Output is real national income in constant dollars from U.S. Department of Commerce, *Survey of Current Business* (1949–1980). Wages equal national income times ratio of employee compensation to national income, from U.S. Department of Commerce, *BCD* (April 1981). Capacity utilization for manufacturing (FRB), from U.S. Department of Commerce, *BCD* (August 1981).

could explain why the profit rate doesn't move still more rapidly in the opposite direction. Only just before the peak does it decline while the profit rate is declining; only just before the trough does it rise while the profit rate is rising—so the potential output-capital ratio *may* have some explanatory power at those points.

Still assuming that this data is meaningful, it is necessary to ask, *Why* does this ratio move down in business expansions and up in business contractions? Since most economists would think of this ratio as being technologically determined according to the given productivity of capital, many economists would say that it cannot change in the short run, but only moves in the long run in response to technological changes. Certainly, any theory that relies on long-run technological changes to affect the rate of profit could *not* operate through this variable in the short run.

Many economists, however, have given reasons why this ratio might vary in the short run, reasons not involving long-run technological change.

First, when capacity utilization rises higher and higher in the expansion, the usual neoclassical argument may apply that the marginal output per unit of capital declines because of declining marginal productivity. This could be one reason for a declining ratio of potential output (Z) to capital (K). Most empirical studies, however, have merely shown constant returns in the short run beyond some point, so this factor has not been proved.[8]

A second possible explanation of declining potential output to capital in each expansion holds that there is increased labor militancy when there is less unemployment. This increased labor militancy may lower the productivity of labor, which may then lower the product per unit of capital (since the argument here does *not* hold all other factors constant, as neoclassical economics does). There is only data on strike frequency (which does increase in expansions), but little or none on restrictive practices or slowdown to indicate the importance of this factor.

A third possible explanation of declining potential output to capital in expansions is that unplanned, chaotic capitalist development will tend to lead to disproportions and bottlenecks at such high levels of capacity. It is a truism that bottlenecks will exist at 100 percent of capacity or above, but capitalism is usually far below full capacity even at the peak. Therefore, it is hard to estimate the importance of this factor.

A fourth argument maintains that thousands of new, small, and inexperienced businesses enter the market in the late expansion. Therefore, they tend to lower the average productivity of capital, as reflected in a falling ratio of potential output to capital. In the ensuing depression, the small firms go bankrupt, thereby helping to restore productivity of capital. When their capital is bought up by the large capitalists at very low prices, the ratio of potential output per dollar of expenditure on capital will increase.

Both the theoretical arguments to this point and the empirical results above are limited to *real* potential output and *real* potential capital. Many theories of the business cycle, such as Kalecki's theory,[9] have also paid much attention to the relations between the price of final output and the price of capital goods, including costs of raw materials. Prices of capital goods and raw materials do usually fluctuate more rapidly than final output prices over the cycle.

Before we look at recent price movements (which are distorted by inflation), it is useful to glance briefly at the historical data. A study by Frederick Mills provides data on prices of 22 consumer goods, prices of 48 producers' goods (excluding raw materials), and prices of 32 raw materials.[10] Each of the price series presents a cyclical, NBER-type pattern averaged over many business cycles (from 3 to 20 cycles), all ending in 1938. He found the price of consumer goods rising in the average expansion by 12 percent (as a percentage of the cycle base) and falling by 18 points in the average contraction. The prices of raw materials rose much faster and fell much faster, rising 23 percent in the average expansion and falling 26 percent in the average contraction. The behavior of other producers' goods prices, that is, prices of plant and equipment, was somewhere between, rising 21 percent and falling 25 percent.

---

[8] See Joe S. Bain, "Price and Production Policies," *A Survey of Contemporary Economics,* edited by Howard Ellis (New York: McGraw-Hill, 1948), p. 140.

[9] See Michael Kalecki, *Theory of Economic Dynamics* (New York: Monthly Review, 1954).

[10] Frederick C. Mills, *Price-Quantity Interactions in Business Cycles* (New York: National Bureau of Economic Research, 1948). For detailed evidence on one industry, see Ruth Mack, *Consumption and Business Fluctuations, A Case Study of the Shoe, Leather, Hide Sequence* (New York: National Bureau of Economic Research, 1956).

The main explanation for this price behavior by most writers is a combination of accelerated demand with limited supply in expansions—and vice versa in contractions. In the accelerator theory, the demand for producers' goods (including raw materials) is derived—not from the *level* of demand for aggregate goods and services—but from the *change* in the demand for goods and services. So when there is a rapid rate of growth of demand for consumer goods and services in mid-expansion, the demand for producers' goods (including raw materials) rises far more rapidly. Similarly, when the demand for all goods and services is declining in the contraction, the demand for producers' goods (including raw materials) falls even more rapidly.

At the same time, the supply of raw materials is much harder to expand than finished goods. Increasing the production of shoes and clothing can be done far more quickly than finding and opening a new mine or a new oil well. Moreover, supplies of raw materials from agriculture also have a long time lag because it takes years to increase the number of cows and at least a whole growing season for a new crop. As a result, in each expansion the quantity of output of raw materials rises more slowly than that of finished goods whereas raw materials prices rise faster than the prices of finished goods. The opposite happened in most contractions, when raw material supply declined more slowly than total output, but prices of raw materials declined more rapidly than prices of finished goods.

In recent cycles, of course, prices of most goods have not fallen at all. Nevertheless, the overall cyclical pattern has remained somewhat similar in many respects. In the five cycles of 1949 through 1975, the average price of finished goods rose, not only in every expansion, but also in every contraction. Yet the price of raw materials rose only in expansions while falling in every contraction! The fall in the 1974–1975 contraction is particularly notable because all other prices rose so rapidly and because the average raw materials price includes the price of oil (which, of course, rose very rapidly). As a result, in every contraction of these five cycles there was a dramatic rise in the ratio of all finished goods prices to all raw material prices.

Since all categories of prices rose in the expansions, the ratio of finished goods to raw material prices provides a muddier picture. In two of the expansions (1949–1953 and 1970–1973), the classic pattern was followed: the ratio of finished goods prices to raw materials prices fell in the expansions (and rose in the contractions). But from 1953 to 1970, there was an unusual, long-run rise of the ratio of finished goods prices to raw materials prices in both expansions and contractions (perhaps owing to a growth in the market power of the industrialized countries versus the Third World raw materials producers). Except for that period, the typical cyclical pattern is that the ratio of finished goods prices to raw materials prices falls throughout the expansion and rises during the contraction. This change would hurt the profit rates of all U.S. capitalists except raw materials producers during the expansion while helping the profit rates of all U.S. capitalists except raw materials producers during contractions.

Of course, if we examine only the domestic economy, any losses by capitalists producing finished goods because of the rising prices of raw materials must also lead to new profits for the capitalists producing raw materials, so aggregate profits would remain the same. To show some effect on overall expectations of profitability from these changing price-cost relationships would require a disaggregated sectoral model, which is far beyond what is attempted here (but Hayek's similar model is discussed in Part Three).[11]

If, on the other hand, raw materials are imported from abroad, *as most are,* then a rise in their price relative to the price of finished goods will lower aggregate U.S. profits. If major producers' goods—such as oil—are imported from abroad, there will be obvious effects on domestic profitability if price-cost ratios change. This important effect can only be noted here; it is discussed in terms of international relations in Part Five.

All these theories indicate that rising capacity utilization (or other factors associated with it) may pull down the potential output-capital ratio. Lower capacity utilization may raise that ratio. The relation between the potential output-capital ratio and the degree of capacity utilization does seem to be confirmed in the regression analysis in Appendix 9A. On the other hand, given the extreme problems of defining and measuring this concept, one should not put much trust in the results.

Tentative Conclusions on the Three Components

The results here support those in the pioneering study by Thomas Weisskopf.[12] He found that the rapid rise of profit rates in the early expansion and mid-expansion is mainly due to the rising demand for output, reflected in a rising degree of capacity utilization.

Furthermore, both the data presented here and Weisskopf's study indicate that the strongest factor causing the downturn in profit rates throughout the contraction is the falling ratio of capacity utilization. It declines rapidly throughout every stage of the average recession of the 1950s, the 1960s, and the 1970s. The behavior of capacity utilization closely mirrors the behavior of demand over the cycle, so it reflects the limitations on the capitalist's ability to realize the profits that have been exploited from workers.

The second component of the profit rate, as defined in equation 11.2, is the share of profit in output or income. Both Weisskopf's data and the data used here disclose that in the early and mid-business expansion, the slowly rising profit share is not as important an influence as the rapidly rising degree of capacity utilization. Near the peak, however, Weisskopf found —as shown here—that the main depressing influence on profit *is* probably the decline in the profit share. The profit share decline reflects, he says, the problems of production of profits because wage rates rise (owing to high employment) faster than productivity.

Similarly, in the early contraction and mid-contraction, the decline of the profit share does not appear as important a depressant as the rapidly falling degree of capacity utilization. Moreover, as shown in the last chapter, the rise of the profit share in early expansion and mid-expansion and the fall of it in early contraction and mid-contraction certainly does *not* seem to be affected by unemployment because unemployment is moving in the wrong direction. The theory says that falling unemployment in an expansion should strengthen labor, so higher wages would cause a falling profit share—but the profit share *rises* in early expansion and mid-expansion. The theory says that rising unemployment in a business contraction should weaken labor, so lower wages would cause a rising profit share—but the

---

[11]See Frederick Hayek, *Profits, Interest, and Investment* (London: George Routledge, 1939).
[12]Weisskopf, *op. cit.,* pp. 341–378.

profit share *falls* in early contraction and mid-contraction. Two tentative conclusions are these: (1) capacity utilization and demand are a more important influence on the profit rate than the profit share or wage share for most of the expansion and most of the contraction, and (2) the present level of unemployment is not the most important influence on the profit and wage shares in most of the cycle. (The level of unemployment is obviously a function of output, as shown in Appendix 11A.)

On the other hand, it must be emphasized that (1) at the end of expansion before the peak, the declining profit share is the main depressing influence on the profit rate, and (2) the very low level of unemployment near the peak (and/or previously falling unemployment with a time lag) is the main reason for wages rising faster than productivity, leading to a falling profit share. Furthermore, both Weisskopf's data and the data used here indicate that (3) at the end of contraction before the trough, the rising profit share is the most important factor helping the profit rate to recover and that (4) the very high level of unemployment near the trough (and/or previously rising unemployment with a time lag) is the main reason for wages falling faster than productivity, leading to a rising profit share.

Finally, the third component of the profit rate is the potential ratio of output to capital. Weisskopf found—as shown here—that the potential output-capital ratio moved contrary to the rate of profit in most of expansion and most of contraction, so could only be a constraint at most. It does move the same way as the profit rate just before the peak and the trough, but Weisskopf finds that its rather weak movements make it a minor explanatory factor at best. Since its measurement is also very dubious—and the theories about its effects are very controversial—this variable is ignored in the summary explanation of profit rate movements given later.

Before we summarize, however, there are (in addition to the weaknesses of the data) three warnings that must be taken very seriously in interpreting the preceding picture. The warnings concern (1) the problem of cause and effect, (2) the facts of time lags, and (3) the facts of different behaviors in different cycles.

First, the fact that two things move together does not prove which one affects the other. For example, the profit share may be affected by the profit rate rather than vice versa. Furthermore, both variables may be determined by a third variable, not mentioned in this schema.

Second, some effects may not operate simultaneously, but with a time lag. Suppose that the rapid rise of the profit share (or rapid decline of the wage share) in the first half of expansion lowers the propensity to consume, but with a time lagged effect, so it limits consumer demand in the last half of expansion. This may be the case, as shown by the continued decline in the growth of capacity utilization before the peak, so it may be one of the factors limiting the profit rate. Thus, the profit rate at each point may be mostly affected by factors operating in a previous period.

Finally, each cycle is different, so the average may hide important differences. It is worth looking at the timing of each variable in all six expansions (timing in the contractions cannot be precisely determined because they were mostly too brief). If the data given in the four tables and graphs of this chapter are used, it is revealed that the profit rate, profit share, and capacity utilization all tended to lead the cycle peak by a long time in the 1950s and the 1960s. Remember that there are five stages of expansion, from 1 at the initial trough to 5 at the peak.

If we average for the four cycles from 1949 to 1970, the profit share peaked at stage 2.5, the profit rate at 2.75, and capacity utilization at 3.75. In the 1970s, they led the cycle peak by somewhat less. On the average, the profit share peaked at stage 4; the profit rate peaked at 4; and capacity utilization peaked at 4.5. On the contrary, the potential output-capital ratio moved countercyclically; it reached its peak at each cycle trough and reached its bottom point around the cycle peak (its average trough was at stage 4.8).

SUMMARY

In summary, the rate of profit (Π/K) is equal to its three components: the profit share (Π/Y) times the capacity utilization ratio (Y/Z) times the potential output-capital ratio (Z/K). Any other economic variable may affect the rate of profit through these three. For example, higher wages will tend to increase consumer demand, so higher wages tend to raise the capacity utilization ratio; but higher wages may also reduce the profit share. Therefore, higher wages have both a positive and negative effect on the rate of profits. (Thus, each capitalist wants to lower costs by lowering wages in his or her own business, but wants all other capitalists to have higher wages to raise demand.)

It is useful to tell the tale in words of how the profit rate is determined in each phase of the cycle. In the early expansion, the profit rate rises rapidly because (1) the profit share is rising (since hourly wages change little whereas productivity rapidly increases), but mostly because (2) the utilization of capacity is rapidly rising (owing to rising demand for both consumer and investor goods). These two factors ensure a rapid rise in the profit rate, which causes a rapid rise in investment.

In late expansion, the profit rate falls because (1) the utilization of capacity is falling or changing very little—owing to the previous fall in the propensity to consume, caused by the previous fall in the wage share. The profit rate also falls because (2) the profit share in national income is falling—owing to falling or stagnant labor productivity, caused partly by more labor militancy, but also owing to a declining growth in the use of capacity.

The rate of profit thus declines before the peak because of rising unit costs due to stagnant or falling labor productivity (and perhaps rising material costs) *and limited demand* (reflected in declining or stagnant capacity utilization). The combined assault from the cost *and* demand sides is always fatal to the rate of profit, whose fall eventually causes less investment, which sets off the depression.

Notice that, in late expansion, the fall in the profit share will bring a rising wage share, which will begin to raise the consumption-income ratio and would eventually bolster the sagging consumer demand. But it is too late; by the time the average propensity to consume rises by a significant amount, the economy is already in a contraction where total consumption must fall because income is falling. The rising average propensity to consume can only cushion the decline and help prepare for the next expansion.

In the early contraction and mid-contraction, the profit rate falls rapidly. Part of the fall is due to the fact that (1) the profit share is falling (since hourly wages fall a little, but productivity as measured falls a lot). The profit rate falls mainly, however, because (2) capacity utilization is falling rapidly (owing to declining demand). The falling profit rate causes an additional fall in investment.

By the late part of contraction, the profit rate rises a little because (1) utilization of capacity may be falling a little less swiftly as demand reaches its bottom point (capacity utilization is helped by a rising propensity to consume and by government welfare). The profit rate begins to rise mostly because (2) the profit share is rising. The profit share rises partly because wages are ground down by the weakness of labor with so much unemployment. The profit share also rises partly because productivity starts to rise again, both because of less militancy and an end to falling use of capacity. *It is the combined effect of a floor to demand and the falling costs that restores the rate of profit,* leading to a recovery of investment.

Of course, this is a very stylized description and simplified summary. Many other factors, such as government behavior (discussed in Chapter 7 and Part Six) and international events also affect each cycle. Long-run trends, discussed earlier, in many of the factors that are mentioned in this summary will also eventually lead to changes in cyclical behavior of the profit rate. Nevertheless, this summary does include some of the most important features in common in the past six cycles affecting the rate of profit.

APPENDIX 11A

Analysis of the Components of the Profit Rate

By definition, the profit rate equals the profit share times capacity utilization times the potential output-capital ratio. In symbols: $\Pi/K = (\Pi/Y)(Y/Z)(Z/K)$. Instead of directly analyzing the profit rate, which is explained 100 percent by its components, we may analyze each component to see what determined it.

THE PROFIT SHARE

The profit share equals one minus the wage share. In the last chapter, movements of the wage share were shown to be associated with movements of unemployment, capacity utilization, and output. Output, in turn, may be assumed to be equal to consumption, investment, government, and net exports, each of which is explained in separate chapters in this book. Capacity utilization is analyzed in the next section. That leaves unemployment to be analyzed.

In both a Keynesian and a Marxist approach, the demand for labor derives from the demand for output. It is no surprise, therefore, that unemployment is a negative function of real national income. When real national income rises in the short run, unemployment must be declining. In a recession, when national income declines, unemployment naturally rises. If we use first differences to estimate the regression (with the same data sources as in Table 10.3), the data for 1949 to 1980 reveal that

$$\Delta U_t = 0.21 - \underset{(-9.9)}{0.03 \Delta Y_t} \qquad R^2 = 0.45$$
$$DW = 1.90 \qquad \qquad (11A.1)$$

Unemployment, as expected, does show a negative, statistically significant relation to real national income. Real national income does "explain" a big chunk of the variance of unemployment (45 percent), but there are obviously other factors involved as well.

CAPACITY UTILIZATION

Capacity utilization is correlated to output, but more strongly in a nonlinear form than in a linear form. This is to be expected because, in every expansion, capacity utilization first rises much faster than output. The nonlinear relationship is quite clear in the data of 1949 to 1980 (still using first differences, with the same sources as Tables 11.1 and 11.3):

$$\Delta \frac{Y_t}{Z_t} = -1.24 + \underset{(11.6)}{.44 \Delta Y_t} - \underset{(-7.4)}{0.00015 \Delta Y_t^2} \qquad (11A.2)$$
$$R^2 = 0.75 \qquad DW = 1.82$$

This equation says that capacity utilization has a significant positive relation to real national income—plus a significant negative relation to the square of real national income. The two explanatory variables together explain 75 percent of the variance of capacity utilization (and there is no significant autocorrelation).

It may be emphasized that capacity utilization has both a direct and an indirect effect on the rate of profit. Directly, it has been defined as one of three components. Indirectly, it was demonstrated in Chapter 10 that capacity utilization affects the profit share, which affects the profit rate.

THE POTENTIAL OUTPUT–CAPITAL RATIO

In most of the theories concerning the potential output–capital ratio given in this chapter, a higher degree of capacity utilization plays a major role in lowering the ratio of potential full-capacity output to the capital stock. In other words, for various reasons, a rising level of capacity utilization seems to drive down the ratio of potential output to capital. Conversely, falling use of capacity seems to lead to a rising ratio of potential output to capital. The theory may be tested by examining the data of 1949 to 1980 on the potential output-capital ratio and capacity utilization (using first differences and the same sources as Tables 11.3 and 11.4):

$$\Delta \frac{Z_t}{K_t} = -0.08 - \underset{(-26.5)}{0.58 \Delta} \frac{Y_t}{Z_t} \qquad R^2 = 0.85$$
$$DW = 1.64 \qquad (11A.3)$$

If all these data are to be trusted, there appears to be a very strong, statistically significant, negative correlation between the potential output-capital ratio and the capacity utilization ratio. As capacity utilization rises in the expansion, the potential output-capital ratio declines. As capacity utilization falls in the contraction, the potential output-capital ratio rises. The definitions of the concept and its measurement, however, cause so many difficulties that one should not trust these results.

Part Three

GROWTH AND BUSINESS CYCLES: CAUSES OF UNEMPLOYMENT

Chapter 12

THE DYNAMIC FRAMEWORK: CONDITIONS FOR STEADY GROWTH

The rate of growth of the U.S. economy has fallen very considerably in the 1970s and 1980s. Three sets of reasons have been advanced to explain this phenomenon. First, it is said by some economists that there is a shortage of capital. This theory emphasizes the supply-side aspect of growth; it supports the conclusion that there should be lower taxes on capitalists so that they will save and invest more capital. Second, it is said by some economists that the lower growth rate of output is caused by lower growth of productivity. There is a huge literature on the causes of lower growth of productivity (some of which denies that it exists), ranging from lack of new research to lack of new capital investment to increase of laziness or more militant workers. Again, the supply-side aspect is emphasized; policy conclusions range from subsidies to research to lower taxes on capitalists to outlawing unions to socialist workers' production cooperatives.

Third and last, some economists attribute the slower growth to lack of effective demand (i.e., desire backed by money) for products. Lack of demand causes less investment (even if there is plenty of capital). Less investment in productive facilities means less growth of output and less growth of productivity. Policy conclusions range from more government stimulation of demand (by higher welfare or military spending or both) to higher wages to socialist ownership of production facilities.

Obviously, some of these diagnoses are diametrically opposed (such as too little saving versus too much saving and hoarding). To understand the different views of U.S. growth, we must understand the different basic theories from which they spring. This chapter examines classical supply-side growth theory, Keynesian demand-side growth theory, neoclassical supply-side growth theory, Marxist growth theory, and Post Keynesian growth theory.

CLASSICAL SUPPLY-SIDE THEORY

The classicals (and all supply-siders) assume Say's law. Thus, aggregate demand always equals aggregate supply, and investment demand always equals supply of savings. As a formal equation, in the private domestic economy the supply of output (Y, or real national income) *must* equal intended consumer demand (C) plus intended investment demand (I), so:

$$Y_t = C_t + I_t \tag{12.1}$$

It also follows that intended investment (I) must equal intended saving where saving is—by definition—equal to income (Y) minus consumption (C), so:

$$I_t = Y_t - C_t \tag{12.2}$$

where saving $= S = Y - C$. This equation is a formalization of Say's law when it is expressed in these intended (*ex ante*) terms rather than as mere after-the-fact (*ex post*) accounting.

Given Say's law, the growth of output depends exclusively on (1) the increase of capital and (2) the increase of product per unit of capital. Note that the product per unit of capital reflects the amount and quality of labor, the availability of natural resources, and the level of technology, so none of these are ignored. In this view, output (Y) must equal the ratio of output per unit of capital (Y/K) times capital (K), so:

$$Y = \left(\frac{Y}{K}\right) K \tag{12.3}$$

or $\qquad\qquad$ output $= \left(\dfrac{\text{output}}{\text{capital}}\right)$ (capital)

Notice that there is no difference between actual and potential output in this theory because there is always sufficient demand, so capital is fully utilized, and labor is fully employed.

In the United States about $3 of capital goods are in use for each $1 of annual national product. So the ratio of output to capital is about 1 to 3. Therefore, when the value of capital stock, including all machines and factories, was about $3 trillion, the economy produced annually an output of about $1 trillion.

Now this analysis may be extended to a growing economy. The *growth* of output is determined by the growth of capital, given a certain ratio of output to capital. The additional or marginal output–capital ratio is the change in output (ΔY) to a change in capital (ΔK). The theory then says that:

$$\Delta Y = \left(\frac{\Delta Y}{\Delta K}\right) \Delta K \tag{12.4}$$

or $\qquad$ change in output = marginal output–capital ratio $\times$ change in capital

But remember that the change in capital is, by definition, what economists call net investment. Net investment is all investment minus depreciation; but, for simplicity, depreciation is ignored in this chapter. Let I stand for investment (net or gross makes no difference since depreciation is ignored). Then:

$$\Delta Y = \left(\frac{\Delta Y}{\Delta K}\right) I_{t-1} \tag{12.5}$$

or   change in output = marginal output–capital ratio × investment (of previous period)

To obtain a simple theory, assume that the marginal output–capital ratio is a constant (k). It would complicate things, but make no basic difference, if it were not a constant (so long as it is predictable). Then:

$$Y_t - Y_{t-1} = k I_{t-1} \tag{12.6}$$

or   change in output = marginal output–capital ratio × investment (previous period)

Equation 12.6 is the simplest way of stating the second supply-side assumption for growth. Investment in new capital leads—with a given level of technology, labor supply, and natural resources—to a certain increase in output. For example, if $9 is invested in new capital and if the marginal capital–output ratio is 1 to 3, then output will grow by $3. It is worth noting that this supply-side effect of new investment was seldom discussed in Keynes's *General Theory* because he emphasized the demand-side effect of new investment on employment (a more important issue in the 1930s).

This supply-side equation (12.6) answers the question as to how much new output is produced by new investment. From where does the new investment come? That question has already been answered; investment equals saving (see equation 12.2). Finally, how much saving will there be? Saving is the residual remaining after consumption. Rather than any of the complicated forms discussed in Chapter 8, the point of this theory can be made with the simplest possible assumption: consumption is a constant percentage (b) of income. Using a more complex assumption would complicate the theory, but would not change its main point. Thus:

$$C_t = b Y_t \tag{12.7}$$

or   consumption = a constant × income

Notice that the constant, b, is both the average propensity to consume (C/Y) and the marginal propensity to consume ($\Delta C/\Delta Y$) because there is no difference in this case. The classical economists emphasized that the level of consumption determines how much can be saved—and saving (equals investment in more capital) determines growth.

The conclusion from this simple model of three basic statements (12.2, 12.6, and 12.7) is easy to see. By substituting consumption from equation 12.7 into 12.2, we find that investment equals income minus consumption:

$$I_t = Y_t - C_t \tag{12.8}$$

or

$$I_t = (1-b) Y_t \tag{12.9}$$

Thus, the saved proportion of income is the source for investment; and, of course, all saving is actually invested.

Finally, if investment from equation 12.8 is substituted in equation 12.6, the result is:

$$Y_t - Y_{t-1} = k(1-b)Y_{t-1} \qquad (12.10)$$

or   change in output = marginal capital–output ratio × propensity to save
× income of previous period

This is a very simple growth model. It says that the rate of growth is equal to the marginal capital–output ratio (k) times the propensity to save ($1-b$). For example, if the marginal capital–output ratio is 1 to 3 and the propensity to save is 0.09 (or 9 percent of income), then:

$$\text{rate of growth} = \tfrac{1}{3} \times 0.09 = 0.03 \text{ (or 3 percent per year)} \qquad (12.11)$$

If national income was 100 last period, then—by these assumptions and equation 12.10—income of this period must be 103. (A numerical example over several years is given in Appendix 12A.)

The classical economists used this theory to make an important ideological argument about the two determinants of the rate of economic growth. The one determinant—the propensity to save—is examined to demonstrate the need for high profits and a high ratio of saving. The second determinant—the marginal ratio of output to capital—is seen as a technological ratio, but it is necessary to foster that technology by the proper climate of competition under capitalism.

The classical view of the importance of saving is quite clear (and is opposed to the Keynesian view). The classical economists, concerned as they were about economic growth, called for as much thriftiness and saving as possible. In early nineteenth-century England, they observed that the savings of businesspeople were being used to build more capital. They drew the moral that more thrift and saving lead to more rapid increase of capital and, consequently, to more rapid economic growth.

The classical economists thus interpreted the potential rate of growth only in terms of supply. The supply of savings could be increased by lower wages and higher profits because almost all saving and investment are out of capitalist profits (so this is always a good argument for reducing wages or for reducing the taxes on profits). The supply of savings could also be increased if capitalists had more of the Puritan ethic, so they would consume less and save more.

Second, given the supply of saving, it was assumed that all of it was invested, so production depends merely on the output per unit of capital ($\Delta Y/\Delta K$). This ratio of output to capital could be raised only by better technology. The most rapid technological progress is made under the pressure of competition. Therefore, a system of pure competitive capitalism is the best way to raise the marginal output–capital ratio.

The classical, supply-side, growth model has serious limitations. The assumption that the output–capital ratio is a constant is very unrealistic and produces results in the logical development of the model that are untenable. For example, if capital and output must grow at the same rate (which is implicit if their ratio is to remain constant), then, logically, the labor force must grow at the same rate as well. Allowing the labor force to grow at a *faster* rate of growth while insisting that the output–capital ratio is a constant implies that increases in labor do not add to the level of output—that the marginal productivity of labor is zero!

This point is easiest to see if the extreme case is considered where investment is zero and the supply of labor is growing. If investment is zero, then the capital stock is constant, which implies, given the assumption about a constant output–capital ratio, that output is constant. This forces the conclusion that adding new labor to production from the growing supply of labor adds nothing to production. Consider the same case (no investment) where the growth of labor is negative; again it is implied that the marginal product of labor is zero, for if it were positive, output would drop rather than remain constant at a fixed proportion of the capital stock. Since labor is necessary for production and there is (by assumption) a fixed output–capital ratio, the model is consistent only if labor is growing at the same rate as capital.

This new qualification poses new problems for the classical growth model. This was pointed out by a growth theory pioneer, Evsey Domar.[1] The growth rate of output and capital is determined by the marginal propensity to save. The growth rate of labor is determined by demographic factors. It would be unrealistic to expect them to be equal, so the model has a destabilizing feature built into it. The implications of this destabilizing feature, called the "razor's edge," are discussed in Appendix 12B.

Modern neoclassical growth theorists recognize this problem and have responded to it by dropping the assumption of a constant output–capital ratio. Their contribution is discussed later in this chapter.

KEYNES ON SAVING AND GROWTH

Keynes challenged the classical conclusions about saving and growth. He argued that more thrift and saving lead to more rapid economic growth *only if full employment is assumed.* This means assuming the classical claim that demand is always enough for any supply of goods and that all saving is automatically invested. This assumption, however, is *not* true according to Keynes. During each depression it is painfully obvious to everyone that there is not full employment and that millions of workers are involuntarily unemployed. In each recession or depression, most saving is *not* being invested (except in the statistical sense of investment in unplanned and unwanted inventory pileups).

Keynes showed that, with unemployment and lack of investment opportunities, more saving may actually lead to *less* production rather than any economic growth. This finding constitutes the Alice-in-Wonderland theme of the *paradox of thrift,* which says that greater thrift and saving may sometimes lead to less output, not more. If the economy is faced with a lack of effective demand, then a higher propensity to save will simply lower consumer

---

[1] See E. D. Domar, "Expansion and Employment," *American Economic Review* 37 (March 1947), pp. 34–55. Domar's pathbreaking work underlies a considerable part of this chapter. Domar acknowledges that Marx's work foreshadows his own.

demand still further. The lower consumer demand may then lead to still less output and income, and therefore, to less aggregate saving and investment than there was before individuals tried to save more of their income. Thrift may always be an individual virtue, as Benjamin Franklin preached, but it is not always a social virtue when there is a lack of paying customers in a private enterprise economy.

More saving at a given income level is a benefit to the economy if, and only if, there is an equal increase in investment. Therefore, Keynesians (such as Evsey Domar[2]) see the potential growth rate as *only* a potential, a possibility that will be realized only if all saving really is invested and becomes an increase in capital. So all of the above model of growth should really be restated in terms of potential output at full use of capacity (Z), not in terms of actual output (Y), because there may be insufficient effective demand. In other words, more saving, which could supply more capital to produce more output, is helpful only if business people expect demand to rise by an equal amount. If they do not expect an increase in demand, they will hoard the increased saving and precipitate a recession or depression. Domar emphasized that new investment does eventually increase supply as well as demand. So the condition for steady growth is not merely no hoarding of present income, but also an increase of income and spending proportionate to growth of supply. If demand does not increase in the required amount, then the economy leaves the golden path of steady growth and may never return to it (see Appendix 12B for more on Domar's theory).

In the modern world, neither side of the problem can be ignored. Setting aside more saving to invest in more capital makes it *possible* to raise the rate of growth. But this happy possibility cannot become a reality as long as significant numbers of unemployed persons and unused capacity continue. Such conditions show that all the savings now available are not being invested. More saving would only cause more unemployment in this case. First, one must guarantee a solution to the Keynesian problem of finding profitable investment outlets for all existing savings. Then one can worry about the classical problem of generating a higher rate of saving to allow the possibility of more investment.

NEOCLASSICAL GROWTH THEORY

Neoclassical economists answered some of the Keynesian criticisms by developing more complex growth models with microeconomic foundations. One especially popular model was developed by Robert Solow.[3]

In Solow's model, the level of national output is determined by a production function that recognizes the contribution of capital (K) and labor (L):

$$Y = f(K, L) \tag{12.12}$$

---

[2]Domar, *loc. cit.*
[3]See, e.g., the founder of neoclassical growth theory, Robert Solow, "A Contribution to the Theory of Economic Growth," *The Quarterly Journal of Economics* 70 (February 1956), pp. 65–94.

This production function has the following two properties:

1. The production function has constant returns to scale. In other words, if capital and labor are *both* increased by some proportion, output will increase by the *same* proportion. If, for example, capital and labor both double, output will double.
2. Each of the two inputs is characterized by diminishing marginal physical product. In other words, if one input is held constant and the other is increased by some proportion, then output will increase but by some *lesser* proportion. If, for example, capital is held constant and labor is doubled, output will increase, but the proportion will be less than double.

The one important feature that distinguished Solow's model from earlier models is that it does not assume a constant capital–output ratio. To say it another way, a given level of output does not require a particular, given capital stock. In the neoclassical tradition, capital and labor are *substitutes;* any given level of output can be produced by an infinite number of capital and labor combinations.

Solow's model produces the result that, over time, capital and labor will grow at about the same rate and the ratio of capital to labor will stay roughly constant. The mathematics of Solow's model are complicated and will not be reviewed here, but the model produces an intuitive result that can be offered as a simplistic explanation.

In Solow's model the labor force is assumed to grow at some natural rate (determined by population growth). Suppose that this natural rate is called g. Solow's conclusion is that capital should tend to grow at rate g as well. The reason why is perhaps best illustrated by a counterexample. Suppose the capital stock grows for a while at some rate greater than g. The optimal ratio of capital to labor is passed, so the disadvantage of the diminishing marginal physical product of capital begins to have an effect. Each additional increase in capital produces a smaller increase in output. Solow assumed that the change in capital (investment) was equal to savings, which equaled the marginal propensity to save times the level of output. Therefore, the reduction in the growth rate of output would eventually slow the growth rate of capital. There would be a natural tendency for this to continue until the growth rate in capital *equaled* the growth rate of labor.

To put it another way, if one assumes a production function with constant returns to scale and diminishing marginal physical product in both factor inputs, if one factor (labor) is increased at rate g and the other factor (capital) is increased at a greater rate x, then the resulting growth rate of output will be greater than g but less than x. For example, if labor is doubled and capital is tripled, output will be more than double but less than triple. This ensures that the growth rate of capital for the next period will also be less than x (because it is determined by the marginal propensity to save times output). This process continues until the growth rate of capital converges to g.

Since in the long run both capital and labor must be growing at the same rate g, then, given the definition of constant returns to scale, output will also grow at rate g! Therefore, Solow reaches the interesting conclusion that capital, labor, and output all grow at the same rate g, which is equal to the growth rate of the labor force! Because the concepts explained here are complicated, a numerical example of Solow's model is presented in Appendix 12C.

Although the model is simplistic, it is appealing to conservatives because it produces the result that there is a *natural* tendency toward a steady state growth path, which, in turn, is fixed by the growth rate of labor. Remember that Solow assumes Say's law.

There is one major flaw in Solow's theory. It does not allow for growth in the per capita income of workers! If the labor population and output have a natural tendency to grow at the same rate, then output per worker is a constant. This is counterempirical because the long-run per capita income of workers has grown. It is also the case that the capital stock has grown at a faster rate than the labor force since World War II.

Neoclassical economists who admit this argue that Solow's model applies to the special case when technology is fixed. When technological change is considered, since the productivity of capital and labor is improved, output grows faster than the labor supply, allowing a rise in the standard of living.

MODERN SUPPLY-SIDE GROWTH THEORY

Recently modern supply-side economists have developed a growth theory that is largely embodied in President Reagan's economic program. Essentially, these theorists believe that high investment stimulated by a high level of savings will promote economic growth. Few economists would disagree with this proposition. The controversial area of supply-side economics involves the question of how the growth in investment and savings are to be *financed.*

According to supply-side economists, tax rates in the United States are too high, and, as such, they discourage savings, which, in turn, discourages investment.[4] The low rate of savings contributes to high interest rates, which raises the cost of investment. At the same time, high tax rates lower the rewards of investment by diminishing after-tax profits. If tax rates were cut, these obstacles to investment would be diminished.

The supply-side theory assumes that the marginal propensity to save is very high for very high income earners (an assumption that is probably correct). Since they wish to encourage saving, the actual tax cuts implemented by the Reagan administration were far more advantageous to the wealthy than they were for the middle and lower classes of income earners.

The dominant faction of supply-side theory also argued that even though the government might cut its tax rates, there was no need for the government to cut *expenditures.* The cut in tax *rates* would cause tax *revenues* to rise. This paradox is explained by a device called the Laffer Curve, named after the University of Southern California economist Arthur Laffer. The Laffer curve is shown in Figure 12.1.

Very generally, the Laffer curve asserts that tax revenues (the amount of taxes actually collected) will be equal to the tax rate (the percentage of income that is taxed) times the level of income (or output). However, Laffer asserts, the tax rate and the level of income are not

---

[4]See Arthur Laffer, "Supply-Side Economics," *Financial Analysts' Journal* 12 (September–October 1981); also Jade Wanniski, *The Way the World Works* (New York: Basic Books, 1978); also Don Fullerton, "On the Possibility of an Inverse Relationship Between Tax Rates and Government Revenues," National Bureau of Economic Research Working Paper, no. 467 (April 1980).

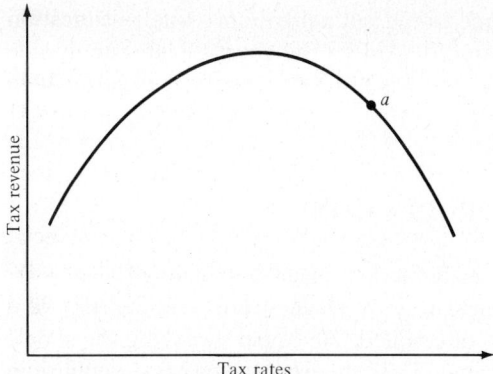

Figure 12.1 The Laffer Curve

independent. As tax rates increase, levels of investment and productivity begin to decline, slowing the growth rate of output. Finally, after tax rates reach a certain level, any further increase causes a *decline* in output. Because tax revenues are the *product* of tax rates and output and because the two are moving inversely, the product slows its growth rate and then finally turns negative. This is the region that is to the right of the peak of the Laffer curve. When tax rates are increased to the right of this peak, such as at point *a* of Figure 12.1, tax revenues actually *drop*. More important, the reverse is also true. At point *a*, when tax rates are *decreased*, government revenues rise. The government is in a no-loss situation. Tax rates could be cut; and expenditures increased; while deficits are eliminated. Laffer hypothesized that the American economy was, indeed, on the right side of the Laffer curve.

The political popularity of such a theory should be obvious. It is one of the few economic theories with no *trade-offs*. Tax rates are cut, but government expenditures can grow, and the economy is more prosperous.

Unfortunately, if modern supply-side economics is wrong, the implementation of supply-side policies can have catastrophic effects. Large numbers of economists really doubt that the American economy is on the right side of the Laffer curve or even doubt that the Laffer curve exists at all.[5] If not, the critics maintain, the reduction in tax rates will result in a reduction in tax revenue. The result will be enormous U.S. government budget deficits. Because the deficits have to be financed by borrowing, this will put upward pressure on interest rates, which will discourage investment rather than encourage it, slowing economic growth rather than causing it to expand.

Furthermore, critics point out that productivity and investment are not abstractions.

---

[5]A good critique of supply-side economics is in Philip Mirowski, "What's Wrong with the Laffer Curve?" *Journal of Economic Issues* 16 (September 1982), pp. 815–828; also see the excellent historical piece by Robert R. Keller, "Supply-Side Economic Policies During the Coolidge-Mellon Era," *Journal of Economic Issues* 16 (September 1982), pp. 773–790.

Genuine programs that emphasize the supply side would put a premium value on education and research and development, including research funded by the government. Supply-side economics, as actually practiced in the United States, has resulted in substantial cutbacks in government funding for education and research.

MARX: EQUILIBRIUM (OR SIMPLE REPRODUCTION)

As a critique of the classical economists, Marx[6] restated their problem of enough savings for growth. Yet he also criticized them n the same way as Keynes did three-quarters of a century later) for their neglect of the problems of demand. He began by asking the simple question: under what conditions of supply and demand will there be an aggregate equilibrium with *no* change of output from period to period? Marx called this the case of simple reproduction.

Marx observed that, in the private domestic economy, the demand for net national product equals consumer spending plus net investment spending. The supply of goods and services comes from the sector producing consumer goods and services and from the sector producing producers' goods and services.

Consumer spending would buy consumer goods and services from that sector of production. The demand for consumer goods must come from the income generated by production of the net national product, namely, wages and profits. *If* there is to be a long-run unchanging equilibrium, then all wages of workers (W) plus all profits of capitalists (Π) must be used to buy consumer goods and services. So:

$$C_t = W_t + \Pi_t \tag{12.13}$$

where C is consumer goods and services produced.

At the same time, *if* there is to be neither increase nor decrease of potential output, then all depreciated capital must be replaced by new producer goods. Moreover, gross investment goods must all be in the form of those replacement goods. There must be *no* net investment:

$$I_t = 0 \tag{12.14}$$

where I is net investment. Likewise, the amount of gross investment goods will have to equal exactly the replacement demand coming from depreciation funds (gross investment = replacement = depreciation). There are no net savings and no net investment. Since there is no net investment—and no net disinvestment—output will remain the same year after year:

$$Y_{1982} = Y_{1981} = Y_{1980} \tag{12.15}$$

where the subscript indicates the year. Demand and supply remain in equilibrium at that level by assumption.

---

[6]See Karl Marx, *Capital* (Chicago: Charles Kerr, 1933; orig. publ. by Engels, 1893), vol. 2, Part 3.

MARX: GROWTH (OR EXPANDED REPRODUCTION)

Marx stated that this simple case would be an unlikely accident, almost impossible under capitalism (a system requiring growth). Next he asked what would the conditions of supply and demand have to be for there to be a steady rate of economic growth with an equilibrium of supply and demand in each period. Marx called this happy possibility—which he emphasized was only an unlikely possibility—a state of expanded reproduction of the capitalist system. Keynesians call it dynamic aggregate equilibrium or steady state growth.

Marx has two insights into the process of saving and investment (or, as he calls it, accumulation of capital) that help to flesh out the Keynesian analysis of investment with greater reality. Keynesians sometime talk about saving by "households," undifferentiated by type of household. One insight of Marx is that workers as a class must spend *all* their income on consumption just to reach culturally given minimum acceptable levels (such as the "low income" budget of the U.S. Department of Commerce). Workers on the average as a whole class—in periods of expansions and contractions and including the highly paid and the miserably paid and the unemployed—do *not* save.

Marx's other insight is that all saving and investment comes from capitalist recipients of large amounts of profits, rents, and interest (hereafter called "profit"). Capitalists use only part of their high incomes to maintain a consumption level well above that of the working class. The rest of their income is saved and *may* be invested.

Assume that capitalists consume a fixed proportion of their profits (a constant, b) whereas workers consume all their wages. Then:

$$C = W + b\Pi \tag{12.16}$$

where b is a constant between zero and one. Notice that, if total income remains constant, a shift of income to wages will increase consumption whereas a shift of income to profits will decrease consumption. For example, let $b = 0.1$. Then assume there is a total income of \$1000. Let the total income be divided, in the first case, half to wages and half to profits; in the second case, three-fourths to wages; in the third case, three-fourths to profits. Then calculate consumption in each case; it will be higher in the second case and lower in the third case. Thus, consumer demand depends not only on total income, but on the distribution of income.

Now, *if there is to be equilibrium* of supply and demand, then what must be the demand for investment goods? Capitalists in this case have saved a proportion of their income $(1 - b)$ in addition to their control of depreciation funds. Therefore, they can (and must to preserve equilibrium) *invest* that percentage of their income in new net investment. (Of course, they must also spend the depreciation funds for replacement investment.) Thus, net investment must equal the saved percentage of profits:

$$I = (1 - b)\Pi \tag{12.17}$$

if there is to be steady equilibrium growth. With this growth of net investment demand (equal to the supply of new investment goods), there will now be a growing output year by year. (A full Marxist growth model is stated in Appendix 12D.) Marx did *not* believe that the capitalist system would meet these stringent conditions for smooth growth.

POST KEYNESIAN GROWTH MODELS

The Post Keynesians—such as Joan Robinson[7] and Nicholas Kaldor[8]—have made many contributions to growth theory. They follow Marx in the assumption that all investment must come out of profits and that saving out of wages is close enough to zero that it may be neglected. They follow Keynes in the emphasis that investment is *not* determined by saving. Saving may differ from investment in the short run; and in the long run it is the level of saving —not investment—that adjusts (and that adjusted level may be below full employment). Investment is primarily an induced or derived demand from the growth in aggregate demand for goods and services. If there is insufficient growth in the demand for all goods and services, investment will decline.

SUMMARY

In a supply-side model based on capital, the potential rate of growth may be stated as the ratio of saving to output times the marginal output–capital ratio. This assumes that all saving is invested in the expansion (or replacement) of capital and that all capital is fully utilized. The classical economists assumed that actual growth would follow these assumptions because of Say's law.

Keynes did not accept Say's law, so he showed that all saving would be invested only under certain unusual circumstances; therefore, actual output would be much less than the potential output under capitalism. The actual and potential outputs are both determined by (1) the saving-income ratio—which differs according to human relationships and institutions. The actual and potential outputs are also determined by (2) the marginal output–capital ratio— which also depends on how human relations and institutions affect technological progress. Finally, the actual output under capitalism differs from the potential because the actual output is also determined by (3) the gap between saving and investment, which leaves unused capacity—and which also depends on human relations and institutions. Keynesian and Marxist models emphasize the stringent conditions (hardly ever met under capitalism) under which it is possible for the actual output to live up to the potential.

Many decades before Keynes, Marx stated the conditions for steady growth, what growth would be if they are met, and why they are not likely to be met under capitalism. One important difference between Marx and Keynes in the analysis of economic growth is that Marx adds the class distribution of income to the factors determining growth. This leads Marx to two insights into the process of saving and investment of capital. First, workers as a class spend all their income on consumption just to maintain a minimum acceptable standard of living, so on the average they do no saving and no investment. Second, all saving and investment come from that part of profit that capitalists do not consume and that they choose to invest.

[7] See Joan Robinson, *The Accumulation of Capital* (London: Macmillan, 1956).
[8] Nicholas Kaldor, *Essays on Economic Stability and Growth* (New York: Free Press, 1960).

Therefore, the Marxist growth model concludes (assuming for the moment that all saving is invested) that the rate of growth under capitalism may be increased (1) if the marginal output–capital ratio is increased, (2) if the wage share is decreased, or (3) if capitalist consumption is lowered. But Marx also noted that reduction of wages and reduction of capitalist consumption would reduce consumer demand, which would cause investment to fall below saving. Only under socialism would investment always equal saving (since both are done by the same public agency), so growth would be at full employment and with no drain for the luxury consumption of a few capitalists. Hence growth would be higher and smoother under socialism.

Robert Solow's economic growth model is strictly in the neoclassical tradition. Solow assumes a typical microeconomic theory production function allowing substitutability between capital and labor. The change in the capital stock (investment) is equal to the marginal propensity to save times the level of output. When it is assumed that labor grows at a constant rate, there is a natural tendency for the growth of capital and output to converge on this rate. Modifications to Solow's model to include technological change allow for the rate of growth of capital and output to exceed the rate of growth of labor, allowing a rise in the standard of living for workers.

As is typical throughout macroeconomic theory, the Keynesian and Marxist models illustrate the possible barriers to growth whereas the neoclassical models give attention to the automatic tendency toward economic harmony.

It is probably the case that growth theory is one of the more inadequate areas of macroeconomics where much remains to be done. The behavior of the economy over long periods of time where future decisions are yet to be made, resource availability is uncertain, and new technology cannot be predicted is difficult to predict with any degree of confidence.

APPENDIX 12A

Classical Supply-Side Growth Model

Table 12A.1 illustrates the arithmetic of a supply-side growth model for a few years' time. The table begins at an arbitrary level of $100 for convenience in calculation. The table is purposely incomplete so that the reader may finish it. Start with the output of the latest year. First, divide this output into 9 percent saving and 91 percent consumption (or a propensity to consume of 91 percent). Second, having found the amount saved or invested (the increase of capital), then find the increase of output for the next year by applying a marginal output–capital ratio of 1 to 3. For example, because saving or increase of capital was $9 in Year 1, the increase of output in Year 2 is one-third of that, or $3. The table is completed by merely repeating these two steps year after year. As long as the propensity to save and the marginal output–capital ratio remain unchanged (and saving equals investment), this economy will continue to grow at a steady 3 percent per year.

Table 12A.1

EXAMPLE OF ECONOMIC GROWTH

Year	Output (or National Product)	Saving = Investment = Increase in Capital	Increase in Output
1	$100.00	$9.00	$3.00
2	103.00	9.30	3.10
3	106.10	9.55	3.18
4	109.28	—	—
5	—	—	—
6	—	—	—
7	—	—	—

ASSUMPTIONS:

1. $\frac{\text{increase in output}}{\text{increase in capital}} = \frac{1}{3}$
2. $\frac{\text{saving}}{\text{output}} = 0.09$

APPENDIX 12B

Domar's Growth Model and the Razor's Edge

Evsey Domar[9] and Roy Harrod[10] were both early pioneers in neo-Keynesian growth theory. Using models similar to the classical supply-side model presented in this chapter, their research exposed the serious limitations of models that assumed a constant ratio of output to capital. The models tend to generate a feature that economists now refer to as the "razor's edge."

First, as was stated in the text, the model implies that the marginal physical product of labor is zero. If the following national production function is assumed (where Y, K, and L represent national output, capital, and labor):

$$Y = f(K, L) \tag{12B.1}$$

then the marginal physical product of labor is defined as:

$$\frac{\Delta Y}{\Delta L} \text{ when } \Delta K = 0 \tag{12B.2}$$

The assumption of a constant output–capital ratio is represented in the equation:

$$\frac{Y}{K} = k \tag{12B.3}$$

---

[9] See Domar, *loc. cit.*
[10] See Roy Harrod, "Domar and Dynamic Economics," *Economic Journal* 69 (September 1959), pp. 451–464. This essay cites all of Harrod's earlier relevant work and compares his with Domar's work.

where k is a constant. The equation implies that when ΔK equals zero, ΔY also equals zero. Therefore, when

$$\Delta K = 0, \frac{\Delta Y}{\Delta L} = 0 \tag{12B.4}$$

which means the marginal product of labor is zero.

Since labor contributes to production, labor must be growing at the same rate as capital. This further implies that the production function in equation 12B.1 has the property of constant returns to scale with no *substitutability among* the two inputs. (In other words, labor cannot be substituted for capital, and if both grow by some proportion, output will grow by the same proportion.)

Given this, if the output–capital ratio (k) is constant through time, then the rate of growth of output must equal the rate of growth of capital:

$$\frac{\Delta Y}{Y} = \frac{\Delta K}{K} \tag{12B.5}$$

Since ΔK is investment, which, according to Say's law must equal savings,

$$\Delta K = S = (1-b)Y \tag{12B.6}$$

(where b is the marginal propensity to consume and $1-b$ is the marginal propensity to save). If equation 12B.6 is substituted into equation 12B.5, the following result is obtained:

$$\frac{\Delta Y}{Y} = (1-b)\frac{Y}{K} = (1-b)k \tag{12B.7}$$

This implies that the rate of growth of output (and capital) is equal to the marginal propensity to save times the constant output–capital ratio.

The rate of growth of labor, however, is also supposed to be equal to this ratio. In other words, the restrictions on this model imply that:

$$\frac{\Delta Y}{Y} = \frac{\Delta K}{K} = \frac{\Delta L}{L} = (1-b)k \tag{12B.8}$$

But the rate of growth of labor is determined by demographic factors whereas $(1-b)$ is determined by the psychology of the public, and k is determined by technology! There is no reason why the rate of growth of labor should equal $(1-b)k$!

What if these differ, as one might expect them to? Suppose that

$$\frac{\Delta L}{L} > (1-b)k \tag{12B.9}$$

In this situation, the economy is not expanding rapidly enough to employ all labor fully, and so long as the growth rate of labor does not fall, the economy falls endlessly into an ever deeper depression (with higher and higher unemployment).

In the case where

$$\frac{\Delta L}{L} < (1-b)k \qquad (12\text{B}.10)$$

there is a chronic labor shortage, resulting in spiraling wage inflation.

The economy is on a razor's edge in the sense that equation 12B.8 must be satisfied if growth stability is to be achieved. If there is any deviation, the economy moves on a noncorrecting path to disaster.

APPENDIX 12C

Solow's Growth Theory

Solow's growth model assumes a production function with constant returns to scale and diminishing marginal physical product of both labor and capital. The change in the capital stock is equal to the level of investment. The level of investment is equal to the marginal propensity to save (a constant) times the level of output. Solow also assumes that the labor force grows at a constant rate, and he concludes that there is a *natural* tendency for the growth rate of capital and output to converge to the growth rate of labor.

Such a proposition can be shown through an example. Assume the following production function:

$$Y = K^{1/2} L^{1/2} \qquad (12\text{C}.1)$$

This production function has the properties of constant returns to scale and diminishing marginal physical products.

The level of investment in any time period is equal to the marginal propensity to save (s) times the level of output (Y):

$$I = \Delta K = sY \qquad (12\text{C}.2)$$

Assume that the marginal propensity to save (s) is equal to 0.10. Likewise assume that at the beginning of the growth period the capital stock is equal to 25 and the labor stock is equal to 100. If we use equation 12C.1, the level of output will be equal to 50. Assume additionally that the labor force grows at 10 percent per year.

Given all of these assumptions, Table 12C.1 shows what would happen to growth over ten periods.

Column 6 represents the level of output. It is calculated by taking the level of capital and labor from columns 3 and 5 and plugging them into equation (12B.2), the production function. Column 7 is the rate of growth of capital, calculated from column 5. Column 8 is the rate of growth of output, taken from column 6.

The model's results are gleaned from a comparison of columns 2, 7, and 8. As can be seen, even if at the beginning of the growth period the capital stock growth rates exceeds that of labor, it will gradually converge to that of labor (the entire convergence is not shown because it converges at a diminishing rate). As explained in the text, the growth rate of output will always be *between* that of labor and capital if they are different, as can be seen by a comparison of columns 2, 7, and 8 for any time period. Because the future growth of capital depends upon this growth rate of output from the previous period, this guarantees that the growth rate of capital gradually drops until both converge to the growth rate of labor. Hence, in this economy, the long-run growth rate of labor, capital, and output will eventually be 10 percent.

APPENDIX 12D

A Marxist Growth Model

The main difference from Keynes to Marx with regard to growth is that Marx examines the effects on growth of the class distribution of income (ratio of profit to wages, which Marx calls the rate of exploitation). Since Post Keynesians also distinguish these categories, the model presented here is similar to theirs in some respects. For simplicity, the potential national product (Z) and potential investment (I) are assumed to be net of depreciation. This abstraction is appropriate because depreciation is a relatively secondary complication when the emphasis is on growth possibilities.

Any growth model must determine the increase in national product. Marx saw the increase in national product at any particular time in a given relationship to the accumulation of capital or amount of net investment in productive capacity. This proportional relation—

Table 12C.1

GROWTH IN SOLOW MODEL

(1) Time t	(2) Growth of Labor $\Delta L/L$	(3) Labor Stock L	(4) Investment ΔK	(5) Capital Stock K	(6) Output Y	(7) Growth of Capital $\Delta K/K$	(8) Growth of Output $\Delta Y/Y$
0	0.10	100		25.0	50.0		
1	0.10	110	5.0	30.0	57.4	0.20	0.15
2	0.10	121	5.7	35.7	65.8	0.19	0.15
3	0.10	133	6.6	42.3	75.0	0.18	0.14
4	0.10	146	7.5	49.8	85.3	0.18	0.14
5	0.10	161	8.5	58.4	96.9	0.17	0.14
6	0.10	177	9.7	68.0	109.7	0.16	0.13
7	0.10	195	11.0	79.0	124.1	0.16	0.13
8	0.10	214	12.4	91.4	140.0	0.16	0.13
9	0.10	236	14.0	105.4	157.7	0.15	0.13
10	0.10	259	15.7	121.2	177.2	0.15	0.12

the change in potential output at full capacity to net investment—may be represented by the constant k. Then:

$$\text{(potential growth)} \quad Z_t - Z_{t-1} = kI_{t-1} \qquad (12\text{D}.1)$$

Since this model shows potential growth *if* capitalism operated at full capacity, Marx lets investment equal all of potential national income at full capacity (Z) minus workers' wages (W) and consumption out of profits ($b\Pi$).

$$\text{(investment)} \quad I_t = Z_t - W_t - b\Pi_t \qquad (12\text{D}.2)$$

Needless to say, Marx did *not* believe that investment could remain at this potential without socialism (in socialism, b would be the percentage of profit spent for collective consumption).

Consumption, for Marx, included all of wages, but only a small part (b) of profits:

$$\text{(consumption)} \quad C_t = W_t + b\Pi_t \qquad (12\text{D}.3)$$

Under capitalism, growth of consumption is limited by the limited growth of wages, which depend on the rate of exploitation of workers.

The national income, for Marx, is divided between the share going to workers in wages and the property (unearned) income, that is, all of the exploited income going to capitalists, called profits here. So, given that there is sufficient demand to realize all profits produced by workers at the full-capacity level by sales in the market, profits equal the entire potential national income at full capacity minus wages.

$$\text{(profits)} \quad \Pi_t = Z_t - W_t \qquad (12\text{D}.4)$$

Finally, some percentage of national income goes to wages—according to the market value of workers' labor power, determined by the power of workers versus capitalists under given conditions of supply and demand. Call the percentage going to workers e because the rest of the product is exploited by the capitalist. Then:

$$W_t = eZ_t \qquad (12\text{D}.5)$$

This completes the model.

This model, with five equations and five variables, may be reduced by successive substitutions to one equation in one variable, potential national income. Thus:

$$Z_t - Z_{t-1} = k(1-b)(1-W)Z_{t-1} \qquad (12\text{D}.6)$$

Given any level of Z at period $t-1$, the reader can calculate future Z for any desired number of years. The rate of growth is $k(1-b)(1-W)$.

This model faithfully reflects the logic of capitalism. It assumes here that the potential at full capacity is reached with demand equal to supply (an assumption that is later dropped). The *potential* output at full capacity under capitalism will be higher (1) if there is a higher product per unit of output (reflected in k), (2) if profits are increased at the expense of wages (reflected in $1-W$), or (3) if capitalists save a higher percentage of their income (reflected in $1-b$). This rule is true *provided* that all saving continues to be invested, as will not generally be the case under capitalism.

Since savings will generally equal investment under socialism, this rule is really a normative rule for socialist growth plans. It says that the rate of growth of output under socialist planning may be increased by (1) increasing the marginal output–capital ratio. There is no capitalist consumption, but there is consumption out of wages, public consumption out of social profits, and investment out of social profits. Then the rate of growth of output may also be increased by (2) lowering the wage share (W/Z), all of which goes for consumption, or by (3) lowering public consumption ($b\Pi$) out of social profits.

Chapter 13

CLASSICAL AND KEYNESIAN CYCLE THEORIES

Until the Great Depression of the 1930s, the main body (or majority) of neoclassical economists did not try to explain, but rather tried to explain away, the business cycle. In the first place, it was argued that the amount of unemployment was exaggerated, that there were only partial and frictional fluctuations of production. In the second place, each depression was said to be the last; especially in the twenties depressions were said to be gone forever —after more than a hundred years of business cycle phenomena. Again, in the 1960s there were many economists who declared that the business cycle had disappeared. Now high unemployment has forced even neoclassical economists to produce a large number of new books and articles on the business cycle.[1]

THE NATURAL RATE OF UNEMPLOYMENT

The latest reincarnation of the theory that most unemployment is "frictional," that is, just movement between jobs, is the *search theory*. In this view, many workers *voluntarily* quit their jobs to search for other jobs with higher pay. Some advocates of this theory indicate that women and young people are most prone to leave one job voluntarily to look for another

---

[1] See, e.g., Robert E. Lucas, "An Equilibrium Model of the Business Cycle," *Journal of Political Economy* 83 (December 1975), pp. 1113–1144; also Richard Stoken, *Cycles* (New York: McGraw-Hill, 1978); also Werner H. Stigel, ed., *Problems and Instruments of Business Cycle Analysis* (New York: Springer-Verlag, 1978); also Carl Dauten and Lloyd Valentine, *Business Cycles* (Los Angeles: Southwestern, 1968).

—but every empirical study shows that women and young people are less likely to leave the same job than adult men (because they are less certain of getting any other job). In the search theory, the problem causing unemployment is not lack of demand, but a lack of information on just what jobs are available. When there are sudden economic changes, such as a recession, perfect information becomes more difficult to obtain, so this explains sudden surges in voluntary unemployment. If all workers had perfect information as to wages and job locations, this theory claims that there would be perfect adaptation to changes, so there would be no search unemployment.

The *natural rate of unemployment* is defined as that rate which would exist in a labor market that has pure competition and no government regulation. So the "natural" rate would only include (1) frictional unemployment (changing job locations or occupations or both) and (2) search unemployment (voluntary searching for a better job).

Apparently, the natural rate of unemployment is increasing according to many mainstream economists (perhaps increasing complexity is making information worse and worse). In the administration of Harry Truman, White House economists said that from 1.5 percent to 2.5 percent was frictional or natural unemployment (and this was greeted with skepticism because unemployment had been only 1 percent in 1943 and 1944). Eisenhower's economists said from 2.5 percent to 3.5 percent was natural whereas Nixon's economists said from 4.5 percent to 5.5 percent was natural. In October of 1982, Reagan's secretary of the Treasury, Donald Regan, said that 6.5 percent unemployment is now the "full employment level." Many conservative economic models also predict over 6 percent unemployment as normal.[2]

Similarly, Frank Wykoff reports that many economists believe that unemployment actually hurts less than it appears because "slightly fewer than half the unemployed today were actually fired or dismissed. The rest are either new entrants into the labor force or those who quit or were voluntarily laid off."[3] Wykoff gives two other reasons why many conservative economists say that unemployment may not hurt so much today. One is the "safety net," as President Reagan calls it, of unemployment compensation, welfare, social security, medical insurance, and progressively less tax burden as income drops—but it is worth noting that conservatives fought the introduction of all these measures and that the Reagan administration has now drastically reduced several of them. Another reason that unemployment doesn't hurt so much now is that there are usually two paid workers in each family—but the reason that wives as well as husbands now work for pay is that it is absolutely necessary to maintain an adequate income!

As this book is being written, official unemployment figures have reached 12 million human beings or 11 percent of the officially defined labor force. But this is an understatement.[4] First, the official definition does *not* include 1.8 million people who are "discouraged

---

[2]For details of the arguments on the natural rate of unemployment, see the excellent article by Robert Cherry, "What Is So Natural About the Natural Rate of Unemployment?" *Journal of Economic Issues* 15 (September 1981) pp. 729–744. The argument that young people and women may have higher natural rates of unemployment appears in George L. Perry, "Changing Labor Markets and Inflation," *Brookings Papers on Economic Activity* 3 (1970), pp. 411–441.

[3]Frank Wykoff, "How Big Is A 10% Unemployment Rate?" *Los Angeles Times* (October 4, 1982), Part 4, p. 2.

[4]All data from the U.S. Department of Labor, reported in Robert Rosenblatt, "10.1% Jobless Rate Highest Since 1940," *Los Angeles Times* (October 9, 1982), Part 1, pp. 1, 20.

workers"; that is, after months or years of futile searching, they have given up. Second, the official definition considers as "employed" 6.6 million people who want to work full-time, but are able to get only part-time work. With these two corrections, the unemployment rate would be much higher. Furthermore, some groups are hurt much worse because of job discrimination. At this time, 9.0 percent of white workers are unemployed, but 20.2 percent of black workers are unemployed. In addition, millions of people are "underemployed," doing work far below their qualifications. As Wykoff observes, "Also beneath the surface are the underemployed: the recent M.B.A. retailing for Gemco, the Ph.D. working in a bookstore, the legal secretary doing odd jobs."[5]

Some people who are quick to suggest unemployment as a cure for inflation, do not seem to count the human misery from unemployment. For every 1.0 percent increase in unemployment sustained over a five-year period, (1) there is a 4.1 percent increase in suicides, (2) there is a 4.3 percent increase in male first-time admissions to mental hospitals, (3) there is a 2.3 percent increase in female first-time admissions to mental hospitals, (4) there is a 4.0 percent increase in state prison admissions, and (5) there is a 5.7 percent increase in homicides.[6]

OTHER NEOCLASSICAL THEORIES OF UNEMPLOYMENT

Early neoclassical theories dealt mainly with demand for particular products based on the subjective utility to individual consumers, which utility must obviously be limited and must begin to decline at the margin after some given quantity is consumed. Thus the very famous D. H. Robertson asserts: "... it is natural ... that after the brisk demand of the Indian ryot for braziers in 1910, or of the American public for motor cars in 1922–23, the intensity of the desire for these articles should fall away."[7] This approach leads naturally to thinking of the problem as one of absolute overproduction, of "too much" production. When, however, the entire economy is examined rather than each individual product, it becomes clear that the problem in a major depression is not that more is produced than people subjectively desire to consume. On the contrary, there is not nearly enough to fulfill the desires or even minimum health needs; there is only "too much" relative to the objective circumstances of the lack of effective purchasing power.

As long as most economists accepted Say's law, there were only a few logically possible explanations for the fluctuations of aggregate output. One such explanation is that "external" or noneconomic forces may limit supply or bring sudden demands. For example, sunspots may cause bad weather, and bad weather leads to bad harvests; unions may go on strike; governments may foolishly interfere with production activities; wars may stop the flow of raw materials or bring sudden demands for military production; et cetera ad infinitum. Thus, Duesenberry declares: "Major depressions have been produced by a variety of different types

---

[5] Wykoff, *op. cit.*, p. 2.

[6] See Harvey Brenner, "Estimating the Social Costs of National Economic Policy," *Achieving the Goals of the Employment Act*, U.S. Congress, Joint Economic Committee (Washington, D.C.: U.S. Government Printing Office, 1976), vol. 1, Paper 5.

[7] D. H. Robertson, *Banking Policy and the Price Level* (New York: Augustus M. Kelley, 1949), p. 10.

of "shocks," not by a regular cycle-producing mechanism."[8] Robert Lucas states that "the cyclical movements of output are generated by unsystematic monetary-fiscal shocks, the effects of which are distributed through time due to informational lags and an accelerator effect."[9] Certainly, such shocks as wars and bad weather do affect the economy, but their happenings do not always coincide with the major swings in the economy, some of which occur with no apparent outside shock at that time. Therefore, it is necessary at least to ask what mechanisms in the economy give rise to cyclical movements as a result of these shocks that occur at random with respect to the business cycle.

One theory does concentrate on the reaction of the economy to accidental or external shocks. It is observed that enterprises tend to react to changes in the economic situation by going much farther than necessary in the new direction—for example, a small rise in demand may cause an excessive increase in supply. Then, to compensate for the excessive movement in one direction, they react excessively in the opposite direction, always swinging beyond the point of "equilibrium" in a sort of "cobweb" pattern woven about that point. This cobweb theory, when applied to the dynamic development of the whole economy, sees it swinging like a pendulum past "equilibrium," always reacting to new random shocks to maintain the length of the swing.[10] This theory has been successfully used to explain the behavior of some individual products; it does not explain anything when applied to the whole economy (except that random shocks aggravate the cycle).

Another theory that emphasizes one kind of "external" shock is Schumpeter's theory of the impact of technological innovations on the economy. In fact, he explicitly declares, "The business cycles with which we are concerned . . . are not analogous to the oscillation of an elastic string or membrane . . . which, once set into motion, would but for friction, go on indefinitely . . . [cycles are not self-generating, but] are due to the intermittent action of the 'force' of innovation . . ."[11] According to this theory, economic expansion begins when an invention is used as an innovation in industry by some one bold entrepreneur, who is then followed by others owing to imitation or competition. The boom is brought to an end when the impetus of this innovation expires. Schumpeter's discussion of the process of innovation is profound and insightful, but it does not answer the cycle puzzle. It is certainly true that the uneven development of technology combines with entrepreneurial psychology to influence the course of economic events, but innovation itself may be determined by economic conditions though it may then intensify the course of events. It should be noted that Schumpeter concentrated on the 30- to 50-year Kondratieff cycles though he also tried to explain the shorter cycles (all other theories in this chapter concentrate on the shorter 4- to 10-year cycle).

Another type of theory reaffirms Say's law to the extent that aggregate demand cannot be deficient for very long. It is argued that it is never rational to hoard money because if it is not used for consumption, it is always most profitable to lend it at interest for further

---

[8] James S. Duesenberry, *Business Cycles and Economic Growth* (New York McGraw-Hill, 1958), p. 11.
[9] Lucas, *op. cit.*, p. 1113.
[10] See Ragnar Frisch, "Propagation and Impulse Problems," *Essays in Honor of Gustav Cassel* (London: George Allen and Unwin, 1933).
[11] Joseph A. Schumpeter, *Business Cycles* (New York: McGraw-Hill, 1939), p. 175.

investment. Yet there may be temporary panics with hoarding of money and withholding of credit caused by irrational pessimism. Typical of these "explanations" is this statement of Marshall's: "The chief cause of the evil is a want of confidence."[12] The defect of these theories lies in the fact that no one has ever demonstrated cycles of optimism and pessimism in business people independent of the economic cycle. In fact, the height of optimism is always reached, as in 1929, at the peak of the business cycle. Only *after* economic conditions have objectively worsened are there irrationally large reactions by business people, which intensify the economic downturn. Similarly, irrational reactions may intensify an economic expansion after conditions have objectively improved.

Closely related to the preceding explanation is the notion that the main fault of the system lies in a banking structure that irrationally brings any industrial expansion to an end. The theory is that the boom is brought about by the expansion of bank credit, but that the bankers cannot or will not continue to expand credit indefinitely at the necessary rate.[13] Certainly, speculative expansion followed by excessive restriction of credit may magnify any disturbance (as shown in detail in Part Four), but banks have generally continued to increase credit rapidly until *after* profit expectations begin to fall. *What must be explained is why these profit expectations change.* The similar monetarist theories of the cycle are discussed in Part Four. To the extent that the monetarists believe that the private economy always stays at full employment equilibrium until disturbed by incorrect government monetary policies, they are hard-core followers of Say's law and the classical analysis.

Some neoclassical theories, relying on changes in expectations, are also discussed in Part Four on monetary cycle theories because they are closely related. One much discussed theory by Otto Eckstein[14] may be used to illustrate the current state of most neoclassical-Keynesian synthesis cycle theories. He concludes that both unemployment and inflation are due to external shocks. He lists the energy shortage and energy crisis (foreign-induced), worldwide crop failures, and various government-caused problems, stemming from the Vietnam War. The government actions include dollar devaluation, monetary policies, price decontrol, and fiscal policies. Eckstein's view that there is *no internal* cyclical or inflationary mechanism, but that mistaken government policies are a major cause of downturns, is very similar to the monetarist view of cycles. He does find three reactive mechanisms in the economy that magnify the unemployment and inflation caused by shocks: the reactions and mistakes of the financial system, the reactions and errors of consumers, and the exaggerations and errors in business expectations.

Eckstein also argues that stagflation (unemployment and inflation) is self-perpetuating once it begins. Inflation leads to high interest rates and loss of confidence, which causes more unemployment. Unemployment leads to less investment, which leads to less productivity growth, which causes more inflation. This vicious circle, which is self-perpetuating, is now the main cause of stagflation in his opinion. One should be skeptical of all perpetual motion

---

[12] M. P. and Alfred Marshall, *The Economics of Industry* (London: Collier-Macmillan, 1881), book 3, p. 155.
[13] See R. G. Hawtrey, "The Trade Cycle," *Readings in Business Cycle Theory* (New York: McGraw-Hill, 1944), pp. 330–350.
[14] Otto Eckstein, *The Great Recession* (New York: North-Holland, 1978).

machines. Will it really continue forever? What can cause the process to speed up or to end? These questions are not answered.

WESLEY CLAIR MITCHELL AND JOHN MAYNARD KEYNES

Wesley Mitchell was one of the first important and relatively orthodox economists to view business cycle phenomena as other than accidental or "external" to the economy. The burden of all Mitchell's works is to show that the business cycle is a self-generating series of "normal" phases of business, each leading into the next under the conditions given by present economic institutions. Although he never reached the comprehensive theory at which he was aiming, his immense empirical research forms the basis for all further scientific investigation of this field.

Until the 1930s, however, few economists paid more than lip service to the facts presented by Mitchell. Those who mentioned these facts at all did so as a special problem beyond the confines of the proper area of economics, which was to describe the process of making minor adjustments by individual firms and individual consumers in a basically stable economy. In the Great Depression of the thirties that complacency was forever shaken though it raises its head anew in every expansion period.

The economist whose name is connected with the theoretical "revolution" of the thirties is John Maynard Keynes. Keynes's main contribution was the demolition of Say's law within a sophisticated theoretical structure acceptable to mainstream economics. He recognized the possibility that the economy as a whole may be in equilibrium at other than full employment —that is, that more or less may be demanded than is supplied at full employment at the present price level. Most of his theory is to be found in some form in earlier economists, such as Malthus or Marx or Wicksell. Furthermore, his theory can at best explain a new "equilibrium" position of the economy at less than full employment *after* there has been a once-and-for-all change in profit expectations and other variables; he does not explain the origins of disequilibrium and the movements caused by it. Hicks comments that "Keynesian economics, in spite of all that it has done for our understanding of business fluctuations, has beyond doubt left at least one major thing unexplained; and that thing is nothing less than the business cycle itself."[15] Keynes's popularity lay in saying in a striking manner the right thing at the right time—for he not only explained the possibility of depressions and inflations, but also laid down possible solutions for these problems within the bounds of the private enterprise economic system.

Keynes focused attention on the fact that all income derives from either consumers' purchases or purchases for investment purposes. The two principal contenders among cycle theories (both pre-Keynesian in origin) are now usually phrased in terms of the reasons for an upturn and a downturn of these two categories of purchases. On the one side, the theory of *underconsumption,* as in the writing of John Hobson, argues that consumption turns

---

[15] John R. Hicks, *The Trade Cycle* (Oxford: Clarendon, 1950), p. 1.

downward to cause the end of prosperity because the distribution of income is so concentrated among a few that there is little purchasing power available to most of the population.[16] In this explanation, investment declines because the lack of consumer demand causes manufacturers to reduce their own demand for investment goods. This theory is often interpreted, mainly by trade unionists, to mean that higher wages are the cure-all for depressions.

On the other side, the theories of *overinvestment,* such as the works of Frederick von Hayek, claim that it is "excessive" investment that precipitates the crisis.[17] They argue that there has been "too much" investment attempted on the basis of the available resources, with a resulting excess demand for labor, machinery, and credit. These are cost or supply-side difficulties. The problem, they allege, is that not only are the producers' goods industries expanding, but also the consumers' goods demand is rising, so that the latter industrial group is trying to bid factors of production away from the former, with the result that wages, prices of machinery, and interest rates are rising. When costs rise far enough, the rate of profit is lowered, and, as a result, investment declines. The recovery begins when costs of production have fallen far enough to raise the rate of profit again. These theories are often interpreted, mainly by managerial personnel, to mean that lower wages are a cure-all for depressions (not to speak of inflations).

Variants of the underconsumption and overinvestment theories are considered in detail in the next two chapters. First, however, it is important to understand the simplest Keynesian-type theory, the so-called multiplier-accelerator theory. It is much too simple, but it is immensely important in the history of macroeconomic thought. It integrates the multiplier and accelerator approaches, so it brings Keynesian consumption and investment theory together. It also sets the formal form followed ever since by most cycle theories in economics. Although it does not give a persuasive answer as to the turning points, it is a good framework for describing the cumulative expansions and contractions.

THE SIMPLEST KEYNESIAN MODEL

John Maynard Keynes never constructed a full cycle theory, but many of his followers have presented Keynesian-type theories. Although many of these are very complex, the earliest and most famous was a very simple model by Paul Samuelson (done while he was still a graduate student under Alvin Hansen.)[18] All demand for goods and services is divided into two parts: demand for consumer goods and services (C) and demand for investor or producer goods and services (I). If there is to be equilibrium between supply and demand, then it is

---

[16]See the works cited in Gottfried Haberler, *Prosperity and Depression* (Cambridge, Mass.: Harvard University Press, 1960), chap. 5.

[17]See *Ibid.,* chap. 3.

[18]See Paul Samuelson, "Interactions Between the Multiplier and the Principle of Acceleration," *The Review of Economics and Statistics* 21 (May 1939), pp. 75–78.

necessary in the aggregate that net national product (Y) be exactly equal to consumer plus investor demand:

$$\text{(output equilibrium)} \quad Y_t = C_t + I_t \tag{13.1}$$

where t is a time period. This model shows the movement of *demand* at each time period. Unlike Say's law, it assumes that supply, represented by net national product, follows demand. There is equilibrium at each time period (though not in between as supply is adjusting to demand), but the equilibrium may be below the full employment level of supply.

As a first approximation, this model of Samuelson's assumes government to be exogenous. (In economics, *exogenous* means determined outside the model whereas *endogenous* means determined by the internal operation of the whole model.) Samuelson's model ignores depreciation, so investment demand (I) is *net* investment and does not include replacement investment. The supply of output is likewise *net* national product, which is also equal to national income here—since government taxes are ignored. The model also ignores changing prices, so all variables are in real terms, that is, in dollars of constant purchasing power.

Samuelson adopts the usual Keynesian consumption function, which describes consumer behavior on the basis of psychological propensities of consumers. It says that consumer demand rises and falls when national income rises and falls, *but* that consumption rises and falls more slowly than income.

$$\text{consumption} = f^1 \text{ (income)} \tag{13.2}$$

where f^1, the function, is positive. In the usual linear form (shown in Appendix 13A), the marginal propensity to consume or the marginal consumption–income ratio is constant. Also, in the usual linear form, there is an additional constant term, so the average propensity to consume (C/Y), or the average consumption–income ratio, falls when income rises and rises when income falls. This consumption function has numerous weaknesses, all of which were discussed in detail in Chapter 8.

The third relationship considered by Samuelson is investment behavior based on the so-called accelerator principle. This principle says that investment is determined by the change in demand rather than by the level of demand. The *change* in capital is related to the *change* in output demanded, but investment is defined as the change in capital. Thus, he argues that investment behavior is a function of the previous change in consumer demand:

$$\text{investment} = f^2 \text{ (change in consumption, lagged)} \tag{13.3}$$

where the functional relation, f^2, is a positive constant coefficient, called the "accelerator" coefficient. The investment function based on an accelerator coefficient also has many defects, which were discussed in detail in Chapter 9.

Equation 13.3, given earlier, is the weakest part of Samuelson's model. One defect may be remedied to an extent by making investment a function of the change in national product or income (Y) rather than a function of the change in consumption (C). This way, at least the effects of investment demand in the investment goods industries are included in the function as well as the effects of investment demand in the consumption goods industries. The function would then be

$$\text{investment} = f^3 \text{ (change in income, lagged)} \tag{13.4}$$

where the functional relation, f^3, is some other positive constant coefficient. Output is lagged because of the considerable time lag between changes in demand and actual investment.

Although the consumption function and investment function used in Samuelson's model have many weaknesses, the model derived from them is an extremely useful analytic tool even though it is very far from reality. (Its mathematical form is presented in Appendix 13A.)

Workings of the Model

Three relationships have been discussed: that consumption plus investment determines income, that consumption is a lagged function of the level of income, and that investment is a lagged function of the change in income. If these three are accepted as correct approximations of reality for the moment, what kind of cyclical behavior results? A description might run as follows. As income grows in prosperity, the proportion spent on consumption declines; as a result, total demand for output eventually rises less rapidly. Then, however, as the increase in demand for output declines in each succeeding period, net investment must accordingly decline absolutely. This causes a decline in aggregate income, leading to a decline in consumption, which leads to a further decline in net investment, thus initiating a depression. As income declines in the depression, the reverse process takes place. Consumption does not drop as rapidly as income, the decline in demand proceeds more and more slowly, eventually some net investment is necessary, and recovery begins.

SUMMARY

Most neoclassical economists believe in Say's law (though often in very complex, sophisticated forms), so they do not believe that large-scale involuntary employment is possible for any length of time. Therefore, many of them believe that most of present unemployment is simply frictional (moving to new jobs created by new technology) or voluntary searches for better jobs (because people lack perfect information). Together these constitute the "natural rate of unemployment." Neoclassical economists acknowledge temporary unemployment only as the result of external shocks, without which the capitalist system would function perfectly. The external shocks may include wars, droughts, government mismanagement of the money supply, irrational actions by bankers, or general irrational loss of confidence.

On the contrary, Wesley Mitchell found that the capitalist system itself produced business cycles. Keynes proved that the system could operate for some length of time below full employment without any automatic return, so he disproved Say's law. Keynes's followers, like Samuelson, produced endogenous models of the business cycle. In Samuelson's model, consumption is based on a percentage of income, with a time lag, whereas investment is based on the change in consumer demand, with a time lag. Given the appropriate parameters, this model does produce cycles. But it is very much oversimplified, so many other writers have created more complex models, expanding greatly or changing the demand-side relations or the supply-side relations (which are explored in the next two chapters).

APPENDIX 13A

A Formal Model of the Simplest Keynesian Theory

Assume that consumption is equal to some minimum plus a constant proportion of the income of the previous time period. Assume that new investment is equal to a constant proportion of the change in income from two periods ago to one period ago. Then it is possible to show the exact time paths that national income or product, aggregate consumption, and net investment will pursue over the business cycle in this model of the economy. A formal model of the simplest Keynesian theory may be formulated as follows:

$$\text{income} = \text{consumption} + \text{investment}$$

$$Y_t = C_t + I_t \tag{13A.1}$$

$$\text{consumption} = f^1 \text{ (income, lagged)}$$

$$C_t = a + bY_{t-1} \tag{13A.2}$$

$$\text{investment} = f^2 \text{ (change in income, lagged)}$$

$$I_t = v(Y_{t-1} - Y_{t-2}) \tag{13A.3}$$

Substituting equations 13A.2 and 13A.3 into equation 13A.1, the reduced form equation is

$$Y_t = a + bY_{t-1} + v(Y_{t-1} - Y_{t-2}) \tag{13A.4}$$

or

$$Y_t = a + (b+v)Y_{t-1} - vY_{t-2} \tag{13A.5}$$

This reduced form equation gives national product in terms of certain constants and the lagged values of national product.

Equation 13A.5 is a second order difference equation (*second order* just means two differences or two time lags). Solving a difference equation means being able to state the time path of the variable (national product) in terms of its initial values (called initial conditions). If there are two differences, as in a second order equation, two initial values of national product must be given.

If we ignore the constant, a, to obtain the simplest case (a homogeneous equation), then:

$$Y_t - (b+v)Y_{t-1} + vY_{t-2} = 0 \tag{13A.6}$$

To solve such an equation, consider a constant, q, such that

$$q^2 - q(b+v) + v = 0 \tag{13A.7}$$

This is a simple quadratic equation. From high school algebra, the quadratic formula says that

$$q = \frac{(b+v) \pm \sqrt{(b+v)^2 - 4v}}{2} \tag{13A.8}$$

When the quantity under the square root sign is negative, the solution is a triogonometric function, which oscillates as the angle goes around the circle. In short, *there will be cyclical fluctuations* in the time path of national product *if the parameters are in a certain range,* namely, if $(b + v)^2$ is less than $4v$. In another range of the parameters, namely, if $(b + v)^2$ is greater than $4v$, then there will be no fluctuations, but constant growth (constant decline is also mathematically possible).

In the range in which there are fluctuations, if $v = 1$, then the fluctuations are of constant magnitude. If v is less than 1, the cycle is damped and converges toward some value (see Figure 13A.1). If v is greater than 1, the cycle is explosive with larger and larger fluctuations (see Figure 13A.2).

Only v and b affect fluctuations. If the constant, a, is included in the equation, it does not change the fluctuations. The constant, a, only affects the level around which fluctuations will occur. Within the cyclical range of the equation, the economic behavior will be exactly that which was described in the text of this chapter. A numerical example of the operation

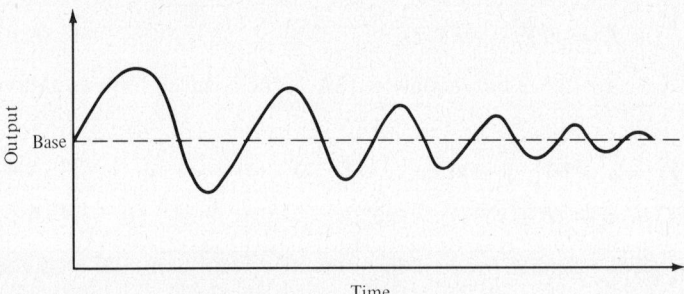

Figure 13A.1 Damped Cycles

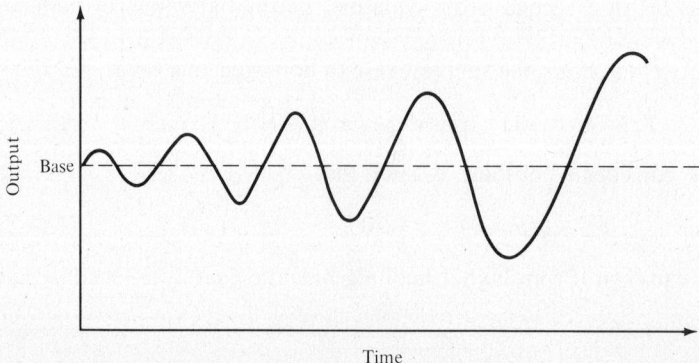

Figure 13A.2 Explosive Cycles

Chapter 13 CLASSICAL AND KEYNESIAN CYCLE THEORIES   255

of the whole model is as follows. Suppose that national product moves upward initially from $Y_0 = 99.6$ to $Y_1 = 100.0$. This is the assumption in Table 13A.1.

For this table, the constants are set at the arbitrary values $a = 9.6$, $b = 0.9$, and $v = 1$. Then the peak will be 100.0, output will decline for 10 periods to a trough at 92.0, then output will rise for 10 periods to a peak at 100.0, and so forth. The fluctuations will have a constant magnitude in this case because the constant v happens to equal 1 in this case.

Table 13A.1 shows how the net national product moves over time, beginning with the assumed levels in periods 0 and 1. The arrow shows that the level of national product in period 1 is multiplied by b to determine consumption in period 2. The product level in period 2 is multiplied by b to determine consumption in period 3, and so forth. The other arrow shows that the *change* in output from period 0 to period 1 is multiplied by v to determine investment in period 2, and so forth.

Table 13A.1

ARITHMETIC EXAMPLE OF SIMPLEST CYCLE MODEL

Time Period	Net National Product	Consumption	Net Investment
0	99.6		
1	100.0		
2	100.0	99.6	0.4
3	99.6	99.6	0.0
4	98.8	99.2	−0.4
5	97.7	98.5	−0.8
6	96.5	97.5	−1.0
7	95.2	96.5	−1.3
8	94.0	95.3	−1.3
9	93.0	94.2	−1.2
10	92.3	93.3	−1.0
11	92.0	92.7	−0.7
12	92.5	92.4	0.1
13	93.3	92.9	0.4
14	94.4	93.6	0.8
15	95.6	94.6	1.0
16	96.9	95.6	1.3
17	18.2	96.8	1.4
18	99.1	98.0	1.1
19	99.6	98.8	0.8
20	100.0	99.2	0.8
21	100.0	99.6	0.4
22	99.6	99.6	0.0
23	98.8	99.2	−0.4

Assume: $Y_0 = 99.6$, $Y_1 = 100.0$, $a = 9.6$, $b = 0.9$, and $v = 1$.
(Remember that $C_t = a + bY_{t-1}$ and that $I_t = v(Y_{t-1} - Y_{t-2})$.
For example, $C_2 = 9.6 + 0.9(100.0) = 99.6$ and $I_2 = 1(100.0 - 99.6) = 0.4$.)

As stated earlier, the Samuelson model has many weaknesses, so it is only an analytic toy. It is extremely useful, however, as an introduction to all cyclical models. All the cycle models in this book have a similar form (with increasingly realistic content), so they follow the same mathematical rules.

DAMPED AND EXPLOSIVE CYCLES

It was noted above that v, the coefficient of the output at $t-2$, must be equal to 1 for constant cycles. If it is less than 1, then cycles are damped and slowly disappear. If it is greater than 1, then cycle amplitudes get larger and larger until the economy explodes. Since the business cycle has not disappeared and the economy has not exploded, it appears that the cycle and the economy exist only because—by some cosmic miracle—the coefficient happens to equal exactly 1. Something must be wrong with this reasoning or the assumptions.

There are several possible solutions. One suggestion is that the business cycle is damped in its endogenous system of equations, but that there are exogenous shocks to it that keep it going. There is a considerable and complex literature on whether the shocks can be purely random or how they must be spaced, and so forth. But the solution does not seem satisfying because it brings back the viewpoint that the cycle is due to purely random accidents. Yet many neoclassical economists do hold this view because of their tendency to deny the endogeneity of the business cycle.

Another solution assumes that the endogenous system is explosive, but that there are so-called floors and ceilings holding it within bounds at every turning point. The *ceiling* is usually described as the limit of production at full-capacity level, which could increase only very slowly over a long time. The *floor* is usually described by the fact that capital can be disinvested only to the amount of depreciation. In other words, the biggest decline that can occur in aggregate capital in one year is the amount of wear and tear of capital. A problem with this solution includes the fact that under capitalism the economy at the peak of the cycle seldom reaches full capacity. Another problem is the fact that even at the trough of the cycle, the economy seldom reaches zero net investment, much less zero gross investment. In other words, it is not obvious that the economy comes anywhere near the floors and ceilings in most cycles.

Another solution lies in the fact that most of the functions mentioned here—including the consumption and investment functions—really do not have one short time lag. Rather, they are influenced by the explanatory variables from several past time periods. The result is then a difference equation with many time lags. Such a higher order equation allows for a much more complex solution of cycles and growth in a wide range of the parameters.

Finally, it has been assumed that the relations are all linear, but that is not true. If nonlinear relations are included (for example, by using Y^2 and Y^3), then this more complex equation can also generate cycles and growth over a wide range of the parameters.

Chapter 14

DEMAND-SIDE CYCLE THEORIES: MARXIST, POST KEYNESIAN, AND INSTITUTIONALIST VIEWS

This chapter examines theories that attribute recessions and depressions to lack of effective demand. These include underconsumptionist, Marxist, Keynesian, Post Keynesian, and institutionalist types, each of which is discussed in the following pages either separately or as part of a more general model.

UNDERCONSUMPTIONIST THEORIES

All underconsumptionist theories include, by definition and tradition, two main components.[1] The most important shared belief is that insufficient consumer demand for goods and services is the main cause of recession, depression, and unemployment. The second belief is that this lack of consumer demand is always a drag on the economy, so there would be long-run stagnation if there were not some external or exogenous events pulling the economy upward at times (it is shown later, however, that there are demand-side theories that are

---

[1] See, e.g., the comprehensive but hostile history in Michael Bleany, *Underconsumption Theories* (New York: International Publishers, 1976).

purely cyclical in nature). Other than these two characteristics, various underconsumption theories are quite different.

There have been many nonsocialist, non-Marxist, underconsumption theories, ranging from the earliest beginnings with Lord Lauderdale and the Reverend T. R. Malthus to later ones such as the theories of Foster and Catchings.[2] In many of these theories, the emphasis was that, on the one side, industry turns out an increasing flood of commodities. On the other side, some people save part of their income. As a result, consumer demand does not keep up with the flood of commodities, there is a pileup of unsold goods, and production is cut. Less production leads to unemployment, which means still less income and less consumer demand. The result is stagnation. The Reverend Malthus recommended that society maintain a class of parasites, such as landlords, who are magnificent at the art of consumption but do not produce anything. Others have recommended schemes to ensure that people be forced to respend all their income rapidly.

Another form of underconsumption theory was popular with liberal reformers, such as John Hobson.[3] Hobson stressed that the cause of the deficient consumer demand is not a general tendency toward too much saving, but a maldistribution of income. Most wage workers are poorly paid, so their income and consumption are very limited. On the other hand, the rich have incomes that are far above their consumption needs, so they save increasing amounts of income. There is a lack of consumer demand because those that have money don't need more consumption and those that need it don't have the money. Hobson's solution was a more equal distribution of income. Almost all trade unions agree that the way out of any recession or depression is more wages to workers (or government welfare or unemployment payments), so they will have the income to spend on consumption.

Early socialist writers, such as Sismondi or Rodbertus,[4] had similar theories. They argued that the worker is not paid his or her "full product," but is limited to a subsistence wage. Therefore, as production expands, the workers' share in national income must decline. As a result, consumer demand must inevitably decline relative to production, so a crisis of overproduction must follow, leading to economic stagnation.

Such theories were expanded by many later Marxists, such as the brilliant Rosa Luxemburg.[5] Luxemburg argued that the exploitation of workers and consequent lack of consumption tend to lead to long-run stagnation. The only reason it has not done so thus far has been the global expansion of capitalism. Capitalists conquer new markets by expanding their trade and their colonial empires. When all the world is conquered by capitalism, stagnation must eventually result.

In the 1930s, when the U.S. economy suffered ten years of stagnation, theories of stagnation naturally became very popular. Alvin Hansen, who was a president of the American

---

[2] See discussion in G. Haberler, *Prosperity and Depression,* 4th ed. (Cambridge, Mass.: Harvard University Press, 1960), chap. 5.

[3] John A. Hobson, *The Economics of Unemployment* (London: George Allen and Unwin, 1922).

[4] See Karl Rodbertus, *Overproduction and Crisis* (New York: Scribner's, 1898); also J. C. L. Simonde de Sismondi, "Industrial Crisis: The Result of Laissez-Faire," in Donald D. Wagner (ed.), *Social Reformers* (New York: Macmillan, 1946), pp. 151–153.

[5] Rosa Luxemburg is discussed very thoroughly and sympathetically in Paul Sweezy, *Theory of Capitalist Development* (New York: Monthly Review, 1942, 1970).

Economic Association, argued that stagnation was held off before the Great Depression only by certain unique historical factors, including the U.S. expansion on its frontier, rapid population growth, and rapid technological innovation (such as the railroad, automobile, and electricity).[6]

An excellent Marxist work, in which underconsumption was one theme, was written by Paul Sweezy in the late 1930s, followed by other important works by Sweezy and Paul Baran in the 1950s and the 1960s.[7] Within the framework of a Marxist underconsumption theory, Sweezy and Baran made some incisive and impressive contributions, well worth reading even today. They argued that the capitalist system puts off stagnation mainly by private wasteful expenditures (such as pyramids or advertising) and public wasteful expenditures (such as military spending). These wasteful or unproductive expenditures constitute demand, but produce no supply of goods or services for consumers or for investors. Stagnation is ended and prosperity arises sometimes for two main reasons: new technological innovations and major wars (such as the two world wars, the Korean War, or the Vietnam War).

There have been many criticisms of underconsumption theories. First, there is no explanation of the recovery process, which is necessary to understand business cycle reality. It is not sufficient to bring in *ad hoc* factors, such as major innovations or wars. Second, a theory is incomplete if it leaves out the fact that the savings of capitalists may be used for new investment. Saving is *not* a problem *if* there is equal investment. Most underconsumptionists have no explanation as to why investment should not fill the gap between output and investment demand. Sweezy, however, does explain it by an accelerator theory, in which there is a fixed relation between net investment and consumer demand. If consumer demand is limited by exploitation of workers to a slower growth, then net investment must decline. Weaknesses of this theory were discussed in Chapter 9.

MARX AND UNDERCONSUMPTION

Karl Marx gave the first balanced appraisal of underconsumption, which pointed out certain errors, but also emphasized its strong points. Marx began with a systematic discussion of the problems capitalists face in making profits, which, in turn, affect their investment.

In Marx's *Capital,* he shows a process whereby the capitalist (1) uses money to buy inputs of labor-power and physical capital; (2) uses these inputs to produce an output, in the process of which profit is produced by the exploitation of workers; and (3) sells the output at the going price to realize the profit embodied in it. Marx emphasized that capitalists may have troubles in making profits either because of problems in the process of *production* of profit (the supply side) *or* in the process of *realization* of profit (the demand side). *Production of profit* depends on both (1) the price the capitalist must pay for labor and physical capital and (2) how efficiently the capitalist uses the physical capital and how intensively the capitalist exploits

---

[6]Alvin Hansen's theory and similar ones are discussed in R. A. Gordon, *Business Fluctuations,* 3d ed. (New York: Harper & Row, 1961).
[7]See Sweezy, *op. cit.;* also Paul Baran, *The Political Economy of Growth* (New York: Monthly Review, 1957); also Paul Baran and Paul Sweezy, *Monopoly Capital* (New York: Monthly Review, 1966).

the workers in the production process. The profit is then embodied in the output, but *realization of the profit* means that the capitalist must sell the output at its long-run price (including cost plus the average profit).

In explaining business cycles, some theorists emphasize one of these two problems while excluding the other. A careful theory must emphasize both sides of the capitalist dilemma: both the production of profit and the realization of profit. It is a dilemma because every capitalist has two conflicting desires. One desire is to pay as low a wage as possible to workers in the capitalist's own enterprise in order to produce as much profit as possible. The other desire is for all other capitalists to pay high wages so that workers will have as much buying power as possible to enable them to purchase the products at the price that has been set.

This dilemma for capitalist employers also means that governments under capitalism have a policy dilemma. Government policy should attempt to lower wages to increase the production of profit, but government policy should attempt to raise wages to increase the realization of profit. For a correct political economic analysis, economists must try to keep in mind both horns of the dilemma.

Marx criticized the earlier underconsumptionists for neglecting the issues of production of profit as well as its realization. Furthermore, in his reproduction schema in Volume 2 of *Capital,* Marx showed that equilibrium at full employment is theoretically *possible* even with exploitation. He also noted that total wages are rising, not falling, during expansion all the way to the peak. He further stressed that there are *no* long-run crises of continuous decline in capitalism.[8] Rather, capitalism grows in a cyclical manner by booms, followed by contractions, followed by another boom.

Marx attacked the liberal solution of higher wages to bolster consumer demand by showing that higher wage costs reduce profit per unit. These lower profits per unit have a depressing effect on capitalist investment. In addition, Marx pointed out that demand consists of both consumer demand and investment demand and that a precipitous decline in capitalist investment is usually the immediate cause of economic contractions. A general rise in the share of wages in output could cause investment to decline even sooner. (Marx favored higher wages, of course, but he did not think it a panacea for capitalist depressions.)

The fact that Marx criticized the earlier simplistic underconsumption theories has been interpreted by some Marxists to mean that Marx dismissed all theories focusing on lack of consumer demand or lack of effective demand in general. In recent years, a number of Marxists have thus made strident attacks on all demand or underconsumption theories. Some Marxists deny that there could be anything Marxist about any theory with a main focus on effective demand. These Marxists, such as Shaikh,[9] seem to be worried that acknowledgment of demand problems must lead to a Keynesian type of reformist solution to business cycle downturns. Robert Cherry even makes the assertion that "Marx believed that deficient demand would not create fundamental problems for capitalist societies."[10] Yet Marx himself wrote that "the ultimate cause of all real crises always remains the poverty and restricted

---

[8]See Karl Marx, *Theories of Surplus Value* (Moscow: Progress Publishers, 1968), part 2, p. 497n.

[9]Anwar Shaikh, "An Introduction to the History of Crisis Theories," in Union for Radical Political Economics, *U.S. Capitalism in Crisis* (New York: Monthly Review, 1978), pp. 219–240.

[10]Robert Cherry, *Macroeconomics* (Reading, Mass.: Addison-Wesley, 1980), p. 331.

consumption of the masses."[11] Marx also argued that the realization of profits "is limited not only by the consumption requirements of society in general, but by the consumption requirements of a society in which the great majority are poor and must always remain poor."[12]

It was Marx, not Keynes, who first systematically dissected Say's law by showing that lack of effective demand can cause mass unemployment in capitalism.[13] Marx notes three institutional conditions of capitalism that make possible crises caused by lack of effective demand: (1) production for the market, not self-sufficient units (such as Robinson Crusoe or primitive tribes or feudal manors); (2) production for private profit, not social use; and (3) use of money, not barter, so hoarding (nonspending) is possible.

It was Marx, not Keynes, who first demonstrated in his famous reproductive schema that dynamic equilibrium is theoretically *possible* in capitalism if, and only if, effective demand grows at a certain rate. Marx shows that realization crises are possible if this rate of growth of effective demand is not achieved.

It was Marx, not Keynes, who first showed that capitalists face not one but two problems: (1) the problem of producing profit and (2) the problem of realizing profit in the marketplace.[14] Keynes concentrated on the realization problem, which was natural in the depths of the Great Depression. Marx tried to examine *both* problems.

A REALIZATION THEORY

If the term *underconsumption* is to be restricted to theories of secular decline in consumer demand, then a short-run theory attributing the business cycle to problems of effective demand must have another name—let it be called a "realization" theory. For a framework, the realization theory divides national income into wages and profits

$$Y_t = W_t + \Pi_t \tag{14.1}$$

where Y is national income in constant dollars, W is wages (or total employee compensation in constant dollars), Π is profits (i.e., all property income, or national income minus wages), and t is a time period.

The supply of national output must also equal investment spending plus consumer spending *if there is to be equilibrium* at a given point (with supply following demand, contrary to Say's law). In the private, domestic economy:

$$Y_t = C_t + I_t \tag{14.2}$$

where C is aggregate consumption and I is aggregate net investment.

A realization model of the cycle requires only four main behavioral relationships. First, investment is based on the rate of profit. Second, the rate of profit is based on changes in output demanded (both for consumption and investment). Third, the rate of exploitation

---

[11] Karl Marx, *Capital* (Chicago: Charles Kerr, 1907), vol. 3, p. 568.
[12] *Ibid.*, vol. 2, p. 363.
[13] See Karl Marx, *Theories of Surplus Value* (Moscow: Progress Publishers, 1968), part 2, pp. 492–535.
[14] See Karl Marx, *Capital* (Chicago: Charles Kerr, 1907), vol. 3, p. 286.

(Π/W) rises as output rises in each expansion and falls as output falls in each contraction. Fourth, consumer spending is a positive function of national income, but a negative function of the rate of exploitation.

The first alleged relationship, that investment is based on the rate of profit, was explored and found to be realistic in Chapter 9. A function reflecting this theory would be:

$$\text{investment} = f^1 \text{ (profit rate)} \tag{14.3}$$

where the function, f^1, is positive, with a time lag. The past profit rate presumably reflects capitalist expectations of future profit rates. It was found, however, that the profit rate affects investment with a long time lag. Furthermore, it is really the profit rate of several previous periods that affects investors' expectations of the future. Moreover, it was found that other variables—such as total profits and interest rates—also have an influence on investment. Nevertheless, one reason that investment rises in expansion and falls in contraction is that it follows the rate of profit.

The second alleged relationship is that the profit rate is determined by the change in output demanded (represented by national income). In Chapter 11, it was discovered that demand influences the degree of capacity utilization, which affects the rate of profit. Thus, it is not unreasonable to assert that

$$\text{profit rate} = f^2 \text{ (change in output demanded)} \tag{14.4}$$

where the function, f^2, is positive, with a time lag. Though this relation has some validity, other variables also influence profit rates. Still it is true that the rate of profit rises in early and mid-expansion partly because the rate of growth of output demanded is rising. The decline of the rate of profit in late expansion may be partly due to the decline in the rate of growth of output demanded. The decline of the profit rate in most of contraction is traceable in large part to the decline in output demanded. To be symmetrical, the rate of growth of output should also rise before the end of the contraction, leading to a rise in the rate of profit —but the relative briefness of contractions must often hide this movement in the data, if it occurs.

The third alleged relationship is that the rate of exploitation (Π/W) rises and falls with the level of output. The equation would be:

$$\text{rate of exploitation } (\Pi/W) = f^3 \text{ (output)} \tag{14.5}$$

where the function, f^3, is positive. In Chapter 10, it was found that the wage share (W/Y) does move opposite to the movements of output though it is probably a nonlinear relationship. Since the rate of exploitation must move opposite to the wage share, it must move the same direction as output. This theory claims that the rising output in expansion is associated with a rising rate of exploitation because (1) capitalists own the product, so the rising output goes to the capitalist until labor contracts are renegotiated; (2) labor contracts have a fixed duration; (3) capitalists resist hourly wage increases; and (4) the real hourly wage rises more slowly than productivity (productivity rises partly because of a falling ratio of overhead workers to output). The theory claims that the falling real output in contraction is associated with a falling rate of exploitation because (1) falling product hurts the capitalist share until new labor contracts can be negotiated; (2) labor contracts have a fixed duration;

(3) capitalists, the state, and the media are all less able and willing to force cuts in hourly wages; and (4) the real hourly wage does not fall as much as productivity (productivity falls partly because of a rising ratio of overhead workers to output).

The fourth and last alleged behavioral relationship is that consumption is positively related to national income, but negatively related to the rate of exploitation. The equation is this:

$$\text{consumption} = f^4 \text{ (output, rate of exploitation)} \tag{14.6}$$

where the function, f^4, is positive with respect to output but negative with respect to the rate of exploitation, with time lags for the reaction to both variables. Chapter 8 found that consumption has statistically significant positive relation to national income, but a statistically significant negative relation to the rate of exploitation (or a positive relation to the wage share). Consumption moves contrary to the rate of exploitation (Π/W) because workers have higher propensities to consume than capitalists. In the business expansion, the rising level of national income raises the consumption level. The rising rate of exploitation, however, creates a falling average propensity to consume, so eventually consumption rises more and more slowly. In the business contraction, the falling national income pulls down consumption, but the falling rate of exploitation raises the average propensity to consume, so consumption falls more and more slowly. Since consumption is the largest part of demand, the rate of growth of total output demanded is strongly influenced by the rate of growth of consumption.

The business cycle, according to the realization theory, looks this way: As economic expansion occurs, the rate of exploitation rises—or, equivalently, the share of wages declines. A rising rate of exploitation or falling wage share reduces the growth of consumer demand and aggregate demand. A decline in the growth of output demanded causes a decline in the rate of profit. A falling rate of profit causes a decline in investment. Lower investment demand means still less output, less employment, less income, less consumer demand, and so forth.

On the contrary, in the contraction (recession or depression) as output declines, the rate of exploitation falls. A falling exploitation rate eventually means that consumer demand declines more and more slowly. When demand stops falling so fast and begins to flatten out, investment again rises, and recovery begins.

Evaluation. It has been shown that a logically consistent Marxist demand-side theory can be stated. Empirical investigation showed that this theory does not contradict reality. Effective demand, limited by exploitation of workers, is definitely *one* important component of a realistic business cycle theory.

On the other hand, there are many weaknesses in the realization model. The four main behavioral functions—consumption, investment, distribution, and the profit rate—each has problems. What are the proper time lags? Are the parameters constant? Are other important independent variables omitted? Some other important variables that would be included by any demand-side theorist are (1) the importance of international economic relations, (2) the role of government in the macroeconomy, and (3) the role of money and credit.

Government and Demand

In the eyes of most demand-side theorists, the main reason that there was no major depression between 1940 and 1980 was the role of government in stimulating demand. Whereas total federal spending was only 1 percent of gross national product (GNP) in 1929, military spending alone has been estimated at 13 percent of GNP for the period from 1950 to 1965. Demand-side theorists visualize the government raising spending or lowering taxes or both every time there is a recession. The spending directly stimulates demand whereas the lower taxes increase disposable income, so they indirectly stimulate demand.

On the other hand, if there is an expansion with rapid inflation, then government will depress demand to end the inflation. This means that government spending should fall relative to taxes in an expansion in order to reduce inflation. All this will reduce the amplitude of fluctuations. Of course, if the U.S. government depresses demand too much in an expansion, then it may itself set off a recession or depression. What actually happens will be seen in Part Six.

Money, Credit, and Demand

Most demand-side theorists heavily emphasize credit, which can bolster consumer and investor demand above where it would have been if only current income were used. According to the data in Chapter 8, consumer debt rose rapidly in most of this period. More precisely, it rose very rapidly in expansions, raising consumer demand. Debt still increased in the first period of contraction, helping consumers stay afloat. Then debt decreased, leading to a more disastrous decline of consumer demand.

In each expansion, the bank rate of interest on short-term business loans is still falling in the first stage of expansion, then rises very rapidly. The rapid rise of the interest rate in late expansion helps choke off investment demand. The interest rate continues to rise in early contraction, pushing down investment demand still more. In late contraction, interest rates finally decline, so credit becomes a factor helping investment demand to recover.

International Demand

As noted earlier in this chapter, many demand-side theorists have put a heavy emphasis on international demand. Net demand for U.S. products abroad is equal to the amount of U.S. exports minus U.S. imports (the difference is called net exports). For example, after the Second World War most other countries were devastated, so there was a tremendous increase in U.S. exports. Most demand-side theorists would say that this was an important factor for expansion of the U.S. economy in the 1950s and the 1960s. Now the competition of other countries (for example, Japanese and German autos) is depressing net U.S. demand.

If the whole capitalist world expands and contracts together, then both exports and imports would rise in expansion and decline in contraction. The net effect would depend on whether U.S. prices and production fluctuated more or less than others. Some underconsumptionists believed that the increase of net exports in each contraction was a major factor in getting the advanced capitalist countries out of contractions (by dumping their excess goods in the colonial countries). What actually happens to the relation of exports to imports will be seen in Part Five.

SUMMARY

In early expansion, consumer demand rises because (1) total income is rising, (2) consumer debt (as a ratio to income) is rising rapidly, and (3) exports are rising. Holding back consumption will be (4) falling average propensity to consume (because of rising rate of exploitation), (5) falling government deficit, and (6) rising imports. In early expansion, investment rises because the expected rate of profit rises owing to (1) rising rate of growth of domestic consumer demand, and (2) rising exports of machinery. Investment is restrained a little by (3) declining government deficit spending and (4) (after the first stage of expansion) a rising interest rate on bank loans.

Near the peak, each of the positive factors weakens, and most of the negative factors get stronger. Therefore, the growth of consumer demand is much slower, the expected rate of profit declines, and investment goes more and more slowly until it declines at the peak.

Throughout the contraction, consumer demand falls (though more slowly near the trough) because (1) income is falling; (2) the ratio of consumer debt to income is falling (after the first stage of contraction); and (3) exports are falling. These negative factors are not fully offset, but are partially offset, by (4) rising government deficit spending for welfare and unemployment compensation, (5) rising average propensity to consume (with falling rate of exploitation), and (6) falling imports. Investment is pulled down by a falling profit rate, caused by (1) declining domestic demand and (2) declining exports of machinery (unless underconsumptionists are correct about dumping in colonies). Investment is held up a little by (3) rising government deficit spending and (4) (after the first half of contraction) declining interest rates on bank loans.

APPENDIX 14A

The Formal Realization Model

For simplicity, the formal model leaves aside government, foreign trade, and credit (readers who like complicated mathematics are free to add these relations, as indicated in the summary). In this model the fact that national income (Y) is divided into wages (W) and profits (Π) is implicit in the rate of exploitation (Π/W). The other five explicit relationships together constitute a complete cycle model.

National income equals consumer demand plus investment:

$$Y_t = C_t + I_t \qquad (14\text{A}.1)$$

Investment is determined by the profit rate (lagged):

$$I_t = r + p\frac{\Pi_{t-1}}{K_{t-1}} \tag{14A.2}$$

The profit rate is determined by the change in output demanded (lagged):

$$\frac{\Pi_t}{K_t} = m + v(Y_t - Y_{t-1}) \tag{14A.3}$$

The rate of exploitation rises and falls as national income rises and falls:

$$\frac{\Pi_t}{W_t} = g + zY_t \tag{14A.4}$$

Consumer demand is positively influenced by national income, but negatively influenced by the rate of exploitation:

$$C_t = a + bY_{t-1} - c\frac{\Pi_{t-1}}{W_{t-1}} \tag{14A.5}$$

These are five variables (Y, C, I, Π/K, and Π/W) with five independent equations. By successive substitutions, the reduced form of this equation is

$$Y_t = a + r + pm - cg + (b - cz + pv)Y_{t-1} - pvY_{t-2} \tag{14A.6}$$

This is a second order difference equation, so there will be cycles[15] if, and only if, $(b - cz + pv)^2$ is less than $4pv$. If the estimates of these coefficients are based on the data from the earlier chapters, it is likely that this model would produce cycles (with the qualifications about damped or explosive cycles discussed in the last chapter).

One cannot say for sure, however, because some parts of the model involve simplifications that put it too far from reality. In reality, the equation for output (equation 14A.1) must include more than consumption and net nonresidential investment; it should add net residential investment, government spending, and net exports while subtracting indirect business taxes. If these variables are all exogenous, the model doesn't explain much. If they are endogenous, then each must be explained. Then all the equations should be recalculated simultaneously and finally tested on data for a later period.

APPENDIX 14B

A Simpler Demand Model

It must be stressed that there are many ways to state the mathematics of cyclical demand models. The following model is very simple. It is also less Marxist-sounding and is perhaps more similar to some underconsumptionist writing and some Post Keynesian theories.

---

[15] See R. G. D. Allen, *Mathematical Economics* (London: Macmillan, 1957), chap. 5.

As usual, in equilibrium:
Output (Y) equals consumption (C) plus investment (I)

$$Y_t = C_t + I_t \tag{14B.1}$$

and income (Y) equals wages (W) plus profits (Π)

$$Y_t = W_t + \Pi_t \tag{14B.2}$$

Then the behavioral equations are these.
Consumption is a function of profits and wages

$$C_t = a + b\Pi_{t-1} + W_{t-1} \tag{14B.3}$$

Wages rise and fall with national income, but less rapidly:

$$W_t = c + dY_t \tag{14B.4}$$

Investment is a function of the change in output demanded

$$I_t = v(Y_{f-1} - Y_{t-2}) \tag{14B.5}$$

For a still more underconsumptionist flavor, this equation could state investment as a function of the change in consumer demand alone, but that is obviously inaccurate.

Like the earlier models, the reduced form equation (obtained by successive substitutions) is a second order difference equation:

$$Y_t = a - bc + c + (b - bd + d + v)Y_{t-1} - vY_{t-2} \tag{14B.6}$$

There will be cycles if, and only if, $(b - bd + d + v)^2$ is less than $4v$. This model, however, leaves out even more of reality than the preceding one.

Chapter 15

SUPPLY-SIDE AND COMBINED CYCLE THEORIES: MARXIST AND CONSERVATIVE VIEWS

hose economists called "supply-siders" contend that business cycle downturns are caused by excessive government taxation, which removes private incentives to invest. This is another theory of external or exogenous causes, which was discussed in general in Chapter 13 and is discussed specifically in Part Six on government. Similarly, monetarists worry about the supply-cost of capital, that is, the interest rate, also allegedly causing problems because of the exogenous monetary actions of government (it is discussed in Part Four).

In this chapter, however, several other theories are reviewed that make cycles depend mainly on supply-side or production problems, but are very different from what is known as "supply-side" economics. These include the *overinvestment* theory of Hayek, the *reserve army* theory of Boddy and Crotty, and the *organic composition* theory of Shaikh. Each of these is examined in detail.

OVERINVESTMENT THEORIES

The basic idea of overinvestment theories is that an excessive amount of investment in a business cycle expansion will mean that the demand for producers' goods and raw materials will outrun the supply.[1] This excess demand raises the cost of supplying these goods. Suppose that the price of the product made with this investment is constant or rises very slowly. The overinvestment theorists all assume that the price of finished goods rises more slowly than their costs. In this case, the margin of profit per unit must fall. This could account for the fact that profit margins are a leading indicator of cycle terms, usually turning down before the cycle peak and usually turning up before the cycle trough. Geoffrey Moore writes: "Of course, like the two blades of the proverbial scissors, both prices and costs determine margins, but costs have generally been the widely moving element accounting for the leads in margins."[2]

Frederick Hayek pictures production as being ordered in a series of stages; each stage feeds the next one and is part of the cost of the next stage.[3] Production of raw materials may be considered the first or earliest stage. The raw materials are then used, at a certain cost per unit, to produce plant and equipment in the second stage. The plant and equipment plus more raw materials—all called producers' goods or capital goods—are used to produce consumers' goods at the third stage.

In every expansion, in Hayek's theory, the rising demand for consumer goods generates an even greater demand for producers' goods. The greater demand for these capital goods, that is, investment, may be explained by the accelerator mechanism (discussed in detail in Chapter 9). The large demand for plant and equipment at the second stage is transmitted to an even stronger demand (by a further accelerator) for raw materials.

The rapid rise in demand for plant and equipment, when it eventually outruns the supply, brings a rise in prices, which are costs to the consumer goods industries. Since demand for raw materials rises even faster, so do the prices of raw materials, which then become higher costs for both latter stages. Furthermore, it is more difficult to increase the supply of raw materials than of manufactured goods because of the constraints of nature. Therefore, there is even more upward pressure on prices.

As a result of these pressures, the data in Chapter 11 revealed that in most expansions the price of consumer goods has risen least, the price of plant and equipment has risen further, and the price of raw materials has risen most of all. Hayek argues that the higher costs coming from the earlier stages eventually reduce profit margins in the later stages, thus causing a contraction.

In each contraction, the accelerator works in reverse, causing a small decline in consumer goods to be reflected in a much larger decline in investment in plant and equipment. Therefore, the price of plant and equipment must fall more than the price of consumer goods. Because of a further accelerator, the demand for raw materials falls even faster than the demand for plant and equipment. In addition, it takes time to reduce the supply of raw materials from agricultural operations (because planning must take place so far in advance). With a more rapid fall in demand and a slower fall in supply, the price of raw materials must fall much faster than the price of manufactured goods.

---

[1] For a discussion of monetary and monetary overinvestment theories of the cycle, see Gottfried Haberler, *Prosperity and Depression*, 4th ed. (Cambridge, Mass.: Harvard University Press, 1960), chap. 3.

[2] See Geoffrey H. Moore, "Tested Knowledge of Business Cycles," *42nd Annual Report of the National Bureau of Economic Research* (New York: National Bureau of Economic Research, June 1962), p. 11.

[3] See Frederick Hayek, *Profits, Interest, and Investment* (London: Routledge, 1939).

Chapter 11 did find that in most contractions, prices of consumer goods fell least, plant and equipment prices fell more, and raw materials prices fell most of all. This supports Hayek's argument that declining costs help stabilize profit margins at some point in the contraction, and this sets the stage for economic recovery.

Hayek's model is not easy to formalize because it disaggregates the economic process into several stages of production. A complete model would require output, prices, costs, and profit margins for each stage of production. This type of model has been neglected by economists because of the Keynesian focus on the components of aggregate demand in the national income accounts.

If Hayek's model were reworked today, it would also require a heavy emphasis on the international sector. The U.S. economy, like all industrialized capitalist economies, imports most of its raw materials from other countries. Those import prices also tend to rise more rapidly than most U.S. prices in expansions, while they fall much more than most U.S. prices in contractions (or rise much less when there is inflation during a contraction). Thus, the cyclical effect of raw materials' prices affects the whole U.S. economy, raising costs (relative to prices) and reducing profit rates in expansions, while lowering costs (relative to prices) and increasing profit rates in contractions.

Although this effect clearly exists, it is not very important quantitatively for the whole U.S. economy—except for a few dramatic changes, such as in oil prices (which was not a cyclical phenomenon). The effects on other industrialized countries and on raw material producers will be discussed in Part Five.

Finally, there are those overinvestment theories that emphasize physical productivity rather than prices. As discussed in detail in Chapter 11, the physical productivity of capital might be lowered near the peak if full capacity levels are approached. There may be bottlenecks and shortages. There may be use of capacity beyond optimal levels. Yet neither of these two possibilities seem to have happened in most expansions.

Another aspect of capital productivity (in dollar terms) is the fact that many small, inexperienced enterprises enter the economy during an upswing. They probably lower the average productivity of all invested capital near the peak. They certainly go bankrupt in the contraction, when their assets (or "capital") are bought for low prices by larger firms, thus raising the average profit per dollar of investment. These issues of small business and big business are further discussed in Part Five.

SUPPLY-SIDE MARXISM: THE RESERVE ARMY THEORY

Another business cycle theory that emphasizes supply-side costs of production is the *reserve army* theory, which has been given its fullest exposition by Boddy and Crotty[4] (and in a secular stagnation form by Glyn and Sutcliffe[5]). This theory argues that, in every expansion, the increasing employment slowly reduces the reserve army of unemployed workers. As full

---

[4]Raford Boddy and James Crotty, "Class Conflict and Macro-Policy," *Review of Radical Political Economics* 7 (Spring 1975), pp. 1–17.

[5]Andrew Glyn and Bob Sutcliffe, *British Capitalism, Workers, and the Profit Squeeze* (London: Penguin, 1972).

employment approaches, there is greater demand for labor relative to the supply. Therefore, the bargaining power of labor improves, and the militancy of labor increases. For this reason, workers are able to get higher wages and to prevent further speedup of work (reducing the growth of productivity). The lower rate of exploitation, or higher wage share means a decline in the profit share (but this happens only at the end of the expansion). The decline in the profit share (Π/Y), all other things being equal, reduces the profit rate. The reduced profit rate lowers expectations, which causes a fall in investment, setting off a recession or depression.

In a recession or depression, unemployment rises. This eventually lowers the bargaining power of labor and reduces labor militancy. Therefore, there are lower wages and more productivity—leading to a higher profit share (but all this happens only toward the end of a contraction). The higher profit share, all other things being equal, causes a higher profit rate, which leads to a recovery.

The theories of the exhaustion of the reserve army of unemployed emphasize some important behavioral functions. It is a fact that the rate of unemployment has fallen in the expansion phase of all business cycles. This fact of rising employment does have some influence on the behavior of wage rates. Wage costs are the largest single element of costs, so this may be a significant cause of higher costs. Likewise, in the depression, unemployment rises, helping to cause a fall in wage rates, so this element of costs does decline.

On the other hand, higher money wage rates may *not* cause a decline in profits per unit *if* prices rise equally (or if productivity rises enough). Since higher wages lead to more consumer demand, prices *may* rise equally if consumer demand rises rapidly enough. Higher wages have both cost and demand effects, so it is necessary to analyze which effect is stronger and more rapid. It is a mistake in economic analysis to concentrate on costs to the exclusion of demand. If all the blame for a recession is put on higher wage costs (where it does *not* belong), this is a good excuse for business to oppose all wage increases—and an excuse for government to help business against labor.

The Basic Framework. The strong points—as well as the weaknesses—of the reserve army theory can best be seen by using a formal model to emphasize its main points. Its basic framework begins with the statement that national income (at each equilibrium point) must equal consumer spending plus investment spending:

$$\text{income} = \text{consumption} + \text{investment}$$

or
$$Y_t = C_t + I_t \tag{15.1}$$

where C is consumption and I is investment. National income also equals "wages" (wages, salaries, and fringe benefits) plus "profits" (profits, rents, and interest).

$$\text{income} = \text{wages} + \text{profits}$$

or
$$Y_t = W_t + \Pi_t \tag{15.2}$$

where Y is national income, W is wages, and Π is profits.

Unemployment Function. There is no controversy about the fact that, over the cycle, unemployment declines as output and income expand whereas unemployment rises as output and income contract. This relationship may be reflected in the function:

$$\text{unemployment} = f^1 \text{ (output)} \tag{15.3}$$

where the function, f^1, is a negative one. It was found in Chapter 10 that the data indicate that this relationship is negative—as is obvious in the cyclical pattern of unemployment over the business cycle.

Income Distribution. The most important behavioral relationship in the reserve army theory is its statement about the wage share (W/Y). The reserve army theory states that the wage share rises and the rate of exploitation (Π/W) falls in the last half of expansion. The reason given is that the decline of unemployment puts labor in a better bargaining position.

The argument was spelled out earlier. In formal terms, it says that the wage share is a negative function of unemployment; that is, lower unemployment causes a higher wage share, but greater unemployment means a lower wage share.

At first glance, the reserve army theory seems to stand in direct contradiction to the factual assumptions of the realization theory. The realization theory assumes a *rise* in the rate of exploitation (and fall in the wage share) in the expansion. The reserve army theory seems to predict a *fall* in the rate of exploitation (and rise in the wage share) because unemployment is falling in the expansion period.

To represent income distribution in this model, it is more convenient to speak of the wage share (W/Y) than the rate of exploitation (Π/W). As unemployment falls or rises, how does the wage share behave? In Chapter 10, it was found that, if there is no consideration of a time lag, then the relationship between unemployment and the wage share is positive. In other words, the wage share falls when unemployment falls in the expansion, but rises when unemployment rises in the contraction. This result is consistent with the findings of the realization theory (that the rate of exploitation rises in expansion and falls in contraction), but seems to contradict utterly a simple version of the reserve army theory.

The more sophisticated formulation of the reserve army theory stated by Boddy and Crotty, however, emphasizes only that the wage share rises in the *latter* part of expansion (and falls in the *latter* part of contraction). These theorists are quite willing to state that the wage share falls in early and middle expansion and rises in early and middle contraction. So a finding that the wage share and unemployment move together in most of the cycle does not necessarily contradict their thesis.

What the sophisticated theory postulates is a long time lag. Why does the wage share continue to fall in early and middle expansion? According to these theories, there is an objective reason for a time lag: the fact that wage contracts are normally fixed for three or four years. Second, there is a subjective reason for a time lag: both bosses and workers remember vividly the high unemployment condition of the recession or depression. Therefore, bosses are still unyielding, and workers are still cautious. In the early contraction, the same reasons create a time lag holding the wage share up: wage contracts are fixed, bosses are still used to yielding to wage demands in high employment conditions, and workers are still militant.

Empirically, it was demonstrated in Chapter 10 that the regression coefficient for the wage share (W/Y) with unemployment does become negative when there is a time lag.

$$\text{wage share} = f^3 \text{ (unemployment) with a time lag} \tag{15.4}$$

where the function, f^3, is negative. Thus, it was found that the wage share rises significantly when unemployment declines at the end of expansion and falls significantly when unemployment rises at the end of contraction. The relationship is most significantly negative with a three-quarter time lag. (The theory could also argue a nonlinear relationship, such that unemployment strongly affects the wage share only when it is very high or very low, but that is more complex.)

Simplifying Assumptions. First, since consumer demand is not discussed by the theory, it is assumed to be in a constant proportion to income—or at least changing so much less than costs that it can be ignored. Second, the theory specifies that investment is related to the rate of profit, but no time lag is specified. Third, the profit rate (Π/K) is broken down into two components: the profit share (Π/Y) and the output-capital ratio (Y/K):

$$\Pi/K = \Pi/Y \cdot Y/K \tag{15.5}$$

which is an identity, always true by definition. Since demand is no problem, the degree of capacity utilization may be ignored. Fourth, since the output–capital ratio plays no role in the theory, it may be assumed constant. Of course, reserve army theorists do not believe such simplifications; they simply do not focus on these areas.

The strengths of the reserve army theory lie in the fact that it reflects some important aspects of reality. It does appear that (1) investment is a function of the profit rate; that (2) the profit rate is, by definition, partly a function of the profit share; that (3) unemployment moves countercyclically; and that (4) unemployment affects the profit share with a long time lag—by affecting the bargaining position of labor.

On the other hand, the theory is weakened by the fact that it ignores effective demand. How can one explain the movements of real wages and the wage share without explaining price movements? Also, the theory does not really explain why the wage share declines for most of expansion (when unemployment is declining) and rises for most of the contraction (when unemployment is rising). To merely acknowledge a time lag—or postulate a nonlinear relation—is not an adequate explanation.

Another important contribution of Boddy and Crotty was bringing government squarely into the story since it is obviously important in the modern world. They argued that, in the late expansion, the rise of wages and decline in the growth of productivity threaten profits—and a low profit rate would lead to less investment and a recession. Therefore, near the peak of the cycle, capitalists urge the government to restrain wage gains by any means. Government sometimes does this by restrictive monetary and fiscal policy, which leads to unemployment, which reduces the bargaining power of workers. There is certainly some truth to the notion that capitalists do not like the strength of labor that comes with full employment. There may also be some truth to the idea that all the yelling about inflation is just a fig leaf for a policy that tries to restrict wages by direct controls, by voluntary controls, or by restrictive monetary and fiscal policy.

Yet this is not a complete theory of the role of government and raises many more questions than it answers. Capitalists do not want a really big depression because that is even worse for profits than are high wages. How do capitalists influence the government so carefully that it stays away from full employment, but does not cause very high unemployment? For that matter, even if government decides to do this on its own, how can government act in such a fine-tuning sort of policy manner? Furthermore, if the only problem is high wages causing contractions, then why does government usually act in the contraction to stimulate demand by more spending, by more unemployment compensation, and so forth? These questions are reserved for Part Six, where they are discussed in detail.

SUPPLY-SIDE MARXISM: ORGANIC COMPOSITION THEORY

Another Marxist theory oriented toward explaining the economy from the supply side is the organic composition theory.[6] The *organic composition of capital* is the ratio of all material inputs (the value of the plant, equipment, and raw materials used up in the production process) to labor inputs (the value of the living labor exerted in the production process). The theory contends that technological change tends to produce a higher and higher ratio of material inputs (such as bigger and bigger blast furnaces) to labor inputs. Yet, according to Marx, only living labor can produce profits, that is, a surplus of value above the value of the workers' own subsistence. With living labor able to produce only so much profit, larger and larger amounts of physical capital per worker must lower the rate of profit.

There is a huge and controversial literature on whether this theory is right or wrong in theory and in historical fact. But it is not necessary to go into that literature because the theory does not appear relevant to the present issue. It has mostly been used to explain long-run trends or long Kondratieff cycles of 50 to 60 years. For one thing, it explains only a continual downward pressure on profits, not a recovery. Most of those arguing the relevance of the theory to long cycles argue that the upturn is caused by exogenous factors such as wars and war spending or by new innovations. In this sense, it has little or no endogenous theory of the upturn and is in the same boat as long-run underconsumption theory in expecting constant stagnation.

A few writers have tried to apply the theory to shorter-run business cycles (3- to 10-year cycles) by arguing that the contraction is caused by rising organic composition whereas the recovery is caused by the destruction of the value or price of capital that comes by bankruptcies. The theory, however, is not a good explanation of the causes of business cycle contractions because technological change takes place very slowly, so its effects cannot account for the rapid decline into a business cycle contraction. Profit rates decline very rapidly at the peak whereas this effect could explain only a tiny decline in a whole year. The explanation of the recovery is also not persuasive because this lowering of the price of capital (by purchase

---

[6]See, e.g., Anwar Shaikh, "An Introduction to the History of Crisis Theories," in Union for Radical Political Economics," *U.S. Capitalism in Crisis* (New York: Monthly Review, 1978), pp. 219–240.

of assets of bankrupt firms) is not important enough quantitatively compared with many other factors.

A COMBINED PRODUCTION-REALIZATION THEORY: THE TWO-HORNED DILEMMA

A general model can be forged by combining the best features of both the realization or demand theories and the production or supply theories of the cycle. Demand and supply both play a role in the determination of prices, output, and profit rates, so they must both be present in every major behavioral relationship. The controversial issue is only the amount of change and impact of each side in each phase of the cycle; this issue is an empirical question. The same framework is common to all of these theories as stated in this book. First, in the private domestic economy, national income equals in equilibrium consumer spending plus net investment spending.

$$\text{income} = \text{consumption} + \text{investment} \qquad (15.1)$$

More generally, the national product must equal consumption plus investment plus government plus net exports. Second, all income equals wage income (wages, salaries, and bonuses) plus profit income (profits, rent, and interest).

$$\text{income} = \text{wages} + \text{profits} \qquad (15.2)$$

The distribution of income, reflected in the wage share, seems to be a negative function of *both* the rate of unemployment—as the reserve army theorists contend—*and* the level of output demanded—as the realization theory holds. The effect of output demanded on income distribution seems to be immediate, but the effect of unemployment is strongest with a time lag. Chapter 10 showed that

$$\text{wage share} = f^1 \text{ (output, lagged unemployment)} \qquad (15.6)$$

where the function, f^1, is negative. It was found in Chapter 10 that *both* factors are important. So the wage share (W/Y) in the expansion moves down as output rises, but—with a time lag—will tend to move up again with declining unemployment. In contractions, the wage share moves up as output declines, but—with a time lag and not in every cycle—it will move down again at the trough with rising unemployment.

So far, investment has been best explained by the profit *rate,* which reflects the motivation for investment. Because it takes time for the corporation to learn and evaluate this information, to make decisions, and to execute them, the time lag is about three-quarters between the movements of the profit rate and the movements of actual investment. Investment, however, is also affected by *total* profits, which are a major component of the funds available to corporations. Here the time lag is only from one to two quarters. Of course, the profit rate normally turns before total profits at each cycle turn. Therefore, after trying many functions, Chapter 9 found that the best fit of investment to profit rates and total profit is:

$$\text{investment} = f^2 \text{ (profit lagged 1 quarter, profit rate lagged 3 quarters)} \qquad (15.7)$$

where the function, f^2, is positive. Investment is a positive function of both total profits (lagged one quarter) and the rate of profit (lagged three quarters), though other variables also influence it.

As shown in Chapter 8, consumer demand is a function of both national income and the distribution of national income (represented here by the wage share).

$$\text{consumption} = f^3 \text{ (income, wage share)} \tag{15.8}$$

where the function, f^3, is positive. Consumption is a positive function of both national income (lagged) and the wage share (lagged). Given the level of national income, there will be more consumption if the wage share of national income is higher.

The rate of profit may be given by the identity:

$$\frac{\Pi}{K} = \frac{\Pi}{Y} \cdot \frac{Y}{Z} \cdot \frac{Z}{K} \tag{15.9}$$

By definition, the rate of profit (Π/K) equals the profit share (Π/Y) times the ratio of capacity utilization (Y/Z) times the ratio of potential full-capacity output to capital (Z/K).[7]

The profit share equals 1 minus the wage share. The wage share was explained earlier.

According to the findings in Chapter 11, the ratio of capacity utilization is a significant function of output demanded, though the relation is nonlinear.

$$\text{capacity utilization} = f^4 \text{ (output, output squared)} \tag{15.10}$$

Capacity utilization *(which reflects demand)* is shown in this equation as a function, f^4, of national income and of national income squared. With the proper parameters, capacity utilization will rise rapidly in early expansion, then slow down, then actually fall just before the peak, and continue falling for most of the contraction, beginning to rise slightly just before the end of contraction.

Again, in Chapter 11 it was found that unemployment is a significant, negative function of output.

$$\text{unemployment} = f^5 \text{ (output)} \tag{15.11}$$

where the function, f^5, is negative. Unemployment falls as output rises, and it rises when output falls.

Finally, data in Chapter 11 indicated that the ratio of potential output to capital falls in expansions and rises in contractions. This means that the potential output–capital ratio is a negative function of the level of output.

$$\frac{\text{potential output}}{\text{capital}} = f^6 \text{ (output)} \tag{15.12}$$

where the function, f^6, is negative. But the data were untrustworthy, and the theory was not fully developed, so the reader is warned to accept this addition to the theory with skepticism, if at all.

---

[7] See Thomas Weisskopf, "Marxist Perspectives on Cyclical Crisis," in *ibid*, pp. 241–260. Also see Thomas Weisskopf, "Marxist Crisis Theory and the Rate of Profit in the Postwar U.S. Economy," *Cambridge Journal of Economics* 3 (December 1979), pp. 341–378.

EVALUATION OF THE COMBINED MODEL

In early expansion, output demanded is rising, so capacity utilization rises whereas unemployment begins to decline. The rapid rise of output demanded and capacity utilization produce an enormous rise in productivity, mainly because of a declining ratio of overhead labor to output. The wage rate, on the other hand, rises very slowly, partly because wages usually do not change without a struggle and partly because of the still high level of unemployment (which means that workers are not yet very militant and employers are still offering strong resistance). The wage rate also rises very slowly because the declining unemployment is recognized only with a time lag and because of fixed wage contracts. Since productivity is rising rapidly, while wage rates rise very slowly, the wage share declines.

A falling wage share (or rising rate of exploitation) lowers the average propensity to consume even though total consumption is climbing. The rate of profit is raised by (1) higher capacity utilization and (2) a rising profit share. Both higher profit rates and higher total profits push up investment. Since both consumer demand and investment demand are rising, total output also continues to rise.

What happens in late expansion? Output rises very slowly, partly because consumer demand is limited to a very slow increase by the still declining average propensity to consume (affected by the declining wage share with a time lag). Investment demand also rises more and more slowly because of stagnant total profits and declining profit rates—though the latter effect has a long time lag. Why does the profit rate decline? First, wage rates continue to rise (because of declining unemployment) whereas the growth rate of productivity slows very considerably. Therefore, the profit share slowly declines. Second, the growth rate of total actual output declines, mainly owing to limited consumer demand. This leads to a declining growth rate—or even actual decline—in the ratio of capacity utilization. (It is also possible that there is a decline in the ratio of potential output at full capacity to capital stock, mainly because of increased numbers of inefficient firms and the rising cost of capital goods, including raw materials.) *Thus, capitalist profit rates are caught in a two-horned dilemma of rising costs and limited demand.*

In the first half of contraction, output, consumption, and investment are all declining rapidly. Consumption declines because of declining income even though the marginal propensity to consume is rising slowly because the wage share is rising slowly. Investment declines because profits and profit rates are declining. The profit rate declines mainly because capacity utilization is falling rapidly (because demand is falling). It also falls because the profit share is falling—which is due to slowly declining wage rates and *rapidly declining* productivity (mostly because of a rise in the proportion of overhead labor costs to output).

Finally, in late contraction, the profit rate stops falling (and may rise). One reason is that wages are still falling, but productivity stops falling and may rise, so the profit share stops falling and may rise. A second reason for the end of the decline is that capacity utilization stops falling as demand reaches a floor, partly caused by a rising wage share. (It is also possible that the potential output–capital ratio is rising because the inefficient firms have gone bankrupt and because of falling costs of capital goods, including raw materials.) Thus, the conditions are laid for a new expansion as improving profit prospects lead to new investment.

Limitations of the Production-Realization Model. What has been described is a bland average of cycles. In reality, both the exogenous conditions and the parameters change somewhat in each cycle, partly reflecting long-run secular changes or new stages in capitalism. Therefore, even this rather complex combined production-realization model is still far simpler than reality. To begin to get a comprehensive model to explain modern business cycles, we must consider at a minimum (1) government spending and taxation; (2) money, credit, and government monetary policy; and (3) international relationships.

Government Fiscal Behavior in the Combined Model. Chapter 7 showed that government spending and government deficits have tended to increase gradually over the last 30 years. This has tended to stimulate demand and help the climb out of recessions. Briefly, government taxes rise in expansions faster than spending, so deficits decline in expansions and may turn into surpluses (which depress the economy) by the cycle peak. In contractions, government spending rises slowly whereas taxes are falling. Therefore, in most cycle contractions in the last 30 years, deficits have risen. This has been a stimulating factor to demand, helping to get the economy out of depressions. The reasons for this behavior are discussed in Part Six.

Money, Credit, and Government Monetary Policy. Part Four will show that, during most expansions, money and credit tend to expand because of various endogenous forces in the economy. Chapters 8 and 9 noted the expansion of consumer credit and investor credit. Thus, demand is stimulated beyond what it would otherwise be by the operation of credit. At the same time, the Federal Reserve System tends to take a more and more restrictive policy, though it is not usually very effective (see Part Six). For this reason and other reasons, the rate of interest on business loans keeps rising in the expansion, so this becomes a depressing cost factor for investors by the cycle peak.

Part Four also will show that, during most contractions, money and credit tend to contract because of various endogenous depressing forces in the economy. Chapters 8 and 9 noted the contraction of consumer and investor credit in recessions and depressions. When credit contracts rapidly and dramatically and banks look unsafe so that money is withdrawn, a monetary or credit panic may greatly accelerate the downturn. The Federal Reserve System usually (though not always) becomes more expansionary in its monetary policy. For this and other reasons, interest rates usually (but not always) decline in contractions. As the cost of credit declines at the end of the contraction, it becomes a factor stimulating the recovery of investment.

International Relations. Chapter 21 will show that the United States dominated trade in the 1950s, but was suffering from competition by the 1970s. So net exports were a stimulating factor in the 1950s and early 1960s, but became a depressing factor by the late 1960s. Cyclically, Chapter 21 will show that imports rise in expansions because U.S. income is rising, but fall in contractions because U.S. income is falling. On the other hand, U.S. exports rise in expansions because the income of the rest of the world usually rises at the same time (but not always). U.S. exports decline in contractions because the income of the rest of the world usually falls at the same time (but not always). As exports fluctuate more than imports, net exports tend to be procyclical, stimulating in expansions and depressing in contractions. On the other hand, the import prices of raw materials tend to rise faster than the prices of all U.S. goods in expansions and to fall more (or rise less) than the prices of U.S. goods in contractions—so this is a countercyclical factor, helping to end expansions and also helping to end contractions. In addition, U.S. profits from abroad tend to rise in expansions and fall in contractions because the cycles of other capitalist countries parallel U.S. cycles. Thus, the effects of international relations move in quite differing directions, so the net effect on expansion or on contraction is hard to predict. These relations are more fully explored in Chapter 21.

SUMMARY

The first half of this chapter discussed supply-side theories of the cycle, including the reserve army theory and the organic composition theory. The last half of the chapter presented a model that combines demand-side and supply-side elements.

APPENDIX 15A

A Reserve Army Model

To summarize the reserve army model, the following relationships are necessary and sufficient:
National income equals wages plus profits:

$$Y_t = W_t + \Pi_t \tag{15A.1}$$

National income equals consumption plus investment:

$$Y_t = C_t + I_t \tag{15A.2}$$

Unemployment is negatively related to real national income:

$$U_t = n - hY_t \tag{15A.3}$$

The wage share is a negative function of lagged unemployment (through its effect on labor militancy and labor's strength):

$$\frac{W_t}{Y_t} = a - gU_{t-2} \tag{15A.4}$$

Consumption is a constant proportion of lagged income:

$$C_t = bY_{t-1} \tag{15A.5}$$

Investment is a positive function of the profit rate:

$$I_t = r + p\frac{\Pi_t}{K_t} \tag{15A.6}$$

The profit rate equals the profit share times the output-capital ratio:

$$\frac{\Pi_t}{K_t} = \frac{\Pi_t}{Y_t} \cdot \frac{Y_t}{K_t} \tag{15A.7}$$

The capital-output ratio is constant:

$$\frac{Y_t}{K_t} = k \tag{15A.8}$$

These eight equations and eight variables produce a fully determined model. By successive substitutions, the reduced form equation is:

$$Y_t = r + pk(1 - a + gn) + bY_{t-1} - pkhgY_{t-2} \tag{15A.9}$$

which will produce cycles if the parameters are in the correct range.

It would be misleading to calculate these parameters, however, because some of the equations are simplifications that no one believes. One simplification is the fact that the model is only of the private domestic economy whereas Boddy and Crotty contend that government plays an essential role. The model does prove, however, that it is possible to construct a logically consistent cycle model based solely on supply- or production-side wage costs.

APPENDIX 15B

A Very Simple Overinvestment Model

A complete cycle model of the overinvestment theory is too complex to show here because it should be disaggregated into the stages of production. A pale reflection of the overinvestment model, in aggregate terms, would have to spotlight the argument that the potential output–capital ratio falls as output rises and rises as output falls:

$$\frac{Z_t}{K_t} = q - kY_t \tag{15B.1}$$

where q and k are constants. The other relations in it are all familiar.

National income equals consumption plus investment:

$$Y_t = C_t + I_t \tag{15B.2}$$

National income equals wages plus profits:

$$Y_t = W_t + \Pi_t \tag{15B.3}$$

Consumption is a constant proportion of lagged income:

$$C_t = bY_{t-1} \tag{15B.4}$$

Investment is a positive function of the lagged profit rate:

$$I_t = r + p \frac{\Pi_{t-2}}{K_{t-2}} \tag{15B.5}$$

The profit rate equals the profit share times capacity utilization times the potential output–capital ratio:

$$\frac{\Pi_t}{K_t} = \frac{\Pi_t}{Y_t} \cdot \frac{Y_t}{Z_t} \cdot \frac{Z_t}{K_t} \tag{15B.6}$$

The profit share is constant (because it is ignored in this theory):

$$\frac{\Pi_t}{Y_t} = w \tag{15B.7}$$

Capacity utilization is constant (because it is ignored in this theory):

$$\frac{Y_t}{Z_t} = z \tag{15B.8}$$

This model of eight equations may be reduced to one equation in one variable to show the time path of output:

$$Y_t = r + wzpq + bY_{t-1} - wzpkY_{t-2} \tag{15B.9}$$

This is a second order linear difference equation, which may produce cycles if the parameters are in the correct ranges.

APPENDIX 15C

Actual Behavior at Different Stages of the Average Cycle

NOTE: all variables are in real terms.

1. *Early expansion* (stages 1 to 2)
    a. Output, income, and total wages—rapid rise
    b. Consumer and investment demand—rapid rise
    c. Capacity utilization and productivity—rapid rise
    d. Profits and profit rates—rapid rise
    e. Wage share—declines
    f. Average propensity to consume—declines
    g. Unemployment—declines

2. *Mid-expansion* (stages 2 to 4)
   Same directions continue, but less rapidly.

3. *Late expansion* (stages 4 to 5)
   a. Output, income, and total wages—very slow rise
   b. Consumer and investment demand—very slow rise
   c. Capacity utilization and productivity—constant or slightly falling
   d. Total profits and profit rates—falling
   e. Wage share—very slight rise
   f. Average propensity to consume—constant or very slight rise
   g. Unemployment—slight decline

4. *Early contraction* (stages 5 to 6)
   a. Output, income, and total wages—falling
   b. Consumer and investor demand—falling
   c. Capacity utilization and productivity—falling
   d. Profits and profit rates—falling rapidly
   e. Wage share—rising
   f. Average propensity to consume—rising
   g. Unemployment—rising

5. *Mid-contraction* (stages 6 to 8)
   Same directions, but moving less rapidly

6. *Late contraction* (stages 8 to 9)
   a. Output, income, and total wages—falling very slightly
   b. Consumer and investor demand—falling very slightly
   c. Capacity utilization and productivity—constant or slightly rising
   d. Profits and profit rates—falling very slightly or constant or even very slightly rising
   e. Wage share—approximately constant
   f. Average propensity to consume—approximately constant
   g. Unemployment—rising more slowly

APPENDIX 15D

The Combined Model in Equations: A Production-Realization Model

A model combining production (supply-side) behavior and realization (demand-side) behavior is as follows:

Income equals consumption plus investment.

$$Y_t = C_t + I_t \qquad (15D.1)$$

Income equals wages plus profits.
$$Y_t = W_t + \Pi_t \tag{15D.2}$$
Wage share equals function of output and unemployment (lagged).
$$\frac{W_t}{Y_t} = w - jY_t - eU_{t-3} \tag{15D.3}$$
Investment equals function of profits and profit rates.
$$I_t = i + p\Pi_{t-1} + r\frac{\Pi_{t-3}}{K_{t-3}} \tag{15D.4}$$
Consumption equals function of income and wage share.
$$C_t = a + bY_{t-1} + c\frac{W_{t-1}}{Y_{t-1}} \tag{15D.5}$$
Rate of profit equals 3 components.
$$\frac{\Pi}{K} = \frac{\Pi}{Y} \cdot \frac{Y}{Z} \cdot \frac{Z}{K} \tag{15D.6}$$
Capacity utilization equals nonlinear function of output.
$$\frac{Y_t}{Z_t} = m + zY_t - qY_t^2 \tag{15D.7}$$
Unemployment equals function of output.
$$U_t = h - gY_t \tag{15D.8}$$
Potential output–capital ratio equals constant.
$$\frac{Z_t}{K_t} = k \tag{15D.9}$$

The entire model has nine equations and nine variables. By substitution, this model may be reduced to one equation showing the time path of output. It is a nonlinear, fourth order difference equation, which can produce both cycles and growth with the appropriate constants. It is too complex to be useful to present visually. If equations explaining the movements of government, credit, and international trade were added, its movements could be simulated to see what cycles and growth they do produce.

Part Four

MODERN MONETARY THEORIES

Chapter 16

THE RETURN OF MONETARISM

The pre-Keynesian economists generally believed that, in a healthy economy with full employment, real output would proceed at a pace determined by the availability of resources and the state of technology. A reasonable growth of the money stock would accommodate this expansion, and any excess would be reflected as price inflation. The Fisherian model of the equation of exchange made a rather direct connection between money balances and the level of spending in the economy. The demand for money was stable in at least the short run, and the supply of the money stock is what mattered when considering the level of nominal spending.

The various Keynesian theories cast considerable doubt upon the stable relationship between money and spending. For a period of time, monetary macroeconomic theories were given less attention and were thought by many to be less important than theories that concerned spending behavior. Monetary theory was out of vogue. Many of the important textbooks on macroeconomics principles downgraded the importance of monetary theory. The Fisherian models were regarded by some as anachronisms. At the University of Chicago, however, economist Milton Friedman was publishing a series of articles in an effort to revitalize the more traditional monetary theories. From this effort an entire school of thought called *monetarism* eventually emerged. Today it is the dominant paradigm in monetary theory.

This chapter begins by briefly discussing some of the general theories that deemphasized the importance of money. It then introduces monetarism as a response critical of these once dominant points of view.

THE DECLINING IMPORTANCE OF MONEY

The stability of the period between 1955 and 1965 seemed to endorse the victory of American Keynesianism, which stressed the wisdom and power of discretionary fiscal policy. It seemed the Keynesians and the neo-Keynesians had finally developed adequate stabilization tools.

Confidence was so high that some economists made the claim that all but minor inventory fluctuations were probably a thing of the past and that the world would likely never again allow the old cycles to degenerate into depressions or galloping inflation.[1]

As we discussed in Chapters 5 and 6, the simplistic Keynesian cross showed up in textbooks everywhere, demonstrating that variations in national spending could be attributed primarily to expectations and exogenous (that is, external to the economy) spending shocks. This most simple and popular Keynesian model also argued that government borrowing produces an equal amount of new savings, so that the impact upon private investment and other areas that rely upon the finance market is *neutral*—that is, government borrowing does not reduce private borrowing.

Because of this, the importance of the monetary sector was substantially de-emphasized. Monetary changes had an influence only to the extent that they were correlated with changing interest rates. In other words, expansionary open market operations were effective only to the extent that they raised or lowered interest rates. Lower interest rates would tend to stimulate investment and perhaps consumer spending, raising the level of aggregate spending in the economy.[2]

Although either expansionary fiscal policy or monetary policy might stimulate growth, fiscal policy was more reliable in times of crisis because the economy did not have to rely upon the voluntary private investment schedule responding to changing interest rates. When the government spent money, demand was directly stimulated. Because of structural imperfections in the economy, attempts to expand output and reduce unemployment would unavoidably be accompanied by some degree of price inflation. This trade-off that policymakers were forced to consider was captured in a theoretical device called the Phillips curve.[3]

THE PHILLIPS CURVE

The Phillips curve hypothesizes a trade-off between the rate of inflation and the unemployment rate. Policymakers supposedly could choose a suitable point on the trade-off line, inflating a bit to raise employment or letting unemployment rise to cool inflation. A Phillips curve is shown in Figure 16.1. If it were desired by policymakers, for example, to reduce unemployment from U_0 to U_1, then prices would have to rise from P_0 to P_1.

The curve identified the unemployment-inflation mix, and policymakers needed to choose the appropriate monetary-fiscal policy that would fix them at the desired location on the curve. With such "fine tuning" expeditiously accomplished, economists could gaze forward

---

[1] Paul Samuelson, *Economics,* 6th ed. (New York: McGraw-Hill, 1964), pp. 337–338.

[2] See Paul Samuelson, "Money, Interest Rates, and Economic Activity," *Proceedings of a Symposium on Money, Interest Rates, and Economic Activity* (New York: American Bankers Association, 1967), reprinted in William Gibson and George Kaufman, eds., *Monetary Economics—Readings on Current Issues* (New York: McGraw-Hill, 1971). Also see Warren L. Smith, "A Neo-Keynesian View of Monetary Policy," *Controlling Monetary Aggregates* (Boston: Federal Reserve Board, 1969), also in Gibson and Kaufman, *op. cit.*

[3] The Phillips curve as a phenomenon was first described by A. W. Phillips, "The Relation Between Unemployment and the Rate of Change of Money Wages in the United Kingdom, 1861–1957," *Economica* 4 (1958). For a good example of its policy application in the neo-Keynesian tradition, see James Tobin, "Inflation and Unemployment," *American Economic Review* 62 (January 1972). For a critical review of its importance to policy, see Thomas Humphrey, "Some Recent Developments in Phillips Curve Analysis," *Economic Review* (Richmond, FRB, January 1978).

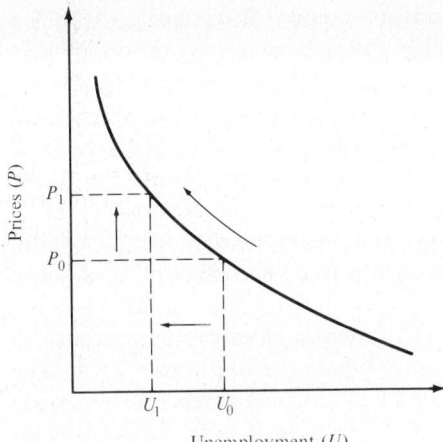

Figure 16.1 The Phillips Curve

to growth policies (such as encouraging innovation) that would allow the expansion of income without inflation.

This textbook approach began to develop a view of money and finance that was somewhat naive. The impact of deficit-financed federal spending upon the finance markets is treated in a simplistic manner in some of these models and distorts the richness of the original Keynesian model, which gives such lavish attention to the financial sector. In the pedagogical Keynesian cross models, any deficit-financed increase in government spending is ultimately financed in its entirety by increased savings, as has already been shown (so it does not raise the demand for borrowed funds).

According to the monetarist critics, such models ignore the fact that government finance needs are *immediate* and that the savings resulting from spending streams generated by the initial government stimulus are not immediate. The rate of borrowing moves faster than the rate of savings necessary to supply the loanable funds. This wouldn't matter if the economy were in a depression with excess savings, because those savings could be borrowed without affecting the interest rate. In that case (for example, at the end of the Great Depression and beginning of World War II), deficit spending would stimulate the economy. But if the economy were at full employment or in a mild recession, interest rates would rise, which might have the effect of discouraging investment, perhaps by as much as government spending rises.

THE CROWDING-OUT HYPOTHESIS

The proposition just given is referred to as the *crowding-out hypothesis*.[4] This hypothesis regards the federal government and private enterprise as competing for funds. In a simple

---

[4]See Roger W. Spencer and William P. Yobe, "The 'Crowding Out' of Private Expenditure by Fiscal Policy Actions, *Review* (St. Louis: Federal Reserve Bank of St. Louis, October 1970).

model, the total demand for funds will consist of private intended investment, which is a function of level of interest rates, plus the federal budget deficit, which is not. The combined total of the demand for funds is shown in Figure 16.2(a).

Assume for the moment that the rate of savings is insensitive to interest rates, as illustrated in Figure 16.2(b). Given the supply and demand for funds, the market clears at interest rate r_0. The government borrows amount a, and the private sector borrows amount b for investment.

Suppose now that the federal government, desiring to stimulate the economy, decides to spend more, increasing the size of the budget deficit from a to c. The effect on the finance market is shown in Figure 16.2(c).

The interest rate has risen from r_0 to r_1. This rise in interest rates caused a decline in investment from b to d. The drop in investment exactly offsets the rise in the deficit. The model attempts to show that a rise in government spending producing a deficit will increase interest rates in such a way as to discourage investment, causing it to be reduced by an amount equal to the increase in public expenditures. Since investment declines by as much as government spending grows, there is no stimulating effect upon the economy. Expansionary fiscal policy can't work according to this monetarist model.

In the preceding model, this result is obviously obtained because the supply of funds to the economy (savings) is fixed and insensitive to interest rates. Obviously, if the supply of funds is fixed, any sector's increase in the use of funds will have to be at the expense of another sector.

What about the case where savings is positively sensitive to interest rates, as shown in Figure 16.3? In this case, the total *amount* of funds available for borrowing will rise because higher interest rates encourage more savings. In this case, if the deficit grows, shifting the

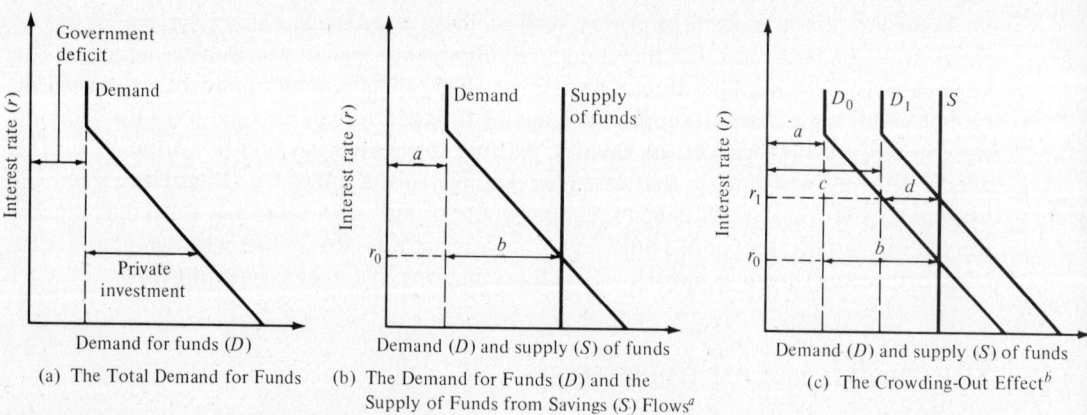

(a) The Total Demand for Funds (b) The Demand for Funds (D) and the Supply of Funds from Savings (S) Flows[a] (c) The Crowding-Out Effect[b]

Figure 16.2 The Crowding-Out Hypothesis

[a] Equilibrium interest rate is r_0. Amount a is borrowed by the government. Amount b is borrowed by the private sector.

[b] When the deficit rises from a to c, the interest rate rises from r_0 to r_1, and investment shrinks from b to d. This is "crowding out."

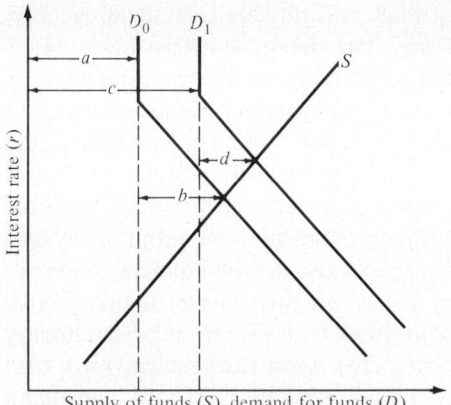

Figure 16.3 The Funds Market When Savings Are Sensitive to Interest Rates

demand line from D^0 to D^1 the higher interest rates might cause investment to fall, but not as much as deficit spending grew. Total debt-financed spending grew larger.

Does this overcome the crowding-out objection? The critics of fiscal policy say no. In this case, if savings grew, it would have to be at the expense of *consumption.* When the drop in consumption is added to the change in investment, the net effect is that government spending has exactly replaced private spending, with no stimulation to the economy.

The impact of fiscal policy, according to the monetarists, is not neutral upon the financial sector. As expansionary fiscal policy became common during the 1960s and 1970s, some of the dominant models of the time were not structured to evaluate the likely impact upon the financial sector of the economy and the resulting repercussions upon national spending and inflation.

Critics of the dominant policies began to coordinate their arguments. Supporters of the Keynesian tradition began to modify their theories and give more importance to the financial economy and the role of money and credit. On the other side were the critics of fiscalism, who wanted primary attention to be given to *money.* They were the monetarists. Their ideas are represented next.

MONETARIST TENETS

Generally, a strict monetarist would agree with the following propositions:

1. Unfettered free markets are efficient, will produce an equitable distribution of goods, will promote growth, and will generally solve their own problems without assistance. Serious economic disturbances are the consequence of random shocks (such as a bad harvest or the formation of a foreign oil cartel), which no one can control—or are due to misguided economic policy from a government that should not be interfering.

2. The expansion and contraction of the money stock will directly and unambiguously affect the level of nominal spending in the economy. The money stock is more closely correlated with that spending than such money-related variables as interest rates or bank credit. A change in the money stock, moreover, will affect *only* nominal variables in the long run (after the passage of a few months). In the short run, real variables are affected, but countervailing forces—after any monetary disturbance—return real variables, such as output and employment, to their old values. Hence, an excessive monetary expansion will generate inflation, but no change in output and employment. Most monetarists would probably also agree that most inflations have excessive monetary expansions as their ultimate cause.

3. There is a lag between changes in the money stock and their impact upon nominal spending, and that lag is variable and unknown. Policymakers trying to use discretionary monetary policy (using monetary policy to attempt to correct short-run problems) will tend to either overreact or underreact and will ultimately end up trying to chase down and stamp out the results of their own misguided policy. Additionally, their behavior will generate destabilizing expectations in the private sector. When all of this is combined with the argument that monetary policy can't influence real income or employment anyway, monetarists have, in their judgment, sufficient reason to rule out the use of discretionary monetary policy. Monetary authorities should do no more than allow the money supply to expand at a fixed rate, perhaps 3 percent or 4 percent per year. This is the so-called monetary "rule."[5]

4. Discretionary fiscal policy cannot be used to solve problems of inflation, unemployment, or sluggish growth. Such policy will merely reallocate the distribution of goods and services, usually in favor of the government at the expense of the private sector (because private investment is "crowded out").

BASIC CRITICISMS OF MONETARISM

The critics have attacked each of the main propositions of monetarism:

1. It is asserted that the market system is distorted by monopoly, so it is not efficient even in the narrowest sense; workers are exploited by employers who make huge profits from the products created by workers, so the distribution of income is not equitable. Moreover, the capitalist market system results in periodic recessions and depressions, so growth is uneven and much slower than it need be. These periodic crises are endogenous to the system as evidenced by the fact that they keep recurring in the same patterns time and again. Particularly in those places where monetarist policy has been tried—such as by the junta in Chile, the Begin government in Israel, the Thatcher government in England, and the Federal Reserve System policies in the United States—the result was more millions of workers unemployed.

2. The critics point out that the money supply does not have any clear effect on spending

---

[5]Certain "mild" monetarists, such as David Laidler, do not accept this monetary rule. For this point and for an excellent review of the "mild" monetarist argument, see David Laidler, "Monetarism: An Interpretation and an Assessment," *Economic Journal* (March 1981).

for two reasons. First, the monetarists use a very narrow definition of money, such as cash and demand deposits. But the critics note that the economy today really operates mainly on credit, so it is the expansion and contraction of the broader credit aggregates that is really important. (The exact definition of the money supply that is used by the Federal Reserve System, as well as definitions the critics suggest might be used, is discussed in detail in Chapter 17.)

Second, whether one speaks of money narrowly defined or of credit, the direction of causation is probably more from economic activity to money and credit than vice versa. When the economy is expanding rapidly, the corporations and the consumers wish to borrow, the banks are happy to comply, and the Federal Reserve System is under pressure to allow it. In the contraction, everyone is afraid to borrow or to lend; this causes the supply and velocity of money and credit to decline.

3. Some critics argue that enough is known so that discretionary monetary policy, combined with fiscal policy, can achieve some short-run success. Others might agree that it is difficult to know what time lags will affect the money supply with a given policy, but they argue that this also undermines the monetarist idea that the money stock directly and unambiguously affects spending. How can it be unambiguous when the time lag is variable and unpredictable? There is obviously no way to test such a relation, so the connection must remain an unscientific assertion.

4. The monetarist argument that fiscal expansionary policies, which lead to deficits, must crowd out private investment, has also been vigorously challenged. It is argued that public spending, through the multiplier mechanism, has a very strong positive effect on the economy and that this positive effect is much stronger than any negative effect on borrowing for private investment. The evidence on this point has been strongly disputed ever since Keynes wrote in the 1930s.

All these points will be expanded in the next chapter. For the remainder of this chapter, however, it is important to give as thorough and sympathetic a statement of the monetarist model as possible, both for fairness and for understanding the issues.

THE PRIMARY MONETARIST MODEL

Monetarism incorporates an inherently conservative set of ideas. It is as much a political philosophy as it is an economic theory. It rejects the notion that fiscal policy can be effective and thus argues that a government using discretionary fiscal policy can only be counterproductive or obstructionist. As a theory, it places faith in the efficacy of the market economy to solve its own problems, so long as an accommodating monetary policy, which greases the wheels of trade but does not fuel inflation, is pursued by the monetary authorities. Such a set of ideas amounts to a return to the laissez-faire ideas of the pre-Keynesian era, and their endorsement of essentially noninterventionist monetary policies.

The intellectual leader of the monetarist paradigm is, of course, Milton Friedman. Although Friedman infers classical and Fisherian conclusions from his monetary models, he uses methods that rely heavily upon modern microeconomic analysis and the Keynesian tradition.[6] Other monetarists deviate from Friedman on particular issues or have contributions of their own, but their ideas are fundamentally consistent with Friedman's. It is appropriate to represent the tenets of modern monetarism by representing the comprehensive ideas of this economist.[7]

Friedman's analytic model is very similar to conventional microeconomic theory models that explain the demand for consumer goods. He identifies money as one of many assets that offers particular services. Utility-maximizing wealth holders will consider the money asset as a candidate when using their income and wealth to purchase goods and add to a portfolio of financial assets and will, therefore, have a demand function for money. When determining the composition of their financial portfolio, wealth holders will consider prices and returns on all assets, their level of wealth and income, and expected values of prices and yields.

Friedman combined wealth and income into a single variable called "permanent income." *Permanent income* is a weighted sum of present income (for example, annual income) measured over past years. The weights are higher in the most recent years. Because permanent income is a weighted moving average, it is much less volatile than immediate income. Friedman argues that the demand for portfolio assets will be at least as sensitive to wealth as to immediate income and that permanent income is a sort of proxy for *both* wealth and immediate income. Therefore, Friedman believed that portfolio asset demand would be *very* sensitive to permanent income and far less sensitive to immediate income. As will be shown later, this subtle belief is critical to an important monetarist argument.

Given current and expected prices and returns on assets, wealth holders will choose the portfolio of assets that maximizes their utility subject to their permanent income constraint. If any prices or returns change, the wealth holder adjusts the portfolio, selling some assets and acquiring others.

This implies, therefore, that there is a demand function for all goods and for *each* of these financial assets, including money. Friedman essentially defined the following demand function of *real money balances* (money demanded divided by the price level):

$$\frac{MD}{P} = f[Ri, ERi, Pi, EPi, (\frac{W}{P})], (i = 1, n) \tag{16.1}$$

where MD is the demand for money, P is the general price level, Ri is the list of present returns on all n assets, ERi is the list of expected future returns on the same assets, Pi is the list of present prices of all n assets, EPi is the expected future prices of the same, and

---

[6] Friedman's debt to Keynes is well argued by Don Patinkin, "The Chicago Tradition, the Quarterly Theory, and Friedman," *Journal of Money, Credit, and Banking* (February 1969).

[7] The ideas set forth in the following pages are contained in the following articles by Friedman. The articles are these: Milton Friedman, "The Monetary Studies of the National Bureau," in William E. Gibson and George Kaufman, eds. *Monetary Economics—Readings on Current Issues* (New York: McGraw-Hill, 1971); idem, "The Role of Monetary Policy," *American Economic Review* (January 1968); idem, "The Quantity Theory of Money: A Restatement," *The Optimum Quantity of Money and Other Essays* (Chicago: Aldine, 1969); idem, and Anna Schwartz, "Money and Business Cycles," *Review of Economics and Statistics* (February 1963 supplement); idem, "Money: Quantity Theory," *The International Encyclopedia of the Social Sciences,* David L. Stills, ed., Vol. 10 (1968); see also David I. Fand, "A Monetarist Model of the Monetary Process," *Journal of Finance* (May 1970); a good summary of Friedman's ideas is well represented by Robert Gordon, *Milton Friedman's Monetary Framework* (Chicago: University of Chicago Press, 1974).

W is permanent income, the proxy for wealth and income. Essentially, this equation says that the demand for real money balances is determined by present and expected future prices and yields of *all* assets, where the demand is constrained by real permanent income.

This is a very complex notion of the demand for money. It implies that the money "inventory" that anyone holds (which is what is meant by the demand for money in this context) might change as prices and yields on other assets (both goods and financial assets) change. It gives considerable importance to the role of expectations about *future* prices and yields.

Friedman constructed this equation because he wanted to test empirically the following three hypotheses:

1. There should be a strong positive correlation between the demand for real money balances and permanent income.
2. There should be a strong negative correlation between the demand for real money balances and *expected* price inflation.
3. There should be no correlation at all between yields on other assets and the demand for money.

The last hypothesis was important, because, as was shown in Chapter 6, if the demand for money is highly sensitive to interest rates, then the connection between money and spending is weakened. Such a proposition is an anathema to monetarism, which imputes a very direct connection between money and the level of aggregate demand.

Friedman felt that he had confirmed all three hypotheses to his satisfaction with the data available. Evidence convinced him that although the demand for money will grow with a rise in permanent income, the growth need not be proportionate. Money, for example, might have so-called economies of scale. As wealth grows, spenders might find ways to economize on cash balances, causing money demand to grow in a lesser proportion than income. In such a case, the velocity of money would show a rising trend over time.

Friedman also tried to show that the *interest elasticity* of the demand for money was nearly zero, which implies that the demand for money was insensitive to interest rates. Friedman's early tests have, however, been disputed. Edgar Feige and Douglas Pearce, in an article in the *Journal of Economic Literature* that surveyed the research of scores of economists that had evaluated the demand for money, reported that there was an empirical consensus of at least a weak relationship between the demand for money and rates of return on other financial assets.[8]

Both Keynesians and monetarists still generally agree that there is an inverse relation between price expectations and the demand for money balances. The reason is intuitively obvious. Anyone caught holding money in an inflation will suffer from a fall in its purchasing power. Consumers would normally shift their portfolio in favor of real goods at the expense of money if they thought that there would be future inflation.

---

[8] Edgar L. Feige and Douglas K. Pearce, "The Substitutability of Money and Near-Monies: A Survey of the Time-Series Evidence," *Journal of Economic Literature* (June 1977).

EXPECTATIONS

Since expectations of future prices and interest rates now play such an important role in monetary theories, it is useful at this point to examine the role of expectations in greater depth. Recently, two schools of thought concerned with the origin and nature of expectations have emerged. One explanation of expectations is called "adaptive expectations" whereas the other is called "rational expectations."[9]

Essentially, *adaptive expectations* models argue that consumers and businesses slowly incorporate expectations into their behavior as they learn from the experience of recent events. Inflationary expectations, for example, are generated gradually as the public begins to feel the impact of an existing inflation.

Rational expectations monetarists argue instead that the public can rationally comprehend the likely impact of discretionary monetary (and fiscal) policy and will formulate their expectations immediately. For example, if the Federal Reserve System increased the money stock sharply, the public would immediately comprehend the inflationary consequences and would rapidly incorporate inflationary expectations into their behavior.

The two models obviously differ in their attitudes about human learning. Adaptive expectations emphasize learning slowly from experience whereas rational expectations impute the ability to learn by logically comprehending and anticipating the impact of policy decisions upon the complex interrelationships in the economy. In the first, the effect of a monetary expansion is not immediately comprehended; in the other, it is.

These two approaches do not merely reflect two academic views about learning, but very strong policy differences. Suppose the government tries to lower unemployment by doing more spending. Both kinds of monetarists would agree that this would cause more inflation in the long run. The price increase would eventually take up all the increase in demand, so there would be no change in output and employment in the long run. But the adaptive expectations theorists agree that the government might outfox the public for a while until the public discovered that the measures were leading to inflation. In the meantime, the policy would work for a while. The rational expectationists disagree. The public learns very quickly and behaves very rationally. So prices will rise so rapidly that the new policy will have no effect on output and will generate no new employment.

These two schools of thought still compete for influence among monetarists and other monetary economists although it is probably the case that a majority of monetarists (and certainly Friedman) tend to favor the adaptive expectations approach.

EXPECTATIONS AND THE MONETARIST "TRANSMISSION MECHANISM"

Given the institutional structure of any economy, a monetary theorist must explain specifically how a change in one variable, such as the nominal money stock, is supposed to affect

---

[9] For a clear delineation of the two approaches, see Thomas M. Humphrey, "Some Recent Controversies in the Theory of Inflation," *Economic Review* (Richmond: Federal Reserve Bank of Richmond, July/August 1976).

another variable, such as the level of nominal spending. Since human beings make the ultimate decisions in the economy, these explanations must describe human behavior. In other words, how do economic agents with certain objectives respond to a monetary stimulus or a change in interest rates? This explanation is called the "transmission mechanism."

In the monetarist explanation, increases in the nominal money stock are exogenous (controlled by the Federal Reserve System). Initially, when reserves are added to the banking system, loans are made, and the proceeds are spent. The connection between money creation and spending is quite obvious at this stage. Monetarists emphasize an equally important secondary effect as well. As the spending surges through the economy, windfall increases in monetary balances are experienced by the recipients of this spending. This temporarily disturbs the portfolio equilibrium of wealth holders, who adjust by reducing their newly acquired money inventory for the purpose of acquiring other assets. In direct contrast to the Keynesians, who might insist that a good part of the newly acquired money would be exchanged for other financial assets, monetarists typically argue that they will instead be spent for real goods and services, contributing directly to nominal spending.

At first, the idea that the windfall monetary gain would be spent on *anything* seems to contradict Milton Friedman's monetary demand model. After all, the model hypothesized a direct relationship between the level of income and the demand for money balances. A windfall money receipt is certainly income. It would seem that if the demand for money is highly correlated to income (as monetarists typically maintain), almost all the windfall monetary gain would be maintained as a cash balance. Income would rise, causing the desired money inventory to rise as well. Spending would stop at this stage, and there would be no secondary effect.

Friedman's model is not afflicted by this dilemma, however, because it uses *permanent* income rather than immediate ("transitory") income. Recall that the permanent income variable is a proxy for both income and wealth. It is a weighted sum of present and past transitory incomes. As such, even when a windfall gain raises *immediate* income substantially, *permanent* income does not rise by nearly as much. Hence, the demand for money, a function of permanent income, does not rise much either. For a short time, available cash balances exceed the demand for them, and the extra cash is spent to restore equilibrium.

The monetarist transmission mechanism is a very simple concept. At the level of the individual wealth holder, the real demand for money (the desired money inventory) is almost purely a function of permanent income and price expectations since it is relatively insensitive to yields on other assets:

$$\frac{MD}{P} = f(EP, \frac{W}{P}) \qquad (16.2)$$

When this wealth holder is the secondary recipient of the money income that results from the initial monetary stimulus, because permanent income is not much affected, the amount of money in the money inventory exceeds the amount actually desired. Such a situation is not optimal for the utility-maximizing wealth holder, so the excess money is exchanged for a good or service; in other words, the money is spent. Consequently, the spending stream continues; the *next* party becomes the recipient of windfall income. (The expression *windfall* is being used here because it must be remembered that *none* of the spending described would have taken place without the initial increase in the money supply.) The next party takes the same action as the previous party, and the process continues.

Once this process is underway, it might seem that this disequilibrium process (where money on hand exceeds the amount demanded) continues indefinitely. This is not, however, what happens. As the spending surges through the economy, prices gradually rise. If the demand for real money balances is roughly a constant in the short run, as has been assumed, then as prices rise, the demand for *nominal* money balances must gradually rise to keep the demand for *real* money balances constant. In other words, each wealth holder wants to keep a money inventory with some given real value. As prices rise, the nominal amount of money in the inventory must rise to maintain the desired real money inventory. Equation 16.2 can be rewritten to express the *nominal* demand for money:

$$MD = f(EP, \frac{W}{P})P \qquad (16.3)$$

Seen this way, it is obvious that the *nominal* demand for money will rise with the price level. When, finally, the aggregate demand for nominal money balances rises high enough to incorporate the new money that has been circulating, then equilibrium is restored, and the spending stimulus terminates.

As we look at this description of the transmission mechanism, it becomes very apparent why monetarists see such a strong connection between the money supply and the price level. When the initial monetary equilibrium is disturbed by an increase in the money supply, the paramount variable that restores equilibrium is the rising price level. Until prices rise high enough, a disequilibrium condition is present, and the disequilibrium stimulates spending until prices rise sufficiently. The price level is the "stopper" that overcomes the disequilibrium and restores equilibrium in this simple model.

This explanation still begs the question of what happens to real values, such as the level of output and real interest rates. Explicit in the monetarist transmission mechanism is the notion that real values are not influenced by the increase in the money supply.

MONEY AND REAL VALUES

Probably the fundamental tenet of monetarism is that changes in the money stock have no permanent effect upon the level of real output. This idea is at least implied in almost all monetarist writings. It is explicit in many of Friedman's works. A robust, growing economy will require gradual increases in the money stock year after year to accommodate expanding trade, but attempts to use discretionary monetary policy to influence either secular changes in real output or offset business cycles will be ineffective at best and counterproductive at worst. Therefore, discretionary monetary policy (manipulating the money stock for the purpose of influencing real output) will affect secular changes in real magnitudes only to the extent that it might be *disruptive,* causing output to fall below a level that would be achieved if such monetary policy were not used. Beyond the amount needed to lubricate trade, differences in monetary policy will be reflected primarily in *prices.*

MONEY AND REAL INTEREST RATES

Germane to the explanation of this hypothesis is the related idea that the money stock does not affect *real* interest rates in the long run. Real interest rates are interest rates adjusted for inflation. Nominal interest rates minus the rate of inflation are a reasonable measure of real interest rates. Since the level of real investment depends upon the level of real interest rates, according to the monetarists, real investment will not be influenced by monetary operations unless it is beaten down by disruptive monetary policy.

This argument depends upon the acceptance of the notion of "natural" rates of interest, unemployment, growth, and so forth. The *natural rate of unemployment* is that rate that would prevail in unfettered and competitive labor markets. If the real rate deviates from the natural rate, it is said to be due to government interference—as with minimum wage laws, for example—and obstacles to competition, such as those imposed by labor unions. The *natural rate of interest* is usually stipulated as that equilibrium rate that would be determined by the interaction of the supply of and demand for loanable funds in the absence of any government intervention in the credit markets. With price stability (which perhaps can be regarded as the natural price level), natural, real, and nominal rates of interest coincide.

Figure 16.4 can be used to demonstrate the monetarist argument about the inability of a monetary stimulus to affect real interest rates.

In phase I, prior to any monetary disturbance, both nominal and real rates of interest are identical at the natural rate r^*. At the beginning of phase II, there is a one-time monetary stimulation. This reduces nominal rates of interest, and because inflation is not immediate, real rates drop as well. In phase III, growing credit demand and inflationary expectations begin to raise nominal rates. Also, somewhere in phase II or III, actual inflation begins to drop the real rate (i) below the nominal rate (r) as is shown by the fact that the solid line is above the dotted line. In phase IV, nominal rates are separated from real rates by the inflation rate. The real rate stabilizes at r^*. If there is no more monetary stimulus, the inflation dissipates, and the nominal rate will gradually drop back to the real rate at r^*.

This explanation depends upon the condition that nominal interest rates are a function

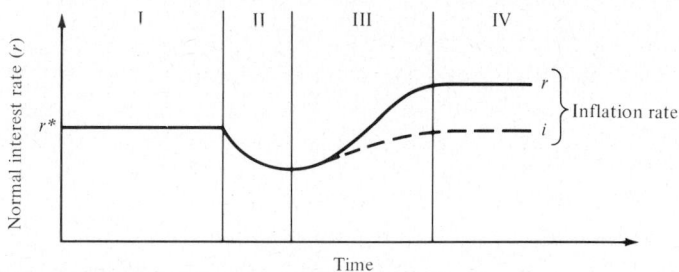

i = real interest rate
r^* = natural interest rate

Figure 16.4 The Behavior of Real and Nominal Interest Rates Over Time After an Increase in the Money Supply

of, among other things, inflationary expectations. These expectations drive the nominal rate to a level higher than the starting point even though real rates return to their old long-run equilibrium level. Inflationary expectations raise nominal rates because savers, realizing that their future interest income stream is being depreciated, attach an inflation premium to the interest rate at which they are willing to loan.

This is an interesting hypothesis. It presents the position that, in the very short run, a monetary expansion will cause market (nominal) interest rates to fall, but, after a period of time, they will actually rise to a level *higher* than their starting point. This counterintuitive reversal is primarily due to inflationary expectations and, again, depends upon the argument that an increase in the money supply causes inflation (otherwise, how would inflationary expectations be explained?). This argument has important long-run consequences as well. It implies that if the money supply growth rate is chronically excessive, market interest rates will continually *rise* along with prices. *Both* will trend upward. In effect, monetarists argue, excessive growth of the money supply causes market interest rates to *rise*. Real interest rates remain unaffected, so real investment is not stimulated.

THE DISTRIBUTION OF MONEY-STIMULATED SPENDING ON PRICES AND OUTPUT

Despite the behavior of interest rates, it still seems intuitive that an increase in the money stock—by increasing spending—will stimulate real output. Monetarists again rely upon inflationary expectations to deny this possibility. Producers, they argue, may observe in any single market that the demand for their product is rising, as is represented in Figure 16.5 by a shift in the demand curve from D_0 to D_1.

Initially, it would seem that producers would *both* raise prices and increase real output.

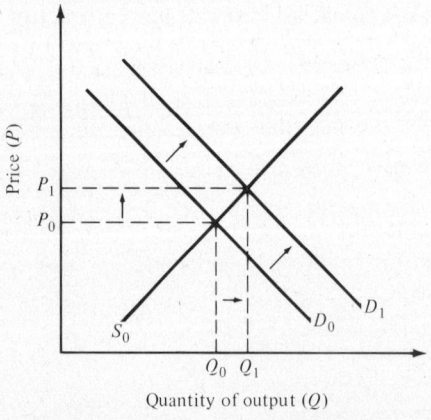

S = supply
D = demand

Figure 16.5 A Shift in a Typical Industry Demand Curve Caused by a Monetary Stimulation

A monetary expansion would stimulate the real economy *as well as real output,* as is shown in the movement of output from Q_0 to Q_1.

As price increases filter through the economy, however, producer costs would rise. Higher costs force an upward shift in supply schedules, such as that represented in Figure 16.6 by the shift from S_0 to S_1. The consequence in the long run is that prices have risen whereas the level of real output remains unaffected. Of course, nominal output $(P \cdot Q)$ has risen.

The speed of this adjustment depends upon whether one uses an adaptive or rational expectations argument. An adaptive expectations argument, which implies that producers will not expect inflation in the short run, would move the equilibrium from a to b to c in Figure 16.6. Equilibrium point c would be realized only when supply curves started to rise when producer costs rise. A rational expectations model would insist that producers anticipate *now* that their supply curves will shift up; hence they respond by moving straight from a to c. They merely raise prices and do not alter the level of real output. As can be seen, the adaptive expectations model generates a sort of cycle where prices ratchet upward and real output first expands, then contracts. The rational expectations model posts an immediate response in prices and no cyclical fluctuation in real output.

THE MONETARIST APPROACH TO THE PHILLIPS CURVE

The conclusions summarized in the preceding section are used in the monetarist battle against the policy applications of the Phillips curve. Moving along the Phillips curve to higher prices and lower unemployment is the equivalent of many thousands of firms moving from point a to point b in Figure 16.6. A monetary or fiscal expansion causes an increase in real output because demand curves are shifted outward, but prices must increase because marginal cost

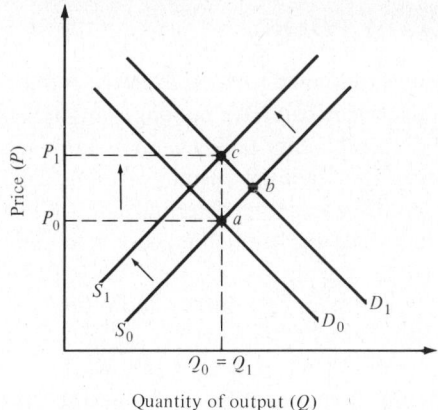

S = supply
D = demand

Figure 16.6 An Upward Shift in the Industry Supply Curve Caused by the Secondary Effects of a Monetary Stimulation

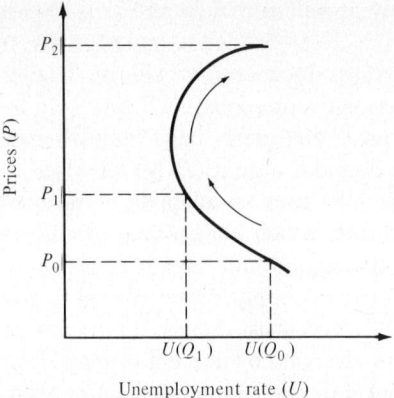

Q = level of output

Figure 16.7 The Adaptive Expectations Version of the Time Path of the Phillips Curve

curves (and hence, supply curves) have a positive slope. Because of this, there is a trade-off between inflation and output, given some fixed technology. But since the monetarist model either involves a movement from a to b to c (adaptive expectations) or directly from a to c (rational expectations), the Phillips curve eventually offers no trade-off. With fixed technology, stimulation induces inflation and nothing more.

The adaptive expectations Phillips curve is shown in Figure 16.7. It simply reflects the fact that there may be a short-run trade-off between unemployment and price inflation where prices, for example, move from P_0 to P_1. Eventually, however, the Phillips curve bends back, with the ultimate result that prices rise to level P_2, but the unemployment rate returns to its original level.

THE FUTILITY OF DISCRETIONARY MONETARY POLICY

These arguments infer that discretionary monetary policy, designed to offset cycles or induce a more rapid rate of growth, is not going to work. That money can have no long-run impact on the level of output makes it obvious why discretionary monetary policy cannot stimulate growth. To the monetarist, growth is the consequence of technology, resource availability, entrepreneurial skills, and the status of human preference. These factors determine a so-called natural rate of growth, which produces a dynamic, optimal, and equitable general equilibrium when markets are allowed to function without interference.

It might appear that because there is a short-run response in real output and other real variables to a monetary stimulus, monetarists might be inclined to support the use of discretionary monetary policy to offset business cycles. The most strict monetarists, however, do not. Sometimes this just seems to be a matter of faith, but it is argued by some that the lags between money changes and income changes are variable and unknown.[10] If the Federal

---

[10] See Michael Hamburger, "The Lag in the Effect of Monetary Policy: A Survey of Recent Literature," *Monthly Review* (New York: Federal Reserve Bank of New York, December 1971).

Reserve System, in other words, expands the money stock, it will not know when the impact will be felt. This uncertainty will generate the propensity to overreact and is, therefore, likely to be counterproductive. Finally, monetarists generally seem to believe that private expectations would be stable and harmless (would not result in disturbing behavior) if the powerful government were not continually engaging in policies that destabilize expectations. This theme is commonly found in the rational expectations literature, where it is argued that many harmful market disturbances and much aberrant market behavior are due to private responses to the *anticipated* consequences of quixotic government policies. Discretionary policies create an environment of uncertainty, and such an environment is more likely to produce troublesome behavior in the private sector.

MONETARISTS' INTERPRETATIONS OF INFLATION

Given the monetarists' attitude about the impact of the growth rate of the money supply upon nominal and real values, their theories of inflation are very easy to discern. Generally, increases in the money stock beyond that level necessary to accommodate the "natural" rate of growth will produce inflation. Furthermore, most actual inflations, certainly including the present, have been caused by excessive money growth.

The story, however, doesn't stop here. Once expectations are included in monetarists' models, they have an impact that compounds the inflationary problem. An excessive money growth rate not only directly contributes to inflation, but also generates inflationary expectations. There is a debate about whether such expectations are the consequence of an excess money growth rate directly or of experienced inflation, but, regardless, inflationary expectations become part of the private sector psychology.

Inflationary expectations reduce the demand for holding a stock of cash. To the extent that the liberated money is used for the purchase of real (rather than financial) assets, spending is stimulated, and velocity rises.

Because of these changes in expectations, monetarists argue that *price inflation can chronically exceed the growth rate of the money supply* after inflation has become pervasive. The difference is due to a chronic rise in velocity owing to inflationary expectations.

THE MONETARIST ATTITUDE ABOUT FISCAL POLICY

Although the crowding-out hypothesis presented earlier in this chapter is not the exclusive intellectual property of monetarists, it is probably safe to say that nearly all of them endorse the hypothesis as a major component of their theoretical opposition to Keynesian-type fiscal policies. As supporters of the crowding-out hypothesis, monetarists generally believe that deficit-financed federal spending merely "crowds out" private investment, having no effect upon the level of output (unless it is an adverse effect because of government inefficiency). Federal spending gradually allows the usurpation of what should properly be in the private domain by the encroaching public sector.

Additionally, monetarists fear that the Federal Reserve System will be inclined to "monetize" the deficits that result from discretionary expansionist fiscal policy. To *monetize* the deficit means that the Federal Reserve System pays money to buy U.S. bonds. Monetarists believe that expansionist policies will lead to monetizing the deficit in the following way: borrowing to satisfy a large deficit will push up nominal interest rates, as the crowding-out hypothesis maintains. The resulting pressure on business borrowing (that is, crowding out) is often politically unacceptable. Therefore, the Federal Reserve System responds to such pressure by buying bonds from banks in open market operations designed to push nominal interest rates down. This provides banks with excess reserves. The resulting increase in bank reserves allows the money supply to expand, which in turn creates an inflation. In addition to this, the monetarists argue, the long-run result of the effort to reduce interest rates eventually causes them to *rise*. (This was explained earlier.) The final effect, therefore, of expansionary fiscal policy will certainly be crowding out, and that is likely to be accompanied by inflation and rising nominal interest rates.

Probably the best-known attempt to verify this hypothesis about ineffectiveness empirically is the oft-cited St. Louis equation. This is a single-equation econometric model developed at the Federal Reserve Bank of St. Louis.[11] The model simply compares changes in the money stock to federal expenditures to see which has the greatest explanatory power in predicting national output. The model typically supports the monetarist position, but not always, and the testing method used has been subject to severe criticism.

MONETARIST RECOMMENDATIONS

Given the anathema that monetarists have for discretionary monetary policy, one might ask what can appropriate monetary policy do? According to Friedman, it can provide a stable background for the economy, especially in the context of flexible prices. It can keep the economic machine "well oiled." Primarily, sound monetary policy can prevent money itself from being a major source of economic disturbance. The Federal Reserve System, to accomplish this, should allow the money stock to grow gradually at a fixed rate and nothing more. Monetarist policy proposals are discussed in greater detail in Chapter 24.

SUMMARY

Monetarism arose as an intellectual response to the neo-Keynesianism that was dominating economic theory after World War II. The neo-Keynesian theories, especially the American versions of them, tended to de-emphasize the importance of money. Monetarism restored a

---

[11]The St. Louis equation first appeared in Leonall C. Anderson and Jerry Jordon, "Monetary and Fiscal Actions: A Test of Their Relative Importance in Economic Stabilization," *Review* (St. Louis: Federal Reserve Bank of St. Louis, November 1968); see also Keith M. Carlson, "The St. Louis Equation and Monthly Data," *Review* (St. Louis: Federal Reserve Bank of St. Louis, January 1975); Benjamin Friedman, "Even the St. Louis Model Now Believes in Fiscal Policy," *Journal of Money, Credit, and Banking* (May 1977); Keith M. Carlson, "Does the St. Louis Equation Now Believe in Fiscal Policy?" *Review* (St. Louis: Federal Reserve Bank of St. Louis, February 1978).

tradition that was very consistent with the conservative monetary theories of the pre-Keynesian era.

Monetarists accept the efficiency of the free market economy and oppose most sorts of government intervention in the economy. They believe that changes in the money supply have no lasting impact upon real interest rates, investment, or national output. Money primarily affects prices, and excessive monetary growth provides the explanation for modern inflation.

Monetarist theory is derived from modern utility theory, where it is hypothesized that the demand for real money balances is primarily a function of permanent income (a proxy for wealth and income) and expectations of future prices. When the recipients of new money receive their windfall money receipts, the money they possess exceeds the amount demanded, so they spend their excess balances. This process continues until inflation rises high enough to restore equilibrium between money supplied and demanded.

Most monetarists believe that the Federal Reserve System should adopt a monetary "rule," providing the economy with a constant money supply growth rate, and avoid discretionary policies. A low growth in the money supply will provide just enough money to promote stable economic growth.

The monetarist paradigm presents a formidable body of opinion that is influential and cannot be ignored. At the present time it is probably the most organized school of monetary theory. It provides serious criticism of vulgar neo-Keynesianism and, even if the entire approach of this inherently conservative political philosophy is not adopted, most monetary scholars borrow something of value from this school.

Monetarism, however, is not without its critics. Modern nonmonetarists provide many criticisms plus a different story, and their ideas are reviewed next.

Chapter 17

MODERN NONMONETARIST MONETARY THEORIES

As was stated in the preceding chapter, monetarism represents the dominant paradigm in modern U.S. monetary theory. Yet it has competitors. Although the purely Keynesian perspective faded from favor during the inflationary period of the 1960s, the diligent efforts of such Keynesians and Post Keynesians as James Tobin and Paul Davidson have kept the tradition alive. It seems that in the 1980s there is a bit of a revival of nonmonetarist, indeed, *anti*monetarist, monetary theory.

REASONS FOR THE NEW CRITICISM

The newly emerging trend can be attributed to a number of sources. First, monetarism tends to endorse a laissez-faire conception of market economics. As an economic philosophy, monetarism is strictly in the tradition of Smith's "invisible hand," Say's law, and the classical free trade advocacy. It has faith in the efficacy of the market to resolve its own problems automatically. Hence, applied monetarism is essentially noninterventionist.

In contrast to this, Keynesians and others influenced by their philosophy view the market system as occasionally afflicted by internally generated problems. As a consequence, they tend to advocate interventionist discretionary monetary and fiscal policies. More radical antimonetarists feel that the system's monetary problems will be one factor leading to its collapse and replacement.

Second, many economists have been impressed by the fact that monetarism has apparently failed wherever it has been applied. Its most consistent application has been in England, where it has resulted in the highest unemployment since the Great Depression.

FOUR NONMONETARIST SCHOOLS OF THOUGHT

Four important competing nonmonetarist theories are given attention in this chapter. It might be said that the critical theories can be fitted into four general schools of thought: the Post Keynesians, the Old Keynesian-Radcliffe theorists, adherents of the "availability doctrine" (including creditists), and Marxists.

The Post Keynesians are the most organized of the non-Marxists. As a group of scholars they have a confederation loosely organized around their *Journal of Post Keynesian Economics*. Through this journal and some of their books,[1] they are attempting, somewhat successfully, to make economists aware of a new critical paradigm in theory. Part of their intent is to interpret Keynes *correctly* (in opposition to what they regard as the *incorrect* interpretations of Keynes), but they are additionally adding new insights and perspectives to modern analysis.

The second group of traditional Keynesians, consisting of a number of English monetary economists supportive of the policies of the Bank of England—and a number of Americans, such as James Tobin—have never deviated much from what they regard as the Keynesian tradition. Although this group is not organized in any formal sense, its members have similar ideas. They have, for years, been outspoken critics of monetarism. Some of the fundamental ideas of the English group are to be found in the controversial Radcliffe Report, which was an English Parliamentary Committee report intending to evaluate British monetary policy.[2] The report summarily dismissed all policies that were monetarist in nature as ineffective. Although the report is ambiguous, it seems that the committee gave primal importance to the total magnitude of liquid assets or the availability of credit or both (all of this they called "liquidity"). Later writers, to be investigated in this chapter, refined the arguments of the Radcliffe Report and still present an essentially antimonetarist position today.

The third group of economists, who give attention to the role of nonbank financial intermediaries, credit conditions, or inclusive monetary aggregates or debt variables, draw from the legacy of the "availability doctrine," first made popular by John Gurley and Edward Shaw.[3] Again, as will be seen later, their opinions distinctly disagree with monetarism.

---

[1] See Paul Davidson, *Money and the Real World* (New York: Wiley, 1978), and Sidney Weintraub, *Keynes, Keynesians, and Monetarists* (Philadelphia: University of Pennsylvania Press, 1978).

[2] *Report:* Committee on the Working of the Monetary System (Radcliffe Committee), Cmnd. 827 (April 1959).

[3] See John G. Gurley and Edward S. Shaw, *Money in a Theory of Finance* (Washington: Brookings Institution, 1960), and "Financial Aspects of Economic Development," *The American Economic Review,* 45 (September 1955).

The fourth school consists of the Marxists and related English and U.S. radicals. This group neglected monetary matters for some time, but are now moving into the area rather strongly. Their views may be seen in the *Review of Radical Political Economics* and in the *Cambridge Journal of Economics.*

MAIN ARGUMENTS OF THE CRITICS

The major arguments of the critics are listed here briefly for the convenience of the reader. The first six arguments have been presented by the three liberal groups of economists—Post Keynesians, Keynesians-Radcliffe, and Gurley-Shaw–creditists. These six arguments are

1. There is a great deal of uncertainty about the future, and this tends to make the finance markets very unstable. Flexible discretionary monetary policies help overcome this instability, whereas inflexible policies such as monetarism contribute to this instability.

2. Because large amounts of money might be hoarded as incomes grow, there might be a permanent leakage from the spending stream that requires ever larger increases in the money supply to offset the leakage. This would invalidate a rigid money rule.

3. Although it is easy to speak of money in *theory,* in *practice* it is very difficult to *define* money. The Federal Reserve is forever unsure about what it should be controlling under monetarism.

4. The expansion of *credit* has a much more direct connection to spending than does the expansion of the money supply, and therefore the control of credit is more important.

5. When the Federal Reserve conducts open market operations, the effect on the economy is via *interest rates* rather than monetary changes. Interest rates have far more of an effect upon spending than does money.

6. The money supply cannot be adequately controlled by the Federal Reserve System. The money supply is primarily determined by conditions and events in the economy over which the Federal Reserve has no control. To use the jargon of economics, the money supply is *endogenous,* therefore it is futile to depend upon policies that attempt to control money.

Most modern Marxists agree with some of these points (especially the endogenous money supply) and disagree with some (such as externally or exogenously given psychological changes determining expectations). They also add some points—such as Federal Reserve policy's being determined by the interests of financial and industrial capitalists as a class and the fact that no monetary policy will simultaneously control both unemployment and inflation.

UNCERTAINTY AND ITS EFFECTS UPON THE FINANCIAL MARKETS

The Post Keynesian economists give considerable importance to the role played by *uncertainty* in the original Keynesian paradigm. Since the economy—and especially private investment—is subject to uncertainty and changing expectations, Say's law does not operate. The unstable economy leads to rapid changes in interest rates. If the Federal Reserve System is to keep the economy stable, it *cannot* maintain a rigid rule for monetary growth. The liberal Keynesians conclude that the Fed must use discretionary policies to counter changes in investment and maintain stability.

Paul Davidson,[4] for example, is careful to distinguish between risk and uncertainty. When considering risk, some economists wish to impute a certain known probability distribution to future events and, indeed, speak of the "expected value" and measures of dispersion for certain variables. Often, it is thought, a reliable estimate of the probability distribution of future events (such as next quarter's interest rates or next year's growth rate in GNP) can be obtained by using accepted techniques in statistical inference, often using time-series data. In effect, one employing such techniques would be using the statistical past to understand or predict the statistical future. Variables representing the "unknown" in economic models become stochastic variables with estimated means and probability distributions. In the portfolio models, for example, the "yield" of a financial asset is its expected return, and the "risk" is either the variance of return or variance of the asset price.[5]

According to Keynes, however, Davidson reminds us, *uncertainty* cannot be estimated by conventional statistical techniques. Because human beings are so complicated, enigmatic, emotional, and even occasionally irrational, there is an extent to which their actions are unexplainable, and there is an extent to which their future behavior is unpredictable.

Decisions that involve costs today in pursuit of uncertain future rewards (such as investment) are made in this uncertain environment. Such decisions rely to some extent upon guessing and intuition, which in turn are aided by experience, knowledge of the market, peer advice, common sense, and probabilistic estimates. The result may be a "best guess," but it is still merely a crude guess. According to Keynes, it is a constraint that all have to live with because the destiny of the economy cannot be predicted.

This observation leads to two important implications. First, even the best-laid plans can end in catastrophe. Lessons from history make this absolutely self-evident. Second, and more important to the theme being pursued here, since the guessing procedures for decisions based on future conditions are so inexact, *such decisions are occasionally very sensitive to even the most subtle influences.*

The Problem of Uncertainty in Investment Decisions: The Unstable Investment Function

What are the implications of the fact that investment decisions are so sensitive to guesses about the future? The statement implies that investment (or the demand for borrowed funds) might occasionally be very unstable. By this it is meant that intended investment might respond dramatically to an unexpected change in economic events that are thought to have some bearing upon future prospects for investment returns. The event might be an unexpected outcome of some previously predicted set of circumstances (such as rising interest rates when falling rates were predicted), an altogether unexpected event (such as an unexpected loan failure), or something that affects the general state of confidence (such as a stock market crash). Such instability could lead to serious problems of economic disequilibrium.

---

[4]Davidson, *op. cit.*, chap. 6.
[5]See Chapter 6, Appendix A.

This view is reflected in Hyman Minsky's major work on Keynes.[6] Quoting Keynes liberally, Minsky demonstrates that Keynes understood that markets for investments are "most clearly based upon tenuous conventions." They are, indeed, "subject to moods of optimism and pessimism and responsive to the vision of soothsayers." Minsky used this theme to develop his "financial instability hypothesis," which is described in the next chapter.[7]

James Tobin pursues a milder version of the same theme in a recent article where he suggests that, despite the popular strength of monetarism, the power of Keynesian thought is here to stay.[8] In that article he states that business expectations of steady prosperity is an important stabilizer of investment. If such expectations are disappointed, a recession has the potential of becoming a prolonged, severe depression.

This general Keynesian point of view, reiterated and emphasized by the Post Keynesians, identifies a salient difference between the Keynesians and the monetarists. A belief in laissez-faire and the sanctity of the free market requires the subordinate belief that important types of human behavior, such as investment, consumption, or the demand for money and other financial assets, are not volatile or highly unstable. The flexible price system is able to accommodate gradual or subtle shifts in supply or demand. But in a world where there are rigidities, long lags, imperfect competition, market imperfection, and a high degree of "price stickiness," a sharp and sudden drop in something like planned investment will cause serious problems. Recognition of this justifies, in the minds of many liberal economists, the use of discretionary policies and provides a reason for supporting large-scale government stabilization programs.

The Unstable Demand for Borrowed Funds and Disequilibrium

In the Keynesian tradition, savings are normally regarded as fairly stable, dependent upon long-established habits and probably highly insensitive to interest rates. Normally, savings also contribute the largest supply of lendable funds to the financial markets. Saved funds, with the exception of undistributed corporate profits that are retained for internal investment, are used to purchase financial assets or are retained in money form. If, for the moment, the supply of nonsaved funds from financial intermediaries is ignored, then the savings function can be regarded as the same as the supply-of-funds function to the credit markets.

The demand for funds primarily consists of investment demand, consumer credit demand, government budget deficits, and corporate liquidity demands. If the Keynesian insights about the power of uncertainty are correct, then it is this demand for funds that is potentially very unstable. Under certain circumstances, the demand for funds might either collapse or expand suddenly, causing serious problems. For example, underlying tensions and disproportions in the economy led to the stock market collapse of 1929. That collapse shattered business confidence, causing an even more dramatic drop in the demand for

---

[6]Hyman P. Minsky, *John Maynard Keynes* (New York: Columbia University Press, 1975), chap. 6.

[7]See Hyman P. Minsky, "A Theory of Systemic Fragility," *Financial Crisis,* edited by E. I. Altman and A. W. Sametz (New York: Wiley 1977).

[8]James Tobin, "How Dead Is Keynes?" *Economic Inquiry* (October 1977). See also James Tobin, "The Monetarist Counter-Revolution Today—An Appraisal," *Economic Journal* 71 (March 1981).

investment funds than would have occurred in a rational response to the underlying depression.

According to these theorists, *in a noncrisis period,* flexible interest rates intermediate the supply of and demand for funds, producing a market equilibrium. If savings shrink or if investment demand or government deficits gradually rise, market interest rates will rise to keep the market in equilibrium. If the marginal propensity to save rises, interest rates will drop to encourage demand.

Interest rates, however, are less effective at intermediating large and sudden shifts in the demand for funds. If investment demand drops suddenly, nominal interest rates might drop to nearly zero percent, but this will neither encourage investment nor discourage savings sufficiently to restore an equilibrium. For a period of time, savings will exceed investment, which implies that aggregate supply will exceed aggregate demand, and the economy will drop into a recession or depression. Some of the savings might remain in a money form rather than be used to purchase financial assets because of the desire to have a large inventory of perfectly liquid financial assets during this period of uncertainty. This would amount to a "leakage" from spending.

If, on the other hand, the demand for funds shot up suddenly because of, for example, a boom in speculation, interest rates would rise sharply. Again, the supply of funds, which tends to be sluggish in the short run, may not rise adequately to meet this new demand. Because of the political unpopularity of high interest rates and the damage done to the economy, the Federal Reserve System might respond by conducting expansionary open market operations, providing banks with new reserves, and bringing rates back down. Since the resulting credit expansion is not financed from savings, this also tends to produce a disequilibrium condition where aggregate supply exceeds aggregate demand at the prevailing price level. If not offset in some way, the result is likely to be inflation. This is one way in which speculation can fuel inflation via its impact upon the demand for funds.

Uncertainty and the Connection Between Monetary "Rules" and Volatile Interest Rates

These theories provide a framework for a Keynesian critique of the monetarist *"rule."* The *monetarist rule* insists that the Federal Reserve System should not conduct discretionary open market operations, but should keep growth of the money supply at some chosen rate. Suppose that investment is volatile whereas savings are relatively stable and do not react much to changes in interest rates. Suppose further that the Federal Reserve System does nothing to dampen interest rate movements by discretionary open market operations. Then interest rates will be volatile. The more insensitive (the more "inelastic") the supply of funds is to interest rates, the more volatile interest rates will be as the demand for funds shifts around.

Indeed, the Keynesians argue, as the Federal Reserve System moves gradually from a credit stabilization policy to rigid "rules," one should expect interest rates to become increasingly volatile. Before the monetary rule is ever achieved, interest rate volatility might reach an intolerable stage. This argument demonstrates why monetarism requires an acceptance of relatively stable human behavior and downplays the problems caused by decision making under conditions of uncertainty.

THE POSSIBILITY OF A PERMANENT LEAKAGE IN THE EXPENDITURE STREAM

By using the Gurley-Shaw theory,[9] one can show, with certain assumptions, that there is a potential for a *constant leakage* from the spending stream in a market economy and that it must be buttressed with a constantly increasing money supply.

Gurley and Shaw divided the economy into three sectors. Each sector is distinguished by the relationship between its receipt flows and expenditure flows. If an economic unit's receipts and expenditures are equal, that unit is part of the balanced-budget sector. In the surplus sector, receipts exceed expenditures whereas in the deficit sector, expenditures exceed receipts. The deficit sector borrows from the surplus sector by selling debt assets to the surplus sector. In a sophisticated economy, intermediaries work between the parties, offering assets and liabilities with a wide variety of features.

As wealth accumulates in a mature economy, the financial portfolios of the surplus sector continue to grow. As they do, Gurley and Shaw argue, the *relative* loss of liquidity makes the surplus sector less willing to absorb additional financial assets at prevailing interest rates. Gurley and Shaw do not use a utility approach in their explanation, instead preferring to discuss the matter in terms of a desire for liquidity. Their result, however, could be obtained by arguing that the marginal rewards of holding financial assets diminish with the growth of the portfolio. To compensate the surplus sector for holding more financial wealth, higher interest rates must be paid. The surplus sector agrees to finance deficits only at ever higher interest rates! Hence, with economic development, there will be a tendency for interest rates to rise, unless the Federal Reserve System takes offsetting action.

It is fortunate, however, that Gurley and Shaw expressed their explanation in terms of "liquidity preference"—the traditional Keynesian approach. It reminds one that as the wealth portfolio of the surplus units grow, *relative liquidity is sacrificed* unless the money inventory grows proportionately.

This means that surplus units might wish to hold money *(M)* as a roughly constant proportion *(k)* of financial assets *(FA)*:

$$k = \frac{M}{FA} \tag{17.1}$$

This device allows the calculation of a simple function in terms of demand for money *(Md)* to hold as balances (liquidity). The money balances will be a function of financial assets:

$$\Delta Md = k\Delta FA \tag{17.2}$$

The implication simply is that as the portfolio grows with income and the accumulation of wealth, the money component grows proportionately. If this is accurate, it introduces the possibility of a constant leakage in the spending stream.

Refer to Figure 17.1. This figure shows the money flow path for the surplus sector. Money receipts (income) flow in from the right. (Numbers are provided as examples.) Most of this

---

[9] Gurley and Shaw, *loc. cit.*, the closest Gurley and Shaw come to the hypothesis stated later is in their book, chap. 5.

is channeled into direct expenditures (consumption, direct investment, and tax-financed government expenditures). A portion, the surplus (savings), is channeled into financial assets. This flow will be used to buy financial assets from the deficit sector. Acquired assets will be added to the surplus unit's portfolio. If, however, the surplus unit requires the portfolio to correspond to demand equation 17.2, where money is held as a constant proportion of the portfolio (in order to maintain liquidity), some part of the money receipt will stay in the money form and sit idle, leaving the spending stream. In Figure 17.1, where $k = \frac{1}{9}$, 1 percent of receipts end up as idle balances. The remainder of the surplus is used to purchase a deficit unit's financial assets, where it is spent. For every $100 that flows in, however, only $99 is ever directly or indirectly spent. There is a leakage in the spending stream.

It is fairly obvious that the constant proportionality assumption is not even necessary to get this result. Even a declining proportion of money held as savings produces the result of the leakage so long as, when the portfolio grows, *some* part of the growth is in money form. *Any* amount of money added to the wealth portfolio is a leakage from the spending stream.

If money inventories are accumulated by surplus sectors in the way described earlier, velocity would gradually drop, so spending would decrease as a percentage of income. To compensate for the depressing effects, the Federal Reserve System would have to allow a gradual expansion of money to replace that which is hoarded. In such a situation, some positive growth rate of money would be required to accommodate even a stationary real income, and a higher growth rate of money would be necessary to accommodate growing real income.

After a period of time, perhaps a decade or two in an era of stability, financial asset wealth would be quite immense. The money component, used to protect "liquidity" would be quite large, and continuing to hold deposits in a sterile from would involve an enormous oportunity cost. In other words, a large segment of financial wealth (the money part) would yield no return. Less liquid financial asset that paid interest would become increasingly attractive.

Recognition of this might encourage the innovation of yield-bearing substitutes for money, or the development of other instruments and devices to protect liquidity. Large corporations, for example, that had been accustomed to maintaining constant cash-to-financial asset ratios or cash-to-total asset ratios might discover new ways to reduce such ratios safely. As evidence

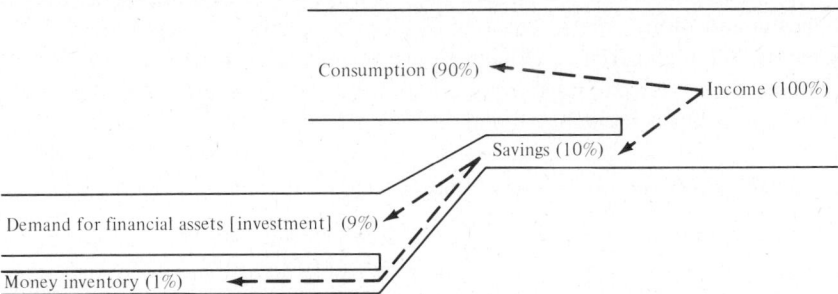

Figure 17.1 A Gurley-Shaw Scenario for a Chronic Leakage from the Income Stream
NOTE: All data are in percentages.
ASSUMPTIONS:
1. Aggregate demand equals 0.99 times aggregate supply. 2. Marginal propensity to consume equals 0.90.

of this, in recent years corporations have reduced their relative money balances by buying lines of credit at commercial banks. Lines of credit allow corporate customers to borrow instantly from banks with a mere telephone call. This protects liquidity while making it unnecessary to hold large liquid money balances.

If such innovations occur, then the large liquid pool of money reserves can be gradually converted to non-money financial assets, stimulating the spending stream to the point where expenditures exceed receipts. Because of this, velocity would rise and inflationary pressures would appear.

There would be two phases, therefore, in the "life" of this phenomenon. In the first phase, the monetary leakage forces the Federal Reserve to expand continually the money supply to protect liquidity. A vast pool of highly liquid but unused funds grows as a result. In the second phase, money inventories have grown so large that the opportunity cost of holding money is prohibitive. Financial entrepreneurs find ways to economize on money holdings, and the release of money back into the spending stream inflates the economy.

This explanation implies that over the long run the connection between money and spending can be very inexact as the surplus sector adjusts its money inventory.

THE PROBLEM OF DEFINING MONEY

To control the money supply, the Federal Reserve System must know what it is. Critics of monetarism, however, maintain that it is very difficult to even *define* money in any practical way. Because this is true, it is useless to speak of controlling something that can't be defined.

In textbooks, money is usually defined in terms of its *functions* rather than as a listing of particular financial instruments. Money, in other words, might be defined to be *anything* that (1) serves as a medium of exchange, (2) is a store of value, and (3) is a unit of account. This is the standard textbook definition. Milton Friedman uses a more general definition: money is a temporary abode of purchasing power. The point is that these are *functional* definitions of money; they do not enumerate actual monetary instruments such as checking deposits or Federal Reserve notes. As was pointed out earlier, the instruments fitting this definition might, at one time, have consisted only of specie, then later included bank notes, then later demand deposits. Perhaps now "money" includes more highly liquid, yield-bearing deposits and money market mutual funds and maybe even credit cards.

That money can be defined in terms of functions rather than instruments poses a serious problem. The Federal Reserve System can only attempt to control *instruments,* or the list of financial assets that perform monetary functions. This is often fairly difficult to do.

Recent Evidence of the Problem of Defining Money

The extent to which defining money is probably a genuine problem is made evident by the continuous changes in the *official* definition of money by the Federal Reserve System since 1978. Between 1978 and early 1982, there were no fewer than *six* definitions of the narrowly conceived money stock. This list does not include any of the menu of wider aggregates, such as M2, M3, L, and so forth.

Prior to October 1978, the narrow money supply was called "M1" and consisted of currency in the hands of businesses and individuals as well as private demand deposits. This definition had endured for decades. In fact, for decades when monetary policy was fairly loose, the Federal Reserve System accommodated general demands for credit. Even then it was felt by some, including Milton Friedman, that the M2 money supply, which included all instruments in M1 plus bank time and savings deposits, was the proper instrument of control.

At any rate, the growing importance of deposits on which checks can be written at nonbank intermediaries caused the introduction of a new aggregate definition called "M1+" into the aggregate monitored by the Federal Reserve System. When M1+ began to misbehave mysteriously, a new aggregate called "M1 adjusted" was introduced. Finally in late 1979, two new aggregates called "M1A" and "M1B" were introduced. M1A was the old M1 and was declining so rapidly that it ceased to draw attention. The growth of nonbank checking deposits became such a problem in 1981 that the Fed began to monitor and target the growth rates of an "M1B adjusted." Finally, in 1982, the narrow aggregate was again redefined as a new M1. At the same time, M1A, which only five years before had been *the* money stock, was dropped as a money aggregate. During this time period, M2 was also redefined three times.

CREDIT MATTERS MORE THAN MONEY

In recent years, a small group of economists have drawn attention to the relationship between credit and spending in the economy. They are continuing in the Gurley and Shaw tradition, but draw more attention to the amount of credit available per se whereas Gurley and Shaw more generally stressed the role played by the growth of financial intermediation.[10]

The creditists, if they can be called that, tend to endorse all that has already been said about the impotence of money. Whatever constitutes money is constantly changing, and money is even difficult to define at any given point in time. What people decide to do with their money varies all the time as well. Some will spend it immediately; others may hold it indefinitely. Some regard money as a financial asset; others regard it as a medium of exchange. How people use their money and the jobs performed by money are in constant flux. Even though a spendable financial asset must flow when spending takes place, there is no stable or reliably predictable relationship between the *stock* of money possessed by economic units and their spending behavior.

Another way of saying this is that velocity is likely to be volatile, will probably follow a rising or falling trend, and is essentially unpredictable. Economists who stress the role of credit demonstrate empirically that various credit and debt velocities (GNP divided by the variables that they favor) are much more stable than money velocities. Some of these

---

[10]See James S. Earley, Robert J. Parsons, and Fred Thompson, "Money, Credit, and Expenditure: A Sources and Uses of Funds Approach," *The Bulletin* no. 3 (New York University Graduate School of Business Administration, 1976).

velocities have, in fact, been close to a constant for these decades whereas the velocity of money has risen in multiples over the same period of time.[11] (Data showing this will be presented in Chapter 24.)

On the other hand, these economists believe, the expansion of credit—especially that credit that is not financed from savings—tends to stimulate the economy. The primary form of credit not financed by savings is, of course, bank credit. Although the extension of bank credit will result in money creation, the new money may go virtually anywhere. Some of it may be channeled into other bank liabilities, in which case it would "disappear." Some may be channeled into other financial intermediaries, where it would be used to generate more credit. Some would be spent, and some would stay idle in the form of demand deposits until the borrower has reason to use it.

As Gurley and Shaw pointed out, the proliferation of financial intermediaries over time provides a very fluid credit system, offering an abundance and wide variety of credit terms. The financial assets of an economy, including whatever is money, can be used far more efficiently and may support an ever higher level of spending. With easy availability of credit, spending units (especially corporations) can maintain a given level of spending, holding fewer and fewer liquid or pure money financial assets. Instead of holding liquid balances for safety reasons, corporations can lend such balances to others. If such lenders are caught in a "liquidity squeeze" (that is, if their cash receipts unexpectedly fall short of their cash obligations), they themselves can borrow in the short-term credit markets. Large corporations, for example, have established lines of credit with their banks, enabling them to borrow automatically if the need arises. Such lines of credit are now in the hundreds of billions of dollars. Creditists are also quick to point out the current asset–total asset ratio and the cash–total asset ratio have dropped markedly for American corporations in the last three decades.

In a sense this argument says that regardless of whatever is used as a spendable asset, it will be used more efficiently as the economy matures. From this perspective, one would expect velocity of money to rise almost constantly, with the speed of the rise occasionally accelerating. Additionally, because high interest rates tend to encourage financial innovation, a restrictive monetary policy might cause such an acceleration, which would undermine the restrictive policy.

INTEREST RATES MATTER MORE THAN MONEY

Many of the critics of monetarism believe that to the extent that monetary policy is effective, it is through variations in interest rates rather than changes in the money supply.

In the strictly orthodox Keynesian paradigm, nonmoney financial assets bear interest because money has a "liquidity premium." In other words, because nonmoney financial assets

---

[11]See Benjamin Friedman, "The Relative Stability of Money and Credit 'Velocities' in the United States: Evidence and Some Speculations," (Harvard Institute of Economic Research, Discussion Paper 824), April 1981. On the velocity of money, see Bryon Higgins, "Velocity: Money's Second Dimension," *Economic Review* (Kansas City: Federal Reserve Bank of Kansas City, June 1978).

are not money (hence, not perfectly liquid) a premium must be offered to encourage people to hold them. The less liquid a financial asset, the higher its yield is likely to be.

This opinion is falling from favor because both theoretically and empirically it is very questionable. There is very little evidence that the term structure of interest rates (which describes the relationship between maturity dates and yields) is determined by the ease or cost of conversion into money. Today, securities that differ considerably in yield are easily sold (converted to money) at very low cost because the finance markets accommodate a huge volume daily in virtually all securities.

Increasingly, monetary economists (including both monetarists and their critics) imply a loanable funds' perspective in their thesis, similar to that used by Irving Fisher 50 years ago. Interest rates are seen as the primary factor that equilibrates the shifting supply and demand curves for different types of borrowed funds. Money, which is provided through bank credit, is just one part of the spectrum of such assets. Yields differ on different financial assets because those who supply and demand these assets realize that the assets provide different services, have different risks associated with holding them, and are associated with different transaction costs.

All monetary economists agree that nominal interest rates are influenced in the short run by Federal Reserve System monetary policy. As explained in the preceding chapter, however, monetarists do not believe that real interest rates are influenced by monetary policy in the long run, and short-run fluctuations are soon canceled out. In the monetarist view, to the extent that spending is influenced by interest rates, it responds only to changes in *real* rates. Hence, any spending changes are due entirely to variations in the spending medium, money.

The critics of monetarism do not accept this interpretation. For one thing, when the Federal Reserve conducts expansionary open market operations, all they can do is provide the banking system with more reserves. For that to be translated into spending, banks must extend bank credit. The lowered interest rate is the mechanism that attracts new borrowing, and new borrowing generates new spending. From this perspective, although the initiative for spending comes from the Fed's easy reserve position, it is the interest rate on credit that translates the spending potential into a spending reality.

The Wealth Effects and Portfolio Effects of Interest Rate Changes

It is argued by some economists that interest rate changes are effective because of *wealth effects* or *portfolio effects*. The *wealth effect* is quite easy to explain. When interest rates on bank loans fall because of expansionary open market operations, competitive pressures depress the yields on other yield-bearing assets in the economy. This drop in yields raises the values of yield-bearing assets, especially longer-term securities. In the minds of the holders of such assets, they are wealthier. The nominal value of their portfolio has risen. To the extent that spending is a function of perceived wealth rather than income, the spending of these wealth holders will rise to reflect this new wealth. A rise in interest rates destroys wealth and would have the opposite, contractionary impact upon spending.

The *portfolio effect* describes how wealth holders change the composition of portfolios in response to interest changes. The portfolio effect can be used to show two things: (1) how an expansionary open market operation changes all interest rates rather than only the rates of instruments used in the open market operation itself and (2) how spending can be stimulated because of the portfolio effect.

When the Federal Reserve System conducts an expansionary open market operation, initially only two interest rates are affected: the yield on the security purchased by the Fed and the rate on bank credit. Both of these drop. Suppose the security purchased is a Treasury bill. Because the yield on the Treasury bill drops (and its market value rises), a disequilibrium condition is introduced into the portfolios of those who own Treasury bills. The Treasury bill component of the portfolio is now too high. Portfolio holders will reduce their demand for Treasury bills and raise their demand for other assets. The resulting equilibrium adjustment tends to spread the interest rate decline to other yield-bearing securities in the economy.

More importantly, the relative attractiveness of yield-bearing securities declines when they are compared to real assets. The demand for real assets rises (especially real assets that are being retained as havens for wealth, such as real estate and durable goods). Hence, spending for real output is stimulated in the long run by the Fed's expansionary operations.

The Sectoral Effects of Interest Rate Changes

Given the terrible performance of the economy in the 1970s and early 1980s, many economists critical of monetarism and sympathetic to these ideas are drawing attention to the sectoral and regional effects of high interest rates. The high interest rates caused by contractionary open market operations do not have an equal impact upon all sectors of the economy. They tend to have a severe impact upon those sectors of the economy that are sensitive to high interest rates, such as housing and the auto industry. They also tend to discourage investment while leaving other areas of demand, such as demand for consumer nondurable goods and services, relatively unaffected. These shifts cause dislocations and inequities in the economy, producing near depressions in certain industries. The economy, in general, begins to be affected only after the secondary linkage effects are felt.

This point of view is germane to the antimonetarist argument because, in the minds of these economists, monetarist anti-inflationary policies, which raise interest rates, tend to destroy industries and severely depress regions of the United States. These events, which purport to describe what *actually* happens to an economy when strong policies are invoked, are due to the *interest rate effects* of tight monetary policy and not to the fact that the growth rate of the money supply has slowed down.

THE ENDOGENOUS MONEY SUPPLY: MONEY CAN'T BE CONTROLLED

One conspicuous feature of *all* of the economists surveyed in this chapter is that they believe, in one sense or another, that the money stock is endogenous. To say that the money stock is *endogenous* means that the magnitude of whatever serves as money in some sense depends upon other activities in the economy over which the monetary authorities have little direct control. Money is a dependent variable. Therefore, whatever actually *serves* as money in a developing economy cannot, under all conditions, be controlled to the extent desired by the

Federal Reserve System. The Fed might affect the nature of that dependence or introduce long time lags in the relationship, but it cannot completely circumvent or overcome the dependent connection between money and activity in the economy over which it has no control. Either in the long run or the short run or both, the Federal Reserve System cannot control the money stock.

This, of course, is a profound argument, and if it has any merit, it shatters the monetarist paradigm. It is one thing to question the influence of money on economic activity; it is another to argue that the money stock cannot be controlled. The monetarist paradigm depends *entirely* upon the notion that the Fed controls money.

The Long-run Relationship

Since the late eighteenth century, there has always been a group of economists who believe that over time the expanding commercial activities of businesses will draw forth an amount of money necessary to accommodate their intentions. With expanding commerce, some device that can function as a medium of exchange or a source of liquid finance will be necessary. If the Fed—or any other central bank—refuses to accommodate this impulse, then innovative entrepreneurs will *eventually* modify the institutional structure and produce a private instrument that begins to serve as money.

This argument is antithetical to the monetarist perspective. In monetarism, money demand adjusts to the controlled money supply through price changes. This argument insists on the opposite: in the long run, the supply of money adjusts to the demand for money. Money responds to the so-called needs of trade.

The Legacy

The notion of the endogenous money stock goes back at least as far as Adam Smith.[12] Smith considered a trading country with currency redeemable in specie (gold or silver). Adam Smith argued that a prosperous trading country would attract specie with a favorable trade balance, supplementing the nation's money stock. Global expansion would raise the price of gold, encouraging more production.

This rather mechanical argument has no relevance today. In his chapter on money in the *Wealth of Nations,* however, Smith has a more subtle argument about the power of financial innovation. He describes a situation in Scotland where merchants had been unsuccessful in soliciting bank loans. In response, the merchants drafted short-term (typically, 90-day) bills of exchange and used them among themselves to finance trade. The practice of *kiting*—where a bill of exchange is redeemed just prior to maturity with a newly written bill—is described as very common. Smith tells his readers that the "practice of raising money in this matter had been long known in England" and was "said to have been carried on to a very great

---

[12]For an excellent review of Smith's attitude on the endogenous money stock, see Thomas Humphrey, "Adam Smith and the Monetary Approach to the Balance of Payments," *Economic Review* (Richmond: Federal Reserve Bank of Richmond, 1981).

extent." Smith, in this example, provided the image of entrepreneurs devising their own medium of circulation when conventional sources refused to accommodate their needs.[13]

With David Ricardo's acceptance of the quantity theory of money, the hypothesis of the endogenous money stock fell from favor. The idea was, in a way, resurrected primarily by Thomas Tooke and John Fullerton in the famous controversy between the Currency School and the Banking School (Tooke, Fullerton, and others) in the 1840s. In that debate, which concerned restrictive legislation affecting the Bank of England, Tooke and Fullerton insisted that bank notes have no effect on prices, but simply accommodate price movements.[14] Bank money appeared only when legitimate commercial transactions required it—that is why banks make loans or offer discounts. Business and commerce, inflationary or not, generate loan demand, and bank money appears in response to this impulse. These economists did concede that *large* increase in specie or government paper money *would* cause inflation. After passage of the Bank Acts of 1844 and 1845, which essentially rejected the Banking School philosophy, the "fact" that the money supply was determined by the monetary authorities was accepted by consensus. Controversy turned to the merits of the gold standard and the proper role of the Federal Reserve System.

The Cambridge emphasis on the demand for money in the Keynesian era established a perspective that made it easier to begin to regard the money supply as endogenous. After all, this perspective makes it apparent that the money stock reflects the interaction of supply and demand forces. Although after Keynes the critical attention was focused on the *demand* for money, the dichotomy made it possible eventually to think about the supply of money.

In *The General Theory*, Keynes accepts the hypothesis of rigid central bank control of the amount of money in circulation.[15] Many of those who have followed in his tradition, however, have brought back the notion of the endogenous money supply.

In the *Report* of the Radcliffe Committee, this attitude was made quite apparent. The committee insists that no sharp distinction can be drawn between money and other financial assets.[16] All financial assets have the monetary quality in varying degrees. If attempts are made to restrict the liabilities of certain financial institutions (such as banks), innovations by private parties will allow new institutions to flourish, and eventually their liabilities will finance spending. Monetary authorities ultimately cannot "stop the private creation of money." Money, in fact, "is the creation of the public that choose to impute certain qualities to certain claims."

Nicholas Kaldor claims that any shortage of money is bound to lead to the emergence of new types.[17] This, he claims, is why the first bank notes and checking accounts appeared. In the long run, the money supply will accommodate itself to the "needs of trade." If, in fact,

---

[13] Adam Smith, *An Inquiry into the Nature and Causes of the Wealth of Nations* (New York: Modern Library, 1974.) Originally published in 1776 (book 2, chap. 2).

[14] See Frank W. Fetter, *Development of British Monetary Orthodoxy, 1797–1875* (Cambridge, Mass.: Harvard University Press, 1965), chap. 6.

[15] See John Keynes, *The General Theory of Employment, Interest, and Money* (New York: Harcourt Brace and Jovanovich, 1936), pp. 230–231, 234–236, 247.

[16] R. S. Sayers, "Monetary Thought and Monetary Policy in England," *Economic Journal* (December 1960). See also John G. Gurley, "The Radcliffe Report and Evidence: A Review Article," *American Economic Review* (September 1960).

[17] Nicholas Kaldor, "The New Monetarism," *Lloyd's Bank Review* (July 1970).

the monetary authorities try to control spending by restricting the growth of certain types of bank liabilities (such as demand deposits), business will gradually be diverted from commercial banks to other financial intermediaries, and business will borrow money from new sources.

Hyman Minsky, the Post Keynesian economist, presents a similar view.[18] According to him, the sort of Federal Reserve System policy designed to control the money supply growth rate will produce new profit opportunities for financial entrepreneurs. This, in turn, causes an evolution of the structure of financial institutions that tends to offset or mitigate the intent of the Fed's policy. Such evolutionary financial changes are likely to occur during periods of high interest rates. Minsky cites the example of banks using reserves more efficiently during periods of high interest rates. Some examples of true "financial innovation" in the 1980s would probably include money market mutual funds, the commercial paper market, federal funds market, the repurchase agreement markets and perhaps even the Eurocurrency markets.[19]

Similar themes are offered by such contemporaries as James Tobin and David Laidler.[20] These writers—and all those cited earlier—have tended to be critical of the purest forms of monetarism (although both Tobin and Laidler predict a blending of monetarism and critical theories in the future). According to the critics, the monetarists, who are devout believers in laissez-faire, impute to entrepreneurs a remarkable capacity for innovation *except* in the area of financial innovation, where they become unimaginative and uninspired victims of the caprice of the Federal Reserve System. Such a paradoxical image of entrepreneurs cannot be sustained, these critics imply. Entrepreneurs innovate in the financial sector as well. The long-run result is circumvention of the Fed. The money supply cannot be controlled in the long run.

The Short-run Endogenous Money Supply

Recently, arguments have emerged that in the short run the money stock is endogenous as well. James Tobin's tendency to identify money as a "dependent" variable in his models classifies him as one who identifies the money supply as endogenous in both the short run and the long run. Kaldor and James Trevithick have a clear explanation of this point of view.[21] According to them, in a credit-money economy, the monetary expansion is the *result* of a desire to increase loan-financed expenditures. The variation in the demand for money-credit is partly autonomous and partly sensitive to interest rate changes.

If, for example, there is an autonomous rise in the demand for bank credit, the potential

---

[18]Hyman Minsky, "Central Banking and Money Market Changes," *The Quarterly Journal of Economics* (May 1957).

[19]For a description of these markets, see Marvin Goodfriend, James Parthemus, and Bruce Summers, "Recent Financial Innovations: Causes, Consequences for the Payments System, and Implications for Monetary Control," *Economic Review* (Richmond: Federal Reserve Bank of Richmond, March-April 1980).

[20]For Tobin, *loc. cit.*, and James Tobin, "Money and Income: Post Hoc Ergo Propter Hoc?" *Quarterly Journal of Economics* (May 1970). See also David Laidler, "Monetarism: An Interpretation and an Assessment," *Economic Journal* (March 1981).

[21]Nicholas Kaldor and James Trevithick, "A Keynesian Perspective on Money," *Lloyd's Bank Review* (January 1981).

borrowers are willing to bid up the interest rate. Using various expedients enabling them to use their reserve position more efficiently, banks meet the new loan demand with money-creating loans. In this situation, the demand for bank credit first rises, resulting in a rise in interest rates, which in turn results in a rise in the growth rate of the money supply.

It is interesting to note that this theory provides another explanation for the positive correlation between the money stock growth rate and the level of nominal interest rates. The classical and monetarist schools believe that the correlation is due to the inflationary expectations generated by an excessive growth of the money supply (and, ultimately, the effect of inflation itself). The critics, on the other hand, view the rising interest rate as the rising *price* of loan money, which encourages the "production," in a sense, of that money.

Basil Moore offers a similar theory, but provides an explanation of the dynamic process involved that more closely corresponds with the original Keynesian tradition.[22] In Moore's scenario, nominal wages rise during a period of lagging productivity. The resulting cash squeeze for producers forces them to demand bank loans to meet their monetary obligations. If no reserves are available, pressure is applied to the Federal Reserve System to provide more reserves. The Fed understands that their failure to act might produce unemployment (because of the distress caused by liquidity problems), which the Fed regards as intolerable. Consequently, they relent, allowing the loans to be made.

The Moore argument is one where the money supply is essentially "politically endogenous," the Fed relents because of the political pressures imposed by unemployment. Monetarists, in fact, might agree with Moore's theory. They would simply insist, in response, that the Fed should not relent when these problems arise.

In addition to this, there are a number of *institutional* reasons for believing that the money supply should be thought of as endogenous. In particular, the money supply is endogenous (not sufficiently controlled by the Federal Reserve) if (1) the Federal Reserve is following a credit market stabilization policy, (2) private banks aggressively use the discount window or the federal funds market, and (3) private banks shift their liabilities from monetary liabilities like demand deposits to high-yield nonmonetary liabilities like certificates of deposit. These three institutional reasons for considering money endogenous are next considered in detail.

The Effect of Credit Stabilization Policies and the Endogenous Money Supply

It may seem, because of the recent inflationary experience, that the Federal Reserve System's singular function is to control inflation. In reality, the Fed has traditionally regarded the promotion of credit market stabilization policies as its primary mandate. Only since the late 1970s, when inflation had reached utterly intolerable levels, was this goal reduced in importance.

A credit market stabilization policy typically has two objectives: keep interest rate

---

[22]Basil Moore, "The Endogenous Money Stock," *The Journal of Post Keynesian Economics* (Fall 1979). See also, Basil Moore, "The Difficulty of Controlling the Money Stock," *The Journal of Portfolio Management* (Summer 1981).

volatility to a minimum, and keep interest rates low. Both goals are thought by the promoters of such policy to produce a healthy investment climate because the first goal minimizes uncertainty and the second keeps investment financing costs low. Additionally, the government is able to finance its deficit at low cost.

Obviously, if such a policy is being used by the Federal Reserve System, then when growing credit demand causes interest rates to rise, the Fed, in the effort to stabilize the rates, will conduct an expansionary open market operation. The Fed buys yield-bearing securities, raising their price and lowering their yields. This act provides the banks with more reserves, which allows an expansion of bank loans (and money).

Therefore, if a credit stabilization policy is in effect, the very policy mechanism itself will ensure that money will be forthcoming to meet the short-run demand of bank-credit money.[23]

The Looseness of Control

A credit stabilization policy is not monetarist policy, obviously, so all that monetarists need to do in response to an argument that uses this policy to explain the endogenous response of money to economic needs is insist that the policy be dropped. In fact they did, throughout the 1970s, and were largely successful in persuasion of other economists.

There *still* remains, however, a final institutional explanation of why even the pursuit of monetarist policies cannot force actual control of the money supply (so that it remains endogenously determined).

Modern banking practices provide part of the explanation. Older monetary textbooks tended to present the image of the "passive" banker; bank loan officers simply sat behind their desks and waited for loan business to come in. They would accept loan business only if reserves were available. Such an image hardly describes modern banking.

Large banks today aggressively solicit loan business, using highly paid loan officers to go into the field and scout out corporate clients. Many banks have elaborate entertainment facilities to court their potential corporate borrowers. Often the banks offer lines of credit, which normally guarantee the right to borrow money up to some contractual limit. After such expensive marketing efforts, such banks are loathe to turn away such valued customers when loans are requested merely because their reserve position is tight. It is more likely that the loans are often made and the reserves are worried about later.

Discount Borrowing and the Federal Funds Market

Banks requiring reserves can borrow directly from their own Federal Reserve Bank, using the so-called discount window. (The *discount rate,* so often referred to in the media, is the interest rate charged for these loans.) Although the Federal Reserve System is supposed to discourage such borrowing unless it is for emergencies, they haven't really done so. Occasionally, such borrowing rises by $1 billion in a single week. Such borrowing will cover loans and

---

[23]See Richard Davis, "The Role of the Money Supply in Business Cycles," *Monthly Review* (New York: Federal Reserve Bank of New York, April 1968).

new money equal to at least six times the amount borrowed. Although the Federal Reserve Banks often pressure borrowing banks to repay the loans when they become excessive, a sudden surge in business loan demand and the resulting rise in the money supply can be sustained by this expedient alone for at least a short period of time and perhaps, upon occasion, even longer.

Banks additionally have the option of borrowing excess reserves from other banks in the federal funds market. Such reserve loans are simply arranged by a series of telephone calls. If loan demand is heavy in New York and weak in the Midwest, New York banks might call midwestern banks and borrow their unused reserves.

Because trade in the federal funds market can be so lucrative, in recent years, certain banks have encouraged their corporate customers with cash deposits to "lend" them their deposits —perhaps for just one or two days—in exchange for a "repurchase agreement." The borrowing bank simply "sells" an instrument like a Treasury bill to the lending corporation while signing a contract agreeing to "buy" it back a few days later. This is really nothing more than a short-term hypothecated loan, where the proceeds are often re-lent by the borrowing bank to the federal funds market.[24] The transaction is treated as a sale of a bank asset with a subsequent repurchase to avoid the reserve requirement on the corporate customer's deposit.

Attracting Funds to High-Yield Liabilities

When business loan demand is high, individual banks successful at making loans will competitively try to attract funds from other banks by raising the yields they offer on their high-yield, large-denomination liabilities, like certificates of deposit. When all banks do this, sometimes the entire banking system will experience a shift in the composition of their liabilities. The ratio of checking deposits to certificates of deposit, for example, will fall. Reserve requirements for checking deposits are much higher than for the high-yield bank liabilities; hence this activity tends to free reserves. This enables banks to make loans that would otherwise not be possible.

A SUMMARY OF THE INSTITUTIONAL EXPLANATION

Given that all of this institutional looseness exists in a complex market, it is argued that one expedient or another will be used by lending banks when loan demand rises. Therefore, even ock. Thus, changes in economic activity lead to changes in the money supply despite the Federal Reserve System's intentions.

The ability of banks to circumvent the Fed's goals is still restrained. The Fed will stop discount window lending once it has reached a certain point. Moreover, using the federal funds market or marketing certificates of deposit merely "tightens up" the credit system. There is a limit to how far banks can go. But the banks do have a great deal of latitude, and

---

[24]See Goodfriend et al., op. cit. 4.

if loan demand is volatile, then bank lending and the money supply will also be volatile even if ultimately constrained by limits. At least in this sense, it is argued, the money supply is endogenous, that is, determined by economic activity and the demand for funds rather than by the Federal Reserve System.

THE RELATIONSHIP BETWEEN MONEY AND SPENDING

As noted earlier, the monetarists and their critics disagree as to the main direction of causation between the money supply and spending. In monetarism, the amount of money in circulation is paramount in explaining the level of spending. Advocates of the endogenous money stock, on the other hand, assert an antithetical proposition, that the level of spending determines how much money will be drawn forth to accommodate trade.

Even to the extent that the money supply can be controlled by the Fed, these critics see little close connection between the amount of money available and the level of demand in the economy. Velocity is seen as highly variable and unpredictable. Since it is unpredictable, attempts to use monetary policy are ineffective at best.

The Radcliffe Committee unequivocally took this position. They insisted that spending depends upon the state of "liquidity" in the economy. Although *liquidity* is never clearly defined in the Radcliffe Report, it seemed to be a measure of the general availability of financial assets or credit or both. In their eyes, it is *not* the money supply narrowly defined but cheap credit that stimulates aggregate demand (and, as we have seen, the cheap credit may be a *result* of the upswing in economic activity). About all of this, the Radcliffe Report is annoyingly ambiguous and imprecise. Critics of the Radcliffe Committee have been quick to point out that their "hypothesis" is nearly impossible to test empirically. Despite this, there may be considerable validity in the committee's general position.

The Radcliffe economists would probably agree that all final payments for goods and services must be made with whatever is serving as money. Regardless of this, however, money can be disposed of rapidly, held a long time, or diverted to financial speculation. Additionally, in a world replete with numerous types of financial assets, a spending transaction can be financed with money simultaneously, before the act, or, more importantly, long after the act. When this is combined with the belief that the amount of money in circulation is loosely controlled, if at all, then the connection between money and spending is very unexact. Moreover, a growing inventory of financial assets or easy availability of credit or both will generate spending. The parties involved, being more "liquid," perceive themselves as faced with fewer constraints on their spending.

As a result of all these mechanisms, the money supply (and credit) expands because an economic expansion occurs—and not because of the intentions of the Federal Reserve System. The money supply (and credit) contracts because an economic contraction occurs—and not because of the intentions of the Federal Reserve System. Some actions of the Fed *may* affect the money supply (and credit)—but the Fed seldom opposes the prevailing will of business for very long.

MARXIST VIEW OF MONEY

Marx was one of the first economists to emphasize the importance of money.[25] Many of the classical economists declared that money only obscured the real and important relation, which was the exchange of commodities for each other. On the contrary, Marx said that the most important form of economic process in capitalism was (1) *money* was spent by capitalists to buy workers' power to labor, materials, plant, and equipment; (2) these *commodities* were used in the production process to produce *more commodities* of a greater value (because labor produces more than it is paid); (3) finally, these new commodities are sold for *more money* than the capitalist had at the beginning. As Keynes argued many decades later, this monetary economy has a delicate circulation process that may break down at any point. When the circulation process breaks down, there may be insufficient demand for goods, so Say's law is false in a monetary economy.

Marx emphasized that capitalists are divided into two groups. *Industrial capitalists* are in charge of production, turning commodities (including labor) into more commodities. But industrial capitalists borrow money from *financial capitalists,* who receive part of the profits exploited from workers in the form of interest returned on loans. (Marx also distinguished a third group, merchant capitalists, but that is not too important here.)

Marx went on at great length about the credit system. He stressed that the existence of credit made the capitalist economy even more vulnerable to economic crises than the mere existence of money. He spoke of the credit system as a complex web in which A owed B, who owed C . . . who owned N. If anyone in this chain could not pay his or her debts, then the whole chain collapsed. Thus, when a contraction occurred in the real economy, people out of work could not pay back consumer credit, and industrialists with unsold goods could not pay back business credit. The financial intermediaries were left holding worthless paper loans, so they too were in trouble. Marx, however, did not believe that it was the credit system that began the downturn; that was due to conflicts and disproportions among real factors. The credit system did greatly intensify the downturn. Similarly, once an expansion began, the speculators would greatly intensify at a frantic pace the amount of new investment in all kinds of risky ventures. Note that Marxists would not agree with the view that irrational changes in capitalist expectations determine the business cycle. These changes in expectations are exaggerated responses to endogenous real changes; they then intensify the change of direction.

Since the credit system was only beginning its incredible development in Marx's day, his own writing on it was limited. Other Marxists, beginning with Hilferding, have developed the view of financial capital and its close interrelations with industrial capital to a much greater extent.[26] Modern Marxist writers have also emphasized that there are today three major spheres of credit: (1) loans to industrial capitalists (as Marx observed); (2) loans to consumers (very little developed in Marx's day); and (3) loans to government (also relatively

---

[25]Marx's views are well documented in Suzanne de Brunhoff, *Marx on Money* (New York: Urizen, 1976).
[26]See Rudolf Hilferding, *Finance Capital* ed. Tom Bottomore, trans. Morris Watnick and Sam Gordon (London: Routledge and Kegan Paul, 1981). Also see the brilliant discussion in Kenneth Woodward, "*Finance Capital* by Rudolph Helferding: A review article," *Social Concept* (Spring 1983).

small in Marx's day). Although borrowing by industrial capitalists has grown immensely, the borrowing by consumers and government is actually much larger.

Most modern Marxists agree with some of the other alternative schools mentioned in this chapter on the most basic criticism of the monetarists.[27] The expansion and contraction of money and credit are very important to the economy, but they are determined by other economic activity; they are not determined outside the economy by some government agency (such as the Federal Reserve System). In other words, the movements of the money supply and credit are determined endogenously by the economic system—and are not exogenously determined shock factors. Of course, once there is a powerful expansion or contraction of money and credit, this has an enormous effect on the real factors of the economy. Marxists are more monetarist than the monetarists in the sense that they do believe that changes in money and credit (endogenously determined) can and do affect real factors as well as price levels whereas the monetarists believe that only price levels are affected in the long run. As noted earlier, Marxists are also more monetarist than the monetarists in the belief that a monetary economy will prevent Say's law from operating as it might have in a barter economy. On the contrary, the monetarists follow the classical economists in the belief that Say's law continues to operate unaffected by the existence of a money and credit economy.

Finally, Marxists have analyzed an area where Marx said hardly anything, namely, the operation of a central bank—which is usually dominated by finance capital, as we saw in Chapter 7. These views are further developed in Chapter 24 on monetary policy. We shall find that the Marxist view of monetary policy is that *no* monetary policy will be successful in an economy suffering from both unemployment and inflation.

SUMMARY

Although monetarism is now the dominant paradigm in monetary theory, it has many critics. A loose coalition of traditional Keynesians, Post Keynesians, creditists, Marxists, and independent critics are making their voices heard, and their influence is likely to grow. Drawing from the original orthodox Keynesian paradigm and the traditions established by the Radcliffe Committee and Gurley and Shaw, the liberal critics decry the inflexibility of monetarism.

Whereas monetarists regard the economy as efficient and stable, the liberal critics see the economy as afflicted with uncertainty, resulting in unstable and volatile spending behavior.

Money is just one of many financial assets, and the public that possesses it can use it in myriad ways. Their decision to hold it as part of their growing financial assets portfolio can

---

[27]Some modern presentations of Marxist monetary views include Gerald Epstein, *Bank Profits and the Political Economy of Monetary Policy in the United States, 1956–1977* (Ph.D. diss., Princeton University, 1981); Nai-Pew Ong, "An Inquiry into the Logic of Marx's theory of Money," *Economics Department Working Paper Series, no. 56* (University of California, Riverside, 1981); Robert Pollin, *Corporate Financial Structures and the Crisis of U.S. Capitalism* (Ph.D. diss., New School for Social Research, New York, 1982); John T. Roche, *Marx's Theory of Money and the Accumulation of Capital* (Ph.D. diss., University of Massachusetts, Amherst, 1981); Kenneth Woodward and Christopher Niggle, "Marx's Theory of Credit, *Economics Department Working Paper Series, no. 62* (University of California, Riverside, 1982).

cause a leakage in the spending stream. If, because of a change in expectations, they decide to spend it suddenly, it can cause a spurt in aggregate demand. In any case, the connection between money and spending is ever-changing and difficult, if not impossible, to predict.

The unreliability of any rules about money is compounded by the fact that the assets that actually constitute money are forever changing. The innovative private sector can circumvent attempts to control money by providing close money substitutes that eventually become money or new credit arrangements that make the use of money unnecessary. Not only is the connection between money and spending questionable, but the ability to control money is questionable as well.

Many of these critics believe that Federal Reserve policy influences the economy only to the extent that it influences interest rates or the availability of credit. Either or both of these variables have a more direct influence on the level of spending than variations in the narrowly defined set of financial assets that economists, at any given point in time, call money.

More important, all of the critics—including the Marxists—agree that the dominant direction of causation is the opposite of the monetarist model. In other words, economic activity determines the rise or decline of the money supply and credit. Money and credit change direction because endogenous real factors have changed direction. This happens either directly through the behavior of bankers and corporate executives (who frustrate Federal Reserve goals) *or* through the political pressures that the economic changes cause to be exerted on the Federal Reserve System.

Marxists emphasize that the political control of the money supply (in so far as that is technically possible) is shaped endogenously by the enormous power of the capitalist economic interests in and over the government (see Chapter 22). Marxists also emphasize that, once the political-economic factors cause a downturn in the money supply and credit, *then* these monetary factors intensify the recession or depression. Finally, Marxists have always emphasized the broader point that a monetary (and credit) economy destroys any possibility of Say's law's operating and opens the door to economic crises.

Chapter 18

MONETARY THEORIES OF THE BUSINESS CYCLE

Although most of monetary theory is oriented toward the development of monetary policy, extensions of the theories described in the last two chapters are often provided to explain business cycles. These theories are typically assigned secondary importance, perhaps because monetary theorists have been so preoccupied with inflation in recent years. Business cycle theories became less exciting during the deceptive tranquillity of the 1960s. That was the decade of "fine tuning," when economists mistakenly believed that enough was known about the economy to control it.

Undergraduate textbooks tended to emphasize the mechanical accelerator models of the business cycle.[1] Whether explained in prose or mathematically, these were dynamic structural models where money played no role in explaining the cyclical behavior of national output. In such models, cyclical behavior comes from oscillating investment demand. Fluctuating investment contributes to the cycle directly because investment is a component of output. It contributes indirectly as well because it influences the income stream on which consumption depends, causing the initial effect to "multiply" its impact throughout the economy.

This clever model is insightful, but the turbulent financial markets, which *must* have something to do with business cycles (or at least the episodic crises experienced by the economy), play no part. With the more amplified cycles of the 1970s and the 1980s, however, there is bound to be growing interest in the *financial* theories of the business cycle. Even the most superficial acquaintance with history makes it evident that major business downturns are at least made worse by, if not initially caused by, serious disturbances in the financial sector. It cannot be forgotten that the Great Depression was accompanied by a stock market crash near its beginning and bottomed out with a collapse in the nation's banking system.

---

[1] These models are explained in detail in Chapter 13.

In this chapter, a select group of monetary theories of the business cycles are presented. The selection is not intended to be comprehensive because there are many other theories that are subtle variations on the same theme. Instead, these types of theories have been chosen because they are conspicuously different from each other. The first represents a combined Fisherian and modern monetarist model. Monetarists today have an explanation of the business cycle that is very similar to Irving Fisher's most popular explanation (he had more than one). This model blames the business cycle on attempts to use discretionary monetary policy.

Fisher also developed a theory of the business cycle that derived from the consistent tendency of decision makers in the economy to miscalculate under conditions of uncertainty in different phases of the cycle. Hyman Minsky developed a model that is similar in theme, but different in structure from Fisher's. These two theories will be presented as well. Finally, we present Marxist views of the role of money in the business cycle.

In evaluating the importance of these theories, one should note that the latter three impute an *inherent* instability over time to market economies whereas the first attributes the instability to well-meaning but interfering policymakers. The monetarists, ever consistent, do not believe that a market economy will generate its own business cycles because of structural defects or free market behavior.

THE FISHERIAN-MONETARIST THEORY OF THE BUSINESS CYCLE[2]

Irving Fisher identified business cycles as primarily a "dance of the dollar." Using less poetic language, modern monetarists maintain that economic fluctuations are primarily caused by variation in the rate of growth of the money stock. Monetary behavior is the "star performer," according to Milton Friedman and Anna Schwartz, whereas the credit market is a "supporting player."

Monetarists remind their readers that unexpected exogenous shocks, like bad weather or an oil embargo, can disturb the economy. Aside from these uncontrollable events, however, there is no structural reason in a market economy for business cycles. Monetarists reject the orthodox Keynesian notion that business cycles are caused by variations in spending. The flexible price system—assumed by monetarists—protects against variations in investment, categories of consumer spending, or government expenditures. A fluctuation in one of these categories will cause the composition of spending to change, but not the aggregate level. Business cycles are the result of attempts to use discretionary monetary policies. Ironically, they argue, business cycles are the result of attempts to cure business cycles! (This particular proposition is at least the position taken by the more rigid monetarists, like Milton Friedman. "Mild" monetarists, like David Laidler, would not go this far. The "pure" monetarist theory is being presented here.)

In his chapter on business cycles in *The Purchasing Power of Money,* Irving Fisher provides the legacy for the theme. The business cycle is initiated by a surge in the money

---

[2]See Milton Friedman and Anna Schwartz, "Money and Business Cycles," *Review of Economics and Statistics* (February 1963 Supplement); and Irving Fisher, *The Purchasing Power of Money* (New York, Kelley, 1971).

supply, presumably because of a decision made by the Federal Reserve System (or some other form of central bank). This rise in the money supply causes aggregate demand to grow. Producers find themselves depleting their inventories and selling at higher prices.

Producers' revenues rise immediately, but their costs do not. Wage earners, who often have fixed wage contracts and are slow to respond to inflation, do not immediately press for higher wages. Because of this dynamic spread between revenues and costs, profits rise.

Because of the growth in profits, business confidence surges. Producers' spending remains high, and investment demand rises. If the money supply continues to expand at its accelerated pace, this "boom" can continue for a long time, providing the illusion of permanent prosperity. The result, of course, will be ever higher inflation, especially when labor decides that it will try to catch up to rising prices with higher nominal wages.

Regardless of what happens to the money supply after the initial stimulus, nominal wage rates will finally begin to rise. This puts pressure on producer costs. Simultaneously, savers begin to attach an inflationary premium to their saved funds. When this pressure by savers is combined with growing investment demand, this puts upward pressure on nominal interest rates.

Eventually, the monetary expansion must stop. Then aggregate demand ceases to rise. The lagged catch-up wage cost continues to rise for a time, putting severe pressure on profit margins. Confidence declines. Some of the more marginal borrowers are unable to honor their debt obligations, and some even are bankrupted. If the scare is serious enough, some banks might call in loans, exacerbating the situation. Credit becomes expensive and hard to obtain. Investment atrophies. Ultimately, the level of spending drops off, putting downward pressure on prices and real output. The cycle is complete.

This is an appealing explanation of a boom-to-bust type of business cycle. In terms of what it says about human behavior, it relies upon an acceptance of two general propositions. The first is that decision makers are somewhat shortsighted. If this is a general theory of business cycles, where the experience is repeated over and over, perhaps once every decade or so, then the parties involved don't remember their unfortunate experiences of the past. If government learned, it would prevent monetary surges. If business people learned, they would generally tend to raise prices, rake in their temporary windfall profits, and wait for their costs to rise. Business people would certainly not become optimistic or raise their investment demand.

Second, the Fisher model implies that producers are able to act faster than wage earners in an inflationary environment. Wage cost increases are lagged behind finished good price increases. This is not hard to accept because it means either that labor reacts slowly to inflation or that wages are fixed by contracts that extend into the future. Since evidence indicates that wages do tend to be sticky in the real economy, this is a credible proposition.

Fisher's model can be shown in a simplified form by using a graph borrowed from Chapter 16. It is reproduced below as Figure 18.1.

The initial increase in the money supply causes the demand curve in a particular industry to shift from D_0 to D_1. The supply curve, which is fixed by costs and available technology, remains initially at S_0 because costs don't rise immediately. A disequilibrium exists at P_0 because demand exceeds supply at that price. As inventories are depleted, both prices and output adjust to equilibrium point b. This is the boom phase of the cycle.

Because of rising costs, the supply curve ultimately shifts to S_1, and the equilibrium shifts

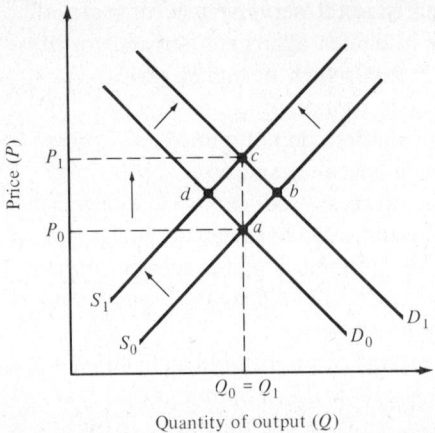

S = supply
D = demand

Figure 18.1 Fisher's Business Cycle Represented at the Micro Level

to c. In Fisher's model, the inflation (represented by the move from P_0 to P_1) is not permanent. Demand contracts because of declining investment, perhaps back to somewhere near the original level, D_0. Prices ease, and there is a sharp reduction in output. The equilibrium during the bust might be somewhere near d. Finally, as costs drop, restoring supply to its old level, the initial equilibrium returns. Fisher's model is not nearly as mechanical as this. Because of optimistic or pessimistic expectations, the supply and demand curves might drift about in a way that makes the cycle a little less smooth and more uneven, but the dynamic shown here captures the essence of Fisher's cycle.

The Modern Monetarist Variation

The modern monetarist version of the cycle model is very similar to Fisher's although it relies more heavily on a portfolio approach to explain the dynamics of the cycle. In the Friedman and Schwartz model, cyclical fluctuations are the outcome of balance sheet adjustments, reflecting the flows between desired and actual stocks of assets.

In Chapter 16 it was shown that Friedman's model posits a demand function for all financial assets, including a demand function for real money balances:

$$\frac{Md}{P} = f(Y_p, P_e \ldots) \qquad (18.1)$$

where Md is nominal money demand, P is the price level, Y_p is permanent income, and P_e is future price expectations. The demand for real money balances was primarily a function of the level of *permanent* income (a weighted moving average of transitory income) and future price expectations. This demand was thought to be insensitive to interest rate changes.

Given some initial equilibrium, a windfall increase in the money *supply* will cause a disequilibrium for the recipient of the money because the windfall money receipt will not affect price expectations or prices (yet) and will barely affect permanent income. In other words, the increase in the money supply causes nothing to change that affects the *demand* for money. Hence, for the recipient of the money receipts, the real money supply exceeds the real money demand:

$$\frac{Ms}{P} > \frac{Md}{P} \tag{18.2}$$

This is not an optimal condition, so the holder of these funds disposes of them through spending. Some might be channeled to other financial assets, but since monetarists do not see money and other financial assets as close substitutes, most money is likely to be channeled into normal spending.

As the money is spent and respent in the effort to restore equilibrium, the price level rises, and there is likely to be a temporary expansion of output, where resources are being used beyond their long-run optimal utilization rate. For example, machinery might be used more intensively and resources depleted more rapidly than justified by natural market conditions. This is the *boom*.

The eventual rise in prices, however, finally increases the demand for *nominal* money balances if the original level of *real* balances is to be maintained. In other words, the P denominator in equation 18.1 begins to rise, forcing up the nominal money demand (Md) if the desired level of real money balances (Md/P) is to be maintained. If the movement in prices (P) is lagged (and the monetarists insist that it is lagged by at least a few months) behind the original increase in the money supply, a large number of early spenders will have "overshot" this true equilibrium position by spending too much. When their demand for nominal money balances finally rises, they satisfy that increase in demand by restricting spending from their current income stream. This drop in demand causes a moderation in prices and a retraction in output. This is the *bust*.

The overspending and contraction, it will be noted, is due to the fact that, in this theory, the price acceleration is *lagged* behind the monetary stimulus. Otherwise, this would primarily be a theory of inflation (which it also is).

There is an extension of the theory just provided that explains cyclical investment. An increase in the money supply lowers nominal interest rates initially. Because the rise in prices is slow to respond to the monetary stimulus, the real interest rate drops as well. Because real investment responds to real interest rates, investment is temporarily stimulated. After a time, however, inflation begins to exert itself, stimulating inflationary expectations. Because of this, lenders of funds to the financial markets attach an inflation premium to their lending, and nominal interest rates rise. They will rise high enough to restore the real rate to its old equilibrium and, with overcorrection, might even temporarily raise the real rate above its old level. In response to this, real investment will contract.

In recent years, some monetarists have emphasized the cyclical problems caused by variable lags in those factors affected by discretionary monetary policy.[3] If the Federal Reserve System attempts to use countercyclical discretionary monetary policy, they argue

---

[3] See Michael Hamburger, "The Lag in the Effect of Monetary Policy: Survey of Recent Literature," *Monthly Review* (New York: Federal Reserve Bank of New York, December 1971); also see William Poole, "The Relationship of Monetary Decelerations to Business Cycle Peaks," *Journal of Finance* 30 (June 1975), pp. 697–712.

that harm may result because the Fed is unable to guess correctly the lag between the variable that the Fed controls and whatever it is that the Fed is trying to influence. Because of this, the Federal Reserve System will constantly overstimulate or understimulate, and because the targets are missed, the so-called corrective action does more harm than good.

For example, suppose the Fed feels that the full impact upon inflation of a reduced growth rate in the money supply will occur within six months because in the past that seemed to be true. Suppose that this lag is actually variable and in this case the full effect will not be felt for a full year. After six months, the Federal Reserve System is disappointed in its inflation fight, and it contracts the growth rate more severely. In the second half of the year, the bottom drops out of the economy. The Fed then pours on the fuel, and so forth. The point being made by these monetarists is that since the lags between what the Fed controls and what it wants to influence are unknown and variable, any attempts to chase the desired results all over the place are so disruptive that the Fed causes business cycles.

Despite subtle differences, the monetarist explanation of the business cycle has changed little since Irving Fisher. The cycle is caused by attempts to use discretionary policies.

Irving Fisher's Debt-Deflation Theory of Business Cycles[4]

Fisher at times was a little skeptical of the laissez-faire attitude of the conventional theories. Sometimes, it seems, his belief in the magic of Smith's "invisible hand" faltered. Such was the case in 1933. In that year, he published his other theory of depressions.

In *this* theory, the cycle is not caused by the folly of the Federal Reserve System. It is caused by the folly of the private investor operating in the marketplace. For this reason alone, this is a distinctly antimonetarist theory because it is a condemnation of the efficiency of markets. It argues for discretionary policies rather than condemns them.

With constant innovation in a market economy, new opportunities for investment periodically appear. A legitimate potential for gain will attract investment dollars into a promising area. When this happens, there is often a rise in equity and real asset values because of the environment of optimism. A good part of the acquisition of assets is debt-financed, which provides credit to the investors on the basis of the anticipated gains.

Conventional equilibrium theories predict that capital is attracted in this way until such time that, at the margin, the value of the expected income stream is equaled by the cost of claiming the income stream. Debt will not be used beyond the point where the income stream from the debt is not sufficient to redeem the obligations of the debt contract.

This might be so were it not for the activities of the speculator. Rising asset values attract speculative funds interested purely in capital gains. Speculators will borrow to buy assets with little of their own money, hoping simply to be able to sell them at a higher price. The participants in this gamble are indifferent to the value of the income stream of these assets.

Because large profits are to be made in the merchandising of such projects, promoters—who themselves take no risk—attract the naive public with promises of great expectations.

---

[4] See Irving Fisher, "The Debt-Deflation Theory of Great Depressions," *Econometrica* (October 1933).

Ultimately, debt-financed assets are greatly inflated in value, far beyond the capacity of the assets to produce an income stream sufficient to meet the debt obligations.

Debt servicing finally becomes a problem. Ultimately, there is a severe deflationary liquidation of assets, causing a market collapse and producing many additional problems. As the deflation becomes a reality, the debt servicing problems are compounded because falling prices make it ever harder to service a debt contract that is stipulated in nominal terms. Without assistance from the monetary and fiscal authorities, such a downturn can easily become a financial depression if debt-financed speculation has been widespread.

In this model, Fisher does not explain variations in real output. The model merely explains why there are a boom and a bust in the financial markets. One would expect, of course, that wild cycles in the financial markets are going to have strong effects on expectations and the general state of confidence, which in turn will translate into cyclical spending behavior. It is hard to imagine that the economy would move along smoothly when the financial markets are collapsing. The actual mechanics of this process, however, are not provided by Fisher. Hyman Minsky, inspired by Fisher's theory, provides a more complete explanation.

HYMAN MINSKY'S FINANCIAL BUSINESS CYCLE THEORY

In his book on Keynes,[5] Minsky resurrected Fisher's old theory and synthesized it with some of Keynes's original thoughts on speculation and economic fluctuations. Minsky's model is perfectly consistent with Fisher's although it is much more refined and complicated. The model is far more complex than the explanation that follows, which is presented as a simplification that—one hopes—captures the essence of the model, albeit, perhaps, with some loss of fidelity.

In the tradition of Keynes, Minsky constructs an environment of uncertainty, speculation, investment, and debt finance. Decisions are made about a future that is unknown. Capital assets are purchased because it is believed that they will produce a profitable income stream. Investment involves the financing of the purchase. The capital assets are directly or indirectly represented by corporate stocks, which are marketable and are sold in secondary markets for securities. Fluctuations in the market values of these stocks amount, *in part,* to constant revaluations of the earning power of the existing stock of capital assets.

In an ever-changing economic environment, such revaluations constantly take place. Security values rise and fall. This provides a fertile environment for the *speculator,* who is uninterested in the income stream earned by capital assets. The speculator, instead, desires to "make his fortune by correctly betting on the turn of the market." The speculator wants to buy at a low level and sell at a higher level. Speculators also want to borrow to finance their speculation. The speculator buys a large amount of corporate stock, with very little of the speculator's own money and with the prospects for higher rates of return.

In his theory, Minsky pays close attention to the behavior of three categories of people:

---

[5]Hyman Minsky, *John Maynard Keynes* (New York: Columbia University Press, 1975); also see several relevant articles (including one by Minsky) in Edward Altman and Arnold Sametz (eds.), *Financial Crises* (New York: Wiley, 1977).

the owners of corporate equity shares, the owners of capital assets (the corporations themselves) who often borrow money to finance their investment, and the lenders who finance investment. Minsky claims that all three of these categories of participants are potential speculators. This means that they often try to profit from changing market conditions, which involve variations in prices and yields of financial assets. Their decisions to buy, lend, borrow, and invest are often heavily influenced by expected price appreciation, yield spread, and so forth.

The speculative activities of owners of corporate stock are well known. Often stockholders actively trade in the market, trying to buy low and sell high. Their decisions are sometimes only remotely connected to a corporation's prospects for profit or present corporate earnings. Stock exchanges often resemble casinos, with a great deal of gambling on security prices. A good part of the activities of the stock speculator are typically debt-financed.

The debt financers—especially the financial intermediaries—also engage in speculation. The financial intermediaries speculate because the maturities of their assets (primarily loans) are not matched with the maturities of their liabilities. Assets have longer maturities. Financial intermediaries often finance long-term loans with deposits that have to be rolled over constantly. For example, the assets of many large banks in recent years include large numbers of real estate loans at fixed interest rates with maturities of 20 or 30 years. Most of their deposits, on the other hand, have maturities of 30 days or less, with such liabilities as federal funds typically maturing in 1 or 2 days. The largest type of deposit is demand deposits, which can be withdrawn at any time.

When lending is aggressive, the lenders are often counting on favorable markets in the future to refinance their liabilities in a way that maintains or increases their profitability. When banks speculate, they raise the ratio of their liabilities to their reserves. They do this by attracting money from demand deposits with high reserve requirements to the various time deposits with lower reserve requirements. The money is attracted by offering higher yields on the latter. They also use the federal funds market, borrowing surplus reserves from other banks. These practices enable the speculative banks to extend their loan assets. In this sense, Minsky argues, the money supply and credit are *endogenous*. The credit side of the boom can be financed by banks without the compliance of the Federal Reserve System.

The corporate owner of capital assets is also a potential speculator. The market value of capital assets will fluctuate, just like the equity values that represent those assets. A mood of optimism may inflate the value of existing capital assets. This identifies two sources of wealth from owning capital assets: the income stream (margin over costs) from owning such assets and any capital gains that accrue from inflated asset values. If the investor incorporates anticipated capital gains in the investment decision by anticipating future market conditions, then this is a form of speculation. This is important, because such decisions can easily affect the level of investment demand and the demand for credit to finance investment.

For example, suppose the business community expects a world oil boom. Some anticipate that supertankers are going to be needed to transport oil. They become *bullish* on supertankers. The rising demand for supertankers, promoted by shipbuilders and financed by banks, might be as much the consequence of an anticipated rise in the value of supertankers as it is the result of the anticipated business that supertankers will handle. If this *bullishness* becomes excessive, there may be overinvestment in supertankers, eventually causing a market shakeout.

In the absence of speculation, investors are influenced by (1) the price of capital assets, (2) the anticipated net revenue flow from investment, (3) the cost of borrowed funds, and, given their attitudes about risk, (4) the extent to which their assets are financed by borrowed capital. If the owners of corporate assets are willing to ignore risks, they will buy assets if the expected value of the income stream from such assets exceeds their cost, including finance cost. The borrowing investor, however, realizes that the cash obligations associated with debt are certain whereas the future yield from capital assets are uncertain. The greater the level of borrowing, the higher the leverage and the greater the impact of an unexpected variation in future revenues upon profits. Hence corporations concerned about risk may tend to discount their estimates of future yields to play it safe. Because borrowing increases their leverage and they are concerned about risk, corporations will borrow ever larger amounts only at lower interest rates or lower prices of capital.

Lenders favor diversification to dilute risk and are concerned about the safety of the borrower. They are willing to loan ever larger amounts to a single borrower, only at higher interest rates. Given their objectives and constraints, the borrowers and lenders meet in the market and settle upon a level of lending at interest rates agreeable to both parties. Given the amount of internal finance, that level of lending determines the level of investment.

If a mood of optimism becomes pervasive in the economy, however, perception about risk and expected future yields is revised. Risk is de-emphasized, and expected yields are revised upward. Borrowers are willing to invest more and pay higher interest for loans. Lenders are enthusiastic about accommodating loan demand at higher rates. The values of capital assets are reevaluated upwards, and equity shares may reflect the optimism with a rise in values. If assets are appreciating and capital gains are being realized, the setting is ripe for speculation.

Now the framework is established. All parties involved are not only passive borrowers and lenders of money, but potentially speculators as well. In an environment of enthusiasm, these speculative tendencies are likely to emerge.

The Boom

The public mood is a major factor influencing spending behavior. In a fertile environment, a mood of extreme optimism or bullishness might gradually emerge. This might be at the micro level, occurring in a small number of markets, such as real estate or petroleum. In such a case it might be due to a new technology or a robust demand condition influenced by population growth, changes in tastes, political developments, new technologies elsewhere that demand new resources, or any number of things. It might also be a pervasive phenomenon that encompasses an entire economy. In this case, the cause might be attributed to the recent experience of a sustained prosperity, a presidential election, a series of new technologies with many linkages, or whatever affects the public mood. In this latter case, the new *euphoria,* as Minsky calls it, is likely to emerge only after the memory of the last catastrophe has gradually faded away.

In this optimistic environment, potential investors either raise their expectations of the value of the income stream associated with newly acquired capital assets or they lower their estimation of the risk associated with such investments. (Minsky implies that the latter attitude is more likely.) Their demand for investment rises. Since their capacity for internal financing is limited, their demand for borrowed funds rises as well.

Banks, operating in the same "healthy" environment, see the demand for their services rising, which they are quite willing to accommodate. If the Federal Reserve System is not cooperating by providing a sufficient level of new reserves, then banks begin their "speculation." They begin to switch from one kind of liability to another (requiring less reserves) so as to expand the ratio of their liabilities to reserves, or else they borrow the free reserves of other financial institutions. The result is that an endogenous expansion of credit takes place. This turns desired investment into realized investment.

If the Fed is conducting expansionary operations, then banks' switching liabilities to those with lower reserve requirements (and higher interest rates) is unnecessary, so the investment impulse is financed at lower interest rates than would otherwise be the case. Under certain circumstances, active Fed expansionary policies could be the *cause* of the boom. An easy credit policy, for example, might make borrowing so easy and inexpensive that speculation flourishes.

The very important point being made here is that *the Federal Reserve System may play an active, a passive, or a negative role in the speculative boom.* It will be active if the Fed's expansionary policies produce and then feed the optimistic environment. The Fed will be passive if the optimistic climate has an independent cause, which is then accommodated by easy credit policies. It will be negative if the Fed is pursuing "tight" policies. In the latter case, the banks will circumvent the Fed by switching to liabilities with lower reserve requirements. *Only in the active case can it ever loosely be said that the expansion phase of the business cycle is caused by the "dance of the dollar."*

As the prosperity escalates, the optimistic emphasis becomes more pervasive. There is a consensus of optimism. This accelerates existing trends. John Maynard Keynes once remarked (this is a paraphrase) that the stability of speculative markets depends upon a continuing state of confusion. If there is a consensus of either optimism or pessimism, a runaway market results. The market rises strongly when optimism prevails and falls when pessimism is the dominant mood. With the consensus of optimism, security values and the value of capital assets will rise. When capital gains are realized through sales and when this happens many times over a lengthy period, it provides a heady experience. The new wealth provided by held assets is often used as collateral to finance new loans. This occurred in the late 1970s in the residential real estate boom. Homeowners borrowed, using their equity from rising real estate prices, as collateral.

The speculative motivation eventually becomes the dominant motivation. Capital-asset owners expand their acquisition of capital goods because of their sheer appreciation in value. There is often a so-called merger madness when corporations swallow whole the assets of other corporations. Speculators hurry into the booming stock markets, buying high and selling even higher yet. Meanwhile, the investment bankers promote this frenzy, and the commercial bankers finance it. Investment booms, security values rise, and debt expands rapidly.

The Bust

When the speculative motivation becomes dominant, the economy has entered a dangerous phase. J. M. Keynes, in a famous passage quoted by Minsky, makes this point quite clear:

> Speculators may do no harm as bubbles on a steady stream of enterprise. But the position is serious when enterprise becomes the bubble on a whirlpool of speculation. When the capital development of a country becomes a by-product of the activities of a casino, the job is likely to be ill-done.[6]

The speculation ignores the fact that the actual income streams generated by capital assets must be capable of honoring all debt obligations that are attached to them. With speculation, capital asset values and corporate stock values become overvalued. Additionally, excess investment has probably taken place, which means the future income stream from sales must be shared by an ever-larger group of investors. To use the examples cited before, there may simply be too many supertankers, or agricultural real estate may have escalated in value far beyond the capacity of farming operations to redeem the debt.

As the boom reaches maturity, some of the more mature speculators begin to realize this. They remember the old Malthusian dictum that financial wealth cannot possibly exceed the capacity of the economy to provide it in real terms. (This is why economics is called the "dismal science." It keeps reminding people of these hard realities.) These speculators begin to withdraw from the markets, and the markets experience a phase of price stability. The mood has passed from a consensus of optimism to a mixture of optimism and guarded caution. Because values stabilize, some marginal speculators who had counted on continuing appreciation are damaged, and this becomes part of the experience of the market.

The markets may dance around for a while in this transition period, but sober reality scares more speculators in its grip. More speculators realize that their assets are overvalued and that too much debt has been extended. Gradually, a mood of caution becomes pervasive, and it rapidly erodes into a consensus of pessimism. If at this time there are any debt-servicing problems or bankruptcies, the news of this can contribute to a climate of fear. Speculators who have gone greatly into debt in order to buy assets near the end of expansion might panic. There is an accelerating liquidation of assets accompanied by a deflation. The bust is on.

The fear of capital losses, downward-scaled expectations of future income streams, and the fear that there may be excess capital goods inventories all produce a sharp contraction in investment. This important component of aggregate demand has itself now gone through a full cycle.

Although in this particular presentation, the cycle is presented as a macro phenomenon, the same cyclical phenomenon can also be isolated in individual markets. The linkage effects to the rest of the economy will depend upon how important the individual market happens to be. Recent candidates for this type of cycle at the single-market level might include the markets for gold, diamonds, residential real estate, airlines, and supertankers. The best

---

[6]John M. Keynes, *The General Theory of Employment, Interest, and Money* (New York: Harcourt Brace Jovanovich, 1936), p. 159.

historical candidates for this type of cycle at the macro level would be the financial panics of the nineteenth century and, of course, the Great Depression.

CONTRASTING THE TWO TYPES OF MONETARY THEORY

The models discussed do not constitute an exhaustive survey of monetary theories of the cycle. Instead, they are presented as representative of essentially antithetical points of view. The monetarist models attribute the business cycle to governmental attempts to interfere with the economy. Minsky's Post Keynesian model emphasizes the role played by the actions of capitalist speculators and investors. In the first, the Federal Reserve System (or other central bank) causes the business cycle. In the second, the Federal Reserve System (or other central bank) can do nothing about the cycle.

Ironically, both theories are derived from the same eminent scholar, Irving Fisher. His own versatility can perhaps exist as a sound lesson for modern scholars. There is probably a considerable degree of truth in both theories. They are mutually exclusive when compared in their entirety. But if they are considered as perspectives, both can be illuminating to important aspects of some cycles.

Business cycles differ from each other in many respects. In fact, different business cycles are often quite different. Some business cycles are dominated by speculation, so they do seem to correspond to Minsky's scenario.[7] Still others, like the slump of 1937 or the recession of 1980, were probably greatly influenced by that kind of discretionary monetary policy that helps to depress the economy.

AN INTEGRATION OF REAL AND MONETARY FACTORS: MARXIST AND OTHER THEORIES

Is money important in causing the business cycle? That question is too imprecise to answer in that form. More narrow and precise questions can be answered in order to get at the broader question (the answers by Marxists to these questions are similar to those by many other nonmonetarist theorists.)

Could there be a business cycle if the capitalist system ran by barter rather than money? No, but one cannot imagine a modern industrialized capitalist system without money. As demonstrated in Chapter 2, the institutional preconditions for a business cycle are (1) market exchange, (2) production for private profit, and (3) *the existence of a monetary system.* Whereas the classical and neoclassical economists paid no attention to these institutions of the modern capitalist economy as necessary conditions of the business cycle, the institutionalists (such as Wesley Mitchell), the Post Keynesians, and the Marxists consider them essential. Since conditions (1) and (2) are fairly obvious, there is an enormous literature on the necessary role of money by these schools of thought.

[7]See Charles P. Kindelberger, *Manias, Panics, and Crashes* (New York: Basic Books, 1978).

This conclusion is very different, however, from the monetarist insistence on governmental monetary policy as the villain in all recessions and depressions. There have been many cycles in U.S. history in which governmental monetary policy played little or no role, much less a negative role.

Is the monetary system always the main initiating cause of cyclical upturns and downturns? The rapid expansion or drastic contraction of credit for speculative reasons does not seem to be the main initiating player in most cycles (nor is government monetary policy). In most cycles, it appears that the money stock and credit continue expanding till after the peak is reached; then—*after* real variables have led to a downturn—the monetary variables play a major role in deepening the downturn. For example, in 1929 the profit rate was declining for several months before the stock market crash. The collapse of the credit system and the banks came much later in the process. Similarly, in most cycles it appears that monetary and credit factors lead to a much more exaggerated boom than would have occurred without them, but only after the real variables (such as demand, cost, and profit rates) begin the expansion; the monetary variables do not initiate the expansion any more than they initiated the contraction. Actually, talking about what the initiating causes are may still be an imprecise question; what really exists is an integrated process of monetary and real factors in which it is only possible to isolate some of the aspects in a particular sequence.

The sequence may be something like this. In early expansion, output and profit rates are rising rapidly because demand is increasing while costs are low (see Chapter 15 for a detailed description). The high expectations of future profits lead to a vast expansion of consumer and investor credit and speculation of all kinds. This is an endogenously caused expansion of the money supply and of money velocity (as discussed in detail in Chapter 17 and in Minsky's theory). This expansion can occur even if the Federal Reserve System puts up barriers to it —which it usually does not do at this point in the cycle.

By late expansion, the profit rate is stagnant or declining because demand is limited and costs are rising (see Chapter 15), leading to an eventual decline in investment. In addition to real costs, there are rising costs owing to increasing prices; these cut into the profit rate and tend to hasten the cyclical downturn. As shown in Chapters 8 and 9, consumer and business credit do continue to increase right up to the peak. Therefore, the use of credit usually strengthens demand and postpones the cyclical downturn (but the central bank may try to limit credit at the end of expansion).

Once the decline is under way, all sectors of the economy conspire to keep it declining. Real demand, costs, and profits fall. But it is the money and credit system that determines whether it will be a mild recession or a terrible depression. If the financial system survives in good working order, it can support some portions of business through the worst times. But the financial system is very fragile, and it becomes more so whenever there is a rise in the ratio of credit to corporate assets or consumer income or both. In such cases, where A owes B and B owes C substantial sums, if C cannot pay back B, then B cannot pay back A, so they all collapse together. These chains of creditors and debtors are very long and intricate in our society—and sometimes, as at present, the percentage of debt outstanding is very high by historical standards—so collapse of the financial system becomes a real possibility. When this happened in the early 1930s, the Great Depression resulted.

Recovery from a business contraction normally occurs when demand has stabilized and costs have declined, so profit expectations again become optimistic (see Chapter 15). If the financial system is back in good working order, it will normally finance the recovery beyond what the (low) current income could achieve. If the financial system has not recovered, then the economic recovery may be very weak. For example, in mid-1983, there were still high interest rates acting like a damp rag to stop any strong recovery.

SUMMARY

Some theories of the cycle allow no role for money and credit and have been heavily criticized for that reason. Some theories of the cycle blame everything on the monetary and credit system—often blaming governmental mismanagement or financial speculation. These theories have been heavily criticized for allowing no role for real nonmonetary factors such as demand, costs, or income distribution.

Theories now emerging tend to argue that (1) money is one of the preconditions of the business cycle; (2) money and credit play a role, along with real factors, at every point in the cycle; and (3) money and credit certainly intensify cyclical fluctuations, sometimes helping to cause deep depressions or wildly speculative expansions.

Part Five

INFLATION

Chapter 19

DEMAND-PULL AND COST-PUSH INFLATION

There are many different theories as to the causes of inflation, which may be separated into demand-side and supply-side explanations. This chapter first examines the demand-side explanations, the situations in which demand-side explanations seem to apply, and the situations—like the present one—in which demand-side explanations do not seem to apply. Then it examines supply-side or cost-push explanations.

THE KEYNESIAN FRAMEWORK

According to Keynes, the "effective demand" for goods and services is that amount of desire or need that is backed up by money in the hands of those with the desires or needs. When effective demand exceeds the full-employment level of supply at present prices, there will be inflation. When effective demand is greater than supply at present prices, but the economy is below full employment, then there may be a rise in output or inflation or both. If demand is less than supply, then there may be a decline in output or deflation or both.

The sources of aggregate demand are defined exhaustively to be (1) consumer spending, (2) investment spending, (3) government spending, and (4) net exports. This chapter ignores net exports (discussed in Chapter 21). Leaving money and credit aside (discussed in detail later), we may say that there will tend to be inflation when the planned amount of real consumption, investment, and government spending exceeds the planned amount of real supply. The Keynesian approach thus leads us to examine the sources and behavior of consumer, investor, and government spending. One would expect that demand exceeds supply in every war and during most of every economic expansion. These two situations are discussed in the next two sections.

INFLATION IN WARTIME

Most of the spectacular inflations in U.S. history have occurred during wars. As shown in Figure 19.1, there were very rapid price increases in the Revolutionary War, the War of 1812, the Civil War against slavery, and World War I. There were similar rapid price increases in the Korean War and the Vietnam War. It is worth emphasizing that there was very little inflation *between* the Korean and Vietnam wars, with several years of near-zero price changes. The present inflationary trend began in 1965 during the Vietnam War.

The apparent exception that proves the rule is World War II. As shown in Figure 19.2, there was very little price increase in World War II. There were enormous inflationary pressures in that war. The reason there was very little inflation, however, was that there were very strict wage and price controls combined with rationing that held the inflation in check. When the controls were lifted in 1947, the strong inflationary pressures immediately revealed themselves in rapid price increases.

Why do prices tend to rise in wartime? First, there is a vast rise in government spending, employment by government, and income paid by government. The increased government spending competes with private dollars for consumer goods, such as shoes for soldiers, and

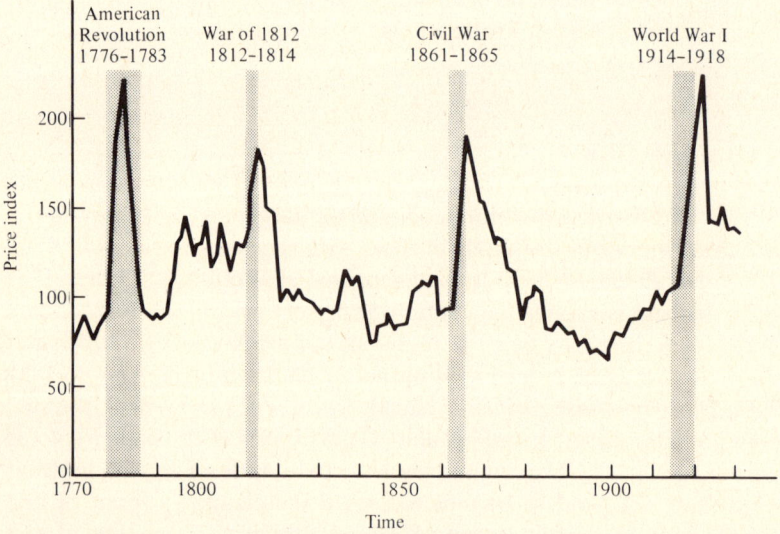

Figure 19.1 War and Inflation in U.S. History
NOTE: Wholesale price index, 1770–1929.
SOURCE: U.S. Department of Commerce, *Historical Statistics of the United States, 1789–1945* (Washington, D.C.: G.P.O., 1949).

Chapter 19 Demand-Pull and Cost-Push Inflation   347

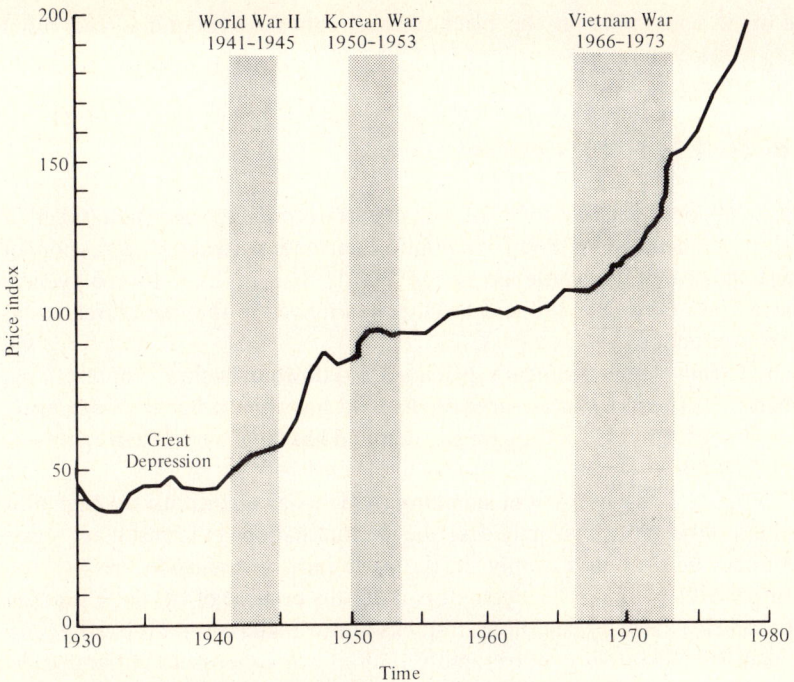

Figure 19.2 Recent Price Movements in the United States
NOTE: Wholesale price index, 1929–1975.
Base: 1957–1959 = 100.
SOURCE: U.S. Department of Commerce, *Statistical Abstracts of the United States, 1964* (Washington, D.C.: U.S.G.P.O., 1964) p. 351; and *Federal Reserve Bulletin* (May 1980), p. A-66.

for producer goods, such as steel for ships in government shipbuilding yards. Second, private firms receive military contracts, with a large flow of government funds and guaranteed high profit rates. Therefore, these firms wish to expand their investment in producer goods by a large amount. Finally, the vast increase in government income to capitalists raises the demand for luxury goods whereas the vast increase in government income to workers raises the demand for all consumer goods.

Thus, aggregate consumer and investment demand are both rising rapidly, but the supply of consumer and investor goods is restricted by the huge drain of purchases by the government. All other things being equal, there must be severe pressures for price inflation.

Of course, the inflationary pressures may be reduced by increased taxes or by increased sale of treasury securities, discussed in Part Six, but these steps have never been sufficient for various reasons. For one thing, governments in wartime wish to be popular and inspire extra work, so they cannot make enormous tax increases. And governments are usually unable to get people to buy, voluntarily at least, enough treasury securities to soak up all the new income—because people who have just achieved the possibility of a decent standard of living do not want to give it up. Wage and price controls may hide the inflation for some time, but at the cost of corruption in the black market, physical rationing, and other problems.

INFLATION IN BUSINESS EXPANSIONS

The normal or usual behavior of prices is to be inflated in every economic expansion (whether mild or boom) and to be deflated in every economic contraction (whether recession or depression). The best index of U.S. wholesale prices reveals that, in 23 of the 26 cyclical expansions and contractions between 1890 and 1938, prices moved in the same direction as business activity and production.[1]

Why do prices tend to move up in business expansions and down in business contractions? What happens is that in most expansions aggregate demand has risen faster than aggregate supply, so prices rise. In most contractions, aggregate demand has fallen faster than aggregate supply, so prices tend to fall.

Leaving aside net exports and government spending (which was quantitatively negligible in peacetime cycles before the 1930s), we may describe the fluctuations in terms of aggregate consumer and investment demand and supply. In the early part of expansion, output rises more rapidly than at any other time in the cycle. It can do this because of the large supplies of unemployed labor, unused capacity, and unused stacks of raw materials. At the same time, however, national income is also rising more rapidly than at any other time in the cycle—and consumers have held back from purchases in the preceding contraction. Therefore, consumer demand rises even faster than consumer goods and services, thus inflating prices. Since the outlook is very optimistic, investment demand also rises faster than the supply of investment goods.

In the later part of expansion, productive facilities may operate near capacity, so output could rise only at its maximum long-run speed. Demand for consumer goods is still rising, though less than income, but income is still rising faster than supply. In many expansions, moreover, capitalists become overoptimistic near the peak of the boom, so investment demand remains higher than the supply of investment goods. Thus, prices normally continue rising to the peak.

In the usual business contraction, supply of output declines as workers are fired and factories are shut down. There is, however, a time lag in the response of production, so the supply of consumer goods declines more slowly than the demand all the way down to the trough. The supply of investment goods also declines more slowly than the demand for investment goods down to the trough. The fact that demand falls more rapidly than supply is revealed by the rising ratio of (unwanted) inventories to sales throughout the contraction (as explained in Part Four). The result has been falling prices in most depressions and recessions up through the 1948 recession.

---

[1]See Frederick Mills, *Price-Quantity Interactions in Business Cycles* (New York: National Bureau of Economic Research, 1946).

MONETARY CONTRIBUTIONS TO DEMAND-PULL INFLATION

Most economists agree that rapid expansion of the money supply or credit will accompany every inflation. The hyperinflations of this century, such as those experienced in Germany in the early 1920s (when inflation exceeded 1000 percent per *day*) and in Argentina in 1976 (900 percent per year) were accompanied by an exploding money supply. For even more moderate inflations, the correlation is quite obvious. For example, in Brazil between 1979 and 1980, the annual rate of change of consumer prices was 83 percent. Over the same period the money supply grew 75 percent. In Mexico, consumer prices rose 26 percent in 1980. The money supply growth rate has not been below 30 percent since 1977 in Mexico. Between 1979 and 1980 consumer prices rose 21 percent in Italy, and the money supply growth rate averaged over 21 percent annually between 1977 and 1980.

Table 19.1 shows the average annual compounded growth rates of the money supply and consumer prices for the decade between 1971 and 1981 for 12 developed capitalist nations. They are arranged in ascending order of money supply growth rates. There is obviously a loose correlation between the money supply and inflation although the correlation allows some variation. The United States is plagued with an unusually high inflation rate, given that it has the second lowest money supply growth rate of the 12 nations listed. Japan, on the other hand, had an inflation rate barely higher than what was experienced in the United States even though its money supply growth rate was 73 percent higher. This can be partly explained by the fact that Japan's average growth rate for real GNP for the same period was higher than that experienced in the United States (4.9 percent compared to 3.2 percent).

Of course, the money supply is not the only financial variable that has grown in this period.

Table 19.1

AVERAGE ANNUAL COMPOUNDED GROWTH RATES OF THE MONEY SUPPLY (M1) AND CONSUMER PRICES (CPI) FOR 12 CAPITALIST NATIONS (PERCENTAGES), 1971–1981

	Money Supply	CPI
Switzerland	3.9%	5.0%
United States	6.7	8.4
Belgium	7.4	7.7
West Germany	8.1	5.2
Netherlands	8.6	7.3
Canada	9.5	9.0
France	11.1	10.4
Japan	11.6	8.9
United Kingdom	12.7	13.9
Sweden	13.4	9.7
Italy	17.7	15.1
Spain	18.1	15.7

SOURCE: *International Economic Conditions* (St. Louis: Federal Reserve Bank of St. Louis, 1982).

All debt aggregates have grown as well. In the United States, the average annual compounded growth rate for all debt owed by the nonfinancial sector grew by 10.5 percent over the same decade. There has, in other words, been a general liquidity expansion over the recent decade that is at least correlated with inflation.

The theoretical connection between the expansion of financial aggregates and price inflation should be fairly obvious. An extravagent expansion of credit that is not financed from savings or excessive growth in the money supply or both (often but not always the same phenomenon) will expand aggregate demand. Although there might be some capacity in the economy to meet the growth in aggregate demand with an expansion of real output, ultimately constraints upon production will ensure that a nominal supply-demand equilibrium cannot be maintained at the prevailing price level. The eventual shortage of goods at the prevailing price level provides an incentive to producers to raise prices.

This phenomenon can easily be explained at the microeconomic level. In microeconomic theory, the demand curves of consumers and businesses are constrained by purchasing power —usually, the sum of income, liquidation of previous savings, and new credit. The availability of new credit shifts demand curves outward, allowing more claims upon goods for sale. Because of rising marginal costs in production, supply curves slope upward so that any new demand resulting from shifting demand curves produces a new equilibrium in the micro markets that involves higher prices. The demand curve has shifted "up" the supply curve.

This disarmingly simple explanation of monetary inflation is in at least general conformity with the theories of the monetarists and creditists explained in earlier chapters. Even the most fervent critic of monetarism would agree that this explanation is sufficient for extraordinarily high inflations. If the authorities in a country like Mexico, Argentina, or Brazil allow the money supply to grow at a 20 percent, 40 percent, or 100 percent rate, runaway inflation will unavoidably be the result.

The more subtle inflations of the developed countries are another matter, however. The critics of monetarism discussed in Chapter 17, such as James Tobin, conceded that the money supply growth rate and inflation are *correlated,* but this does not imply *causality* running from money to prices. Tobin specifically argues that the direction of causation is often the other way around; surges in nominal national income, including the price component, draw forth an accommodating increase in the money supply. Those Post Keynesian and Marxist economists who support the endogenous money stock argument believe essentially the same thing.

Inflation, according to these economists, might still be demand-dominated. The demand for investment and consumer goods might be chronically high because of expectations of prosperity, a strong desire for a higher standard of living (promoted by a barrage of advertising propaganda), or speculation. The rising demand from all these sources forces an accommodating growth in money or credit or both. This accommodation might be due to political pressure on the Federal Reserve System or by their desire to maintain stable interest rates. Because of private innovation in the financial sector, it may occur without the compliance of the Federal Reserve System. These theories were discussed in detail in Chapter 17. The point being made here is that many critics deny that causality runs from money (or credit) to prices. Inflation and a high growth rate of financial aggregates simply rise together, the behavior of both being caused by a third factor, a temporary or chronic rise in effective demand.

There is another criticism of the elementary monetary demand-pull theories of inflation. In the theory, one would expect ever higher prices, but a high level of employment would also be the natural result. As aggregate demand expands because of a monetary expansion, production will not continue at the prevailing price level. Prices will rise. But production should rise as well. At worst (at absolute full capacity if such a thing exists) production should remain unchanged. Whatever the case, it should not fall.

The reality of recent years has introduced a profound mystery into traditional theories of inflation, invalidating the elementary monetary demand-pull theory as an explanation for at least the inflation since 1970 in the United States. This reality may be referred to as *stagflation*.

Stagflation: Inflation During Stagnation

The simplest kind of Keynesian demand-pull theory—or an equally simple monetary explanation—suffices to explain wartime inflation, the usual inflation in expansions, and the usual deflation in contractions. In the last three decades, however, a new phenomenon has been witnessed. Even in contractions, with rising unemployment and *falling demand,* prices have continued to rise.[2] Because we witness inflation in the midst of a stagnant economy, it has been called *stagflation*. Whatever the phenomenon is called, it requires a new theory. Various new theories are presented in this chapter and the next, but the exact dimensions of the problem must first be outlined.

On the basis of the earlier historical data, Professor Phillips drew a graph relating high growth of wages to low unemployment and low growth (or decline) of wages to high unemployment. Later economists generalized the Phillips curve to picture a negative relation between unemployment and inflation. Many economists still accept the Phillips curve trade-off as valid, at least in the short run.

In the 1950s and the 1960s, prices no longer declined in recessions, and the rate of inflation was zero or somewhat positive in recessions. Nevertheless, it was still the case that the rate of inflation was lower in recessions than in expansions. Therefore, it is possible to draw a Phillips curve for the 1950s and the 1960s even though it no longer goes into the negative range. In Figure 19.3, there is a neat and continuous Phillips curve for the period 1960 to 1969 in annual data for the percentage of unemployment and the percentage change in the consumer price index. The relationship is clearly *negative*.

In the 1970s, however, the *rate of inflation was higher in economic contractions* than in expansions. As a result, a straight line between the points for each year's inflation and unemployment from 1970 to 1978 shows a clearly *positive* relationship. Both curves are merely descriptions of the relation in particular time periods.

For a more precise empirical description, quarterly data can be examined. The cyclical pattern for unemployment is clear, simple, and very consistent. In almost every segment of the five expansions from 1949 to 1973, unemployment declined. In almost every segment of the five contractions from 1953 to 1975, unemployment rose. Table 19.2 shows the average cyclical pattern for the five cycles. As expansion continues, unemployment declines (usu-

---

[2] One good empirical description of the historical change in price behavior is Jeffrey Sachs, "The Changing Cyclical Behavior of Wages and Prices," *American Economic Review* 70 (March 1980), pp. 78–90.

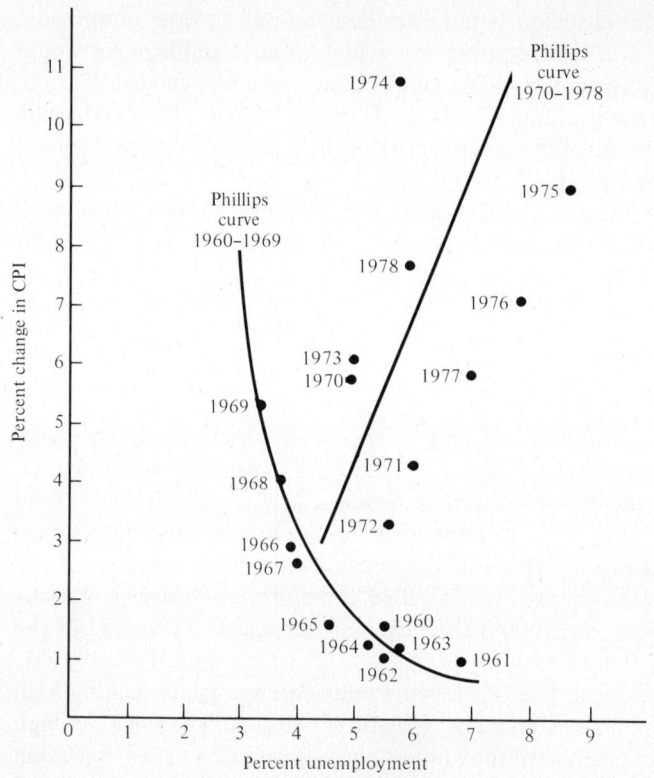

Figure 19.3 Unemployment and Inflation
SOURCE: Council of Economic Advisors, *Economic Report of the President* (Washington, D.C.: GPO, 1979).

Table 19.2

CYCLICAL PATTERN OF UNEMPLOYMENT, 1949–1980

CHANGE FROM STAGE TO STAGE PER MONTH, IN CYCLE RELATIVE

	1–2	2–3	3–4	4–5 Peak	5–6	6–7	7–8	8–9
Average	−1.36	−1.79	−.59	−.19	3.28	5.18	5.18	4.55

NOTE: This table represents an average of six cycles, in quarterly data.
SOURCE: U.S. Department of Commerce, *Business Conditions Digest* (Washington, D.C.: GPO, 1980).

ally at a slower rate near the peak). In the contraction, unemployment rises. (See Figure 19.4.)

For price behavior, quarterly data for the GNP price deflator are used.

Table 19.3 presents the monthly rate of change of the GNP price deflator, that is, the rate of inflation, in eight different segments of the cycle, four in expansion and four in contraction. In the first three cycles (1949–1961), the inflation rate is much higher in the expansions than

Chapter 19 DEMAND-PULL AND COST-PUSH INFLATION

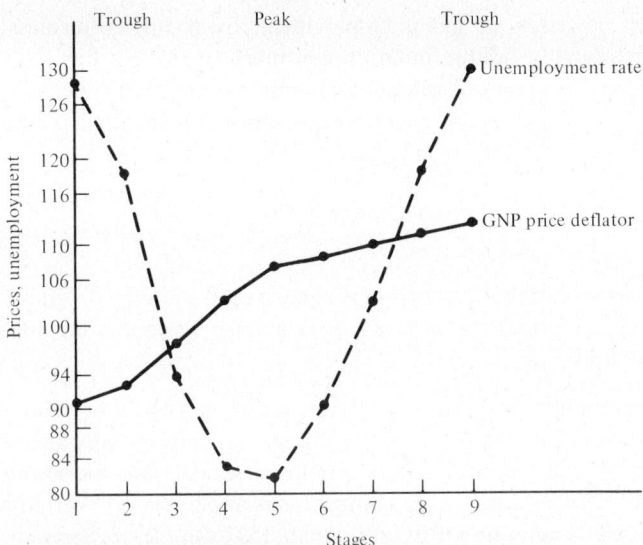

Fig. 19.4 Unemployment Rate and Price Deflator
NOTE: This figure represents an average of six cycles, from 1949 through 1980, with the average value at the cycle stage as a percentage of the cycle base.
Source: Department of Commerce, *Business Conditions Digest* (April 1981).

Table 19.3

CYCLICAL PATTERN OF GNP PRICE DEFLATOR, 1949–1980

CHANGE FROM STAGE TO STAGE, PER MONTH, IN CYCLE RELATIVES

Cycle	1–2	2–3	3–4	4–5 Peak	5–6	6–7	7–8	8–9
		Expansion				Contraction		
1949–1954	0.28	0.45	0.12	0.15	−0.06	0.16	0.19	−0.01
1954–1958	0.17	0.21	0.31	0.28	0.16	0.00	0.19	0.05
1958–1961	0.13	0.22	0.16	0.15	0.10	0.08	0.06	−0.05
1961–1970	0.12	0.15	0.28	0.44	0.53	0.51	0.36	0.55
1970–1975	0.40	0.32	0.40	0.64	0.70	1.01	0.97	1.12
1975–1980	0.41	0.44	0.65	0.66	0.09	1.86	0.00	1.18
Average	0.25	0.30	0.32	0.39	0.25	0.60	0.30	0.47

NOTE: Quarterly data divided by 3 to get monthly data.
SOURCE: U.S. Department of Commerce, *Business Conditions Digest* (Washington, D.C.: GPO, 1980).

in the contractions. In fact, in two of the contractions, there are segments where there is a negative inflation rate or deflation. In the next two cycles (1961–1975), on the contrary, the inflation rate is much higher in the contractions than in the expansions! Thus, in those two cycles inflation rose just as unemployment was also rising—and demand was falling. (See Figure 19.4 for the average over 6 cycles.)

These data provide the basis for a good part of the criticism of elementary demand-pull theories. It shows that as inflation has risen, so has unemployment. Even during business cycle contractions when output is actually falling, inflation continues to rise. In fact, the inflation rate was higher during some contractions than during some expansions. Although demand-pull theories of inflation have considerable merit, they cannot explain this.

COST-PUSH THEORIES

To replace the demand-pull theories, a number of cost-push theories have emerged. These theories emphasize problems in supply. Prices rise because, for whatever reason, costs rise. Costs can rise for a number of reasons:

1. In countries that rely heavily upon imports or in countries where certain imports are critically important in manufacturing, a rise in the price of the import may substantially affect domestic inflation rates. The most obvious recent example is, of course, oil. The rise in oil prices after 1973 certainly contributed to inflation in the United States and had a very serious impact upon smaller nations that rely heavily on OPEC oil. Japan, for example, imports all of its oil.

On commodities as important as oil, there is a direct effect. The prices of petroleum products rise, and that fact alone makes a contribution to the rises in price indices. There is usually a secondary effect as well. If the inflated product is used in the production of finished goods or services, it will raise the costs of providing these goods and services. In the case of oil, secondary price increases were seen in electricity rates, in transportation costs, and in areas of manufacturing that use large amounts of electricity. Because energy is so important in economic life, virtually no one was exempt from the inflationary penalty of rising oil prices throughout the 1970s.

The impact upon general inflation of a rise in the price of a few critical imported commodities depends also upon the availability of substitutes for those commodities and, in the long run, upon the ease and cost of developing substitutes. A price rise in copper, for example, would have little lasting impact because many materials can be substituted for copper. In the short run, however, there are few substitutes for petroleum even though over a period spanning a few decades, numerous substitutes might be developed. If the development of such substitutes is costly, however, even this can contribute to inflation.

2. If critical resources are being exhausted, costs may rise, resulting in higher prices for finished goods. Industrial nations like the United States use raw physical resources intensively. As these are depleted, if few substitutes are available, then costs must rise. Not only are fossil fuels and minerals likely candidates for such depletion, but such commodities as lumber, fertile agricultural land, and even fresh water can also cause problems. The exhaustion of farm lands in the southern United States in the last century raised costs of production substantially in that area. There is considerable concern today about the depletion of water resources in the western United States and the impact that can have on farming costs.

Even when resources are abundant, if they are extracted from the earth, the costs of extraction will rise as the most economical deposits are extracted first. The United States is still abundantly endowed with natural resources, but the most accessible deposits for some resources have undoubtedly been exhausted.

==Heavy utilization of resources can contribute to higher costs as well.== The military in the United States, using sophisticated resource-intensive technology, irretrievably use vast amounts of material, especially fuels and metal alloys. Given the number of aircraft, ships, vehicles, missiles, and buildings that the military use, the resulting demand for resources not only contributes to demand-pull inflation, but because resources are ultimately depleted, in the long run it also contributes to cost-push inflation as well.

3. If a nation's productive resources are obsolescent, deteriorating, not adequately maintained, or simply wearing out, the variable costs of using such resources often tend to rise. Breakdowns and inefficiency in use can contribute to rising costs. Manufacturing obsolescence will either raise costs or will prevent costs from being *lowered* in spite of improving scientific knowledge. One of the major benefits of technological innovation is to *reduce* costs while allowing workers some share of their increased productivity. Thus, innovation has allowed a rise in the standard of living while holding inflation in check.

In recent years there is some evidence that in some major industries, such as steel, railroads, and autos, obsolescence has become a problem. The auto industry, for example, seems to have fallen behind the Japanese in the implementation of cost-saving production techniques, which probably explains some of the Japanese success in markedly increasing their share of the American auto market in the early 1980s.

There is mounting evidence that *public* (government-owned) capital goods are overused and poorly maintained as well. As the spending reductions of the new conservative era begin to be felt, public buildings, highways, and capital projects are being underfunded for maintenance. Newspapers commonly refer to the deterioration of highways in the eastern United States. Estimates of the costs of repairing potholes alone run into the billions of dollars. In 1981 it was estimated that Chicago might be leaking as much as 40 percent of its water supply owing to faulty pipes. In the case of public goods, maintenance is neglected because the funds to finance maintenance are not made available by conservative governments. Ironically, part of the reason is because taxpayers are trying to save money, and the resulting economy moves are likely cost to more in the long run.

4. Throughout the 1970s there was a growing awareness that many areas of the United States were becoming rather unpleasant. There was a greater concern for the problems of pollution. Air and water quality was becoming unacceptable in many regions, and chemical pollution was reaching scandalous proportions.

The costs of pollution are often difficult to see and measure. Air pollution undoubtedly affects human health (not to mention state of mind), which raises health costs. Water pollution destroys fisheries and mars the beauty of some of the world's most magnificent resources.

==Because the decision to combat pollution was delayed so long, the cost of curbing the harm has been quite high.== Substantial progress has been made in reducing water and chemical pollution, and the deterioration of air quality has been slowed (although air quality has probably not improved). The equipment necessary to contribute to this effort has been expensive, and the costs are certainly reflected in prices of finished goods. Without doubt, such expenditures are providing benefits (many of them nonmarketable), but the costs nonetheless have contributed to higher prices. Had the pollution abatement efforts been initiated earlier, present generations would probably be paying a far lower cost for environmental quality.

5. Costs of finance are rising. If money must be borrowed to finance the purchase of a factory, an automobile, or a home, and the interest charged on the borrowed amount rises, this raises costs because the loan payment to service the debt rises.

This is especially obvious in the case of housing. To a consumer, the true cost of owning a home is the monthly payment. When interest rates rise to record levels as they have in recent years, then the "price" of one of the three basic commodities (shelter) has risen. To the consumer it makes no difference whether monthly payments rise because of a rising market price for homes or because of higher interest rates. The effect is the same.

Businesses financing capital expenditures during periods of rising interest rates face the same cost pressures. If, on a house, a rise in interest rates of 1 percent raises the monthly payment by $100, then a piece of capital equipment priced the same and financed along the same terms will also cost $100 per month more. Although the business might absorb some of the cost, the better part of the cost increase will be passed on to consumers by higher-priced finished goods.

6. Cost-push inflation might be due to concentration among producers. Because this topic needs special treatment, it is dealt with in the next chapter.

7. A final set of cost-push theories has alleged that this type of inflation may be primarily caused by the monopoly power of unions. There is no question but that the power of a union in an industry can keep wages higher than they would be if individual workers faced the giant corporations alone.

The point to be explained, however, is not why wages and prices are at some given level. The question is one of inflation, increasing prices (and increasing wages, usually at a lesser speed)—and why U.S. capitalism has the new phenomenon of inflation during depression. This new condition did not exist at all before the 1950s and got much worse in the 1969 and 1974–1975 depressions. Therefore, this new situation must be explained by some new variable or by a large and continuing increase in some old variable.

It is shown in the next chapter that the monopoly power of business is not only high, but has drastically increased since 1950. What about the power of unions? Has it increased? Probably the best indicator of union power in the economy is the percentage of workers who are in unions. If unions represent 90 percent of all workers, they are undoubtedly more powerful than if they represent 10 percent of all workers. The available data are presented in Table 19.4.

These data show that, excluding agriculture, in which area unions have had few members, the percentage of unionized workers was at a low of about 7 percent in the Great Depression. The militant organizing drive of the Congress of Industrial Organizations (CIO) rapidly raised union membership in the late 1930s and in World War II to a high of 25 percent in 1955. The CIO organized many millions of unskilled and semiskilled workers whom the AFL had always ignored.

In the 1950s, union leaders became less militant (and some were corrupted by power or bribes), so the drive by labor diminished. Moreover, in the repressive period of the 1950s,

Table 19.4

UNION MEMBERSHIP, 1930–1978

Year	Percent Unionized	Year	Percent Unionized
1930	6.8%	1960	23.6%
1935	6.7	1965	22.4
1940	15.5	1970	22.6
1945	21.9	1975	20.7
1950	22.3	1978	19.7
1955	24.7		

NOTE: Union members as percentage of total labor force.
SOURCE: U.S. Department of Labor, Bureau of Labor Statistics, *Handbook of Labor Statistics 1980* (Washington, D.C.: GPO, 1980), p.412.

Table 19.5

UNIONIZATION IN MANUFACTURING BY INDUSTRY

Industry	1958	1972	Change, in Percentage Points, 1958–1972
All manufacturing	52.4%	47.1%	−5.3%
Food, beverages, and tobacco	55.1	53.4	−1.7
Clothing, textiles, and leather	50.1	41.6	−8.5
Furniture, lumber, wood, and paper	50.3	50.1	−0.2
Printing and publishing	39.7	32.7	−7.0
Petroleum, chemicals, and rubber	39.6	34.7	−4.9
Stone, clay, and glass	44.6	48.0	+3.4
Metals and machinery	52.3	47.1	−5.2
Transportation equipment	78.7	59.1	−19.6

NOTE: Union Members as Percentage of Employees on Payrolls
SOURCE: U.S. Department of Labor, Bureau of Labor Statistics, *Handbook of Labor Statistics, 1974* (Washington, D.C.: GPO, 1975), p. 367.

labor was split by Red-baiting, and the left-wing unions were driven out, with some destroyed. Finally, under the pressure and leadership of business, a reactionary Congress passed the Taft-Hartley Act, which was designed to accomplish—and did accomplish—a chaining down and further weakening of labor. For these reasons and others, union membership dropped from 25 percent of the nonagricultural labor force in 1955 to only 20 percent in 1972.

Of course, unions are stronger in the manufacturing sector than in the rest of the economy. The manufacturing sector, however, has declined in importance relative to other sectors, especially service industries. Moreover, union power has been declining even in the manufacturing sector. The changes in percent of unionization in manufacturing are shown in Table 19.5.

Table 19.5 shows that union strength declined by 5.3 percentage points in all manufacturing from 1958 to 1972. When manufacturing is divided into eight industrial groups, the percentage of workers in unions rose slightly in only one group whereas it fell in seven groups. The loss of bargaining strength, with a lower percentage of the labor force enrolled in unions, helps to explain the weakening position of labor versus capital.

Cost-Push Inflation as an Explanation for Stagflation

Cost-push inflation is a much better candidate for explaining stagflation than demand-pull inflation. Demand-pull inflation is hard pressed to explain high unemployment or even an actual decline in output during contractions.

When *costs* rise, however, the response that is theoretically expected is for producers to (1) raise prices and (2) reduce output. This is because producers face *downward-sloping demand curves* for their products. In other words, if an industry has to absorb rising costs, it will try to pass some part of the cost, if not all of it, on in higher prices. However, if there is a downward-sloping demand curve for the industry's products, the quantity demanded of the industry's output will drop. The equilibrium for the industry is, in a sense, moving up the demand curve. If the quantity demanded drops, then the level of production must ultimately drop. Workers must be laid off, and excess capacity will appear.

Consider a real example. After the OPEC embargo, prices of petroleum rose dramatically. The prices of petroleum products rose rapidly to reflect the higher cost of crude petroleum. In response to this, the actual quantity demanded of petroleum declined in the late 1970s.

There is a second reason why cost-push inflation might result in lower output. According to microeconomic theory, producers will reduce their demand for raw materials, labor, and the other inputs in production if the price of those inputs rises. Therefore, there is not only a decline in the demand for final products, but there is also a decline in the demand for intermediate goods used in production.

Theories of cost-push inflation are very consistent with the nonmonetarist theories of inflation offered by economists like James Tobin and the Post Keynesians. Monetarist theories are essentially demand-pull theories; the growth in the money supply stimulates demand, which causes inflation. Nonmonetarist theories have their demand-pull component as well (where demand surges and is merely accommodated by a growth in liquidity), but their belief in how the financial system works is also very consistent with cost-push inflation.

Suppose, for example, that costs rise for any of the reasons stated earlier. That alone is sufficient to explain inflation and even stagflation regardless of the behavior of the money supply or other liquidity measures. In other words, the OPEC cartel, technological obsolescence, higher interest rates, or resource depletion would have and may have contributed to inflation even with a constant or modestly growing money supply. With a constant money supply, had nothing been done, output in the economy might have suffered severely. Because of downward-sloping demand curves and the constraints imposed on fixed nominal incomes, the higher price level would have resulted in *lower real* aggregate demand, having a depressing effect upon the economy. Because such a set of circumstances is both politically and economically unacceptable, the Federal Reserve System becomes expansionary, allowing the money supply (or liquidity in general) to grow, offsetting, at least in part, the recessionary tendencies of cost-push inflation. Ultimately, both the rate of inflation and the money supply grow, but the direction of causality is reversed; cost-push inflation seriously disturbs the economy, drawing forth the expansion of liquidity as a *response*.

This seemingly subtle distinction is important. If the monetarists are right and inflation is primarily a demand-pull phenomenon caused by an excessive growth of the money supply, then the inflationary cure involves little more than slowing the growth of the money supply. If, on the other hand, inflation is due to a structural problem and the growth of the money supply has only *eased* the gravity of the problem by stimulating demand enough to keep the economy from severely declining, then a monetary contraction will solve no problems. On the contrary, the decline in nominal demand will have more impact upon real output than inflation since the causes of inflation are not overcome with a monetary contraction.

SUMMARY

Demand-pull inflation is caused by anything that stimulates aggregate demand in such a way that production in the economy will not continue at the prevailing level of prices. Expanded demand exhausts inventories, reduces unused capacity, results in fuller utilization of capacity, and creates an environment where producers find it profitable to raise prices.

One candidate for explaining demand-pull inflation is a monetary expansion. Monetarists point to the strong correlation between money supply growth rates and modern inflation as evidence that the inflation that has plagued capitalism in recent years is primarily demand-pull monetary inflation. Critics of this point of view insist that the causality moves in the opposite direction; either increases in demand from other sources or cost-push inflation explain inflation, and money merely plays an accommodating role, if that.

Cost-push inflation is caused by any factor that tends to raise costs. Cost-push inflation can be caused by increased import costs, resource depletion, obsolescence in productive capacity, higher interest rates, legislated costs like pollution controls, or increased economic concentration. Cost-push inflation is consistent with stagflation and does not necessarily require a growth in the money supply or credit. In the absence of a monetary expansion, the conditions that produce cost-push inflation can produce depressing conditions. For that reason, it is argued by critics of monetary demand-pull theories of inflation, political economic pressures have forced the money supply to grow during periods of inflation.

Given that the American economy is so complex, modern inflation probably has both a demand-pull and a cost-push component, especially if the economy is divided into sectors and regions. As monetarists and creditists point out, there has been a rapid expansion of financial assets in recent years, and this has likely made it easier for consumers, business, and the government to maintain and even expand their level of expenditures. On the other hand, there is no doubt that such important areas as energy and housing inflation are adequately explained by cost-push inflation. Both theories seem to provide a partial explanation. In the following chapters, we explore in detail (1) the cost or profit-push by concentrated industries, (2) the international aspects of stagflation, and (3) the role of government in stagflation (including the inflation caused by the Vietnam War spending).

SUGGESTED READINGS

There is a vast literature on the subject of inflation, so it is worthwhile highlighting some of the works from different schools of thought:

A monetarist view is presented in Philip Cagan, *Persistent Inflation* (New York: Columbia University Press, 1979).

A supply-side view is given in Norman Ture, "Forecasting the Supply Side of the Economy," Hearings before the Joint Economic Commission, U.S. Congress (Washington, D.C.: U.S. Government Printing Office, May 21, 1980).

A theory of inflation caused by supply-side shocks (such as OPEC) is presented by Alan S. Blinder, *Economic Policy and the Great Stagflation* (New York: Academic Press, 1979).

Some typical neo-Keynesian views are found in Walter Heller, "Shadow and Substance in Inflation Policy," *Challenge* (January-February 1981), pp. 5–13, and Otto Eckstein, "Economic Choices for the 1980s," *Challenge* (July-August 1980), pp. 15–27.

One Marxist view is given in Ernest Mandel, *Late Capitalism* (London: Verso, 1978).

A collection of diverse views, with emphasis on the role of socioeconomic interest groups, is in Fred Hirsch and John Goldthorpe, *The Political Economy of Inflation* (Cambridge, Mass.: Harvard University Press, 1978).

Another interesting collection of views, from neo-Keynesian to Post Keynesian to radical, is in James H. Gapinski and Charles E. Rockwood, *Essays in Post Keynesian Inflation* (Cambridge, Mass.: Ballinger, 1979).

A thorough institutionalist approach is in Wallace C. Peterson, *Our Overloaded Economy: Inflation, Unemployment, and the Crisis in American Capitalism* (Armonk, N.Y.: M. E. Sharpe, 1982).

Chapter 20

PROFIT-PUSH INFLATION: MONOPOLY POWER

The excess of demand above supply was an adequate explanation of inflation during wars and of inflation during most normal business expansions in the past. Yet, in recent business cycles, inflation has occurred even in contractions in a declining or stagnant economy (stagflation). This phenomenon indicates that it is a new type of inflation not caused by excess demand, but by supply-side conditions. The cost push may come from higher wage rates or high nonwage costs or less productivity per unit of input (all discussed in the last chapter). Yet there may also be higher prices owing to efforts at higher profits by capitalist suppliers under new structural conditions. This chapter argues that one major cause of the new phenomenon of inflation in the midst of unemployment is the structural change in the U.S. economy toward more business monopoly power.

THE INCREASE OF MONOPOLY POWER

As late as 1860, small farms and small businesses produced most of U.S. output. After the Civil War had wiped out the slave owners, the capitalist class had no more rivals for power to rule. The northern industrialists ran the government through the Republican party and used government power to penetrate into the South and the West. For example, huge parcels of land—equal in total to more than many European countries—were given to the railroads. At the same time, technological improvements made a much larger scale of production more profitable, so there was strong motivation to expand. Furthermore, improvements in transportation and communication made nationwide firms quite feasible.

By 1929, the 200 largest manufacturing corporations held 45.8 percent of all manufacturing assets.[1] Except for a slight decline in the Second World War (when medium-sized corporations did very well), this index of overall concentration has been rising steadily. The share of the 200 largest manufacturing corporations rose from 47.1 in 1949 to 54.8 in 1959 and to 60.3 in 1973.[2]

Some of this increase in concentration was due to internal growth of the largest corporations, and some of it was due to mergers. Since 1950, 1 out of every 5 of the 1000 largest manufacturing corporations has been swallowed by an even larger giant. The nature of these mergers has changed over time. In the 1890s and the 1900s, there was a wave of horizontal mergers, that is, mergers between competitors in the same industry. In the 1920s and the 1930s, there was a wave of vertical mergers, that is, mergers between a manufacturer and its suppliers or its retail dealers. There has been only a very small increase in horizontal and vertical concentration in recent decades. But there has been an enormous wave of conglomerate mergers in the late 1960s, 1970s, and 1980s, that is, mergers of unrelated firms. These conglomerate mergers have not been limited to manufacturing, but have occurred in every sector of the U.S. economy.

By 1963 (before most of the conglomerate mergers) just four firms had over half the sales in 40 percent of U.S. manufacturing industries.[3] In another 32 percent of U.S. industries, just four firms sold between 25 and 50 percent of all sales. Only 28 percent of the industries had less than 25 percent of the sales controlled by four firms. These data on concentration are very impressive, but they still greatly underestimate the concentration of economic power.

One problem is that the census industries are too broadly defined; that is, they include products that are not substitutes and do not compete. This reduces the reported degree of concentration. On the other hand, the reported concentration is increased by not including international competition. Adjusting for these two contrary biases (and some other less important biases), W. G. Shepherd found that in most industries concentration is higher than reported.[4] A *concentration ratio* may be defined as the percentage of total industry sales controlled by 4 firms. In 1966, the unadjusted concentration ratios were lower than the adjusted ratios in all major industry groups except 1. The changes were substantial; for example, the adjusted ratios rose from 16 to 46 in lumber, and from 32 to 64 in petroleum and coal products.

Second, each of 100 largest conglomerates controls some of the biggest firms in several industries, so their power goes far beyond the recorded concentration ratios. Using that census definition that best fits economic theory, there are 1014 individual manufacturing industries. The concentration ratio was defined earlier by the percentage of sales controlled by the 4 largest firms in each of these industries. Yet, in a majority of the manufacturing industries, at least 1 of the 4 largest firms in that industry is controlled by a large conglomerate.[5] By *large conglomerate* is meant one of the 100 largest firms in all of manufacturing.

---

[1] Federal Trade Commission data, discussed in John Blair, *Economic Concentration* (New York: Harcourt Brace Jovanovich, 1972), p. 64.
[2] Federal Trade Commission data discussed in Blair, *loc. cit.*, and in David Penn, "Aggregate Concentration," *Anti-Trust Bulletin* (Spring 1976).
[3] See Blair, *op. cit.*, p. 14.
[4] William G. Shepherd, *Market Power and Economic Welfare* (New York: Random House, 1970), pp. 274–280.
[5] Blair, *op. cit.*, pp. 53–54.

Table 20.1

ALL U.S. CORPORATIONS, 1977

Size of Assets	Number of Corporations	Amount of Assets (in $ millions)	% of Corporations	% of Assets
Less than $100,000	1,274,318	$ 40,593	57.0%	1%
$100,000–$500,000	650,754	149,072	29.0	3
$500,000–$5 million	269,301	353,199	12.0	6
$5 million–50 million	38,262	580,012	1.6	11
$50 million–250 million	6,443	662,666	0.3	12
over $250 million	2,239	3,563,433	0.1	67
Total	2,241,317	$ 5,348,974	100.0%	100%

SOURCE: U.S. Internal Revenue Service, *Preliminary Report, Statistics of Income, Corporation Income Tax Returns for 1977* (Washington, D.C.: GPO, 1981).

Third, there are many interlocking directorates amongst the largest conglomerates, so one person sits on several boards to oversee their collusion or cooperation. In 1965, the 250 largest corporations had a total of 4007 directorships, but these were held by just 3165 directors.[6] Among the directors, 562 held 2 or more directorships, and 5 men held 6 each. There are also various groupings of corporations; for example, large blocks of stock in one group are held by the Rockefellers, whereas large blocks of stock in another are held by the Du Ponts.

Furthermore, banks are interlocked with many industrial corporations to form other important groups that work in a unified manner. Within the banking system itself, there is concentration of assets. In 1968, there were 13,775 commercial banks. Of these, a mere 14 banks (*not* 14 percent, but just 14) held 25 percent of all deposits. The 100 largest banks held 46 percent of all deposits.[7]

Finally, it is necessary to examine all U.S. corporations, including all sectors of business. Table 20.1 shows the most recent available data. The corporations below $5 million in assets include 98 percent of all corporations (2,194,373 corporations), but they have only 10 percent of all corporate assets. The corporations above $250 million in assets include only one-tenth of 1 percent of all corporations (2,239 corporations), but they hold 67 percent of all corporate assets! All of this data leads to two conclusions. Economic concentration among U.S. corporations is very high. Aggregate economic concentration among U.S. corporations, as defined by the percentage held by the 1000 largest corporations, increased considerably in the 1970s. Industrial concentration, defined as the percentage of sales held by the top 4 in *each* industry, is much less clear in its trend, but did show a slight average increase in the last available data (though even this is controversial and depends on definitions). With these facts in mind, one can understand some of the evolution of price behavior of U.S. corporations.

---

[6] See *ibid.*, p. 76.

[7] House of Representatives, Committee on Banking and Currency, *Commercial Banks and Their Trust Activities* (Washington, D.C.: GPO, 1968), p. 5.

MONOPOLY POWER AND ADMINISTERED PRICES

In the Great Depression of the 1930s (and in the smaller depression of 1938), Gardiner Means found what he called "administered" prices in the monopoly sector.[8] In the more concentrated industries, Means discovered, prices were not set in a competitive market, but were carefully administered or set in the best interests of the monopolies. He found that the competitive prices changed frequently, but that the administered or monopoly prices changed very seldom.

More specifically, prices in the competitive sector registered large declines in the depression contractions, but the administered prices in the monopoly sector declined very little. Means defines the competitive sector as the 20 percent least-concentrated industries whereas the monopoly sector is defined as the 20 percent that is most concentrated. From 1929 to 1932, prices in the more competitive sector fell 60 percent, but prices in the monopoly sector fell only 10 percent.[9] A few prices in the monopoly sector even rose a little in the face of the Great Depression.

In the expansion of 1933 to 1937, competitive prices rose by 46 percent whereas monopoly prices rose only 10 percent. In the depression of 1937 to 1938, competitive prices fell again by 27 percent whereas monopoly prices fell only 3 percent! Monopoly prices are clearly more stable and are very resistant to the decline of demand during depressions. It will be shown that the stability (or increase) of monopoly prices is achieved at the expense of large price declines for small and competitive business, lower purchasing power for consumers, and high unemployment of workers.

Table 20.2 shows that even in the Great Depression the industries with great monopoly power lowered their prices very little. They kept prices from dropping farther only by reducing their production by very large percentages. The more competitive sectors had no choice but to let their prices be forced down by lack of demand. Production in the competitive sector declined less, because the lower prices brought greater demand. The monopoly sector thus held up its prices (and profit per unit) at the expense of great decreases in production and large-scale unemployment. The competitive sector lowered production less, fired fewer workers, but suffered much greater declines in prices and profits per unit. A highly monopolized economy is thus more apt to produce high rates of unemployment in every decline.

Data for more recent business cycles show similar patterns, becoming most dramatic in the latest depression. The competitive sector is defined as all those industries in which concentration of sales by eight firms is *under* 50 percent. The monopoly sector is defined as all those industries in which concentration of sales by eight firms is *over* 50 percent. (This definition, like any definition with a particular dividing point, is purely arbitrary. A more accurate—but far more complex analysis—would look instead at the whole spectrum from

---

[8] See, for example, Gardiner Means, "Inflation and Unemployment," in John Blair (ed.), *The Roots of Inflation* (New York: Burt Franklin, 1975). Also see the summary of Means's findings in Blair, *Economic Concentration, op. cit.*, pp. 64–80.

[9] Means, "Inflation," pp. 8–9. Means's methods and findings are criticized by the conservative economists George Stigler and James Kindahl (cited and themselves criticized in Blair, *Economic Concentration*, p. 465). Means is upheld against Stigler and Kindahl by Douglas Bohi and Gerald Scully, "Buyers Prices, Sellers Prices, and Price Flexibility," *American Economic Review* 65 (June 1975), 517–526.

Table 20.2

PRICE AND PRODUCTION BEHAVIOR IN DEPRESSION,
1929–1932

Industry	Decline (As a Percentage of 1929 Figures)	
	Prices	Production
Motor vehicles	12%	74%
Agricultural implements	14	84
Iron and steel	16	76
Cement	16	55
Automobile tires	25	42
Leather and leather products	33	18
Petroleum products	36	17
Textile products	39	28
Food Products	39	10
Agricultural commodities	54	1

SOURCE: National Resources Committee (under the direction of Gardiner Means), *The Structure of the American Economy* (Washington, D.C.: GPO, 1939), p. 386.

the least concentrated to the most concentrated for every statement about corporate performance.)

The hundreds of individual industries may be aggregated—by averaging all their concentration ratios, weighted by the value of shipments of each industry—into the major industry groups. Those industry groups with *less* than a 50 percent concentration ratio of sales by the largest eight firms to all sales in the whole period, 1949 to 1975, include Pulp, Paper and Allied Products; Textiles and Apparel; Hides, Skins, and Leather; and Lumber and Wood Products (though even these industry groups were all over 40 percent, except for Lumber and Wood). Those industry groups with concentration ratios *over* 50 percent by eight firms in the whole period include Tobacco Products; Motor Vehicles and Equipment; Photo Equipment and Supplies; Refined Petroleum Products; Machinery and Equipment; and Chemicals and Allied Products.

The *expansion amplitude* of a price index is defined as its rise from initial trough to cycle peak as a percentage of its average level over the cycle. The average expansion amplitudes for all the prices in the monopoly sector and for all the prices in the competitive sector are given in Table 20.3 for five recent expansions.

The results for the two cyclical expansions of 1949 to 1953 and 1954 to 1957 are somewhat unusual in that prices in the monopoly sector rose faster than prices in the more competitive sector. In the three later expansions, 1958–1960, 1961–1969, and 1970–1973, the prices in the more competitive sector rose faster than prices in the monopoly sector. This is the same pattern as in the expansion of 1933 to 1937. It will usually be the case that, in expansions, prices in the more competitive sector rise somewhat faster than prices in the monopoly sector. The theoretical reasons for this behavior are discussed in the next section.

Of most interest, however, are the relative price behaviors in recent contractions. As noted

Table 20.3

EXPANSION AMPLITUDES OF PRICES IN MONOPOLY AND COMPETITIVE SECTORS

Dates of Expansion	Prices in Monopoly Sector	Prices in Competitive Sector
October 1949–July 1953	13.6%	11.1%
May 1954–August 1957	11.0	4.6
April 1958–April 1960	2.1	3.0
February 1961–December 1969	8.3	16.3
November 1970–November 1973	10.2	23.4

NOTE: Expansion amplitude means rise from trough to peak as a percentage of cycle average.
SOURCE: From the dissertation by Kathleen A. Pulling, *Market Structure and the Cyclical Behavior of Prices and Profits* (University of California, Riverside, 1977), p. 194.

Table 20.4

CONTRACTION AMPLITUDES OF PRICES IN MONOPOLY AND COMPETITIVE SECTORS

Date of Contraction	Prices in Monopoly Sector	Prices in Competitive Sector
November 1948–October 1949	− 1.9%	− 7.8%
July 1953–May 1954	+ 1.9	− 1.5
August 1957–April 1958	+ 0.5	− 0.3
April 1960–February 1961	+ 0.9	− 1.2
December 1969–November 1970	+ 5.9	− 3.0
November 1973–March 1975	+32.8	+11.7

SOURCES: Price changes for 1948–1959, 1953–1954, and 1957–1958 from Robert Lanzillotti, Hearings before the Joint Economic Committee of the U.S. Congress, *Employment, Growth and Price Levels* (Washington, D.C.: GPO, 1959), p. 2238. Price changes for 1969–1970 from John Blair, "Market Power and Inflation," *Journal of Economic Issues* 8 (June 1974), pp. 453–478. Price changes for 1960–1961 and 1973–1975 from Kathleen Pulling, *Market Structure and the Cyclical Behavior of Prices and Profits, 1949 to 1975* (Ph.D. diss., University of California, Riverside, 1978).

earlier, average prices for all sectors have behaved differently in recent contractions than in all previous recessions or depressions. They have risen instead of falling, so depression and unemployment no longer guarantee an end to inflation. For this reason, significant inflation has been continuous since 1967, though at different rates. The inflation began in the "normal" way with the spending during the Vietnam War, but its persistence through periods of falling demand indicates a new kind of animal. How much of this new phenomenon is associated with the competitive sector, and how much with the monopoly sector?

Various investigators have studied competitive and monopoly price behavior in the contractions since 1948. Their findings are presented in Table 20.4

Table 20.4 reveals that the pattern of the 1948 recession was the same as in the 1929 and 1937 depressions. In all three cases, monopoly prices declined a little whereas competitive prices declined an enormous amount. In the 1954, 1958, and 1961 recessions, the first indications of the new stagflation behavior appear. Competitive prices decline as usual, although by a small amount, but monopoly prices actually *rise* in the recessions, although again by a small amount. The new situation is very clear in the 1970 recession, in which competitive prices decline by a significant amount, whereas monopoly prices rise by a considerable amount. A finer division indicates even stronger price declines in the more competitive industries. Whereas prices in all industries under a 50 percent concentration ratio fell 3 percent, prices in industries under a 25 percent concentration ratio fell by 6.1 percent.

Price data on the 1973–1975 depression indicate that monopoly prices *rose* in the depression by an astounding percentage. This very large price increase throughout the now-dominant monopoly sector caused even competitive prices to show a small *rise* in the depression for the first time on record. This undoubtedly caused great disruption in the competitive sector, decreased production, increased bankruptcies, and increased unemployment.

Prices of Automobiles, Oil, and Food

Before we give a systematic analysis of such price behavior, it is worth looking at three of the most important examples of monopoly pricing and restriction of production. The most obvious is the automotive industry, in which the Big Three control over 90 percent of U.S. domestic production. (Of course, the degree of monopoly power has been drastically reduced by the competition of German and Japanese imports; the issues raised by this fact are discussed in the next chapter.) The largest automobile producer, General Motors, is usually the price leader. In the early part of the 1973–1975 depression, from the third quarter of 1973 to the third quarter of 1974, demand for automobiles fell rapidly, and GM sales were *down* 22 percent. Yet GM did not lower its prices as traditional economics would predict, but raised its prices by $900 to $1000; the lower sales were met by further restriction of production and the firing of thousands of GM workers.[10]

Oil prices rose dramatically during the 1973–1975 depression. The companies blamed the price rises on the Arab oil producers, but there is evidence that the U.S. companies had artificially restricted oil production for many years before that time. Internationally, almost all oil in the Arab countries was owned by Anglo-U.S. companies, which carefully controlled the flow (and made profit rates over 100 percent every year from 1950 to 1970 on the oil from that region).[11] In the United States, with immense oil deposits of its own, the oil companies had not built a new refinery since 1965, and they had cut back exploratory drilling by 60 percent since 1956.[12] Even during the so-called shortage, the U.S. oil companies held immense amounts of oil off the market in reserve-holding areas. U.S. oil companies contributed to the "shortage," raised U.S. prices, and made enormous profits from it.

Finally, U.S. consumers have been badly hurt by rising food prices and restricted food

---

[10]See Richard Edwards, "The Impact of Industrial Concentration on Economic Crisis," in David Mermelstein (ed.), *The Economic Crisis Reader* (New York: Random House (Vintage Books), 1975), pp. 217–218.

[11]See Farouk Akhdar, "Multinational Firms and Developing Countries: A Case Study of the Impact of the Arabian-American Oil Company (Aramco) on the Development of the Saudi Arabian Economy" (Ph.D. diss., University of California, Riverside, 1975).

[12]See Bennett Harrison, "Inflation by Oligopoly: Two Case Histories," *Nation* (30 August 1975), pp. 145–148.

production. Myth has it that food production is a purely competitive area, so the high prices could not possibly be the result of monopoly. The argument is that high food prices must be due to Russian wheat deals (a very small percentage of the crop), a drought or flood, or some other random factor, but not to monopoly because there is none. The fact is that the number of small farmers is shrinking whereas the number of giant agribusiness corporations is rising. On the supply side, farmers must buy most of their implements and fertilizers from monopolies. On the selling side, Campbell sells 90 percent of soups, four firms sell 90 percent of breakfast cereals, Gerber sells most baby food, Del Monte sells most canned fruits and vegetables, and only 20 supermarket chains sell 40 percent of all food.[13]

The power of the monopolies in food sales was accurately summed up by one investigator of the high prices of our Thanksgiving meals: "The Smithfield ham comes from ITT, the turkey is a product of Greyhound Corporation, the lettuce comes from Dow Chemical Company, the potatoes are provided by the Boeing Company, and Tenneco brought the fresh fruits and vegetables. The applesauce is made available by American Brands, while both Coca-Cola and Royal Crown Cola have provided the fruit juices."[14] In the 1973–1975 depression, prices received by farmers *dropped,* but intermediaries (canners, packers, and distributors controlled by conglomerates) increased their share of the food dollar to 60 cents, so retail prices actually rose!

EXPLANATION OF PRICE BEHAVIOR

In all previous recessions (before the 1950s), prices fell. That behavior was predictable and easily explained by traditional economic theory. Neoclassical theory leads us to expect that falling demand will cause *both* output and prices to decline. By a reduction of supply and also of prices in order to sell more of the supply, the amount of output supplied is brought back into equilibrium with the demand in each industry.

Similarly, in the aggregate, neo-Keynesian theory predicts that an excess supply will lead to falling production, unemployment, and falling prices (or stable prices if there are "institutional rigidities" or monopoly power). Neo-Keynesian theory predicts price inflation only when there is an excess demand above the supply at full employment.

Neither neoclassical nor neo-Keynesian theory predicts price inflation in the face of falling demand and unemployment, but this is what has occurred in the monopoly sector in the recessions or depressions of 1954, 1958, 1961, 1970, 1975, 1980, and 1982. Of course, traditional theory would admit that firms with monopoly power can always set prices higher if they wish to restrict their supply enough to do so. But *why,* in the face of falling demand, should monopolies find it profitable to reduce their production so drastically as actually to increase prices?

Only a few economists, mostly in the Marxist, Post Keynesian and institutionalist tradi-

---

[13]See David Mermelstein's introduction to the section entitled "Food Inflation," in Mermelstein (ed.), *Crisis Reader, op. cit.,* p. 326.
[14]William Robbins, *The American Food Scandal,* quoted in Mermelstein (ed.), *Crisis Reader, op. cit.,* p. 325.

tions, have provided some answers to this question.[15] In most of the monopoly sector, a single large firm in each industry sets prices; others simply follow this price leader. These large firms generally set prices at a certain margin of profit above their cost level. This "cost-plus" pricing by the large corporations has been confirmed by many empirical investigations.[16]

The giant corporations do *not* maximize their short-run profit by setting prices as high as possible at any given moment. Rather, they set prices with a profit margin such as to ensure their maximum long-run growth—and maximum long-run profits. This profit margin must, therefore, be enough to meet fully their expected needs for growth and expansion. Each corporation sets a *target* profit level based on its previous record and the record of the leaders in its industry.

In a business expansion, to achieve their best long-run growth of profits, the giant corporations usually set their prices *below* what the market would pay so as (1) to discourage entry by rivals, (2) to gain acceptance of new products in a wider market, (3) to stop unions from claiming they have the ability to pay much higher wages, (4) to discourage government antitrust actions or attempts to put price controls on their products, and (5) to stabilize dividend payments (and stock prices) by preventing them from rising too high so that they won't fall as much in the next recession. This holding down of prices thus gives the monopoly or oligopoly firms more power to maintain or even raise prices in the following contraction —because the giant firm has acquired a larger market, fewer rivals, less government control, and so forth.

What happens if a giant corporation finds its sales revenue falling in a recession or depression? The firm will try to obtain enough revenue to reach its target profit by means of a higher price markup on the remaining sales. This process has been ably illustrated in an arithmetic example in an excellent article by Howard Wachtel and Peter Adelsheim.

> For example, say a firm operating in a concentrated industry has direct costs (raw material and labor) of $200 per unit of output and sets its profit markup above direct costs at 20 percent, therefore selling the product for $240 per unit and making a profit of $40 per unit. Let us say the firm has a target level of profits of $40,000; to realize this profit level it will have to sell 1,000 units at $240 per unit. Now we have unemployment and a recession which causes the volume of sales to fall, say, to 960 units. But if the firm still has a target profit level of $40,000, which it wants to attain, it will have to raise its prices to slightly over $242 per unit from the previous level of $240 per unit. It does this by raising its percentage markup over costs to 21 percent compared to the previous 20 percent. Having increased their profit per unit, the firm now achieves its target profit level, but the resultant manifestation in the economy is the simultaneous occurrence of inflation and unemployment.[17]

---

[15]The basic theory was first stated in Michal Kalecki, *Theory of Economic Dynamics* (New York: Monthly Review, 1968). It is applied to the present situation in John Blair, "Market Power and Inflation," *Journal of Economic Issues* 8 (June 1974), pp. 453–478, and in Alfred Eichner, "A Theory of the Determination of the Mark-up under Oligopoly," *Economic Journal* 83 (December 1973), pp. 1184–1199.

[16]See the citations and discussions in Eichner, "The Mark-up," *op. cit.*, p. 1184. Also see the discussion in Joan Robinson, "Solving the Stagflation Puzzle," *Challenge* (November-December, 1979), pp. 40–46.

[17]Howard Wachtel and Peter Adelsheim, "The Inflationary Impact of Unemployment: Price Markups During Postwar Recessions, 1947–1970" (for U.S. Congress, Joint Economic Committee, forthcoming). Wachtel and Adelsheim also give the most complete theoretical explanation of this phenomenon.

This illustration assumes little or no further decrease in demand when the price is marked up. But Wachtel and Adelsheim point out that their conclusion, that monopolies will raise prices in a recession with these policies, holds true even if the price increases cause some further decline in demand. Of course, even the tightest monopoly in reality will lose a few customers from any price rise, but most of them have a strong enough market control—and a strong enough image from advertising—to ensure that they will not lose many customers. Just how high a price they can set is a function of their degree of monopoly, which power is roughly reflected in their high degrees of industrial concentration.[18]

More specifically, their degree of monopoly power over price has three main constraints.[19] First, if the industry raises its prices (led by the price leader), how many customers are willing or able to switch to a substitute product? Second, if the price and profit margins are raised, how many new firms will be able to enter the industry, or how high are the barriers to such new entrants? Third, what is the realistic likelihood of any government intervention if the price-gouging becomes too obvious to be overlooked?

It follows from this "cost-plus" behavior that such oligopoly firms do not change their prices as frequently as competitive firms. Even if there is rapid inflation of prices and costs, these firms usually keep one price for quite a while, then raise it to the new level dictated by their usual profit margin above costs. Thus, there is considerable evidence that in periods of business expansion and rapid inflation, it is the prices of the more competitive firms that rise more rapidly and change from day to day.

In a recession, however, the small, competitive firms are forced to drop their prices rapidly as demand falls (because no one of them can restrict the industry supply) *regardless* of the effect on their profit rates. Not so the large, oligopoly firms. In the recession, if costs per unit of oligopoly firms remain the same (as they do in physical terms over a wide range of output), then the oligopolies may keep their prices the same so as to maintain a profit rate as near constant as possible. Of course, that entails extra reduction of production and the unemployment of many more workers than in a similar competitive industry, but that is not their worry.

Indeed, in recent recessions or depressions, when total sales were declining, the firms with monopoly power actually raised prices as far as they believed necessary to maintain their profit margins and total profit. In order to make these price increases in the face of declining demand, they very drastically reduced their production, thereby worsening unemployment.

MONOPOLY AND PROFIT RATES

If our economy operated under pure and perfect competition, then capital would flow immediately from areas of low profit rates to areas of high profit rates. It follows that the rate of profit would be equal in all industries. The rate of profit, however is *not* equal in all industries. It is consistently higher in industries with greater monopoly power.

---

[18] See this concept in Kalecki, *Economic Dynamics, op. cit.,* chap. 1.
[19] See these concepts in Eichner, "The Mark-up," *op. cit.,* pp. 1190–1191.

Table 20.5

MONOPOLY POWER AND PROFIT RATES, 1972

Industry Group	Concentration Ratio	Profit Rate
Monopoly Sector		
Motor vehicles	88%	8.7%
Tobacco	87	11.3
Instruments	65	13.9
Primary nonferrous metals	64	5.6
Electrical machinery	62	7.1
Primary iron and steel	56	5.0
Chemicals	55	11.3
Petroleum and coal products	55	8.3
Average		8.9%
More Competitive Sector		
Food	49%	4.7%
Paper	47	6.8
Textiles	46	4.7
Leather	41	5.1
Fabricated metals	39	6.5
Apparel	33	4.3
Lumber	31	8.0
Furniture	29	6.7
Printing and publishing	29	8.7
Average		6.2%

SOURCE: U.S. Federal Trade Commission data on profits and U.S. Census Bureau data on concentration, compiled by Kathleen Pulling, *Cyclical Behavior of Prices and Profits, 1949–1975* (Ph.D. diss., University of California, Riverside, 1977).

Once again, define a *concentration ratio* as the percentage of industry sales controlled by the eight largest firms. The ratio for each industry group is a weighted average of the ratios in each of its component industries. The *monopoly sector* is defined as all those industry groups over 50 percent concentration in all the census years from 1949 to 1973 whereas the *more competitive sector* is all those groups under 50 percent concentration in all the census years from 1949 to 1973. The *rate of profit* used here is the percentage of profit to sales in each industry group. Other studies have found the exact same results when the rate of profit is defined as the percentage of profits to owner's capital or to all capital (including borrowed capital).[20] Table 20.5 shows the results for 1972.

The average rate of profit on sales for the monopoly sector (over 50 percent concentration) was 11.2 percent for the average of the years from 1949 to 1973. The average rate of profit

---

[20] See, e.g., Howard Sherman, *Profits in the United States* (Ithaca, N.Y.: Cornell University Press, 1968), chap. 3.

on sales for the more competitive sector (under 50 percent concentration) was only 6.2 percent for the average of the years from 1949 to 1973.[21]

Why does the monopoly sector have higher profit rates than the competitive sector? In the first place, monopoly power means the ability to restrict supply and keep prices higher than in the competitive sector (within the limits discussed in the preceding section). The higher prices mean lower real wages for all worker-consumers. The profits of small, competitive business and farmers are also hurt by monopoly prices to the extent that they must purchase producer goods from the monopoly sector. Some large firms in the monopoly sector also have extra market power as large buyers of commodities from small competitive business, forcing down the prices charged by these small suppliers.

Large firms in the monopoly sector may also have extra power in the labor market, so they may add to profits by buying labor at a rate lower than the average wage. This factor may, of course, be somewhat offset by trade union action. In the modern world, wages are not automatically determined by supply and demand in the market. They are determined by the bargaining strength of capital and labor (under given conditions of supply and demand), with monopoly capital usually in the stronger position. Workers are thus squeezed from both sides by monopoly. On the one hand, the monopolies can pay lower money wages by exerting their power in the labor market. On the other hand, monopolies can charge workers higher prices as consumers.

Additional monopoly profits come from lucrative government military contracts, which are financed from the workers' tax money, thus again increasing total profits. Extra-high returns from foreign investments abroad also add to monopoly profits; that is, profits are extracted from workers in foreign countries. In summary, monopolies or oligopolies make profit far above the average rate in several ways: (1) selling at higher prices to consumers, thereby lowering the real wage; (2) selling at higher prices to small business and farmers; (3) buying at lower prices from small business and farmers; (4) buying labor power at lower wages from workers; (5) selling to the government at higher prices; and (6) buying labor power and materials at lower prices in foreign countries. Through these relatively high prices and low costs (always relative to a competitive firm in the same situation), the monopoly or oligopoly firms extract more profits from the worker-consumer-taxpayer here and abroad; they also transfer some profits from small business and farmers to themselves.

Table 20.6 shows the profit rate on the capital investment of all stockholders averaged for the years 1956 through 1975. Each group of corporations is shown by the size of total assets, from the smallest (below a million) to the largest (over a billion). The relationship in Table 20.6 is very clear. The profit rate on investment rises monotonically as the size of the corporation increases.

The higher profit rate with size is explained by all the reasons given earlier for the higher profit rate resulting from monopoly power. To a large extent, large size means monopoly power—though there are industries where there are so many giant firms that the concentra-

---

[21]See Kathleen Pulling, *Market Structure and the Cyclical Behavior of Prices and Profits, 1949–1975* (Ph.D. diss., University of California, Riverside, 1977). Also see Kathleen Pulling, "Cyclical Behavior of Profit Margins," *Journal of Economic Issues* 12 (June 1978), pp. 1–24.

Table 20.6

LONG-RUN PROFIT RATE ON INVESTMENT
For All U.S. Manufacturing Corporations, 1956–1975

Size (by Assets)	Profit Rate (Profit Before Taxes Divided by Stockholders' Capital)
$0–$1,000,000	3.7%
1,000,000– 5,000,000	5.3
5,000,000– 10,000,000	6.7
10,000,000– 50,000,000	7.4
50,000,000– 100,000,000	8.1
100,000,000– 250,000,000	8.5
250,000,000– 1,000,000,000	8.8
$1,000,000,000 and over	11.7

Source: U.S. Federal Trade Commission, *Quarterly Reports of U.S. Manufacturing Corporations* (Washington, D.C.: GPO, 1956–1975).

tion ratio by four or eight appears low, and there are industries small enough for a medium-sized firm to have monopoly power. Moreover, when we examine behavior by size alone, this eliminates some of the distortion of the concentration ratios caused by one conglomerate's controlling subsidiaries in a number of different industries. The large size also directly affects profitability through economies of scale in production, in distribution, and in nationwide advertising. The large manufacturing corporation may also own its own natural resources. Moreover, the large corporation may have much cheaper access to finances either by its credit rating or by a direct tie-in with a financial institution.

Monopoly Profit Rates over the Cycle

We have seen that the large monopoly corporations have higher profit rates in the long run than small competitive firms. We have also seen that, in expansions, the large monopoly firms raise their prices more slowly in order to increase their share of the market. In contractions, the large monopoly firms keep their prices from falling or actually raise them whereas competitive firms have to reduce prices or raise them much, much less than the monopolies. Given this difference in price conduct, what is the difference in performance of profit rates in the two sectors over the cycle? Table 20.7 shows the cyclical amplitudes of the monopoly and competitive profit rates.

In Table 20.7, the monopoly sector includes all major industry groups with concentration ratios greater than 50 percent in all of the Census of Manufactures years, 1954, 1958, 1967, and 1972. The competitive sector includes those groups of less than 50 percent in all the same years. An expansion amplitude measures the peak value minus the initial trough value as a percentage of the cycle average. The contraction amplitude is the final trough minus the peak as a percentage. The profit rate is the total profit divided by sales (but very similar results

Table 20.7

AMPLITUDES OF MONOPOLY AND COMPETITIVE PROFIT RATES

Cycle	Monopoly Sector		Competitive Sector	
	Average Expansion	Amplitude in Contraction	Average Expansion	Amplitude in Contraction
1949–1954	32.1	−30.8	45.8	−56.9
1954–1958	21.6	−41.3	32.1	−47.8
1958–1961	33.5	−28.6	36.6	−47.1
1961–1970	25.0	−35.1	49.0	−32.3
Average	28.0	−34.0	40.9	−46.0

Source: Federal Trade Commission data compiled by Kathleen Pulling, *Market Structure and Cyclical Behavior of Prices and Profits, 1949–1975* (Ph.D. diss., University of California, Riverside, 1977).

have been found using the profit rate on capital[22]). All manufacturing corporations are included in the groups examined.

Table 20.7 shows quite clearly that the profit rates in the more competitive sector normally rises and falls more violently than profit rates in the monopoly sector—which parallels their price behavior. Profit rates in the more competitive sector of manufacturing rose faster than in the monopoly sector in four out of four expansions from 1949 to 1970. And profit rates in the more competitive sector fell further in three out of four contractions.

If we examine the cyclical amplitude of profit rates by size of corporation, the pattern is very similar. Table 20.8 shows the profit rate on sales by size of assets of corporations for two periods, the three cycles of 1949 to 1961 and the most recent full cycle of 1970 to 1975. This division into period was forced on us by changes in government categories and has no other significance in this case.

Table 20.8 reveals that the profit rates of the larger corporations rise less in expansions and fall less in contractions than the profit rates of the smaller corporations. When we combine these findings with the similar findings of Table 20.7 on monopoly and competitive sectors, the conclusion is that the profit rates of large monopoly corporations are far more stable than those of small competitive corporations.

Why do the large monopoly corporations have more stable profit rates in both boom and bust? First, they attempt to set their prices so as to maintain a stable profit rate. Second, their monopoly power allows them to set their prices at those levels. They maintain those prices in contractions by restricting their production (and employment). In expansion, they raise prices only slowly while rapidly increasing their production (and employment) to obtain or keep a high share of the expanding market. Third, the costs per unit of the largest corporations remain fairly constant over a wide range of output below full capacity.[23] The unit costs of small corporations rise rapidly when they drop below optimum capacity. Fourth, the

---

[22] See Sherman, *op. cit.*, chap. 7.
[23] See, e.g., Joe S. Bain, "Price and Production Policies," in Howard S. Ellis (ed.), *A Survey of Contemporary Economics* (New York: McGraw-Hill, 1948), p. 140.

Table 20.8

AMPLITUDE OF PROFIT RATES BY SIZE

A. Average of Three Cycles, 1949–1970

Asset Size	Expansion Amplitude	Contraction Amplitude
(lower limit)	+83%	−83%
$250,000	+39	−55
$1 million	+37	−52
$5 million	+28	−27
$100 million	+22	−27

B. Cycle of 1970–1975

Asset Size	Expansion Amplitude	Contraction Amplitude
$0	+87	−22
$1 million	+36	−24
$5 million	+22	−13
$10 million	+27	−18
$50 million	+29	−10
$100 million	+12	− 5
$250 million	+13	− 8
$1 billion	+22	− 5

NOTE: Profit on Sales of All U.S. Manufacturing Corporations
SOURCE: Federal Trade Commission, *Quarterly Financial Reports of Manufacturing Corporations* (Washington, D.C.: GPO, 1949–1976).

unchanging interest burden of small as compared to large corporations is greater both because they pay higher interest rates and because they borrow a higher percentage of their capital. Fifth, and very important, the small corporations have all their eggs in one basket (with no reserves) whereas the large conglomerates are very diversified, with some investments in industries that may happen to grow despite a contraction (and an ability to shift reserve capital from one area to another).

There is also some evidence that crises hit the small competitive firms long before they hit the large monopoly firms. In the business expansions in the period 1949–1961, the profit margins of the competitive industries (defined as those with below 50 percent concentration of sales by eight firms) turned down 6.7 months before the expansion peak on the average. Yet the profit margins of the monopoly industries (defined as those with over 50 percent concentration of sales by eight firms) did not feel the squeeze for another four months, turning down on the average only 2.2 months before the expansion peak. It appears that the increased monopolization of the economy increases the stability of the sector of high monopoly power, but further destabilizes the competitive sector. And the instability of the competitive sector is the prime factor setting off each new crisis of overproduction and contraction.

SUMMARY

The cycle of boom and bust, with periodic high levels of unemployment, is inherent in capitalism. In every expansion, demand is limited by the limited purchasing power of the worker-consumer whereas costs of new equipment and raw materials rise as capitalists in these areas find supply always below the rising demand. In every contraction, the excess supply, or overproduction relative to effective demand, is cured by wiping out many smaller capitalists, with the monopolies buying their capital cheaply; by drastic reduction of all supply; by unemployment lowering labor costs; and by stagnation lowering the costs of raw materials and equipment.

The phenomena of inflation appear in recessions now because of the vast increase in concentrated monopoly power. In several recessions of the 1950s and 1960s, though competitive prices dropped in each contraction, monopoly prices rose. In the depression of 1973–1975, general inflation increased competitive prices a little whereas monopoly prices soared. As a result of the monopolists' control over prices—as well as some other factors associated with absolute size—the monopoly profit rates are relatively stable, declining very little in recession or depression. The small competitive firms, however, bear the full burden of the profit decline in depression (although workers shoulder an even larger burden through reduced real wages). Hence, increasing monopoly has caused greater declines of production and unemployment while raising prices through that very restriction of supply.

Monopoly, however, is not the only factor whose increase has led to both more inflation and greater unemployment. The government of the United States is more strongly influencing the economy than ever before and is in part responsible for the current stagflation (discussed in Part Six). In addition, the international scene has shifted against U.S. capitalism so as to intensify these problems (discussed in the next chapter). Occasional factors influencing costs were discussed in the preceeding chapter.

SUGGESTED READINGS

A very thorough radical study of monopoly (and prices and profits) is Joseph E. Bowring, *The Dual Economy: Core and Periphery in the Accumulation Process in the United States* (Ph.D. diss., University of Massachusetts, Amherst, 1982).

A beautifully and clearly written, popular book by a left-wing liberal is John Case, *Understanding Inflation* (New York: Penguin Books, 1981).

A very interesting and useful discussion of monopoly and inflation is Malolm C. Sawyer, *Macro-Economics in Question: The Keynesian-monetarist Orthodoxies and the Kaleckian Alternative* (Armonk, N.Y.: M. E. Sharpe, 1982).

One kind of Marxist view is in Ernest Mandel, *Late Capitalism,* trans. Joris de Bres (London: Verso, 1978).

APPENDIX 20A

Monopoly in a Cycle Model

To add the issue of monopoly power to the cycle models of Part Three in an explicit fashion, we would have to disaggregate the variables into monopoly and competitive sectors. For empirical purposes, the *monopoly* sector might be defined as all industries with over 50 percent concentration whereas the *competitive* sector might be defined as all industries at or under 50 percent concentration—obviously a crude and arbitrary distinction. Then, for example, there would be investment in the monopoly sector (I^m) and investment in the competitive sector (I^c).

$$I = I^c + I^m \qquad (20A.1)$$

Investment in both sectors might be a function of profit rates and total profits, but the two functions would be quite different.

$$I^c = f^1 \left(\Pi^c, \frac{\Pi^c}{K^c} \right) \qquad (20A.2)$$

and

$$I^m = f^2 \left(\Pi^m, \frac{\Pi^m}{K^m} \right) \qquad (20A.3)$$

where Π^c is profit in the competitive sector, Π^m is profit in the monopoly sector, K^c is capital in the competitive sector, and K^m is capital in the monopoly sector.

In addition, one would have to specify the functions determining the total profits and profit rates in the two sectors. The explanatory variables might be the same, but it is clear that the profit rate reacts far more strongly to changes in the competitive sector than in the monopoly sector. This is the reason that profit rates of small business fluctuate more and may have a longer lead at both the peak and the trough.

Effects of monopoly on income distribution could be shown by examining separately the wages and the profits in each of the two sectors.

A complete model of inflation would also need to show the prices in each of the two sectors (P^c and P^m) separately, with different functional relations.

Chapter 21

INTERNATIONAL ASPECTS OF INFLATION AND UNEMPLOYMENT

In this chapter we remove the assumption of an isolated, self-sufficient economy and inquire how the U.S. economy behaves in the real world of international trade and investment. We shall examine the facts and theory of the international propagation of cycles, as well as the facts and theory on the international spread of inflation.

THEORY OF BUSINESS CYCLE SPREAD

The main channels for transmission of business cycles are the same internationally as they are nationally, namely, the demand for consumer and investment goods and the relative changes in prices and costs. Yet there are certain important differences.

The most obvious and important channel of transmission of cycles is international trade. Suppose there is a growth in U.S. exports, so that exports become greater than imports (a *favorable* balance of trade). This means a net increase in demand for U.S. products; it will raise income and output if the economy has been below full employment. Of course, if there already was full employment, the increased demand could lead only to higher prices. If, on the contrary, the United States increases its imports till it has fewer exports than imports, then it loses buying power to foreign countries. It is always possible, therefore, for a shift in demand from one area to another to produce depressing effects in country A and equal expansion effects in country B. This phenomenon was apparent in the post-World War II period in the shift in demand caused by the use of substitutes for certain natural products, for example, synthetic rubber for natural rubber.

Suppose the U.S. economy is in a depression and the rest of the world is not. Then since U.S. citizens have less income, the United States will import less from other countries. In that case, the other countries have a decrease in the demand for their commodities, causing depressive effects on their industries. Since the rest of the world then has less income, part of their adjustment will be made by getting fewer imports from the United States. Thus, the process is cumulative. Just the opposite process occurs if one country begins to recover from a depression. If U.S. income begins to rise, U.S. citizens have more money to spend, and foreign goods look more attractive. Therefore, the United States imports more of both consumer and investment goods, leading finally to increased income and increased imports in other countries. Of course, in either expansion or depression, we should keep in mind that the cumulative process, whereby changes in imports and exports have a multiple effect as they pass from country to country, requires a finite amount of time for each new round of trading. Moreover, not all the increased income that a country gets from increased net exports will be respent for imports; some of it will leak into internal spending and will not rebound to increase the exports of another country.

The big differences between national and international spread of business cycles arise from the fact that space as well as time enters the picture. Since the distances are so great, it is easier for merchants to make mistakes of over- or underestimation of the market demand; goods may be in short supply or pile up at a whole series of places along the trade routes. On the other hand, the fact of transport costs reduces the volume of international trade and therefore lessens the depth of this channel of cycle transmission. Likewise, any governmental trade barriers that permanently lessen trade between countries will tend to localize the effects of cycles. Of course, there are other government measures to stimulate or lessen trade that arise from the fact of separate national currencies; for example, a government may temporarily stimulate exports and decrease imports by devaluing its money vis-à-vis that of other countries. Finally, in the labor market, the two facts of high transport costs and high artificial travel barriers make labor among the most immobile of commodities, thereby lessening the direct spread of unemployment.

There is also a more controversial theory that if country A is in a depression, then its prices will decline relative to those in other countries. Therefore, its goods will look more attractive to foreign buyers. So country A's exports will increase in a depression. When its prices rise in a domestic expansion, its goods will be less attractive, so its exports will decline. Thus, this theory concludes that exports will move counter to the cycle. Exports will therefore help bring the economy back to equilibrium. This theory is analogous to Say's law, it helps support Say's law, and it is about as accurate as Say's law.

In reality, as described in Chapter 1, the economies of most capitalist countries tend to move up and down together. Since all other countries have falling income, their demand for the exports of country A declines in every contraction. When there is a worldwide expansion, the demand for the exports of country A rises. Thus, the demand effect greatly outweights any price effect, so we expect exports (like imports) to move with the cycle. We shall see in later sections that U.S. exports do mostly move with the cycle.

Investment and the Spread of Cycles

The second major means of transmitting the business cycle is via international investment. If country A loans or invests in country B, then usually part of the money is spent in A on equipment and part is spent in B on installation and operation. This transaction will have several effects. It will immediately result in some increase in demand in A and some in B. To the extent that the money is respent, there will again result cumulative and multiple effects, which may increase a boom or aid a revival from depression. We may note that there will be secondary effects not only on imports and exports of goods and capital, but also to some extent on internal consumption and investment.

Some observers have stressed that investment abroad means less excess of savings at home; thus, "the stability of capital-exporting countries with high rates of saving has . . . been dependent on the recurrent appearance of new opportunities for investment abroad."[1] But this very important source of investment opportunities is also very fluctuating and cyclical in nature. The fact that it has even greater fluctuations than domestic investment is due to the greater sensitivity of investment abroad to changes in the business outlook in the world. The greater sensitivity is due, in turn, to the greater uncertainty because of distances, different laws, customs, and political trends. Among the most often mentioned problems of international investment are (1) difficulties of management owing to long lines of communication and transportation, (2) inadequate legal protection, (3) ignorance of language and customs, and (4) risk of transfer restrictions on profits or outright confiscation. These factors account not only for the wide cyclical fluctuation of foreign investments, but also for the low supply of international investment funds and the high interest rates.

The approach of the classical as well as the Marxist economists stresses the ability of foreign investments to raise the average rate of profit of the home country, which all these economists felt to be in danger of declining for various reasons. J. S. Mill mentions this avenue of investment as

> . . . the last of the counter-forces which check the downward tendency of profits . . . This is, the perpetual overflow of capital into colonies of foreign countries, to seek higher profits than can be obtained at home . . . In the first place, it . . . carries off a part of the increase of capital from which the reduction of profit proceeds. Secondly, the capital so carried off is not lost, but is chiefly employed . . . in founding colonies which become large exporters of cheap agricultural produce . . .[2]

Thus, the rate of profit of the capital-exporting country would be raised by having less competition at home, higher profits from abroad, and a supply of cheap raw materials for its industries. In this context it is possible, if a depression started in a capital-importing country, that the lesser returns on investment would have depressing effects abroad.

The income from investments abroad also has an effect on demand because it is equivalent

---

[1] League of Nations, Report of the Delegation on Economic Depression, *Economic Stability in the Post-War World* (Geneva: League of Nations, 1945). Also see Alan Severn, "Investor Evaluation of Foreign and Domestic Risk," *Journal of Finance* 29 (March 1974), pp. 545–550; Norman Miller and Marina Whitman, "Alternative Theories and Tests of U.S. Foreign Investment," *Journal of Finance* 28 (December 1973), pp. 1131–1150.

[2] John Stuart Mill, *Principles of Political Economy* (London: Longmans, Green, 1920 reprint; W. L. Ashley ed.), book 4, chap. 4, p. 736.

to an invisible export. The receiver has that much accounts receivable credit against the debtor. If that money or credit so obtained is immediately reinvested in the debtor country, then the effect will be expansionary. In a depression period, however, the more likely course is for the creditor to withdraw those funds from the debtor country back to his or her own country and there to hoard it. In passing, we may note that if the loan or investment were made in a boom or during inflation and had to be paid back in a depression or deflation, then the funds pulled out of the debtor would be worth more in buying power than those put into it.

Every investment must eventually produce a supply of goods on the market. Thus, though the original effect of an international investment will be to increase demand for the factors of production, it is often claimed that its later effect will be to compete with the industry of the home country. This depends on the type of goods produced and where they are marketed. If the goods are of the same type as already produced by either the capital-exporter or importer and are sold in the same market as the previously established industries, then, of course, the effect may very well be deflationary at the future time. This does not deny that much income and demand were generated in the capital-exporter country for the entire time before the new goods reached the market. On the other hand, if the goods are raw materials needed by the capital-exporter, then their production and sale may even cause the marginal profitability of capital in the capital-exporter country to rise. Then, in turn, its investment may rise; and, eventually, if it imports more raw materials, there may be still further expansionary effects on the capital-importing country as well. In a depression, however, there may be no buyer for any kind of goods, whether finished or raw materials; and so the only result of increased production will be further depressing effects on the industry of the capital-importer and eventually on the industry of the capital-exporter.[3]

There does seem to be a considerable degree of agreement on the main points of the transmission mechanism, which might be summed up as follows: If a depression begins in a country that imports a large amount of goods, then the rest of the world feels a sudden decline in the demand for many kinds of goods. This seems initially to be the main instrument of spreading the depression. Then, however, in the exporting countries the lower demand for their goods lowers their income, their consumption, and the investment opportunities in their lands. When the effects reach back to the initiating countries, not only may there be some drop in demand for their finished goods exports, but usually, more importantly, the demand for their capital export drastically declines in view of the drying up of investment opportunities abroad.

Behavior of Investment and Trade in the Great Depression

In the Great Depression, for example, the flow of U.S. investment abroad declined from over $1.3 *billion* in 1928 to $1.6 *million* dollars in 1932.[4] Countries may still desire most intensively during a depression to find or conquer new markets for goods and capital export, as

---
[3]See the argument in Gottfried Haberler, *Prosperity and Depression* (Geneva: League of Nations, 1937), pp. 406–451.
[4]League of Nations, *Statistical Yearbook, 1932–1934* (Geneva: League of Nations, 1934), pp. 220–230.

Britain did in the nineteenth century, but this easy road to recovery has seldom been open in the twentieth century. In fact, markets have narrowed with the increase of government ownership in large areas of the world as, for example, in the nationalization of the Suez Canal. If recovery begins or new investment opportunities do develop in the capital-importing countries, this will greatly stimulate recovery in the rest of the private enterprise world. Perhaps more often, however, we must await the expansion of income and increase of imports in the industrially advanced countries before expansion begins cumulatively spreading around the world.

As might be expected, the U.S. depression of the thirties had the worst effect on (1) those in debt to the United States, who had been paying back principal, interest, and dividends by U.S. imports or by new U.S. loans or new U.S. investments (2) exporters of producers' goods (especially raw materials) because these had constituted 85 percent of U.S. imports in the previous period; and (3) those who exported the consumer's goods to the United States (mostly food) that constituted the other 15 percent of U.S. imports. For this reason, Argentina and Australia, large exporters of raw materials, were immediately among the hardest hit and were the first to go off the gold standard.

When there is a period of expansion in the United States, it also appears that some of the increased income is used for increases both in the import of finished products for consumption, which are mostly luxuries, and in the import of producers' goods for new investment, most of which are raw materials. Though U.S. imports are a small proportion of U.S. income, an *increase* (or *decrease*) of U.S. income means a larger than proportional increase (or decrease) of imports. This is because a larger part of the increase in income is devoted to investment in raw materials (because of the acceleration principle) and to consumption of luxuries (because demand for these items reacts most strongly to changes in income). Therefore, in the boom of the twenties, imports increased faster than national income, and in the depression of the thirties, imports decreased even faster than the rapidly falling national income.[5] Furthermore, it is the underdeveloped countries that are hardest hit by these wide flutuations. Since international investment and international trade in primary products—that is, in raw materials, both agricultural and mineral—show the greatest fluctuations, "it follows that any country whose economy is intimately dependent on foreign investment or whose trade is greatly dependent on primary commodities will be seriously affected by swings of business arising outside its own borders."[6]

The physical output of agriculture was stable or showing a slow rise during the entire twenties and the thirties. Manufactures, on the other hand, rose up to 1929, then dropped off rapidly. In 1933 world output was only about 40 percent of that of 1929, then rose slowly till manufacturing reached the 1929 level in 1938, only to fall off again. Mining activity and the output of minerals in world statistics show even greater fluctuation. In the period from 1918 to 1939, minerals rose about as fast as manufacturing in expansions, but minerals fell faster than manufacturing in depressions.[7] In price terms also, the fluctuations of raw materials are much greater than those of finished products. During the expansion of the twenties,

---

[5]League of Nations, *Economic Stability in the Post-War World* (Geneva: League of Nations, 1945), p. 103.
[6]*Ibid.*, p. 92.
[7]*Ibid.*, p. 80.

raw material prices rose faster than finished goods prices, then dropped much faster to the depression trough of 1933, and rose more slowly till 1938; in the 1938 recession, raw material prices again dropped faster. In the world market, the *prices* of iron and steel had quite small fluctuations in this period, but the *prices* of both nonferrous metals and farm products had very large cyclical variations.[8] Since raw materials are relatively expensive in the boom, the agrarian countries tend to have a favorable balance of trade and good terms of trade; in the depression, the opposite is true. And it should be remembered that although their exports are cut back in the depression, most of their imports are necessities, which cannot be cut back so easily.

The drop in demand for commodities exported can have one of two effects, either lowering the price or lowering the amount or both. The physical output and amount taken of most agricultural products for consumers is relatively stable because on the demand side they are necessities of life and on the supply side they are largely governed by nature and produced under extremely competitive conditions. Therefore, almost the total drop in food products, such as crops and livestock, is a drop in prices, so that there is a proportionate drop in the people's income in these areas though they still do the same amount of production.

The situation with minerals and industrial crops, which are used as raw materials for which the demand fluctuates very greatly, is quite different. In the case of raw materials—minerals most obviously—there is a great drop in output and employment as well as in price and income. It should be emphasized that in the case of raw materials, their rise or decline is accelerated twice because the demand for raw materials is derived from the demand for producers' goods, which is derived from the demand for consumer's goods. In the brief recession of 1937 to 1938, for example, not only did the amount of tin exported from Bolivia (their main export) drop precipitously, but the price of tin fell by 45 percent.

Facts of U.S. Export and Import Cycles from 1949 to 1980

The actual behavior of U.S. exports, imports, and net exports (exports minus imports) is shown in Table 21.1 and in Figures 21.1 and 21.2.

U.S. imports (in constant dollars) rose in every segment of the average U.S. business expansion. U.S. imports fell in every segment of the average business contraction. Obviously, imports are a direct function of rising and falling U.S. national income. This factor tends to push all other capitalist and dependent countries toward conformity with the U.S. business cycle.

At the same time, U.S. exports also rose in every segment of the average business expansion. In an earlier section, we noted the theory that U.S. exports will rise in a contraction because falling prices make goods easier to sell. The opposing theory said that exports will fall in a U.S. contraction because other countries also have declining income. In reality, exports continued to rise in early contraction, but fell in most of the contraction, and then rose again in late contraction. Exports are not as closely tied to the U.S. cycle as imports because (1) they depend on foreign demand, which is not always closely synchronized; and

[8]*Ibid.,* pp. 81 and 82.

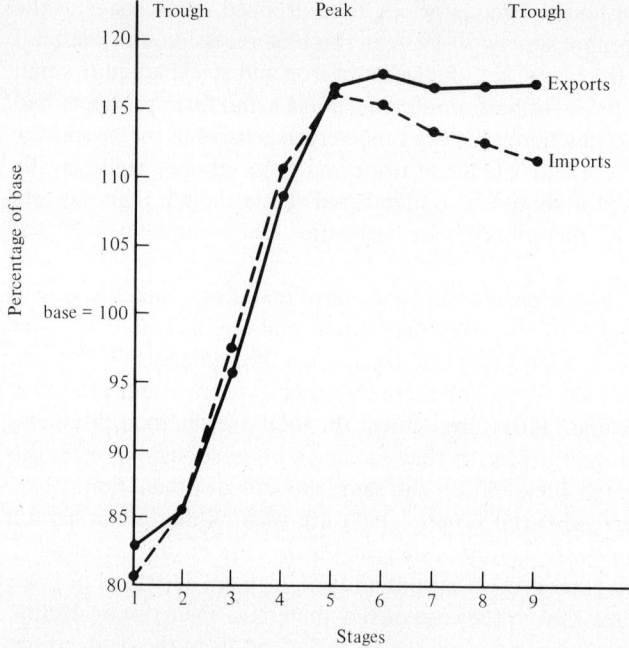

Figure 21.1 U.S. Exports and Imports

NOTE: This figure represents an average of six buiness cycles, from 1949 through 1980, in a quarterly data and in constant 1972 dollars, in percentage of cycle base.
SOURCE: Quarterly data, in constant 1972 dollars, from U.S. Department of Commerce, *Business Conditions Digest* (May 1981).

Table 21.1

U.S. EXPORTS AND IMPORTS

CHANGE FROM STAGE TO STAGE, PER MONTH, IN PERCENTAGE OF CYCLE BASE

Stage	Expansion				Peak	Contraction		
	1–2	2–3	3–4	4–5	5–6	6–7	7–8	8–9
Exports	0.32	0.55	0.90	0.87	0.47	−0.39	−0.33	0.05
Imports	0.61	0.78	0.69	0.42	−0.16	−0.69	−0.63	−0.71
Net Exports	−0.79	−0.88	1.68	2.94	3.13	1.55	1.17	2.84

NOTE: This table represents an average of six cycles, from 1949 to 1980, in quarterly data and in constant 1972 dollars.
SOURCE: U.S. Department of Commerce, *Business Conditions Digest* (May 1981).

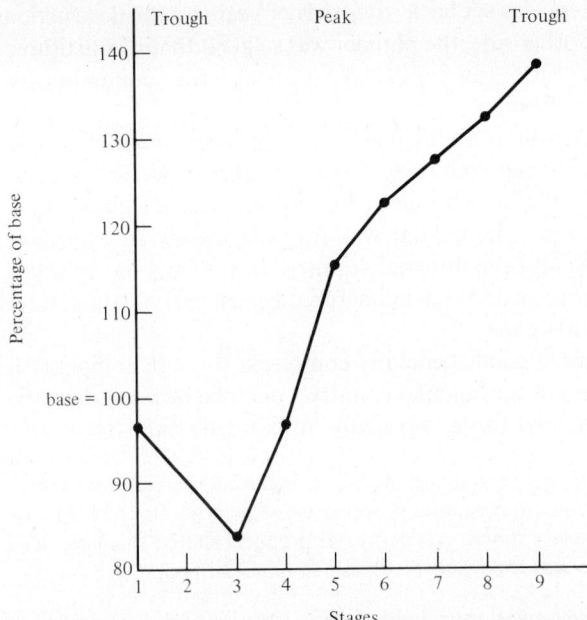

Figure 21.2 U.S. Net Exports (Exports Minus Imports)
NOTE: This figure represents an average of six cycles, from 1949 through 1980, in quarterly data and in constant 1972 dollars, in percentage of the cycle base.
SOURCE: Quarterly data, in constant 1972 dollars, from U.S. Department of Commerce, *Business Conditions Digest* (May 1981).

(2) they depend, to a less extent, on relative U.S. prices, which usually decline in a U.S. contraction.

Because exports fluctuate less than imports, net exports tend to fall in expansion and rise in contraction, so they are a countercyclical factor.

IMPERIALISM AND MULTINATIONAL FIRMS

So far, we have described international relations as if they were between completely independent firms in independent countries. To understand fully the present situation of giant multinational firms, a brief historical sketch will prove very useful. Only then can one comprehend how a small number of giant corporations have come to dominate the international economy and what their impact has been.

From the fifteenth century onward, the developing capitalist economies of Europe grew economically and militarily at a rate then unparalleled in human history. From the fifteenth to the nineteenth centuries, they slowly came to dominate much of the rest of the world. They plundered, enslaved, and ruled so as to extract the maximum from their subjects.

Such havoc was created that ancient and culturally advanced civilizations disappeared, as in Peru and West Africa, and progress was set back hundreds of years by the destruction of native industries, as in India. On the other side, the plunder was so great that it constituted the main element in the formation of European capital and provided the foundation for prosperous trade and eventual industrialization.

By the end of the nineteenth century, almost all the present less developed countries were under the colonial rule of the more advanced countries. The imperialist countries invested in the colonial countries at astoundingly high profit rates, primarily because of a cheap labor supply and enforced lack of competition. The capital was invested mainly in extractive industries, which exported raw materials to the imperial country. In the imperial country, the cheap raw materials were profitably turned into manufactured goods, part of which were exported back (tariff-free) to the colonial country.

The tariff-free imports of manufactured goods generally completed through competition the destruction (often begun by plunder) of the colonial country's manufacturing industries. An example of this may be seen in colonial India, especially in its textile industry:

> India, still an exporter of manufactured products at the end of the eighteenth century, becomes an importer. From 1815 to 1832, India's cotton exports dropped by 92 percent. In 1850, India was buying one quarter of Britain's cotton exports. All industrial products shared this fate. The ruin of the traditional trades and crafts was the result of British commercial policy.[9]

The development of the colonial areas was thus held back by the imperialist countries whereas the development of the imperialist countries was greatly speeded by the flow of plunder and profits from the colonies. The exception that proves the rule is Japan. Japan escaped colonialism as a result of several more or less accidental factors. Thus, it was able independently to industrialize and develop its own advanced capitalist economy. Japan achieved this alone among the countries of Asia, Africa, and Latin America because the others had all been reduced to colonies and had their further development prevented.

The half century from 1890 to World War II was the peak period of colonialism, when all the world was divided among the Western European and North American powers. In the late 1940s and 1950s, a new era began, with formal independence achieved by hundreds of millions of people throughout Asia and Africa as a result of struggles fomented by the impact of two world wars, the Russian and Chinese revolutions, and long pent-up pressures for liberation. The day of open colonialism is over, but the pattern still holds by which the ex-colonial countries export food or raw materials. In fact, the less developed countries are often dependent mainly on exports of just one product, and they still import most of their manufactured goods. Foreign investment still dominates their industries. Because of the continuance of the underlying colonial economic pattern, we are justified in describing this situation as *neocolonialism* in spite of formal political independence.

In fact, formal independence has changed the essential economic relationships very little. On the one side are all the less developed, newly independent countries, still under foreign economic domination, still facing all the old obstacles to development. On the other side are

---

[9] Charles Bettleheim, *India Independent* (New York: Monthly Review, 1968), p. 47. Also see Romesh Dutt, *The Economic History of England,* 7th ed. (Boston: Routledge & Kegan Paul, 1950), pp. viii–x.

the advanced capitalist countries, still extracting large profits from the dependent Third World. The imperialist group includes all the countries that extract profits by trade and investment. Thus, it includes most of Western Europe, Japan, and the United States.

Although military power is occasionally used (as in Vietnam), most neocolonial control comes through economic and monetary penetration. This ranges from blatant forms such as subsidies and military supplies to highly complex monetary agreements. It also seems to be characteristic to grant independence to small territories, tiny divisions of former colonial domains. Thus, they have no political or economic power with which to resist continued domination.

It should also be noted that the economic control often is not direct but built up in a complex pyramid. For example, some American companies directly invest in northeast Brazil. More control of that area, however, is achieved through American domination of major southern Brazilian companies, which in turn buy controlling interests in companies in the northeast. Still more control is achieved through American domination of some Western European companies, which in turn own some major Brazilian firms or directly own some of the local firms in the northeast.

INFLATION AND MONOPOLY IN WESTERN EUROPE AND JAPAN

Western Europe and Japan have suffered as much from stagflation, the combination of inflation and stagnant production, as has the United States (though West Germany and Japan encountered stagflation later than the others). The reason these economies perform basically in a similar way in the macrosphere as the U.S. economy is that they have basically similar structural problems (with, of course, many specific differences). By the 1950s, all the leading capitalist countries showed high levels of concentration of output and sales by a few firms in each industry. In Great Britain in the 1950s, for example, the top four firms had the following percentages of total sales in various industries: 91 in explosives, 56 in electric lamps, 73 in distilled liquors, 47 in aircraft, 93 in petroleum refining, and 90 in cement. In Japan the top four firms had the following percentages of total sales in various industries: 65 in electric lamps, 52 in steel ingots, 49 in cement, 98 in beer and ale, 42 in petroleum refining, and 56 in pharmaceutical products. In France, the top four firms had the following percentages of total sales in various industries: 57 in aircraft, 76 in shipbuilding, 72 in petroleum refining, and 53 in cement.[10]

Since the 1950s, concentration has increased in each of the leading capitalist countries. The share of the 100 largest manufacturing firms in all manufacturing output in the United Kingdom rose from 21 percent in 1948 to 38 percent in 1963 to 51 percent in 1970![11] Similarly, in France by 1962 in 56 industrial groups, just 4 firms had over 50 percent of the sales in 21 of these groups. "French industry, since 1962 appears to have a market structure more

---
[10] Joe Bain, *International Differences in Industrial Structure* (New Haven: Yale University Press, 1966), p. 130.
[11] P. Sargent Florence, "Stagflation in Great Britain," in John Blair (ed.), *Roots of Inflation* (New York: Franklin, 1975), p. 88.

concentrated than American industry itself."[12] Finally, in the entire European economic community (excluding the United Kingdom), the share of total output produced by the 50 largest firms was 35 percent in 1960, 35 percent in 1965, and 46 percent in 1970.[13] During the process of integrating several economies in the early 1960s, concentration held steady. When integration was completed in the mid-1960s, however, there was a large number of mergers, and the share of the largest 50 corporations rose rapidly.

Similar industrial structures lead to similar economic behavior and performance. For example, an important study in Japan finds that monopoly prices fluctuate much less than competitive prices, so that, in recessions, monopoly prices in Japan have fallen less (or risen more) than competitive prices.[14] It is, therefore, no surprise that increasing monopoly power in Europe and Japan has helped produce—as in the U.S. economy—the strange phenomenon of inflation in the midst of depression. Of course, this is not the only reason for the new phenomenon, but it is an important one.

There are also plenty of defenders of big business who put the whole blame for Japanese and European stagflation on the workers. One economist makes his class viewpoint very clear: "To put the case bluntly, the British labor movement has been independent, parochial, generally oblivious to modern economic thinking, and moreover, apparently unaware of what policies will serve its own long-run interest, much less that of the general economy."[15] It is easy to see, however, why British labor, like American labor, is oblivious to that "modern economic thinking" that tells it to lower its own wages in its own interest? And since workers are 80 percent to 90 percent of the population, what is the interest of "the general economy" that is different from labor's interest?

There is no good evidence that high wages in Britain—rather than low wages and low demand—have led to Britain's current unemployment and inflation. Moreover, one serious research study shows that a long-run falling profit share in England is a myth and that the profit share (after taxes) in national income was constant from 1950 to 1973.[16] On the contrary, there is plenty of evidence that business monopoly power *has* increased in England.

The increase of business monopoly power in Western Europe is the first factor explaining stagflation there. The second factor is the policy pursued by European governments. In England it is called the *stop and go policy*. At the peak of the cycle, the government tries to stop the rise of wages by direct controls or even by general restrictive policies. In the trough of the depression, the government tries to stimulate the economy, to make profits go upward by various means. These policies, which constitute a political business cycle of capitalism, are likewise pursued by all the other Western European governments.[17] (Of course, during the Thatcher administration, England pursued a drastic policy of cuts in social services and

---

[12]Data and quote from French National Institute of Statistical and Economic Studies, reported in Joel Dirlam, "The Process of Inflation in France," in Blair, *op. cit.,* p. 114.

[13]See H. W. de Jong, "Experience Within the European Economic Community," in Blair, *op. cit.,* p. 187.

[14]Yoshihiro Kobayashi, "Movements of Price and Profit in the Periods of Rapid Growth in the Japanese Economy," *Economic Studies Quarterly* (August 1971), in Japanese.

[15]Florence, *op. cit.,* p. 76.

[16]M. A. King, "The United Kingdom Profits Crisis: Myth or Reality," *The Economic Journal* 85 (March 1975), pp. 33–54.

[17]See the description of the most recent depression policies country by country in "World-wide Depression Policies," *Riverside Press-Enterprise* (September 14, 1975), pp. A2, A4.

restriction of the money supply, which succeeded in pushing unemployment to record heights.)

The third factor explaining stagflation is the international situation. In the following sections, we examine (1) the degree of international concentration by the multinational corporations, (2) the profits extracted by the multinational corporations from developed and less developed capitalist countries, (3) the changing power of the U.S. economy vis-à-vis Western Europe and Japan, (4) the problems of trade balances and supposed shortages caused by these changes, and (5) how international problems worsen stagflation in each country.

CONCENTRATION BY MULTINATIONAL (OR GLOBAL) FIRMS

The new degree of economic concentration of assets in the whole capitalist world by a few enormous multinational or global corporations constitutes a new structural stage of international capitalism. The term *multinational* suggests management from many countries whereas the truth is that each firm is governed mostly by the nationals of one developed capitalist country. The term *global corporation* may be less misleading. The one proposition uniting all these corporations is the notion that the whole globe is their oyster, that vast profits may be made by control of markets in several countries.

In pursuit of profit, U.S.-based global corporations have been rapidly expanding abroad. In terms of total assets of U.S. industries, by 1974 about 40 percent of all consumer goods industries, about 75 percent of the electrical industry, about 33 percent of the chemical industry, about 33 percent of the pharmaceutical industry, and over half of the $100 billion petroleum industry were located outside the United States.[18] Moreover, this expansion trend has increased and perhaps accelerated in recent years. In 1957, investment in plant and equipment by U.S. firms abroad was already 9 percent of total U.S. domestic investment in plant and equipment; but by 1970 that investment abroad rose to 25 percent of domestic investment. In 1961, sales of U.S. manufacturing abroad were only 7 percent of total sales by all U.S. manufacturing corporations, but that figure rose to 13 percent by 1970. In 1960, the foreign dollar deposits of the largest U.S. banks were only 8.5 percent of domestic deposits, but by 1970 foreign deposits rose to 65 percent of domestic deposits.[19]

The pattern of ownership by foreign-owned global corporations is most striking in the less developed countries. In Chile, before Allende's socialist government, global corporations controlled at least 51 percent of the 160 largest firms. In Argentina, global corporations control more than 50 percent of the total sales of the 50 largest firms. In Mexico, global corporations control 100 percent of rubber, electrical machinery, and transportation industries. Moreover, in Mexico, foreign ownership in the metal industry rose from 42 percent in 1962 to 68 percent in 1970, and foreign ownership in tobacco rose from 17 percent in 1962 to 100 percent in 1970. In Brazil, global corporations own 100 percent of automobile and tire production, their share of machinery rose from 59 percent in 1961 to

---

[18] See Richard Barnet and Ronald Muller, *Global Reach* (New York: Simon & Schuster, 1974), p. 17.
[19] Ronald Muller, "Global Corporations and National Stabilization Policy," *Journal of Economic Issues* 9 (June 1975), pp. 183–184.

67 percent in 1971, and their share of electrical equipment rose from 50 percent in 1961 to 68 percent in 1971.[20]

A more complex case is Canada, which invests much money in less developed countries, but is itself largely foreign-owned. Thus, in 1968 in Canada 54 percent of all manufacturing industry was directly owned by foreigners, including 97 percent of automobile production, 97 percent of rubber, 78 percent of chemicals, and 77 percent of electrical apparatus. In addition, foreigners owned 62 percent of mining and smelting and 64 percent of the petroleum and natural gas industry. About 80 percent of the foreign ownership was lodged in U.S.-based global corporations.[21]

It is also important to note that many transactions within and between capitalist countries are conducted solely between subsidiaries of the same parent corporation. A large-scale sample found that over 50 percent of total foreign trade transactions in the capitalist world are of this nonmarket intracorporate variety between subsidiaries of the same company.[22] This means that taxes can be shifted to those countries where the rates are lowest. It also means that fiscal policies may not operate—or may operate mainly to the benefit of the global giants. Several studies show that the global corporations based in the United States absorb a disproportionate part of all government spending and tax reductions designed to stimulate the economy.[23]

The global manufacturing corporations are served by global banks with tentacles almost everywhere. At their urging, additional credit has been created as a new currency, the $110 billion dollar pool of Eurodollars (and the special drawing rights, which act as currency). Since there are no reserve deposit requirements on the Eurodollars, they are particularly unstable and contribute a strong impetus to inflationary pressures by further credit creation. This international credit expansion plus rapid monetary flows between corporate subsidiaries across borders make it less possible than ever for any capitalist nation to control its money supply by any conceivable monetary policies.

It should also be noted that union bargaining power has been further weakened by the power of the global corporations to shift production rapidly from areas of high wages to low wage areas. For example, if the United States has high wages, they shift to Mexico, and if even Mexican wages are considered too high, they shift to Hong Kong.[24]

Finally, the international concentration of investment decision making in a relatively small number of corporations plus the very intimate ties of international trade and investment among all the capitalist countries bind these economies closely together. Therefore, a contraction begun in one country or in just a few global corporations spreads at lightning speed to the others. If investor demand declines in several countries at once, then their import trade in raw materials declines, lowering demand for exports in several other countries. If unemployment rises in several countries at once, then their demand for consumer goods from abroad also declines. Thus the entire capitalist world tends to move in the same direction

---

[20]Barnet and Muller, *op. cit.,* p. 147.
[21]Canadian Privy Council Report, *Task Force on the Structure of Canadian Industry* (Ottawa: Queens Printer, January 1968).
[22]See Muller, *op. cit.,* p. 194.
[23]See *Ibid.,* p. 188 and footnote 6.
[24]See Barnet and Muller, *op. cit.,* chaps. 10 and 11.

in its investment decisions as well as its demands from trading partners. This encourages either explosive expansion amid spiraling optimistic speculations or universal contraction amid a downward spiral of lower profits and pessimism.

Profits and Multinational Firms

The multinational or global firms are the present instrument whereby enormous profits are extracted from the neocolonial countries and sent back to the imperialist countries. U.S. firms' profits from abroad were only 7 percent of total U.S. corporate profits in 1960, but rose to 30 percent by 1974.[25] The top 298 U.S.-based global corporations earn 40 percent of their entire net profits overseas, and their rate of profit from abroad is much higher than their domestic profit rate. In office equipment, for example, the overseas rate was 26 percent; and the domestic rate, only 9 percent. There is dramatic evidence for specific companies: In 1972, the overseas profit rate was 72 percent for United Brands, 51 percent for Parker Pen, and 53 percent for Exxon.[26]

In the neocolonial countries, the global corporations skim off a very large percentage of all profits for themselves. For example, in 1971 in Brazil the global corporations grabbed 70 percent of the total net profits of the five important sectors of rubber, motor vehicles, machinery, household appliances, and mining.[27] Moreover, a considerable part of these corporate investments is not U.S. funds at all, but is provided by local capitalists. In all of the Latin American manufacturing operations of U.S.-based global corporations from 1960 to 1970, about 78 percent of the investments were financed by local funds. Yet the same corporations, between 1965 and 1968, sent 52 percent of all their profits back to the United States.[28]

As a result of the use of local funds for investment, plus high profit rates and the sending of most profits to the United States, the neocolonial or Third World countries actually have a net outflow of capital to the United States. This surprising fact has been documented by the U.S. Department of Commerce for the period 1950–1965, in which there were striking differences in the flow pattern to and from the advanced capitalist countries and to and from the less developed Third World.[29]

U.S. corporations made direct investments of $8.1 billion in Europe and transferred $5.5 billion of profit from their European investments to the United States for a net flow of $2.6 billion (U.S.) into this advanced capitalist area. Similarly, U.S. corporations invested $6.8 billion in Canada and extracted $5.9 billion of profit for a net flow of $900 million (U.S.) into that advanced capitalist area.[30]

In the less developed Third World, the situation was different. In Latin America, U.S. corporations invested $3.8 billion but extracted $11.3 billion for a net flow of $7.5 billion

---

[25]Muller, *op. cit.,* p. 183.
[26]Barnet and Muller, *op. cit.,* pp. 16–17.
[27]*Ibid.,* p. 147.
[28]*Ibid.,* p. 153.
[29]U.S. Department of Commerce, *United States Business Investments in Foreign Countries* (Washington, D.C.: GPO, 1970), p. 85.
[30]*Ibid.,* p. 86.

(U.S.) from that area to the United States. Yet profit rates were so great that at the same time the value of U.S. direct investments in Latin America rose from $4.5 billion to $10.3 billion. In fact, in the period 1957–1964, only 12 percent of direct U.S. investment in Latin America came from the United States; 74 percent was a reinvestment of profits or depreciation funds from Latin American operations. Similarly, in Africa and Asia in the period 1950–1965, American corporations invested only $5 billion but transferred to the United States $14 billion of profits for a net flow of $9 billion to the United States. Yet enough profit remained for reinvestment so that U.S. direct investments in Africa and Asia rose from $1.3 to $4.7 billion.[31]

Two facts are blatantly obvious from these data: (1) The rate of profit in U.S. investments abroad is several times higher in the less developed than in the advanced capitalist countries, and (2) the less developed neocolonial countries generously make a good-sized contribution to U.S. capital accumulation.

Stagflation and the Multinationals

What is the impact on the U.S. economy of the extraordinarily high profits that flow in from the neocolonial countries? When each U.S.-based global firm finds and grabs a new market, its excess investment funds can now be invested abroad. Moreover, the new investment can be expected to yield high profits year after year. The problem is that for the economy as a whole, these new profits pour in from overseas faster than the new investment areas can be found for the mounting funds. This capital accumulation is in excess of the investment opportunities domestically or abroad. Therefore, in a depression the situation is worsened by adding to savings when there is already a surplus of savings beyond what can be invested profitably.

For the less developed Third World countries, the outflow of immense amounts of capital (in the form of profits) is disastrous for their growth and feeds their own peculiar type of stagflation. These neocolonial countries have long suffered the odious combination of inflation and unemployment. In September 1974 inflation rates in the advanced capitalist world averaged a high 12.6 percent, but inflation rates in the less developed capitalist countries averaged 19.1 percent.[32] The rates of unemployment in the less developed capitalist countries have been scandalous for many years, often over 30 or 40 percent of the urban labor force.

To understand their type of stagflation, one must realize that the less developed neocolonial countries suffer from a tremendous lack of capital. This is quite unlike the advanced capitalist countries, who usually suffer from a surplus of capital far beyond the profitable investment opportunities. Lack of capital means not only a small amount of new factory construction, but also little new equipment, very little in research funds, and very slow technological improvement. Lack of capital also means few funds for the education and training of human beings, the most important lack in the long run.

The Third World countries lack capital because of the institutional-structural arrangements within most of them and vis-à-vis the capitalist world. First, most have an internal

---
[31]*Ibid.*, p. 87.
[32]First National City Bank of New York, *Monthly Economic Letter* (September 1974).

ruling class that spends much of its income on luxuries, spends government revenues on unnecessary public monuments or on vast military establishments, and banks much of its wealth in Switzerland or the United States. Second, most of them have very poor terms of trade for large parts of each business cycle because prices of raw materials from the Third World fall much faster in depressions than prices of finished goods from the advanced capitalist world. Thus, in the 1973–1975 depression, prices of most raw materials rose very slowly (with the exception of oil prices) whereas prices of finished goods went sky high.

Finally, as shown earlier, the outflow of profits and interest from the Third World countries is much, much larger than the flow of foreign investment into them. For all these reasons, there is a horrendous lack of plant and equipment, a lack of technological progress, and a lack of highly trained workers.

The lack of plant and equipment means that millions and millions of workers have little or nothing with which to work. Therefore, these millions cannot be profitably employed. Since the rate of profit would be insufficient, these millions of human beings are left unemployed. Because it is due to lack of capital, this unemployment continues even in the face of demand for products and severe shortages leading to inflation.

The stagflation in the less developed capitalist world is thus characterized by lack of capital whereas stagflation in the advanced capitalist world is characterized by surplus capital. This difference is reflected in the fact that mass unemployment of workers in the advanced capitalist countries is accompanied by high rates of nonutilization of capital (idle machines and factories).[33] Mass unemployment of workers in the less developed capitalist countries, on the contrary, often coexists with full utilization of their tiny supply of capital plant and equipment.

Of course, stagflation in the neocolonial countries is worsened by their dependent position. The global corporations generally have little competition and exercise their monopoly power to keep prices of goods within these countries high even during global depressions. Moreover, the global corporations often reduce all their investments during a depression (though not as much as competitive firms must do), but they continue to extract and return to their home countries as much profit as possible throughout the depression, thus intensifying the lack of capital. Finally, it is worth repeating that the raw material products of the Third World suffer the greatest price declines or the smallest price rises in depression periods, so they bear a considerable part of the international burden of the slump.

RISE AND DECLINE OF THE U.S. EMPIRE

Until the Civil War, American capitalism was far behind European capitalism. It had the advantage, however, of having no feudal or semifeudal encumbrances. After the Civil War, it also abolished slavery and opened the whole country to capitalism. Moreover, the U.S. economy was relatively short of labor, so it was forced to use the most advanced technology. As a result, U.S. industrialization proceeded very rapidly after 1870, and it eventually

---

[33] There is a detailed description of the underutilization of capacity in the United States and Western Europe in Ernest Mandel, *Europe vs. America: Contradictions of Imperialism* (New York: Monthly Review, 1970), p. 145.

overtook and passed British and other European industry. Finally, the two world wars devastated much of Europe, but stimulated the U.S. economy. By 1945 the United States emerged completely dominant in the capitalist world.

Between 1945 and 1950 the U.S. gross domestic product (GDP) was equal to that of the whole rest of the world combined. Thus in 1950 the French GDP was only 10 percent of the American; West Germany's, only 8 percent; Italy's, only 5 percent; Japan's, only 4 percent; the United Kingdom's, only 13 percent—and all five only 39 percent of the American GDP. In 1950, the United States produced 82 percent of all the world's passenger vehicles, produced 55 percent of the world's steel production, and consumed 50 percent of the world's energy consumption.[34]

Throughout this period U.S. firms also extended their control over much of European industry. By 1965 American firms or their subsidiaries owned 80 percent of computer production, 24 percent of the motor industry, 15 percent of the synthetic rubber industry, and 10 percent of the production of petrochemicals *within* the entire European Common Market. Furthermore, it is well to remember how concentrated this ownership is. About 40 percent of all U.S. direct investment in Britain, France, and Germany is owned by Ford, General Motors, and Standard Oil of New Jersey.[35]

American firms have maintained a relative superiority over Western European firms because of (1) greater size of capital assets and (2) greater technological advances. The size advantage of U.S. corporations is indicated by the fact that, of the hundred largest global corporations, 65 are based in the United States, 11 in the United Kingdom, 18 in other Common Market nations, and 5 in Japan. Because they have greater size and financial power, U.S. firms are able to do more technological research. Furthermore, the continued enormous U.S. military spending has subsidized much technological research for U.S. firms. U.S. spending on research per capita is still three to four times European research spending. Finally, the United States has drained away many of the best brains in Europe (after they were trained in Europe). Between 1949 and 1967, about 100,000 of the best doctors, scientists and technicians left Western Europe for the United States.[36]

In spite of all these initial and continuing advantages, the absolute superiority of the U.S. economy in world production has slowly faded away. It was restricted and then reduced by three main factors. First, the Soviet Union broke away from the capitalist world in 1917 and has steadily gained on the U.S. economy since the late 1920s. Despite the one awful hiatus of the Second World War, Soviet production now rivals U.S. production in many areas.

Second, the old colonial empires were overthrown at the end of World War II. At first, the new "independent" neocolonial countries turned to the U.S. economy for aid and investment, so U.S. power expanded further. Later, however, wars of liberation (as in Vietnam) spread and were focused against the United States as the main policepower of imperialism.

Finally, as a counterweight to the Communist countries and the increasing resistance of

[34]Albert Syzmanski, "The Decline and Fall of the U.S. Eagle," in David Mermelstein, *The Economic Crisis Reader* (New York: Random House (Vintage Books), 1975), pp. 65–70.
[35]Mandel, *op. cit.,* pp. 22–23.
[36]The data and most of the ideas for this section on "Rise and Decline of the U.S. Empire" come from *ibid.,* pp. 30–43.

Chapter 21 INTERNATIONAL ASPECTS OF INFLATION AND UNEMPLOYMENT

the Third World, the United States was forced to give strong support to the rebuilding of the capitalist economies of Japan and Western Europe. These economies began in 1945 with a skilled labor force but devastated factories. As their industry was rebuilt from scratch, they used the latest technology and began the long march to catch up with the U.S. economy. Whereas the data show that the United States ruled supreme in the early 1950s, it was being challenged by the growing power and competition of Japan and Western Europe in every market by the early 1970s.

The United States was still the largest, but it no longer was far larger than the combination of all the rest. Thus, by 1972 the French gross domestic product (GDP) had risen to 17 percent of American GDP, West Germany's rose to 22 percent, Italy's rose to 10 percent, Japan's rose incredibly to 24 percent, the United Kingdom's to 14 percent—all five of these together now had a GDP equal to 86 percent of American GDP. In specific areas of basic production, the U.S. share of the world total fell between 1950 and 1972 from 82 to 29 percent of passenger vehicles, from 55 to 20 percent of steel production, and from 50 to 33 percent of world energy production. The competitive position of Japan and Western Europe was also strengthened by the fact that their productivity per labor-hour, especially Japanese productivity, rose much faster than U.S. productivity. On the other hand, Japanese and West European wage levels also rose faster than U.S. wage levels, which hurt their competitive position a little, but they are still somewhat lower than U.S. wage levels.[37]

All this has several obvious results. First, U.S. corporations can no longer easily sell excess production abroad, so unemployment is increased. Second, U.S. corporations have lost some degree of control in some of the Third World, so prices of some raw materials—mainly oil—have increased, so inflation is exacerbated. This weakness is also related to the alleged "shortages" discussed in the next section. Third, foreigners have now vastly increased their investments in the U.S. economy. Foreign investments rose to $481 billion or almost half a trillion dollars by 1980.[38] These investments were held 50 percent by West Europeans, 7 percent by Canadians, 7 percent by Japanese, and 21 percent by others, including Middle Easterners. Since profits from these investments fluctuate with the U.S. economy, they also help transmit U.S. depression abroad.

A fourth reflection of the reduced U.S. strength versus West European and Japanese competitors is the deficit in the U.S. balance of payments. In the 1950s, the United States exported vastly more than it imported, so all other countries complained of a "shortage of dollars" whereas the United States had big surpluses. Then the surplus of dollars from exports was used up by (1) huge U.S. investments abroad plus (2) enormous military spending abroad and military aid abroad. When the competition of Europe and Japan reduced the share of U.S. exports in world exports while U.S. imports of oil rose in value, a deficit developed in U.S. payments abroad that has persisted and grown.

---

[37]Syzmanski, *op. cit.,* pp. 66–69.
[38]Data from U.S. Department of Commerce discussed in Karen Tamalty, "Foreigners' Investments in U.S. Rise," *Los Angeles Times* (November 15, 1981), p. 1.

SHORTAGES

International shortages—that is, supply less than demand at present prices—certainly played a part in the inflationary spiral. These shortages, however, were not natural accidents (except in a few minor cases) nor were they acts of God; they were clearly contrived by human actors. In the case of foods and fuels, the two most important categories, conservative economists have blamed Soviet wheat buyers and Arab oil sheikhs.

The evidence, however, indicates that the blame for the oil "shortage" must be placed much closer to home than Arabia. One careful investigator writes indignantly that it is hypocritical to blame the raw material–producing countries for inflation. He stresses the fact that

> The major imperialist powers control the marketing of raw materials—so that even when nationalizations are undertaken, profits are not seriously threatened. But most of the world's raw materials continue to be owned by the major imperialist monopolies, above all by U.S. firms.[39]

For many decades, U.S. and Western European-based multinational corporations controlled all the oil production and made astonishingly high rates of profit. In the late 1960s and early 1970s, it was those global corporations that decided to restrict the expansion of supply—by reducing oil exploration or the building of new refineries—and thereby created an artificial shortage designed to raise prices. The Arab oil embargo was used as an excuse to make rapid price increases.

It is true that in recent years some of the oil-producing countries have taken larger shares of revenue by taxes or even by nationalization. They were able to do this by the increased power of the whole Third World and the Communist countries, so this *does* represent a shift of power that accounts for some small part of the U.S. and Western European inflation. It has meant the rise of a new ruling class in the Arab countries, Iran, and Venezuela that is a peculiar combination of semifeudal attitudes, capitalist production, and some financial capitalist power—though they still act closely in coordination with the multinational corporations to the benefit of both parties.

Nor have the multinational corporations lost much, if anything; they are simply getting some new stockholders and new forms. Most of the production and financing companies in the oil-producing countries are not publicly owned even today (and most other raw materials are purely private). For example, in Kuwait one investment company is 24 percent privately owned, and the other is 50 percent privately owned, with about half the private stock being foreign-owned.[40] But even if production is all nationalized, the fact—as pointed out in the quotation just given—is that the multinational corporations continue to control all the distribution and marketing of oil. Therefore, it is the multinational corporations who set the market prices, determine their profit margins, and continue to make enormous profits.

There are several facts indicating that the Arab oil boycott was nothing more than an excuse for the monopolies to raise prices. First, 60 percent of U.S. oil is produced at home

---

[39]Dick Roberts, "Ripening Conditions For Worldwide Depression," in Mermelstein, *op. cit.*, p. 97.
[40]Ernest Mandel, "The Emergence of Arab and Iranian Finance Capital," in Mermelstein, *op. cit.*, p. 316.

and is unaffected by Arab production costs, yet the price of U.S. crude oil rose from $3.50 to $7.00 a barrel. Second, from March 1973 to March 1974, Arab oil producers raised their taxes by 17 cents a barrel, but U.S. gasoline prices rose almost 30 cents a gallon for all gas, regardless of origin. Third, the U.S. government allows the oil companies to deduct all payments to foreign governments from their U.S. taxes, so this cost was passed on to all other U.S. taxpayers (in addition to passing it on to consumers at the pump). Finally, the minute the embargo was over, the companies suddenly found large reserves of oil on hand, so they didn't need to buy any more, but did not lower the prices.[41]

The high price of U.S. food was blamed on a shortage created by sales to the Soviet Union. Yet the main blame seems to fall on agribusiness and the U.S. government. First of all, for many years the U.S. government paid large farm subsidies to get farmers *not* to plant food over large areas of the best farmland. "As late as 1973, after the shortages of 1972, the government was still paying over $3 billion to keep roughly 50 million productive acres out of farming use."[42] Then, when deficits in the balance of payments became a problem, the U.S. government reversed itself and tried to stimulate production, not for domestic consumption, but for exports. The government encouraged the export of food as fast and as fully as possible in order to get foreign currency to pay for U.S. investment and military spending abroad. Thus, exports of U.S. food on the world market tripled between 1969 and 1973 as a result of careful planning by agribusiness and the government.[43] Of this enormous planned outflow of food for profit, the Soviet wheat deal formed a very minor part even of the sales of wheat.

SUMMARY

In conclusion, the inflation and the so-called shortages have several not surprising bases. The inflation was not caused by accidental natural calamities because these tend to even out over a few years' time. The inflation, however, has not evened out, but has picked up over some years. A small part was caused by a shift in power toward the Arab ruling classes away from the oil companies. But this was fairly minor and cannot account for the long inflation. Most of the inflation and "shortages" were caused by the multinational monopolies.

In the next part of this book, we shall see that the U.S. government began the inflation by spending for the Vietnam War and made it worse by the continued outflow of money for domestic military purchases and for military aid abroad.

---

[41] Dave Pugh and Mitch Zimmerman, "The 'Energy Crisis' and the Real Crisis Behind It," in Mermelstein, *op. cit.*, pp. 278–279.
[42] Union for Radical Political Economics, National Food Collective, "The Capitalist Food System," in Mermelstein, *op. cit.*, p. 351.
[43] *Ibid.*, p. 359.

Part Six

THE ROLE OF GOVERNMENT

Chapter 22

THE ENDOGENOUS SHAPING OF GOVERNMENT POLICIES

All books on macroeconomics discuss the impact of government on the economy. Before one can discuss that subject intelligently, however, it is necessary first to have a theory of how the socioeconomic system shapes the government. Only when the motivations and interests behind the behavior of government are understood can one integrate government into the entire model of the macroeconomic system.

Unfortunately, there are three different views among economists (and political scientists) concerning how the U.S. government is shaped and operates. So this chapter must begin by stating each of these three views in some depth: the conservative, liberal, and radical views. Most books on macroeconomics do not state explicitly even their own view, but it becomes crucial as their implicit and unstated assumption. Complete chapters on fiscal, monetary, and wage and price control policy will follow.

CONSERVATIVE VIEW OF GOVERNMENT

Implicit in almost all conservative and liberal books on macroeconomics is the view that the U.S. government intends to operate in the best interests of all U.S. citizens. For example, if welfare payments to the poor are reduced, conservatives claim it is necessary to reduce inflation. Inflation hurts the poor more than anyone, so cutting welfare benefits to the poor is in the best interests of the poor. The job of economists is to tell the government what is the most rational thing to do in everyone's best interests—and the government will do it to the best of its ability. In this sense, government actions are determined by rational thinking;

they are *not* shaped by the socioeconomic system itself, so they are exogenous to any economic model.

This view of government is based on the usually implicit assumption that our government under capitalism is a perfect democracy in which each person's views carry equal weight. Milton Friedman, in his *Capitalism and Freedom*,[1] makes explicit his assumption that the economic system of capitalism tends to produce a perfect political democracy. Friedman contends that the capitalist system is an economic democracy because anyone can start a business and because consumers vote with their dollars on what shall be produced. This economic democracy of capitalism is the perfect base for a political democracy because it does away with all interfering bureaucrats. Thus, the United States enjoys a political democracy based on capitalism. Every citizen has an equal vote. Every citizen has an equal right to publish a newspaper or own a TV station without interference or censorship.

The Friedman position has frequently been criticized. "Anyone" cannot start a business in the United States because most people do not have the capital to start a business. Consumers vote with their dollars, but consumers with a million dollars outvote consumers with a thousand dollars by a thousand times! Consumer votes reflect the enormous inequality of our society, so a few can "vote" successfully for mink coats and Cadillacs whereas many do not have enough votes for sufficient milk and shoes for their children.

Less than 1 percent of Americans control a majority of corporate stock. One thousand corporations control two-thirds of corporate assets. Those thousand corporations make most of the economic decisions in the United States on hiring and firing workers, what products to produce, where to locate, and what prices to charge. Those thousand corporations are controlled by boards of directors that are mostly old, white, and male. Most directors are on several boards, so the total number of directors on these boards constitute a remarkably small number of decision makers. In this sense, the United States is an economic oligarchy, a small number of decision makers selected only because of their wealth.

Moreover, this economic oligarchy has *not* produced a perfect democracy. Although all citizens may have a vote, their political power is *not* equal, but is weighted by their wealth, as described in detail later. Nor is there equal freedom of the press. Most citizens can *not* publish a newspaper or own a TV station because this requires millions of dollars. Thus, it will be argued that capitalist economic power places severe limitations on political democracy, even in the few capitalist countries where the forms exist.

As evidence that capitalism leads to political democracy, conservatives like Friedman argue that political democratic forms do exist in the capitalist countries of North America, Western Europe, and Japan. They repeat the fact that the so-called socialist countries of Eastern Europe, the Soviet Union, China, and Cuba, have undemocratic forms of government. They ignore, however, the contrary evidence. *The overwhelming majority of all capitalist countries are political dictatorships.* These countries—mostly developing countries in Asia, Africa, and Latin America—are either military dictatorships or one-party dictatorships. These capitalist countries with dictatorships, such as Chile, are no more democratic than many so-called socialist countries, such as China. There have also been dictatorships in

---

[1]Milton Friedman, *Capitalism and Freedom* (Chicago: University of Chicago Press, 1957).

developed capitalist countries, such as Japan, Germany, and Italy. Moreover, there are some countries with self-defined socialist governments, such as France or Sweden, that have democratic political processes.

Conservatives like Milton Friedman do make some major exceptions to the rule that the U.S. government serves the best interests of everyone. Government makes many mistakes. For example, government may reduce the money supply, causing the Great Depression of the 1930s, and may repeat this mistake periodically, causing recessions. Or government may increase the money supply too rapidly over many years, causing inflation. The mistakes are usually made by misguided liberals. Liberals act for political gain based on the short-run interest of corrupt unions or of the lazy unemployed. Conservative economists claim that the actions of liberal governments hurt everyone in the long run, including even union members and the unemployed (e.g., by easy money leading to inflation).

It is natural for conservatives to think that misguided government itself is the cause of most macroeconomic problems because they believe (1) Adam Smith's theory that competition in the market produces the highest quality, the best mix, the most productivity, and the most growth and (2) Say's law that in an unregulated market aggregate demand must always adjust to aggregate supply in the private sector. As everyone knows, this results in their view that the best government role in the economy is *no* government role. One should note, however, that there are many, many exceptions, including a huge military complex, a large police force, harsh sentences for not following social dictates (e.g., smoking marijuana), prohibiting some choices (e.g., women's choice of abortion), punishment for dissenting views (e.g., anti-Communist oaths), welfare payments to business (e.g., subsidies), and correction of liberal mistakes (e.g., cutting government spending and taxes or reducing the growth of the money supply). The economic exceptions, which allow conservative governments to practice a great deal of active intervention, are discussed in detail in the next chapter.

THE LIBERAL VIEW: KEYNESIANS AND PLURALISTS

Liberal economists like John Maynard Keynes have seldom considered what motivates government activity. As a result, liberal economists have tended to accept the naive view that government economic activity is devoted to the best interests of everyone. Liberal economists tend to reject the extreme Adam Smith view, and they reject Say's law, so they do believe there are many inequities and many macro problems generated by capitalism. They fervently hope and believe, however, that government can and will solve these problems.

In the liberal view, Herbert Hoover simply lacked the knowledge of how to eliminate unemployment, which liberal economists can now furnish the government. Liberal economists, therefore, tend to be much greater defenders of the virtues of government and its programs than are conservative economists. They implicitly accept the popular American myth that the U.S. government results from a perfect democracy and serves the best interests of everyone. If pushed, they will agree that some politicians (like Ronald Reagan) serve "special interests." They strongly defend the notion, however, that all such "political" problems should be left to political scientists (in spite of the all-important role of government in the U.S. economy) and should not be considered by economic theory.

The dominant school in American political science is the *pluralist* school. It is a liberal viewpoint, but somewhat more sophisticated with regard to government than the typical view of liberal economists. The pluralists assert that the U.S. government is not a class dictatorship but a democracy reflecting many different interest groups, that power is not held by one group but plurally by many groups. They assert that the "power structure of the United States is highly complex and diversified (rather than unitary and monolithic), that the political system is more or less democratic . . . , that in political processes the political elite is ascendant over and not subordinate to the economic elite . . ."[2] Notice that in arguing for the proposition that America is democratic in nature, the pluralists find it necessary to emphasize that political power is *to a large degree* independent of and superior to economic power. The reason for this insistence is that economic power is so extremely unequally distributed. If political power exactly followed economic power, the degree of inequality would leave little to be called "democracy."

The interest groups discussed by the pluralists are very different from the classes discussed by Marxists. Pluralists have a long list of interest groups, including not only rich and poor, debtors and creditors, unions and big business, but also advocates of gun control and the National Rifle Association, women's rights groups and antifeminist groups, Protestants, Jews, Catholics, and so forth. The pluralist view is that all of these compete in the political arena. The democratic process chooses representatives from among them all according to their success with the voters. The resulting government compromises and reconciles all the competing interests.

For those pluralists who stop at this point, it is a complex way of arriving at almost the same conclusion as the simplistic view that the U.S. government serves everyone's interests. Most sophisticated pluralists, however, do go somewhat further. They ask why one group is more successful than another. Most of those asking this question more or less agree that economic power has something to do with the political results. Some of these political scientists then edge closer to a Marxist position.

THE RADICAL OR MARXIST VIEW

Radicals recognize that one cannot study political power without studying economic power, and vice versa. The most vulgar and dogmatic Marxists go to the other extreme, arguing that economics determines everything and that politics is completely subordinate. They love to quote one line that Marx and Engels wrote in *The Communist Manifesto:* "The executive power of the modern state is simply a committee for managing the common affairs of the entire bourgeois class." In the literal, dogmatic interpretation, this statement says that freedom of speech does *no* good, that elections can change nothing, that workers can have *no* influence and can achieve *no* major reforms in capitalism.

---

[2]Arnold Rose, *The Power Structure* (New York: Oxford University Press, 1967), p. 492. A powerful critique of pluralism and complete alternative view is presented in Charles Lindblom, *Politics and Markets* (New York: Basic Books, 1977).

Chapter 22 THE ENDOGENOUS SHAPING OF GOVERNMENT POLICIES

Marx himself had a very sophisticated and complex view of political sociology.[3] It is a view quite different from some of the vulgarized versions that often pass for Marxism. Where vulgar Marxists usually speak of only two classes fighting for political power, every one of Marx's own analyses—including detailed political studies of France, England, Germany, and the United States—specified numerous subclasses, remnants of classes, in-between or middle classes, and strife between factions of a single class. Where vulgar Marxists assume that capitalist governments bear a one-to-one relation to the economic interest of "the capitalist class," Marx shows that governments do have a certain limited autonomy from the dominant class and that politics represent a tangled skein of long-run and short-run interests of a wide variety of different classes and different factions within classes.

To begin with, Marx argues that there are two sides to the origin and functioning of the state. He uses the term *the state* to mean all the power structures of government (everything from the police functions to the propaganda functions of "public relations" personnel). Marx contends that one source of the origin of state power was the need for control of some common functions in the interest of the whole community; for example, in ancient Egypt it was necessary to control the Nile and irrigation. A second source of the origin of state power was the need by the ruling class, as in ancient Egypt, to hold down and repress the slave class in order to exploit the slave's labor. All U.S. government functions today still have these two aspects: common functions for the community and class functions for the ruling class. For example, the building of highways serves the whole community, but the question of which highways and how many highways is largely determined by the profit goals of the automobile industry and the construction industry (both of which maintain huge lobbies at the federal and state levels).

Marx was also very critical of theorists who insist that there always has been and always will be an elite of rulers and an oppressed mass of ruled. Marx and Engels were among the first to take seriously the findings of anthropology that many primitive societies are built around the extended family or clan, have no government in the modern sense, and certainly no police or other repressive forces. Marx said that this absence of a repressive state was due to the fact that there was no class division. People were elected for temporary leadership of community functions, but there was no need for repression because there was no exploited class.

The goal of Marxists is a communist society in which there will again be no classes, no ruling elite, voluntary cooperation by all, and no repressive state machinery. As the first step in this direction, Marx advocated democratic socialism as the only consistent form of democracy. He pointed out that capitalist states have the forms of democracy in the political sphere, but that the dictatorship of a small number of capitalists in the economic sphere extends their power in substance to the political sphere as well. Socialism means a society of democracy

---

[3] Marx's views, critique of other views, and applications to the present reality are presented in Albert Szymanski, *The Capitalist State and the Politics of Class* (Cambridge, Mass.: Winthrop, 1978); also Hal Draper, *Karl Marx's Theory of Revolution* (New York: Monthly Review, 1977); also Shlomo Avineri, *The Social and Political Thought of Karl Marx* (Cambridge: Cambridge University Press, 1968); also Ralph Miliband, *The State in Capitalist Society* (New York: Basic Books, 1969); also G. William Domhoff, *Who Rules America?* (Englewood Cliffs, N.J.: Prentice-Hall, 1967).

in substance as well as in form because the democratically elected government will own and control the economy. This direction over the lives of the people is taken away from a few capitalists and exercised by all of the people (that is, the working class).

Vulgar Marxists argue as if the capitalist class directly runs the government of capitalist countries. Marx, on the contrary, emphasized that the actual day-to-day running of the government is usually left to a specialized group (politicians, employed in the same way that engineers are employed) and that capitalist control is indirect. Nor is the control exercised by a conspiracy, but by the built-in structural features of the whole system and its institutions. Marx emphasized in his writings a long list of means by which capitalists and the capitalist state exercise control. These means are mostly indirect and mostly accomplished by peaceful propaganda and economic means.

The radical view emphasizes that economic inequality does lead to political inequality. The institutions of the United States are democratic in form but not in content because of differences in economic power. Thus, a millionaire owning a newspaper chain has only the same formal political rights as an unemployed poor worker, but surely their actual political influence is very different. One careful study discovers "the existence of a national upperclass that meets generally accepted definitions of social class . . . that this upperclass owns a disproportionate amount of the country's wealth and receives a disproportionate amount of its yearly income, and that [its] members . . . control the major banks and corporations, which . . . dominate the American economy . . . that [its] members . . . and their high-level corporation executives control the foundations, the elite universities, the largest of the mass media, . . . the Executive branch of the federal government . . . regulatory agencies, the federal judiciary, the military, the CIA, and the FBI."[4]

The Importance of Class

The radical hypothesis is that (1) class interests play a major role in political behavior; (2) the most powerful economic class, the capitalist class, dominates the political system; (3) most of those elected are capitalists or, more importantly, subservient to capitalist interests; and (4) the outcomes of the political process are mostly favorable to the capitalist class because of (a) their domination of the process and (b) the structural features that set the limits of policy. But assertions are not proof. A full-scale attempt at proof from primary sources would add one more thick book to the many already written on the subject—and the "facts" would still be controversial. Instead, in the following brief sections we use as "facts" the statements in a widely used pluralist text by Marian Irish and James Prothro,[5] which in turn is based on all the standard pluralist references.

Membership in a class may be defined roughly according to the relationship a group has to the means of production, that is, plant and equipment. Capitalists are that group that own the means of production. Workers do not own any of the means of production (or very little of them), but are paid a wage for working with the means of production to produce products,

---

[4]G. William Domhoff, *Who Rules America?* (Englewood Cliffs, N.J.: Prentice-Hall, 1967), pp. 10–11.
[5]Marian D. Irish and James W. Prothro, *The Politics of American Democracy* (Englewood Cliffs, N.J.: Prentice-Hall, 1965).

Chapter 22 THE ENDOGENOUS SHAPING OF GOVERNMENT POLICIES

which are sold by the capitalists. While using this as a first approximation, keep in mind in this section that many social and psychological factors may also affect class identity (or at least self-identification).

The standard text by Irish and Prothro, summarizing a great deal of empirical data, says that "class, whether determined by personal feelings or by educational and occupational status, is an essential concept for understanding political differences."[6] Of course, a great many other socioeconomic factors affect political differences, including racial and religious background, friends and community, union membership (obviously related to class), and family tradition and upbringing in one political ideology or party affiliation. Family influence has been shown in a study that found that 80 percent of American voters cast their first vote for the same party as their parents did.[7] Furthermore, the amount of education, which is partly determined by class, has a striking effect on opinions, changing them quite significantly.[8]

Class affects political behavior in many ways, of which the most obvious is voting behavior. A leading liberal sociologist writes: "More than anything else the party struggle is a conflict among classes, and the most impressive single fact about political party support is that in virtually every economically developed country the lower income groups vote mainly for parties of the left, while the higher income groups vote mainly for parties of the right."[9] In fact, class background goes beyond voting patterns to affect the entire political outlook. Class differences cut across regional and other lines. Thus, "the banker in California has more in common with another banker in New England than he has with a fruitpicker in his own county."[10]

In the late 1940s, a pioneering study (confirmed many times since) based social class on the respondent's own self-identification.[11] On this basis of "class consciousness" it was found that, on social welfare issues, class makes a vast difference. In the self-defined "upper" class, 42 percent were ultraconservative; and another 24 percent, conservative. In the self-defined "middle" class, ultraconservatism declined to 35 percent, but conservatism was a huge 33 percent. In the self-defined "working" class, ultraconservatism was only 12 percent; conservatism, 23 percent. In the self-defined "lower" class, ultraconservatism was far less than 1 percent; conservatism, 23 percent, and radicalism and ultraradicalism were 46 percent!

Just how class conscious are people, and how many people think of themselves as working class? Popular polls, such as Gallup, always report 80 or 90 percent of Americans consider themselves "middle class." But these polls use loaded questions and have many other inaccuracies. Therefore, much careful research on the issue "tells quite a different story."[12] In a 1964 study, 56 percent said they thought of themselves as working class! Some 39 percent considered themselves middle class. (It is true, though, that 35 percent of all those questioned

---

[6] Irish and Prothro, *op. cit.,* p. 175.
[7] *Ibid.,* p. 170.
[8] *Ibid.,* p. 174.
[9] Seymour Lipset, *Political Man* (Garden City, N.Y.: Doubleday (Anchor Books), 1963), p. 234.
[10] Irish and Prothro, *op. cit.,* p. 242.
[11] R. Centers, reported in Irish and Prothro, *op. cit.,* p. 174.
[12] Irish and Prothro, *op. cit.,* p. 37.

said they had never thought of their class identification before that moment.) In addition, 1 percent said they were upper class. And only 2 percent rejected the whole idea of class.[13]

How Economic Power Determines Political Results

We have seen that an individual's political behavior is strongly influenced by class background. But that leads to a puzzle. If a majority identify with the working class and everyone has one vote, how is it that parties favorable to the working class don't win every election? How come government policies usually do not represent working class desire, but the overwhelming influence of the capitalist class? More precisely, given formal democracy and capitalism, exactly how does the extreme economic inequality tend to be translated into inequality of political power?

In the first place, there is the simple fact that the degree of political participation tends to vary with class background. "The average citizen has little interest in public affairs, and he expends his energy on the daily round of life—eating, working, family talk, looking at the comics [today, TV], sex, sleeping."[14] More exactly, in a 1964 study, 86 percent of those identified as middle class voted, but only 72 percent of the working class voted (and that percentage has declined since then). Similarly, 40 percent of the middle class had talked to others about voting for a party or candidate, but only 24 percent in the working class had. Among the middle class people interviewed, 16 percent gave money to a political cause, 14 percent attended political meetings, and 8 percent worked for a party or candidate; in the working class, figures on the same activities were only 4, 5, and 3 percent.[15]

Thus, political participation of all kinds rises in the higher income groups and drops in the working class. Some of the reasons are obvious. Lower income workers have less leisure time, less money above minimum needs, and more exhausting jobs. Furthermore, detailed studies show that the workers' lower participation also reflects less knowledge of how important the issues are because of (1) less education and (2) less access to information. The same studies show more "cross pressures" on workers—for example, the racial antagonisms that conveniently divide and weaken their working class outlook.[16]

Second, unequal political power is also achieved by control of the "news" media. Even if the average worker "had an interest in politics, he would have great difficulty getting accurate information; since the events of politics unfold at a great distance, he cannot observe them directly, and the press offers a partial and distorted picture."[17] Even the quantity of news is limited. Although 80 percent of Americans read newspapers and 88 percent have TV, political news is only 2.8 percent of total newspaper space and less on TV.[18]

The quality of political news is worse than its quantity. The first problem is that only one view is available to most people because of the increasing concentration of newspaper ownership. In 1910 some 57 percent of American cities had competing daily newspapers, but in

---

[13] *Ibid.*, p. 38.
[14] *Ibid.*, p. 165.
[15] *Ibid.*, p. 38.
[16] *Ibid.*, p. 193.
[17] *Ibid.*, p. 165.
[18] *Ibid.*, p. 183.

1980 only 3 percent had competing dailies! Furthermore, news media tend to have a conservative bias for three reasons. First, they do not want to offend anybody. Second, they especially do not want to offend major advertisers, all of whom are big businesses. Third, and most important, "since the media of communication are big businesses, too, the men who control them quite naturally share the convictions of other businessmen."[19]

A third factor in favor of unequal political power is the vast difference in the influence of different pressure groups according to their economic power. Thus, the standard text by Irish and Prothro says that status is the most important factor in determining the influence of a pressure group. After listing other sources of status, they conclude: "Finally, since status is so closely tied to money in the United States, the group with greater status will almost automatically be able to command greater financial resources. And it costs money to engage in pressure politics..."[20] Of course, pressure groups employ lobbyists who persuade and bribe members of Congress as well as those in the executive branch, including presidents. The largest lobbies in Washington represent the military contractors and the oil companies. Yet lobbying is nowhere near as important as other means mentioned here (such as control of the media).

Furthermore, advertising is now a vital component of politics: "... Pressure groups ... are now spending millions of dollars every year on *mass propaganda*. Not only broad groups like the National Association of Manufacturers, but even individual companies maintain elaborate bureaucracies to sell 'correct' ideas on general policy questions along with favorable attitudes to the company."[21] The largest amount of political contributions now comes from political action committees (PACs), mostly set up by corporations.

The vast amount of business advertising reinforces the general ethos of capitalism. It says that material luxuries are the highest priority, and implies that everyone can have them. A certain percentage of advertising is also specifically devoted to political issues, as we saw earlier. Yet all advertising is counted as a "cost," so it can be deducted from income when computing taxes! Of course, labor unions are not allowed this tax deduction for political advertising.

Specifically, the unequal distribution of economic power means a very unequal distribution of the power to control political parties and their choice of nominees, as well as to influence elections. Thus, in America upper income classes have a very disproportionate power in campaigns. Two other pluralist writers state that "because campaigns are exceedingly costly, the wealthier a person is, the more strategic his position for bringing pressure to bear on politicians. . . . When it is remembered that a campaign for a congressional seat can easily cost $15,000 to $25,000, and a senatorial campaign can cost half a million dollars or more, it is not difficult to see why 'money talks.' "[22]

There is nothing new about this situation. In 1900, Senator Boise Penrose said to a meeting of business people: "I believe in a division of labor. You send us to Congress: we pass laws

---

[19] *Ibid.*, p. 184.
[20] *Ibid.*, p. 245.
[21] *Ibid.*, p. 249.
[22] Robert Dahl and Charles Lindblom, *Politics, Economics, and Welfare* (New York: Harper & Row, 1953), pp. 313, 315.

under . . . which you make money; . . . and out of your profits you further contribute to our campaign funds to send us back again to pass more laws to enable you to make more money."[23] The only thing that has changed is the amounts of money involved.

By 1980, many candidates for the House of Representatives were spending over $500,000; and many candidates for the Senate, over $3 million! In total in the 1980 election, $250 million was spent in the presidential campaign, and $300 million was spent electing people to Congress, including $60 million spent directly by corporate political action committees.[24] Moreover, the influence of money on elections has become still more crude and obvious as politicians hire professional advertising or public relations firms to campaign for them. Whom you can hire and how much they will do depends on how much money you are willing to spend.

Another line of control of considerable importance in the modern United States are the private foundations, which spend money to support education and research. Naturally, the big businesspeople who set them up have some say over the content of the education, propaganda, and research on which their money is spent. Moreover, many of these foundations get direct help from government, at least in their beginnings, and many of them are closely connected with the espionage and "intelligence" network.[25]

Finally, the fact that upper income groups exercise a disproportionate political power naturally allows them to use the government itself to increase their power further. In a later section we shall examine these political feedback effects on political behavior and the economic structure. They include such things as the educational system, the police, the army, "intelligence" services, and even the announcements of the president. Also not to be overlooked is the effect on people's political behavior by the control over their jobs, both private and public.

CLASS BACKGROUND OF POLITICAL LEADERS

Because of their disproportionate political influence, upper income individuals of the capitalist class have a disproportionate percentage of the top political positions. From 1789 to 1934, fathers of U.S. presidents and vice-presidents were 38 percent professionals, 20 percent proprietors and officials, 38 percent farm owners, and only 4 percent wage earners or salaried workers.[26] Similarly, fathers of U.S. senators in the period from 1947 to 1951 were 22 percent professionals, 33 percent proprietors and officials, 40 percent farm owners, and only 4 percent wage earners or salaried workers. By 1978, there were 21 millionaires in the U.S. Senate. Finally, fathers of members of Congress (House of Representatives) in the period 1941–1943 were 31 percent professionals, 31 percent proprietors and officials, 29 percent farm owners,

---

[23] Quoted in Mark Green et al., *Who Runs Congress?* (New York: Bantam, 1972), pp. 7–8.
[24] See Terence Smith, "If Nothing Else, Recent Campaign Was at Least the Costliest," based on Federal Election Commission reports, *Riverside Press-Enterprise* (November 27, 1980), p. B6.
[25] David Wise and Thomas B. Ross, *The Invisible Government* (New York: Random House, 1964), passim.
[26] Irish and Prothro, *op. cit.*, p. 39.

and only 9 percent wage earners or salaried workers.[27] By 1978, at least 153 members of Congress (House of Representatives) owned corporate stock worth over $100,000.

In the executive branch, aside from the president and vice-president, upper income business-oriented individuals have had a majority of all the important positions throughout U.S. history. This includes the members of the cabinet, their assistants and department heads, and heads of most regulatory agencies. They quite naturally, with no conspiracy, tend to consult big businesspeople and groups as experts (such as the Committee for Economic Development or the Council on Foreign Relations). Wealthy families have also contributed a majority of our federal judges, top military men, and top leaders of "intelligence agencies." Last, we may note that there is much crossing-over at the top: ex-generals often get to be corporate executives, and corporate executives often get to be cabinet members.

THE STRUCTURAL BASES OF CONTROL

Unlike the vulgar notion of a conspiracy by a small number of nasty capitalists, we have emphasized that the very structure of capitalism means that wealthy capitalists have the means to hire most lobbyists, to do most advertising, to make the largest political contributions needed to buy candidates, and—quite naturally—control the flow of information in the press, the radio, and on television. *In addition, the capitalist structure constrains the policy options of any government,* even one elected with a strongly working-class base and honest intentions.

For example, when Chrysler Corporation started to go bankrupt in 1980, the U.S. government gave it a welfare handout in the form of loan guarantees. If public ownership is ruled out as a solution, then the only thing to do with a large corporation going bankrupt is to put it on public welfare. The alternative is a large downward pull on the economy. It is not surprising that a capitalist-oriented government rode to the rescue (though Chrysler's competitors did *not* cheer the action). What seems at first glance to be a surprise is that the lobbying in favor of welfare to Chrysler was led by a very liberal union, the United Auto Workers. Yet if a socialist solution is ruled out, the UAW position makes good sense. If Chrysler goes down the drain, tens of thousands of UAW would lose their jobs. Given the reality of heavy unemployment under capitalism, there is no guarantee that they would soon get other jobs.

This case could be multiplied a thousand times. Very liberal members of Congress and very liberal unions frequently support welfare in the form of subsidies to corporations in their localities. For example, all the liberals in Congress from Hawaii support subsidies to the sugar companies in order to keep jobs for sugar workers. Some unions resist environmental controls for corporations in their industry because of fear of losing jobs. These are real political facts of life, and cannot be changed as long as the structure of capitalism exists.

Even where a government, such as the socialist government of Allende in Chile, was

[27] *Ibid.,* p. 39.

committed to ending capitalism, the structural facts are a barrier to transition. As soon as some part of industry was nationalized, a great deal of capital fled the country with a naturally depressing effect.

These structural constraints apply very strongly and clearly in the realm of macroeconomic policy. John Maynard Keynes stressed the need for "business confidence" to maintain investment and get out of a depression. Business confidence is achieved by policies that give tax cuts to business, shift income distribution toward the wealthy, cut spending programs that would help the poor, restrict union wage increases, and so forth. Given the structure of capitalism, it is perfectly true that there will be no new investment—and consequently high unemployment—if business is not confident of making profits. High profit rates are the only road to prosperity under capitalism—but we must remember that this requires policies designed not only for high rates of exploitation of workers, but also policies to ensure that workers have enough income to buy the mass of commodities embodying the high profits.

QUALIFICATIONS TO THE CLASS ANALYSIS

So far, we have stated the radical thesis that (1) class differences determine much of political behavior, that (2) the wealthy capitalist class has a disproportionate amount of political power, to the extent that (3) it occupies or controls most key political positions, and that (4) the structural features of capitalism put narrow constraints on policy, forcing it to be procapitalist. Now we must turn to some other very definite qualifications to this thesis.

First, although the capitalist class has a strong influence on Congress, the Congress is not fully controlled or dominated by the capitalist class. The direct representation of the capitalist class is disproportionate, but still a small minority.[28] Influence must rather be exerted indirectly through pressure from the executive branch, paid lobbyists, and big campaign contributions to the parties and candidates. Second, although strongly influenced by the capitalist class, most state governments and most city governments are not controlled or dominated directly by that class.[29]

Third, although the old middle class of independent small-farm owners, small businesspeople, and self-employed artisans is no longer the vast majority, but only a tiny percentage of the labor force, U.S. society has *not* polarized into two classes with no middle. In addition to low-paid manual workers, there is a very large and growing percentage of high-paid technical workers—"a new working class" (or "new middle class" if you prefer) of engineers and teachers and such.[30] Even though they are workers in a purely economic sense, they see themselves mostly as middle class, and their political behavior follows that pattern to some extent. On the other hand, teachers and even college professors are now organizing and even striking in some places, so the behavior of at least some of the new working class approximates that of the old working class rather than the old middle class.

Fourth, although the capitalist class controls some areas of government and strongly

---

[28] See, e.g., Domhoff, *op. cit.*, pp. 111–114.
[29] *Ibid.*, pp. 132–137.
[30] C. Wright Mills, *White Collar* (New York: Oxford University Press, 1956).

influences others, "the control is not complete; other groups sometimes have their innings, particularly when these groups are well organized and angry."[31] Thus, farmers won reforms in the late nineteenth century against monopoly pressures, and angry workers won many reforms in the New Deal of the 1930s. The power of numbers and *organization* can defeat the power of money in some extraordinary circumstances.

Fifth, there is disagreement and factionalism within the capitalist class. "Nor is the power elite always united in its politics; there are long-standing disagreements between its moderate and conservative wings..."[32] They disagree partly because of opposed interests. Thus, most large corporations benefit from and favor military spending, but a significant minority does not benefit from it and is opposed to much military spending. The large corporations also have major tactical disagreements over the best way to handle current macro problems.

Sixth, business people and those who follow their view in government do not always have a perfect grasp of their own best interests: "... To read case studies of specific decisions is to be aware that lack of information, misunderstandings, and personality clashes may lead to mistakes on issues that must be decided in a hurry."[33] Thus, no one should predict that government policy will always represent an optimal solution from the capitalist view.

Seventh, critics of the class analysis sometimes point out that in America there are real conflicts over policies, that decisions are made by shifting coalitions, that these coalitions usually include some worker or farmer organization. True, but "the shifting coalitions are dominated ... by members of the American upperclass."[34] Thus, one cannot simply say that a certain small capitalist group decides government policy. On the contrary, there appear to be several conflicting capitalist groups, and some of them are loosely allied with some farmer or worker groups. But the ruling coalition does always end up dominated by a major capitalist group—though, as in the New Deal, it may have to grant many reforms to its coalition partners.

Eighth, another qualification to the class analysis is that "most businessmen are not part of the group that controls the government."[35] Certainly, most businesspeople are small businesspeople and have little, if any more, power than workers or farmers. A ruling coalition may sometimes include small business, but it is usually dominated by a small group of big capitalists. In fact, the U.S. economy is dominated by very large corporations, exercising vast amounts of monopoly power. In this era of monopoly there is extreme concentration of income, wealth, ownership of the means of propaganda ... and political power. Two liberal economists comment that "with every advance of monopoly toward greater economic power and more social acceptance, the federal government becomes more subservient to it, more dependent on it."[36]

Last, the political behavior of individuals is guided at any given time by many factors besides pure economic motivations. A politician may simply be power-hungry rather than

---

[31]G. William Domhoff, in Domhoff and Ballard (eds.), *C. Wright Mills and the Power Elite* (Englewood Cliffs, N.J.: Prentice-Hall, 1969), p. 277.
[32]*Ibid.*, p. 277.
[33]*Ibid.*, p. 277.
[34]*Ibid.*, p. 3.
[35]*Ibid.*, p. 154.
[36]Walter Adams and Horace Gray, *Monopoly in America* (New York: Macmillan, 1962), p. 35.

consciously acting in favor of class interest. If a white male worker is infected with racism, he may vent his anger at bad conditions against black workers rather than against the capitalist owner. Yet it may be that both power drives and racism themselves can be ultimately explained by the socioeconomic structure.

FEEDBACK MECHANISMS OF CONTROL

We have seen how—with many qualifications—extremely unequal economic power tends to lead to extremely unequal political power in the United States. On the other hand, once the state apparatus is controlled via economic power or other means, it may then function as a feedback mechanism to secure political power more firmly. Thus, the Egyptian slaveholders (including Pharaoh and the priests) used their control of the state apparatus—the police, army, courts—to control the slaves by laws supported by force.

Similarly, given a large measure of political control by those with the most economic power in America, the wealthy naturally tend to use the government apparatus to further strengthen their power. Thus, the police or the National Guard or the army may be directly ordered to support "law and order" by force, as law and order is interpreted by those with political control. Many, many times in American history police or even soldiers have shot down American workers trying to strike for better conditions (police have even been used recently against the relatively conservative construction workers). Most courts have always cooperated by issuing injunctions against strikes by labor unions.

There is also that means of feedback control that is a mixture of propaganda and force, namely, the various espionage and "information" agencies. These include in America the Central Intelligence Agency, Defense Intelligence Agency, National Security Agency, Army Intelligence, Navy Intelligence and Research, and the Federal Bureau of Investigation. "By 1964 the intelligence network had grown into a massive hidden apparatus, secretly employing about 200,000 persons and spending billions of dollars a year."[37] This so-called invisible government is still only an instrument of political power, but does exert its own semi-independent, malevolent influence once it is activated, especially in foreign policy. Frequent publicized scandals have taught us that its corruption and paid agents reach down into every private organization (one outstanding case was the subsidized foreign activities of the AFL-CIO).

Another important feedback is the use of the *prestige* of the state. Thus, while police try to break a strike by construction workers, the president tells the nation that their wages are too high. Every department of the government, particularly the military, also does its own massive advertising in favor of business and government policies, particularly military spending.[38]

Education is the last avenue of feedback control considered here. Children are brought up to believe in the righteousness of a value system that preserves the status quo. Even if one looks at university boards of regents and trustees, it is astounding to find that they are almost wholly composed of capitalists, corporate lawyers, military officers, and their wives. Much of the funding (and direction) of research comes from military expenditure. The important

---

[37]Wise and Ross, *op. cit.,* p. 4. Also see Fred Cook, *The Warfare State* (New York: Macmillan, 1962), passim.
[38]Senator J. William Fulbright, *The Pentagon Propaganda Machine* (New York: Liveright, 1970), passim.

schools of law and business administration take the capitalist system for granted and work to improve (or have their students improve) its efficiency—mainly in the making of private profits.

Finally, if all else fails, the capitalist class may use outright repression or even force and violence to prevent governments from using drastic anticapitalist macro policies. Many countries have suffered from military coups and ended with military dictatorships. In a very large number of the underdeveloped countries of the "free" capitalist world, there are now such dictatorships, mostly dedicated according to their leaders "to the protection of democracy." Also in the twentieth century a number of semideveloped capitalist countries (Spain, Mussolini's Italy, Portugal, Greece, Tojo's Japan) and at least one developed capitalist country (Nazi Germany) have had fascist or military-fascist dictatorships. In most cases, they were instituted because of the threat that the Left might win power in a peaceful democratic election (or in Spain after such an election). In these cases, the feedback control of vested interests is manifested directly through the dictatorship of an extreme right-wing individual or party (though they may claim to be anything but a class dictatorship).

Much of this chapter has emphasized how economic power allows the capitalist class an enormous influence on even the most democratic of political processes. Nevertheless, it must be stressed that a liberal democratic process is *not* the same as a Fascist or military dictatorship, either politically or in macroeconomic policies. As long as there is a liberal democratic political process, it allows the working class to exercise its influence and to win very significant reforms.

There is always a potential or actual conflict between the popular participation in the liberal democratic process and the control of the economy by a small group of capitalist owners.[39] For example, the gains won by workers in the 1930s and 1960s included union recognition, unemployment compensation, social security, some health programs, some welfare programs, and expanded education programs. All these put certain constraints on the capitalist economy and add to the expenses of business. True, some enlightened parts of capital have welcomed each of these reforms as a necessary cost of making the system workable, acceptable, and legitimated for most citizens. Yet it is also true that the constraints posed by labor's strength in the political process make it impossible to solve all the current macroeconomic problems simply by putting the burden on labor. The capitalist system rules out some solutions to macroeconomic crises, but the liberal democratic process rules out others.

SUMMARY

The decision-making process of the U.S. government (including macroeconomic decisions) is heavily influenced by the economic power of the capitalist class and the structure of capitalism. Yet that power is far from complete and is hedged about by a long list of qualifications, many of which stem from the participation of other classes in the liberal democratic process.

---

[39]See the very careful discussion in Samuel Bowles and Herbert Gintis, "The Crisis of Liberal Democratic Capitalism," *Politics and Society* 11, no. 1 (1982), pp. 51–93.

Chapter 23

FISCAL POLICY

Within the political context discussed in the last chapter, this chapter examines fiscal policy, that is, government spending, taxing, and borrowing policies. We present the conservative, liberal, and radical viewpoints on all the main issues of fiscal policy.

THE CONSERVATIVE VIEW OF FISCAL POLICY

Most conservative economists—especially supply-side economists—believe in Say's law, which claims that supply creates its own demand. It follows that (1) in the aggregate and (2) after time for adjustment, demand and supply are equal. Inadequate demand cannot cause a depression—and excess demand cannot cause inflation. All of this is true only so long as the capitalist system of competition in the market is allowed to work by itself. Therefore, interference by government may cause unemployment or inflation, but government cannot cure unemployment or inflation. Therefore, the best fiscal policy for preventing or curing unemployment or inflation is no fiscal policy.

In this context, conservatives tend to favor no government intervention, no government regulation, no government spending (or "as little as possible"), no government taxation (or "as little as possible"), and a balanced budget. Milton Friedman is the most consistent; he wishes to cut almost all government spending for public education, almost all government spending for welfare for the poor, almost all government spending for the elderly, and almost all other government peaceful spending for anything that gives food, clothing, shelter, education, or medical care to the population.[1] Private business and charity will handle all these functions.

On the other hand, to their general rule of the less government the better, conservatives

---

[1] See Milton Friedman, *Capitalism and Freedom* (Chicago: University of Chicago Press, 1957).

have a long list of exceptions. The conservative rules—with the exceptions discussed here—were followed from the founding of the United States until the Great Depression of the 1930s.

First and foremost, their belief in the necessity of "law and order" leads conservatives to favor astronomical amounts of military spending.

Conservatives would also abolish all taxes on property income, capital gains, profits, interest, rent, and inheritance (as done in California in 1982). This would give more money to the wealthy, which the wealthy would (or should?) save. Assuming Say's law, there is always enough demand, so all the savings will be invested. This will increase jobs, increase productivity, and—assuming business passes on the lower costs to the consumer—reduce inflation. According to this plan, the cuts in government spending for the poor plus the reduced taxes on the rich will eventually trickle down to benefits to the poor. So the conservative government policies are, in their view, not motivated by class interest, but rather help everyone.

Another conservative exception to lower government spending is welfare to business, known as subsidies or tax breaks or both. Although many conservative economists might oppose even these, most conservative lawmakers always find reasons to support them. For example, in the nineteenth century, when the government did nothing for the poor, enormous subsidies were given to the railroads for "national security." U.S. railroads were given more land as gifts (or welfare) than makes up the entire country of France! For example, at present, national security demands big subsidies (or welfare) for the merchant marine, for the nuclear industry, for the dairy industry, for the sugar industry, for the tobacco industry (!), and for many other vital industries.

Another major conservative exception to the removal of government barriers to business and trade is the existence of tariffs and quotas for imports. A truly conservative economist, like Adam Smith, might oppose all trade barriers. Again, however, most conservative U.S. lawmakers find reasons to support high tariffs and quotas. For the entire period of their dominance, from the Civil War to the Great Depression, Republicans supported very high tariffs, such as the infamous Smoot-Hawley tariff. They claimed that these barriers were necessary for national security to protect industries that were only infants from the world competition. Apparently, such U.S. industries as steel and auto are still infant industries requiring protection from the "unfair" competition of the Japanese (any successful competition from other countries is unfair).

THE LIBERAL VIEW

In economics, liberals see the need to guide, cajole, and control the market to guarantee that it serves the social need. Liberals usually vote to protect the poor and workers, but they also vote to protect and encourage businesses in their particular localities. Thus, liberal members of Congress from Hawaii vote for sugar subsidies, and liberal members of Congress from Michigan vote for guarantees on loans to failing auto companies.

Beginning with the Great Depression of the 1930s, liberal lawmakers have differed with conservatives over macroeconomic policy. To combat unemployment, they have generally supported increased government spending to stimulate demand. To combat unemployment, liberals have also supported tax cuts for the poor, who have the highest propensity to consume. Also in the name of combating unemployment, however, liberals have frequently pushed for tax cuts to big business. To combat inflation, at least some liberals would be for less military spending and for closing tax loopholes for the wealthy (though some liberals have always been for more military spending to combat unemployment).

The greatest liberal economist was John Maynard Keynes, who first formulated most of these liberal principles of demand management by government during the Great Depression. A book by John Hotson, who is in the liberal Post Keynesian school, summarizes the measures proposed by Keynes to deal with unemployment and inflation.[2] According to Hotson, Keynes prescribed (1) "a somewhat comprehensive socialization" of investment through government spending on public works, (2) low interest rates, that is, "the euthanasia of the *rentier,*" and (3) an income policy of direct controls to combat inflation and to redistribute income more equally. These points emphasize the Left-liberal element that does exist in Keynes.

Hotson also summarizes the views dominant among many American Keynesians, whom he calls Bastard Keynesians because they deviate so far from Keynes's own proposals. The American Keynesians advocate higher military spending to reduce severe unemployment. To combat inflation, the American Keynesians would reduce aggregate demand, causing some unemployment, which would cause lower wages. The American Keynesians ignore Keynes's program for (1) curing income maldistribution, (2) the euthanasia of the rentier, and (3) the socialization of investment.

Liberal Keynesianism was dominant in U.S. fiscal policy from the 1930s to the 1970s.[3] Obviously, enormous government spending in the Second World War got the United States out of its worst depression. Obviously, continued high levels of government spending, especially in the Korean War and Vietnam War, helped stimulate employment. This made most economists into Keynesians. The dominant view was that "a private enterprise economy using an intangible money *needs* to be stabilized, *can* be stabilized, and *should* be stabilized by appropriate monetary and fiscal policy."[4]

The grim fact of both high unemployment and high inflation in the 1970s destroyed the liberal Keynesian consensus. The greatest defender of the liberal consensus was Paul Samuelson, who renamed the American "Bastard Keynesian" view to call it the "neoclassical Keynesian synthesis." He boasted that economists now could solve either unemployment or inflation—but sadly admitted that there was no liberal policy to solve both at the same time. Samuelson wrote: "Experts do not yet know . . . an income policy that will permit us to have simultaneously . . . full employment and price stability."[5] Liberals in Congress and the Democratic president, Jimmy Carter (1977–1980), had no consistent fiscal policies to defeat the simultaneous high unemployment and high inflation.

---

[2]John Hotson, *Stagflation and the Bastard Keynesians* (Waterloo, Canada: University of Waterloo Press, 1976), pp. 13–14.
[3]See David Gold, "The Rise and Decline of the Keynesian Coalition," *Kapitalistate,* 6 (Fall 1977), pp. 1–18.
[4]Franco Modigliani, "The Monetarist Controversy Or, Should We Forsake Stabilization Policies?" *Economic Review* (San Francisco: Federal Reserve Bank of San Francisco, Spring 1977), p. 27.
[5]Paul Samuelson, *Economics,* 9th ed. (New York: McGraw-Hill, 1973), p. 823.

SUPPLY-SIDE FISCAL POLICY

The decline and fall of liberal, neoclassical Keynesian economics opened the door to new doctrines on the Right and the Left. The Left-liberal Post Keynesians, who advocate wage and price controls as well as demand management, showed a rising strength. Radical economics, which advocates democratic socialism, grew in numbers. And two new conservative schools, monetarists and supply-side economists, found enormous support among big business and right-wing politicians. In fiscal policy, supply-side economics dominated government decisions of the early 1980s. (Actual fiscal policy from 1949 to 1981 was outlined in Chapter 7 and is discussed in detail later in this chapter.)

There are actually now three major conservative trends among economists. They all agree on the main ideological points just discussed, but they disagree on many specific points of analysis and policy. First, the monetarist view sees the problem as lying in mistaken government monetary policy. Their analysis was detailed in Chapter 16, and their policy proposals are discussed in Chapter 24.

Second, there is the "old time religion of fiscal orthodoxy." Inflation is the most dangerous and vital problem. Inflation is caused by extravagant government spending, which stimulates the economy, allows higher wages and prices, and generally lets people live beyond their means for a while. The only cure is sacrifice, cutting back government spending, and living with the consequences until the economy returns to a stable price system. One of the consequences of cutbacks in government spending is recognized to be unemployment. Says Martin Feldstein: "Unemployment is the price we must pay to undo more than a decade of inflationary policies."[6] (But Feldstein has not volunteered to be unemployed.)

Otto Eckstein has estimated that it would take five to seven years of over 8 percent unemployment to cure inflation.[7] Not surprisingly, we have mostly rejected this conservative economic cure—most politicians refuse to endorse publicly a program of encouraging unemployment to end inflation (though they may vote for measures designed to do just that). The attractiveness of the supply-side solution is that it promises to reduce inflation without increasing unemployment. In fact, unemployment will also be reduced. Both of these objectives are achieved by the magic of tax cuts, which is a popular political program by itself.

In the supply-side view, as shown later, the tax cuts should be primarily in the taxes of the rich. The reason is that they wish to stimulate investment, for which they believe—on the usual classical grounds—that all that is necessary is plenty of saving to provide capital. Cutting the taxes of the rich will provide the necessary saving and investment. In their view, this does not hurt the poor. On the contrary, it leads to rapid growth of the economy, from which the poor benefit immensely (as wealth trickles down from the rich). So not only will supply-side economic policies reduce both inflation and unemployment, they also will—in the long run—help both rich and poor. This is not a new viewpoint. The millionaire Secretary of the Treasury, Andrew Mellon, said in 1924: "The prosperity of the middle and lower

---

[6] Martin Feldstein, "Supply-side Economics," *Wall Street Journal* (March 28, 1981), p. 1.
[7] Otto Eckstein, "Stagflation: Is There a Way Out?" in Cullen Sanderson (ed.), *DRI Readings in Macroeconomics* (New York: McGraw-Hill, 1981), p. 292.

classes depends on the good fortune and light taxes of the rich."[8] And in 1981 a supply-sider said: "Regressive taxes help the poor! . . . To help the poor and middle classes, one must cut the tax rates of the rich."[9]

Although most of this viewpoint has appeared in newspapers, such as the *Wall Street Journal,* there now are a considerable number of books and articles supporting it, including Gilder,[10] Keleher,[11] Kemp,[12] Laffer,[13] Mellon,[14] Meyer,[15] Roberts,[16] Tatom,[17] Ture,[18] and Wanniski.[19] There is also an excellent critical survey of the literature by Campen and MacEwan as well as a sympathetic essay by Hailstones.[20] On the basis of these works, it is now possible to state the supply-side theory in a systematic way, with its assumptions and their criticisms.

The supply-side view advocates a tax cut, particularly for the rich. This tax cut will provide more capital for investment. The new investment will provide more jobs. It will also mean more factories with lower costs and higher productivity, which will bring down inflation. The implicit assumptions in this scenario are as follows: (1) The tax cuts for the rich will provide more saving by giving income to people who have a high propensity to save. (2) All of the saving will be invested. Because the supply-siders assume Say's law, they do not even admit that saving might not be invested; the two acts are one and the same. "In the "supply-side" analysis, there is no conceptual distinction between the act of saving and investment."[21] (3) The investment results in new and more productive production facilities, which can supply products at lower cost. (4) The lower costs are passed along to the consumer.

The critics have disputed each and every one of these assumptions. First, the supply-siders follow the usual neoclassical picture of saving done by individual entrepreneurs. The reality, however, is that individuals do only a small part of saving, and most business is not run as an individual enterprise. Most saving in the United States is done by the giant corporations. This assumption can be made more realistic if it says that tax breaks are given to both rich

---

[8]Andrew Mellon, *Taxation: The People's Business* (New York: Macmillan, 1924), quoted in James T. Campen and Arthur MacEwan, "Crises, Contradictions and Conservative Controversies in Contemporary U.S. Capitalism," mimeographed (Boston: Department of Economics, University of Massachusetts, 1981), p. 35.

[9]George Gilder, *Wealth and Poverty* (New York: Basic Books, 1981), quoted in Campen and MacEwan, *op. cit.,* p. 35.

[10]Gilder, *op. cit.*

[11]Robert Keleher, "Supply-side Tax Policy," *Economic Review* (Atlanta: Federal Reserve Bank of Atlanta, April 1981).

[12]James Kemp, *An American Renaissance* (New York: Harper & Row, 1979).

[13]Arthur Laffer, *Supply-Side Economics* (Pacific Palisades: Goodyear, 1982). Also see Arthur Laffer and J. P. Seymour, eds., *The Economics of the Tax Revolt* (New York: Harcourt Brace Jovanovich, 1979).

[14]Mellon, *op. cit.*

[15]L. H. Meyer, *The Supply-Side Effects of Economic Policy* (St. Louis: Federal Reserve Bank of St. Louis, 1981).

[16]Paul Craig Roberts, "The Breakdown of the Keynesian Model," *Public Interest* 5 (Summer 1978), pp. 25–46.

[17]J. A. Tatom, "We Are All Supply-siders Now," *Review* (St. Louis: Federal Reserve Bank of St. Louis, May 1981).

[18]N. B. Ture, "Forecasting the Supply Side of the Economy," U.S. Congress Joint Economic Committee, *Hearings* (Washington, D.C.: GPO, May 21, 1980).

[19]Jude Wanniski, "Taxes, Revenues, and the 'Laffer Curve,' " *The Public Interest* 5 (Winter 1978), pp. 22–49.

[20]Campen and MacEwan, *op. cit.,* present a thorough and comprehensive survey of recent conservative economics. For a sympathetic survey, see Thomas J. Hailstones, *A Guide to Supply-side Economics* (Richmond, Virginia: Robert F. Dame, 1982).

[21]Ture, *op. cit.,* quoted in Campen and MacEwan, *op. cit.*

individuals and the corporations. In fact, the Reagan administration has given enormous tax cuts to the corporations (with the agreement of most of the Democrats), so more savings are available.

Second, the main deficiency of supply-side economics is its acceptance of Say's law. All the advance made by Keynes (see Chapter 5 of this book) has been tossed away. As Keynes pointed out, it is a strange notion that corporations (or individual entrepreneurs) will invest their savings when there is no expectation of a profit. Regardless of how low costs may be (including both wages and taxes), if there is no prospect of demand for a commodity, then the reasonable expectation is for a zero or negative rate of profit. Therefore, if there is not enough demand, there will be no investment, regardless of how much savings exist. In the 1981–1982 recession in the United States, for example, automobile makers had plenty of productive capacity, but they didn't use much of it because there was insufficient demand for their product. They were closing many plants, so they would laugh at anyone who told them to use their savings to build more plants. Any tax cuts they received were used to pay for immediate operating costs or were hoarded; they were not used to build new productive facilities.

Third, the supply-side theory assumes that the new investment results in higher productivity. One problem is that, even if factories are planned with higher productivity, it takes several years to build new factories and get them into operation. Assuming technological improvement and the desire to use it, there will still be several years before industry significantly reduces the average cost level.

Fourth, the assumption that the lower costs will be passed on to the consumer is built on the neoclassical picture of thousands of small enterprises in each industry engaged in pure and perfect competition. It was shown in Chapter 20 that that is not the case. Monopoly power is the rule, so there is no reason to believe that lower costs must be passed on to the consumer.

THE RADICAL VIEW OF FISCAL POLICY

Part Four of this book demonstrated how the private sector of the U.S. economy by itself has always tended to produce a business cycle of boom and bust. On the eve of the Great Depression in 1929, federal government spending was only 1 percent of gross national product. Since federal government expenditure had always been minuscule (except in wartime), fiscal policy did not cause the Great Depression or any of the previous approximately 20 contractions.

Part Five of this book demonstrated that the present inflationary tendency is closely associated with the increasingly monopoly structure of the economy. Military spending in the Vietnam War began the current inflation, but it is only one relatively minor cause of its continuation (because there has *not* been excess demand in the economy in the 1970s and 1980s).

Radicals (and many liberals) conclude that fiscal policy may now influence the business cycle at all points, but the cycle of boom and bust would still exist if federal government spending, taxation, and borrowing were all zero. (State and local fiscal policy does not cause cycles because its tendencies are relatively stable and long-run.) The present type of inflation would probably also exist if federal spending, taxation, and borrowing were zero.

Fiscal policy, in the radical view, has influenced unemployment and inflation in recent decades. Government, however, has not been the main determinant of the cycle in peacetime, contrary to extreme advocates of a political business cycle theory (which sees government as "causing" the cycle).[22] Deficit spending, as will be demonstrated, has mostly behaved in a countercyclical manner, with the deficit declining in expansion and rising in contraction. If these countercyclical policies depress the economy at the cycle peak when the economy is ripe for a contraction, then it may be the catalyst for a contraction. If government stimulates the economy at the trough when it is ripe for a recovery, then government may be the catalyst for a recovery.

LIMITATIONS OF LIBERAL FISCAL POLICY

As noted earlier, some radicals (and some conservatives) view government under capitalism as a main cause of unemployment and inflation—and some radicals claim there is an intention to cause economic downturns to discipline labor and hold down wages. Most radicals would simply say that government policies against unemployment and inflation have severe limitations—and sometimes are one cause of what they are claiming to cure (whether intentional or not). There are three kinds of limitations on liberal fiscal policy: (1) administrative inadequacies, (2) political constraints based on class interests, and (3) inherently conflicting economic goals.

The basic liberal (American Keynesian or neoclassical Keynesian synthesis) fiscal policy sounds very simple to administer. If there is unemployment, increase government spending, and reduce government taxes. This allows a higher deficit to inject more demand into the system. If there is inflation, cut government spending, and raise taxes. This allows a surplus, which will take excess demand out of the economic system.

ADMINISTRATIVE CONSTRAINTS

In reality, administration of these policies is difficult (as conservatives frequently note) because it requires precise and prompt government planning within a chaotic and unplanned capitalist economy. First, there is the information-gathering problem. There is always delay before available data can reveal changes in unemployment and inflation. Second, there is a much longer delay for interpretation of the data. Some government economists must determine that rising unemployment or inflation or both exist before something can be done about it. Third, there is a further delay to plan what to do about it. Economists must estimate how much of an increase or cut in spending or an increase or cut in taxes or both is required to meet the goals. This is not only time-consuming, but very, very difficult. No two economists

[22]See, e.g., Duncan C. Macrae, "A Political Model of the Business Cycle," *Journal of Political Economy* 85 (April 1977), pp. 239–263.

agree on the amounts, and government estimates are always totally inaccurate (a conclusion for which past evidence is overwhelming). If there is to be spending for the purchase of equipment or construction, engineers must also make plans.

A fourth administrative delay must occur while Congress goes through the lengthy process of deliberation (that is, class conflict in more or less polite debates) and legislation. A fifth administrative delay must occur before the plans can be put into effect. A plan to build a new battleship does not put money into immediate circulation, but slowly over many years. An "immediate" tax cut still requires a year for the estimated annual amount to remain in the pockets of consumers or investors.

As a result of these five delays (information, interpretation, planning, legislation, and execution) as well as the gross mistakes in planning, the results seldom have any resemblance to the plans. In fact, it has frequently happened that new spending, designed to end a recession, actually helps overstimulate an expansion. Similarly, tax cuts to stimulate the economy may occur in time to increase inflation.

POLITICAL CONSTRAINTS

The political constraints on fiscal policy are much worse for the process than the administrative constraints. As shown in the last chapter, capitalist class interests are dominant in the Congress and in the president's cabinet. These interests frequently conflict with the pleasant goals assumed by liberal economists. For example, real full employment—with no one unemployed—would mean a much greater power for labor to raise wages, so it is *never* an actual goal of U.S. fiscal policy (though liberals have gotten Congress to adopt some pious statements, with no enforcement procedure).

Increases or decreases in government spending hurt some groups and help others. Increases or decreases in taxes hurt some groups and help others. There is no class-neutral fiscal policy—just as there is no button marked "government waste" to push for painless cuts. The question is always this: spending or cuts *for whom?* The ability to ignore this issue is the greatest weakness of liberal fiscal policy.

Not only is the distribution of income directly affected, so also is the allocation of resources. Fiscal policies determine the use of private resources (such as Cadillacs) versus public resources (mass transit). They decide on spending for hospitals or schools versus bombs or battleships. Again, none of this is class-neutral, but strongly affects distribution of income.

Suppose by some miracle that everyone agrees on a certain amount of government spending to combat unemployment. The prime political question, however, is spending on what, for it is here that vested interests come into play. Thus, even small vital expenditures on medical care have sometimes been defeated by the American Medical Association. Powerful vested interests oppose almost every item in the civilian budget as soon as expansion proceeds beyond the necessary minimum. What kind of interests must be defeated to have the necessary spending to fill the present enormous deficiency in demand? Constructive projects such as the Missouri Valley Authority could develop dams, irrigation, and cheap power, but these have been fought tooth and nail by the private power interests because they might lower profit rates. There could be large-scale public housing, but private contractors have long kept such programs to a minimum.

There might be other welfare spending—for example, on hospitals and schools. The rich, however, see these as subsidies to the poor for things that the rich can buy for themselves out of their own pockets. Proposals to increase unemployment compensation or lower taxes paid by the poor encounter even greater resistance because they would transfer income from the rich to the poor. Likewise, billions could usefully be spent in aid and loans to the less developed world, where poverty and human suffering are so widespread. That, however, could be passed on a massive scale only over the bodies of hundreds of members of Congress, who well represent the wishes of their self-interested constituents and have no concept of the long-run gain to world trade and world peace. If any of these measures is to some extent allowed, it is only after a long political fight and certainly not promptly enough to head off a developing depression.

The dominant capitalist interests will not tolerate government competition with private enterprise, measures that undermine the privileges of the wealthy, or policies that significantly alter the relative distribution of income. They therefore tend to oppose all government nonmilitary spending—except business subsidies. The only major exception to this generalization is government spending on highways, which is actively promoted by the largest lobbying effort of any single industry after defense: the automobile producers.

From all of the facts just given, it must be concluded that welfare or constructive spending on a large enough scale for full employment is opposed by too many special interests to be politically feasible. On the other hand, military spending does not violate any vested interests. Military spending is considered an ideal antidepression policy by big business for three reasons. First, such expenditures have the same short-run effect on employment and profits as would expenditures on more socially useful projects. Second, military spending means big and stable profits whereas welfare spending may shift income from rich taxpayers to poor recipients. Third, the long-run effect is even more favorable because no new productive equipment is created to compete with existing facilities. (On the other hand, most studies conclude that military spending provides fewer jobs per dollar than nonmilitary spending.)

It is a historical fact that only the military spending of the Second World War brought the United States out of the Great Depression. It is a historical fact that the strong expansions and mild contractions of the 1950s and the 1960s were strongly supported by the high level of cold war spending, by the Korean War, and by the Vietnam War. Yet writing just after the Vietnam War, the liberal Paul Samuelson claimed that it would be easy to replace military spending by nonmilitary spending. He claims, "However true it might have been in the turn-of-the-century era of Lenin . . . it is definitely no longer the case in the age of Keynes that prosperity of a mixed economy (i.e., capitalism plus government) depends on cold-war expenditures and imperialistic ventures . . . Does building missiles and warheads create jobs? . . . Then so too will building new factories, better roads and schools, cleaning up our rivers, and providing minimum income-supplements for our aged and handicapped."[23] Certainly it

[23] *Ibid*, pp. 823–824.

is true that jobs could be created in all these constructive ways rather than the destructive ways of warfare.

But—and it is a big *but*—vested interests can and will obstruct government programs that might harm them. For the government to build new factories means direct competition with private industry. Free public education means a use of money for the education of poorer citizens. To clean up the rivers means forcing private industry to spend money on purifying its wastes. Giving to the aged and handicapped means shifting income to the poor. The political reality is that vested interests oppose each of these programs with violent rhetoric and successful political pressure.

Paul Samuelson says that radicals have asked: "Politically, will there be as much urgency to spend what is needed for useful, peacetime full-employment programs as there is urgency and willingness to spend for hot- and cold-war purposes?" And he answers: "It was proper to ask this question back in the 1950s. But . . . experience since then has shown that modern electorates have become very sensitive to levels of unemployment that would have been considered moderate back in the good old days. And they do put effective pressure at the polls on their government."[24] But in the first place, the pressure is only to get jobs—not necessarily to get welfare rather than warfare jobs. So both Republican and Democratic administrations continue military spending to avoid unemployment—and do not do large amounts of constructive spending.

In the second place, Samuelson just assumes that "the people" or "the electorate" put on successful pressure for their needs and interests. In the last chapter we showed that this has not been true, that the U.S. government has been dominated by capitalist interests opposed to the interests of the majority. Since Samuelson wrote, the Nixon, Ford, Carter, and Reagan administrations have surely not shown any anticapitalist tendencies. The U.S. government did *not* replace Vietnam War expenditures with a new flood of income supplements to the aged and handicapped, government-built factories, roads and schools, or huge expenditures to clean up our rivers. The historical record shows, contrary to Samuelson's expectations, that there was high unemployment in most of the 1970s and early 1980s and that the U.S. government did *not* eliminate it by vast increases in peaceful government spending.

On the contrary, Nixon, Ford, and Carter all talked about the need for fiscal conservatism, and—in the midst of high unemployment—cut various social programs. The fiscal policies of the Democratic Carter administration differed very little from those of the previous Republican administrations—and the Carter administration clearly bears part of the blame for the sharp increase of unemployment in 1980.

The Reagan administration merely followed the same policies in a more drastic manner. The 1981 budget is a classic example of class interests at work. It made huge increases in military spending. At the same time (with continued high unemployment), the largest cuts in spending were in public service job programs, and the job-producing Young Adult Conservation Corps was eliminated. Other spending cuts tending to reduce employment were in the

[24]*Ibid*, pp. 824–825.

following: education programs, aid to disadvantaged children, specific health programs, medicaid payments to states, medicare for the elderly, public housing (with increases in rents), food stamps, mothers' and infants' nutrition, school lunches, day care, aid to families with dependent children, the Economic Development Administration, the Appalachian Regional Administration, urban development action grants, the Consumer Product Safety Commission, mass transit aid, funds for water cleanup projects, funds for more parks, funds for arts and humanities, funds for legal services for the poor, funds for the postal service, funds for public broadcasting, and funds for community action programs. There were no cuts in subsidies to big business (a point mentioned to a reporter by David Stockman, head of the Office of Management and Budget).

On the tax side, there was an equal percentage cut in all personal income taxes, which means that the rich got much larger cuts than the poor. When all was finished, the personal income tax system had more loopholes and was less progressive than before. Representative Robert Michel, Republican leader in the House, while on national television just before the tax cuts were voted, told a conference of House Republican members to be sure to remind their wealthy constituents that the new tax law would be less progressive than the old. At the same time, many kinds of business taxes were reduced to an enormous extent. The acceleration of depreciation schedules tremendously reduced the taxation of corporate profits. An immense extra tax cut was given to the oil companies. Finally, to help the "truly needy" wealthy (though Reagan talked about helping the truly needy poor), all gift and inheritance taxes suffered huge cuts.

Some lessons are clear. Instead of increases for the spending items that Samuelson thought would be easy to increase, these types of spending were cut. All the cuts in spending were types that tend to hurt the poor and the working class—and some spending cuts even hurt the middle class. Most of the tax cuts, as well as the increase in military spending, increased the aftertax profits of the whole capitalist class. A cautious summary of the tax bill said: "Although the bill contains massive tax cuts for business and a host of tax breaks for special interests, there are only a handful of changes to help the average worker."[25]

It is important to remember that this anti–working class, procapitalist budget was written by the conservative Republican Party. Yet it is also important to remember that the budget proposal of the liberal Democratic leadership had the same class bias, though a little less in degree. The Democrats' spending proposal made enormous cuts in all nonmilitary pro-working class programs, though not as much as the Republican cuts. Even Tip O'Neill, the Speaker of the House, admitted that the Democratic proposal cut off the working class at the knees, but argued that the Republican proposal cut off the working class at the waist. The Democrats' tax proposal gave somewhat larger cuts to the middle class than the Republicans (indicating their somewhat different class support). But the Democrats' tax proposal also gave big business just as incredible a cut as did the Republicans. These giveaways to big business are clearly the only widely agreed-upon program for stimulating the economy, which is completely understandable given the structural basis of capitalism. The liberal Democratic

[25] United Press International, "Tax Cut Seen Having Small Initial Impact," *The Honolulu Advertiser* (August 5, 1981), p. 1.

leadership not only went along with most of the Republican program, but had no alternative program.

ECONOMIC CONSTRAINTS

To understand why both conservatives and liberals end up with remarkably similar fiscal policies in most periods, we must be clear on the economic constraints set on policy by the structure of capitalism. The three major constraints are limits on the redistribution of income, competition with private enterprise, and the conflict of anti-unemployment and anti-inflation policies.

If drastic redistribution of income toward equality were seriously legislated by a strongly liberal or mildly radical government, then capitalists might refuse to invest. This sabotage of the economy, as Thorstein Veblen called it, has *not* occurred in the past with minor tax reforms or increased welfare spending (as in the 1930s or 1960s). But a really drastic redistribution policy might "lower business confidence" and make capitalists hoard or flee the country with their capital. This did occur, for example, with the socialist Allende government of Chile. It did occur with the socialist government of France. Of course, capital needs places to go that are safer or give higher returns or both. Such places might be difficult to find for large amounts of capital fleeing redistribution policies from the United States (it can't all go to South Africa).

If the U.S. government sponsored a successful energy corporation, the lower prices would compete with present private energy corporations. These private energy corporations might then go on strike by not investing or by fleeing overseas. As conservatives frequently and correctly point out, *any* peaceful constructive direct investment by government does compete with private capital. Therefore, enough government investment might cause an investment strike or capital flight. Of course, one remedy would be still more government investment, but that would lead to socialism, would it not?

The same constraint may apply to competition with elite professionals. If free national health care were instituted, doctors might get reasonable payments instead of outrageous monopoly revenues. Doctors might also flee, but where would they go? Every other industrialized country (except South Africa) already has free national health care—and how many doctors could fit into South Africa?

Finally, fiscal policies for higher employment may conflict with anti-inflation policies because one requires higher demand and the other requires lower demand. Only the supply-siders claim that their panacea of tax cuts will cure both, but we have indicated why that is a very questionable claim. It is true that unemployment and inflation sometimes moved together in the 1970s, so under some circumstances it would appear at first glance the two could be cured together. Closer examination, however, reveals that they sometimes increased at the same times, but almost never decreased at the same time, so there is little or no symmetry. A drastic enough rise in demand to cause full employment would also probably lead to much more inflation. A drastic enough fall in demand to cause stable prices (zero inflation) would also cause much more unemployment. If the inflation is cost-push or profit-push, then it possibly could be curbed by controls without causing unemployment, but such controls are outside the realm of fiscal policy.

AUTOMATIC STABILIZERS

Excessive or deficient demand can be combated in two ways: with *automatic* fiscal devices and with *discretionary* fiscal policies. Discretionary fiscal policies are changes in the fiscal structure made by current and conscious government decisions. Since World War II, the government has placed more reliance on automatic than on discretionary fiscal measures. An automatic stabilizer is a government device built into the fiscal system that automatically increases or decreases government flows to or from the rest of the economy in response to changes in economic conditions.

In a depression, when the GNP tends to drop, the stabilizers should automatically increase government money flows to businesses and households or decrease money flows from businesses and households to the government or both. This will prevent disposable personal income from dropping as rapidly as otherwise, and thus investment and consumption expenditures can be maintained at a higher level. Similarly, in an inflation, the automatic stabilizers are supposed to decrease the amount given and increase the amount taken away from businesses and households, thus decreasing the total amount of consumer and investor spending. In either case, the net changes in government flows should have a multiple effect.

Now what are the magic devices by which the government is supposed to keep the economy automatically stable? On the spending side of the ledger, the government makes many types of welfare payments that automatically increase in depressions and automatically decrease in expansions. For example, as full employment is approached, there will be very little unemployment compensation. But in a depression, with growing unemployment, this may become a significant source of buying power.

On the taxation side, the total amounts of federal income tax collected had declined in most recessions faster than personal income, so it usually left people with more to spend. The federal income tax acted this way because the individual automatically pays a lower tax rate if his or her income declines. Therefore, the federal tax system was an important automatic stabilizer.

Unfortunately, the depression of 1973–1975 was in a continued price inflation. Therefore, personal income rose in the depression in money terms though it fell in terms of purchasing power. Thus, the amount and the percentage of taxes rose in the 1973–1975 depression. For middle-income taxpayers, with an intermediate income by government standards, in 1974 personal income taxes went up 27 percent and social security taxes went up 22 percent over 1973. As a result of the inflation, this was the first depression in American history in which the burden of personal income taxes actually increased. Instead of being the most important automatic stabilizer, the federal income tax operated as a major automatic destabilizer.

The automatic stabilizers are a clear failure when both rising unemployment and high inflation are present. In smaller recessions with less unemployment, when there happened to be no inflation, the automatic stabilizers did have a positive impact according to most studies. When a downturn is longer and deeper, however, even with no inflation, the auto-

Table 23.1

U.S. FEDERAL GOVERNMENT REVENUES

Change from Stage to Stage, Per Month, in Percentages of Base

	Expansion				Peak	Contraction		
Stages	1–2	2–3	3–4	4–5	5–6	6–7	7–8	8–9
Revenues	0.78	0.79	0.39	0.53	−0.52	−1.09	−0.72	−0.29

NOTE: This table represents an average of six cycles, from 1949 to 1980, in quarterly data and in constant 1972 dollars.
SOURCE: U.S. Department of Commerce, *Business Conditions Digest* (May 1981), deflated by GNP price deflator. GNP price deflator also from *Business Conditions Digest* (May 1981).

matic stabilizers will tend to have less and less impact. For example, unemployment compensation terminates after 26 weeks. Moreover, the millions of unemployed cannot be taxed less than 0 percent.

The actual effects of both automatic stabilizers, discretionary fiscal policy, and objective conditions in the private sector are traced in the next few sections.

CYCLICAL BEHAVIOR OF GOVERNMENT REVENUE

To ascertain the impact of fiscal variables on the economy, we must know their cyclical behavior. On the revenue side, the picture is quite clear, as revealed in Table 23.1 and Figure 23.1

Federal revenues rose in every one of the six expansions, the average rise being 0.61 percent per month. Federal revenues fell in every one of the six contractions, the average decline being −0.66 percent per month. Government revenues rise in expansions because income rises, and most taxes rise with income. Government revenues fall in contractions because income falls, and most taxes fall with income.

The only partial exceptions were the continued rise of revenues in the first stages of the 1973–1975 recession and the first stage of the 1980 recession. Why did these partial exceptions occur? Real wages and real profits both fell rapidly during these recessions. Yet price inflation was so strong that nominal wages and nominal profits continued to rise during the early parts of these two recessions and only fell in the last half of these two recessions. Therefore, taxes moved in the same direction.

When total federal revenues are broken down into separate components, the picture is still quite clear. For the average of all five *expansions* from 1949 to 1973, the monthly rate of change (as a percentage of the cycle average) was +0.48 for the federal personal income tax, +0.53 for the federal corporate profit tax, and +0.94 for the federal social security tax.[26] For the average of all five *contractions* from 1953 to 1975, the monthly rate of change was −0.33 for the federal personal income tax, −1.78 for the federal corporate profit

---

[26]Data for these five cycles come from John Ray, Jr., *Government Fiscal Policy and the Business Cycle in the United States, 1949–1975* (Ph.D. diss., University of California, Riverside, 1980).

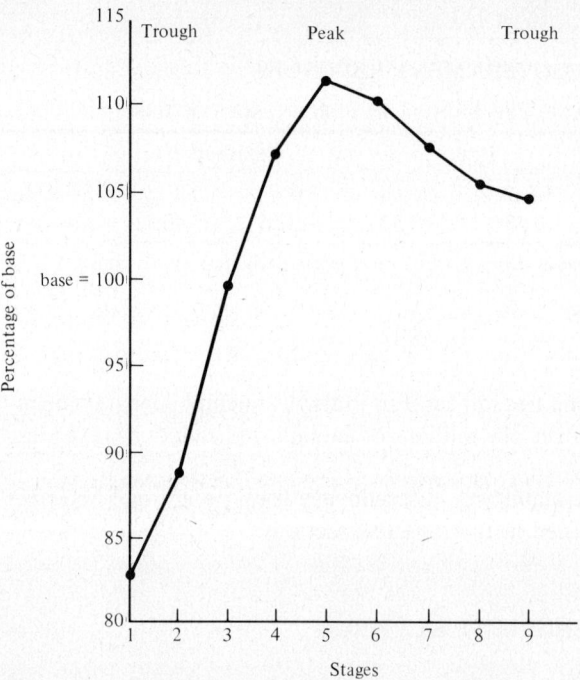

Figure 23.1 U.S. Federal Government Revenues
NOTE: This figure represents an average of six cycles, from 1949 through 1980, in quarterly data and in constant 1972 dollars (deflated by GNP price deflator) in percentages of cycle base.
SOURCE: U.S. Department of Commerce, *Business Conditions Digest* (May 1981).

tax, and -0.09 for the federal social security tax. Thus, all the main types of federal revenues rose in expansions and fell in contractions (except for the early stages of the inflation-ridden 1973–1975 and 1980 recessions).

The state and local level is more complex because there was, as shown in Chapter 7, a powerful upward trend (including tax rate increases in contractions). In the average of the five cycles (1949–1975), total state and local revenues rose $+0.53$ per month in expansions, but continued to rise (though more slowly) by $+0.47$ per month in contractions. Of the tax components at the state and local level in the average of the five *expansions*, personal income taxes rose $+0.75$, corporate taxes rose $+0.80$, and indirect business taxes rose $+0.43$. Of the same state and local components in the average *contraction*, personal income taxes rose $+0.43$, indirect business taxes rose $+0.30$, and only the corporate profit tax fell at -0.81 per month. (Note that most states are prohibited from deficit spending by their constitutions.) But the biggest difference was in the federal grants in aid to states and localities, which rose an average 0.71 in expansions, but continued to rise an amazing $+1.49$ in contractions.

GOVERNMENT SPENDING OVER THE BUSINESS CYCLE

It is worth remembering that the largest single component of federal spending is military spending. That is true even for the restricted definition in official series on "U.S. Government Purchases of Goods and Services for Defense," which we use here (notice that not a penny is spent for offense, according to the official definition). Military expenditures have, as one would expect, a quite different pattern in cycles dominated by wars and those cycles that are mostly peaceful. Table 23.2 and Figure 23.2 show the different behavior of military spending in war and peace.

In terms of the usual political myths, this table is surely confusing. Military spending rose when Democrats were in power, but fell when Republicans were in power (except for a slight rise in part of Eisenhower's term). The truth is that military spending had little to do with who was in power.

During both cycles dominated by war—the Korean and Vietnam wars, the rate of growth of military expansion was very high (even the 0.26 per month rate in the cycle including the Vietnam War was very high because it is an average for *nine* years). In the contraction at the end of each war, military spending fell. It is obvious in these two cycles that growing

Table 23.2

MILITARY SPENDING
PERCENTAGE RATE OF CHANGE PER MONTH

A. Two War Cycles

Expansion (Trough to Peak)			Contraction (Peak to Trough)		
Years	Rate	Politics	Years	Rate	Politics
1949–1953	2.09	(Truman, Korea)	(1953–1954)	−1.99	(Eisenhower)
1961–1969	.26	(Johnson, Vietnam)	(1969–1970)	−0.96	(Nixon)
Average	1.18		Average	−1.48	

B. Four Peace Time Cycles

Expansion (Trough to Peak)			Contraction (Peak to Trough)		
Years	Rate	Politics	Years	Rate	Politics
1954–1957	0.01	(Eisenhower)	(1957–1958)	0.09	(Eisenhower)
1958–1960	−0.29	(Eisenhower)	(1960–1961)	0.42	(Kennedy)
1970–1973	−0.44	(Nixon)	(1973–1975)	−0.13	(Ford)
1975–1980	0.15	(Carter)	(1980)	0.37	(Carter)
Average	−0.14		Average	0.19	

NOTE: This table represents two war cycles and four peacetime cycles, in quarterly data and in constant 1972 dollars. Peaks and troughs are also quarterly. All data divided by 3 to make it monthly.
SOURCE: U.S. Department of Commerce, *Business Conditions Digest* (May 1981), deflated by GNP price deflator from U.S. Department of Commerce, *Business Conditions Digest* (May 1981).

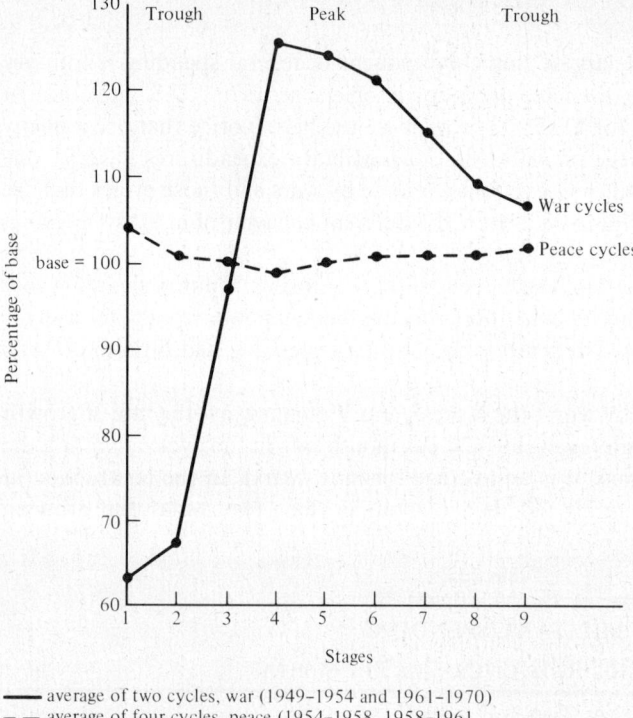

——— average of two cycles, war (1949–1954 and 1961–1970)
— — average of four cycles, peace (1954–1958, 1958–1961, 1970–1975, and 1975–1980)

Figure 23.2 Military Spending
NOTE: This figure represents an average of four peace cycles and an average of two war cycles, in quarterly data and in constant 1972 dollars (deflated by GNP price deflator), in percentage of cycle base.
SOURCE: U.S. Department of Commerce, *Business Conditions Digest* (May 1981).

military spending was a major cause of expansion, especially the exceptionally long Vietnam expansion. It is also obvious that the decline in military spending was a major cause of the following contraction.

During the four (mostly) peaceful cycles, military spending played a lesser role. It appears, however, that military spending was used for the most part as a tool of counter cyclical planning. In the average peacetime expansion, it fell an average −0.14 percent per month. In the average peacetime contraction, it rose 0.19 percent a month. In peacetime, military spending is the most controllable and the largest of the budget items. Radical theory expects it to move countercyclically, and it does! There are, of course, many exceptions owing to external and other internal pressures.

Now consider total federal spending, including both military and nonmilitary, shown in Table 23.3 and Figure 23.3.

Table 23.3 reveals that in the average wartime cycle, there was a rapid rise of real federal spending in the business expansion during the war. Then there was a decline (or slower

Table 23.3

ALL FEDERAL SPENDING
PERCENTAGE RATE OF CHANGE PER MONTH

Two War Cycles

Expansion			Contraction		
Years	Rate	Politics	Years	Rate	Politics
1949–1953	1.07	(Truman, Korea)	1953–1954	−1.16	(Eisenhower)
1961–1969	0.39	(Johnson, Vietnam)	1969–1970	0.33	(Nixon)
Average	0.73		Average	−0.42	

Four Peacetime Cycles

Expansion			Contraction		
Years	Rate	Politics	Years	Rate	Politics
1954–1957	0.16	(Eisenhower)	1957–1958	0.85	(Eisenhower)
1958–1960	0.07	(Eisenhower)	1960–1961	0.68	(Kennedy)
1970–1973	0.27	(Nixon)	1973–1975	0.50	(Ford)
1975–1980	0.32	(Carter)	1980	0.84	(Carter)
Average	0.21		Average	0.72	

NOTE: This table represents two war cycles and four peacetime cycles, from 1949 to 1980, in quarterly data and constant 1972 dollars.
SOURCE: U.S. Department of Commerce, *Business Conditions Digest* (May 1981), deflated by GNP price deflations from *Business Conditions Digest* (May 1981).

growth) during the contraction following the war. In these cycles, military spending dominated total spending.

In every one of the peacetime cycles, there is also a consistent pattern, but it is a different one. In the business expansions, real federal spending rose very slowly. In the four business contractions, real federal spending rose much more rapidly (regardless of the political party in power!). Obviously, a contraction automatically generates more spending from the so-called automatic stabilizers. There are more unemployment compensation, more farm subsidies, more welfare, more subsidies to business. Little, if any, of the increased spending in contractions was a discretionary spending in addition to the automatic increases. Note that the rate of growth was highest (and identical) in the Eisenhower recession and the Carter recession.

Finally, it is worth noting that state and local purchases of goods and services rose (in constant dollars) in almost every cycle phase in this period. State and local expenditures rose by 0.31 percent per month during all the long years of cyclical expansions from 1949 to 1980.[27] In the five cyclical contractions from 1953 to 1975, spending rose (in constant dollars)

---

[27] Data on state and local purchases from U.S. Department of Commerce, *Business Conditions Digest* (May 1981).

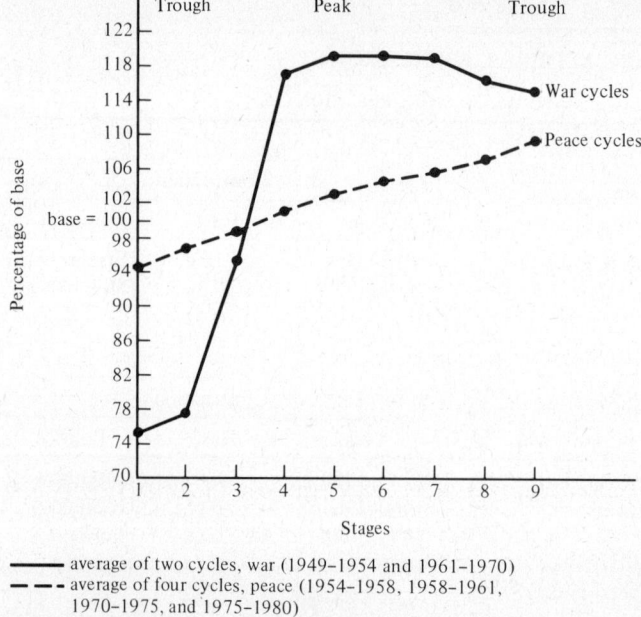

——— average of two cycles, war (1949–1954 and 1961–1970)
– – – average of four cycles, peace (1954–1958, 1958–1961, 1970–1975, and 1975–1980)

Figure 23.3 All Federal Spending
NOTE: This figure represents and average of four peace cycles and an average of two war cycles, in quarterly data and in constant 1972 dollars (deflated by GNP price deflator), in percentage of cycle base.
SOURCE: U.S. Department of Commerce, *Business Conditions Digest* (May 1981).

even faster, at a rate of 0.60 percent per month! This was because state and local governments must also automatically spend more in some categories in recessions, for example, welfare payments. Only in the recession of 1980 did state and local purchases of goods and services actually fall, at a rate of -0.11 percent per month. This happened because of the increasingly tight budget constraints, which have become even more dramatic in the early 1980s.

Since state and local expenditures rose more rapidly in all contractions (except 1980) than in the preceding expansions, they helped increase total government spending rapidly in all contractions—even in the postwar contractions when federal expenditures fell or didn't rise so fast. Thus, the pattern of all government spending—state, federal, and local—has been slow increases in business expansions and more rapid increases in business contractions.

CYCLICAL BEHAVIOR OF GOVERNMENT DEFICITS

Government revenues mostly rose in expansions and fell in contractions. Government spending mostly rose slowly in expansions and faster in contractions. Therefore, we can predict the behavior of the deficit. In constant dollars, the federal deficit *fell* in every one of the six

Table 23.4

FEDERAL AND TOTAL GOVERNMENT DEFICITS

Change from Stage to Stage, per Month, in Percentage of Base

	Expansion				Peak	Contraction		
Stage	1–2	2–3	3–4	4–5	5–6	6–7	7–8	8–9
Federal deficit	−1.90	−1.87	−0.06	−1.64	3.59	8.24	3.51	5.73
Total deficit	−2.27	−2.99	−1.21	−0.44	4.49	8.29	8.53	7.47

NOTE: This table represents an average of six cycles, from 1949 through 1980, in quarterly data and in constant 1972 dollars. *Total* means federal plus state plus local. A constant $20 billion was subtracted every quarter to eliminate surpluses and make all figures into deficits.
SOURCE: U.S. Department of Commerce, *Business Conditions Digest* (May 1981), deflated by GNP price deflator from *Business Conditions Digest* (May 1991).

business expansions from 1949 through 1980. It fell quite a bit slower in the Korean War and Vietnam War cycle expansions, but it did fall. In constant dollars, the federal deficit *rose* very rapidly in five of the six contractions—while falling slightly in the post-Korean War contraction (because of the rapid decline in military spending).

Now add in the effect of state and local government spending and taxation, which were not much affected by the wars. Then it is found that, in constant dollars, total federal, state, and local deficits *fell* in every one of the six business expansions (but less rapidly during the Vietnam and Korean wars) and *rose* rapidly in every one of the six business contractions (but slowest in the post-Korean War contraction).

Since the pattern was fairly similar in all the cycles, with the exceptions just noted, it is enough to show the average cyclical behavior for the federal deficit and for the total deficit in Table 23.4 and Figure 23.4. (The cyclical behavior of government spending, revenue, and deficits in the 1920s and 1930s has been described and analyzed in an excellent study by John Miller.[28])

A positive figure in Table 23.4 means an increasing deficit (or decreasing surplus); a negative figure means a decreasing deficit (or increasing surplus). An increasing deficit tends to stimulate the economy, reduce unemployment, and increase inflation. A declining deficit tends to mean less stimulation (or even depressing effects on the economy if it becomes a surplus), more unemployment, and perhaps less inflation.

The pattern shown in the average of the six cycles is quite clear. The federal deficit declines in the average expansion. The federal deficit rises in the average contraction. Similarly, the total federal, state, and local deficit falls in every expansion and rises in every contraction.

The overall conclusion appears to be that the federal, state, and local government deficit usually moves in a countercyclical direction (at least in peacetime), falling in expansions and rising in contractions. The reasons why lie in the detailed analysis of spending and taxation in earlier sections. Briefly, in most expansions, government spending rose very slowly whereas

---

[28] John A. Miller, *The State, Cycles, and Crises: A Critical Examination of the Fiscal Revolution in the United States* (Ph.D. diss., University of Pittsburgh, Pittsburgh, 1982).

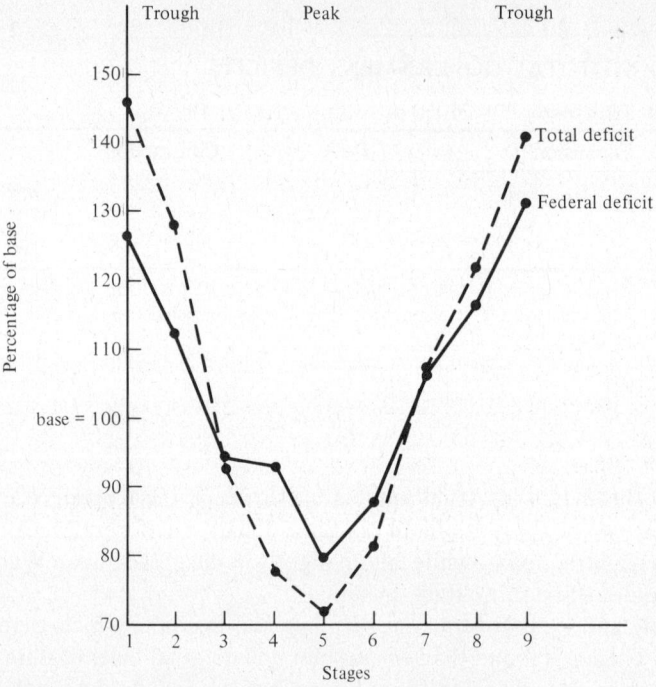

Figure 23.4 Federal and Total Government Deficits
NOTE: This figure represents an average of six cycles, from 1949 through 1980, in quarterly data and in constant 1972 dollars (deflated by GNP price deflator), in percentage of cycle base. *Total* means federal, state, and local.
SOURCE: U.S. Department of Commerce, *Business Conditions Digest* (May 1981).

taxes rose more rapidly; therefore, the deficit fell (or the surplus rose). In most contractions, spending rose rapidly whereas taxes fell, so the deficit rose (or the surplus fell).

CONFLICTING INTERPRETATIONS OF THE FISCAL DATA

In the aggregate, government deficits—federal, state, and local—tend to fall in expansions and rise in contractions (with exceptions in periods of drastic movements in military spending or very strong inflation in a contraction). Liberal Keynesians will applaud this countercyclical behavior of the deficit. The rising surplus in the last half of expansion will tend to prevent overheating and inflation in an expansion. The rising deficit in contractions will tend to decrease unemployment and encourage a recovery.

On the other hand, conservatives will point out that the rising deficit in contractions may lead to inflation. This is certainly true in the present situation of chronic high unemployment and chronic high inflation—with the inflation continuing into the contractions. It is for this reason that *no* aggregate fiscal policy is correct in the face of these downturns with both unemployment and inflation. Conservatives will also point out that, in the expansions of

1970–1973 and 1975–1980, the deficit did fall, but it never became a surplus. Therefore, it created *less* inflationary pressure, but still had some inflationary pressure.

Those Marxists with a strong underconsumptionist orientation should praise the fact that there have been only deficits since 1970, thus helping bolster the inadequate demand (but they would condemn the *type* of spending, which is mostly military). They should also approve of the fact that the deficit did increase in all of the contractions, presumably aiding recovery. The underconsumptionists would tend to argue, however, that the countercyclical spending was never anywhere near enough to produce full employment.

Some conservatives—and some Marxists—believe that the government helps cause the business cycle contraction. Some conservatives would argue that government does not reduce the deficit enough in expansions, so continued inflationary pressure pushes up wages, causing lower profits, leading to a downturn. Some Marxists argue—contrary to the conservatives—that the capitalist-dominated government does not want full employment because it leads to high wages, so the government intentionally uses depressive fiscal measures to reduce expansion or start a downturn. The Marxists may point to the fact of rising surpluses before three peaks (1957, 1961, and 1969), which would cause rising unemployment and a recession or depression. They may also point to the fact of a rapidly declining deficit at the last two peaks (1973 and 1980), which would give less and less support to employment long before full employment was reached.

Some other conservatives, the supply-siders, do not seem to worry so much about big deficits. They do wish to cut government spending for the usual conservative reasons: it causes inflation, redistributes income to workers, and competes with private capital; and it could be done more efficiently by private capital (all very debatable reasons). But they wish to cut taxes even more, regardless of the effect on the deficit. As we have noted, they believe that lower taxes on the wealthy will increase saving, which will increase investment. More private investment will directly cure unemployment, which is caused by high taxes that hold down investment. More private investment will also indirectly cure inflation (even though it increases demand) because it will lead to higher productivity, which will be passed on to consumers in lower prices (either by competition or the goodwill of the monopolies).

SUMMARY

It is true that fiscal variables move countercyclically. At the peak, there is a rising surplus (or at least a declining deficit), which does indicate that capitalist governments have no desire for full employment. At the trough, however, capitalist governments do use a rising deficit to stimulate recovery because recessions and depressions also lead to rapidly declining profits.

The capitalist-dominated government fiscal policies do seem to be one of the factors precipitating downturns and also precipitating upturns. The extreme political business cycle theorists take this to mean that government is the sole cause of the business cycle. This theory appears to be quite incorrect for several reasons. There was a business cycle long before government fiscal variables were quantitatively important enough to have any effect. There is good evidence as to the important role of government only since the late 1930s.

Even when government has had some effect in precipitating downturns and upturns (the grain of truth in the political business cycle theory), it is only one factor if one considers the greater quantitative importance of others. Most important, it appears that the usual range of government fiscal policies could not set off a contraction until the private sector is ripe for it; then the slightest nudge sets it on a downward course in which the private sector plays the major role (while government policies try to reverse it). Depressive fiscal policies early in expansion will not cause a downturn unless they are very extreme. Similarly, early in a contraction government fiscal policies can achieve little. Toward the end of the contraction, however, a small push from government may set off a recovery because the private sector was ready to expand again. One must first understand the business cycle in the private economy and only then investigate how government strongly influences it in the present era.

APPENDIX 23A

An Endogenous Model of Fiscal Policy

If it is true, as radicals assert, that government fiscal policy is an endogenous function of the needs of the capitalist system (as interpreted by the dominant capitalist groups), then it should be possible to insert an equation explaining government fiscal policy in the cycle models of Part Three. The simplest explanatory factor is the gross national product (GNP). When GNP is rising, governments do less and less; but when GNP is falling, capitalist governments do more and more stimulation.

Another obvious explanatory element for Marxists is the rate of profit (Π/K). When the rate of profit is rising in an expansion, capitalist governments do less and less stimulation. As costs threaten profits at the end of expansion, governments may even attempt to depress the economy. When profit rates fall in the contraction, capitalist governments do more to stimulate the economy.

The equation for net government spending (G), or spending above revenue, with these two factors would be:

$$G_t = f\left(\frac{\Pi}{K}, Y\right)_{t-1} \tag{23A.1}$$

where the function f is negative and Y represents GNP. Thus G would rise in contraction and fall in expansion. There has been very little research so far in this framework to determine the exact causal mechanisms involved, other significant variables, and the size of the parameters.

APPENDIX 23B

Deficits and Balanced Budgets

Most politicians argue that an unbalanced budget is always bad. This has an intuitive appeal because the average person knows that if he or she has a deficit in his or her own personal budget, that is terrible.

But the Keynesian argument is that the federal budget of the United States is very different from a personal budget. In the first place, the U.S. government cannot go bankrupt. If it cannot tax or borrow enough, it can always print money. Moreover, the claim is that the debt is owed to ourselves (this is very different for countries with a debt owed to foreigners). Second, Keynesians argue that a deficit expenditure will stimulate the economy (prime the pump), so—though the multiplier—it will generate far more income than the new expenditure. Therefore, the expenditure will soon return to the government in the form of new taxes (supply-siders make a similar argument about lowering taxes).

Conservatives make two arguments against unbalanced budgets (besides the false intuitive one). One argument is that deficit spending floods the economy with money demand, so it causes inflation. Of course, in the Great Depression, this argument was irrelevant because the problem was deflation.

The other conservative argument, much more common at the present time, is the "crowding-out" thesis. It says that deficit spending means borrowing by the government in the bond market. This borrowing reduces the funds remaining for private investors, raises the interest rate, and therefore depresses the economy. Keynesians have argued that there is no strong evidence for the crowding-out effect. Many countries have had high deficits with low interest rates at various periods. It is also questionable how much of effect rises in interest rates have on investment (except in obvious cases like housing and autos).

It must also be noted that the two conservative arguments contradict each other to some extent. The first says that deficit spending expands demand and so is inflationary; the second says that deficit borrowing crowds out private borrowing, so it depresses demand (and is deflationary). The net effect may be one way or the other, but not both.

Finally, there is one radical argument against deficit spending that does not dispute its macro effect, but points to its income distribution effect. Almost all federal bonds are bought by upper-income individuals, who therefore receive all the interest on the debt. So the higher the debt, the more money is transferred from all taxpayers to upper-income interest receivers.

Chapter 24

MONETARY POLICY

Most of the monetary theory discussed in earlier chapters is oriented toward the development of proper monetary policy. In the American economy, our central bank, the Federal Reserve System (or Fed) is responsible for implementing monetary policy. The Federal Reserve System has traditionally had a mandate with multiple objectives. These objectives have generally tended to fall under four categories.[1] The Fed must try to do the following:

1. Protect the banking system from the kinds of financial emergencies that episodically did enormous damage.
2. Promote price stability.
3. Promote interest rate stability (sometimes called credit market stability).
4. With the cooperation of other central banks, promote international financial stability.

The Federal Reserve System accomplishes the first objective by regulating and auditing the activity of the nation's private commercial banks. The Fed is the depository for member bank reserves (hence, the name) and can act as a *lender of last resort* to troubled banks. In other words, if there is a run on a bank for any reason, where depositors make heavy withdrawals, the Fed can lend the troubled bank as much money as is needed to prevent a liquidation of the bank's assets.[2]

In recent years the Federal Reserve System has tended to give priority to the second objective, the promotion of price stability. Today the expression *price stability* translates into anti-inflation policy, of course, but it should not be forgotten that in other eras, such as the 1930s, deflation was probably more dreaded than inflation is now. That is why this particular objective is described as price stability rather than as anti-inflation policy. The Fed in

---

[1] See *The Federal Reserve System, Purposes and Functions* (Washington, D.C.: Board of Governors, 1963).
[2] For a good explanation of the importance of this "lender of last resort" function, see Charles P. Kindleberger, *Manias, Panics, and Crashes, A History of Financial Crises* (New York: Basic Books, 1978).

pursuing its policies, must not only ensure that prices don't inflate, but also that they don't deflate as well.

The objective of interest rate stability primarily compels the Federal Reserve System to keep interest rates reasonably low and nonvolatile. The Fed believes that investment is likely to be healthier in an environment where unexpected wild interest rate swings are not likely to be present.

Finally, the world's central banks are supposed to promote international financial stability. They assist in the exchange of foreign currency and often intervene in the foreign exchange market—where the currencies of different countries are traded—to protect the exchange value of a currency (such as the dollar price of the British pound or the Japanese yen price of the West German mark).

The successful pursuit of *all four* of these objectives is sometimes impossible. Often one objective is temporarily sacrificed so that another can be emphasized. For example, during a serious financial crisis, the Fed would certainly abandon an anti-inflation or foreign exchange stabilization policy if it felt the financial system needed a large dose of bank reserves at lower interest rates.

As will be emphasized strongly later in this chapter, sometimes the simultaneous pursuit of price stability and interest rate stability is mutually exclusive. During a period of high inflation, an anti-inflation policy is likely to wreak havoc with interest rates. In recent years, the "battle against inflation" has been given highest priority. As a result, the Fed's tight money policies have greatly increased unemployment. Because of the attention given to the fight against inflation, recent observers of the Fed might get the impression that the easing of inflationary pressures is their singular objective. That is not, however, their own view of their goals. Yet when one objective is being strongly emphasized, another may be harmed.

In the effort to fulfill its mandate, the Board of Governors of the Federal Reserve System has devised continually evolving policies that rely heavily upon the long tradition of monetary theory. It would be a mistake, however, to believe that actual policy is simply theory in practice or, to use another expression, theory put to work. The Fed is a political institution playing an important role in a complex and enigmatic world. Because of this, theory only *contributes* to policy and is only one ingredient in the strange mixture that also includes intuition, political judgment, and pressures from the banking system (remember that bankers control the regional banks according to the law, and bankers have a major influence in the whole system[3]).

Nonetheless, it is still probably the case that theory is an important factor influencing policy. Because of this, the remainder of this chapter is divided into roughly two parts. In the first, a brief review of monetary policy since the end of World War II is presented. This section, which is primarily descriptive, simply explains what the Fed has done over those four decades.

The second part of the chapter provides an overview of what the various critics insist the Federal Reserve System *should have done* and *what it should be doing.* It will be quite obvious

---

[3] For a very careful Marxist analysis of the Federal Reserve System, see Gerald Epstein, "Domestic Inflation and Monetary Policy: The Federal Reserve and the Hidden Election," in Tom Ferguson and Joel Rogers (eds.), *The Hidden Election* (New York: Pantheon, 1981), pp. 141–195.

that the competing *policy recommendations* are nearly perfectly aligned with the competing *monetary theories* discussed in earlier chapters. Because of this, the different policy recommendations are arranged according to the major competing schools of thought in monetary theory. We present monetarist, liberal, and radical views.

MONETARY TOOLS

A detailed description of Federal Reserve System policy tools was provided in Chapter 7. The three major tools are (1) reserve requirement changes, (2) controlling the discount rate, and (3) open market operations.

Reserves must be held against all liabilities of banks, with the legal minimum set by the *reserve requirement*, which is expressed as a certain percentage of each type of liability. Raising or lowering this reserve requirement will substantially affect the amount of new bank lending and money–credit creation that results from new reserves' being provided to the banking system. For example, when the reserve requirement on demand deposit liabilities is raised, this reduces the amount of new bank loans and demand deposit liabilities that can be extended when the Fed provides banks with new reserves. (Since the original writing of this text, laws have been passed requiring *all* federally insured financial institutions to keep reserves at the Fed.)

Banks are also allowed to borrow reserves from the Federal Reserve System through the discount window. The interest rate charged on such loans is called the discount rate. By raising or lowering the discount rate, the Fed can discourage or encourage the borrowing of bank reserves.

Neither of these two policy options has been used much by the Federal Reserve System in the past. Reserve requirement changes are thought to be too drastic and have seldom been used for policy reasons. Reserve requirements have gradually been lowered over the years, partly in response to pressure applied by commercial banks. The Fed does change the discount rate periodically, but this usually merely reflects changes in market interest rates. Often the discount rate is below competing market rates because, ideally, banks are supposed to borrow only emergency loans from the discount window, and it is felt that this rate should not be a penalty rate. The discount rate has never been used aggressively for policy reasons.

Open market operations are the true vehicle for implementing monetary policy. These operations are used daily by the Federal Reserve System with the explicit intent of accomplishing policy objectives. Open market operations are overseen by the Federal Open Market Committee (FOMC), and all open market transactions take place at the open market trading desk (actually a huge operation involving scores of traders) at the Federal Reserve Bank of New York. It is here that traders buy and sell U.S. Treasury securities. When they buy them, bank reserves are increased, and when they sell them, reserves are decreased. An increase in reserves allows bank loans to be made and bank liabilities, including demand deposits, a component of the money supply, to grow. These operations, therefore, influence levels of credit and money and interest rates in the economy.

In the policy discussions that follow, the primary tool of implementing policy will be open market operations. These have been used almost exclusively in the past and, because they are so effective, will certainly continue to be the paramount tool for implementing policy, whatever that policy happens to be, in the future.

MONETARY POLICY BETWEEN 1946 AND 1951

World War II was primarily debt-financed. In every year from 1942 to 1945, U.S. government borrowing exceeded tax receipts. The total U.S. government gross public debt, which was only $45 billion in December 1940, grew to $278 billion by December 1945. Yet despite this colossal growth in federal borrowing, interest rates on U.S. Treasury securities remained at exceptionally low levels. The average annual yield on three-month Treasury bills never exceeded 0.5 percent during this entire period. The yield on long-term bonds never exceeded 2.5 percent and was often well below that figure.

The Treasury's success in keeping interest rates low was due in part to the unusually high savings rate during the war. The Treasury, for example, managed to sell nearly $50 billion of the little Series-E savings bonds, typically with maturity values of only $25. But a good part of the success is also explained by the Fed's explicit policy of using open market operations (buying U.S. Treasury securities) to keep those rates down.

In fact, by the end of the war, the Federal Reserve System and private commercial banks held over half of all marketable Treasury debt outstanding (the Fed held about 12 percent, and banks held about 40 percent).[4] The Fed stood ready throughout the war to assist the Treasury in its financial operations. When interest rates showed any sign of rising, the Federal Reserve System would buy Treasury securities, which suppressed their yield. By doing this, the Fed absorbed only 12 percent of Treasury debt directly. Because this action increased bank reserves, however, there was a multiplier effect that allowed four to five times this amount of credit to be created (for example, the nation's money supply increased from $42 billion in December 1940 to $102 billion in December 1945).[5] Hence, there was plenty of new liquidity to "demand" the Treasury debt, and interest rates remained at low levels.

Up until the early 1950s, the U.S. Treasury had taken pride in the fact that government debt financing had always been orderly and nondisruptive. Even during the costly Civil War a century before, interest rates were seldom above 4 percent. The policy of keeping interest rates low and stable had been referred to as an "even-keel" policy. Aside from the international prestige that such policies offered (presumably "strong" governments could always maintain orderly finance markets even in times of adversity), it was generally thought that such stable markets promoted a very healthy investment climate.

Because of the critical need for cooperation during the war effort, the Federal Reserve System allowed itself to be subservient to the Treasury. The Treasury wanted an even-keel policy, and the Fed complied. The Treasury's dominance, however, did not end with the war. They still expected the Fed to remain a residual buyer of U.S. Treasury securities when there

---

[4] All preceding data are from *Banking and Monetary Statistics, 1941–1970* (Washington, D.C.: Board of Governors of the Federal Reserve System, 1971).

[5] Milton Friedman and Anna Schwartz, *A Monetary History of the United States, 1867–1960* (Princeton: Princeton University Press, 1971), Appendix A, Table A-1.

was no market for such securities at their prevailing low rates. Although three-month bill rates were allowed to drift upward gradually, three-to-five-year notes were kept at about 1.5 percent, and long term bonds were kept below 2.5 percent.

Through the late 1940s, the Federal Reserve System was becoming alarmed at the inflationary consequences of continuing this even-keel policy. Inflation emerged as a serious problem after the war, with the wholesale price index rising in excess of 50 percent between 1945 and 1948. In the eyes of the Fed's critics, the expansionary open market operations used to maintain the even-keel policy were adding far too much liquidity (be that money or credit; both expanded dramatically) to the economy.

After the outbreak of the Korean War in the summer of 1950, the Treasury again announced that it would be selling Treasury securities at low interest rates. This time the Board of Governors of the Federal Reserve System balked, insisting that these even-keel policies could not continue because of their inflationary implications. This resistance led to a series of meetings, which culminated in the Federal Reserve–Treasury Accord of March 4, 1951. This Accord was essentially a compromise. The Federal Reserve System reasserted its independence from the Treasury and announced that it would abandon policies designed to keep yields on Treasury securities at very low levels. They did agree, however, to promote "orderly markets" in government securities. This last concession effectively meant that the Fed would still heavily intervene in the security markets, preventing sizable movements in interest rates. If market forces were putting upward pressure on interest rates, they were allowed to drift upward very gradually. Rates did start to rise slowly after the Accord, and the long-term bond rate finally exceeded 3 percent for the first time in two decades in 1953.[6]

INTEREST RATE STABILIZATION POLICIES, 1952–1970

After the Accord, the Federal Reserve System kept its policy essentially unaltered for a decade. The Fed used open market operations to keep interest rates very steady throughout the 1950s although they allowed them to creep up gradually. Long-term U.S. Treasury bond rates rose from about 2.5 percent at the time of the Accord to about 4 percent in 1960. After 1960, the open market policy arm of the Fed, the Federal Open Market Committee (FOMC), began to emphasize strongly what they called "money market conditions" in their monthly meetings. They monitored the performance of a wide range of variables, including the growth rate of bank reserves, the federal funds rate, and the three-month Treasury bill rate. They did *not* monitor or attempt to control the money supply. During these years, the FOMC in their monthly meetings simply tried to get a feel for how the economy was performing in round-table discussions where anything of relevance, from housing starts to the rate of unemployment, was introduced. After discussion they would decide whether "money market conditions" should be "eased," "tightened," or left alone. If they decided to tighten, for example, they might have instructed the open market trading desk at the Federal Reserve Bank of New York (where open market operations are conducted) to trade in Treasury bills at a rate sufficient to raise their yield by 0.25 percent.

[6]For background on events leading to the accord, see New York Clearing House Association, *The Federal Reserve Re-examined* (New York: 1953).

These older operating procedures were a good example of purely discretionary monetary policy. During a recession, prevailing money market conditions in that environment might be interpreted as too tight, and instructions would be sent to the trading desk to ease conditions. Through open market operations, reserves were pumped into the banking system, dropping interest rates and stimulating credit, which, in turn, it was hoped, would stimulate the sagging economy.

After 1966, the FOMC began to monitor bank credit. They made projections about acceptable growth rates, and if the actual growth rate deviated from projections, they regarded that as a signal that conditions might be too tight or too easy. Deviations from projected growth rates did not *necessarily* generate any policy response, however. When bank credit growth deviated from projections, that was simply regarded as information by the FOMC. Sometimes they reacted, and other times they did not.

Regardless of the nature of their reactions to economic performance, the Fed never allowed interest rates to fluctuate very much. Their policy moves were typically very subtle.

MONITORING MONETARY AGGREGATES, 1970–1979[7]

Two developments in the late 1960s eventually forced the Fed to alter its procedure. One was the recognition that both the rate of inflation and nominal interest rates were creeping upward. The other was the growing popularity of monetarist theories, which provided appealing theoretical explanations for inflation. As was explained in Chapter 16, monetarists identified the money supply as the paramount variable influencing the level of nominal spending in the economy. It was natural, therefore, for them to advocate control of the money supply as appropriate central bank policy.

In 1970, these monetary aggregates (M1, M2, and M3) began to receive the attention of the FOMC. M1, the narrowest definition of the money supply, consisted of currency in the hands of the public plus demand deposits. M2 consisted of M1 plus small time deposits at commercial banks. M3 consisted of M2 plus time deposits at savings and loans and mutual savings banks. (All of these aggregate definitions have since been redefined numerous times).

Despite the new emphasis on monetary aggregates, the FOMC did not abandon its interest rate stabilization policies. Instead, as the new policy evolved, the FOMC developed multiple targets. In their monthly meetings, they would first consider the state of the economy. Then they would periodically attempt to determine growth rate ranges for M1 and M2 (they tended to ignore M3) and interest rate ranges consistent with their policy objectives. After 1975, every quarter the FOMC set an acceptable annual growth rate range for the year beginning in that quarter for M1, M2, M3, and bank credit (the acceptable range was 2 to 3 percentage points in width). Additionally, each month the FOMC set short-run, two-month growth rate ranges for the same aggregates.

Combined with this plethora of monetary aggregate growth rate range targets, the FOMC also set an allowable monthly trading range for the federal funds interest rate. Since the federal funds market is the market where banks lend and borrow excess reserves from each

---

[7]See Staff, "Monetary Aggregates and Money Market Conditions in Open Market Policy, *Federal Reserve Bulletin* (February 1971).

other, open market operations, which add reserves to the banking system when expansionary and subtract them when contractionary, can be used to control the federal funds interest rates directly.

This rather complicated strategy is perhaps easier to understand if the logic used to justify it is explained. The Fed does not have the ability to control the money supply *directly*. In its open market operations, all it can do is control the rate at which reserves are provided to the banking system. That will be *correlated* with the rate of growth of the money stock, of course, but there is no exact connection between reserves and the creation of monetary aggregates. Reserves can be applied against *any* bank liability, resulting in the growth of those not included in M1 or M2, or banks might choose to hold excess reserves.

Open market operations *can,* however, directly control the federal funds interest rate. Experience has shown that the open market trading desk at the Federal Reserve Bank of New York can peg the rate exactly where it wants it on a daily basis. Since the monetary aggregates couldn't directly be controlled and the federal funds rate could, the FOMC tried to choose a federal funds rate consistent with their targeted monetary aggregate growth rates. They relied upon experience to determine these pairings of interest rate and aggregate targets. For example, in the April 1975 FOMC meeting, it was believed on the basis of experience that if the federal funds rate stayed within the 4.75 to 5.75 percent trading range, M1 would grow at an annualized rate between 6.5 to 9 percent for the next two months.

At every monthly meeting, the FOMC would set this federal funds rate range and then would instruct the system account manager of the open market trading desk at the Federal Reserve Bank of New York to conduct open market operations in a way that would keep the federal funds rate within its target range. Throughout the late 1970s, because of growing credit demand, the trading desk had to expand bank reserves gradually in order to meet these targets. If, after a period of time, the monetary aggregates were growing above or below their target ranges, the federal funds rate range would be adjusted to compensate for the discrepancy. If, for example, M1 had been growing at a rate above the upper limit of its target range, then market conditions would be "tightened" by raising the federal funds rate range by some amount.

These operating procedures allowed the Federal Reserve System to continue their interest rate stabilization policies. They were still using open market operations primarily to control interest rates. As mentioned before, the allowable trading range on the federal funds rate was typically narrow between 1975 and 1979. The performance of the monetary aggregates was primarily used to adjust the interest rate ranges up and down. If M1 consistently exceeded its targets, then the federal funds rate range would be revised upward.

Because of this procedure, credit markets were, in fact, quite stable. Although interest rates gradually crept up between 1975 and 1979, they fluctuated very little (at least when compared to the period after 1979—they fluctuated more than they had in the 1950s and 1960s). The federal funds rate was almost always within its trading range. Tables showing both the short-run and long-run targets and performance of the monetary aggregates and the targets and performance of the federal funds rate are presented in Appendix 24A. Reference to those tables show that the monetary aggregates missed over half of the short-run targets set in the four-and-a-half-year period between 1974 and 1980, with the majority of misses being on the high side. The long-run targets were also usually missed, with the majority of misses being on the high side.

These results demonstrate that even though the FOMC had become more serious about monetary targets, they were still more effective in controlling interest rates because the monetary targets were often missed and typically exceeded, and the interest rate targets seldom were.

THE VOLCKER PLAN—OCTOBER 1979

The Federal Reserve System interest rate stabilization policies began to have serious problems after the recession of 1974–1975. The usual policy was becoming inherently inflationary. Generally, when credit demand is consistently very high, in the absence of central bank intervention, interest rates would rise to reflect this growth in credit demand. With an interest rate stabilization policy, however, the central bank is compelled to inject reserves continually into the banking system in order to meet their interest rate targets. Because of this, growing credit demand is automatically satisfied at low interest rates, and the amount of liquidity in the economy substantially grows. When the economy is running at near full capacity, inflation is the likely result. (Inflation is not *automatically* the result. If the borrowed funds are used for the sort of intensive capital investment that markedly raises productivity, production costs might decline, working against inflation.)

An elementary model of this explanation is shown graphically in Figure 24.1. In that graph, the initial demand for funds, which consists primarily of investment, consumer, and government deficit demand, is represented by line $DF1$. The initial supply of funds, which consists of private savings, gross business savings, and any new credit provided by financial intermediaries not related to savings (such as bank credit extended when excess reserves are available), is represented by the line $SF1$. The SF line has a positive slope because savings are assumed to be positively related to interest rates. The DF line has a negative slope because investment is assumed to be negatively related to interest rates. The interest rate trading range allowed by the monetary authorities is represented by the horizontal band. The Fed conducts open market operations with the explicit intent of keeping interest rates within this band. Given the initial demand and supply of funds ($DF1$ and $SF1$), the market equilibrium is represented by point a, and the equilibrium level of credit is represented by amount e_1.

Suppose the demand for funds rises from $DF1$ to $DF2$. This might be due to a rise in business, consumer, or government credit demand or to a combination of all these. Without any intervention in the credit markets by the Federal Reserve System, the new equilibrium would be point b, and the level of credit would expand from e_1 to e_2. Without intervention, the increase in the supply of funds (represented by movement *along* the $SF1$ line from a to b) would primarily result from an increase in savings. If this equilibrium prevailed, the level of credit-financed spending would rise, but it might be offset by a decline in consumption because the growth in the supply of funds is due to a growth in savings at the expense of consumption.

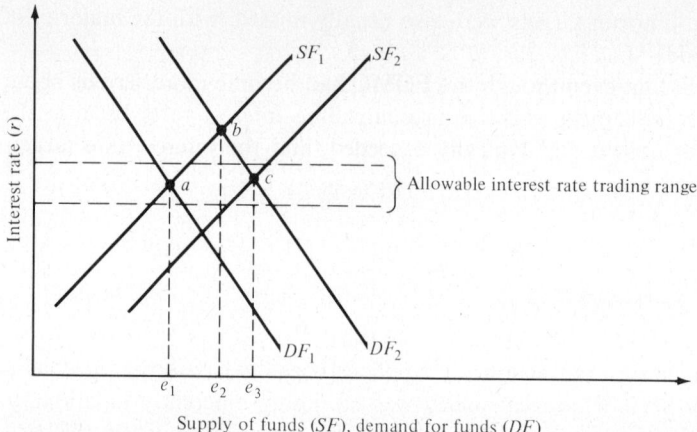

Supply of funds (*SF*), demand for funds (*DF*)

e = equilibrium values

Figure 24.1 The Effect of Interest Rate Stabilization Policies on the Level of Credit and Interest Rates

The new interest rate represented by point *b*, however, violates the upper limit of the interest rate trading range. If the Fed is using an interest rate stabilization policy, the open market trading desk will automatically inject reserves into the banking system. With the new excess reserves, the banking system can extend bank loans. This has the effect of moving the supply of funds line from *SF*1 to *SF*2. The final equilibrium is at point *c*. As can be seen, the interest rate target has been maintained.

The effect of this policy is to expand credit far more than would have otherwise been the case, from e_1 to e_3 (instead of e_1 to e_2). Furthermore, since the level of interest rates is roughly unchanged from the initial equilibrium level (at *a*), very little of the funds supply increase is financed by savings (why would savings grow if interest rates are ultimately unaltered?). This implies that almost all the increase in credit from e_1 to e_3 is funded by the newly created credit. Because savings did not grow, consumption did not drop, so the level of spending will likely rise rather substantially. The inflationary implications of this are quite obvious.

If the growth in credit demand persisted, the Federal Reserve System would soon discover that its monetary aggregate targets were being exceeded. After a time they would likely conclude that the original perceived correlation between their interest rate targets and their monetary targets were incorrect, and they would likely raise their allowable interest rate trading range. If the growth in credit demand *continued* to persist, however, over time the monetary authorities would discover that they needed to *continue* raising the interest rate bands time after time.

The final result over a long period of time, in the presence of a relentless growth in the demand for credit, is likely to be high growth rates in credit actually made available and in the money supply and also a gradual, albeit erratic, rise in nominal interest rates. Unless the productive capacity of the economy is dramatically expanding all during this period, inflation is likely as well.

By 1979, it was apparent that this was happening. As can be seen on Table 24.1 and Figure

Table 24.1
AMOUNTS AND ANNUAL RATES OF GROWTH OF SELECT MONEY, CREDIT, AND OUTPUT VARIABLES

	M1 Stock		Corporate Debt Net Total		Consumer Credit		Total Funds Owed by NP sectors[a]		Total Bank Credit		Nominal GNP	
	Amount	%Δ	Amount	%Δ	Amount	%Δ	Amount	%Δ	Amount	%Δ	Amount	%Δ
1965	187.5		350.1		89.9		1047.5		310.6		713.3	
1966	191.7	2.2	385.4	10.1	96.2	7.0	1114.2	6.4	327.6	5.5	771.7	8.2
1967	206.6	7.8	416.0	7.9	100.8	4.8	1194.4	7.2	365.0	11.4	818.8	6.1
1968	221.5	7.2	468.1	16.9	110.8	9.9	1292.2	8.2	405.1	11.0	894.7	9.3
1969	229.4	3.6	521.6	11.4	121.1	9.3	1381.0	6.9	422.4	4.3	953.3	6.5
1970	241.8	5.4	561.7	7.7	127.1	5.0	1477.5	7.0	459.0	8.7	996.4	4.5
1971	259.3	7.2	609.6	8.5	140.1	10.2	1620.2	9.7	510.3	11.2	1091.2	9.5
1972	283.7	9.4	679.8	11.5	157.2	12.2	1786.2	10.2	585.6	14.8	1219.4	11.7
1973	301.1	6.1	791.4	16.4	181.0	15.1	1981.3	10.9	669.0	14.2	1355.1	11.1
1974	308.7	2.5	833.5	5.3	191.3	5.7	2163.9	9.2	731.4	9.3	1452.4	7.2
1975	324.3	5.1	863.4	3.6	200.6	4.9	2363.5	9.2	761.1	4.1	1598.0	10.0
1976	347.0	7.0	932.8	8.0	224.2	11.8	2625.8	11.1	826.2	8.6	1749.8	9.5
1977	375.7	8.3	1035.4	11.0	259.2	15.6	2963.1	12.8	912.7	10.5	1958.1	11.9
1978	401.7	6.9	1175.3	13.5	339.9	31.1	3358.4	13.3	1030.3	12.9	2210.8	12.9

[a]Excluding equities.
NOTE: Data are for the last quarter of the year listed. The percentage change is annualized.
SOURCE: Federal Reserve System, *Flow of Funds* (Washington, D.C.: GPO, 1980).

24.2, the rates of growth of many credit and money measures grew dramatically after 1965. Corporate debt in most years after 1965 grew at a rate exceeding 10 percent. Consumer credit virtually exploded, rising an amazing 31 percent in 1978.

Net government borrowing was very high as well throughout this period. As was described in Chapter 7, after 1970 the government began running consistently large deficits, which were debt-financed.

As was discussed earlier, the federal funds rate target ranges were also gradually drifting up. After the recession of 1974–1975, the federal funds rate was typically between 4.5 percent and 5.5 percent. After 1978, the same rate typically exceeded 10 percent. The performance of the Treasury bill rate and the regulated ceiling on savings deposits are shown in Figure 24.3. Again it can be seen that interest rates have exhibited a volatile upward trend.

Prices were rising as well. As was shown in Chapter 3, the consumer price index and producer (wholesale) price index both rose markedly and erratically after 1960.

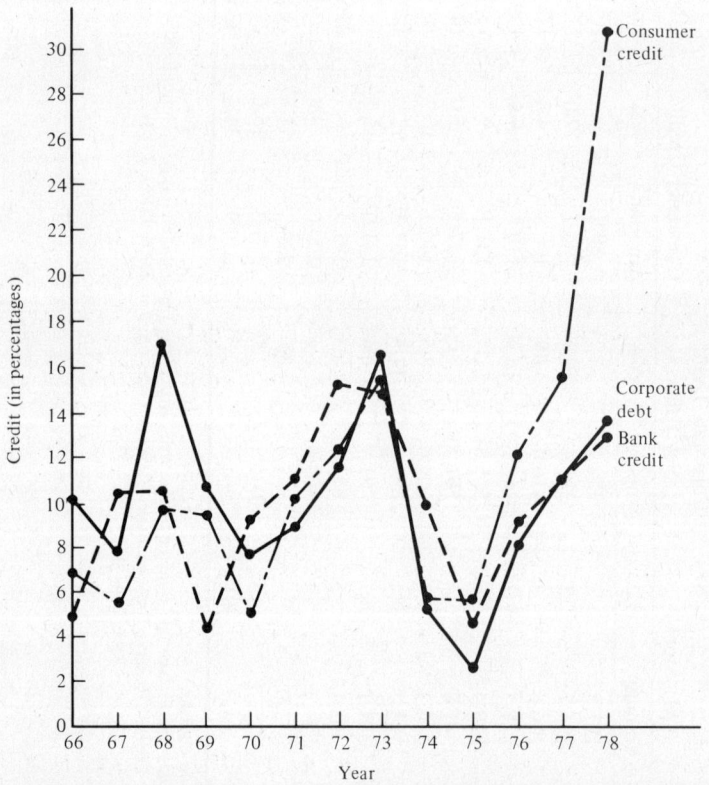

Figure 24.2 Annual Rates of Growth of Select Debt and Credit Variables
SOURCE: Federal Reserve System, *Flow of Funds* (Washington, D.C.: U.S.G.P.O., 1980)

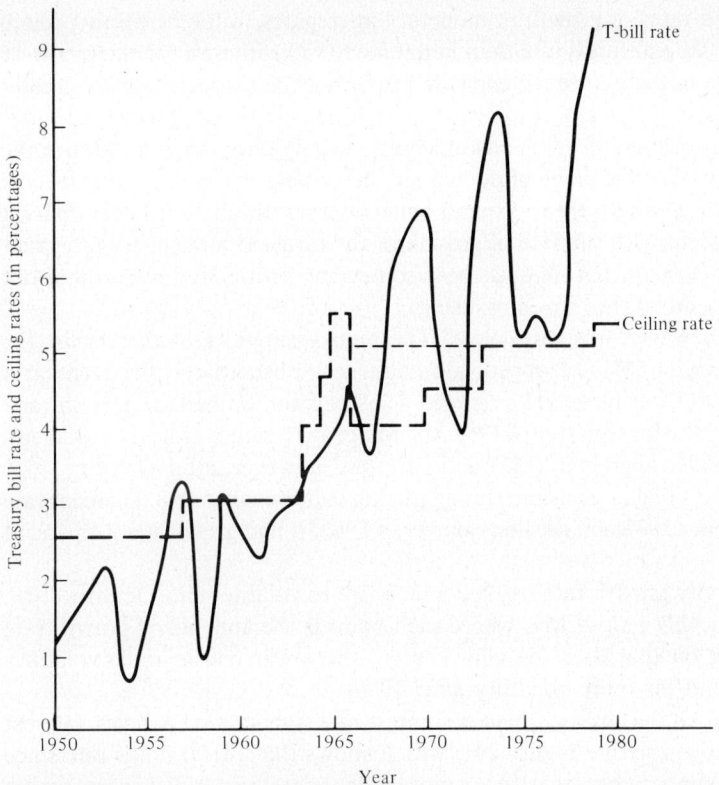

Figure 24.3 Treasury Bill Rate (3-month original issue) and "Regulation Q" Ceiling on Savings and Time Rates for Commercial Banks

NOTE: Interest rates on T-bills are June figures for each year shown. In 1970, ceilings were set for maturity categories. The graph represents ceilings for bank savings deposits and time deposits of shortest maturity. Time deposit ceiling was higher from 1965 to 1973 and is represented by the dotted line. In September 1966, ceilings were extended to other thrift institutions and were typically .25 percent higher than these shown here.

Source: Federal Reserve System, *Flow of Funds* (Washington, D.C.: U.S.G.P.O., 1980)

The Volcker Decision

By the autumn of 1979, the Federal Reserve Board of Governors and the Federal Open Market Committee (FOMC), under the stewardship of their newly selected chairman, Paul Volcker, had concluded that their monetary policies simply were not working. The decision was made to abandon the interest rate stabilization policy and to substitute in its place a policy that was more monetarist in structure. It was announced after an FOMC meeting in October 1979 that the Federal Reserve System would give priority in its monetary policy to controlling the growth rate of the monetary aggregates. This decision amounted to a switch in emphasis from controlling the federal funds within narrow ranges to targeting and controlling specific monetary aggregates by carefully managing bank reserves. The FOMC, it was promised, would place emphasis "on supplying the volume of bank reserves estimated to be consistent with the desired rates of growth in monetary aggregates, while permitting much greater fluctuations in the federal funds rate than heretofore."[8] The interest rate targets were not to be dropped entirely, but were instead expanded to very wide ranges, typically greater than 4 percent.

Since this new policy was announced, it has not been entirely clear how in practice the policy is supposed to work. The language of documents describing the policy make it seem as if the open market trading desk were to expand bank reserves gradually in open market operations at a rate consistent with the rate of growth of the targeted monetary aggregates. The growth of bank reserves since that time has been somewhat erratic, however, so it is not clear what operating procedures they are now using.

A number of results, however, are quite clear. The money supply growth rate for the narrowest monetary aggregate (M1)[9] dropped, although not substantially. Between early 1977 and the time of the Volcker plan, M1 averaged a 7.8 percent annualized growth rate. Between October 1979 and the first quarter of 1982, the M1 growth rate averaged 6.6 percent. The growth rate of the wider aggregate (M2) actually *rose*, however, after October 1979. Between early 1977 and the Volcker decision, this aggregate had grown at an 8.9 percent rate annualized. Between October 1979 and the first quarter of 1982, it had grown at a 9.4 percent annualized rate.

The narrow money supply growth rate has become far more volatile since October 1979. Figure 24.4 shows the monthly plot of M1, where each point is the annualized growth rate for the 12 months ending on that date. As can be seen, there was considerable volatility between 1970 and 1975, but far more volatility after 1979.

As might be expected, with the abandonment of interest rate stabilization policies, interest rates have also become more volatile. Figure 24.5 which shows the federal funds rate since 1970, again confirms that the rate has become far more volatile at a much higher level since the 1979 decision.

By *most* criteria, it can be said that the Federal Reserve System was conducting policies leading toward a contraction after late 1979. The narrow money supply growth rate dropped (albeit somewhat modestly), and the general level of interest rates rose. *Real* interest rates (adjusted for inflation) rose to very high levels. Adjusted bank reserves, which had risen at an annualized rate of 6.4 percent between early 1977 and late 1979, rose at only a 4.7 percent rate after 1979. On the other hand, the growth of the M2 money stock actually rose after October 1979.

The rate of inflation did abate after mid-1980 with the deceleration being at first gradual,

---

[8]This quote and the description of these policies are found in "Record of the Policy Actions of the Federal Open Market Committee, *Federal Reserve Bulletin* (December 1979), pp. 972–978. For a detailed discussion of the new policy produced shortly after the policy was devised, see The Board of Governors of the Federal Reserve System, *Monetary Policy Report to Congress Pursuant to the Full Employment and Balanced Growth Act of 1978,* February 19, 1980.

[9]The narrow money supply, M1, is defined, as of April 1982, as currency and demand deposits held by the nonbank public, traveler's checks, and other checkable deposits at financial institutions. M2 is defined as M1 plus savings and small time deposits at all depository institutions, commercial bank overnight repurchase agreements, overnight Eurodollars, and money market mutual fund shares.

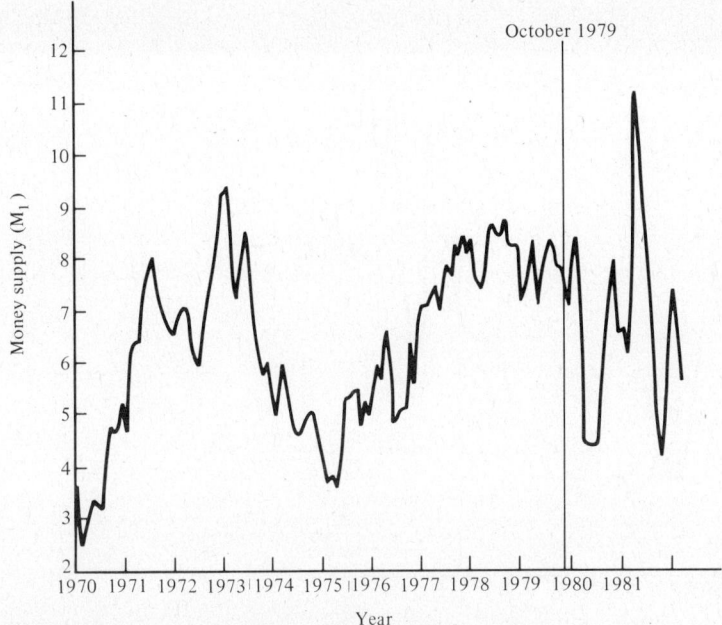

Figure 24.4 Rate of Change of Money Supply (M1)
SOURCE: Federal Reserve Bank of San Francisco.
NOTE: Percentage rate of change of money supply per month.

then dropping more sharply with the deep recession of 1982. The reduction in inflation was, of course, accompanied by and perhaps caused by the double-dip recession of 1980–1982. It is too simplistic to attribute the *cause* of the recession and the corresponding drop in the inflation rate to the Fed's contractionary policies, but there is no doubt that the persistent high interest rates after 1979 took a heavy toll on certain sectors of the economy that are sensitive to interest rates.

In 1982, the Board of Governors was reasonably confident that the new monetary policy was accomplishing its intended objective, the reduction of inflation. The board was also receiving a lot of criticism for the severity of the recession in 1982 as well, but the board seemed to regard the recession as a necessary trade-off in the war against inflation.

STRICT MONETARIST POLICIES[10]

Even though the new Federal Reserve System policies are the closest thing to monetarism yet seen in the economy, they have not received the endorsement of those economists who

---

[10] For a succinct explanation of strict monetarist policies, see Milton Friedman, "The Role of Monetary Policy," *The American Economic Review* (January 1968). See also references in Chapter 16.

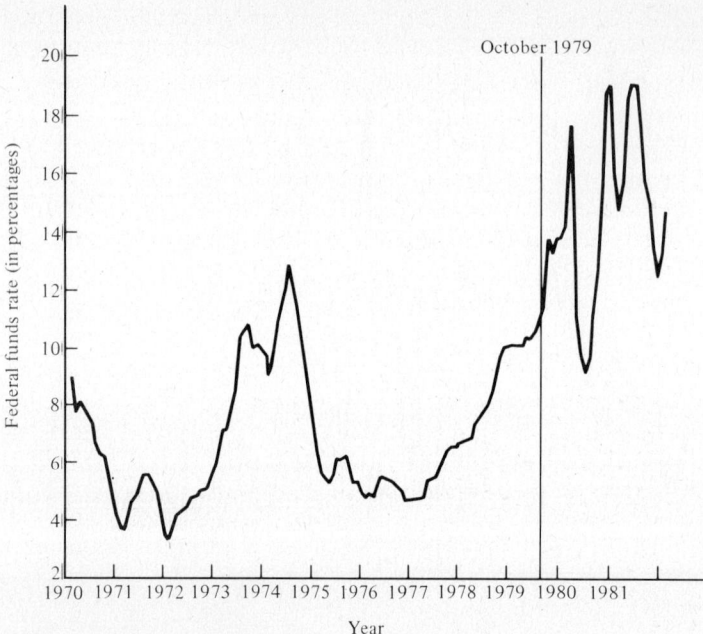

Figure 24.5 Federal Funds Rate
SOURCE: Federal Reserve Bank of San Francisco.

are in the strictest monetarist tradition. This new policy still allows discretionary responses to economic conditions and continues to give attention to the level of interest rates, although to a lesser degree.

Strict monetarism advocates the adoption of a monetary "rule." The rule means that the money supply should be forced to grow at some designated rate, say 4 to 5 percent, regardless of economic circumstance. A monetary expansion should not be used to counteract a recession. Interest rates should be determined entirely by the market.

The money supply, according to this school of thought, will be controlled by either carefully controlling the level of bank reserves or the monetary base (bank reserves plus currency in the hands of the nonbank public) through open market operations. Through empirical research, the *money multiplier,* which establishes the connection between reserves or the base and the money supply will be determined. Once determined, open market operations will be conducted at a pace sufficient to allow reserves or the base to grow at the rate sufficient to produce the desired growth in the money supply.

For example, the FOMC might decide to control total bank reserves in their open market operations. Staff economists might conclude, in their research, that if reserves grow at a 3.5 percent annual rate, then the M1 money supply would grow at 4 percent. Presumably, the trading desk at the Federal Reserve Bank of New York would be instructed to purchase Treasury securities gradually at a rate that would allow bank reserves to expand 3.5 percent annually. This they would do faithfully and passively regardless of market conditions.

If, after a period of time, they discovered that they had guessed incorrectly about the multiplier and the money supply growth rate was too fast or too slow, they would presumably adjust the reserve growth rate to compensate. For example, if the FOMC were controlling reserves and the growth rate of reserves was 3.5 percent, but the money supply was growing at 5 percent instead of the desired 4 percent, then the allowed growth rate of reserves might be dropped down a bit until the money supply target would be approximately reached.

To be practical, if the FOMC were using a strict monetarist policy, they would probably use narrow target *ranges* for both their control instrument (the base or reserves) and their monetary target. They might, for example, want the money supply to grow between 3.5 percent and 4.5 percent annually. Since the money multiplier does vary, this is probably the only practical policy.

Regardless of the practical operating plans of strict monetarism, the policy has one fundamental feature that separates it from the Volcker monetarism: in the conduct of open market operations, there is to be no response whatsoever to prevailing economic conditions. It is *not* the job of the central bank to pursue stabilization or countercyclical policies. This is the purest form of a laissez-faire policy. The free market economy is to work without intervention.

The Theoretical Justification for Strict Monetarism

The theoretical justification provided by monetarists for their own policies is described in Chapter 16. What is offered here is a summary of some of their most salient arguments.

First, monetarists see their policy as the most *workable* monetary policy. In their opinion, the Federal Reserve System can't hope to control interest rates and the two or three measures of monetary aggregates simultaneously, for example. Furthermore, monetarists argue, variations in the money supply growth rate will undoubtedly produce variations in the level of spending, but the lags and amplitudes between money and spending are very variable, so an expansionary discretionary monetary stimulus might overstimulate or understimulate, producing more confusion and harm than assistance. It is far simpler to have one easy target meet with one simple procedure in pursuit of a very elementary objective—to make it easy for the private sector of the economy to solve its own problems.

Second, a strict monetarist policy distinctly avoids the temptation to inflate. Strict monetarists contend that discretionary policy unavoidably ends up being inflationary policy. There is simply too much political and economic temptation to keep credit terms easy and interest rates low. Expansionary open market operations are used during a recession, but contractionary operations are not used during the boom phase of the business cycle because they are so unpopular. Because the long-run connection between money and spending in the economy is so exact, an inflation is utterly impossible when a monetary rule is in effect. Inflation, monetarists insist, would absolutely be a thing of the past in the presence of a monetary rule.

On a related matter, monetarists argue that strict monetarist policies would make the U.S. Treasury entirely responsible for its own fiscal activities. Even after the Federal Reserve–Treasury Accord of 1951, the Fed with its interest rate stabilization policies tended to monetize a good part of the Treasury debt. Such activity was politically expedient for the Treasury even though economically inadvisable, because the Treasury was not forced to borrow at market interest rates. Because interest rates were artificially low until inflationary expectations drove them higher, the damaging effect of chronic deficits was not easily apparent to the general public until years after the deficits. With strict monetarism, the advocates argue, the impact of deficits becomes *immediately* apparent; they result in high interest rates.

In recent years monetarists have stressed that monetary rules will eliminate uncertainty over monetary policy. They see the presence of uncertainty as very damaging for the economy. With investors and consumers uncertain about future levels of inflation and interest rates and not knowing when monetary authorities are going to intervene arbitrarily in the markets, they tend to become more cautious and somewhat unpredictable themselves in their behavior. This has the long-run effect of tending to depress both savings and investment (because the rewards of such activity are less certain) and place a risk premium on interest rates.

Implicit in the justification of strict monetarist policy is the notion that the finance markets would be reasonably *stable* if monetarist policies were in effect. This implies that both saving and borrowing activity would not be volatile. If, on the contrary, investment demand for borrowed funds is volatile, then the monetary rule is going to produce very volatile interest rates. If investment demand should shift suddenly downward, then in the absence of intervention by the Fed, interest rates would drop precipitously. If business loan demand shot up sharply, interest rates would jump. Monetarists acknowledge that the demand for borrowed funds is occasionally volatile, but they attribute that volatility to the fact that discretionary policies produce an unhealthy environment of uncertainty.

DISCRETIONARY MONETARISM

Advocates of a discretionary monetary policy[11] also identify money as the most important financial variable influencing the level of nominal spending in the economy, and it is the primary, if not the exclusive, variable that the Federal Reserve System should attempt to control. These monetary theorists also have considerable faith in the free enterprise system, but they regard it as less stable than their conservative colleagues and occasionally in need of countercyclial stabilization policy.

The Volcker policy that has existed since 1979 is certainly a type of discretionary monetarism although some "mild" monetarists may disapprove of certain aspects of the new policy. Volcker's policy gives primary emphasis to the control of monetary aggregates, with most attention given to M1. Secondary attention, however, is given to the behavior of interest rates. Strict monetarists would not allow this.

An ideal discretionary monetarist policy would always state its objectives in meeting monetary targets, as is the case with the Fed now. Explicit secondary interest rate targets might or might not be utilized. The monetary targets, however, rather than being held constant, would be raised and lowered as economic conditions dictated. They would be

---

[11]For typical examples of discretionary monetarism, see Paul Volcker, "The Role of Monetary Targets in an Age of Inflation," *Journal of Monetary Economics* (1978–1979) and David Laidler, "Monetarism: An Interpretation and an Assessment," *Economic Journal* (March 1981).

raised, for example, at the outset of a recession and lowered if inflation became a problem. In the presence of an inflationary recession, such as those that were experienced in 1975 and 1980, the anti-inflation goal would be given priority until such time as damage to the economy from the recession became politically unbearable. Then the Fed would likely pursue a "tightrope" policy, providing enough of a stimulus to prevent unemployment from rising more but still keeping the financial system safe.

Discretionary monetarist policies recognize that the Federal Reserve System has a mandate with *multiple* and often contradictory objectives and find some merit in credit market stabilization policies. The advocates of discretionary policy do not impute to the finance markets the sort of stability that strict monetarists believe is there, but they are confident that *properly conducted* discretionary monetary policy can productively smooth out market disturbances. At critical times the finance markets are victimized by all sorts of shocks and disturbances; they are often disrupted by the harmful activities of speculators and damaged by occasional episodes of irrational behavior. At such times, the discretionary monetarists argue that the Fed must step in and do whatever is necessary to restore order even if it means abandoning monetary targets for a period of time.

THE CRITICISM OF MONETARIST POLICIES

The critics of monetarism[12] have a number of complaints against monetarism and especially the monetarist "rule." Generally, the rule is regarded as too inflexible. The critics, often in the Keynesian tradition, believe that one of the many roles of the government is to implement countercyclical stabilization policies and that the government can do this successfully if appropriate policies are implemented. Rather than regard the economy as a smoothly running machine needing an occasional few drops of monetary oil, they see the private sector as prone to all sorts of disturbances, calamities, and economic mishaps. The monetary rule simply ties the hands of one of the most potentially potent public agencies, rendering it ineffective during times of economic crises.

In the Keynesian view, it may have been the case that the discretionary policies of the 1950s, 1960s, and 1970s led to inflation and related problems, but this cannot imply a condemnation of *all* discretionary policies. It merely demands that the mistakes of the past be recognized and that better discretionary policies be devised.

If the finance markets are inherently unstable, with volatile demands for credit, episodic bursts of harmful speculation, and lapses of rational decision making, then monetarist policies are ill-advised. The closer the Fed moves toward emphasis on narrow monetary growth rate targets, the greater the interest rate volatility is going to be. Any sudden jump in credit demand is likely to drive interest rates up without the intervention of the Fed. The extreme volatility in interest rates since the Fed adopted a discretionary monetarist policy in 1979 is cited as evidence of this. If a monetarist rule were in effect, with open market operations providing a daily trickle of new reserves regardless of market conditions, interest rates would

---

[12]See references in Chapter 17 for some of the many articles critical of monetarism.

be wildly volatile. There is, in other words, a trade-off involved with monetarist policies. The closer a central bank gets to a monetarist rule, the more volatile interest rates become.

Volatile interest rates can do some serious economic damage. Because the market value of long-term securities, such as bonds, move inversely with interest rates, volatile interest rates introduce the possibility of enormous capital losses. Such losses were, in fact, experienced in 1979 and after with the rise in interest rates. In healthy markets, the lender is willing to assume the market risks of lending over long periods if promised the reward of slightly higher interest rates on long-term debt. But when interest rates are volatile (or there is some fear of future increase in rates), lenders want to shift more of the risk to borrowers and are not willing to lend long-term unless it is at *very* high interest rates. In the presence of volatility, long-term financing becomes very expensive and, in some cases, impossible. Since many types of economic projects, such as large-scale plant and equipment and both residential and commercial construction, are best financed with long-term loans, a disorderly long-term finance market may seriously curb investment in these areas.

Economists who have been influenced by the argument that the money stock is endogenous, such as the Post Keynesians and creditists, are also highly critical of monetarism. In the long run, monetarist policies will simply be ineffective, they argue. If a monetary rule is adopted, for example, and either private or government credit demand continues to grow, the resulting high interest rates will introduce a fertile environment for the development of financial instruments that initially are money substitutes and eventually begin to serve money functions, at least at some levels of commerce. With such a development, the list of instruments that the Fed actually controls (such as M1) become increasingly irrelevant to the level of spending. This phenomenon might "mysteriously" appear as a rise in velocity—the ratio of spending to the officially defined money supply will shoot up as whatever the Fed is controlling with its rule becomes less important to the level of spending in the economy.

MONETARY ECLECTICISM

One general type of nonmonetarist policy proposal that might receive a revival if discretionary monetarism yields disappointing results in the 1980s might be referred to as *monetary eclecticism*. This sort of policy proposal is consistent with the spirit of the Radcliffe Committee Report and the economists with whom that document found favor.[13]

Economists who might favor monetary eclecticism would tend to believe that the connection between any *single* monetary target, be that M1, M2, some credit aggregate, or some interest rate, and the level of spending in the economy is very inexact. The Radcliffe Committee implied this when they stated that the health of the economy is greatly influenced by the "state of liquidity." The committee was criticized for the obvious ambiguity in this opinion, but perhaps unfairly so. They simply believed that a central bank (they were concerned primarily with the Bank of England) could do little more than *contribute* to a healthy financial environment conducive to noninflationary economic growth. In conducting policy,

[13] See references to the Radcliffe Committee in Chapter 17.

the central bank should continually reevaluate the status of the financial sector by monitoring and considering the performances of a *wide spectrum* of financial variables and other economic variables.

If this sort of monetary policy were being used by the Federal Reserve System, the Federal Open Market Committee would meet frequently and discuss the state of the economy and the status of the variables that they monitor. They might identify trouble spots in the finance markets, such as an excessive expansion of certain credit measures or high long-term interest rates. They might decide that an economic slump is too serious and requires an expansionary stimulus. They would then communicate to the open market trading desk that an expansion or contraction is desired.

From the viewpoint of monetary eclecticism, certain lessons from the past should aid in the avoidance of old mistakes. The FOMC should pay far more attention to *real* interest rates (adjusted for inflation) than they have in the past. If discretionary policies are to be used then it would be appropriate to run an expansionary policy during a recession, allowing real interest rates to drop and the aggregates to grow at higher levels. Equally important, however, is the need to begin to contract after the recovery is underway. If the second step is forgotten, then the lopsided stabilization policy will be afflicted with the same problem that beset the old interest rate stabilization policy; it will be inflationary.

Monetary eclecticism denies the importance of any single monetary variable. Instead, in the Radcliffe tradition, it feels that the central bank should assist in the maintenance of overall financial stability. This approach obviously endorses the liberal use of discretionary policy. It would be successful as *anti-inflation* discretionary policy only if the FOMC were resolved to run a genuine recession or depression in the face of inflation regardless of the political criticism that such a policy might generate. Some monetarists have claimed that this particular requirement might destroy the effectiveness of the policy when actually applied in a real political world.

CONTROLLING INTEREST RATES

An interest-rate-control policy would operate in a way similar to the old interest rate stabilization policies with one major exception: the FOMC would monitor and attempt to control a *real* rather than a nominal interest rate. The authorities might adopt an interest rate rule, keeping, for example, the federal funds rate three percentage points above the consumer price index, or they might choose to pursue a discretionary policy, raising real rates when inflation threatened and dropping them during a recession. Suppose, for example, that the nominal federal funds rate is 6 percent with a 3 percent rate of inflation. If the inflation rate gradually rose to 7 percent, the FOMC might want to raise the federal funds rate to 2 percent above the inflation rate at 9 percent. If inflation continued into the double-digit range, the FOMC might wish to widen the gap between inflation and nominal rates, pushing the federal funds rate to perhaps 4 percent above the inflation rate.

Implicit in a real interest rate policy is the acceptance of the hypothesis that a high enough real interest rate will *automatically* act to discourage the sort of borrowing that leads to inflation. An accelerated discretionary policy (when the *real* interest rate target is raised at higher levels of inflation) would tend to be more effective as an anti-inflation tool. The policy is compatible with the Post Keynesian and similar critiques of monetarism in that it implies that the *real price* of borrowing rather than the amount of money is the critical variable influencing the sorts of marginal spending that generate inflation and contribute to business cycles. It also avoids the inflationary bias of *nominal* interest rate stabilization policies, but also assures considerable stability in the *real* cost of borrowing. There is a trade-off in considering which policy to adopt. The rigid interest rate rule assures a stable real cost of borrowing, which reduces uncertainty when there is price stability, but a discretionary policy is more likely to be successful if the connection between real interest rates and inflation is inexact.

Such a policy requires that there be a very strong connection between real interest rates and the level of spending in the economy—or at least between real rates and those *changes* in spending that produce either inflation or business cycles. Economists not convinced of this strong connection will be critical of this policy proposal.

CONTROLLING WIDE AGGREGATES AND CREDIT[14]

Some monetary economists critical of monetarism's focus on narrow monetary aggregates advise the monitoring and targeting of much wider liquidity aggregates, such as M3 or some measure of credit. It is felt by these theorists that these inclusive aggregates of credit are much more closely correlated to levels of spending than money.

Such ideas are certainly consistent with the endogenous money stock argument. If near money substitutes that begin to function as money are developed, wide aggregates that include more financial instruments are likely to include those instruments (such as money market funds) that begin to serve as money. Hence, a wide aggregate policy is less likely to be "surprised" by inflation if the endogenous money stock argument is correct. Advocates of these policies point out that the velocities of wide aggregates have tended to be nearly constant for two decades whereas the velocity of money has risen sharply. This provides strong evidence, in their opinion, that the long-run relationship between wide aggregates and spending is far more exact.

Creditists, as they might be called, stress that both the level of spending and the extension of new credit are both *flows* (whereas the monetary aggregates are stocks), and any variation in credit flows will *directly* cause a variation in spending whereas expenditures can grow without changes in the money stock, and changes in the money stock need not necessarily lead to changes in spending. A rise or fall in the demand for money as a financial asset can disturb the connection between money and spending, but a rise in the amount of credit extended will almost certainly generate new spending. When inflation is a problem, the creditists believe that controls over credit are more likely to succeed than a reduction in the rate of growth of the money supply.

[14]For a clear articulation of this policy, see James S. Earley, Robert J. Parsons, and Fred A. Thompson, "Money, Credit, and Expenditures; A Sources and Uses of Funds Approach," *The Bulletin* 3 (New York: NYU Graduate School of Business, 1976).

SOME CRITICISMS OF THE NONMONETARIST POLICIES

The wide aggregate and credit policies are most vulnerable on the issue of *controllability*. Even though it may be the case that these aggregates are more closely correlated to spending than money, there is some question about whether the Federal Reserve System can control them.

The Fed's primary tool is the open market operation, which changes the level of bank reserves. Since the narrowly defined money supply consists of a Fed liability (currency) and a bank liability (demand deposits), which must meet reserve requirements, monetarists insist that only with money is there a reliable connection between what the Fed can actually control (reserves or the monetary base) and what it is trying to influence (money). Inclusive aggregates or credit might work better than money if they could be controlled, but they can't, so there is no point in giving them so much attention. Ultimately, advocates of the wide aggregate and credit policies must be confident that a contraction in reserves reduces general credit availability or slows the growth of financial assets if open market operations are to be effective in implementing their policies.

The interest-rate-control policy fares a little better on the issue of controllability. Experience has already shown that nominal interest rates can be controlled with open market operations. The control of real interest rates, however, would be more difficult. Policymakers would probably have to set a *nominal* target rate that is adjusted for a recent observation of a price index. For example, if the most recent consumer price index rose at an annualized rate of 6 percent, the FOMC might set a nominal interest rate target of 9 percent (or 8.5 percent to 9.5 percent) and consider this to be a 3 percent real target rate. The nominal target rate could easily be met. Again, however, it should be remembered that not all monetary economists think the connection between interest rates and spending is very exact.

As has already been mentioned, economists critical of discretionary policies in general are afraid that such policies are inherently inflationary. It is feared that using any policy that emphasizes interest rates or monetary eclecticism will reintroduce inflation through the back door. There is simply too much political pressure to keep credit terms easy and interest rates low. Expansionary policies during recessions would be virtually automatic, but anti-inflationary policies during the recovery would be strongly resisted. Such critics, indeed, seem to have history on their side. For two, perhaps even three decades, the Federal Reserve System has been lax in their anti-inflation effort and undoubtedly contributed substantially to the recent inflation. No discretionary policy will work unless the Federal Reserve System is absolutely *resolved* to tighten credit conditions through open market operations at the appropriate times. Without that resolve, no discretionary policy can work.

Finally, monetarist critics believe that discretionary policies, tightening here and easing there, introduce an element of uncertainty into the finance markets because one can never be sure of what the Federal Reserve System is going to do. Interestingly enough, the advocates of discretionary policies believe that uncertainty will be *reduced* if monetarism is abandoned. It is easy to see why they differ. With discretionary nonmonetarist policies, the rate of growth of the money supply becomes very variable, which the monetarists claim introduces extreme uncertainty about the future state of the economy because money is so important in determining the level of spending. On the other hand, with monetarist policies, the money growth rate is likely to be stable, but interest rates and perhaps the growth of other variables will be volatile. Since economists in the Keynesian and other critical tradition downplay the importance of money, *this* situation is seen as introducing more uncertainty.

THE PROBLEM OF SIMULTANEOUSLY HIGH RATES OF INFLATION, INTEREST RATES, AND UNEMPLOYMENT

As has already been indicated, policymakers have been confronted with an unusually sticky problem in the late 1970s and early 1980s. During this period of stagflation, the economy has been afflicted with very high rates of inflation, interest rates, and unemployment *simultaneously.* This is very unfortunate because the policies discussed in this chapter almost certainly involve *trade-offs* among these variables. For example, once an inflation is under way, an anti-inflation policy of any description will in the short run almost certainly cause unemployment and interest rates to rise. The consequences might be politically or economically unbearable, which bodes very ill for a genuine anti-inflation policy.

If policymakers rely on any of the policies described in this chapter, they will have to decide upon the balance of evils they desire in the outcome of their policy. Given the complexity of the political and economic structure in the United States, it is difficult to know if any anti-inflation policy can truly be successful when there is high unemployment.

THE NEED FOR MONETARY AND FISCAL POLICY COORDINATION

The power of monetary policy, regardless of which plan is favored, will be seriously diminished if the policy is not integrated with a sound fiscal policy. For example, a tight monetary policy designed to cure inflation is incompatible with an expansionary fiscal policy running large budget deficits.

If a traditional interest-rate-stabilization policy is being used, the large federal deficits will simply be monetized. Increased federal borrowing will put upward pressure on interest rates, forcing rates to exceed their targets. The Federal Reserve System must respond by conducting expansionary open market operations to lower nominal interest rates, and the resulting increase in bank reserves will generate an expansion of money or credit or both, fueling future inflation.

If a real interest-rate-stabilization policy is being used, the short run effect will be the same. Real interest rates will rise initially, forcing an open market expansionary operation. As inflation emerges; however, nominal interest rates will have to be forced upward to maintain the real interest rate target. The final result will be very high nominal interest rates.

If either monetarist or wide aggregate and credit control policies are being used, the Federal Reserve System will not accommodate Treasury borrowing, and interest rates are bound to rise, producing the crowding-out effect. The effect of high interest rates during a tight monetary policy and easy fiscal policy can be very damaging to an economy. It will have the tendency to polarize the economy. Those industries that are sensitive to interest rates, such as residential construction, consumer durables, and durable investment goods, and all linkage industries such as raw materials, might be severely damaged. Simultaneously, those industries that are the direct and indirect recipients of the Treasury's heavy spending, such as defense, might prosper. The economy can be polarized into simultaneous depression and prosperity side-by-side, which not only affects industries inequitably, but also geographical regions that depend heavily upon particular industries. Such polarization is an extremely unhealthy state of affairs because it can produce political polarization, is unfair to the victims, and seriously harms those industries that contribute so much to long-run economic growth.

Liberals are now emphasizing these points because such polarization policies have been emerging in the early 1980s. The Reagan administration, in a move of political expediency, decided that it was the job of monetary policy to cure inflation and the job of fiscal policy to generate real growth. Consequently, through 1981 and 1982, the Federal Reserve System was using a tight discretionary monetarist policy while the Treasury, after some tax cuts, began to run large deficits. Such a strange policy mix is likely to have this polarizing effect unless the Fed abandons its policies, in which case inflation will return.

RADICAL MONETARY POLICY

Radicals advance three reasons why liberal fine-tuning of monetary policy will *not* work to solve U.S. economic problems.[15]

First, take the case of inflation. It is true that sufficiently strong measures will cure inflation. For example, in the winter of 1980, both the Carter administration and the Federal Reserve System agreed to strong measures to reduce credit. These measures succeeded in reducing inflation from about 18 percent to 8 percent in a few months. The trouble is that such measures must be so harsh to have any effect on inflation that they depress the economy. In 1980 the result was a recession and a very considerable rise in inflation. (The same policies appear to have had the same results in England under the Thatcher administration and in the United States under the Reagan administration.)

Second, take the case of severe unemployment. Many Keynesians would support low interest rates and easy credit. Yet liberal Keynesians themselves admit that the interest rate required for a full-employment equilibrium may be so low as to be unattainable. That interest rate might be below the minimum level for speculation, so speculative investors will hold back because they expect it to return to a higher level. The equilibrium (full-employment) interest rate might even be negative if profit expectations are negative—that is, if losses are expected, a business will borrow only if a bank pays it to borrow! For these reasons, the Post Keynesians see monetary policy at best as an adjunct to (or copartner with) fiscal policy in a deep depression. Marxists don't see how low interest rates can alleviate unemployment at all if expected profit rates are below zero.

Finally, the realistic situation in the early 1980s is the existence of *both* inflation and unemployment in U.S. capitalism. Does monetary policy ease credit to stimulate the economy and reduce unemployment? Or does monetary policy restrict credit, so as to lessen economic

---

[15]See the excellent radical discussion of monetary policy in Epstein, *loc. cit.*

activity and reduce inflation? If these are the only alternatives, then it appears that curing unemployment must worsen inflation whereas curing inflation would worsen unemployment. Radicals do not like either choice and believe that other alternatives are available.

SUMMARY

Monetary policy relies very heavily upon monetary theory. Given that there is considerable disagreement on theory, there are, as would be expected, numerous competing monetary policy proposals.

The Federal Reserve System has altered its applied policies numerous times since World War II. Prior to the Federal Reserve–Treasury Accord of 1951, the Fed was subservient to the Treasury, using open market operations to keep interest rates on U.S. Treasury securities very low. After the Accord, the Fed asserted its independence and allowed interest rates to rise gradually as credit demand grew. Nonetheless, for nearly three decades the Fed pursued interest rate stabilization policies, allowing very little fluctuation in interest rates.

In the 1970s, because of concern about inflation and the growing popularity of monetarism, the Fed attached growing importance to controlling money aggregates. Finally in 1979, interest rate stabilization policies were essentially abandoned, and primary emphasis was given to the control of money aggregates such as M1 and M2.

The new policies are the closest thing to monetarism yet seen even though many monetarists are critical of the new policies. Strict monetarists still promote the adoption of a monetary rule. Discretionary monetarists emphasize the importance of controlling money, but believe that the targeted growth rate of money should be adjusted to accommodate changing economic conditions.

There are many critics of monetarism. Most regard monetarism as too inflexible and do not accept the notion that there is a reliable and easily understood connection between money and spending in a complex economy. Some advocate monetary eclecticism, where a wide spectrum of financial variables is monitored and, in the Radcliffe tradition, an effort is made to control the general state of liquidity in the economy. Others emphasize the control of real interest rate targets or inclusive measures of credit and debt. The liberal critics all agree that even the best of monetary policies are doomed to failure if monetary policy is not coordinated with a sensible fiscal policy.

Regardless of the policy chosen, the effectiveness of monetary policy is limited or nil when inflation, unemployment, and interest rates are at high levels simultaneously. Under these circumstances, one conservative policy is to concentrate on bringing down inflation regardless of the increases in unemployment. The monetarist view is to have a steady growth of the money supply at some particular rate with no discretionary policy. According to the monetarists, this will *eventually* cure both inflation and unemployment; in practice, this seems very similar to the first alternative. Liberals advocate all the fine-tuning of monetary and fiscal policy discussed earlier, but they do not explain how any amount of fine-tuning will end both inflation and unemployment simultaneously because the necessary policies for both fiscal and monetary policy are directly opposite for curing each of the evils.

The radical view says that there is no conceivable combination of monetary and fiscal policies that will simultaneously cure inflation and unemployment, given the structure of the present capitalist system. Monetary policies to stimulate the economy in order to cure unemployment will cause inflation. Monetary policies to depress the economy in order to cure inflation will cause unemployment.

APPENDIX 24A

Targets of the Federal Reserve System

The Federal Reserve System monetary growth rate and the federal funds growth rate targets and performance are shown in Tables 24A.1, 24A.2, and 24A.3.

Table 24A.1 shows the federal funds allowable trading range. As can be seen, the federal funds targets were almost always hit. Equally obvious, however, is the fact that the FOMC had to raise the target continually. It was typically below 6 percent prior to 1977, but began to rise after that date. The target *ranges* were substantially widened under the new Volcker plan after October 6, 1979. Before that time they were 0.75 percent or narrower. After that time they were 4 percent.

Table 24A.2 shows the annual targets and performance of the monetary and credit aggregates. As can be seen, these targets were often missed, with the majority of misses on the high side. There was not a single period where all targets were met simultaneously.

Table 24A.3 shows the short-run (two months) targets and performance of M2. Again, the targets were missed a majority of the time, with most misses being on the high side.

Table 24A.1

THE ALLOWABLE TRADING RANGE FOR THE FEDERAL FUNDS RATE

FOMC Meeting Date	Federal Funds Allowable Trading Range	Actual Federal Funds Rate	FOMC Meeting Date	Federal Funds Allowable Trading Range	Actual Federal Funds Rate
10/15/74	9 to 10½	9.45	4/19/77	4½ to 5¼†	5.35
11/19/74	8½ to 10	8.53	5/17/77	5¼ to 5¾	5.39
12/16/74	7½* to 9	7.13	6/21/77	5¼ to 5¾	5.42
*lowered to 7⅛ on 1/9/75			7/19/77	5¼ to 5¾*	5.90
1/20/75	6½* to 7¼	6.24	*raised to 6 on 8/5/77		
*lowered to 6¼ to 2/5/75			8/16/77	5¾ to 6¼	6.14
2/19/75	5¼ to 6¼	5.54	9/20/77	6 to 6½	6.47
3/18/75	4¾ to 5¾	5.49	10/17/77	6¼ to 6¾	6.51
*lowered to 5½ to 3/27/75			11/15/77	6¼ to 6¾	6.56
4/14/75	4¾ to 5¾	5.22	12/19/77	6¼ to 6¾	6.70
5/20/75	4½ to 5½	5.24	1/17/78	6½ to 7	6.78
6/16/75	5 to 6*	6.10	2/28/78	6½ to 7	6.79
*raised to 6¼ on 6/26/75			3/21/78	6½ to 7	6.89
7/15/75	5½ to 6¾	6.14	4/18/78	6¾ to 7½	7.36
8/19/75	5¾ to 7	6.24	5/16/78	7¼ to 7¾	7.41
9/16/75	6 to 7*	5.82	6/20/78	7½ to 8	7.68
*lowered to 5¾–6⅛ on 10/2			7/18/78	7¾ to 8	7.88
10/21/75	5¼ to 6¼§	5.22	8/15/78	7¾ to 8¼*†	8.45

Table 24A.1 (Continued)

FOMC Meeting Date	Federal Funds Allowable Trading Range	Actual Federal Funds Rate	FOMC Meeting Date	Federal Funds Allowable Trading Range	Actual Federal Funds Rate
11/18/75	4½ to 5½	5.20	*raised to 8½ on 9/8/78		
12/16/75	4½ to 5½	4.87	9/19/78	8¼ to 8¾†	8.85
1/20/76	4¼ to 5	4.77	10/17/78	8¾ to 9¼	9.76
2/17/76	4¼ to 5¼	4.84	11/21/78	9¾ to 10	10.03
3/15/76	4¼ to 5¼	4.82	12/19/78	9¾ to 10½	10.07
4/20/76	4½ to 5¼	5.03			10.06
5/18/76	5 to 5¾	5.48	2/6/79	9¾ to 10½	10.09
6/22/76	5¼ to 5¾	5.31	3/20/79	9¾ to 10½	10.01
7/19/76	4¾ to 5¾	5.29	4/7/79	9¾ to 10½	10.24
8/17/76	5 to 5½	5.25	5/22/79	9¾ to 10½	10.29
9/21/76	4¾ to 5½	5.03			10.47
10/19/76	4½ to 5¼	4.95	7/11/79	9¾ to 10½†	10.75
11/16/76	4½ to 5¼	4.65	8/14/79	10¾ to 11¼	11.43
12/20/76	4¼ to 5	4.61	9/18/79	11¼ to 11¾	11.61
1/17/77	4⅝ to 4¾	4.68	10/6/79	11½ to 15½	13.18
2/15/77	4⅝ to 5	4.69	11/20/79	11½ to 15½	13.78
3/15/77	4¼ to 5¼	4.73			13.82
			1/8/80	11½ to 15½	14.13

SOURCE: *Federal Reserve Bulletin* (issues from 1974 through 1981).

Table 24A.2

FEDERAL OPEN MARKET COMMITTEE'S ANNUAL GROWTH RANGES FOR MONETARY AND CREDIT AGGREGATES

Period	Month established	M1	Actual	M2	Actual	M3	Actual	Bank Credit	Actual
Mar 75 to Mar 76	4/75	5 to 7½	5.3	8½ to 10½	9.7%	10 to 12	†12.3%	6½ to 9½	§ 3.2%
Jun 75 to Jun 76	6/75	5 to 7½	§4.4	8½ to 10½	8.8	10 to 12	11.3	6½ to 9½	§ 3.2
75/II to 76/II	7/75	5 to 7½	5.4	8½ to 10½	9.6	10 to 12	12.0	6½ to 9½	§ 3.1
75/III to 76/III	10/75	5 to 7½	§4.6	7½ to 10½	9.3	9 to 12	11.5	6 to 9	§ 3.7
75/IV to 76/IV	1/76	4½ to 7½	5.8	7½ to 10½	†10.9	9 to 12	†12.7	6 to 9	§ 4.3
76/I to 77/I	4/76	4½ to 7	6.5	7½ to 10	†11.0	9 to 12	†12.8	6 to 9	§ 5.0
76/II to 77/II	7/76	4½ to 7	6.8	7½ to 9½	†10.8	9 to 11	†12.5	5 to 8	5.8
76/III to 77/III	11/76	4½ to 6½	†8.0	7½ to 10	†11.1	9 to 11½	†12.7	5 to 8	†11.4
76/IV to 77/IV	1/77	4½ to 6½	†7.9	7 to 10	9.8	8½ to 11½	†11.7	7 to 10	†11.3
77/I to 78/I	4/77	4½ to 6½	7.7	7 to 9½	8.8	8½ to 11	10.5	7 to 10	†11.3
77/II to 78/II	7/77	4 to 6½	†8.2	7 to 9½	8.6	8½ to 11	10.0	7 to 10	†12.0
77/III to 78/III	10/77	4 to 6½	†8.1	6½ to 9	8.6	8½ to 10½	9.6	7 to 10	†11.9
77/IV to 78/IV	2/78	4 to 6½	†7.3	6½ to 9	8.5	7½ to 10	9.4	7 to 10	†11.3
78/I to 79/I	4/78	4 to 6½		6½ to 9		7½ to 10		7½ to 10½	
78/II to 79/II	7/78	4 to 6½		6½ to 9		7½ to 10		8½ to 11½	
76/III to 79/III	10/78	2 to 6		6½ to 9		7½ to 10		8½ to 11½	

NOTE: The § and † denote periods where the actual growth rate fell below or exceeded the target, respectively. The table shows seasonally adjusted annual percentage rates.

SOURCE: Federal Reserve Bank of New York *Quarterly Review*, 4, no. 1 (Spring 1979), p. 57. Prior to April 1977, the Board of Governors used an adjusted bank credit proxy for the Bank Credit variable.

Table 24.A3*

SHORT-RUN (TWO MONTHS) TARGETS AND PERFORMANCE OF M1 AND M2

FOMC Meeting[a]	M1 Range[b]	Actual M1[c]	M2 Range[d]	Actual M2[e]
10/15/74	4¾ to 7¼	6.2	5¾ to 8¼	8.2
11/19/74	6½ to 9½	§ 6.0	8 to 10½	§ 5.8
1/20/74	3½ to 6½	§ −1.9	7 to 10	§ 6.6
2/19/75	5½ to 7½	† 8.3	6½ to 8½	†10.6
3/18/75	5 to 7½	† 7.6	8 to 10	9.8
4/14/75	6½ to 9	7.5	9½ to 11¾	10.4
5/20/75	7 to 9½	† 14.4	9 to 11½	†16.0
6/16/75	6½ to 9½	9.0	9 to 12	†13.1
7/15/75	3 to 5½	4.5	8 to 10½	§ 7.7
8/19/75	4½ to 7	§ 3.5	8¼ to 10¾	§ 5.0
9/16/75	5 to 8	§ .04	7 to 9½	§ 4.8
10/21/75	3 to 7	4.1	5½ to 8½	8.5
11/18/75	6 to 10	§ 2.9	7½ to 10½	7.8
12/16/75	4 to 7	§ −1.0	7 to 10	7.3
1/20/76	4 to 9	§ 3.5	7 to 11½	†12.8
2/17/76	5 to 9	5.9	9 to 13	†11.8
3/15/76	4 to 8	† 10.5	7 to 11	†11.4
4/20/76	4½ to 8½	† 10.7	8 to 12	11.5
5/18/76	4 to 7½	§ 2.8	5 to 9	6.7
6/22/76	3½ to 7½	§ 2.8	6 to 10	8.4
7/19/76	4 to 8	6.3	7½ to 11½	10.6
8/17/76	4 to 8	§ 2.8	7½ to 11½	9.4
9/21/76	4 to 8	6.7	8 to 12	†12.7
10/19/76	5 to 9	6.9	9 to 13	13.0
1/16/76	3 to 7	4.0	9½ to 13½	11.3
12/20/76	2½ to 6½	† 6.75	9 to 13	10.9
1/17/77	3 to 7	3.1	7 to 11	8.0
2/15/77	3 to 7	3.45	6½ to 10½	7.4
3/15/77	4½ to 8½	† 12.9	7 to 11	10.6
4/19/77	6 to 10	† 10.05	8 to 12	9.1
5/17/77	0 to 4	2.8	3½ to 7½	6.5
6/21/77	2½ to 6½	† 11.4	6 to 10	†12.35
7/19/77	3½ to 7½	† 11.9	6½ to 10½	†11.5
8/16/77	0 to 5	† 6.6	3 to 8	7.15
9/20/77	2 to 7	† 9.65	4 to 8	† 9.0
10/17/77	3 to 8	6.9	5½ to 9½	7.3
11/15/77	1 to 7	3.1	5 to 9	5.2
12/19/77	2½ to 8½	7.4	6 to 10	6.9
1/17/78	2½ to 7½	4.25	5 to 9	6.65
2/28/78	1 to 6	1.2	4½ to 8½	4.85
3/21/78	4 to 8	† 11.1	5½ to 9	8.2
4/18/78	4 to 8½	† 13.5	5½ to 9½	† 9.65
5/16/78	3 to 8	6.96	4 to 9	7.8
6/20/78	5 to 10	5.7	6 to 10	8.2
7/18/78	4 to 8	6.65	6 to 10	9.2

*Table continues on page 270. All footnotes for this table appear on page 270.

Table 24.A3 (Continued)

FOMC Meeting[a]	M1 Range[b]	Actual M1[c]	M2 Range[d]	Actual M2[e]
8/15/78	4 to 8	† 11.3	6 to 10	†11.45
9/19/78	5 to 9	8.9	6½ to 10½	9.75
10/17/78 (M1+)	5 to 7½	§ −2.65 (M1+)[f] −.45 (M1)	5½ to 9½	5.65
11/21/78	? to 5	−.15 (M1) −3.15 (M1+)	6 to 9½	§ 3.7
12/19/78	2 to 6	§ −1.8 (M1) −4.7 (M1+)	5 to 9	§ .75
2/6/79	3 to 7	§ −1.5 (M1) −4.35 (M1+) 1.5 (M1adj)[g]	5 to 9	§ 3.0
3/20/79	4 to 8	† 9.5 (M1) 5.0 (M1+) 12.5 (M1adj)	3½ to 7½	† 8.95
4/17/79	4 to 8	† 9.2 (M1) 4.5 (M1+) 10.7 (M1adj)	4 to 8½	† 9.75
5/22/79	0 to 5	† 7.75 (M1) 4.9 (M1+) 9.25 (M1adj)	4 to 8½	† 9.8
7/11/79	2½ to 6½	† 8.6 (M1) † 8.35 (M1+) † 9.1 (M1adj)	6½ to 10½	†13.55
8/14/79	4 to 8	† 9.0 (M1) 6.85 (M1+) † 10.5 (M1adj)	7 to 11	†11.6
9/18/79	3 to 8	6.85 (M1)	6½ to 10½	10.4
10/6/79	0 to 4½ (Sept.–Dec.)	† 4.97 (M1A)[h] (Sept.–Dec.)	0 to 7½ (Sept.–Dec.)	N/A
11/20/79	0 to 5	† 5.7 (M1A)	? to 8½	N/A
1/8/80	4 to 5	N/A	? to 7	N/A

[a] The first date of the meeting. Minutes of the meeting are reported in the *Federal Reserve Bulletin* usually two months after the meeting.

[b] The acceptable range for the annualized rate of growth of M1 over the two months including the month of the meeting and the month that followed.

[c] The actual annualized rate of growth of M1 over the two months including the month of the meeting and the month that followed. For meetings including and since 11/16/76 this was calculated by taking the average annualized rate of growth for the appropriate two months from table 1.10 of the *Federal Reserve Bulletin*. For meetings prior to 11/16/76, this rate was calculated using M1 data. The † and the § denote those periods where the actual rate exceeded and fell below the target range, respectively.

[d] The acceptable range for the annualized rate of growth of M2 over the two months including the month of that meeting and the month that followed.

[e] Calculated the same as M1.

[f] At this one meeting alone a range was set for the newly developed M1+.

[g] It was recognized in mid-1978 that the creation of ATS and NOW accounts would depress the growth rate of M1. It was later thought that the existence of these accounts reduced M1 by 3% in the first quarter and 1½% afterwards. These figures are shown to demonstrate what the FOMC thought was roughly the "real" M1 growth rate.

[h] The FOMC set a three-month target at this meeting. That M1A slightly exceeded the targets for October and November does not necessarily mean that they missed their target.

SOURCE: *Federal Reserve Bulletin* (issues from 1974 through 1981).

Chapter 25

DIRECT CONTROLS AND PUBLIC EMPLOYMENT

Since the 1950s, the American economy has experienced a first in the nation's history: simultaneous unemployment and inflation. This situation appears impossible, according to elementary Keynesian analysis, because inflation implies an excess of demand over supply, whereas unemployment implies an excess of supply over demand. Part of the answer to the riddle, as demonstrated earlier, lies in the monopoly power of American capitalism (but also changes in government and the international sphere). In spite of a certain amount of unemployment, the largest corporations actually still have the power to continue to raise their prices, which might be called *profit-push* inflation.

No aggregate monetary or fiscal policy can remedy or prevent both inflation and unemployment in these circumstances. To end unemployment by increasing aggregate demand sufficiently to affect output in all sectors allows the monopoly sector to set off another inflation spiral. To end inflation by reducing aggregate demand sufficiently to affect monopoly prices causes catastrophic unemployment in the whole economy. The capitalist-oriented governments of America and Europe have generally chosen to combat inflation at the expense of more unemployment. Yet even high levels of unemployment have failed to end inflation; only truly catastrophic levels of unemployment would end inflation given the present monopoly structure of the economy.

WAGE-PRICE CONTROLS

Since neither monetary nor fiscal policy is much good against stagflation, even the conservative Nixon administration was forced to try the drastic solution of direct wage-price controls.

On August 15, 1971, Nixon announced a new economic policy designed to save America and increase corporate profits.

Phase 1 ran for 90 days from August to November 1971. All wages, prices, and rents were frozen.[1] Profits were not frozen. In actuality, all wage increases were prevented, but some prices continued to creep upward. Nixon explained that the controls were necessary because we had combined inflation and unemployment, and all other monetary and fiscal policies had failed.

Phase 2 lasted from November 1971 until January 1973. The freeze was ended, but there were mandatory controls of wages, prices, and rents, though not for profits. Under this system, inflation continued, though at a reduced rate of "only" about 4 percent per year. Unemployment, according to the official definition, fell from its highest level of about 6 percent in the 1971 recession down to about 5 percent. When one realizes that the official data leave out many people and do not even try to count part-time unemployment, this is still a very high level. Wages were successfully kept to a very, very slow increase in this period, but profits rose spectacularly (as we shall see in detail).

Phase 3 was supposed to "phase out the economic stabilization program back to the free market, since the price target was being achieved," according to administration spokesmen. It removed all controls over prices in all industries except food, health, and construction and substituted voluntary controls. The voluntary controls were no controls at all because they had no enforcement procedure. Therefore, business paid no attention to them, so prices skyrocketed, rising at about 8 percent a year. In the end, even the administration admitted failure in holding down prices and had to institute a new freeze. Phase 3 lasted only from January to June 1973. A striking feature of it was the pressure kept on the unions to abide by voluntary controls and the extent to which the unions did restrain workers from asking for wage raises. As a result, there was a very slight rise in money wages, and the earning power of workers declined. Again there were no controls on profits, which continued to soar.

Phase 3½ was a second freeze. All prices were frozen, but there were no controls on unprocessed food or on rents. Neither wages nor profits were frozen, but wages remained under Phase 3 controls. This phase lasted only 60 days, from June to August 1973.

Phase 4 began in August 1973 and ended in April 1974. It was again a mandatory system of controls over prices, wages, and rents, but not over profits. It was very effective in holding down wages, but prices continued to rise at about 10 percent per year. The lack of enforcement on the price side was apparent in the case of the oil industry. The Cost of Living Council allowed the price of "old oil" (from existing wells, averaging less than $1 to produce) to rise from $4.25 to $5.25 a barrel. The council allowed the price of "new oil" (which costs no more than $2 a barrel to produce) to rise to $10.50. Then during the (alleged) shortage winter of 1973, the Federal Energy Office allowed the retailers' profit margin to rise from 7.25 cents a gallon to 11 cents—and this increase was not rescinded in the later period of surplus.[2]

In all of 1973, the actual buying power of workers declined by 4 percent whereas profits

---

[1] Much of this description comes from a dissertation by Joe Harris, *The Impact of the 1971–1974 Wage and Price Controls on Profit Levels and Distribution of Income* (Riverside, Calif.: University of California, Riverside Library, 1978).

[2] See Bennet Harison, "Inflation by Oligopoly," *The Nation* (August 30, 1975), p. 147.

rose rapidly. In the first half of 1974, unemployment rose to 6 percent, real gross national produce declined, and the rate of inflation rose to 12 percent. According to the usual definitions, the U.S. economy was in a recession in the midst of an unprecedented inflation. Nixon, however, denied it was a recession, preferring to call it a slight readjustment. Much later, President Ford finally admitted it was a recession, but not a depression, even though unemployment was over 9 percent. Ford still resisted any attempts to cure unemployment until late 1974; even in October 1974, he was still talking about *raising* taxes.

We have seen that 1975 was a year of recession, high unemployment, and declining real wages owing to inflation. In late 1975 and 1976, the economy recovered somewhat, corporate profits rose, but unemployment continued very high while inflation also continued at a slower pace. Because of the wage-price controls and the continued inflation and unemployment, the actual buying power of workers (real wages in constant 1967 dollars) reached a peak in 1972 and declined during the next four years. Thus, the real weekly wages of an urban worker with three dependents (after adjustment for higher prices and after Federal Income taxes) were $96.64 in 1972, $95.73 in 1973, $90.97 in 1973, $90.53 in 1975, and $90.36 in April 1976.[3] This 1976 level of real wages was actually below the 1965 level (which was $91.32)!

CONTROLS, INEFFICIENCY, AND CORRUPTION

Economists of all ideological views criticized the controls, but for different reasons. The conservatives, such as Milton Friedman, were horrified at the violation of the First Commandment of laissez-faire economics: Thou shalt not interfere with the market process of setting wages and prices.[4] They have always argued that resources, including capital and labor, cannot be efficiently allocated if prices are not set by competition in the market. If the government arbitrarily sets prices, how can a businessperson calculate most efficiently what to produce or what technology to use? If a businessperson does follow the arbitrary prices set by the government, then he or she will not produce what consumers desire and will not produce it in the cheapest possible way. It will not be produced as cheaply as possible because those prices do not correctly reflect the true scarcities of resources. Moreover, it will not be the combination of goods that consumers desire because those prices do not correctly reflect true consumer preferences. Thus, wage-price controls doom a capitalist economy to inefficiency.

Radicals agree with this insight. Radicals—and some conservatives—go further along these lines to point out that a huge bureaucracy would be needed really to enforce these controls. Not only would that bureaucracy have enormous repressive power, but it would also be wide open to corruption. After all, if businesspeople cannot freely raise their prices when opportunity arises, then they are better off spending their time and money bribing a bureaucrat to raise their prices than worrying about producing a better quality product. If capitalists cannot freely raise prices, then they will either bribe the bureaucrats as described

---

[3] U.S. Labor Department data, reported in Fred Burton, "The Economic Squeeze on the Workers, 1976," *AFL-CIO American Federationist* (June 1976), p. 1.

[4] See Milton Friedman, *Newsweek* (August 30, 1971), p. 45.

or else evade the controls by selling illegally (that is, on a black market, the way much gasoline was sold during the crisis). In this sense, comprehensive wage-price controls in a capitalist system combine the worst aspects of capitalism and Soviet-style socialism: a huge and inefficient bureaucracy plus private greed.

CONTROLS AND INCOME DISTRIBUTION

When the conservatives, such as Friedman, argued against the controls, their own solution was an unregulated private capitalism. The liberals, such as Paul Samuelson, pointed out politely that it was private capitalism that had resulted in our present unpleasant mixture of inflation and unemployment.[5] Moreover, they pointed out that even the usual monetary and fiscal policies could not cope with inflation and unemployment at the same time. In fact, it was the liberals who first advocated the controls; they expected controls to hold down prices while welfare spending would increase demand to eliminate unemployment. At first, the liberals applauded Nixon's controls. Even then, however, their reactions were a little doubtful on two points: Would Nixon actually hold down prices or just wages? And would he actually spend enough on welfare programs to end unemployment?

They were right to worry and wrong to applaud at all. Nixon actually (1) held down wages, (2) allowed prices to continue to rise, and (3) did nothing to cure unemployment, except some military spending. The important thing to understand is that this was not accidental, nor would Nixon be the only president to do such a thing. It was shown above that all U.S. governments have been strongly probusiness for many reasons. Any wage-price controls under a business-dominated government can be expected to favor business.

The only difference with Nixon is that there was a great deal of evidence in his case that he accepted business bribes (such as those of ITT and the dairy industry) beyond the usual legal election campaign contributions, and he was much more blunt about his probusiness biases than most presidents have been. For example, in his speech announcing the wage-price controls, Nixon said, "All Americans will benefit from more profits. More profits fuel the expansion . . . More profits mean more investment. . . . And more profits mean there will be more tax revenues. . . . That's why higher profits in the American economy would be good for every person in America."[6] Vice-President Agnew repeated the theory, saying: "Rising corporate profits are needed more than ever by the poor."[7]

President Nixon and Vice-President Agnew succeeded quite well in their objectives of limiting wages and raising profits. Thus, in all of Phase 1 and Phase 3½, wages didn't rise at all. During the longer Phases 2 and 3, average hourly earnings rose only 5.9 percent a year. At the same time the cost of living rose by about 4 percent yearly in Phase 2, 8 percent yearly in Phase 3, and about 10 percent yearly in Phase 4. Since the cost of living rose faster than wages in 1973, for the first time on record in a year of economic expansion, the buying power of workers declined. In 1973, during Phases 3 and 4, wages rose by about 5 percent; and retail

---

[5] See Paul Samuelson, *Newsweek* (August 30, 1971), p. 46.
[6] President Richard Nixon in TV speech, August 15, 1971.
[7] Vice-President Agnew at National Governors' Conference, 1971.

prices, by about 9 percent, so real wages (that is, what the worker can buy) declined by 4 percent.

One way Nixon achieved these results was by appointing a probusiness Pay Board to make wage decisions. The big unions first joined it, hoping to salvage some crumbs, then withdrew when they found they were to be allowed nothing. The AFL-CIO said: "We joined the Pay Board in good faith, desiring—despite our misgivings—to give it a fair chance. . . . The so-called public members are neither neutral nor independent. They are tools of the Administration, and imbued with its viewpoint that all of the nation's economic ills are caused by high wages. As a result, the Pay Board has been completely dominated and run, from the very start, by a coalition of the business and so-called public members. . . . The trade union movement's representatives on the board have been treated as outsiders—merely as a facade to maintain the pretense of a tripartite body."[8]

While real wages were declining in Phases 3 and 4, profit rates were actually climbing. Profit rates on investors' equity (before taxes) in all of manufacturing were 16.5 percent in 1971, but rose to 18.4 percent in 1972; then—under Phase 3—rose to 21.6 percent in 1973; then—under Phase 4—rose to 23.4 percent in 1974 in the first year of the depression.[9] A strange depression!

Finally, in the first quarter of 1975, the profit rate fell to 15.0 percent (not seasonally adjusted). When this fall in the profit rate occurred, Congress and President Ford took immediate action to stimulate the economy by lower taxes, and the profit rate jumped back up to 19.2 percent in the second quarter of 1975.

One must conclude that the inevitable results of wage-price controls under a pro-capitalist government are additional corruption and inefficiency, as well as a shift in income distribution away from wages and toward profits. Yet there is no obvious combination of aggregate monetary and fiscal policies that can cure both unemployment and inflation at the same time. So what cures are available?

THE LIBERAL SOLUTION TO STAGFLATION

Liberal Keynesians, Post Keynesians, and institutionalists have all emphasized wage and price controls as a cure to inflation. John Kenneth Galbraith has consistently advocated them, and the AFL-CIO has advocated controls at various times. It was a liberal Democratic Congress who gave the control powers to Nixon, though it did it only because it did not expect him to exercise the powers (and could then have blamed him for doing nothing).

The conservative Nixon had always opposed controls, but saw them as necessary for his short-term goals. It is the structural needs of the system rather than expressed ideology that determines presidential actions. It is important to understand that Nixon was successful in his short-term goals of lowering unemployment *and* preventing inflation until the election. He not only used direct controls to hold down inflation (and distribute income to capistalists).

---

[8] AFL-CIO Executive Committee in *The National Economy* (AFL-CIO, 1973), p. 7.
[9] Federal Trade Commission, *Quarterly Financial Report for Manufacturing Corporations* (First quarter 1974 and first quarter 1975), pp. 12–16.

He also used a a proper fiscal policy to stimulate the economy, namely, an increase in military spending. These policies were successful from August 1971 to the election of 1972.

During the 1980 primary elections, Senator Edward Kennedy advocated the same basic stabilization policies, with different distribution and allocation policies (and he and the AFL-CIO still are supporting these policies in the early 1980s). A coherent statement of this policy might be as follows. First, in order to achieve full employment, use higher government spending on peaceful, constructive programs. Second, in order to achieve full employment, reduce taxes of the poor, the workers, and the middle class, so as to stimulate consumer demand. Third, in order to achieve full employment, use monetary policy to lower interest rates. Fourth, in order to eliminate inflation completely, put on direct controls on the prices of all monopoly corporations with stiff enforcement penalties. No controls are needed for small business prices, which will follow monopoly prices. No controls are needed for wages, which only try to catch up to prices. Controls only on the prices of the top thousand corporations could be efficiently administered and involve less bureaucracy—while the lack of controls on wages would make it difficult to have anti–working class distribution effects.

PUBLIC EMPLOYMENT

The type of government spending used to stimulate the economy is very important. The only consensus for many years was higher military spending; the political pressure for that type of spending will continue to be enormous (for all the reasons given in Chapter 23).

At the other extreme, the most liberal form of public spending would be a very strong Full Employment Act (to replace the act sponsored by Senator Humphrey and Representative Hawkins, which was weakened till in its final form it had no effect). A real Full Employment Act would provide that *any unemployed person could get work with the government* (local, state, or federal) as an employer of last resort. The wage would automatically be set equal to the wage for comparable work in the private sector.

This liberal reform can be argued on the basis that, if and only if private enterprise fails to provide jobs, then the government would be forced to provide jobs. It should appeal, however, to some conservatives in that (1) unemployment compensation could be ended forever (so people would no longer be paid not to work), and (2) all welfare payments to people who are able to work could be ended forever. (Of course, child care payments would be needed for working women with children.)

The work done need *not* be wasteful work. The United States badly needs to replace old bridges, replace old roads, replace and expand mass transit, replace old sewer systems, clean up rivers and lakes, build new hospitals and provide more health care personnel, expand and better maintain national parks, provide more educational personnel, and so forth. There are plenty of jobs to be done; it is just that these are not areas for big private profits.

This is a liberal reform with some radical implications. It would have meant—at the bottom of the 1982 depression—that as many as twelve (12) million people could claim government jobs. Actually, the multiplier effect of putting even six million people to work might stimulate the private sector to provide six million more jobs. It would also give workers and unions more bargaining power to get a larger piece of the pie, thus shifting income distribution toward more equality. The higher wages and less submissive behavior of workers are the reasons that big business has always vociferously and successfully opposed any real full employment legislation.

PROBLEMS WITH PUBLIC EMPLOYMENT AND PRICE CONTROLS

Such a program could be relatively successful for some length of time. *But,* in the first place, political reality will result in wage-price controls on all prices *and all wages,* if there are to be any controls. Even Senator Kennedy and the AFL-CIO favor this compromise, provided, of course, that there are strong promises that the controls will not be used to distribute income in an anti–working class manner. This is probably the best possible liberal program that could be enacted. It probably would work for a while.

For how long could such a program successfully move toward full employment, stable prices, class-neutral income distribution, and a reasonably efficient economy? Suppose a liberal administration enacted such a program. All of our experience with controls—in World War II, the Korean War, and the Nixon controls—as well as all economic theory, indicates that it could succeed to some degree for six months to a year. Then it reaches a crossroad.

First, the conservative issue of efficiency becomes more and more difficult. Prices can be almost frozen for six months to a year, but by then domestic supply and demand conditions, technology, and foreign conditions will have changed very considerably, so big readjustments become more and more necessary. One choice is to dismantle controls slowly, as Nixon did. The other choice is to move toward central planning.

Second, since the economy has been stimulated to full employment, with much higher government spending and much higher resulting consumer demand, the inflationary pressures would be enormous. Again, one answer is to (1) end price controls and (2) end guaranteed full employment. This means going back to the same old business cycle in which inflation is eventually "cured" by depression and large-scale unemployment. The other alternative is some form of central planning.

A third problem is the battle over income distribution. Imagine an economy at full employment, but where wages and profits are determined by government boards. Labor and capital would have to fight in the political arena to control these boards. Given a continuing capitalist system, one would expect capital to win—so wages would be frozen while prices rose. This situation could only be enforced against labor by a very repressive government.

If, on the other hand, labor developed enough political power to get strong price controls, but continuous wage increases, this would mean reducing the rate of profit. Falling rates of profit would make capitalists react by reducing their investments. This would further lower employment in the private sector. The loss of business "confidence" and collapse of the private sector would again lead to enormous pressure to dismantle the controls. The alternative is more public employment and some form of national economic planning.

THE CHOICES OF PLANNING MODES

One mode of national economic planning is done in Japan, where big business and government agree on a direction to go without consulting anyone else. The "plan" is only indicative and voluntary. Business is prompted in that direction by tax breaks, low interest loans, and direct subsidies. A number of Wall Street economists and corporate executives (such as Felix Rohatyn) do favor this type of planning. As the U.S. economy moves toward more controls, with resulting difficult decisions, it is easy to predict more support for this type of planning.

On the other hand, a strong labor movement may support a democratic type of planning by the elected government, with policy inputs from workers and consumers. This implies spreading public employment—and perhaps spreading public ownership of some productive facilities. These issues are discussed in the next chapter.

SUMMARY

A consistent liberal program to combat stagflation would have to include (1) expansionary fiscal and monetary policy to end unemployment plus (2) price controls to eliminate inflation. The most liberal form would include guaranteed public employment for all unemployed workers. Compromise in the present political reality would most likely include wage as well as price controls.

In the short run, this solution was proven successful by Richard Nixon. After a time, however, it means (1) violent political struggles over income distribution; (2) enormous inflationary pressure, repressed by the wage-price controls; and (3) increasing distortion of allocation in the economy.

These problems would lead to three possible choices: (1) dismantle the program and go back to the private business cycle; (2) use corporate planning in a symbiosis of big business and government, with repression to hold down criticism; or (3) some form of democratic planning.

Chapter 26

PUBLIC OWNERSHIP

France, under a democratically elected socialist government, has decided to extend public ownership to about 28 percent of the economy. When that change is complete and when the new structure has operated for a few years, then we will be able to evaluate the macro effects of a significant degree of public ownership in a democratic framework. Until then, we can only look at the question theoretically (with a few insights from those countries that have government ownership and no democracy).

MACRO BALANCE UNDER PLANNING

Public ownership may be accomplished by central planning, or decisions may be left to each enterprise in a market context. Planning may be conducted for the whole world or several countries or one country or one region or even one locality. If decision making is at the plant level, then control may be exercised by a government-appointed manager or by a workers' council or by a council of workers, consumers, and public representatives. Let us begin with the simplest case of a single isolated country with 100 percent public ownership, central planning, and democratic political control.

Suppose the public representatives appoint a central planning board. The board will be responsible for most saving and for most investment. It saves out of income taxes, sales taxes, taxes on enterprises, government bonds sold to savers, savings in government-owned banks, depreciation allowances, and all profits of enterprises flowing to the treasury. It invests the money in new enterprises or expansions of old ones. A small amount of saving and investment might be done by individual firms out of depreciation allowances to replace depreciated capital. Since almost all saving and investment are controlled by one agency, it should always be possible to set investment equal to saving or aggregate demand equal to supply. Hence, there should be no involuntary unemployment.

If, by accident, there is not enough demand owing to inaccurate planning, this may always be corrected by increasing the demand. Since public interest and not profitability is the main rule for operation of the economy, firms can always be ordered to pay out more wages to increase demand. In fact, wherever there is public ownership and central planning, it is much more likely that planners will make mistakes in the other direction, trying to produce more than can be produced at full employment. The result of those mistakes will be shortages of labor.

What are the possibilities of inflation under planning with public ownership? If supply is set equal to demand and saving is set equal to investment, once again there is no reason to expect inflation of prices. There are situations, however, where inflation is possible. First, planners may be put under enormous political pressure to set targets higher than is physically possible, especially in developing countries. In that case, demand for both producer goods and consumer goods may be higher than the supply, there may be a shortage of capital goods, and a shortage of labor. This situation will create inflationary pressures. These situations will occur either when there is an all-out drive to industrialize a previously underdeveloped country or when there is a war. In a war, there is usually an all-out attempt to produce an infinite amount of military commodities.

Second, there may be external shocks leading to inflation. If a planned economy must import goods and the prices of those goods rise, then inflationary pressures must occur.

Thus, the theoretical conclusion is that unemployment need not ever occur, but that there may be some tendency to labor shortages if there is a plan calling for production beyond current capacity. Second, those same mistakes of overcapacity planning may lead to inflation. But without mistakes and without external cost increases, there need be no inflation.

Some of this may be illustrated in a very simple model. Suppose that planners are able easily to control saving and investment in the producer goods sector. Inflation may show up in consumer goods unless there is a balance of consumer goods and wages paid out. An attempt to overproduce may show up in higher wages being paid out. The simplest balance that must be maintained is

$$\$C = \$W \tag{26.1}$$

where $\$C$ is the money value of all consumer goods and $\$W$ is the total amount of money wages paid. Since everything is publicly owned, there is no private rent, interest, or profit. Therefore, wages (including salaries and bonuses) are the only type of income. Moreover, investment does not come out of private income, but out of the government revenue. Thus $\$C = \$W$ is the correct condition of equilibrium though it must also be true that investment equals saving.

As a second approximation, we may separate quantities and prices. Let $\$C = C \cdot P_c$, where C is the real amount of consumer goods and P_c is the price of consumer goods. Let $\$W = W \cdot N$, where W is the wage rate per worker and N is the number of workers. Then the condition for price equilibrium is

$$C \cdot P_c = N \cdot W \tag{26.2}$$

The real amount of consumer goods times its price must equal the hourly wage rate times the number of workers (in labor hours).

As a third approximation, we may divide up the total number of workers into four sectors, workers in consumer goods (N_c), workers in investment goods (N_i), workers in military goods (N_m), and workers in collective welfare goods (N_w). This emphasizes the point that under planning the problem may be the competition of different sectors for the finite labor force. If workers are taken from the production of consumer goods and switched to the production of investment goods, military goods, or collective welfare goods, then the same amount of wages are paid, but the amount of consumer goods has declined. This is a common problem of real-life planned economies. The balance that must be maintained for price stability is

$$C \cdot P_c = W \cdot N_c + W \cdot N_i + W \cdot N_m + W \cdot N_w \qquad (26.3)$$

Thus, the demand for consumer goods must equal the total wages generated in all four sectors.

As a final approximation, we may bring in the fact that workers may have personal savings (S), that workers pay income taxes (T_i), and that consumer goods have sales taxes on them (T_s). Therefore, the condition for price stability becomes

$$T_s \cdot C + P_c \cdot C = W \cdot N_c + W \cdot N_i + W \cdot N_m + W \cdot N_w - S - T_i \qquad (26.4)$$

On the one side is the sales price of consumer goods plus the sales taxes. On the other side are the wages paid in all four sectors minus the personal savings of workers minus the income taxes paid by workers. Obviously, a planning authority may create price stability by raising sales taxes or raising personal income taxes or encouraging saving. The other obvious way to achieve price stability, if the problem is that wages are higher than the value of available consumer goods, is to lower wages. That may not be politically possible, however, in the midst of an all-out industrialization drive or in a war period.

GROWTH CYCLES AND CENTRAL PLANNING

In the actually existing centrally planned economies of the Soviet Union and Eastern Europe, there has been no general unemployment during the entire period of central planning. There has, however, been an economic cycle of high growth followed by low growth (with actual decline only in one year in Czechoslovakia and the last couple of years in Poland). What causes these growth cycles? It is not lack of demand because demand by public agencies has been unlimited in the aggregate.

The causes of the growth cycles (and recent low productivity) seem to be mainly overcentralization and rigid political dictatorship. The usual cycle behaves something like this:

1. The economy is progressing smoothly and at a good rate of growth. Then the political leaders get overly enthusiastic and optimistic, so they order a more rapid growth.
2. Because it is a dictatorship, the planners are afraid to tell the leaders that this is impossible in reality. Therefore, the planners do their best to plan a more rapid growth.
3. The more rapid growth entails production of many new factories and other construction across the land.
4. But since the economy was already progressing as rapidly as possible at full employment

and full use of capacity, it follows that the extra construction cannot be completed. Therefore, the countryside is dotted with many half-finished factories and other construction projects.

5. Since much labor and capital are tied up trying to produce additional factories that cannot be completed, this removes labor and capital from actual operation. The result is a lower growth rate. If the mistakes are extreme enough, it could even produce negative growth.
6. At this point, even the leadership is forced to recognize the reality. So the leadership orders a moratorium on starting new plants until the old ones are completed.
7. Finally, after several years, the new plants are completed and begin to add to production. The rate of growth rises dramatically.
8. After a short time at the higher rate of growth, the leadership again becomes overly optimistic, orders an even higher rate of growth—and the whole cycle repeats itself.

This is literally a *political* economic cycle, exacerbated by an overcentralized planning system, such that there is insufficiently detailed information at the center on which to base decisions. It is extraordinarily different in mechanism from the capitalist business cycle and should not be confused with it. Moreover, except in the case of Poland, it has not created actual downturns of any extended length. Furthermore, it continues to operate at full employment even while the growth rate is dropping. In fact, those are periods of greater than normal labor shortage. Clearly, the cure lies in democratizing these systems so that (1) inept political leaders can be tossed out by elections and (2) economists are allowed to speak the truth, even when it is less optimistic than leaders desire.

In addition to the cyclical growth, it also appears that there may be a long-run growth decline in recent years, based on a long-run decline in the rate of growth of productivity. Again, the reasons are very different from those mentioned earlier for the capitalist economies. Dictatorial control of the means of production by a small group does tend to restrict the incentive to invent or innovate in Soviet industry. This condition is worsened by the very short-run nature of Soviet incentives to managers, which encourage managers to look only at the next few months and discourage them from making major changes (which might reduce production in the short run). It is also worsened by the overcentralization of decision making in the Soviet Union, so that technological decisions are made at the center for all plants, based on scanty information on local conditions. The overcentralization is itself a natural result of dictatorship. Again, the cure is democratization.

Since no socialist in Western Europe or the United States proposes dictatorship or even a high degree of centralization, these problems would not exist under democratically run public ownership in those areas. The alternatives to centralization are discussed in the next section, and the relation of public ownership to democracy is discussed in a later section.

MACRO BALANCE UNDER DECENTRALIZED PUBLIC OWNERSHIP

It is perfectly possible, as is true to some extent in Yugoslavia, to have public ownership, but to have control lodged in the hands of workers' councils in each enterprise. If that control includes setting prices and production decisions, then there must be some mechanism for the coordination of the millions of decisions made in all the separate enterprises. Only two modes of coordination have ever been discovered. One is the use of central planning. The other is the use of the market. Therefore, control of decisions in each enterprise by a local workers' council implies the use of the market for coordination of decisions.

The use of the market, in turn, implies all the macro problems of market capitalism. Therefore, one expects to find monopoly power affecting prices, cyclical unemployment, and inflation. Certainly, all these problems have been seen in the experience of Yugoslavia.

The arguments in favor of workers' councils have included more incentive for workers to produce and innovate, more efficiency at the local level, less central bureaucracy, and so less alienation and less tendency toward dictatorship. Even if these arguments are true, one must still recognize the trade-off that brings back the problems of competitive capitalism. Most advocates of public ownership, as in France, advocate some compromise mixture of central planning with worker-consumer-public councils at the enterprise level. There has never been a simple answer given to the most difficult question, which is what functions should be centrally planned and what functions should be determined by the market.

OTHER PROBLEMS OF PUBLIC OWNERSHIP

In the macro sphere, especially in relation to unemployment and inflation, public ownership with central planning offers the most direct and complete solution. When considering alternative solutions, however, one must always ask what other problems are generated. The main problems with public ownership alleged by the critics are (1) lack of incentive, (2) inefficiency, (3) alienation from a faceless bureaucracy, and (4) a tendency to dictatorship.

Incentives. The allegation about lack of incentive relates to the fact that public ownership is intended to reduce inequality of income distribution. Public ownership does eliminate private rent, interest, and profit, which have been the main causes of inequality in U.S. income distribution. The critics assume that a very high degree of income inequality is needed to guarantee incentives to work.

One answer to this criticism is that equality of income distribution is an important goal even if it reduces incentives to some degree. A second answer is the fact that there is little or no evidence that inequality is a major incentive to work. Certainly no one needs a million dollars a year as an inducement to work. Moreover, most people with high property incomes in the United States inherited most of it, and many of those do not work very hard. On the other hand, many people with very low incomes work very hard at dirty, dangerous jobs.

Moreover, public ownership need not mean any reduction in the inequality of labor incomes (though it eliminates property incomes). In the Yugoslav case, in which each firm competes in the market and workers receive shares of firm income according to skills, there is great inequality of labor income between workers in different firms and different skill levels. Even in the Soviet Union, during the industrialization drive of the 1930s, the distribution of labor income was more unequal than in the United States. The point is that wages are planned, so they may be very unequal or—at some point in the far future—may be made completely equal. More equality could only be accomplished when (1) there are very high levels of productivity and (2) there are very high levels of social consciousness of the need to produce for the good of society.

Efficiency. A primary argument of the critics of public ownership is that rational prices (reflecting preferences and scarcities) are required for rational planning. But rational prices can only be generated by a market. Therefore, rational planning is impossible under a system of public ownership.

In the first place, this argument ignores the possibility of using the market with public ownership. Individual firms may compete in the market and maximize profits under public ownership, either under the control of workers' councils (as in Yugoslavia) *or* under the control of state-appointed managers who are instructed to maximize profits (as in Hungary).

Second, the problem of optimum, rational planning for efficiency can be solved so long as certain information is known. The information is (1) the available, human and nonhuman resources, (2) the preferences of consumers (including government), and (3) the ratio of each output to inputs required under existing technology. The set of all possible required input-output ratios must be furnished by engineers under either private or public enterprise. The available resources and preferences are given by prices under private enterprise, but can be estimated independently under centrally planned public enterprise. There is no purely theoretical reason for more optimization and efficiency under one system than the other.

The practical issue involves balancing the monopoly distortions and imperfections of market competition against the problems of information gathering and large number of calculations under central planning. This is a vast and controversial empirical issue, which cannot be discussed here.

Alienation and Bureaucracy. Central planning implies a vast bureaucracy. Critics see this as a cause of alienation among workers, consumers, and citizens, who may feel helpless to influence decisions and threatened by bureaucracy. It is probably true that most Soviet citizens feel helpless and threatened by their vast undemocratic bureaucracy. But is this true because of central planning and "public" ownership or because of dictatorship? The "public" ownership in the Soviet Union is really governmental ownership, with a small group controlling the government and the public having no voice at all.

In countries with democratically controlled public enterprises, the situation is different. Individuals may feel helpless to change decisions of the U.S. post office, but not threatened by it. Postal workers may organize unions, and postal consumers may organize political parties to change post office policies. Similarly, the French do not feel threatened by the publicly owned Renault auto firm; many French are even proud of its performance.

It must also never be forgotten that the giant monopoly firms of the United States also have vast bureaucracies, which are beyond the influence of most citizens. If an individual worker or consumer is confronted by General Motors, the person feels helpless and sometimes threatened. Furthermore, there are no democratic processes whereby the voter can directly control the operating policies of General Motors; only its stockholders have a vote proportionate to their money invested.

Democracy. Conservatives argue that, because capitalism disperses power among millions of entrepreneurs and many millions of consumers, it is the ideal basis for political democracy, freedom to discuss, and freedom to elect whatever representatives the people desire. The criticism of this view and an alternative view were presented at great length in Chapter 22 and will not be repeated here.

Conservatives also argue that public ownership means that the government employs a huge bureaucracy and controls every aspect of the economy. It thus directly controls the media and controls the employment of all persons. Therefore, it must tend to produce a political dictatorship. The Soviet Union, Cuba, and China are examples of such dictatorships.

The answers to this argument may be stated very briefly. First, what is the empirical relation of socialism and capitalism to dictatorship? Socialism has been the official government policy of Sweden, England, and France. Yet these are also among the most democratic countries in the world. On the other side, most capitalist countries in the world (particularly in Africa, Latin America, and Asia) *are* political dictatorships.

Certainly, in many underdeveloped countries (from czarist Russia to Algeria) both government ownership and dictatorship have been utilized together. This is because it has appeared that only harsh, Draconian measures would lead to rapid development—and because there was no tradition of democratic processes in their semifeudal past (with mostly illiterate populations). Whether this perception is true or not, we are only discussing public ownership as a tool for full employment and price stability in countries—such as the United States and Western Europe—with highly developed economies, democratic traditions, and highly educated populations. In these areas, steps toward public ownership have gone hand in hand with a deepening of the democratic process. In fact, public ownership has been presented as a way of extending the democratic process to the economic sphere.

Control of the economy by the public may increase democracy in the national sphere as well. The argument is that the main power limiting, distorting, and controlling our present democratic processes is the concentrated economic power of the large monopoly corporations. If these concentrations of wealth are eliminated, then all of us are much closer to equal participants in the democratic process. That improved democratic process can then exercise control over the economy.

As to the specific issue of control of the media, no one ever said that all the media must be publicly owned. First, some private ownership of the media could remain. Second, cooperative, nonprofit ownership of the media (such as radio stations KPFA in Berkeley, KPFK in Los Angeles, or WBAI in New York) could be strongly encouraged. Third, in the publicly owned area, the traditional U.S. "fairness" doctrine could be used to prevent political bias—or the system of the British Broadcasting System that allocates time to political parties according to their strength in Parliament.

Obviously, these brief arguments on incentives, bureaucracy, efficiency and democracy only scratch the surface of an enormous and controversial literature. It is not possible to pursue them further in this book, but the reader may follow up the citations suggested in our footnote.[1]

---

[1] For a complete discussion of these issues with a very extensive bibliography, see Howard J. Sherman, *Radical Political Economy* (New York: Basic Books, 1972); also see Andrew Zimbalist and Howard J. Sherman, *Comparative Economic Analysis* (Orlando, Florida: Academic Press, forthcoming).

SUMMARY

Monetary and fiscal policy offer no easy solutions to the simultaneous problems of unemployment and inflation. Wage-price controls may work for a short time, but then must be ended or go forward to extensive planning. Extensive planning can be done only under extensive public ownership. Both theory and historical experience indicate that public ownership with planning can eliminate both unemployment and inflation (except for externally caused inflation). The problems that may be raised by public ownership were discussed briefly above.

INDEX

Page references to illustrations are printed in **boldface** type.

Accelerator theory of investment, 158–161, 215, 250, 251, 269
Adelsheim, Peter, 369–370
AFL-CIO, 475, 476, 477
Aggregate supply and demand
 in classical model, 8–9, 48–51
 defined, 58–59
 at equilibrium, 59–60
 in Keynesian model, 60–63, 71–72
  with demand side orientation, 72–75
Ando, A., 134
Automatic stabilizers, 428–429
Automobile industry
 monopoly price behavior in, 367
 obsolescence in, 355
Average propensity to consume, 61, 132–138
 cyclical pattern of, 142–143

Bain, J. S., 175
Balance of payments, deficit in, 395
Bank(s). *See also* Federal Reserve System
 in business cycle, 248
 credit, 314, 316, 321–322, 323–324
 global, 390
 and monopoly power, 363
Banking School versus Currency School, 320

Baran, Paul, 259
Barter system, 15, 16, 80
Baumol, William, 99–100
Blinder, Alan, 137
Boddy, Raford, 270, 273
Brazil, 349
Britain. *See* Great Britain
Burns, Arthur, 20
Business cycles, 11. *See also* Contraction; Depression; Expansion; Recession
 classical theory of, 244–249
 combined demand-supply model of, 275–279, 282–283
 damped and explosive, 256
 defined, 20
 demand-side model of
  realization, 261–266
  underconsumption, 249–250, 257–261
 export-import behavior over, 383–385
 external shocks in, 246–247, 248, 256
 first appearance of, 20–21
 foreign influences on, 21–22
 government deficit over, 114, 115 (table), 434–437
 government revenue over, 429–430
 government spending over, 148, 264, 278, 431–434
 income distribution over, 187, 188–200
 consumption and, 139–149
 interest rates over, 169–171

international spread of, 378–383, 395
 in Great Depression, 382–383
 investment in, 380–381
 multinationals in, 390–391
 trade in, 378–379
investment over, 155–156, 162, 163 (table), **164**, 180–181
 accelerator theory of, 158–161, 215, 250, 251
 inventory, 166–169
 replacement, 174–176
Keynesian model of, 249, 250–252, 253–256
monetary theories of, 329–342
price behavior over, 214–219
 monopoly versus competitive, 364–367
profits over, 163, **164**, 205–218
 in monopoly sector, 373–375
supply-side model, 268–275, 279–281
timing of, 24–27
 in different industries, 164–165
types of, 20, 27
in United States history, 21–24

Cambridge Journal of Economics, 308
Canada, foreign investment in, 390, 391
Capacity utilization
 cyclical behavior of, 198, 199–200
 defined, 198–199

487

Capacity utilization *(Continued)*
   output-capital ratio and, 216, 220–221, 276
   profit rate and, 205, 210–212
Capital
   defined, 36, 37
   and labor ratio, 7
   marginal efficiency of, 61, 62–63
   measurement of, 206
   and output ratio, 212–216, 220–221, 228–229, 231, 270, 276
Capital (Marx), 259–260
Capitalism
   of Adam Smith, 4–5
   defense of. *See* Say's law
   defined, 19
   Malthus on, 6–7
   market production under, 14–15
   Physiocrats on, 5–6
   and political democracy, 402–403. *See also* Political power
   in United States, 393–395
   and use of money, 16–18
Capitalism and Freedom (Friedman), 402
Carter, Jimmy, 418, 425, 463
Checking accounts, 81
Cherry, Robert, 260
Chrysler Corporation, 411
Civil War, 443
Class. *See* Social class
Classical theory. *See also* Say's law
   equilibrium conditions in, 8–9, 43–44, 46–53
      unemployment and, 67–68, **69**
   growth models in, 226–229, 230–234, 237–238
   money supply and demand in, 82, 83, 95–96
   unemployment in, 9, 43–44, 46–48, 67–68, **69**, 244–249
Class income hypothesis of consumer demand, 138–139, 144–146, 152
Cobweb theory, of business cycle, 247
Colonialism, 386
Commerce Defended (Mill), 8
Communist Manifesto, The, 404
Competitive sector
   cyclical price behavior in, 365–367
   defined, 364
Construction, residential, 157–158

Consumer debt. *See* Credit
Consumer Price Index (CPI), **25**, 39, 450
Consumption
   categories of, 131
   defined, 37
   and income, 6–7, 132–139
      cyclical behavior of, 139–149
      functional relation of, 151–154
   investment and, 158–161, 215, 250, 251
   in Keynesian economics, 61, 132–133, 345
   long-run trends in, 149–150
   Say's law on, 8–9
   social class and, 6–7, 76–77, 144–147, 138–139
   transitory, 135
   and underconsumption theory, 257–261
Contractions. *See also* Business cycle
   average, 25
   indicators of, 25
   inflation in, 24
   price behavior in, 365–367
   in United States history, 26 (table)
Corporations. *See* Industry; Monopoly power
Cost-push inflation, 354–359
Credit, 17
   bank, 314, 316, 321–322, 323–324
   in business cycle, 248, 278, 264
   and consumption-income ratio, 147, **148**, 149
   controls over, 460
   growth of, 350, 447–450, 468–470
   Marxist view of, 326–327
   and spending, 315–316
   stabilization policy and, 322–323
Creditists, 315–316, 460
Crotty, James, 270, 273
Crowding-out hypothesis, 289–291, 303
Currency School versus Banking School, 320
Cypher, James, 110, 111

Davidson, Paul, 309
Debt-deflation theory, of business cycles, 334–335
Demand-side cycle theory, 266–267

   in combined supply model, 275–279, 282–283
   of inflation, 345–354
   realization model in, 261–266
   of underconsumption, 257–261
Democracy
   in capitalist countries, 402–403
   public ownership and, 484–485
Democratic socialism, 405–406
Depreciation, 32–33, 34–35, 37, 39
   in business cycle, 174
   and replacement spending, 175
Depression. *See also* Business cycles; Contraction; Great Depression; Stagflation
   defined, 19
   external shocks in, 14
   financial panic and, 18
Diffusion indexes, 165
Discount rate, 120, 323
Discount window borrowing, 120, 323–324, 442
Discouraged worker, 245–246
Disequilibrium
   defined, 60
   role of expectations in, 65–67
Dishoarding, 65
Disposable personal income, 34
Domar, Evsey, 229, 230
   growth theory of, 238–240
Duesenberry, James, 134, 246

Eastern Europe, growth cycles in, 481–482
Eckstein, Otto, 248, 419
Economic growth. *See* Growth theory
Education, as feedback control, 414–415
Eisner, Robert, 161
England. *See* Great Britain
Equation of exchange, 52, **53**, 81–82, 87
Equilibrium
   in classical model, 8–9, 43–44
   for income and expenditures, 48–51
   for labor market, 46–48, 52–53
   defined, 59
   in finance market, 64–65
   financial hoarding and, 59–60
   with unemployment, 67, **68**
Essay on the Principle of Population (Malthus), 6
Eurodollars, 390

Index

Europe. *See also specific country*
  monopoly price behavior in, 387–389
  multinationals in, 391
Even-keel policy, 443–444
Expansion. *See also* Business cycle
  average, 25
  indicators of, 25, 27
  inflation in, 348
  price behavior in, 365, 366 (table)
  in United States history, 26 (table)
Expectations
  adaptive and rational, 296, 301
  inflationary, 295, 300, 303
  in investment decision, 61, 62, 65–67, 161, 162, 310
  of profit, 248, 341
  of sales, 70
Exploitation, rate of, 184, 241, 261–263
Exports. *See* Trade

Federal funds market, 324, 444–446, 450, 466–467
Federal Open Market Committee (FOMC), 119, 442, 444–445, 446, 451, 454, 455, 468–470
Federal Reserve Bank of New York, 444, 446, 454
Federal Reserve System, 278
  control operations of, 119, 318–319, 321, 322–323, 325
  creation of, 117–118
  and monetary policy, 440–441
    even keel, 443–444
    interest rate stabilization, 444–445, 446–450
    monetary aggregates in, 445, 468–470
  money defined by, 314–315
  objectives of, 440–441
  policy tools of, 119–121, 128–130, 442. *See also* Open market operations
  structure of, 118–119
Federal Reserve–Treasury Accord (1951), 444
Feige, Edgar, 295
Feldstein, Martin, 419
Feudal economy
  production in, 14
  Say's law in, 12
  use of money in, 16
Finance market
  disequilibrium in, 65–67

equilibrium in, 64–65
  with unemployment, 67, **68**
speculative motive in, 84–85, 336–337
  in boom, 337–338
  in bust, 339–340
Fiscal policy. *See also* Government, spending
  automatic stabilizers in, 428–429
  conservative, 416–417, 436–437
    supply-side, 419–421, 437
  discretionary, 292, 428
  endogenous model of, 438
  expansionary, 291, 293, 304
  liberal, 417–418, 436–437
    constraints on, 422–428
  monetarist, 303–304
  radical, 421–422
Fisher, Irving, 81–82, 317, 340
  cycle theory of, 330–332, 334–335
Food prices
  monopoly power and, 367–368
  shortages and, 397
Ford, Gerald, 425
Foreign exchange stabilization, 441
Foreign trade. *See* Trade
Foundations, 410
France
  monopoly price behavior in, 387–388
  public ownership in, 479, 483, 484
Frictional unemployment, 244–245
Friedman, Milton, 10, 135, 144–145, 287, 314, 330, 332, 402, 416, 473
  monetarist model of, 293–295
Full employment
  in classical model, 9, 44, 48
  legislation on, 476–477
Fullerton, John, 320

Galbraith, John Kenneth, 139, 475
Germany, inflation in, 349
Global corporations, 389–393, 396–397
Gluts, Malthus's theory of, 6–7
Glyn, Andrew, 270
Government. *See also* Public ownership
  conservative view of, 401–403
  deficit, 278
    versus balanced budget, 438–439

    cyclical behavior of, 434–437
    federal versus state and local, 114, 115 (table)
    financing of, 117
  liberal view of, 403–404
  Marxist view of, 404–406
  radical view of, 406–415
  revenue. *See also* Taxation
    cyclical behavior of, 429–430
    Laffer curve of, 232–233
    state and local, 114, 430
    trends in, 112–114
  spending. *See also* Fiscal policy; Military spending
    business subsidies in, 411, 417
    cyclical behavior of, 148, 264, 278, 431–434
    deficit-financed, 116, 128, 289–291, 303, 422, 439
    defined, 30
    effect of changes in, 123–128
    federal versus state and local, 107–110
    on Full Employment Act, 476–477
    growth factors in, 115–116
    income distribution and, 116, 423
    Reagan cuts in, 425–426
    total, 107
    vested interests in, 423–425
    in wartime, 346–347
Grants-in-aid, federal, 108–109, 114
Great Britain
  business cycle appearance in, 20
  monopoly price behavior in, 387
  Say's law in, 7–8
  stagflation in, 388–389
Great Depression, 24
  foreign investment in, 381–382
  income distribution in, 188–189
  interest rates in, 171
  international impact of, 21
  investment in, 157, 310–311
  Keynes on, 77
  monetary theory and, 82–83
  monopoly prices in, 364, 365 (table)
  phases of, 22–23
  profit rate in, 207
  trade in, 382–383
Gross business savings, 37
Gross investment, 37
Gross national income (GNI), 31

Gross national product (GNP)
  circular flow of, 30–32, **37**
  consumption in, 131, **132**
  defined, 29–30
  government spending in, 108–110, 111
  housework exclusion from, 41
  income side of, 31–32
  per capita, 40–41
  post-1955, 35–36, **38**
  potential, 40
  in real terms, 39–40
  value added concept and, 38–39
  as welfare measure, 41
Growth cycles, under central planning, 481–482
Growth theory, 225–226
  of Keynes, 229–230
  Marxist, 234–235, 241–243
  neoclassical, 230–232
  neo-Keynesian, 238–240
  Post Keynesian, 236, 241
  supply-side, 226–229
    classical, 237–238
    modern, 232–234
Gurley, John, 316

Hansen, Alvin, 258–259
Harrod, Roy, 238–240
Hayek, Frederick, 269–270
Hicks, John, 88, 100, 249
Hilferding, Rudolf, 326
Hoarding, 59–60, 66, 67, 77
  liquidity preference and, 85–86
  motives for, 83–85
Hobson, John, 249–250, 258
Hotson, John, 418
Housework, exclusion from GNP, 41
Housing industry
  economy and, 157–158
  finance costs in, 356
Human nature, self-interest in, 3–4
Hyperinflations, 349

Imperialism, 385–386
Implicit price deflator (IPD), 39–40
Imports. *See* Trade
Income
  in gross national product (GNP), 31–32
  national, 33, 36t
  permanent, 294, 297
  personal and disposable, 33–34, 36 (table)
  and spending, **32**
    in Say's law model, 48–51
  transitory, 135

Income distribution
  and consumption, 6–7, 132–139
    cyclical behavior of, 139–149
    functional relation of, 151–154
  cyclical behavior of, 187, 188–200, 272–273
  data collection on, 185–186
  fiscal policy and, 427
  functional, 183
  government spending impact on, 116, 423
  long-term trends in, 149–150
  measurement of, 183–185
  theories of, 187–188, 194–198
  in United States, 182–183
  wage-price controls and, 474–475, 477
Income tax
  loopholes in, 112–113
  regressive, 113
  trends in, 113–114
Industry(s). *See also* Monopoly power
  business cycle timing in, 164–165
  competitive versus monopoly sectors in, 364–365, 371
  government subsidies to, 411, 417
  and labor union strength, 357–358
  obsolescence in, 355
  United States, in world production, 392–395
Inflation, 23, 24. *See also* Stagflation
  consumption and, 150
  cost-push, 354–359
  demand-pull, 345–354
    in expansions, 348
  monetary, 349–354
  in wartime, 346–348
  information sources on, 360
  monetarist interpretation of, 303
  public ownership and, 480–481
  and unemployment trade-off, 288–289, 301–302
Inquiry into the Nature and Causes of the Wealth of Nations (Smith), 3–5
Interest groups
  economic power and influence of, 409
  and fiscal policy, 423–425
  pluralists on, 404
Interest rates
  in classical theory, 50
  control policy for, 459–460, 461

  cyclical behavior of, 169–171, 278
  equilibrium, 50–51
  even-keel policy on, 443–444
  in federal funds market, 446, 450, 466–467
  Federal Reserve System and, 120, 121, 318
  flexible, 9, 311
  and investment, 289–291, 311
  inventory, 168–169
  in Keynesian model, 62, 63, 64
  and monetary policy, 316–318
  and money supply, 299–300
  on mortgage loans, 158, 356
  natural, 299
  stabilization policy, 444–445, 446, 462
  inflationary effects of, 447–450
Interlocking directorates, 363
International demand. *See* Trade
Inventory
  change, 34
  investment, 27, 30, 31
    cyclical behavior of, 166–169
    intended and unintended, 156
Investment
  categories of, 156–158
  and consumption, 251
  cyclical behavior of, 155, 156, 162, 163 (table), **164,** 165, 180–181
  accelerator theory of, 158–161, 215, 250
  inventory, 166–169, 251
  overinvestment theory in, 250, 268–270, 280–281
  defined, 30, 36–37, 60, 155
  foreign, 394
    in cycle transmission, 380–381
    during Great Depression, 381–382
    in less developed countries, 386–387
    by multinational corporations, 389–392
    in United States, 395
  gross, 37
  growth rate in, 171–172
  interest rates and, 289–291, 311
  inventory, 27, 30, 31, 156, 166–169
  in Keynesian model, 61–63, 64
  multiplier, 176–180
  net, 155–156

INDEX 491

in plant and equipment, 157
problem of uncertainty in,
  308–311
and profit rate, 161, 273,
  275–276
replacement, 37, 173–176
role of expectations in, 61, 62,
  65–67
and savings, 60, 63–65, 77
  in Classical theory, 8, 50–51,
    226
  hoarding and, 59–60
  interest rate-income levels
    and, 89–93
  Keynes on, 229–230
  Marx on, 235
  in supply-side policy, 419–421
speculative, 336–340
theories of, 161–162, 173
  accelerator model, 158–161
Irish, Marian D., 407, 409
IS-LM model, 88–97
  criticism of, 96–97
  interest rate-income levels in,
    89–93
  money demand functions in,
    88–89
  uses of, 93–95
Italy, inflation in, 349

Japan
  industrial development in, 386
  monopoly price behavior in,
    387, 388
  planning modes in, 477–478
*Journal of Post Keynesian
  Economics,* 307
Juglar, Clement, 27
Juglar cycle, 27

Kaldor, Nicholas, 236, 320–321
Kalecki, Michael, 165
Kalecki's theory, 214
Kennedy, Edward, 476, 477
Keynes, John Maynard, 421
  background of, 58
  on consumer demand, 132–133,
    345
  contribution of, 77–78, 249
  fiscal policy proposals of, 418
  growth theory of, 229–230
  on money demand, 82–87, 101,
    320
  on Say's law, 9–10
  on speculative markets, 338, 339
Keynesian economics. *See also*
  Neo-Keynesian school; Post
  Keynesian school
  factions in, 97–98

and fiscal policy, 418, 422–428,
  439
on governmental role, 403
models of, 60
  of business cycle, 250–252,
    253–256
  consumption function in, 61,
    251
  disequilibrium conditions in,
    60, 65–67
  financial market in, 63–65
  investment function in, 61–63,
    64
  IS-LM, 88–93, 96–97
  Keynesian cross, 72–75, 288
  labor demand in, 67, **68,**
    70–72
  monetary theory of, 287–288,
    307
Kitchin, Joseph, 27
Kitchin cycle, 27
Klein, Lawrence, 144
Klein, Philip, 147
Kondratieff, N. D., 27
Kondratieff cycles, 274
Korean War, 431, 433, 435, 444
Kuznets, Simon S., 27, 174
Kuznets cycle, 27

Labor. *See also* Productivity
  and capital ratio, 7
  hoarding theory, 188, 196
  supply and demand. *See also*
    Unemployment
    in classical model, 45–48,
      52–53, 67–68, **69**
    in Keynesian model, 70–72
  reserve army theory of,
    270–271
Labor unions
  in manufacturing sector,
    357–358
  membership of, 356–357
  monopoly power of, 356–358
  multinationals and, 390
Laffer, Arthur, 232
Laffer curve, 232–233
Laidler, David, 292, 321, 330
Latin America, foreign investment
  in, 391–392
Lauderdale, Lord, 258
Legal tender, 81
Less developed countries
  business cycle in, 21
  feedback control in, 415
  foreign domination of, 386–387
    multinationals and, 389–390,
      391–392
  stagflation in, 392–393

Life cycle hypothesis, of consumer
  demand, 134–135
Liquidity premium, defined, 101,
  316–317
Lucas, Robert, 247
Luxemburg, Rosa, 258

Malthus, Thomas Robert, 6–7, 9,
  258
Manufacturing sector
  labor unions in, 357–358
  monopoly power in, 361–362
Marcet, Jane, 7
Marginal productivity theory, 187
Marginal propensity to consume,
  61, 124–125, 126–127
  cyclical behavior of, 134, 135,
    144–145, 146 (table)
  in inflation, 150
  from profit versus wage income,
    144–145
Marginal propensity to save,
  124–125
Market pricing system, 30
Market system. *See* Capitalism
Marx, Karl, 9, 32
  on consumer demand, 138–139
  on credit system, 326
  on government power structure,
    405–406
  growth theory of, 234–235,
    241–243
  Say's law critique of, 75–77
  underconsumption theory of,
    259–261
Marxism, 308
  monetary theory of, 326–327
  supply-side cycle theories of,
    270–275
Means, Gardiner, 364
Media
  and political power, 408–409
  public ownership and, 485
Medium of exchange, money as,
  80
Mellon, Andrew, 419–420
Mergers, conglomerate, 362
Mexico, inflation in, 349
Michel, Robert, 426
Military dictatorships, 415
Military spending, 189, 414
  over business cycle, 431–433
  and business profits, 111–112,
    372
  size of, 110–111
  and vested interests, 424
Mill, James, 7, 8
Mill, John Stuart, 380
Mills, Frederick, 214

Minsky, Hyman, 310, 321, 330
  business cycle theory of, 335–340
Mirabeau, Marquis de, 5
Mitchell, Wesley, 9, 20, 21, 144, 164–165, 188, 249
Modigliani, Franco, 134
Monetarism, 10
  business cycle theory of, 330–335
  criticisms of, 292–293, 308
  versus discretionary policy, 298–303
  on fiscal policy, 303–304
  inflation theory of, 303, 358, 359
  and monetary policy, 304, 453–458, 461–462
  noninterventionist nature of, 306
  primary model of, 293–295
  role of expectations in, 296
  tenets of, 291–292
  transmission mechanism concept in, 296–298
Monetary aggregates, 445–447, 451–453, 460, 468–470
Monetary eclecticism, 458–459
Monetary policy. *See also* Federal Reserve System, and monetary policy
  credit controls in, 460
  discretionary, 293, 298–303, 310, 461
    cyclical problems of, 333–334
    monetarist, 456–457, 463
  of interest rate control, 459–460, 461. *See also* Interest rate, stabilization policy
  Marxist, 327
  monetarist, 453–458, 461–462
  of monetary eclecticism, 458–459
  radical, 463–464
  in stagflation, 462–463
Monetary rule, 311, 454, 457–458
Monetary theory. *See also* Monetarism
  of business cycle, 329–342
  classical, 82, 83, 95–96
  creditist, 315–316
  crowding-out hypothesis in, 289–291
  equation of exchange in, 81–82
  Great Depression and, 82–83
  Gurley-Shaw, 312–314
  implications of, 79–80
  importance of money in, 287–288
  inflation-unemployment trade-off in, 288–289, 301–302
  Keynesian, 82–87, 101, 288, 289, 308–311. *See also* IS-LM model
  Marxist, 326–327
  money defined in, 80–81, 314–315
  of money inventory, 99–100
  nonmonetarist schools of, 307–308
  portfolio theory model of, 100–104
Money
  demand for, 294–295
  functions of, 80, 314
  liquidity of, 63, 85
  types of, 81
  use of, 15–18
  velocity of, 81, 82, 86–87, 315–316
Money multiplier, 454
Money supply
  changes in, 93–94
  control of, 445, 451–456
  defined, 293, 314–315, 445
  endogenous, 308, 318–324
  growth rate for, 349–350, 359
  interest rates and, 299–300
  output and, 298
  price level and, 298
  spending and, 81–82, 85–86, 292–293, 297–298, 325
    constant leakage from, 312–314
Monopoly power, 361–362
  and administered prices, 364–370
  abroad, 387–389
  conglomerate mergers and, 362–363
  cycle model of, 377
  of global corporations, 389–392
  shortages and, 396–397
  stagflation and, 392–393
  profit rates and, 370–375
Monopoly sector, defined, 364, 371
Moore, Basil, 322
Moore, Geoffrey, 269
Mortgage loans, interest rates on, 158
Multinational corporations, 389–393, 396–397
Multiplier
  government, 123–128
  investment, 176–180
  Keynesian, 75
  money, 454
Mutual funds, 81

National Bureau of Economic Research (NBER), 139–140
  business cycle dating by, 24–27
National health care, economic constraints on, 427
National income
  categories of, 183
  and consumption, 139–141, 142 (table)
  defined, 33, 36 (table)
National income accounts. *See also* Gross national product (GNP)
  circular flow concept in, 30
  consumption in, 131
  income approach to, 31–32
  national income defined for, 33
  net national product in, 32–33
  for 1981, 34–36, 35 (table), 36 (table)
  personal-disposable income in, 33–34
Neocolonialism, 386–387
Neo-Keynesian school
  on consumer demand, 134–139
  growth theory of, 238–240
  on inflation, 368
  IS-LM model of, 88–97
  versus Post Keynesians, 97, 98
  and Say's law, 10
Net economic welfare (NEW), 41
Net export spending, defined, 30
Net investment, defined, 155–156
Net national product (NNP), 32–33
News media. *See* Media
Nixon, Richard, 425, 471
  wage-price control policy of, 471–473, 474–476

Obsolescence, in industry, 355
Oil prices
  inflationary impact of, 354
  output decline and, 358
  monopoly power and, 367
  shortages and, 396
O'Neill, Tip, 426
Open market operations, of Federal Reserve System, 121, 128–130, 304, 308, 317, 442–443, 444, 446, 454–455, 461
Organic composition theory, 274–275

Index

Output
    and capital ratio, 212–216, 228–229, 231, 270, 276
    cyclical movements of, 198–200, 246–247
    growth of, 226–227
    money supply changes and, 298
Overhead labor theory, 188, 196
Overinvestment, theory of, 250, 268–270, 280–281

Paper money, 17
Pearce, Douglas, 295
Penrose, Boise, 409–410
Permanent income, 135–136, **137**, 294, 297
Personal income
    calculation of, 33–34
    and consumption, 142–143
    disposable, 34
Personal savings, 37
Phillips curve, 288–289, 301–302, 351
Physiocrats, 5–6
Pigou, A. C., 70
Planning
    central, 479–482
    democratic, 477–478
    and public ownership, 484
Plant and equipment investment, 157, 269, 270
Pluralists, 404
Political power
    capitalism and, 402–403
    economic inequality and, 405–406, 408–410
    feedback control in, 414–415
    interest groups and, 404
    social class and, 406–408, 410–411, 412–414
    structural bases of, 411–412
Pollution, cost of, 355–356
Portfolio assets, demand for, 294
Portfolio effects, of interest rate change, 317–318
Portfolio theory, 100–104
Post Keynesian school, 10–11, 307, 419
    on consumer demand, 138
    growth theory of, 236, 241
    monetary theory of, 308–309
    business cycle in, 335–340
    versus Neo-Keynesians, 97–98
Power. *See* Monopoly power; Political power
Pressure groups. *See* Interest groups
Price(s). *See also* Wage-price controls
    cyclical behavior of, 214–219, 269–270
    of imports, 270
    expectations, 295, 296
    flexible, 9
    monopoly, 364–370
        abroad, 387–389
    in Say's law model, 51–52, **53**
    stability, 440–441
Price index, 39–40
    expansion amplitude of, 365
Primitive society
    barter in, 15
    production in, 13
Principles of Political Economy (Malthus), 6
Producer price index (PPI), 39
Production
    for market, 13–15
    for private profit, 18–19
    in Say's law model, 44–45
    for use, 13
Productivity
    capital, 212–216, 220–221, 223–229, 231, 270
    cyclical behavior of, 191–192, 194
    defined, 184
    determinants of, 195, 202–203
    lower growth of. *See* Growth theory
    measurement of, 186
Profit(s)
    cyclical pattern in, 163, **164**, 165, 269
    expectations of, 248, 341
    measurement of, 185
    in monopoly sector, 370–375
    of multinationals, 391–392
    production of, 259–260
    profit rate components in, 219–221
    realization of, 260
Profit motive
    government policy and, 405
    in production, 18–19
Profit rate
    capacity utilization and, 205, 210–212
    components of, 204
    cyclical pattern in, 163, **164**, 205–208, 341
    defined, 204
    investment and, 161, 273, 275–276
    output-capital ratio and, 212–216
    theories of, 205
Profit share
    cyclical behavior of, 208–210
    defined, 208
Propensity to consume *See* Average propensity to consume; Marginal propensity to consume
Prosperity. *See* Expansion
Prothro, James W., 407, 409
Public employment, 476–477
Public goods, maintenance costs for, 355
Public ownership
    bureaucracy in, 484
    central planning in, 479–481
        growth cycles and, 481–482
    decentralized, 482–483
    democracy and, 484–485
    efficiency and, 484
    incentives and, 483–484
Purchasing Power of Money, The (Fisher), 330–331

Radcliffe Committee, 307, 320, 325, 458
Rational expectations, 296
Reagan, Ronald
    and monetary policy, 463
    spending cuts of, 425–426
    taxation cuts of, 113–114, 426
    and unemployment, 245
Realization theory, of business cycle, 261–266
    in combined production model, 276–279, 282–283
Recession. *See also* Business cycle; Contraction
    defined, 19
    disequilibrium conditions and, 65–67
    mild, 22
Relative income hypothesis, of consumer demand, 134, **137**
Replacement investment, 37, 173–176
Reserve army theory, 188, 197, 270–274, 279–280
Reserve requirements, of Federal Reserve System, 119–121, 442
Residential construction, 157–158
Resource depletion, inflationary impact of, 354–355
Revenue. *See* Government revenue
Review of Radical Political Economics, 308
Ricardo, David, 7, 8–9, 16, 320
Robinson, Joan, 75, 97, 98, 236
Robinson Crusoe economy, Say's law in, 12

Rodbertus, Karl, 258
Roman Empire
  production in, 13–14
  use of money in, 15–16

St. Louis equation, 304
Sales, and inventory ratio, 167–168
Samuelson, Paul, 97, 418, 424, 425, 474
  accelerator theory of, 158–159, 160
  cycle model of, 250–252
Savings
  defined, 59
  economic glut and, 7
  flow, 85–86
  gross business, 37
  and growth
    in classical theory, 228
    Keynes on, 229–230
    Marx on, 235
  and investment, 311
    in classical theory, 8, 50–51, 226–228
    hoarding and, 59–60, 77
    interest rate-income levels and, 89–93
    Keynes on, 63–65, 229–230
    Marx on, 77, 235
    in supply-side policy, 419–421
  money as, 63, 65, 66
  personal, 37
Say, J. B., 7, 8
Say's law, 403, 416, 421. *See also* Classical theory
  and conservative theory, 10
  criticism of, 9–11
    Keynesian, 60–75
    market production and, 14–15
    by Marx, 75–77
    by Neo-Keynesians versus Post Keynesians, 97–98
    profit motive and, 18–19
    use of money in, 16–18
  formulation of, 7–8, 43–44
  model of, 44, 52–57, 226
    commodity market in, 48–51
    labor market in, 45–48
    national production function in, 44–45
    price levels in, 51–52
    real output in, 48, **49**
  in precapitalist economies, 12
  refinement of, 8–9
Schumpeter, Joseph, 27, 247
Schwartz, Anna, 330, 331, 332
Search theory, of unemployment, 244–245

Self-interest, and human nature, 3–4
Shaikh, Anwar, 260
Shaw, Edward, 307, 312, 316
Shepherd, W. G., 362
Shocks, external, in cyclical movements, 246–247, 248, 291, 330
Shortages, international, 396–397
Sismondi, J. C. L. Simonde de, 258
Smith, Adam
  on human nature, 3–4
  market system of, 4–5
  on money supply, 319–320
Smoot-Hawley tariff, 417
Social class
  consciousness of, 407–408
  fiscal policy benefits and, 426
  and political behavior, 406–407, 412–414
  of political leaders, 410–411
  and political participation, 408, 413
  spending behavior and, 6–7
Solow, Robert, growth model of, 230–232, 237, 240–241
Soviet Union, growth cycles in, 481–482
Speculative demand motive, for holding money, 84–85, 95
  portfolio theory of, 100–104
Spending. *See also* Consumption; Government spending; Investment
  credit and, 315–316
  and income, **32**
  in Say's law model, 48–51
  money supply and, 81–82, 85–86, 292–293, 297–298, 325
  constant leakage in, 312–314
  planned, 59
  types of, 30–31
Stagflation, 24, 248–249
  cost-push theory of, 358–359
  demand-pull theory and, 351–354
  and fiscal policy, 427–428
    automatic stabilizers in, 428–429
  and monetary policy, 462–463
  and monopoly power
    abroad, 387–389
    multinationals in, 392–393
    prices in, 364–370
    shortages in, 396–397
  public employment against, 476–477

wage-price controls and, 471–476
Stagnation, theories of, 258–259
State and local government
  revenues of, 114
  spending by, 108–109
Stockman, David, 426
Stock market. *See* Finance market
Store of value, money as, 80
Supply and demand. *See* Aggregate supply and demand; Labor, supply and demand
Supply-side economics, 10, 32
  criticism of, 420–421
  cycle theory of, 268–275
    in combined demand model, 275–279, 282–283
    Marxist, 270–275
  and fiscal policy, 419–421
  growth theory of, 226–229
  modern, 232–234
Sutcliffe, Bob, 270
Sweezy, Paul, 259

Tableau Economique (Quesnay), 5
T-account, 128–130
Taft-Hartley Act, 357
Taxation. *See also* Government revenue
  as automatic stabilizer, 428–429
  and consumption, 148
  cuts in, 157, 232–233, 264
    by Reagan, 426
    supply-side theory on, 419–421
  loopholes, 112–113, 185, 186
  regressive effects of, 113, 116–117
  revenue trends and, 113–114
Technological innovation, economic impact of, 247
Third World. *See* Less developed countries
Tobin, James, 100, 307, 310, 321, 350
Tooke, Thomas, 320
Trade
  barriers, 417
  over business cycle, 264–265, 278–279, 383–385
  under colonialism, 386
  in cycle transmission, 378–379
  neocolonialism and, 386–387
Transactions demand, for money, 83, 84, 95–96, 100
Transfer payments, 34

Trevithick, James, 321
Trickle-down theory, 419–420
Trough, defined, 25

Uncertainty, in investment decision, 308–311
Underconsumption theory, 249–250, 257–261
 Marxist, 259–261
Unemployment. *See also* Stagflation
 in classical theory, 9, 43–44, 46–48, 67–68, **69**
  search model of, 244–245
 cyclical behavior of, 198, 199–200, 219–220
  reserve army theory and, 188, 270–271, 272
 in equilibrium conditions, 67, **68**
 human costs of, 246
 and inflation trade off, 288–289, 301–302
 monetarist policy and, 292
 natural rate of, 299
 official definition of, 245–246

 voluntary, 53, 68, 244–245
 wage level and, 67–68, **69**, 71–72, 76–77, 273
Unions. *See* Labor unions
Unit of account, money as, 80

Value-added concept, 38–39
Veblen, Thorstein, 9, 139, 427
Vietnam War, 431, 433, 435
Volcker, Paul, 451, 456
Voluntary unemployment, 68, 244–245
Voting behavior, social class in, 407

Wachtel, Howard, 369–370
Wage(s)
 hourly
  cyclical behavior of, 190–194
  determinants of, 194–195, 201–202
 measurement of, 185
 in monopoly sector, 372
 restraints on, 273–274
 share
  cyclical behavior of, 187–188, 189, 190–194, 272, 275

 in income distribution, 184, 272–273, 275
 measurement of, 186
 regression analysis of, 200–201
 unemployment and, 67–68, **69**, 71–72, 76–77, 273
Wage lag theory, 187–188, 195
Wage-price controls, 189, 346, 347, 471–473
 criticism of, 473–474
 income distribution and, 474–475, 477
 and liberal policy, 475–476, 477
Wartime
 inflation in, 346–348
 military spending in, 431–433
Wealth, defined, 36
Wealth effect, of interest rate changes, 317
Wealth of Nations (Smith), 319
Weisskopf, Thomas, 216–217
Welfare spending, vested interests against, 424
World War II, 346, 443
Wykoff, Frank, 245, 246

Yugoslavia, 428, 483

83 84 85 86 9 8 7 6 5 4 3 2 1